Business Law

Related titles in the series

Accounting
Auditing
Book-Keeping
Business and the European Community
Business Environment, The
Business French
Business German
Business Italian
Business Spanish
Business Studies
Commerce
Cost and Management Accounting
Economics
Elements of Banking
Financial Management
Human Resource Management
Law
Management Theory and Practice
Marketing
Organizations and Management
Statistics for Business

Business Law

Fourth edition

Abby Kadar, LLM, BA(Hons) in Law, FBSC, CertEd
Ken Hoyle, BSc(Econ)
Geoffrey Whitehead, BSc(Econ)

MADE SIMPLE
BOOKS

Made Simple
An imprint of Butterworth-Heinemann Ltd
Linacre House, Jordan Hill, Oxford OX2 8DP

A member of the Reed Elsevier plc group

OXFORD LONDON BOSTON
NEW DELHI SINGAPORE SYDNEY
TOKYO TORONTO WELLINGTON

First published 1984
Reprinted 1985
Second edition 1987
Reprinted 1988
Third edition 1991
Reprinted 1992, 1993
Fourth edition 1996

© A. Kadar, K. Hoyle and G. Whitehead 1984, 1987, 1991, 1996

All rights reserved. No part of this publication
may be reproduced in any material form (including
photocopying or storing in any medium by electronic
means and whether or not transiently or incidentally
to some other use of this publication) without the
written permission of the copyright holder except in
accordance with the provisions of the Copyright,
Designs and Patents Act 1988 or under the terms of a
licence issued by the Copyright Licensing Agency Ltd,
90 Tottenham Court Road, London, England W1P 9HE.
Applications for the copyright holder's written permission
to reproduce any part of this publication should be addressed
to the publishers

British Library Cataloguing in Publication Data
Kadar, Abby
　Business Law – 4Rev.ed
　I. Title
　344.20666

ISBN 0 7506 2551 1

Composition by Genesis Typesetting, Laser Quay, Rochester, Kent
Printed and bound in Great Britain by Martins the Printers Ltd,
Berwick-upon-Tweed

Contents

Preface — xi
Acknowledgements — xiii

Part One The Framework of Business Law

1 Elements of English law — 3
 1.1 A definition of law — 3
 1.2 A definition of business law — 3
 1.3 About this book — 4
 1.4 The divisions of the law — 6
 1.5 The sources of English law — 8

2 The courts of law — 25
 2.1 The structure of courts in the UK — 25
 2.2 The House of Lords — 25
 2.3 The Court of Appeal — 27
 2.4 Divisional Courts of the High Court — 28
 2.5 The High Court — 29
 2.6 The Crown Court — 30
 2.7 The County Court — 31
 2.8 The Small Claims Court — 32
 2.9 The Magistrates' Court — 33
 2.10 Special courts — 34
 2.11 The doctrine of binding precedent and its effect on litigation — 38
 2.12 Personnel of the law — 39
 2.13 Legal aid — 40

Part Two The Law and Business Entities

3 The legal environment for business entities — 47
 3.1 The concept of business entity — 47
 3.2 Sole trader enterprises — 48
 3.3 Partnerships: definition and name — 51
 3.4 Formation of a partnership — 51
 3.5 Relationship of partners with third parties — 53
 3.6 Interrelationship of partners — 54
 3.7 Partnership property — 55
 3.8 Assigning a share in a partnership — 56
 3.9 Limited partnerships — 56
 3.10 Dissolution of a partnership — 56
 3.11 Advantages and disadvantages of operating as a partnership — 58

4 Business entities: unincorporated associations — 62
 4.1 Introduction — 62
 4.2 Organization of a club — 62
 4.3 Legal liability of unincorporated associations — 63
 4.4 Unincorporated associations and the ownership of land — 63
 4.5 Legal actions affecting unincorporated associations — 64

5	**Business entities: limited companies**	66
	5.1 The nature of a limited company	66
	5.2 Basic characteristics of a public company	67
	5.3 The formation of a company	67
	5.4 The consequences of incorporation	72
	5.5 Share capital of a company, and debentures	74
	5.6 The management of companies	76
	5.7 Company directors	77
	5.8 Other officers of the company	84
	5.9 Meetings and proceedings	85
	5.10 Winding up of a company	86
	5.11 Advantages of the limited company as a form of business entity	88
	5.12 Disadvantages of limited companies	89

Part Three   The Law of Contract

6	**The nature of contracts**	95
	6.1 Agreement as the basis of contracts	95
	6.2 A definition of a contract	97
	6.3 The elements of a contract	98
	6.4 Capacity to contract	98
	6.5 Intention to create legal relations	103
	6.6 Agreement to the same idea (*consensus ad idem*)	106
7	**Offer, acceptance and valuable consideration**	110
	7.1 A clear offer, communicated to the offeree	110
	7.2 Termination of the offer	114
	7.3 Acceptance	116
	7.4 Communication of acceptance	117
	7.5 Other points on acceptance	119
	7.6 Valuable consideration	120
	7.7 General requirements of valuable consideration	120
8	**Circumstances affecting the validity of contracts**	129
	8.1 Introduction	129
	8.2 Duress and undue influence	129
	8.3 Mistake	132
	8.4 Illegal contracts	139
	8.5 Contracts illegal at common law	140
	8.6 Illegality declared by statute	141
9	**The terms of the contract**	144
	9.1 Introduction	144
	9.2 Express terms: conditions and warranties	145
	9.3 Implied terms	148
	9.4 Excluding and limiting terms	150
	9.5 The *Unfair Contract Terms Act, 1977*	156
10	**Misrepresentation**	160
	10.1 What is misrepresentation?	160
	10.2 Types of misrepresentation	162
	10.3 Remedies for misrepresentation	165
11	**The discharge of contracts**	171
	11.1 The meaning of discharge	171
	11.2 Discharge of the contract by performance	171
	11.3 Discharge by express agreement	173

11.4	Discharge of a contract by frustration	174
11.5	Discharge of a contract by breach	177
11.6	Assignment of contracts	179
11.7	Other assignments	181

12 How the law enforces contractual obligations — 184
- 12.1 The nature of contractual enforcement — 184
- 12.2 Common law remedies — 184
- 12.3 Equitable remedies — 189
- 12.4 Limitation of actions — 192
- 12.5 The *Contracts (Applicable Law) Act, 1990* — 193

13 Agency — 197
- 13.1 The nature of agency — 197
- 13.2 The appointment of agents — 198
- 13.3 The nature of contracts made under agency — 201
- 13.4 Subsequent ratification of an unauthorized act — 202
- 13.5 Breach of warranty of authority — 203
- 13.6 The duties of the agent — 204
- 13.7 The duties of the principal — 204
- 13.8 The agent as servant or independent contractor — 206
- 13.9 The doctrine of the undisclosed principal — 207
- 13.10 The termination of agency — 208
- 13.11 The European directive on agent–principal relationships — 210

Part Four Some Specialized Sections of Law

14 Contracts for the sale of goods — 219
- 14.1 Development of the law of the sale of goods — 219
- 14.2 The meaning of 'goods' — 220
- 14.3 The contract of sale — 220
- 14.4 Conditions and warranties in the contract — 222
- 14.5 Effects of a contract for the sale of goods — 226
- 14.6 The duties of the seller in the performance of the contract — 231
- 14.7 Exclusionary clauses in contracts — 234
- 14.8 The duties of the buyer in the performance of the contract — 235
- 14.9 The remedies of the buyer — 235
- 14.10 The remedies of the unpaid seller — 236
- 14.11 The *Trade Descriptions Act, 1968* — 238
- 14.12 The *Supply of Goods and Services Act, 1982* — 239
- 14.13 The *Sale of Goods (Amendment) Act, 1995* — 240

15 Insurance — 244
- 15.1 The nature of insurance — 244
- 15.2 The principles of insurance — 245
- 15.3 Life assurance — 248
- 15.4 Fire insurance — 249
- 15.5 Marine insurance — 251
- 15.6 Accident insurance — 255
- 15.7 Liability insurance — 260
- 15.8 The *Policyholders' Protection Act, 1975* — 261
- 15.9 The *Insurance Companies Act, 1982* — 261

16 Law of carriage by land, sea and air — 264
- 16.1 Carriage and the concept of the common carrier — 264
- 16.2 Carrying as a private carrier — 265
- 16.3 Aspects of carriage which are important in law — 266

16.4	Statutory modifications to the law of carriage	271
16.5	Carriage by road	272
16.6	Carriage by rail	273
16.7	Carriage by inland waterways	276
16.8	Carriage of goods by sea	276
16.9	Charterparties	284
16.10	Carriage by air: the Warsaw Rules	287
16.11	Multimodal movements by a Combined Transport Operator (CTO)	289
16.12	Comparison of conventions on international carriage	294

17 Negotiable instruments — 297
17.1	The concept of negotiability	297
17.2	Definition of a bill of exchange	298
17.3	The use of bills of exchange	299
17.4	The parties to a bill of exchange	303
17.5	The acceptance of a bill	304
17.6	Negotiation of a bill	306
17.7	The payment of a bill	306
17.8	Dishonour of a bill	306
17.9	The discharge of bills	307
17.10	Forgeries	308
17.11	Cheques	309

18 Arbitration — 316
18.1	The nature of arbitration	316
18.2	The advantages and disadvantages of arbitration	316
18.3	The *Arbitration Acts, 1950, 1975* and *1979*	317
18.4	The *Consumer Arbitration Agreements Act, 1988*	321

Part Five Public Law

19 Administrative law — 327
19.1	Introduction	327
19.2	Judicial control of administrative powers	328
19.3	Grounds for judicial intervention	328
19.4	Rules of natural justice	334
19.5	Methods of judicial review	336
19.6	Administrative justice	337

Part Six The Businessman and the Law of Tort

20 Introduction to the law of tort — 349
20.1	The nature of the law of tort	349
20.2	Definition of tort	349
20.3	General defences in tort	352
20.4	Capacity of the parties	357
20.5	Remedies for torts	360
20.6	Limitation of actions	363
20.7	Vicarious liability	365
20.8	Joint tortfeasors	369

21 Negligence — 371
21.1	The meaning of 'negligence'	371
21.2	The duty of care	371
21.3	Breach of duty and the standard of care	374

	21.4	Liability for negligent misstatements	376
	21.5	*Res ipsa loquitur* (the thing speaks for itself)	378
	21.6	Contributory negligence	378
	21.7	Negligence and economic loss	379

22 The liability of occupiers of premises — 382
- 22.1 The *Occupiers' Liability Act, 1957* — 382
- 22.2 The *Defective Premises Act, 1972* — 384
- 22.3 Strict liability — 385
- 22.4 Liability for animals — 389

23 Trespass to property — 392
- 23.1 Trespass to land — 392
- 23.2 Trespass to chattels — 394

24 Nuisance — 400
- 24.1 Types of nuisance — 400
- 24.2 Private nuisance — 400
- 24.3 Public nuisance — 404

25 Defamation — 408
- 25.1 What is defamation? — 408
- 25.2 Forms of defamation — 408
- 25.3 The standard of proof required — 408
- 25.4 Defences to defamation — 411
- 25.5 Remedies for defamation — 414

26 Miscellaneous torts — 417
- 26.1 Introduction — 417
- 26.2 Conspiracy — 417
- 26.3 Deceit or fraud — 417
- 26.4 Injurious falsehood — 418

Part Seven   Business Property

27 The law of property — 423
- 27.1 Ownership and possession — 423
- 27.2 Types of property — 424
- 27.3 Rights over land — 425
- 27.4 The purchase and sale of landed property — 426
- 27.5 Acquiring leasehold premises — 427
- 27.6 Restrictive covenants — 428
- 27.7 Mortgages — 428
- 27.8 Patents, trade marks and copyrights — 429

Part Eight   Consumer Protection

28 The law and consumer protection — 435
- 28.1 Introduction — 435
- 28.2 The *Consumer Protection Act, 1987* — 437
- 28.3 The *Consumer Credit Act, 1974* — 439
- 28.4 The *Unsolicited Goods and Services Acts, 1971–5* — 441
- 28.5 The *Fair Trading Act, 1973* — 441
- 28.6 The *Estate Agents Act, 1979* — 441
- 28.7 The *Data Protection Act, 1984* — 442
- 28.8 The *Weights and Measures Act, 1985* — 442
- 28.9 The *Financial Services Act, 1986* — 442

Part Nine Employment Law

29 Employment law — 449
- 29.1 The field of employment law — 449
- 29.2 Manpower — 449
- 29.3 The rights of employees — 451
- 29.4 The individual rights of employees — 452
- 29.5 The collective rights of employees — 456

Appendix 1: Questions — 461

Appendix 2: Glossary of Latin terms — 477

Appendix 3: Table of cases — 481

Appendix 4: Table of statutes — 492

Index — 497

Preface

Business people today face an extensive range of legal restrictions on their activities, and a climate of business law much less favourable to them than at any time in the past. As one commentator said, the traditional rule of *caveat emptor* (let the buyer beware) has almost been changed into *caveat venditor* (let the seller beware). Not only have the suppliers of goods and services come under enormous pressure in their actual business arrangements, but the climate of legal restraints surrounding these activities, administrative and ecological controls, have become steadily more burdensome.

The title of the book has been changed from *Business and Commercial Law* to *Business Law*. This reflects present trends in syllabus requirements and the increasing interest of the business community generally. Law is no longer an academic subject (if it ever was) but an increasingly powerful influence on every aspect of business life. One only hopes its tentacles will not strangle the life out of the goose that lays the golden eggs.

This book seeks to set out the chief features of all the major branches of law affecting businesses. It covers a multiplicity of vital legal areas such as the various aspects of the legal system, the law of contract, the sale of goods and supply of services, business organizations, transport, banking, insurance, administrative law, the law of tort, the law of property and consumer law. The new edition includes an introductory chapter on employment law. It brings its appraisal of the law up to the end of the year 1994.

The book covers the majority of commercial and business law syllabuses of professional bodies, such as the Chartered Association of Certified Accountants, the Association of Accounting Technicians, the Institute of Chartered Secretaries and Administrators, the Chartered Institute of Bankers, the Institute of Freight Forwarders and the Institute of Commercial Management. It will be particularly useful for colleges offering the business law options of such bodies as BTEC, and universities offering business degrees with a business law module. It has selective but important coverage of many aspects of those areas found in the syllabuses of students taking GCE Advanced Level.

The book will assist anyone studying a business-orientated course at whatever level who is required to appreciate the legal framework relating to businesses. Last but not least, the book forms a valuable reference work for directors, managers, officials in central or local government and others connected with the running or administration of businesses.

In preparing this revision we would like to thank the numerous organizations which have sanctioned the use of their material and agreed to the use of their names, addresses and telephone numbers where these are helpful to students. Every effort has been made to provide a comprehensive and readable account of the legal background to business activity, but this book cannot be entirely comprehensive in covering so broad a field of law. The reader with a particular problem, or interested in an in-depth study of a particular topic, must turn to the more specialist literature. The authors cannot be responsible for actions arising from the use of this book, which is descriptive rather than analytical, and is no substitute for professional legal advice.

ABBY KADAR
KEN HOYLE
GEOFFREY WHITEHEAD

Acknowledgements

In preparing this book the following firms and organizations have been very helpful; their courtesy is gratefully acknowledged:

Clearway Publishing Co. and The Law Society, for permission to reproduce three diagrams of the courts.
Butterworth and Co., for permission to reproduce cases from *Cracknell's Law Students' Companion* (Contract) and (Tort).
Witherby and Co., Ltd, for permission to reproduce the 1.1.82 Clauses (A).
Woodhead Faulkner & Co., for permission to reproduce extracts from their publication *Elements of Export Law*.
Formecon Services Ltd, for permission to reproduce a bill of exchange.

Part One The Framework of Business Law

1 Elements of English law

1.1 A definition of law

Law has been defined as follows:

Law is a body of rules for the guidance of human conduct which is imposed upon, and enforced among, the citizens of a given state.

This enduring definition includes three very important features. First, laws are **imposed upon** the citizens of a given state. This implies that there is some sovereign body, which promulgates laws and imposes them from above upon the general body of citizens. There have been many kinds of sovereign bodies in the past, ranging from tyrants on the one hand to democracies (rule by the people) on the other. In the UK the sovereign body is the 'Queen in Parliament', which makes law by enacting 'Acts' of Parliament.

Second, laws must be **enforced among** the citizens of a given state; without enforcement of the law there is no law. There are several elements in enforcement. First, the criminal laws must be policed by a body of police officers with powers of arrest, so that those in breach of the law may be brought before the courts. The police at one time prosecuted offenders but in 1985 the *Prosecution of Offences Act* set up a Crown Prosecution Service and charged it with the duty of prosecuting offenders. Its titular head is the Director of Public Prosecutions. The courts, whether at high or low levels, decide if a breach of the law has occurred and if appropriate penalties have to be imposed. These can include fines, imprisonment or death on the criminal side, and damages or equitable remedies on the civil side. The penalties imposed by the courts are enforced through the court administration and prison services, who collect fines, or ensure that probation or prison sentences are served in a proper manner.

Finally, laws apply **only within the boundaries of nation states**. The laws apply within the territory of the state to all citizens and non-citizens alike who are resident there, for however short a period. If a breach of the law has occurred, and we can bring the person concerned before the courts, justice can be obtained. It is much more difficult if they are outside the jurisdiction of the courts, for the foreign court may not be prepared to hear the case, or may consider that no breach of the law has occurred. At best we shall be put to extra cost in bringing the case, and finding a lawyer who will represent us. At worst it may be quite impossible to secure justice.

1.2 A definition of business law

The term 'business law' as used in the title of this book, is much wider than the terms more generally used about laws to do with business. In the past the terms 'commercial law' and 'mercantile law' have been used to describe the laws which control the commercial activities of merchants. Today these terms are too restrictive, although the bodies of law which they describe are of enormous importance to businessmen and businesswomen.

4 Business Law

(At this point the authors would like to make a statement about the use of 'sexist' words in this book. It is unfortunate that to date no sovereign body has pronounced on the use of suitable words for describing persons carrying on institutions like businesses who may be both male and female. Long before the present nationwide discussion began, and the Equal Opportunities Commission was appointed, the *Interpretation Act, 1889*, laid it down that 'the male includes the female gender' or, as one wag put it, 'Ever since time immemorial male has embraced female.' The *Interpretation Act, 1978*, re-enacted this same rule. To avoid endless repetitions of the phrases 'business men and business women' and his/her, we have elected to follow the statute. The term 'businessman' should therefore be read as 'businessman/woman' and no slur is intended whatsoever to the female sex.)

Today a businessman is concerned with the whole environment within which he must operate and the laws which govern the various institutions and situations to be found in this environment. The traditional commercial law – of contracts, the sale of goods, the carriage of goods by land, sea and air, payments, etc. – is still a large part of this environment, but there are several other fields to be considered.

Businesses operate within a framework of **administrative law**, which influences many of the things they do. Businesses must observe planning regulations, comply with rules about health and safety at work, and with employment legislation. Another area is that known as the **law of tort**. Torts are civil wrongs. It is a very simple matter for businesses to harm other institutions or individuals, and find themselves facing actions for damages for negligence, nuisance, trespass, defamation and other torts. Another area which has come into prominence in the last half century is the area of **economic law**, which attempts to influence and control the financial and trading practices of firms. Thus the monitoring of restrictive practices, monopoly legislation, the control of prices and incomes, and consumer protection legislation may be considered parts of economic law.

Within the limits imposed by space and cost we shall endeavour to deal with all these topics adequately.

We may therefore define business law as being those areas of law which form the legal environment within which business entities come into existence, enter into business relationships, pursue their industrial and commercial activities and achieve their aims.

1.3 About this book

This book attempts to cover the business law requirements of several bodies of students, particularly those studying for examinations run by professional bodies such as the various accountancy institutions, the Chartered Institute of Bankers, the Institute of Commercial Management and the various institutes in the transport and freight-forwarding fields. Another large group are those students preparing for examinations controlled by the Business and Technician Education Council, particularly the BTEC National and Higher National courses. Many students reading business law as a background subject for degrees in economics, accountancy, business administration, etc., will find this book helpful.

The study of law usually proceeds in the following way. The student first reads elements of English law, an introductory subject, and then proceeds to specialize; in this case in business law. We should therefore assume that the student already has some background in the study of law, and that the present volume can develop this background at once to cover the specialist subject of business law. Unfortunately, there will be many readers who do not already have such a background, and some compromise is necessary. We therefore have some introductory chapters which cover the framework of English law – its development and the system of courts. In addition, wherever necessary throughout what is inevitably a complex book, we begin each part with a restatement of basic principles to assist those who have not pursued a course in elements of law. Such readers are recommended to read *Law Made Simple*, a companion volume to this book.

Cases. The study of cases is an important element in English law. In this volume we have kindly been permitted to quote cases from the series *Cracknell's Law Students' Companion*. This series consists of several volumes, of which the most useful to students of business law are:

- *Commercial Law*, by G. H. H. Glasgow and D. Grace
- *Contract*, by Vincent Powell-Smith
- *Torts*, by M. G. Lloyd
- *Company Law*, by F. E. Smith
- *Conflict of Laws*, by M. R. Chesterman
- *Constitutional Law & English Legal System*, by W. H. Holland

The student is strongly recommended to obtain at least some of these titles, which will be of enduring interest.

Students are often perplexed to know how they are expected to use their knowledge of cases in examinations. Ideally one should be able to name any case that is relevant to the discussion in hand, and quote the year in which it was decided. It is then helpful to be able to give the facts of the case and the *ratio decidendi* (the reason for the decision). A decision has three basic elements: findings of material facts, direct or inferential; the statement of the principle of law applied to these facts; and the judgment based on the combined effects of the two. It is the statement of the principle of law contained in the decision that is the vital element and which is termed the *ratio decidendi*. This is the binding element and in a subsequent case the judge is bound to apply it if the facts are similar. The actual rules about following precedent are explained later (see Chapter 2), because higher courts are not bound to follow decisions made in lower courts so that the hierarchy of courts enters into the picture. The student should therefore be able to show that the facts are similar, and recommend that the precedent is followed. If the facts are not exactly similar the case under discussion may be 'distinguished' from the precedent, but it may still be 'persuasive' even if it is not binding. The student will recommend a decision which is appropriate for the set of facts under consideration in the question he is attempting to answer.

In order to assist students to recall the names of cases, the facts, etc., these have usually been featured in the revision pages at the end of each chapter. They should be learned by heart, using the self-testing pages. Even so, it is possible that in the heat of an examination some detail will not be recalled. In that case, give what you can remember. For example, it is better to say:

> *In one case in 1908 a tailor who had supplied eleven fancy waistcoats to a student failed in his action to secure payment because he could not establish that the waistcoats were necessaries, since the parents of the student proved that their son was already adequately supplied with clothing.*

This does not tell us the name of the case (*Nash v. Inman*) but it does tell us a great deal, and is clearly worth a few marks.

6 Business Law

1.4 The divisions of the law

Law is an enormous subject and some specialization is essential. A complete classification would require a very detailed chart, but the more important branches of the law are displayed in Figure 1.1. This is largely self-explanatory, but a few points require further explanation. These are:

1.4.1 International law

This may be divided into two parts. One is the law about the mutual relationship between states. This may be described as public international law. It is also concerned with international organizations, e.g. the United Nations Organization and its associated bodies. International law consists of

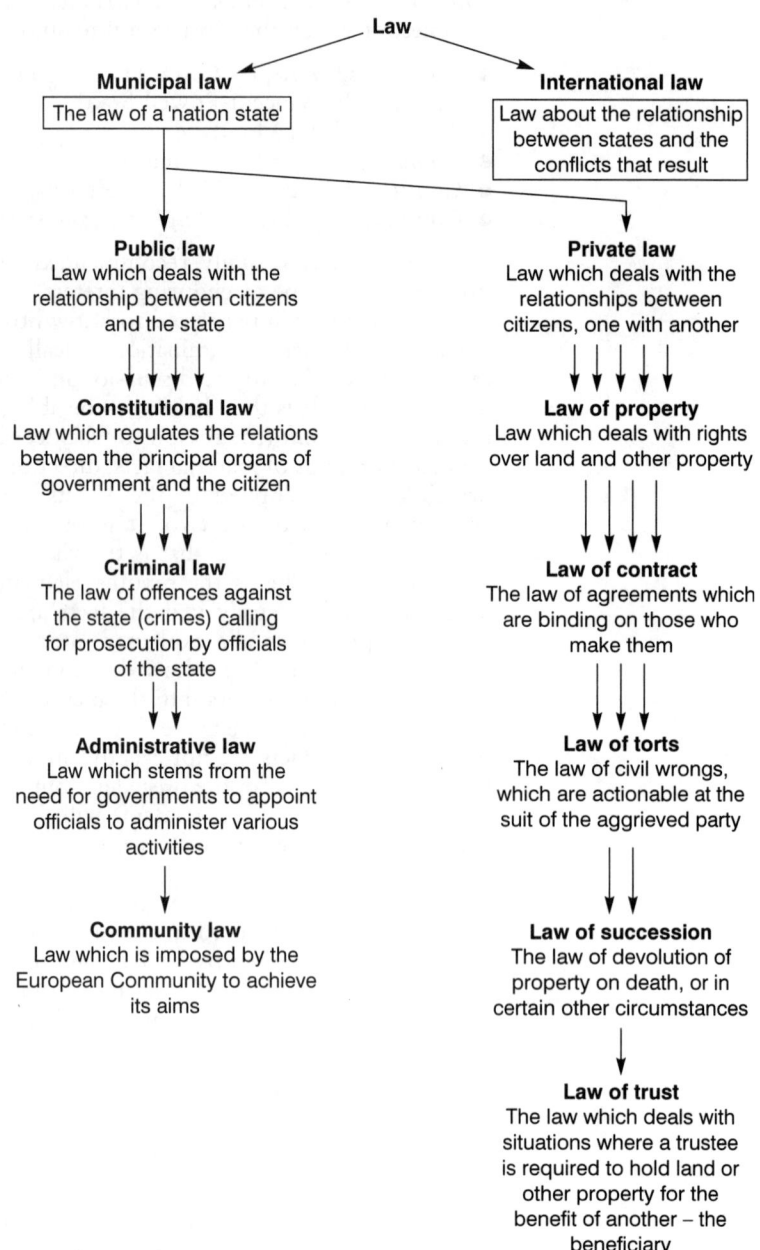

Figure 1.1 The branches of the law

Elements of English law

the general principles of law recognized by civilized nations, and internationally recognized customs, international conventions or treaties, decisions of the World Court and the teachings of the most highly qualified publicists of the various nations.

The other branch of international law, private international law, is sometimes called the 'conflict of laws'. It concerns the difficulties which arise when legal disputes occur between parties from different nations. Thus if an Englishman does business with Japan, which body of laws shall be used to decide any dispute, which courts shall have jurisdiction, to whom should appeals lie, how should damages be decided, in what currency, and how shall payment be compelled? These are difficult problems.

However, some reduction in these difficulties has been achieved by the *Contracts (Applicable Law) Act, 1990* which has incorporated three international conventions into United Kingdom law. These are the Rome Convention on Contractual Obligations where a choice between laws has to be exercised, the Luxembourg Convention (which brings Greece into the system and the Brussels Protocol, which gives the Court of Justice of the European Communities jurisdiction over disputes about the applicable law as laid down in the Rome Convention.

Full details of these conventions cannot be dealt with in this book, and those with a special interest should consult the Act of 1990, obtainable from Her Majesty's Stationery Office, by telephone on 0171 873 9090.

1.4.2 Municipal law

The term 'municipal' in common use refers to the administration of a city or town. Its use in law is wider – it refers to a nation state. It is thus the opposite of international law. Municipal law is the sum total of law that applies in a particular realm, whether constitutional, administrative, criminal or private. Hence all the branches of law mentioned in Figure 1.1 (except international law) are part of municipal law.

1.4.3 Public law and private law

Public law is primarily concerned with those cases in which the state is involved, as representing the public in general. Thus the public is interested in the prevention of crime, so that criminal law is actionable officially by the **prosecution** of **offenders**. The branches of public law are shown in the chart. Private law includes all branches of the law which involve disputes between citizens, where one individual has a complaint against the other. The various matters are said to be 'actionable at the suit of the aggrieved party'. The aggrieved party is called the **plaintiff** who **sues** the **defendant**.

1.4.4 Constitutional and administrative law

Constitutional law is that law which regulates the relations between the principal organs of government and the citizen. It deals with such topics as the monarch and the royal prerogative; the executive in the form of the Prime Minister and the Government; the relationship and functions of the House of Commons and the House of Lords; the position of the courts and the judiciary; the structure of local government; and the status of the police and the armed forces. An understanding of constitutional law enables citizens to appreciate their rights, e.g. freedom of the person, freedom of property, freedom of expression and freedom to hold meetings, processions, etc.

There is no exact demarcation between constitutional law and administrative law, as both are concerned with the exercise and control of governmental powers. While the former is concerned with the structure of the primary organs of government, the latter is concerned with the functioning of official agencies providing various services.

Since most branches of public law involve penalties at one stage or another, which thus involve the prosecution of offenders, we may say that criminal law is an extensive body of law brought into effect wherever there is a breach of public law. By contrast, private law is often spoken of as civil law, because it is available to the general public, civilians, rather than to the authorities.

There are certain basic differences between the two. **Criminal law** is the concern of the state, and a criminal case is normally brought by the state – or rather the police as the agents of the state – against an individual. The case is reported as *R. v. Bloggs* (the surname of the accused). R. stands for *Rex* or *Regina*, in Latin, meaning 'the King' or 'the Queen'. However, in respect of certain crimes, e.g. malicious prosecution or false imprisonment, any member of the public can commence criminal proceedings. **Civil law** is concerned with regulating the relationships of an individual with other individuals and comprises contract law, tort, the law of property and succession, family law, etc. The cases are reported as *Smith v. Bloggs*, Smith being the surname of the plaintiff and Bloggs the surname of the defendant.

It is wrong to confuse criminal and civil terms. One individual does not prosecute another for breach of contract or some other civil matter. 'Prosecution' is a term used in criminal law. The most famous example of confusion is the 'wooden lie' – a notice reading 'Trespassers will be prosecuted'. Since trespass where no damage is done is nearly always a civil matter between private citizens, it is incorrect to say 'prosecuted'. The good law student feels an uncontrollable impulse to amend such a notice to read 'Trespassers will *not* be prosecuted – but they will be sued'.

Lastly, a successful party in a civil case is awarded monetary compensation called **damages**. Other remedies in the form of **injunctions** or an order of **specific performance** are also available. In a criminal case the **accused**, if found guilty, is fined, or imprisoned according to the penalties laid down for the offence in question.

1.5 The sources of English law

Every legal system has its roots, the original sources from which authority is drawn. Sometimes these will only go back as far as some revolutionary overthrow of a previous social order. For example, there cannot be much of Tsarist law which is of influence in Russian society today. Other revolutions have been less complete. American law still has its roots in English law despite the Declaration of Independence, and the law of England was not greatly changed by the Civil War of 1649 except in the field of constitutional law.

The sources of English business law may be listed as follows:

- the ancient custom of the realm
- common law
- equity
- the law merchant
- statute law
- European Community law
- books of authority
- other sources

A short account of each of these is desirable.

1.5.1 Ancient custom of the realm

Before the Norman Conquest in 1066 Saxon England was ruled by kings whose power was based on their acceptability to the broad democratic assembly of a tribal society. Every man could speak at the tribal gathering, though in practice a *witenagemot* (meeting of wise men) acted as a parliament. England at that time was divided into various tribal areas such as Mercia, Kent, Wessex and so on. Each tribal area had its own laws based on the original customs of the settlers in question. There were three distinct legal systems applying to different areas of England: the 'Dane law' applied in the coastal areas of northern and north-eastern England; 'Mercian law' applied around the Midlands; and the 'Wessex law' applied in the south and west of England.

The influence of 'ancient custom of the realm' is not great today, but it is still important in one or two areas of law. In particular, in the law of carriage the concept of the 'common carrier of goods' is still important. Carriage is a very ancient activity and inevitably takes the carrier over the hills and far away with our property. In such circumstances we cannot possibly know what is happening to our goods, and ancient custom held that the carrier was liable for every loss that occurred, whether it was his fault or not. He is said to be like 'an insurer of the goods'. It is true that later the common law developed certain exceptions to this rule, called the 'common law exceptions'. These included Act of God, Act of the King's (or Queen's) enemies, fault of the consignor, fraud of the consignor and inherent vice. If a carrier proved that the loss was due to one of these causes he could escape liability (see Chapter 16).

The Norman kings gradually displaced ancient custom of the realm by a system known as 'common law'. The trouble with ancient custom was that it was not a national system of law, since it depended on the traditions and customs of tribal peoples with different ethnic backgrounds, who were now to be welded into one nation by the Norman nobility who had seized control. The process, which is explained under (b) below, was virtually completed by AD 1189. This year became known as the 'limit of legal memory'. After that date all was clear, recorded and remembered; before that date all was vague and uncertain, because no national system of law prevailed. This period is known as 'time immemorial', a time so ancient that it is beyond memory or record. If you wish to establish that you do something by ancient custom of the realm (for example, walk along a footpath from A to B) you should really prove that your great, great, grandfathers did it before AD 1189. In practice you only need to prove that people have been doing it for as long as anyone can remember. This establishes a 'presumption of antiquity' which shifts the 'burden of proof' to the person who seeks to deny you this ancient right. It is up to this person to prove that the right was not exercised before AD 1189. The case of *Mercer v. Denne (1905)* illustrates the point.

Mercer v. Denne (1905)
D owned part of a beach where local fishermen had for at least 70 years dried their nets. D wished to build houses on the land, but was prevented, since the presumption of antiquity could not be rebutted by proof that the right was not exercised before AD 1189.

To conclude, we may say that custom is in one sense the principal source of English law since it was the original source of common law, and gave it its broad democratic basis which is rather different from foreign, authoritarian, codes of law.

1.5.2 Common law

The mechanism used by the Norman kings to replace ancient custom of the realm by a system of law common to the whole country was the system of assizes, which was only finally abandoned in 1971. The king would appoint judges (originally called 'itinerant justices in Eyre') who travelled round the country, holding sittings (*assises*) whose function was to hear and settle any cases waiting to be tried in the county towns. In so doing they were made aware of many local customs, some of which were better than others. By a process of supporting good customs and rejecting bad customs the general level of law was improved. By making the decisions of judges binding upon other judges a good custom supported in one assizes was bound to be followed if a similar case arose in another area. As a result a 'common law' was formulated and established throughout the country, and inconsistencies between the law in one locality and the law in another locality were overcome. Common law therefore means the law common to all areas of England and Wales. Later it was also applied in Northern Ireland to a very considerable extent, but Scotland has its own, largely distinct, law. The common law is still a vital element in English law today, but it soon became clear that it was not entirely satisfactory. The chief difficulties were as follows:

(a) Shortage of writs

Action was commenced by the issue of a royal writ – a paper on which one of the more common complaints was written. The claim was required to be stated in an acceptable manner, called the 'form of action'. The writ called on the sheriff to summon a jury to hear the case. The variety of complaints for which an action could be commenced was not large and many cases could not be brought to trial at all because a writ of the type required was not available. For example, there were no writs about negligence in the early days.

(b) Inadequacy of money damages

Another defect in the common law was its view that money satisfies all wrongs. The only remedy at common law was, and is, money damages. Although compensation is often all that is required it does not answer every case. Thus if my neighbour's workshop produces unpleasant smells which ruin my enjoyment of my property, it is of no help to me to receive money as compensation. I want him to stop making the unpleasant smells. This requires some sort of court order, an **injunction** to restrain him from continuing the process that is a nuisance.

(c) Equality before the law

The third defect of common law was the pressure that could be exerted by high officials on the legal system. At a time when some barons and earls were as powerful as the king it was often difficult to secure justice against people in high places. Equality before the law is a basic principle of justice, but some people proved to be 'more equal than others' (to use George Orwell's phrase).

The solution was found to lie in bringing such cases before a special court, the Court of Chancery, where equity (Latin *aequitas* = fair) could be achieved.

1.5.3 Equity

If law is to be respected, and trusted, it must be fair. Complaints about the defects in the common law were made to the king, who appointed the Lord Chancellor to deal with them. The word 'chancel' refers to a place in a church closest to the altar. The chancellor was not only the king's legal adviser and right-hand man, but also his spiritual adviser. The link between justice and religion was closer in those days, and since all were equal in the eyes of God, equity in law was also deemed to be a religious affair. Equity (principles of fairness, or natural justice) guided successive chancellors in their decisions, and the sum total of their legal decisions over the years is spoken of in law as 'equity'. The problems of the common law referred to above were solved by the removal of cases where common law was inadequate to a special, powerful court in London, called the Court of Chancery. How did the Court of Chancery solve the three problems outlined above?

First, the chancellor was second only to the king, and could command the appearance in court of even the highest nobles. They could not influence his decisions or avoid the damages or fines he imposed.

Second, the problem of a shortage of writs was overcome by the chancellor ordering new types of writ as required. It is true that this process eventually caused trouble, because litigants soon found that justice could be obtained more easily in London than at their local courts. The nobles therefore lost the lucrative business carried on in their own courts and forced the king to stop the creation of further writs in an enactment called the Provisions of Oxford (1258). This was later modified in the Statute of Westminster II, 1285, which declared that new writs could be developed if they were similar to writs in existence already. This led to a slow growth in the type of writs, since new writs were acceptable only if they could be proved to be similar to writs already in existence.

Finally, the Court of Chancery solved the problem of the inadequacy of money damages by introducing new 'equity' remedies. The chief of these were the **injunction**, to restrain a defendant from continuing the action complained of by the plaintiff, and **specific performance**. This required the defendant to do what he had promised to do.

Other important contributions made by equity to English law involved the creation of new rights where none had existed before. For example, the whole law of trusts owes its existence to the willingness of equity to recognize and enforce the rights of a beneficiary under a trust. Equity also introduced new procedures which enabled witnesses to be subpoenaed, to compel their attendance at court. Another important development was the process known as 'discovery of documents' which enables a party to a case to inspect the relevant documents in the possession of the other party.

Hence there was a time during the development of English law when there were two parallel sets of laws, one under equity and the other under common law. The Court of Chancery administered equity while the other courts, called the Common Law Courts, administered common law. Where two systems of law exist there is bound to be a conflict sooner or later. These conflicts caused delays, particularly in the Court of Chancery – which was overloaded with work anyway – and eventually it became a byword for slowness and procrastination. The major conflict between common law and equity was resolved in 1616, in the Earl of Oxford's case, with the decision that where there was a conflict between the two, equity should prevail. This rule was given a formal, statutory basis in the *Judicature Acts, 1873–5*. These acts also empowered all courts to give both common law and equity decisions in cases coming before them. The separation between the courts, which had lasted more than five hundred years, was ended. All courts now give appropriate remedies: the common law remedy of money damages if this is adequate for the case in hand; if not, the equitable remedies of injunctions, specific performance, etc. The system of courts established in

1873–5 progressively developed into the present system of courts (see Chapter 2) and the availability of both types of remedy in all courts continues unchanged.

1.5.4 The law merchant

Trade is older than nationality. For thousands of years ships have plied the oceans and kings have welcomed merchants, and accorded them rights of passage and exemption from local taxes. From the earliest times a sophisticated cosmopolitan crowd of merchants moved around the known world, dealing with one another in ways which were not fettered by legal concepts imposed upon them. Their commercial principles such as 'my word is my bond', 'bethink you of my poor honesty' and 'goodwill' had evolved commercial practices of the greatest importance today: freedom of contract; freedom to transfer property; assignability and negotiability; the seal; stoppage in transit; the bill of exchange; the charterparty; general average – these are almost as old as time.

The law's delay was anathema to the early merchants, who settled cases in their own courts quickly. These were often based in ports, like Lubeck in the Baltic:

*What can you want more
Than the old Lubeck law*

goes on old German saying. In ports cases were often settled 'between the tides', while in the 'Piepowder courts' at the inland fairs disputes were settled on the last day of the fair. The origin of this name has been suggested as 'dusty feet – *pieds poudreux*'. The judges were senior members of the merchant community, and since disputes were frequently between local people and the foreign merchants it was usual to have equal numbers of each in the panel who settled cases.

Merchant law was cosmopolitan and uniform wherever trade was conducted. Its privileged system was bound to conflict with the newer concept of a 'nation state' ruled by an autocratic king imposing law from above upon the citizens of his state. The problem was to reconcile the 'law merchant' with the 'common law' of the country, and thus bring the merchants under control without killing the goose that laid the golden eggs.

In England the solution was found in the principle that 'the courts will always uphold the reasonable expectations of businessmen'. This principle is sound because it not only supports the existing practices of merchants, but also covers any sensible developments which may be devised. Thus in the City of London, over the years, new markets have been established in all sorts of commodities and monetary instruments, without any legislative activity. If a market is needed in Sterling Certificates of Deposit, or palm oil, or crude oil, etc., it is only necessary for a body of interested persons to come together, lay down agreed guidelines and start to quote prices, for the market to be established and have the full backing of the law. To the extent that it is reasonable the law will uphold the commercial practices of the merchants.

The law merchant, which during the Middle Ages had become the basis for an expanding commerce throughout the Mediterranean, the Atlantic seaboard and the Baltic, became in the next three hundred years an integral part of the law of the separate great trading nations – the English, the French, the Dutch, the Spanish and the Portuguese. In England, for example, by the mid-eighteenth century the Common Law Courts had absorbed almost all the jurisdiction of the local courts merchant, with the exception of maritime law and prize law which was applied in the Maritime Courts. Eventually the whole area of law relating to merchants and traders was absorbed into the common law of England. In the process of absorption by national laws the law merchant lost to some extent its cosmopolitan nature, but in the fields where a conflict of laws between national legal systems was inevitable – in carriage by sea, in international trade, in marine insurance, etc. – there were sufficient threads remaining to settle disputes in peace time, and preserve reasonable behaviour in times of war. Nations had still to behave reasonably if trade was to prosper.

1.5.5 Statute law

In a sovereign state the fountain of law is the sovereign body which promulgates laws which it imposes upon and enforces among the citizens. In the UK this sovereign body is 'the Queen in Parliament', its promulgations are called Acts of Parliament, or Statutes, and they are the major source of all new law today. Acts of Parliament alone can overthrow custom, the decisions of judges, the rules of merchants, earlier Acts of Parliament, etc. One of their most common uses today is to tidy up, or codify, the law when it has become excessively complicated and beset by contradictory decisions over the years or abused by clever businessmen and their legal advisers.

Some celebrated statutes, such as the *Partnership Act, 1890*, the *Bills of Exchange Act, 1882*, and the *Sale of Goods Act, 1893* (now re-enacted as the *Sale of Goods Act, 1979*), are models of what a statute should be – carefully worded to eliminate ambiguity. Students should read the proceedings of the parliamentary committees on legislation to see the quality of the discussion and the detailed consideration given to a bill in its 'committee stage'. We certainly owe much to Members of Parliament who devote months of their time to closing loopholes. One Member of Parliament recently said: 'The Right Honourable Member shares with me the privilege of having debated three major companies bills in five years. It is the sort of exercise for which campaign medals are given in other fields.'

Legislation is the major source of new law. Legislation takes the form of an Act of Parliament, which is a printed document. It represents the will of the sovereign Parliament. Sovereignty of Parliament implies that Parliament can make or unmake any laws, and no person or body has a right to override or set aside an Act of Parliament. The courts must give effect to, and the law enforcement agencies must enforce, legislation. The term 'Parliament' comprises the Queen, the House of Lords and the House of Commons. For a measure that has been drafted (normally called a 'bill') to become an Act of Parliament it must have the approval of the three distinct elements that make up Parliament. Within the legislative process, the House of Commons is the dominant House while the powers of the House of Lords have been severely curtailed as a result of the *Parliament Acts, 1911* and *1949*. The monarch's position in Parliament has long been a formality and Royal Assent has not been refused since the reign of Queen Anne in 1707.

A statute can displace any previous piece of law, repeal former statutes or parts of statutes, impose new rules and lay down principles which will guide judges in the future. It comes into effect on a particular date, after which time businessmen must comply with its rules. Many Acts empower officials at a variety of levels to make **'Orders'** which have statutory effect since their authority is drawn from the Act of Parliament. Some of these are designed to deal with emergencies – like the prohibition of cattle movements in an outbreak of foot-and-mouth disease. Others are not emergency measures, and have time to 'lie upon the table' at the House of Commons for MPs to consider them, and object to them if necessary. This vast body of rules created by subordinate bodies under specific powers delegated to them by the sovereign Parliament are described as **delegated legislation**. Delegated legislation can take the form of:

(a) Orders in Council

Under the *Emergency Powers Act, 1920*, the state can in specified circumstances proclaim a state of emergency and by Order in Council issue rules and regulations to counter the emergency.

(b) Statutory instruments

Most delegated legislation is made in the form of statutory instruments. For example, power is delegated to Ministers of the Crown to make regulations for specific purposes. The paper containing this law is called a statutory instrument and about 2000 of the more important ones are published every year.

(c) Bye-laws

Parliament delegates authority to local authorities and other public bodies to make bye-laws over their respective areas.

The interpretation of statutes

One aspect of statute law that should be mentioned is the need on occasions to interpret the statute, and decide what Parliament actually did enact. If an Act has gone through all its stages in both Houses of Parliament and has been subjected to rigorous line by line examination it should be fairly free from error. By contrast where the 'guillotine' has been applied, the unexamined part of the bill may pass into law full of errors. The 'guillotine' procedure is one used when the opposition is deliberately delaying a bill of which it disapproves. A set time is allowed for further discussion, after which the 'guillotine' cuts off all discussion and the bill passes into law.

There are a number of rules used by the judges when seeking to discover what Parliament meant by the words enacted. The first, and very ancient, rule has always been that the judges must find the true meaning of the document within its four corners, for that is what Parliament has passed, to which the Queen has given the royal assent. The judges have never been free to consult other records, for example Hansard, to clarify their ideas by re-reading the Parliamentary record – what the Houses of Parliament really thought at the time. However this rule has been recently overturned in a celebrated case, *Pepper v. Hart and Others (1992) STC 898*, which is referred to below.

Most Acts of Parliament have an 'Intepretation' section where many of the terms used in the Act are explained. Such assistance is very welcome to the judges. For example the *Companies Act, 1985* has one part that reads: '"Officer" in relation to a body corporate includes a director, a manager or the secretary.'

So where a section says, 'Every officer in default of this shall be liable to a fine of £5000 or imprisonment for up to six months' it will not be possible for them to blame the chief clerk for the error and let him go to prison. The chief clerk is not an officer of the company.

A second, more general, Act is the *Interpretation Act, 1978*. This contains further guidance to their lordships. One famous part of this Act reads:

In any Act, unless a contrary intention appears –
(a) Words importing the masculine gender include the feminine;
(b) words importing the feminine gender include the masculine;

(c) *words in the singular include the plural, and words in the plural include the singular.*

The law does not distinguish between the sexes, who have equal rights, and laws apply to every individual and to all groups.

A third rule is **the literal rule**, which says that words have their ordinary dictionary meaning. This is further supported by the **'ejusdem generis' rule**, which means 'of the same class or genus'. Thus if a general word – such as pet – has been used in an Act about cats, dogs, white mice, hamsters and gerbils we know that the general word is referring to small domestic pets. If a case arises where a citizen is claiming the right to play with his pet lion, pet tiger or pet elephant on the back lawn the court will rule that these animals are not 'pets' under the Act, for they are not of the same genus as the small pets referred to in the Act.

The fourth rule is called **the golden rule**. This rule says that Parliament never intends to enact a manifest absurdity, and if the words used amount to an absurdity the court will modify the wording just enough to avoid the absurdity, but no further. In one case the *Administration of Estate Act, 1925* said that the estate of a dead person should be shared among that person's 'issue'. The deceased only had one child, but that child had murdered her mother. Should she be allowed to inherit the wealth left by the person she had murdered? Clearly it would be a manifest absurdity, and Parliament did not intend it. Had the deceased person left other bequests they would have been allowed, for the failure to inherit of the person at fault would not affect the will as far as other parties were concerned. The Act is modified just enough to stop the absurdity, but not so much as to declare the other parts of the will invalid.

The mischief rule is a rule which allows the judges to use their discretion in a wider way than the 'golden rule' permits. It was laid down in 'Heydon's case', in 1584. It rules that in cases where Parliament has not made itself clear, the judges should follow a train of thought as follows:

- What was the common law on the matter in hand before the Act was passed?
- What was the mischief in the common law which Parliament was seeking to redress by passing the act?
- What is the true remedy? Then we must interpret the Act in such a way that we defeat the mischief and advance the remedy.

In following this chain of enquiry the rules are:

- Look at the whole Act, because only this will enable us to find Parliament's true intention.
- Every Act has a preamble which outlines the intentions of Parliament in passing the Act, so this may help us decide Parliament's true intention.
- Marginal headings, which tell the reader what is contained in a particular section, are inserted by civil servants who draft legislation and get it into final form for publication. They are not really enacted by Parliament, and are therefore disregarded.
- Punctuation varies from person to person, and is not to be regarded, because once again it is often inserted by civil servants, not Parliament.

The mischief rule is an attempt to find out what Parliament thought, but only by looking within the four corners of the Act as passed. The courts could not refer to Hansard to read the wider background, but the important case of *Pepper (Inspector of Taxes) v. Hart and Others* has changed the rule. The importance of the change can be seen by the fact that the House of Lords appointed seven judges to hear the case. It concerned the interpretation of Section 156 of the *Income and Corporation Taxes Act, 1988*, which attempted to tax employees on the fringe benefits arising from their employment. This affected thousands of people often in not very well paid jobs, whose fringe benefits as part of the employment package made their jobs worthwhile. Hart, named in the citation, for example was a teacher at a private school, who was allowed to send his own children to the school at a nominal rate (enough to cover the extra cost to the employer of providing food, educational materials, etc.). Pepper, the tax inspector, argued that the 'cost to the employer – less any amount paid by the employee' at which the fringe benefit was to be valued for tax purposes, should include a fair proportion of the general overhead expenses, such as salaries, heating and lighting, etc. Since these expenses would have to be borne by the employer anyway Hart argued that they were not 'extra expenses of the employer' and should not be included as his income. To adopt Pepper's line would produce some strange anomalies. Airlines frequently make spare seats available to employees and their families, for a much smaller charge than the price charged to passengers. Suppose an employee takes a seat on a scheduled flight that has no paying passenger. Is the benefit to the employee to include a proportion of the overhead of the whole organization?

Where does Hansard come into this picture? It revealed that the Financial Secretary to the Treasury, in the debate on this point, had clearly stated that the intention of the Treasury was to tax only on the basis of the marginal cost to the employer. The clause in the bill which attempted to charge such benefits at the price paid by the ordinary public was actually withdrawn during the debate under pressure from MPs. If a Minister of the Crown actually gave Parliament an assurance on some point that was worrying it, should a lesser person in the organization, at a later date, be able to vary the meaning? The House of Lords thought not. If the Treasury wants to change the rule, and reinstate the original clause let it bring in amending legislation and hear Parliament's views a second time.

The question of whether the courts should be allowed to consider Hansard when resolving a difficulty in the interpretation of a statute goes back to the *Bill of Rights, 1689*. The Bill of Rights was the set of rules which finally established the sovereignty of Parliament over the Crown. It was passed after James II had been driven from the throne and replaced by the joint rulers, William of Orange and Mary. Article 9 of the Bill of Rights says 'The freedom of speech and debates or proceedings in Parliament ought not to be impeached or questioned in any Court or place out of Parliament.' The question is whether reference to Hansard by their Lordships to elucidate what Parliament actually intended in enacting a statute really does question what was said. To discover what was said is not necessarily to express an opinion on it. In *Pepper v. Hart* the Financial Secretary to the Treasury clearly stated that he did not envisage the Act as having the effect which Pepper claimed it had. Will justice be served if this fact is withheld from the panel seeking to know what Parliament did intend? Lord Browne-Wilkinson said he hoped that the Commons would appreciate that the House of Lords was not seeking to impeach its privileges. The right to refer to Hansard would only be used in very special circumstances, where the Act in question was ambiguous, or the House appeared to have enacted a manifest absurdity. It is clearly helpful in interpreting a statute to know how the official responsible for getting the piece of legislation through the procedures of the Houses of Parliament envisaged it would work.

1.5.6 European Community law

By the Treaty of Accession dated 22 January 1972, the UK became a member of the European Community with effect from 1 January 1973. To give legal effect to community law in the UK, the *European Communities Act, 1972*, was passed. By accession to the Treaty of Rome and other specialist treaties, member states have limited their sovereign rights and created a body of law which binds their nationals and themselves. Later the name 'European Community' was changed to European Union (EU) and we now speak of 'European Union law' rather than European Community law. European Union law consists of:

(a) The treaties

The principal sources of Community law are the treaties which established the three Communities, i.e. the European Coal and Steel Community (1951), the European Economic Community (1957) (the treaty known as the Treaty of Rome) and the European Atomic Energy Community (1957). A later treaty, the Maastricht Treaty bound the members to extend their mutual links into a tighter relationship, and at this point the name European Union came into use. These treaties are binding on member states and Community institutions and in certain circumstances they may create rights for individuals which may be enforced in national courts.

(b) Regulations

These are binding in all member states without requiring any implementation or adoption by the national parliament. They apply directly, and prevail over national law. They can create rights enforceable by individuals in national courts.

(c) Directives

Although a directive is binding, it leaves member states a choice of the method by which the result required by the directive must be achieved. This can be done by an Act of Parliament or delegated legislation. In certain circumstances a directive can create rights for individuals enforceable in national courts.

(d) Decisions

A decision is binding in its entirety upon those to whom it is addressed whether it be member states, individuals or companies.

Decisions of the Court of Justice of the Communities are binding on the highest courts in member nations, so that the House of Lords must accept a European Court decision as binding – for example, as to the meaning of a clause in the Treaty of Rome.

(e) The European Communities (Amendment) Act, 1986

This Act introduced certain changes in the law-making procedures of the European Union. It embodied into English law the Single European Act. This Act amended the Treaty of Rome in several important ways. First a new Article 8A formed the basis of the programme to complete the internal market in the Community. In 1992 the European Market became a single market and tariff barriers between member nations came down completely leaving a very competitive atmosphere within the Community. To facilitate these developments there was an increased use of 'decisions' (see (d) above) based on a qualified majority (Article 100A) although the present need for unanimity was not entirely abandoned. There was also a new need for these measures to be agreed by the European Parliament – whereas previously there was only a need to consult Parliament. The intention was to raise the status of the Parliament and give it more of a 'federal' impact. The early results of this second requirement were not rosy, because more than 100 measures were held up by disagreement in the Parliament. The Single European Act provided that any measure amended or rejected by Parliament required unanimous approval of the Council of Ministers, which created a serious backlog in the implementation of some of these directives – even though a very tight timetable (of one month only) is in theory attached to the reconsideration of the directive.

One final point about the Single European Act was that it established the **Court of First Instance** to ease the workload of the European Court of Justice. Its jurisdiction covers competition cases, actions for damages and EU staff cases. These are the sorts of cases which in any national system of law would not require the full panoply of the highest court in the land, but would be handled at lower levels. The court has 15 members, appointed by common agreement of the member states, each for a six year period, which is renewable.

(f) The Maastricht Treaty

This treaty was agreed in December 1991 and finally ratified in 1993. It expands the areas of agreement in the original Treaty of Rome to cover economic and monetary union and defence. The logic of economic and monetary union has been to some extent in conflict with established notions of the 'nation state' and at the centre of the conflict is the concept of **subsidiarity**. This concept holds that regulations of various sorts should not necessarily be imposed by the Commission or the Council from above, but should be handled so far as is possible by organizations lower down in the hierarchy of institutions (i.e. by the member states). If arrangements can be implemented at national level rather than a European Union level they will be implemented more easily, and arouse less antagonism because they will be introduced in a way which the 'local' populations are used to. The implementation of all EU rules from above would mean the appointment of more bureaucrats in Brussels.

The British Government felt so strongly about the importance of subsidiarity that it negotiated 'opt-outs' on two matters. These give it the right to decide at a later date whether it will join the Economic and Monetary Union, with a single European currency based on the ECU. It will also not at present implement the Social Charter, which agrees certain minimum social standards to be achieved by member states, using qualified majority voting for some matters.

The system of qualified majority voting at the time of writing (December 1994) gives the 12 nations differing weights in voting procedures. These are:

Country	*Number of votes*
France	10
Germany	10
Italy	10
United Kingdom	10
Spain	8
Belgium	5
Greece	5
Netherlands	5
Portugal	5
Denmark	3
Ireland	3
Luxembourg	2
	76

Elements of English law

A total of 54 votes is required out of 76 for a proposal to be passed by a qualified majority. Once passed it is binding on all member states, and consequently the opt-outs arranged by the United Kingdom are non-normal arrangements. The Social Charter is concerned with equal opportunities for men and women at work, health and safety, working conditions and workers' rights.

The movement to Economic and Monetary Union has been set to a timetable which envisages a full union (with or without the United Kingdom) by 1 January 1999. The prerequisites are that economies should converge along certain lines. These are:

- Stable prices (i.e. inflation under reasonable control).
- Public debt not more than 60 per cent of gross domestic product.
- Currency remaining within the margins set by the European monetary system (which the UK left) for at least 2 years.
- Interest rates over previous 12 months no higher than 2 per cent above the three member states with the lowest interest rates.

The UK opt-out reserves the UK's right to consult its government and Parliament before deciding whether to proceed, while the Danish government will need a referendum before finally joining the Economic and Monetary Union.

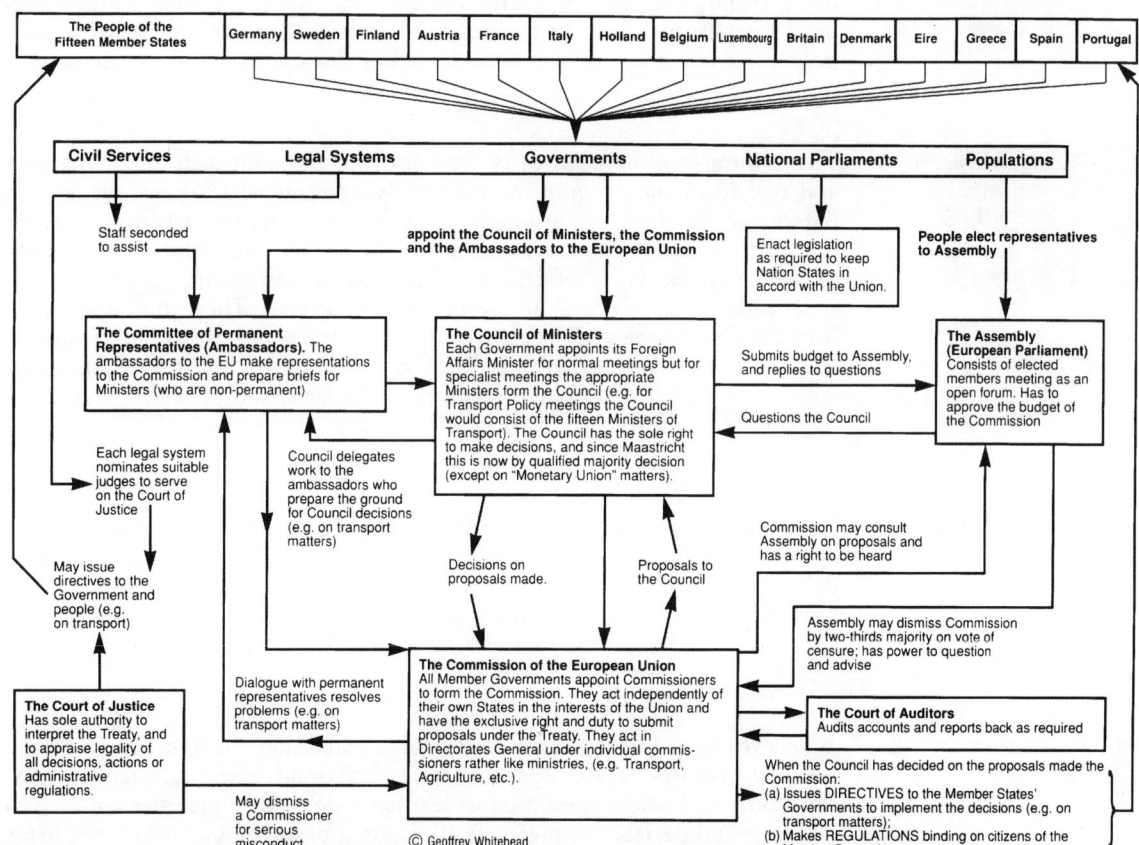

Figure 1.2 The major institutions of the European Union (© Geoffrey Whitehead)

Figure 1.2 shows the major institutions of the European Union. They are described briefly below. There are six of them:

- the Council of Ministers
- the Commission
- the European Parliament
- the Court of Justice
- the Committee of Permanent Representatives
- the Court of Auditors.

Their organization and functions are as follows:

(a) The Council of Ministers

This consists of one Minister from each of the member states. Generally the Foreign Minister is regarded as the appropriate minister, but on special occasions when particular policies are under discussion the Minister for the Department concerned – say fuel and power, or agriculture – would represent his country. Presidency of the Council is taken in turn for six-monthly periods. The Council takes all basic decisions on European Union policy, and is empowered to pass minor matters with a simple majority. On major matters a system of weighted voting is used, and a qualified majority is necessary. The original weighting, before Maastricht, gave four votes to major powers, two votes to lesser powers and one vote to very small powers like Luxembourg. In practice the Council has usually wrestled with matters until unanimity is reached, since, particularly on new and controversial policies, it is not deemed wise to force policies upon unwilling partners.

(b) The Commission

The Commission consists of two commissioners from each major member and one from smaller powers, chosen by agreement. They are pledged to independence of the governments of their countries, and act in accordance with the powers laid down in the Treaty of Rome. They coordinate activity in particular fields, considering issues from a community point of view independent of national interests or aspirations. Their function is to formulate proposals for decision by the Council of Ministers and to supply information to, and answers to questions from, the European Parliament. They have a staff of EU civil servants in Brussels, and provide the day-to-day administration of the Union.

(c) The European Parliament

In June 1979 the first elections were held to the European Parliament. There are 410 members of this directly elected Parliament. Their function is to debate all matters of Union policy, to question both the Commission and the Council of Ministers and to supervise the Community budget. It can compel the Commission to resign en bloc by a two-thirds majority.

(d) The Court of Justice

Whenever rules and regulations are promulgated they must inevitably be the cause of disputes between parties favourably or adversely affected. It is for the Court of Justice, composed of learned judges from member nations, to interpret and declare the meaning of disputed passages. Governments, firms and individuals as well as the Union authorities have a right of appeal to the Court of Justice if they are aggrieved by the application of any EU rule.

(e) The Committee of Permanent Representatives

This consists of the 15 ambassadors to the Union from the member countries. Their function is to act as permanent watchdogs on behalf of the Foreign Secretaries (or other Departmental Ministers forming the Council of Ministers). The latter are essentially part-time and rely on the permanent representatives to prepare briefs, advise on procedures, etc. This body – Coreper, the French abbreviation – has proved very effective in getting practical agreement on all sorts of detailed matters and then having them ratified by the Council of Ministers without difficulty. A proposal to make these representatives of greater importance is being aired at the moment.

(e) The Court of Auditors

Set up as part of the 'Single European Act' the Court of Auditors has the duty of detecting financial malpractices in the European Union, where large sums of money are allocated daily to a whole range of desirable social and economic projects.

There are one or two other EU institutions; the Court of First Instance (referred to above) and the European Investment Bank, which is based in London.

The European law and the general principles of law

Article 215 of the Treaty recognizes that Community law consists in part of 'the general principles common to the laws of member states'. These general principles are clearly a rather mixed bag, and presumably cases might arise where some dispute as to the relevant general principle occurred. Presumably in a case affecting a particular nation, or citizen of a particular nation, the principles of law observed in that country would have greater force.

Article 164 requires the Court of Justice to ensure that 'in the interpretation and application of this Treaty the law is observed'. The members of the court therefore have all the legal traditions of the member states to draw upon, as well as the rulings of the European Court itself, as they develop over the years.

Some important features of European Union law are as follows:

(a) Primacy

EU law takes precedence over national law in any situation where a conflict appears to arise. In deciding to set up a Community (now advanced to a Union) of their nations, the member states recognized that they had limited their sovereign rights to a limited extent and had created a body of law common to all member states which binds both the states themselves and the nationals who are citizens of their states. Although that law amounts only to a treaty, or a series of treaties, and the various interpretations of the treaties developed by the Court of Justice, it nevertheless overrides all national laws and cannot be modified in an individual state without appearing to cast doubt on the validity of the Union itself.

Section 2.1 of the *European Communities Act, 1972* states:

> *All such rights, powers, liabilities, obligations and restrictions from time to time created by, or arising under the Treaties ... are without further enactment to be given legal affect ... and be enforced, allowed and followed accordingly...*

(b) Direct application

The majority of EU laws are directly applicable to all states, institutions and individuals, from the moment they are promulgated as regulations, decisions or directives. They do not require any national legislation to bring them into effect (Article 189). This also applies to provisions of the treaties, provided they are clear, precise, unconditional and self-contained (that is they do not call for national Parliaments to take some action before they can be implemented).

1.5.7 Books of authority

In general, books of authority are not very influential in English law, but some celebrated ones in the past, written by eminent judges, have been widely quoted in the courts. More recently the development of university departments of law has raised the standing of books of authority and some major textbooks are quoted in the courts, or counsel may ask the judge's permission to adopt the arguments in the presentation of their client's case.

1.5.8 Other sources

English law differs greatly from **Roman law**, which is very influential on the Continent of Europe though now largely replaced by modern codes of law developed from the Napoleonic Code. The need to harmonize law under the EU is likely to bring some further Roman influences. **Canon law** is largely ecclesiastical law, but the close link between the Church (in those days a Roman Catholic Church) and the Court of Chancery meant that canon law influenced equity decisions (since equity was to do with morality as much as legality). **Foreign law** can also be an important influence, especially if it comes from a country which has a system of laws developed from English common law. Thus decisions of the US courts might be influential – persuasive precedents – though they cannot be binding. In certain conventions – for example, the Hamburg Rules developed by the United Nations Convention – judges are required to take account of decisions elsewhere. Article 3 of the Hamburg Rules of 1978 reads:

> *In the interpretation and application of the provisions of this Convention regard shall be had to its international character and to the need to promote uniformity.*

Clearly this requires judges to consider decisions of foreign courts in similar cases as persuasive precedents.

Test your knowledge

In this book each chapter ends with a test-yourself section, which acts both as a chapter summary and a revision test. Cover the page with a sheet of plain paper and uncover the first question. Try to answer it from your knowledge of the chapter. Lower the paper and read the answer to question 1. Then read question 2 and try to answer it, and so on.

Answers	Questions
	1 Define law.
1 Law is a body of rules for the guidance of human conduct which is imposed upon, and enforced among, the citizens of a given state.	2 What legal concept is implicit in the term 'imposed upon'?

Elements of English law

Answers	Questions
2 The concept of a sovereign body which alone can promulgate and enforce laws.	3 What body is 'sovereign' in the UK?
3 The Queen in Parliament.	4 Who enforces the law in the UK?
4 In criminal matters the police have powers of arrest. They pass the necessary papers to the Crown Prosecution Service which brings offenders before the judiciary. In civil matters plaintiffs sue the defendants and hearings are held at which defendants may appear to answer the plaintiff's complaint, before a judge.	5 What are the chief branches of public law?
5 Constitutional law, criminal law, administrative law and European Union law.	6 What are the chief branches of civil law?
6 Property law, contract law, tort, succession and trust.	7 What are the sources of English law?
7 (a) Ancient custom of the realm; (b) common law; (c) equity; (d) the law merchant; (e) statute law; (f) European Union law; (g) books of authority; (h) other sources, such as Roman law and canon law.	8 What is meant by 'time immemorial'?
8 A time so ancient that it is beyond memory and record. The year AD 1189 is set as the limit of legal memory.	9 What was *Mercer v. Denne* about?
9 It was a 1905 case in which Denne, who owned a beach on which he wished to build two houses was prevented from doing so because local fishermen proved that since time immemorial they had dried their nets on this piece of beach.	10 How was common law established?

24 Business Law

Answers	Questions
10 By a system of assizes in which judges travelled round the country trying cases according to local law, but overriding bad customs and supporting good ones. Since judges had to follow precedents from other courts a national 'common law' quickly developed.	11 What were the defects of common law?
11 (a) Money damages were the only remedy; (b) actions could only be commenced if a suitable writ was available; (c) privileged people could secure favourable treatment.	12 How did equity improve on the common law?
12 (a) By expanding the range of writs available; (b) by giving other remedies, especially injunctions and specific performance; (c) by the power of the chancellor, who could call even the highest people before the Court of Chancery.	13 How has European Union law affected English law?
13 It has imposed a body of law above national law which takes precedence over all national systems of law in the member states.	14 What is meant by subsidiarity?
14 That the implementation of European rules should be in the hands of the lowest possible level of administration, and not imposed from above by the Council of Ministers or the Commission.	15 What are the rules for interpreting statutes?
15 (a) The literal rule; (b) The ejusdem generis rule; (c) The golden rule; (d) The mischief rule	16 Go over the questions until you are sure of the answers. Then try some of the written questions in Appendix 1.

2 The courts of law

2.1 The structure of courts in the UK

A civilization depends on law and order for its existence. Justice does not depend solely on having a comprehensive set of laws; it also requires machinery for the administration and enforcement of the laws of the land. While the task of enforcing the laws falls primarily on the police and the Crown Prosecution Service, the question of interpreting and applying the laws is the concern of the courts. Hence the courts exist to uphold and interpret the law and undoubtedly occupy a central role in the legal system.

The present-day court system in England consists of a hierarchy of courts each having its own functions, and connected to the courts above and below it by a chain of responsibilities, duties and powers. The structure of the courts today is shown in Figure 2.1, and dates from two fairly recent Acts, the *Administration of Justice Act, 1970*, and the *Courts Act, 1971*. A more recent, major Act is the *Supreme Court Act, 1981*.

The court structure, which is one of the most complete systems in the world for the administration of justice, has developed into its present form as a result of many important changes in the past. These changes were the result of experience. Each of the courts in the hierarchy will be looked at individually from the point of view of such matters as the court's origin and history, its jurisdiction and internal organization.

2.2 The House of Lords

The House of Lords developed from the *Curia Regis* or King's Council, which was the effective governing body of the Norman and Plantagenet kings. As such it had legislative, administrative and judicial powers. These judicial powers were the highest in the land and persist today. The House of Lords is the superior court (except on certain European Community matters). It is the ultimate court of appeal for civil and criminal cases. Until the nineteenth century, an appeal to the House was considered as an appeal to the whole House but today there is a convention whereby lay peers may not participate in the judicial sittings of the House. Today the House of Lords sitting as the final court of appeal is distinct from the House of Lords in its legislative capacity. Because of a shortage of peers who had held high judicial office, the *Appellate Jurisdiction Act, 1876*, provided for the appointment of salaried life peers to hear appeals. The features of this Act were as follows:

- It provided for the appointment of two Lords of Appeal in Ordinary (Law Lords) who had held high judicial office in the UK, or had been practising barristers (or advocates in Scotland) for a period of 15 years.
- The Act declared that appeals should only be heard when at least three of the following were present: the Lord Chancellor, the Lords of Appeal in Ordinary and such peers as have held high judicial office in the UK. A quorum is therefore three.

26 Business Law

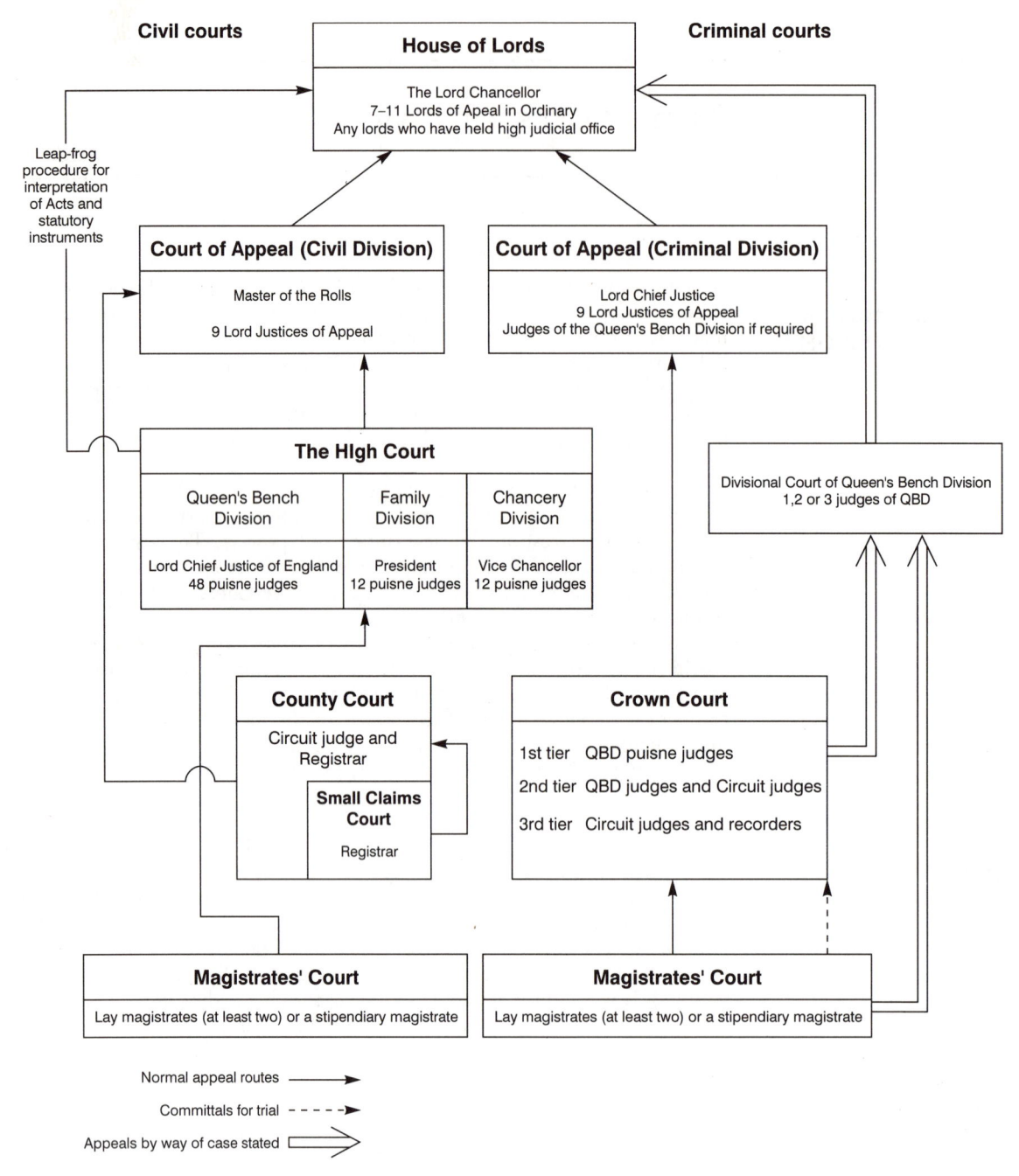

Figure 2.1 The court system

```
Civil courts                                              Criminal courts

                        House of Lords
                      The Lord Chancellor
                 7–11 Lords of Apeal in Ordinary
              Any lords who have held high judicial office

Leap-frog
procedure for
interpretation
of Acts and
statutory
instruments

   Court of Appeal (Civil Division)        Court of Appeal (Criminal Division)
        Master of the Rolls                      Lord Chief Justice
       9 Lord Justices of Appeal               9 Lord Justices of Appeal
                                       Judges of the Queen's Bench Division if required

                        The High Court

      Queen's Bench        Family         Chancery         Divisional Court of Queen's Bench Division
        Division          Division         Division              1,2 or 3 judges of QBD

   Lord Chief Justice of England   President      Vice Chancellor
        48 puisne judges        12 puisne judges  12 puisne judges

        County Court                            Crown Court
     Circuit judge and                 1st tier   QBD puisne judges
        Registrar                      2nd tier   QBD judges and Circuit judges
       Small Claims                    3rd tier   Circuit judges and recorders
          Court
         Registrar

     Magistrates' Court                    Magistrates' Court
  Lay magistrates (at least two)        Lay magistrates (at least two)
   or a stipendiary magistrate            or a stipendiary magistrate

  Normal appeal routes        ———→
  Committals for trial        - - - →
  Appeals by way of case stated ⇒
```

The Lords of Appeal in Ordinary are the senior members of the judiciary and are generally appointed from the ranks of the Court of Appeal. Their number, originally fixed at two, is now usually nine (not less than seven nor more than 11). They are salaried staff and are under an obligation to sit for appellate work. There is also a convention that an ex-Lord Chancellor should serve when requested to do so by the Lord Chancellor. Usually appeals are heard by five judges but in exceptional cases seven judges may sit. By custom, one or two of the law lords are Scots and the Scottish judges generally sit when the House hears appeals from the Court of Session, the Scottish equivalent of the Court of Appeal.

The jurisdiction of the House of Lords is almost entirely appellate. In civil cases it hears appeals from the Court of Appeal (Civil Division) in England, the Court of Appeal in Northern Ireland and the Court of Session in Scotland. The grounds for an appeal are normally that a point of law of public importance is involved, but this does not necessarily have to be the case. A 'leap-frog' procedure was introduced by the *Administration of Justice Act, 1969*, whereby in certain cases an appeal can now be made direct from the trial court to the House of Lords without the need for a prior appeal to the Court of Appeal. It is used when a ruling is required on the construction (interpretation) of an Act of Parliament, or a statutory instrument.

In criminal cases appeal lies from the Court of Appeal (Criminal Division), the Court of Criminal Appeal in Northern Ireland and from the Courts-Martial Appeal Court. The House of Lords has, however, no jurisdiction in Scottish criminal cases. Hearings result in decisions known as 'opinions', which are delivered to the parties in printed form. The case is then remitted to the Appeal Court which translates the 'opinion' into a judgment.

Being at the peak of the hierarchy of courts in the UK, the House of Lords enjoys great authority and exerts a powerful influence on the development of the law. Decisions of the House of Lords are binding upon all other courts trying civil or criminal cases. Previously the House regarded itself as strictly bound by its own earlier decisions. However, since 1966 the House will depart from its own earlier decisions when it appears right to do so. For example, the earlier decision may have been made *per incuriam*. (*Per incuriam* means that the court which made the earlier decision was not in possession of the full facts at the time, or its decision was arrived at through carelessness or oversight.)

In one respect only the House of Lords is no longer the supreme legal authority in the UK. This is in matters regarding the interpretation of the Treaty of Rome, the treaty which is the basis of the European Union. The **Court of Justice of the European Communities (the European Court)** is the final court of authority on the meaning of the Treaty. English courts are bound by the decisions of the European Court on any matters relating to the treaty, and the interpretation of Community legislation.

2.3 The Court of Appeal

The *Judicature Acts, 1873–5*, created a new Supreme Court of Judicature divided into two parts: the High Court and the Court of Appeal. The jurisdiction of the Court of Appeal was gradually extended and by the *Criminal Appeal Act, 1966*, it was divided into two divisions: a Civil Division and a Criminal Division. The Civil Division's jurisdiction is entirely civil and almost entirely appellate. It hears appeals from the High Court, the County Courts, the Restrictive Practices Court and various tribunals – for example, the Lands Tribunal. The Civil Division hears appeals on questions of law and of fact, rehearing the whole of the evidence presented to the court below relying on the notes made at the trial. If the appeal is allowed the court may reverse the decision of the lower court, or amend it, or order a retrial. It can hear appeals about the exercise of discretion – for example, discretion as to costs.

The Criminal Division of the Court of Appeal has no civil jurisdiction and its criminal jurisdiction is solely appellate. It hears appeals from persons convicted on indictment at the Crown Court. It considers references made to the Division by the Home Secretary of cases under Section 17 of the *Criminal Appeal Act, 1968*, and it can hear an appeal against a verdict of 'not guilty by reason of insanity' or against findings of fitness and unfitness to plead. It has powers to dismiss appeals, or to quash convictions and order a new trial. It can substitute an alternative verdict, reduce the sentence or vary it, receive fresh evidence and order a proper trial.

The Court of Appeal is partly composed of the following *ex officio* judges; the Lord Chancellor, the Master of the Rolls (who heads the Civil Division), the Lord Chief Justice (who heads the Criminal Division), the President of the Family Division of the High Court, former Lord Chancellors and the Lords of Appeal in Ordinary. The rest of the judges are Lords Justices of Appeal, who are appointed by the Queen from judges of the High Court or barristers of at least 15 years' standing. There are not less than eight or more than 16 Lords Justices of Appeal, the maximum number being capable of increase by Order in Council. Judges of the Queen's Bench Division may also serve on the Criminal Division.

Normally an appeal is heard by three judges. However, interlocutory appeals (heard during the course of a legal action) may be heard by two judges, while a single judge may hear an appeal in the Criminal Division in regard to certain legal matters. Occasionally five or more judges can sit to hear appeals involving matters of exceptional importance in both the Civil and Criminal Divisions.

Decisions of the Court of Appeal bind all inferior courts trying civil or criminal cases, including the divisional courts. It will be seen later that a divisional court is a hearing at which two or three judges from a division of the High Court hear an appeal sitting together.

In civil matters the Court of Appeal is bound by decisions of the House of Lords and by its own earlier decisions except where:

- There are two earlier conflicting decisions.
- The court's earlier decision cannot stand with a subsequent House of Lords decision.
- The court's earlier decision was given *per incuriam* (through carelessness or oversight).

These principles were laid down by Lord Greene, MR, in *Young v. Bristol Aeroplane Co. Ltd (1944)*.

In criminal matters the court would depart from its earlier decision in the interests of justice. This principle was laid down by Lord Goddard, CJ, in *R. v. Taylor (1950)*.

2.4 Divisional Courts of the High Court

Many appeal matters are not of sufficient importance to merit the attention of the Court of Appeal, and are dealt with by Divisional Courts of the High Court. Thus a divisional court of the Queen's Bench Division hears appeals on criminal matters from the Magistrates' Courts and the Crown Court. It also hears appeals from certain tribunals, and Solicitors' Disciplinary Tribunals. A divisional court of the Family Division hears appeals from the Magistrates' Courts on matrimonial issues, and a divisional court of the Chancery Division hears appeals from the County Court on bankruptcies, and from the Commissioners of Taxes on tax matters.

A divisional court usually consists of two or three judges of the appropriate division, sitting together. An important aspect of such appeals is that the decisions act as precedents for future cases, whereas decisions at a

Magistrates' Court do not. Thus it is quite common for the prosecution to appeal against an acquittal at a Magistrates' Court, not as a matter of vindictiveness against the acquitted person, but in order to get a clear legal precedent. There may be hundreds of other cases of a similar nature in the pipeline. If the divisional court upholds the magistrates' view and gives a clear legal precedent for all the rest, the backlog of cases can be dropped to the very great benefit not only of the many accused but of the courts too.

Divisional courts in civil matters are bound by decisions of the House of Lords, the Court of Appeal (Civil Division) and their own previous decisions. In turn, they bind the High Court in their own divisions, and all lower courts. In criminal matters the divisional courts have a right of appeal to the House of Lords under the *Criminal Justice Act, 1960*, and are not strictly bound by decisions of the Criminal Division of the Court of Appeal.

2.5 The High Court

The lower half of the Supreme Court of Judicature set up in 1873–5 is the High Court. Today its three divisions have been renamed: they are the Queen's Bench Division, the Chancery Division and the Family Division.

All divisions of the High Court have equal competence to try any actions although certain specific matters are reserved for each of them. Details about the divisions are as follows:

2.5.1 The Queen's Bench Division

This is the busiest division, trying the very large numbers of cases about contracts and torts. The division is headed by the Lord Chief Justice and there are about 40–50 puisne (pronounced 'puny' and meaning 'lesser') judges. There is also within the division an 'Admiralty Court' which deals with actions to enforce claims for damages, loss of life or personal injury arising out of accidents at sea, collision between ships, and loss of or damage to goods carried in a ship. There is also a Commercial Court, set up by the *Administration of Justice Act, 1970*. It deals with cases brought by traders and merchants, such as insurance claims, etc. There are three judges nominated by the Lord Chancellor as commercial judges. The aim is to have such cases tried by judges experienced in the general areas of business law. Generally speaking, a quorum in the Queen's Bench Division is one; a judge sits alone and decides both questions of fact and questions of law. A jury may be empanelled to decide matters of fact, the judge then applies the law to the facts as found. There is no limit to the jurisdiction (i.e. damages may be for any amount).

Although contract and tort cases predominate, the Queen's Bench Division has residual jurisdiction over all cases not naturally falling to the Family and Chancery Divisions. The division also provides all the puisne judges trying criminal cases in the Crown Courts. This forms much of the work of the very large body of puisne judges available to the division. The division also has the appellate function referred to in Section 2.4 above, and a supervisory function over all lower courts and tribunals to ensure proper conduct of such bodies.

2.5.2 The Chancery Division

This division has important functions inherited from earlier times, when the old Chancery Court was concerned with all the more difficult and involved branches of law. The administration of estates of deceased persons; trusts; mortgages; sale of property subject to liens and charges; company, partnership and bankruptcy matters; taxation, etc., are typical subjects for its original jurisdiction. It also hears certain appeal matters from County Courts. The division, while nominally headed by the Lord Chancellor and the Master of the Rolls, is actually run by a Vice Chancellor, with the help of about 10–12 puisne judges. Numbers vary, but the names of all serving judges may be found in publications such as the quarterly *Vacher's Parliamentary Companion*.

2.5.3 The Family Division

This consists of the President and not less than three puisne judges. It has jurisdiction over matrimonial cases, dissolution of marriage, validity of marriage, wardship, adoption and the guardianship of minors. It has exclusive jurisdiction over matrimonial disputes and the rights of children.

The High Court normally sits at the Strand in London but there are 15 other towns to which judges of the High Court travel to hear common law claims and divorce cases. All other matters are dealt with in London. In civil matters, the High Court is bound by decisions of the House of Lords, the Court of Appeal and also by decisions of the divisional courts of the same division. The decisions of High Court judges sitting alone at first instance are not binding on other High Court judges, although these decisions do bind inferior courts.

In criminal matters, the position of the High Court is similar to the Court of Appeal – namely, it will depart from its own earlier decisions in the interests of justice.

2.6 The Crown Court

The Crown Court came into existence as a result of the *Courts Act, 1971*, which abolished the ancient system of quarter sessions and assizes. The new Crown Court was expressly stated to be a part of the Supreme Court of Judicature, and Section 1 of the *Supreme Court Act, 1981*, defines the Supreme Court as the Court of Appeal, the High Court of Justice and the Crown Court. Unlike the assizes and quarter sessions, the jurisdiction of the Crown Court is not local, and Section 4(4) of the 1971 Act provides that its sittings may be held anywhere at any time. There are three levels, called tiers, the first tier being served by puisne judges from the Queen's Bench Division and trying the most important cases. The second tier may be served by circuit judges as well as High Court judges, and the lowest tier by circuit judges or recorders. Circuit judges and recorders are appointed by the Queen on the recommendation of the Lord Chancellor. Unlike circuit judges, who have full-time permanent appointments, recorders are part-time judges appointed on a temporary basis. In addition to the judges the Court also consists of 12 members of the jury. Between two and four lay justices of the peace may also be present, especially when the court is hearing an appeal or a committal for sentence from the Magistrates' Court, and triable before a judge and jury.

The three tiers in the Crown Court deal with cases of increasing seriousness. Class 1 offences (murder, treason, etc.) must be tried by a High Court judge. Class 2 offences, which include manslaughter, rape and infanticide, must be tried by a High Court judge unless released by a High Court judge to be tried by a circuit judge or a recorder. This also applies to Class 3 offences, of a less serious nature. Class 4 offences, which include all offences triable summarily if preferred, are usually heard by circuit judges or recorders in the lowest tier of the Crown Court.

The Crown Court has jurisdiction over cases involving indictable offences, i.e. those offences punishable with three months' imprisonment or more. It hears appeals from the Magistrates' Courts and the Juvenile Courts.

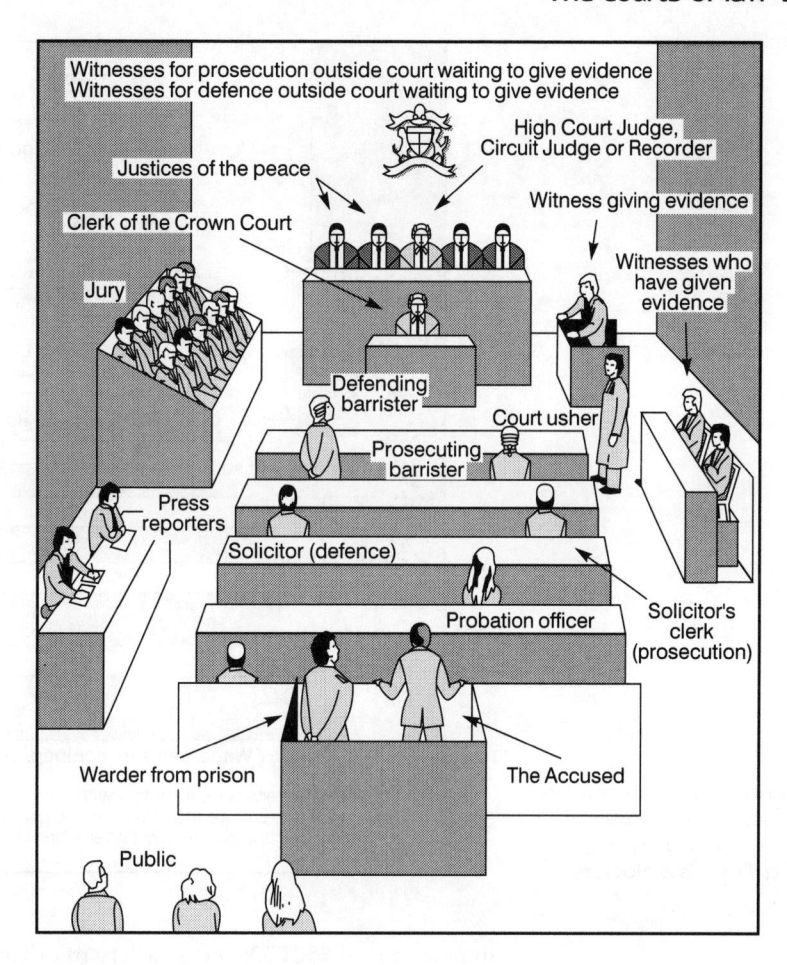

Figure 2.2 The Crown Court (By courtesy of Clearway Publishing Co. Ltd and The Law Society)

The court also sentences offenders committed from the Magistrates' Courts where the lower court has insufficient powers to deal with the offender. Finally, the court has a limited civil jurisdiction, mainly concerned with licensing appeals.

Some idea of the personalities and layout of the Crown Court is given in Figure 2.2.

2.7 The County Court

This court has exclusively civil jurisdiction. County Courts were initially established by the *County Courts Act, 1846*, and their composition and jurisdiction is governed by the *County Courts Act, 1959*. The court is usually presided over by a circuit judge appointed by the Crown on the advice of the Lord Chancellor. The judge normally sits alone, but on rare occasions a jury of eight persons may be empanelled. There are some 300 County Courts in England and Wales, administered by **registrars** who keep the records and carry out the administrative work associated with the court.

The Court's jurisdiction is to deal with all minor civil cases up to certain limits of action, beyond which the case must be tried at the High Court. Actions founded in contract and tort (except defamation) are dealt with up to a limit of £50 000; trusts and mortgages up to £30 000; land matters up to a rateable value of £1000; probate matters for estates up to £30 000; winding up of companies with a paid-up capital up to £120 000; personal injury cases

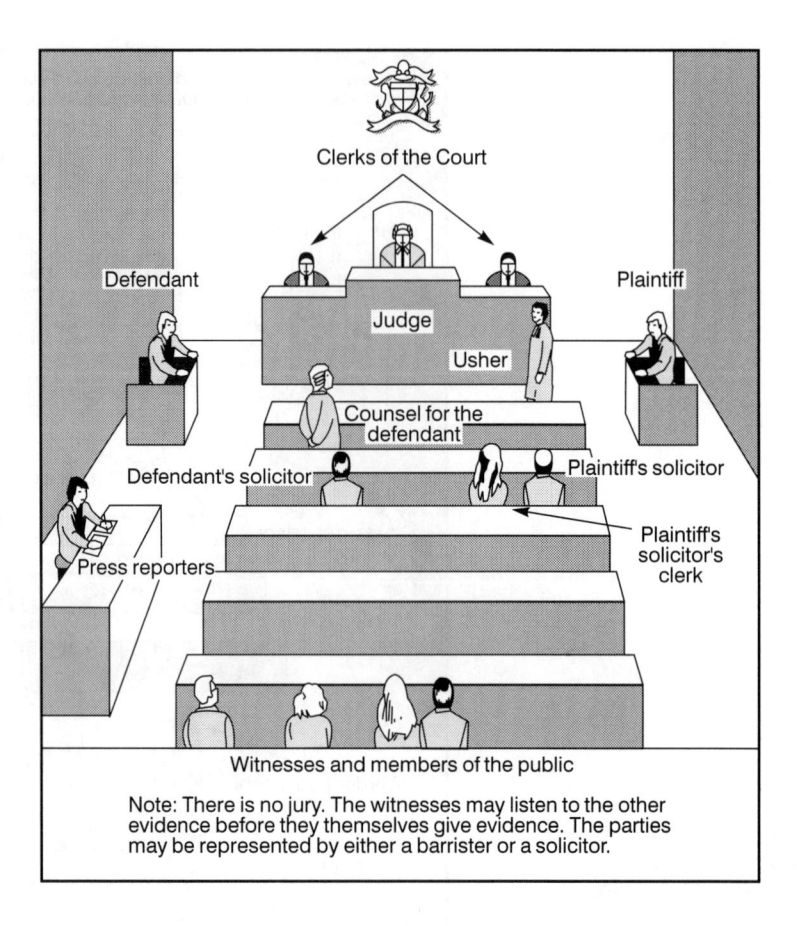

Figure 2.3 The County Court (By courtesy of Clearway Publishing Co. and The Law Society)

[Diagram of the County Court showing: Clerks of the Court, Judge, Usher, Defendant, Plaintiff, Counsel for the defendant, Defendant's solicitor, Plaintiff's solicitor, Plaintiff's solicitor's clerk, Press reporters, Witnesses and members of the public.

Note: There is no jury. The witnesses may listen to the other evidence before they themselves give evidence. The parties may be represented by either a barrister or a solicitor.]

up to a limit of £50 000; and a variety of other matters such as hire purchase, bankruptcy, landlord and tenant and other cases brought into the County Court by a variety of statutes. Certain County Courts are designated as Divorce County Courts and may hear *undefended* matrimonial causes.

Appeal against decisions in the County Court lies to the Court of Appeal.

Some idea of the personalities and layout of the County Court is given in Figure 2.3. The name 'registrar' has been changed to 'District Judge'.

To reduce the litigation coming before the County Court, and enable those with very small claims to bring an action without fear of excessive court costs, a 'small claims' procedure is now available.

2.8 The Small Claims Court

The County Court has been able to offer, since 1974, a 'small claims' procedure which enables plaintiffs who have claims of less than £1000 arising from the sale of goods, the provision of services, the repayment of loans, arrears of rent, possession of property, negligence, etc., to claim with a minimum of legal formality. The majority of small claims are dealt with by District Judges (a new designation for officials known in earlier times as registrars). Circuit judges may occasionally sit in the Small Claims Court to hear some cases. Other cases may be settled by arbitration, usually with the District Judge acting as arbitrator.

Many claims do not come to trial, and of those that do it is the facts which are usually in dispute rather than a question of law. The judge hears both sides and decides which version he thinks is right. A booklet *Small Claims in the County Court* is available from courts, and gives sound advice to both plaintiffs and defendants. Appeal from the decisions of a registrar goes to the circuit judge, at the County Court.

2.9 The Magistrates' Court

These courts deal with more cases than any other courts under the English legal system. A vast amount of criminal work is handled by the Magistrates' Courts since the Crown Court tries only the more serious criminal cases, i.e. cases on indictment with juries. Magistrates' Courts also deal with a variety of civil cases too trivial to be heard in the High Court. Examples are matrimonial matters, affiliation orders, consent of minors to marry, children in care, etc.

A Magistrates' Court consists of between two and seven **justices of the peace**. The justices of the peace are local people with intimate experience of the surrounding area. These people give their time to discharge judicial functions. They are laymen who do not receive a salary but only expenses incurred in the performance of their judicial duties.

Apart from the justices of the peace, whose office is ancient and originated in the thirteenth century, in big cities and towns one also finds **stipendiary magistrates**. Unlike the lay justices, stipendiary magistrates are full-time members of the court appointed by the Queen on the advice of the Lord Chancellor. A stipendiary magistrate is normally a barrister or a solicitor of at least seven years' standing. Unlike the lay Magistrates' Court, where a quorum of two magistrates is required, a stipendiary magistrate may sit alone.

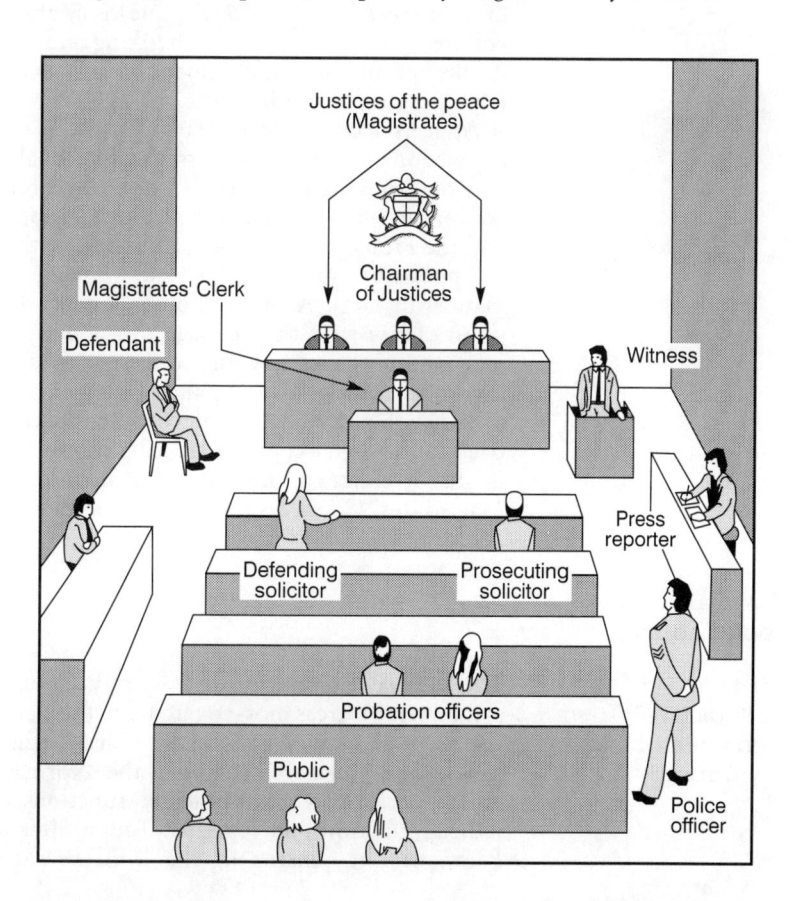

Figure 2.4 The Magistrates' Court (By courtesy of Clearway Publishing Co. and The Law Society)

A Magistrates' Court has a **clerk to the justices**, normally a solicitor or a barrister of at least five years' standing, appointed by the Magistrates' Court Committee (*Justices of the Peace Act, 1949*). Apart from performing the administrative work of the court, the main function of the clerk is to advise the justices on points of law and procedure.

The personalities and layout of the Magistrates' Court are shown in Figure 2.4.

The criminal jurisdiction of the Magistrates' Court is mainly concerned with summary offences, i.e. offences tried without a jury. These are comparatively minor offences and carry a maximum penalty of a £5000 fine and/or six months' imprisonment. Such offences would include minor motoring offences such as speeding, unauthorized parking, driving without a licence and/or insurance, failing to obey traffic signals, etc. Other offences would include petty theft, drunkenness, common assault, wilful damage, begging in a public place, etc.

A Magistrates' Court has jurisdiction to try an indictable offence summarily with the consent of the accused. Where a defendant deserves a greater sentence than the maximum permitted in the Magistrates' Court, the defendant is committed to the Crown Court for sentence.

As a court of preliminary investigation, a Magistrates' Court holds committal proceedings to examine an accused who has committed an indictable offence (offences punishable with a minimum of three months' imprisonment), to establish whether or not a *prima facie* case exists for committal to a Crown Court. The court's civil jurisdiction includes making affiliation orders, separation and maintenance orders, orders under the *Mental Health Acts, 1959–83*, questions about the adoption and custody of children, matters relating to invoking and granting of licences for alcoholic drinks and betting, enforcement of rates and recovery of debts, e.g. income tax, rates, electricity bills, etc.

Appeals from a Magistrates' Court lie to the Crown Court for both conviction and/or sentence, to the divisional court of the Queen's Bench by way of 'case stated' and, lastly, to the divisional court of the Family Division concerning matrimonial orders. Further appeal lies to the Court of Appeal and the House of Lords – in each case with permission only.

Appeals by way of case stated are made on matters of law only (not on matters of fact). A prosecutor or defence lawyer who is dissatisfied on a point of law with the decision of a Magistrates' Court or a Crown Court may require the lower court concerned to 'state a case' for the opinion of the divisional court. This is a panel of judges from the Queen's Bench Division of the High Court. They will consider the case as stated, and send the matter back to the lower court instructing it how to proceed. This is advantageous in that it creates a precedent for all future cases (whereas decisions of a Magistrates' Court do not create precedents).

2.10 Special courts

2.10.1 The Judicial Committee of the Privy Council

The Judicial Committee of the Privy Council has appellate jurisdiction in a number of areas not covered by the appellate powers of the ordinary courts. It has its origins in the Curia Regis (King's Council) of Norman times. The Curia Regis under the Norman kings was an inner cabinet which performed governmental functions, i.e. legislative, executive and judicial functions, all together. Today, after a series of revisionary Acts of Parliament, it consists of the Lord President of the Council, the Lord

Chancellor, ex-Lord Chancellors, the Lords of Appeal in Ordinary (the Law Lords) and Privy Councillors who have held high judicial office in the UK and the Commonwealth countries.

The Privy Council is not part of the Supreme Court and its decisions have persuasive authority only and hence are not binding on English courts. It does not pass a judgment but merely tenders advice to the Sovereign in person. This is followed and implemented by an Order in Council. Matters coming before the Judicial Committee concern appeals from:

- The Isle of Man, the Channel Islands, British Colonies and Protectorates and those independent Commonwealth countries whose domestic laws allow this right of appeal.
- The ecclesiastical courts, i.e. the Canterbury Court of Arches and the Chancery Court of York.
- The prize court, whose jurisdiction is now exercised by the Admiralty Court of the Queen's Bench Division and extends over matters concerning the ownership of ships and cargoes and their capture during time of war.
- Medical tribunals appertaining to doctors, dentists and opticians as when a person's name has been erased from the Medical Register by the Professional Conduct Committee of the General Medical Council under the *Medical Act, 1978*. Similar provisions exist under the *Dentists Act, 1957*, and the *Opticians Act, 1958*.

Lastly, apart from the appellate jurisdiction outlined above, the Privy Council can sometimes be called upon by the Sovereign for advice on matters of law. Exercising this jurisdiction, the Privy Council has tendered advice on diverse matters such as the powers of colonial judges, legislation in Jersey and eligibility of a person for membership of the House of Commons.

2.10.2 The Restrictive Practices Court

This is a court of record created by the *Restrictive Trade Practices Act, 1956*, and reconstituted by the *Restrictive Practices Court Act, 1976*. The court is concerned with restrictive trade agreements (agreements where restrictions are placed on price, quantity, quality or method of distribution of goods) referred to it by the **Director General of Fair Trading**, whose office was set up under the *Fair Trading Act, 1973*.

Matters concerned with restrictive trade practices are covered by the *Restrictive Practices Court Act, 1976*, the *Restrictive Trade Practices Act, 1976*, the *Resale Prices Act, 1976*, and certain provisions of the Treaty of Rome, especially Articles 85 and 86 which deal with rules on competition.

The court, which has equal status to the High Court, consists of three judges of the High Court appointed by the Lord Chancellor, a judge from the Court of Session (Scotland) nominated by the President of that court, a judge from the Supreme Court of Northern Ireland nominated by the Lord Chief Justice of Northern Ireland and 10 lay members appointed by the Crown from industry, commerce or public office. A duly constituted court consists of a judge and two lay members. Appeals on questions of law only lie to the Court of Appeal and its counterparts in Scotland and Northern Ireland.

Over the years very few of the restrictive practices which firms have sought to register under the Acts have been found by the court to be in the public interest, and the vast majority of such practices have been swept away since 1956. The dire consequences which were envisaged as a result of the ending of such practices have in general not followed the court's rulings, and the general public have largely benefited from the greater freedom in the availability of goods and the increased competition in resale prices.

2.10.3 The European Court of Justice

The UK became a member of the European Community from January 1973 and to give legal effect to the Community law in the UK the *European Communities Act, 1972*, was passed. While Section 2 of the Act makes the Community law directly effective in the UK, Section 3 requires local courts to take judicial notice of any decision of the Court of Justice on Community law.

Article 164 of the Treaty of Rome 1957 gives the court authority to ensure that the interpretation and application of the Treaty is observed. The court consists of at least one judge from each member state appointed by the governments of the member states. Judges are appointed for a renewable term of six years. They are assisted by four Advocates General whose prime function is to consider the issues of each case independently of the judges and make reasoned submissions in open court after the parties to the case have completed their submissions. The Advocate General does not participate in the formulation of the judgment and his submissions are not binding on the court. However, the court frequently accepts his conclusions and refers to them in its judgment. A single judgment is given and no dissenting views are given. These judgments are then enforced through the national courts of member states.

2.10.4 Jurisdiction of the Court of Justice

The types of action brought in the Court of Justice are as follows:

(a) Action against member states

Under Articles 169 and 170 of the Treaty of Rome an action may be brought in the Court of Justice against any member state, by another member state, or by the Commission. In fact such actions are not common, because the emphasis is on cooperation, not confrontation, between member states. Where a member state has failed to honour a particular provision of the Treaty, other member states have tended to leave the Commission to bring any action that is required.

(b) Action against Community institutions

If Community legislation adopted by either the Council of Ministers or the Commission is believed to be unlawful for any reason, an action may be brought by a member state, or by the Council, the Commission or even a natural or legal person. There are four grounds for this:

- That the institution is not competent to take the action objected to;
- That procedural rules were not followed;
- That a provision of the Treaty was infringed;
- That a lawful power was misused for an improper purpose.

A successful action leads to a declaration that the legislation is void, in whole or in part.

It is also possible to bring an action against an institution for failure to act where the Treaty imposes a duty to act (Article 175).

The courts of law

(c) Preliminary rulings

Under Article 177 of the Treaty, national courts or tribunals are required to bring certain questions about the interpretation of the Treaty, or the interpretation of acts of Community institutions, before the court for a preliminary ruling. Since the court is the final arbiter on all matters relating to the interpretation of the Treaty, it may sometimes be necessary for a national court to have the Treaty interpreted before they can come to a decision about a particular matter. They usually have discretion in deciding whether to bring the matter before the European Court, but it is mandatory if:

- The national court is the highest in the land, against whose decisions there is no national judicial remedy, and
- Where a decision on the point of Community law is essential if the court is to be able to give judgment.

The point of law is settled by the ruling of the European Court, and referred back to the national court for implementation of its judgment.

2.10.5 UK courts and Community Law

Community law is developed by the Court of Justice, either under Article 177 (preliminary rulings) or cases brought by member states, etc. The decision is then passed back to the national court, which must apply the decision in its national legal system. We thus have a harmonizing influence at work to achieve uniformity in the application of Community law. However, the natural conservatism of English law has not favoured references from lesser courts to the European court. In the interesting case of *H. P. Bulmer v. J. Bollinger SA (1974)*, two English companies sought declarations that they were entitled to manufacture drinks described as 'champagne cider' and 'champagne perry'. The French company disputed this claiming that it was contrary to Community law, and asked the Court of First Instance to refer the matter under Article 177. This was refused. On appeal Lord Denning, MR, suggested certain guidelines for such references. These were:

- *Is the point conclusive?* The English court must consider whether the point is so important that a decision cannot be made on the matter before the court unless the point is resolved. If a judgment can be given without resolving the point then it is not necessary to seek a preliminary ruling.
- *Is there already a precedent?* If the European Court has already decided substantially the same point, the English court need only follow the precedent.
- *Is it an 'acte claire'*. If the point is reasonably clear, we do not need to interpret the Treaty, only to apply it.
- *Decide the facts first*. Before any reference on the law it is best to decide the facts first.
- *Consider the circumstances at the time*. An appeal to the European Court should not be made against the wishes of the litigants, or if the expense or delay was likely to cause hardship, or if it was likely to over-burden the European Court.
- *Article 177(3)*. Section 3 of Article 173 makes an application for a preliminary ruling mandatory only if the highest national court is involved, 'against whose decisions there is no judicial remedy under national law'. Lord Denning held that this applied only to the House of Lords in the UK. Other courts therefore had no duty to apply for a ruling, only a discretion which they could exercise if they wished.

All these guidelines are only *'obiter dicta'* (sayings by the way), not *'ratio decidendi'*. They are therefore not binding precedents, but they have proved very persuasive. However sound this advice may be, the guidelines cannot relieve a court or a tribunal from exercising its own discretion under Article 177, and it is possible that the Article may apply to other English courts and tribunals (see *Miliangos v. Frank (Textiles) Ltd (1976)*).

2.11 The doctrine of binding precedent and its effect on litigation

To recapitulate what was said in Chapter 1 about binding precedent a judicial decision may be divided into three elements: findings of material facts; a statement of the principles of law concerning these facts; and the judgment based upon the principles stated. It is the statement of the principles of law which is the *ratio decidendi* (the reason for the decision), and forms the binding precedent for the future. Judges follow earlier decisions for guidance and apply the law enunciated in those decisions. The *ratio decidendi* always refers specifically to the facts as found in the particular case being tried. Any other statement of law which is not strictly relevant to the facts of the case is termed an **obiter dictum** (something said by the way). An *obiter dictum* is not a *binding* element of a decision but it does have persuasive authority, especially if the statement of law concerned emanates from a court of high authority. A case which illustrates a distinction between a *ratio decidendi* and an *obiter dictum* is:

> *Rondell v. Worsley (1967)*
>
> The House of Lords had to decide on the question whether a barrister could be successfully sued for negligence when conducting a case in court in the performance of his duties towards his client. The House held that no action could lie against a barrister for negligence in the conduct of his duty towards a client. This was the *ratio decidendi* of the case. However, the court went further and expressed opinions not quite relevant to the case in hand and these were that a barrister might be held liable in tort when acting outside the sphere of litigation and that a solicitor acting as an advocate might enjoy immunity. These opinions are *obiter dicta*. They are not binding on any court, but they could be persuasive in any future case where a barrister was sued for negligence on some matter outside his advocacy of a client's case, or where a solicitor acting as an advocate was sued for negligence in his pleading on behalf of his client.

We have seen that there is a hierarchy of courts with a chain of binding precedents imposed from higher upon lower courts. What is the advantage of this system? The answer is that it gives greater certainty in law, and thus reduces litigation. For example, if A has sold goods to B in certain circumstances, and sues for payment of the price, the decision of the court in that case, based on that exact set of facts, will act as a precedent for all similar cases. Suppose that B was a minor and the court held that the contract between A and B was voidable by the minor. If, later, C sells goods to D in a similar way, and approaches a solicitor to commence an action for payment of the price his solicitor will explain that the case of *A v. B* has already decided the point, and an action against D would not succeed. The litigation will not proceed, and C has no redress for his grievance – which was his own fault. He failed to enquire whether D had the capacity to contract.

Even when litigation is commenced, it is frequently only a method of putting pressure on the other party, and forcing him to act sensibly. Thus in a typical recent year more than a million cases were commenced in the County Court, but only about 100 000 actually reached a hearing; the rest were settled out of court. This happens because the party in the wrong, when he takes legal advice, is advised to settle out of court, and thus avoid the costs which will follow from losing the case.

There is the disadvantage about certainty in the law, that bad law becomes just as entrenched as good law. Since a legal precedent can be disturbed only by appeal to a higher court, a case may appear to be good law until someone affluent enough to risk the costs involved appeals against the decision of a judge who followed the precedent. It is true that judges may refuse to follow a particular precedent by 'distinguishing' the case from the one they are trying. This means they hold that the facts of the earlier case were not quite the same as the facts of the case they are trying at present. This gives them an excuse to avoid following the precedent. When a case has been decided wrongly most of the judges 'distinguish' it. As one wag put it, 'Some cases become "very distinguished".'

To conclude, the benefit of precedent is that it increases certainty in law, and thus reduces litigation. In the process we may find that an occasional 'hard case' results – justice is not quite done to everybody. Is it worth destroying the certainty in the law for the sake of easing the odd injustice? In former times the general opinion was that it was undesirable to reduce certainty in the law – 'Hard cases make good law' is an old saying. Today there is usually some sort of review process which leads to a change in the law in these situations, though the change may come too late for the individual whose unjust treatment led to the review.

The other adverse aspect of the system is that case law can be excessively complex, with a vast body of cases to be considered by the court. This complexity is frequently reduced by codifying the law – enacting the present state of the law as a statute which supersedes case law for the present. A further body of case law may then be built up from the interpretation of the statute, over the years.

2.12 Personnel of the law

The legal profession has always been a divided one, with barristers forming a senior rank and solicitors a lower rank. Barristers are people who have been 'called to the bar' in one of the four Inns of Court: the Inner Temple, the Middle Temple, Lincoln's Inn and Gray's Inn. They are qualified both educationally and by experience to act as advocates in the courts of law. An advocate is someone who pleads cases in the courts speaking on behalf of his clients either as plaintiff (or prosecutor in the criminal courts) or to defend the client against the civil or criminal case being presented.

Solicitors are not members of the Bar. They deal directly with the public, giving legal advice and if necessary drawing up writs to commence legal action on behalf of their clients. If the matter is relatively trivial and only a low-level court appearance is needed, the solicitor may plead the case himself, but if the matter is one for the High Court or above the solicitor must brief a barrister with the necessary experience in the particular field in question. A brief is a succinct account of the problem, the facts of the case as told to the solicitor by the client and the client's view of the desirable outcome of the case.

Besides these courtroom activities both branches of the law carry out many other activities. Barristers spend a considerable amount of their time writing 'opinions' – expert guidance for solicitors who are seeking to advise clients what action they should pursue. The result of such an opinion might be that a case will be commenced against some offending party. On the other hand, it may clearly state the barrister's opinion that the action proposed could not be successful, and the aggrieved client will be told either to forget the matter, or to settle out of court. Barristers also write 'pleadings'. These are the clear statements to be made in court when a plaintiff's case is presented, or a defendant's case is made to rebut the claims made by a plaintiff. Very experienced barristers may apply to become Queen's Counsel, (QCs). Called 'taking silk', because the Queen's Counsel wear silken gowns, the QC is likely to be offered the more important cases, earns higher fees, and is also more likely to be offered judicial posts of various sorts.

Solicitors not only have a wide variety of specialist areas of law to which they can give attention – for example conveyancing – but are free to take posts in many areas of industry, commerce, the civil service and local government. The position of company secretary in larger public limited companies is nearly always filled by a solicitor (not necessarily a full-time appointment in the smaller companies).

The reform of the Bar and the legal profession is an endless topic for discussion, but some of the barriers between the two branches of the profession are coming down. The *Courts and Legal Services Act, 1990* is a comprehensive review of the provision of legal services. It provides for a re-allocation of business among the civil courts to match the importance and complexity of cases to the level of court concerned. For example, as a result of an order made under the Act, from July 1991 personal injury claims below £50 000 will have to be started in a County Court and under other measures the small claims jurisdiction will increase, as will the trial jurisdiction of district judges. A plaintiff's solicitor will now be able to serve a County Court summons by post.

The new Act's provisions with regard to rights of audience are interesting. First, the Act will remove all restrictions on rights of audience in some County Court proceedings, such as proceedings about the supply of goods and services, the enforcement of judgment orders, matters concerning consumer credit or in relation to domestic premises. Lay persons will be able to represent the parties (but there is a proviso that the court may refuse to hear them if they behave in an unruly manner). The Act will allow solicitors to gain wider rights of audience, and barristers to gain the right to conduct litigation, and will in due course permit new classes of advocate and litigator to be developed under educational programmes envisaged in the establishment of a **Lord Chancellor's Advisory Committee on Legal Education and Conduct**.

The Act will permit an extension of the classes of person who can do probate and conveyancing work. It will also establish a **Legal Services Ombudsman** and a **Conveyancing Ombudsman**. The Act will introduce procedural changes which will reduce delays and cut the cost of civil litigation. While providing certain safeguards, 'no win, no fee' agreements will be permitted between clients and their legal representatives. Bearing in mind the realities of the single market, established in 1992, solicitors are now able to enter into partnerships with foreign lawyers.

2.13 Legal aid

It has often been said that there is one law for the rich and another for the poor. Legal representation has long been made available to such criminals as murderers, yet many more deserving litigants (for example wives seeking to obtain a divorce from an unsatisfactory partner) find it quite impossible to afford legal advice. The situation was remedied by the *Legal Aid Act, 1974*, now repealed and replaced by the *Legal Aid Act, 1988*, which reviewed the whole position of legal aid, advice and assistance. The problem with a wide system of legal aid is the cost of such services, which tend to increase as more and more categories of disadvantaged persons claim aid from public funds to pursue their 'legitimate' legal aspirations.

The Act sets up a **Legal Aid Board**, with between 11 and 17 members, two of whom must be solicitors and two barristers. The others are people knowledgeable about the provision of legal services, the work of the courts and management. The Board has many powers, including the establishment of a separate legal aid fund. Official funds, contributions from people aided under the Act, costs recovered by those aided who were successful in their actions and other moneys will be paid into the fund, from which barristers and solicitors who take on legal aid cases will be recompensed at a proper level of remuneration.

Legal aid is available at a wide level to those whose impecunious condition makes legal aid necessary. For those making a preliminary enquiry about their legal aid status a small charge (£5) for a 'fixed fee interview' provides them with an opportunity to state their case and if necessary a 'green form' will be completed. This is a clear statement of the applicant's income, and enables an assessment to be made of the applicant's ability to pay. Some may be granted legal aid; some will be asked to make a contribution to the cost and others will be told they are not eligible.

For criminal cases it is for the court to order legal assistance for a person who should not be allowed to go to trial without a legal representative.

Legal Aid Certificates are granted by the Legal Aid Board, which has a prior charge on any money recovered in a successful action for the contribution required from a plaintiff and the costs recovered. The balance goes to the plaintiff. Where a legally-aided person loses a case costs may be awarded against him/her, yet, being poor, the person may be unable to pay. In such cases the court may order the costs to be paid out of the Legal Aid Fund.

Test your knowledge

Answers	Questions
	1 What is the hierarchy of courts for civil matters of a commercial nature? Start from the bottom.
1 (a) County Court; (b) the High Court (Queen's Bench Division); (c) Court of Appeal (Civil Division); (d) House of Lords.	2 What is the hierarchy of courts for criminal matters? Start from the bottom.
2 (a) The Magistrates' Court; (b) the Crown Court (three tiers); (c) the Court of Appeal (Criminal Division); (d) the House of Lords.	3 What is the chain of binding precedents?

Answers	Questions
3 (a) Decisions of the House of Lords bind both divisions of the Court of Appeal and all lower courts. It reserves the right not to be bound by its own earlier decisions. (b) Decisions of the Court of Appeal bind the Court of Appeal itself (except in a few circumstances) and all lower courts. In certain criminal matters decisions of the Court of Appeal do not bind a Divisional Court because appeal lies direct to the House of Lords. (c) Decisions of Divisional Courts bind the Divisional Court itself, and all lower courts. (d) Decisions of High Court judges sitting alone do not bind other High Court judges. They do bind all lower courts.	4 What is the chain for appeals to a higher court on the civil side?
4 (a) Appeals from the Small Claims Court lie to the circuit judge at the County Court. (b) Appeals from the County Court lie to the Court of Appeal (Civil Division). (c) Appeals from the High Court lie to the Court of Appeal. (d) Appeals from the Court of Appeal lie to the House of Lords.	5 What is the chain of appeal on the criminal side?
5 (a) For full appeals we have: (i) From the Magistrates' Court appeal lies to the Crown Court; (ii) from the Crown Court appeal lies to the Court of Appeal (Criminal Division); (iii) from the Court of Appeal (Criminal Division) appeal lies to the House of Lords. (b) For appeals by way of case stated we have: (i) from the Magistrates' Court appeal lies to the divisional court of the Queen's Bench Division; (ii) from the Divisional Court appeal lies to the House of Lords	6 What are the functions of the European Court?

Answers	Questions
6 (a) It is the final arbiter on all matters concerning the interpretation of the Treaty of Rome and other treaties, such as the Maastricht Treaty. (b) It is the final authority on the validity of the acts of Community institutions and the interpretation of Community legislation.	7 What sort of actions may be brought in the European Court?
7 (a) Actions against member states. (b) Actions against Community institutions, i.e. the Council, the Commission, etc. (c) Actions asking for a 'preliminary ruling' under Article 177 of the Treaty.	8 What are the two branches of the legal profession?
8 Barristers and solicitors	9 What are the chief activities of barristers?
9 (a) Advocacy, particularly in the High Court and the Court of Appeal. (b) Writing 'opinions' to assist solicitors with difficult cases. (c) Writing 'pleadings' preparatory to Court proceedings.	10 What are the chief activities of solicitors?
10 (a) Legal advice and the commencement of legal actions on behalf of clients. (b) Representation of clients in both civil and criminal proceedings, particularly in low-level courts. (c) Conveyancing and similar areas of law. (d) Appointments in commerce, industry, local government, etc.	11 Now try some of the questions in Appendix 1

Part Two The Law and Business Entities

3 The legal environment for business entities

3.1
The concept of business entity

Every business exists as a distinct unit separate from all other units, and sometimes even distinct from its owners. This is recognized by law, which accords different rights and duties to those in business as sole traders, partnerships, etc. In the UK a limited-liability company has a separate legal status independent of its shareholders: it is an incorporation, which means it has been given authority to act in a business capacity. Partnerships, sole traders, trade unions and clubs are not corporations and do not have a separate legal status distinct from their owners or members.

A **sole trader** is a person who enters business on his own account; selects a site appropriate to the activities he has in mind; labours in the business with or without the assistance of employees; contributes the original capital by personal saving or borrowing on his own responsibility; and finally receives as his reward the proceeds (if any) of the venture.

A **partnership** is formed when two or more persons (the partners) agree to join together to pursue a particular type of activity. There need not be any formal arrangements, but it is best if a deed of partnership is drawn up at the start. A good lawyer will often suggest many points that the partners should agree on from the start, and if these are put in writing, and witnessed, many later difficulties may be avoided. There is no limit to the arrangements that may be made, but bodies of rules have grown up over the years about partnership behaviour, and these were embodied in an important act, the *Partnership Act, 1890*.

Sole traders and partners are natural, legal persons, and operate as separate entities, with their own rights and obligations. Their businesses do *not* have a separate legal personality from the owner, or owners, as is the case with limited companies.

Trade unions, social and sports clubs, literary societies or arts groups are termed 'unincorporated associations'. The law regards them as a group of persons bearing individual responsibility for their association's actions.

Other legal persons are not natural, but are artificial persons – or corporations. The term means 'formed into a body'. The commonest types of corporations are limited companies registered under the *Companies Acts, 1985–89*. There are also statutory companies set up by private Act of Parliament, and chartered companies. The legal basis of a chartered company is a Royal Charter.

Although this chapter is basically concerned with types of business units in the private sector, large areas of British industry were progressively nationalized after 1945. Most of these have now been re-privatized but there are still a number of **public corporations**, such as the Bank of England, the Post Office, the BBC, etc. and a word about them is not out of place here.

The organizational structure for each nationalized corporation may vary from one corporation to another. However, each is headed by a Minister of the Crown who is answerable to Parliament for the corporation's general policy. Day-to-day management is in the hands of a board headed by a chairman appointed for fixed periods by the appropriate minister. Like any other corporation, a public corporation has the independence of a company but it does not have shares or shareholders. It can enter into contracts, own land, buy property, engage staff, be vicariously liable for the torts of its servants, and can sue and be sued. Although ultimate control of a public corporation rests with Parliament, day-to-day management is in the hands of the board and Parliament cannot interfere. Unlike business enterprises in the private sector, public corporations do not exist solely for making profit. Although they are required to be self-sufficient financially, public ownership implies that they strive to provide an efficient public service and operate in the national interest.

In the next few chapters we shall consider the legal positions of the various types of business unit and demonstrate the chief features of the legal environment in which they operate.

3.2 Sole trader enterprises

A sole trader enterprise is inseparable in law from the individual who set it up and labours in it. Usually the business name is the same as the name of the sole trader. If it is not then certain rules, which are explained below, have to be observed. They are laid down in the *Business Names Act, 1985*. This Act replaces an earlier (1916) Act of the same name which set up a Register of Business Names, to prevent any possibility of confusion between businesses using the same name. This register was discontinued, largely to save administrative expense. However, in order to enable those dealing with such businesses to know the identity of the owners, from that date businesses covered by the new Act must display their owners' names and addresses at business premises and on business stationery, and supply this information on request to any customer or supplier. A leaflet about this, and a specimen notice like the one reproduced in Figure 3.1, are available from the Companies Registration Office, Department of Trade, Guidance Notes Section, 55 City Road, London EC1Y 1BB.

A sole trader's legal personality is not separate or distinct from the business he runs. Just like any other legal individual a sole trader is bound by the ordinary civil and criminal law of the land. It is this law that gives him certain rights and imposes certain obligations on him. These legal rights and duties are adequately explained in the various chapters of this book on contract, tort, administrative law, agency, sale of goods, carriage of goods by land, sea and air, etc.

Anyone can set up in business as a sole trader and no formal procedures are required for setting up. A licence is required for certain types of businesses. With the repeal of the *Registration of Business Names Act, 1916*, the onus is now on the sole trader to ensure that the name of his business conforms with the laws of the land. For example, he cannot use an offensive name or the name of an existing business. He leaves himself open to a civil or criminal action if he does so. If the business name is not the true name or names of the proprietor then, as explained above, his full name and address must be displayed at business premises, on business stationery and be readily available to a customer or supplier on request. For example if you call your business 'Beautiful Gardens' you must include 'Proprietor Tom Greenfingers' on your shop-front, letterhead, etc. The absence of an official register can have unfortunate consequences. For example sole traders all over the country might decide on the name 'Beautiful Gardens'. If a court order is made against the proprietor of such a firm it will be reported by the

The legal environment for business entities **49**

PARTICULARS OF OWNERSHIP

OF

_____ *

as required by section 4 of the Business Names Act 1985

Full name(s) of Proprietor(s)	Address within Great Britain at which documents may be effectively served on the business

* Insert Name of Business

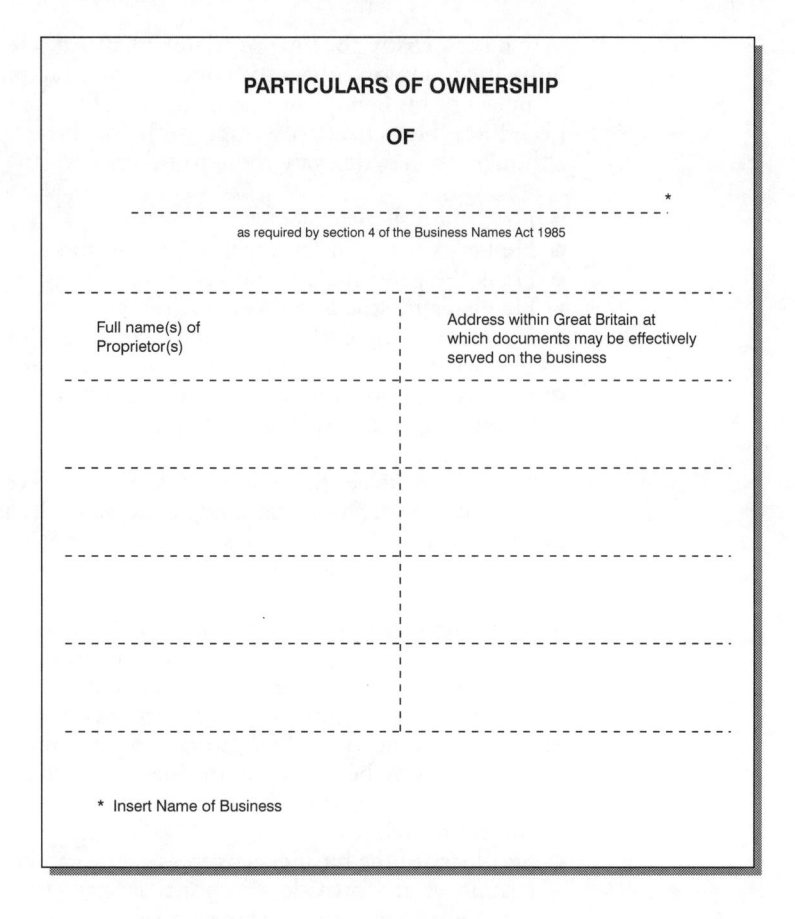

Figure 3.1 A specimen notice of ownership

various credit reference agencies and it is possible that a cautious finance house or bank might close any account on its books with the same name. The withdrawal of credit can be very harmful to a business, destroying its credibility with various suppliers and financial institutions. The insertion of an extra word in the name, for example Beautiful Gardens (Windsor), will reduce the chances of being confused with other firms, and a quick check from time to time in the local telephone directory will confirm that no other firm of that name has been established.

This type of business unit is extremely common today, and official encouragement is being given to budding entrepreneurs in all trades and professions. There are about 1 250 000 sole traders in the United Kingdom at present. However industrialization and large scale production, with the consequent need for larger capital has meant that large businesses run as limited companies are the more significant business units today. In one investigation it was found that 10 per cent of the business units did 84 per cent of the work – with a few large firms dominating the industry – and the much more numerous sole traders commanding only a small fraction of the work.

In this form of business unit it is normally one person who provides all the capital and assumes all the risks associated with a business, e.g. business losses, losses resulting from theft, burglary, fire and other calamities such as public disorder, natural disaster, etc. With the advent of insurance, many of the risks can be minimized although a fully comprehensive insurance policy may be too costly for the proprietor to afford. He may run the business by himself or employ others to work for him. He may call on the services of members of his family. Success or failure of the business depends entirely on his efforts. He is primarily responsible for the following business activities, although he may delegate these to others:

- He is the sole manager.
- He keeps in touch with market trends and customer preferences.
- He is the general clerk and secretary.
- He displays, stocks and orders goods.
- He keeps business records and accounts, though he may require the services of an accountant from time to time for auditing accounts.
- He is responsible for publicity and advertising, often on a small scale only through local newspapers and magazines.

In large businesses these activities are undertaken by different persons and this ensures specialization and increased efficiency. A sole trader is necessarily a 'Jack of all trades and a master of none'.

The **advantages** of operating as a sole trader may be listed as follows:

- He is the master of his own destiny. He does not have to consult others or receive their approval in making business decisions and implementing them. Being the sole provider of capital, he is entitled to all the profits. There is consequently a greater incentive for him to work hard.
- There is no delay in the making and implementing of decisions. Prompt attention can be given to the needs of customers. In big businesses, decision-making and the implementation of management policies are subject to delay.
- Smallness of the business ensures that he can keep in close touch with his customers and provide a personal service. The impersonal nature of the services provided by large businesses is a constant source of irritation and inconvenience for many customers.
- Personal supervision can ensure business efficiency and this is easier for a small business unit.
- He is not required to disclose, or make public, details of his profits or losses to anyone other than the Inland Revenue.

The **disadvantages** of operating as a sole trader are:

- The sole trader has to put in long hours of work and there is little time for vacations. Many have to work at non-business hours, at evenings and weekends. All this may have a detrimental effect on his health. The sole trader cannot afford to be sick as the business might have to be closed or run with difficulty.
- The proprietor carries personal responsibility for all the debts and obligations of the business. In the event of bankruptcy, creditors can call on the personal assets of the proprietor to satisfy their demands.
- Limitation on capital means that the business cannot be expanded and in many cases modernized. Almost all the capital has to be provided from his personal resources and the facilities for borrowing are limited when compared to a company or a partnership.
- The business can only be run as a high-cost enterprise because of limited specialization. It cannot compete with the prices offered by large enterprises since it buys on a small scale, probably from a middleman who adds his commission to the price of the product.

The legal environment for business entities 51

- He is personally responsible for the business. On his death the business is normally inherited by members of his family, but there is no guarantee that the successor will be interested in or able to manage the business.

For the reasons listed many sole traders take a partner and operate as a partnership.

3.3 Partnerships: definition and name

The *Partnership Act, 1890*, is the principal statute that governs all partnerships and Section 1(1) of this Act defines a partnership as 'the relation which subsists between persons carrying on business in common with a view of profit.' The business entity that is created as a result of persons entering into partnership with one another is called a **firm** (Section 4). A key phrase in the definition distinguishes a partnership from other entities which appear similar, e.g. a social or a cricket club, a debating society or a co-ownership. A club or a society is not formed to make a profit and is not therefore organized on business principles: all partners are jointly liable for the debts of a firm whereas members of a club or society are not liable for debts, except that they can be required to pay any part of their individual subscription if it is outstanding. Any debts incurred will be the personal debts of the member who made the contractual arrangement. Similarly a partnership exists to make a profit and this may not be the case with a co-ownership. In deciding whether or not a partnership exists it depends entirely on the intention of the parties to the arrangement. Intention is something that is expressly stated in the contract or it can be implied from the conduct of the parties to the contract. Examples of arrangements that do not necessarily constitute evidence of a partnership since they may not be 'carrying on a business in common with a view of profit' (Section 2, 1890 Act) are:

- Joint tenancies.
- Tenancies in common.
- An arrangement where gross returns are shared.
- Receipt of a share of profits.
- Payment of a debt through instalments out of accruing profits.
- Payment of servants or agents through a share of the profits.
- Payment to money lenders through a share of the profits.
- Annuity payments to a widow or a child of a deceased partner out of profits.
- Payment of a portion of the profits as goodwill.
- Charitable or religious organizations.

In order to safeguard those involved in any arrangement that does not fall into the category of a partnership, documents called 'Heads of Agreement' are usually drawn up. The documents detail the nature of the particular arrangement, state that no partnership exists but give details of the duties, rights and obligations of the parties to the particular arrangement.

Partnerships are often described as 'ships that sink in rough seas' and unless the partners know and trust each other implicitly, with the exception of professional firms, this type of business entity usually fails when partners fall out.

3.4 Formation of a partnership

A partnership is created as a result of a contract between two or more persons. This contract may be either in writing or oral or both. The contract may be signed and sealed, i.e. a deed. A contract in writing creating a partnership is known as the 'Articles of Partnership' and a signed and sealed contract is termed a 'Deed of Partnership'. All partners are bound by the terms mentioned in the Articles or Deed of Partnership and the *Partnership Act, 1890*, will only apply in so far as particular points are not covered by the Articles or Deed of Partnership. The terms of the Act can be varied by the Articles or the Deed.

The Articles or Deed of Partnership will normally include the following matters:

- The business's trading name.
- The nature or purpose of the business.
- Details of the individual capital contributions of the partners.
- The method for sharing profits or losses.
- The powers of the partners.
- Rules about the admission of new partners.
- Rules about the expulsion of a partner.
- Rules about the dissolution of the partnership.
- Rules about the accounts and audit of the books.
- How goodwill is to be determined.
- How the amounts payable to outgoing partners or deceased partners' estates shall be calculated.
- Rules about the use of arbitration in case of disputes between partners.

Goodwill, mentioned above, is important in partnerships because at any time when a change in the relationships between partners occurs – such as the admission of a new partner, the departure or death of an existing partner, a rearrangement of work-loads, etc. – it is necessary to value the goodwill, so that the net worth of the business can be accurately assessed.

A partnership contract may be express or it may be implied by a court from the conduct of the parties – for example, if a person holds himself out as a partner or allows himself to be held out as such, he may incur the liabilities of a partner (*Bevan v. The National Bank Ltd* (*1906*)). Being a contractual arrangement, a partnership agreement is subject to the same principles and rules of contract law that are applicable to any other contract (see Part 3). Some of the consequences that arise are as follows:

- A minor may become a partner. During his minority the contract of partnership cannot be enforced against him. On attaining his majority the contract becomes voidable, i.e. it can be avoided by him within a reasonable period. If no steps are taken to avoid the contract within a reasonable time, it becomes binding on him (*Goode v. Harrison* (*1821*)). A minor is liable for such debts of the firm as are incurred subsequent to his attaining his majority if he does not take steps to avoid the partnership.
- Although an alien may become a partner, upon the outbreak of war the partnership dissolves since he becomes an enemy alien and the partnership contract becomes illegal.
- Mental incapacity of a partner is a ground for dissolution. However, a mentally incapacitated person may become a partner with the consent of existing partners.
- Death or bankruptcy of a partner, unless otherwise agreed, results in the dissolution of a partnership (Section 33(1), 1890 Act).
- A partnership can be terminated by mutual agreement of all the parties.
- The maximum number of partners should not exceed 20 (*Companies Act, 1985*, Section 716), with the exception of professional partnerships – e.g. solicitors, accountants, stock exchange firms – where the maximum

number of 20 can be exceeded (see the same section). Under the *Companies Act, 1948*, the maximum numbers for a banking partnership was 10; the 1967 Act allowed this number to be exceeded up to a maximum of 20 provided the Board of Trade's approval was obtained. The *Banking Act, 1987*, removes the limit on maximum numbers. The upper limit has also been lifted for other professions, such as auctioneers, estate agents and town planners, but at least three-quarters of the partners of such 'unrestricted size' professional partnerships must be members of the relevant professional body, as prescribed in the statutory instrument made under Section 716(2)(d).

The duration of a partnership depends on whether it is formed for a specified time, for a particular business venture, or for an indefinite time (partnership at will, which can be terminated at any time at the discretion of a partner, by giving notice to the other, or others, of his intention to dissolve the partnership (Section 32, 1890 Act)).

3.4.1 The firm's name

The *Registration of Business Names Act, 1916*, has been replaced by the *Registration of Business Names Act, 1985*. Firms that do not operate under their owners' true names do not have to register at a central registry which has now been abolished. In order to enable those dealing with such businesses to know the identity of the owners, the owners' names and addresses must be displayed at business premises, on business stationery and this information must be freely available on request to any customer or supplier. A partnership can use the word '& Company' after its name but it cannot also use the word 'Limited' as a last word.

3.5 Relationship of partners with third parties

According to Section 5 of the 1890 Act every partner (except a limited partner) is considered an agent of the firm and will therefore bind other partners on any transaction within the ordinary course of the firm's business with an outsider. This will not apply if the partner has no authority to act on behalf of the firm and the outsider is aware of this lack of authority or does not know or believe the other party to be a partner. Apart from this limitation, a partner has implied authority to bind the firm in relation to the following transactions:

- Buying and selling of goods that are normally associated with the firm's business.
- Receiving payments from debtors and issuing receipts against them.
- Engagement and dismissal of employees of the firm.

The implied powers just mentioned apply equally to a non-trading partnership as to a trading partnership. However, certain additional powers are imputed to a partner in a trading partnership, i.e. one that is involved in buying and selling of goods (*Higgins v. Beauchamp (1914)*), and these are:

- Accepting, drawing and issuing negotiable instruments on behalf of the firm.
- Borrowing money and pledging the firm's goods or chattels as security. If the credit of the firm is pledged for a purpose not connected with the ordinary course of business, the firm is not bound unless specific authority has been given to the partner and in such a case the partner is

personally liable (Section 7). His action can always be ratified by the firm.
- Hiring the services of a solicitor if an action is commenced against the firm (*Tomlinson v. Broadsmith (1896)*).

In a non-trading partnership the additional powers mentioned above can be expressly provided by the Articles or the Deed of Partnership.

Section 9 of the 1890 Act made every partner jointly liable for the firm's contracts. This means that a partner was liable along with all other partners and not by himself alone. A claim could be made against the private resources of each partner to satisfy a judgment. Joint liability meant that a plaintiff who sued one of the partners on a contract with the firm could not subsequently sue the other partners (*Kendall v. Hamilton (1879)*). However, this position was changed by the *Civil Liability (Contribution) Act, 1978*, which provides that a judgment obtained against one partner does not preclude an action against the other partners. They are therefore jointly and severally liable for contracts.

A firm and its partners are also jointly and severally liable for any torts or wrongs committed by a partner in the ordinary course of the firm's business or with the authority of other partners (Section 12) (*Hamlyn v. Harston & Co. (1903)*).

It would follow that if a tort was committed by a partner outside his apparent or ostensible authority, the firm is not liable and the partner concerned will incur personal liability (*Arbuckle v. Taylor (1815)*). *Joint and several liability of partners means that if an action were brought against one of them for a wrong committed by the firm and the third party obtains a judgment with which he is not satisfied, he can bring an action against the other partners since their liability is joint and several.*

3.5.1 Liability of incoming and outgoing partners

The estate of a deceased partner is liable only for such obligations and liabilities as are incurred by the firm prior to his death. The estate is not liable for any debts contracted subsequent to the death (Section 14(2); *Bogel v. Miller (1903)*). Similarly, the estate of a bankrupt partner is liable only for debts acquired prior to the date of bankruptcy and not those resulting subsequent to the date of bankruptcy. A newly admitted partner is not liable for those debts of the firm that result from acts done prior to his entry as a partner (Section 17(1)). The new partner may acquire this obligation through a contract called 'novation' with the consent of the creditor, the newly constituted firm and the new partner.

A retiring partner is liable for those debts and obligations incurred by the firm prior to his retirement. After retirement he is liable to those previously dealing with the firm who have not been given notice of the retirement (Section 36). To those with no previous dealings with the firm, he is liable unless he has advertised his retirement in the *London Gazette* or given them notice of his retirement. To those with no previous dealings with the firm who are unaware that he was a partner of the firm, he is not liable (*Tower Cabinet Co. Ltd v. Ingram (1949)*).

3.6 Interrelationship of partners

The relations between partners are governed by the provisions of the Articles or the Deed of Partnership. Because partners are *agents* of each other and can bind each other when making contracts on behalf of the firm, it is important for trust to exist between them. The law recognizes this and deems them to be in a **fiduciary** relationship with each other (*fides* is the

Latin for confidence or trust). Each partner is also a **principal** and under normal circumstances the relationship between partners will be governed by the provisions of the Articles or Deed of Partnership. In the absence of a written partnership agreement, their relations with each other may be inferred from the course of dealings between them. The provisions of the *Partnership Act, 1890*, apply only in so far as the partnership agreement does not either expressly or impliedly provide for the relations of partners to each other. The rights and duties between partners as provided in the 1890 Act (Sections 24–30) are as follows:

- All partners are to share equally in the capital, profits or losses of the firm.
- No partner is entitled to interest on his subscribed capital. Interest at the rate of 5 per cent per annum is payable on loans which exceed the subscribed capital.
- No partner is entitled to remuneration for acting on behalf of the firm.
- A partner is to be indemnified for any expenses incurred by him when acting properly on behalf of the firm in the ordinary course of business.
- All partners are entitled to participate in the management of the firm except a limited partner (see Section 3.9).
- To introduce a new person as a partner requires the consent of all the existing partners.
- Ordinary business matters are to be decided by a simple majority but no change to the nature of the partnership business may be made without the unanimous consent of all the partners.
- A partner cannot be expelled by a majority of the co-partners unless this power has been reserved in the partnership agreement.
- The partnership books must be available for inspection by any partner or his agent (*Bevan v. Webb (1901)*).
- Each partner is owed a duty of utmost good faith by his fellow partners in all partnership matters. This means all partners are required:
  - To render true accounts.
  - To provide full information on all aspects of the partnership business.
  - To account for any benefit derived (*Featherstonhaugh v. Fenwick (1810)*).
  - To disclose any secret profit made (*Bentley v. Craven (1853)*).
  - Not to carry on business that competes with that of the firm.
  - Not to use partnership documents and other confidential information elsewhere (*Floydd v. Cheney (1970)*).

3.7 Partnership property

Sections 20 and 21 of the 1890 Act define partnership property to include property originally introduced into the partnership business, property subsequently acquired on behalf of the firm for the purposes and in the course of the partnership business and any property bought with the firm's money. The partnership property is required to be applied exclusively to the business of the firm and in accordance with the terms of the partnership agreement.

The partnership property is distinct and separate from the property belonging to the individual partners. If bankruptcy were to occur, the partnership property forms part of a joint estate whereas each partner's personal property forms a separate estate.

3.8 Assigning a share in a partnership

Under Section 31 of the 1890 Act a partner may mortgage or assign his share in the partnership to an outsider if the partnership agreement does not prevent this. The newcomer (mortgagee or assignee) does not have the full rights of a partner. He is entitled to the share of the profits due to the assigning partner and also to his share of the partnership property on dissolution. He has no right to interfere in the management or administration of the firm or to inspect the books of the firm. The assignee is entitled to an account in the event of dissolution (*Watts v. Driscoll (1901)*).

Although an assignor will remain liable for the firm's debts, normally the assignee agrees to take over this liability. It follows, for example, that if the existing partners entered into a *bona fide* agreement to pay themselves salaries, such agreement would be binding on the assignee (*Re Garwood's Trust, Garwood v. Paynter (1903)*).

3.9 Limited partnerships

Under the *Limited Partnership Act, 1907*, a limited partnership may be formed. The Act allows one or more limited partners with limited liability but there must be at least one general partner with unlimited liability. The maximum number of partners is the same as for ordinary partnerships. A limited partner contributes a certain amount of capital and his liability for the firm's debts is limited to the amount he has contributed. A limited partnership must be registered with the Registrar of Companies, who must be provided with particulars such as the firm's name, place of business, purpose of the business, full names of each partner, a statement that the partnership is limited and the sum contributed by each limited partner.

The following rights and duties are attributed to a limited partner (Section 6):

- He cannot take part in the management of the firm. If he does, he is liable, just like a general partner, for all the debts and liabilities of the firm.
- He cannot bind the firm in dealings with outsiders.
- He can examine the firm's books and advise the other partners accordingly.
- His death or bankruptcy does not dissolve the partnership; mental disorder is a ground for dissolution if his share in the partnership cannot be ascertained or realized otherwise.
- To assign his share, he requires the consent of all the general partners.
- The partnership cannot be dissolved by him by notice.
- The limited partner's consent is not required if a new partner is introduced by the general partners.

Because of the ease with which a limited company may be registered with all participants enjoying limited liability, the popularity of the limited partnership has declined and very few of them are now registered.

3.10 Dissolution of a partnership

Dissolution of a partnership would depend on the terms of the partnership agreement. Subject to this, if a partnership was entered into for a particular business venture, then the completion of this venture would bring the partnership to an end. If the partnership was entered into for a fixed period, the partnership ends at the expiry of this period. Where, however, the partnership is entered into for an indefinite time (partnership at will) then it can be ended by one partner giving notice (Section 32). Apart from the grounds of dissolution just mentioned and subject to the provisions of the partnership agreement, a partnership may be dissolved on any of the following grounds:

The legal environment for business entities

3.10.1 By court order

Under Section 35 any partner may apply to the court for dissolution if:

- One of the partners cannot manage or administer his affairs because of mental incapacity.
- A partner, other than the applicant, becomes permanently incapable of carrying out his duties under the partnership contract.
- A partner, other than the applicant, is found guilty of conduct prejudicial to the business. In *Carmichael v. Evans (1904)*, dishonesty, i.e. travelling on the railway without a ticket, was considered an adequate ground for dissolution of the partnership.
- A partner, other than the applicant, wilfully or persistently breaks the partnership agreement or conducts himself in such a way that it becomes impractical for the other partners to carry on in partnership with him.
- The business can only be carried on at a loss.
- The court considers it just and equitable. In *Re Yenidje Tobacco Co. Ltd (1916)* a deadlock in the management of a private company was held to be adequate grounds for winding up the company. Although this was a case about a company the rule might well be applicable to a partnership in similar circumstances.

3.10.2 Without reference to court

A partnership may be dissolved on the following other grounds, subject to the terms of the partnership agreement:

- On bankruptcy or death of a partner (Section 33).
- When a court orders a partner's share in the firm to be charged to a separate debt, the other partners have an option to dissolve the partnership (Section 33).
- On bankruptcy of the partnership (Section 34).
- On grounds of illegality (Section 34), i.e. a partnership with an alien enemy at the outbreak of a war.
- Through mutual consent of all the partners.

3.10.3 Partnership insolvency

Where a partnership is insolvent (unable to meet its debts as they fall due) the partners can seek a voluntary arrangement of their affairs as an alternative to insolvency. Called a 'composition' with the creditors it amounts to an agreement by the creditors to accept a smaller sum in full settlement of the sums owed. It avoids the need to make the partners bankrupt. The partnership will be dissolved and the assets realized for what they will fetch, and the debts will be settled at the best rate possible – as explained below. If this procedure is not adopted the creditors may apply as follows:

- to wind up the partnership compulsorily, or
- to present a petition for the bankruptcy of one or more partners, or
- both of the above

If the third course is decided upon the court will still allow the bankruptcy of any partner even if the debts are paid in full from the sale of the partnership assets (*Marr (Pauline) re Marr (Robert) re (1989) v. Commissioners of Customs and Excise (1989)*).

On dissolution the partnership property including the goodwill is sold. The proceeds are then applied to pay outstanding debts and liabilities. If the amount realized is insufficient to discharge all the debts, each partner bears personal responsibility to pay for the deficiency in proportion to his entitlement to profits of the firm. If, however, a residual amount is left after discharge of all the debts, this will be divided amongst the partners in proportion to their normal entitlement to profits. In the event of bankruptcy of a partner when the partnership is dissolved, the partnership estate must be applied initially for the payment of partnership debts and it is the individual estate of each partner which must be applied in payment of their separate debts. Any surplus in the partnership estate becomes part of the separate estates of each partner in proportion to their respective entitlement to the partnership estate.

An important case arising from insolvency of a partner in the dissolution of a partnership is *Garner v. Murray (1903)*. The facts were that the partnership was dissolved, and all the creditors were paid, but there were insufficient funds to repay their capital to the partners. The actual figures were:

Assets to repay partners	£	*Liabilities (Capital)*	£
Cash	1916	Garner	$2288\frac{1}{3}$
		Murray	$102\frac{1}{3}$
			$2390\frac{2}{3}$
		Less	
		Wilkins (deficit)	$474\frac{2}{3}$
	£1916		£1916

Wilkins was insolvent and unable to bring in any money to repay his deficit on capital account, so that the other partners could not obtain the return of their funds. The question that arose was how this loss should be shared. It was held that such a loss was not an ordinary trading loss, but a capital loss. The deficit should not be shared in the usual proportions in which profits were shared, but in the ratios of their capitals at the start of the year. The loss therefore fell more heavily on Garner than on Murray, who had only a small amount of capital, although they shared ordinary profits equally.

3.11 Advantages and disadvantages of operating as a partnership

Advantages

- A larger amount of capital can be raised, although this cannot compete with the capital that can be raised by forming a company.
- Responsibilities, expertise and experience can be shared for the common good of the business.
- For some professional businesses (accountants, lawyers, doctors, etc.) partnerships are ideal business entities. There is no need for large capital; the environment is not cumbersome or impersonal as with large companies; everyone knows everyone else and so close contact and cooperation is maintained.
- Partnerships are suitable for small businesses with no need for a large injection of capital and those businesses that prefer operating on a family basis with no need for further expansion.
- Privacy of business affairs can be ensured, unlike a company whose business affairs become public knowledge in that various documents including accounts have to be filed with the Registrar of Companies and are open for inspection.

- All the partners are provided with equal incentives to work for the interests of the firm. They have all provided capital from their personal resources and can participate fully in the management of the firm.
- Less formality, publicity and expense are involved in forming a partnership as opposed to a company.
- Holidays, days off and sickness are easily covered by the partners.

Disadvantages

- Unlimited liability means that in the event of dissolution a partner may be called upon to make good outstanding debts of the firm from his personal assets.
- Business decisions require consultation and agreement of all the partners and this may not be always forthcoming.
- Death or bankruptcy may result in the dissolution of a partnership, unlike a company which enjoys perpetual succession.
- A partnership cannot raise capital by issuing shares or debentures and the facilities for raising capital are more restrictive when compared to a company.

Test your knowledge

Answers	Questions
	1 What is the concept of 'business entity'?
1 The concept that holds each business to be a separate unit distinct not only from other businesses but also from its owner.	2 A sole trader does not trade under his own name but under an invented name. What rules must he observe?
2 He must display on a notice at his premises the 'Particulars of Ownership', and these must also appear on all letterheads, business documents, etc.	3 What is the sole trader's business position?
3 One of unlimited liability; he is the business and the business is him, and there is no separate business legal personality.	4 List the advantages of being a sole trader.
4 (a) Independence; (b) the full profits are available to the proprietor; (c) rapid implementation of decisions; (d) close credit control; (e) personal supervision of work done and therefore maximization of goodwill.	5 List the disadvantages of being a sole trader.

Answers	Questions
5 (a) Long hours of work; (b) no holidays; (c) sickness seriously affects the business; (d) unlimited liability for debts and torts; (e) difficult to accumulate capital; (f) inadequate capital may mean high-cost activities.	6 What Act controls partnerships?
6 The *Partnership Act, 1890*.	7 Define a partnership.
7 A partnership is the relation which subsists between persons carrying on a business in common with a view of profit.	8 What matters should be included in a Partnership Deed?
8 (a) The trading name; (b) the nature of the business; (c) details of capital contributions, sharing of profits, and arrangements about drawings; (d) the powers of the partners; (e) details about admissions, retirement and dissolution of the business; (f) details about accounting and audit procedures; (g) how goodwill is to be revalued.	9 What is the relationship of the partners to one another?
9 Every partner is an agent of the other partners and binds them on all actions he takes which are within the ordinary business transactions of this type of partnership.	10 What liability has a partner for the debts of the business?
10 They are jointly and severally liable for both debts and torts, since the *Civil Liability (Contribution) Act, 1978*	11 The *Partnership Act, 1890*, is often said to have a residual effect only on the relationships between partners. What does this mean?
11 It means that if the partners have agreed expressly or impliedly on a particular procedure this is the procedure to be followed.	12 What does the Act say in this case about the relationship between the partners?

Answers	Questions
The Act only takes effect if no other agreement has been made, or a particular element of disagreement was not foreseen and covered by the Partnership Deed or Articles.	
12 (a) All partners share equally in the capital, profits and losses of the firm. (b) No interest to be given on capital. (c) Interest on loans over and above capital to earn 5 per cent. (d) No partner is entitled to a salary. (e) Ordinary business matters to be decided on a simple majority but matters fundamental to the partnership require the consent of all the partners.	13 Go over the questions again until you are sure of all the facts. Then try some of the written questions in Appendix 1.

4 Business entities: unincorporated associations

4.1 Introduction

An unincorporated association is one where members act together in pursuance of certain aims without taking on any formal separate legal structure. They may take the form of clubs, societies, cooperative societies, trade unions, employers' associations and partnerships. They may be profit-making or non-profit-making units. Their distinctive feature is that no separate legal body (corporation) is created when the association is formed.

The most common form of unincorporated association is the non-profit-making club, which does not exist solely to make a profit in the true sense of the word. In this category come clubs and societies which exist essentially to provide their members with certain benefits, e.g. club facilities, discount trading, etc. Usually membership of the club is obtained by paying a subscription which entitles the member to share in the facilities and services available. If profits are made by the club they are not profits in the usual sense of that word, but over-subscriptions (the members having jointly paid more for the services than was really necessary). The profits are therefore called surpluses. They may be used in improving or expanding existing facilities, buying new equipment, etc. Alternatively, they may be refunded to the membership. The income of the clubs and societies is drawn from the members' subscriptions, hiring of club facilities, and raising funds from activities like club trading, holding festivals or discos. Working men's clubs, social and sports clubs, cricket clubs and debating societies are examples of this type of unincorporated association.

4.2 Organization of a club

A club or society is managed by a committee headed by a chairman. Unlike a corporation, a club or society does not have a separate legal existence from its members. The **rules** of a club may be very important, and lay down not only the way the club is organized, but such legal matters as the responsibility of members for the acts of the committee, the powers of the officials and whether they act as agents of the committee, and their right to act as a tribunal in deciding disciplinary matters, the expulsion of members, etc. At meetings of the club it is common for points of order to be raised, which refer back to the rules of the club and question whether the matter under discussion is being properly considered.

The committee usually consists of a chairman, who conducts the meetings impartially to ensure all voices are heard and all opinions expressed; a secretary who takes a leading role in the organization and deals with correspondence; and a treasurer who deals with the subscriptions and disbursements of funds, and prepares a suitable receipts and payments account for presentation to the members at the annual general meeting. Other members may be appointed to the committee for general purposes (a social secretary, for example). Subcommittees may be appointed to deal with particular matters: their authority comes from the committee, or possibly from the members themselves if the appointment was from a general meeting of a club. Any action taken by such a committee (for example, suspension of a member) is subject to the rules of natural justice and the constitution of the club.

The powers, duties and functions of the management committee are normally contained in the constitution of the club or society.

4.3 Legal liability of unincorporated associations

The law regards these organizations as mere collections of individuals banded together to pursue certain aims, and bearing individual responsibility for the actions of the association. A member making contracts ostensibly on behalf of the club, but without actual authority to act as the club's agent will be personally liable on the contract. If he acts in an official capacity on behalf of the committee, the committee which authorized the agency will be jointly liable, or the members may be jointly liable if they collectively authorized the contract.

With regard to torts, where a tort is committed by an individual member that individual will be liable, as in *Prole v. Allen (1950)*.

> *Prole v. Allen (1950)*
>
> Acting through the committee, all the members of an unincorporated members club appointed a steward who, by his negligence, caused injury to the plaintiff, a club member. **Held**: the steward, but not the members of the committee, was liable to the plaintiff in respect of the injuries which she received. (Courtesy of *Cracknell's Law Students' Companion*)

However, where the committee have approved the employment of an incompetent person to do work they may be held jointly liable, as in *Brown v. Lewis (1896)*.

> *Brown v. Lewis (1896)*
>
> The stand at the ground of the Blackburn Rovers Football Club collapsed and caused injury to the plaintiff. The accident occurred because the club committee had employed an incompetent person to repair the stand. **Held**: the members of the committee were personally liable and the plaintiff was entitled to recover damages from them. (Courtesy of *Cracknell's Law Students' Companion*)

The members are not usually liable, unless the rules make it quite clear that they are liable.

4.4 Unincorporated associations and the ownership of land

Where many people own land jointly it becomes very difficult to transfer landed property, since the agreement of all must be secured. To overcome this type of difficulty the *Law of Property Act, 1925*, restricted the number of people who could own any piece of land to four. Consequently the members of a club may nominate up to four members to hold land as trustees. In any transfer of land the agreement of the trustees is all that is required, and the trustees are also entitled to sue or be sued on any matter affecting the property.

4.5 Legal actions affecting unincorporated associations

When a club is involved in a legal action it is usual for one representative or more to sue, or be selected as a target to be sued, in the courts. The rules of the Supreme Court say that the proceedings may be begun, and continued, unless the court otherwise orders, against one or more representing all. The decision of the court will then be binding on the association.

Where an organization is a trade union recognized as such by inclusion in a special register of trade unions, or is an employer's association included in a special register of employers' associations, it shall be capable of suing in its own name, and being sued in its own name, save that the law has recognized the immunity of such bodies (at present) from actions in tort for damage suffered, caused by action in furtherance of a trade dispute. Secondary action – defined in the *Employment Act, 1980*, as amended by the *Employment Act, 1982* – is not protected by this immunity in certain circumstances.

The Registrar of Friendly Societies is given the task of compiling lists of trade unions and employers' associations and ensuring that they comply with certain administrative and accounting requirements.

Test your knowledge

Answers	Questions
	1 What is an unincorporated association?
1 It is a business unit whose members act together to achieve certain aims without assuming any separate corporate legal status.	2 Give examples of unincorporated associations.
2 Clubs, societies, certain types of cooperatives, trade unions, employers' organizations and partnerships.	3 How may such bodies bring legal actions, or be sued?
3 Representatively, by choosing one or more individuals to bring the action, or be the target for the action.	4 Where does the legal responsibility lie for contracts made by unincorporated associations?
4 If the contract is made by a particular individual it lies with that individual. If the individual can show he was authorized by a committee the committee will be collectively liable.	5 Are the members personally liable?
5 Not usually, unless the rules clearly state that this is so.	6 Who is liable for torts performed by a member acting for the club?

Business entities: unincorporated associations **65**

	Answers		Questions
6	Usually the member will be liable, but if the loss suffered arose from the acts of a committee the whole committee may be jointly liable.	7	How is landed property owned by an unincorporated association?
7	Up to four members may be nominated as trustees to hold the land for the benefit of the club.	8	What is special about the situation of trade unions and employers' organizations?
8	(a) They can sue and be sued in their organization's name, provided they are registered. (b) They cannot be sued in tort for losses suffered in consequence of a trade dispute, except for certain cases of secondary action, i.e. action against an individual not directly engaged in the dispute.	9	Go over the page again if necessary. Then try some of the questions in Appendix 1.

5 Business entities: limited companies

5.1 The nature of a limited company

As industry developed the demand for capital could not be satisfied from profits created in business, and it became necessary to ask other people – not directly involved in the business – to contribute capital. In the early days of the Industrial Revolution those who contributed capital in this way were held to be full partners, with unlimited liability. Since many projects were highly speculative, and collapsed leaving enormous debts, many unsophisticated investors were ruined. Thousands lost their homes when speculative projects collapsed and the partners were required to contribute to pay the debts of the firms concerned. Only in 1855, when the increasing demands for capital met resistance from savers who had already seen others suffer hardship through no fault of their own, did Parliament sanction limited liability for shareholders. Parliament took the view that where a person has funds to contribute which can be used by others for the promotion of business activity, but does not wish himself to take any part in the conduct of the business or the management of the firm, it seems unfair to require him to carry the burden of unlimited liability which attaches to sole traders or partners. The principle of limited liability holds that such a person should be liable to the extent of the capital he has contributed, or agreed to contribute, but no further than this. The limitation of liability in this way unlocks savings which would otherwise merely be hoarded by their owners, and releases them to play a productive part in the industrial and commercial fields.

Companies are also called corporations and are of three types, depending on their mode of creation: chartered companies, statutory companies and registered companies. **Chartered companies** are set up by the granting of a Royal Charter, and the classic examples were the East India Company, the Hudson Bay Company, and certain universities. Today charters are usually reserved for professional organizations like the Chartered Institute of Transport. **Statutory companies** were set up by the passage of an Act of Parliament. This method was used for most of the early companies, such as canal and railway companies. The Act embodied the safeguards Parliament deemed necessary, and accorded the powers to purchase land compulsorily, etc. As the number of such enterprises grew a simpler system was required. The **registered company** system enabled companies to be set up by a simple procedure of registration with the Registrar of Companies. The first Companies Act also accorded limited liability to the shareholders: today the effective Acts are the *Companies Acts, 1985* and *1989*. The 1985 Act consolidated all the earlier Acts of 1948, 1967, 1976 and 1981 into a single comprehensive statute. The *Companies Act, 1989* implements the 7th and 8th Company Law Directives of the European Community but also deals with one or two defects which have become apparent in the 1985 Act. Both Acts are essential reading for any student of business law.

Business entities: limited companies **67**

**5.1.1
Types of registered companies**

Registered companies are of two kinds: **public companies** and **private companies**. Public companies tend to be larger than private companies, and are required to have a name which ends with the words 'public limited company' (abbreviated to plc). It must have a capital of at least £50 000 and one quarter at least of each share shall actually have been paid. The figure of £50 000 may be modified to such sum as the Secretary of State may determine at some future time (to take account of inflation) (Section 118, *Companies Act, 1985*). Public companies may offer their shares to the public, but private companies, whose names must end in the word 'Limited', are not allowed to offer their shares to the public. Provisions exist for a company to convert from one type to the other; for example, for a private company to register as a public company a special resolution must be passed to authorize the company to conform with the requirements mentioned above (Sections 43 and 45, 1985 Act).

At this point it is worth noting that the *Companies Act, 1989* relaxes many of the administrative rules for private companies, many of which are very small. The rules are relaxed on the following matters:

- The passing of resolutions at a general meeting can now be achieved in writing, and by correspondence, rather than at a formally convened meeting, the resolution being signed by, or on behalf of, all the members who would be entitled to vote at the meeting (had one been held) (Section 113).
- An 'elective regime' is introduced by which a private company may elect to dispense with certain formalities (such as annual general meetings, the laying of accounts and reports before general meetings, the annual appointment of auditors etc.)

**5.2
Basic characteristics of a public company**

- It must be incorporated or formed by registration in accordance with the *Companies Acts, 1985–9*.
- It must display the letters 'plc' (public limited company) after its name – for example, on its memorandum of association, in notices on public display at its place of business and on its company stationery.
- It must have a minimum capital of £50 000 of which at least one quarter must be paid before trading commences.
- Where its articles do not provide otherwise, the company may apply for a stock exchange quotation and offer its shares to the public.
- It may transfer its shares freely.
- The minimum membership is two, and there is no maximum, except that the limit is set by the number of shares issued.
- It must have at least two directors.
- Before issuing shares, the promoter of the company must issue a prospectus, or a statement in lieu of prospectus must be filed with the Registrar of Companies at least three days before any shares or debentures are allotted.

**5.3
The formation of a company**

To form a company certain formalities are required to be followed. The law requires that the following documents must be forwarded to the Registrar of Companies for England and Wales along with the requisite fees and stamp duties:

- A memorandum of association.
- A set of articles of association.

- A statutory declaration that the requirements of the Companies Act in respect of registration have been complied with.
- The names of the intended first director or directors and first secretary or joint secretaries with their written consents to take up shares.
- A statement of capital.

When the Registrar receives the documents he examines them to see that they have been completed satisfactorily and that the statutory requirements have been complied with. These are that the memorandum has been signed by at least two persons; that the company is being formed for a lawful purpose; that the proposed name is acceptable; and that the memorandum and articles are in the statutory form. When satisfied, the Registrar issues a **Certificate of Incorporation**, which can be described as the company's birth certificate. A private company may commence trading at this point while a public company has to wait until the Registrar issues a **Trading Certificate** under Section 117 of the 1985 Act. Section 117(6) of the 1985 Act provides that a Certificate of Incorporation is conclusive evidence that all the requirements of the Act in respect of registration have been complied with. The effect of registration is that from the date in the certificate the original subscribers and any others who later become members are a body corporate with the name given in the memorandum.

Before a company begins trading it must secure the capital it needs. With a private company this will be contributed largely by the founders so there is no difficulty. With a public company it must be obtained from the public either directly or indirectly through the institutional investors. In order to do this the company issues a prospectus which tells members of the public about the company and invites them to subscribe for shares in the enterprise. Two of the most important documents connected with registration of a company – namely, the memorandum and the articles of association – will now be considered individually.

5.3.1 The memorandum of association

This document is a deed signed by at least two persons, called 'subscribers' or 'promoters', which states and defines the constitution and powers of the company. The format of a memorandum for each type of company is issued in a statutory instrument under Section 3 of the 1985 Act. The Act requires that a memorandum contains the following pieces of information.

(a) *The name of the company, with 'Limited' as the last word for a private limited company.* A public company's name must end with the words 'public limited company' which is abbreviated to plc. The word 'limited' tells anyone who does business with the company that the shareholders have limited liability. It is a warning to them not to deal with the company unless they are quite sure they can afford the risk. Many people think a company is more reliable to deal with than a sole trader or partnership, but this is not necessarily so, since creditors can only claim against the capital contributed. This may be as low as the members like, and in practice £100 companies are often formed to be available at any time they are required. If the reader consults any newspaper which has a business section he will see companies offered for sale. At the time of writing the cost is about £120 and the companies are usually £100 companies. A businessman wishing to set up a company saves time and trouble by purchasing one ready-made. The objects of a company can be varied by a simple procedure, and so can the authorized capital, and the name. So a company which has been set up by a specialist company promoter can be taken over for a nominal sum and altered to suit the needs of any businessman. Whether a company is taken over in this way or set up in the way being described, the word 'limited' at the end of the name tells everyone dealing with the company that they can only look to that £100, or any authorized increased sum, for satisfaction in the event of difficulties. Although Section 17 of the *Companies Act, 1948*, provided that 'no company shall be registered by a name which in the opinion of the Board of Trade is undesirable', the *Companies Act, 1985*, makes changes in this area. Whereas previously the Registrar of Companies ensured that all proposed names were checked and the undesirable ones rejected, the new Act places the onus on self-regulation. An index of company names is maintained by the Registrar and the Act prohibits certain names, i.e. those of existing companies or offensive names. If an undesirable name is registered and subsequently discovered within 12 months, the company may be required to change its name. Three months is allowed to do this. The Act basically reduces the work of the Registrar, and reduces public costs, but the result is that established companies must do more checking for themselves.

(b) *Whether the registered office is situated in England, Wales or Scotland.* If the address of the registered office does not appear in the memorandum, it must be provided separately within 14 days of incorporation.

(c) *The objects of the company.* The 'objects clause' of a company has always been important in English law and it is desirable for students to know the background to this subject. However, the 7th and 8th Directives on Company Law of the European Community have called for simpler 'objects' clauses, and as we shall see the *Companies Act, 1989* has incorporated a new Section 3A into the *Companies Act, 1985* which recognizes that if a company states that its object is to carry on business as a general commercial company this means that it may carry on any trade or business whatsoever. This will reduce the need for complex and convoluted 'catch-all' objects clauses in future. The background to this subject is as follows.

The objects clause states the powers (*vires*) of the company; what it will do when it is established; and forms the legal basis for its activities within the fields specified. Other activities are *ultra vires* (outside its powers). This is a protection to the shareholders. Suppose I invested £500 in a company that was to develop a revolutionary type of aero engine, which I believed had a great future. I suddenly discover that the directors are using my money to buy sugar, which happens to be rising on world markets. I would naturally feel that this was not the purpose for which I had subscribed my capital, and would be able to obtain an injunction restraining the directors from using my money in this *ultra vires* way. For example, in *Ashbury Railway Carriage and Iron Co. v. Riche (1875)* a statutory company's objects allowed it to make and sell or lend or hire, railway carriages and wagons. However, the company contracted to finance the construction of a railway in Belgium. The company ratified its action subsequently by passing a resolution in accordance with its articles of association. The company later repudiated its contract and when sued by Messrs Riche for breach of contract, the company set up the defence of *ultra vires*. The House of Lords held unanimously that the contract was *ultra vires* the company and hence void; no subsequent agreement of the members could ratify the company's action. According to Lord Cairns, LC: '... it is not a question whether the contract ever was ratified or was not ratified. If it was a contract void at its beginning, it was void because the company could not make the contract.'

In *A.G. v. Great Eastern Railway (1880)* it was held that a company's objects shall include not simply the stated objects in its memorandum but also by implication power to do anything which is reasonably incidental to the carrying out of those objects. Further, *Re Jon Beauforte, Ltd (1953)* provides evidence that where goods are supplied to a company under a *prima facie ultra vires* contract and if the company uses those goods for *intra vires* purposes and the person supplying the goods has no knowledge that the goods will be used for *ultra vires* purposes, then the contract may not be held to be *ultra vires*.

In *Introductions Ltd v. National Provincial Bank Ltd (1969)*, a company was formed and its objects enabled it to provide services and accommodation for visitors to the Festival of Britain in 1951. At a later date, as a result of a change in management, the company began pig-farming contrary to its objects, and borrowed money. The pig scheme failed and when sued by the bank the liquidator put forward the defence of *ultra vires* while the bank placed reliance on an independent objects clause under which the company could borrow for any purpose which in the opinion of the directors could be advantageously carried out either in connection with or as ancillary to the business of the company. The Court of Appeal held the borrowing as *ultra vires* since the power of borrowing could not be exercised independently of the objects of the company. It must be noted, however, that the objects clauses of modern companies are elaborately drawn and may allow a company to engage in numerous types of business activities. The wording used in modern memorandums allows a certain amount of interpretation. Legal advice should be sought by a person dealing with a company whose objectives cannot be clearly identified. However, as mentioned at the start of this section ((c) above) the 1989 Act now permits companies to declare their objects as being 'to carry on business as a general commercial company' which will permit them to carry on any trade or business whatsoever. As companies alter their 'objects' clauses to meet this new situation the problem of knowing what a company may, or may not, do will diminish.

In any case the *ultra vires* doctrine has been considerably weakened as a result of the various directives of the European Community, especially to protect outsiders. The *Companies Act, 1989* introduces revised clauses 35, 35A and 35B into the 1985 Act, the burdens of which are as follows:

- *35(1)*. The validity of an act done by a company shall not be called into question on the ground of lack of capacity by reason of anything in the company's memorandum.
- *35(2)*. A member of a company may bring proceedings to restrain the doing of an act which but for subsection (1) would be beyond the company's capacity but no such proceedings shall lie in respect of an act to be done in fulfilment of a legal obligation arising from a previous act of the company.
- *35(3)*. It remains the duty of the directors to observe any limitations on their powers flowing from the company's memorandum; and action by the directors which but for subsection (1) would be beyond the company's capacity may only be ratified by the company by special resolution.

    A resolution ratifying such action shall not affect any liability incurred by the directors or any other person; relief from any such liability must be agreed to separately by special resolution.
- *35A(1)*. In favour of a person dealing with a company in good faith, the power of the board of directors to bind the company, or authorize others to do so, shall be deemed to be free of any limitation under the company's constitution.

- *35B.* A party to a transaction with a company is not bound to enquire as to whether it is permitted by the company's memorandum or as to any limitation on the powers of the board of directors to bind the company or authorize others to do so.

The essence of these provisions seems to be that while the members of the company can still hold the directors liable for any *ultra vires* acts this does not mean that outsiders dealing with the company in good faith can be affected by the fact that the contracts they made were *ultra vires*, nor are they put upon enquiry as to the validity of any contracts made. The actions of the directors will bind the company as far as outsiders are concerned irrespective of the wording of the 'objects' clause.

It must be noted that protection is also afforded to an outsider under the rule established in *Royal British Bank v. Turquand (1856)*. It was held in this case that in dealing with a company an outsider can assume that all the internal requirements or formalities have been completed by the company (e.g. the passing of a resolution at a general meeting) and a director or directors acting without authority in such circumstances will bind the company on any contracts entered into.

(d) *A statement that the liability of the members is limited.*

(e) *The amount of share capital to be issued and the type of shares.*

Note: Besides the above points a memorandum of association must be accompanied by a statement in the prescribed form giving the names and relevant particulars of the first director or directors, and the first secretary or joint secretaries, and their consents to the appointments.

Alterations to the essential clauses mentioned above may be made provided the statutory requirements laid down in the *Companies Act, 1985*, are satisfied. For example, the name may be changed by a special resolution under Section 18 of the Act; the objects of the company may be changed by special resolution (revised Section 4 introduced in the 1989 Act); alterations of capital must comply with Section 121; the creation of reserve capital must comply with Section 120 and Section 124; reduction of capital with Section 135; if the liability of directors is made unlimited it must comply with Section 307 and in the case of a private company if the limited liability clause is altered Sections 49, 50 and 516 must be complied with.

5.3.2 The articles of association

Having drawn up and signed the memorandum of association, the promoters usually then draw up detailed articles of association which control the internal affairs of the company. Such matters as the procedure to be followed at meetings, appointment and duties of the directors and the managing director, the borrowing powers that may be exercised, and so on, are considered and agreed. A set of model articles, called Table A, is printed as a statutory instrument (at present 1984 No.1717). These articles will be effective and binding on all companies issuing shares, unless the company's own articles specifically invalidate them on some point.

Section 9 of the 1985 Act provides that the articles may be altered by special resolution. The case of *Allen v. Gold Reefs of West Africa Ltd (1900)* suggests that not only the statutory requirements must be fulfilled for any alteration but that the alteration must be '*bona fide* for the benefit of the company as a whole ...' (*per* Lord Lindley, MR). The case is also authority for the proposition that alterations may have retrospective effect.

All the documents relating to a company are kept in a file at the Companies Registry at Companies House. The file is open for inspection by anyone for a nominal fee.

Before we leave the subject of the memorandum and articles of association we should perhaps refer to one controversial aspect. Section 14 of the *Companies Act, 1985* says 'the memorandum and articles, when registered, bind the company and its members to the same extent as if they respectively had been signed and sealed by each member.'

In other words the members have made a contract with one another to form the company and achieve its objects. This is often referred to as a Section 14 contract. However, this contract is of a special type, for it draws its legitimacy from the statute that created it, and not from ordinary contract law. Therefore if it subsequently appears that there is some unsatisfactory feature about the memorandum or articles the Court is powerless to amend it by implying a term into it which would give it business efficacy. The only way it can be changed is by a special resolution as prescribed in the Act. However the Act also says that a company cannot alter its articles if it in any way increases a member's liability to pay money to the company. Since it is the memorandum and articles which an outsider investing in the company consults before doing so, it would be unfair if subsequent alterations could change the amount due from a member.

In an introductory book of this sort is is impossible to go too deeply into company law – it is a subject for detailed study later. Suffice it to say that while the memorandum and articles can be altered in many ways, to pursue different objects or change the name, for example, they cannot be changed to increase the financial obligations of the members. An interesting case where this problem was aired is *Bratton Seymour Service Co. Ltd v. Oxborough (1992) BCC 471.*

5.4 The consequences of incorporation

As a consequence of registration and the issue of a Certificate of Incorporation a company comes into existence. One of the fundamental results of this is that the company acquires its own independent legal personality. The law regards the company as a separate legal entity, distinct from and independent of the persons who manage it (the directors) or those who own it (the shareholders). This separate legal personality of a company was confirmed by the House of Lords decision in *Salomon v. Salomon and Co. Ltd (1897).*

Salomon v. Salomon (1897)

Salomon owned a profitable boot manufacturing business and converted it to a limited company. The company then issued a debenture to Salomon for £10 000, secured on the total assets of the company. Later the company got into difficulties and became insolvent. When the creditors attempted to recover their money an assignee of the debenture in Salomon's name claimed all the assets which were his security for the debenture. **Held:** the debenture took priority. The company was a different person in law from the controlling shareholder and the unsecured creditors could not defeat the assignee's claim.

The principle of separate corporate personality of a company established in Salomon's case is also referred to as 'the veil of incorporation'. As a general rule the courts will not go beyond this veil of incorporation except in some of the following instances where the separate personality of a company may either be ignored or modified:

- In time of war in order to find out who the members of the company are to determine whether or not the company has enemy characteristics (*Daimler Co. Ltd v. Continental Tyre & Rubber Co. (Gt Britain) Ltd (1916)*).
- In circumstances indicating that the company was formed for a fraudulent purpose (*Re F.G. Films Ltd (1955)*). Sections 458 and 630 of the 1985 Act provide that if a company engages in fraudulent trading, any persons who knowingly become partners to the fraud are personally liable for the debts and other liabilities of the company.
- Where a company makes a loan to a director, as in *Wallersteiner v. Moir (1974)*. A director made a loan to another company which was his puppet. **Held**: The loan should be treated as made to the director personally.
- If a company carries on business for more than six months with less than the statutory minimum of members (two for both private and public companies – *Companies Act, 1985*), the person carrying on business may be made personally liable to the creditors for the debts of the company (Section 24, 1985 Act).
- In some cases the courts may want to investigate the control structures of companies to determine the question of residence for tax purposes (*Unit Construction Co. Ltd v. Bullock (1960)*).
- In *Creasey v. Breachwood Motors Ltd (1992) BCC 638*, the corporate veil was lifted to permit justice to be done in circumstances, which would otherwise have left a plaintiff disadvantaged. Creasey had been awarded damages for wrongful dismissal by a company called Breachwood Welwyn Ltd. Welwyn ceased to trade, paying off all its creditors except the plaintiff, and the directors transferred all its assets to a new company Breachwood Motors Ltd. The plaintiff's default judgment against Welwyn could not be enforced because Welwyn had no assets. Although Breachwood Motors was a different company from Welwyn the court decided to 'lift the veil' and see who was really behind Breachwood Motors. It was, of course, the same people and the court gave Creasey the right to proceed against the new company. It appears the courts will not allow the legal principle that incorporation creates a new legal personality to obstruct justice.

5.4.1 Liability for torts

A company is liable for the torts committed by its servants in the course of their employment, e.g. negligence, fraud or libel (*Citizens Life Assurance Co. v. Brown (1904)* and *Houldsworth v. City of Glasgow Bank (1880)*). A company may also be criminally liable for the acts of its organs. In *R. v. I.C.R. Haulage Ltd (1944)*, the fraud committed by the managing director was imputed to the company, although the court accepted that there were some crimes which a company was not capable of committing. The company can own land, buy property and employ people. Company property belongs to the company itself and not to any individual member. A company may enter into contracts, it can sue and be sued. The death of any members of the company does not affect the company since it enjoys perpetual succession unless wound up or dissolved. The liability of the company is limited to the amount of its share capital and the liability of its members is limited to any outstanding amount on the shares the members hold.

In *Richardson v. Pitt-Stanley and Others (1994)* (*The Times, 11 August*) the question was raised whether the directors of a company could be held liable in a civil action for a crime committed by the company. The circumstances were that the company had failed to insure itself against employer's liability, in breach of the *Employer's Liability (Compulsory Insurance) Act, 1969*. The company had thus committed a crime, for which the punishment was a fine. The Act does not impose civil liability on an employer, since civil liability already exists at common law if the plaintiff can prove breach of a duty of care. Civil liability also exists if the employee can prove breach of a statutory duty under the Factory Acts or similar legislation.

The injured employee, Richardson could not prove civil liability under these headings and sought to claim breach of the 'duty to insure' as giving rise to a civil liability of the directors. The Court of Appeal, by a majority decision rejected this. The Act was clearly intended to be a criminal law statute only. It had been passed to compel directors to insure their companies, but could not be construed as imposing unlimited civil liability on the officers of the company.

5.5 Share capital of a company, and debentures

A person will invest in a company either by taking up shares and thus becoming a member of the company or by making a loan to the company usually against a security – he will then be issued with a debenture certificate, thus becoming a debenture holder. A debenture holder is not a member of the company and does not therefore have voting rights. He is a creditor of the company who is entitled to interest at a fixed rate on his loan to the company.

When a person takes up a share he is issued with a share certificate. The basic characteristics of a share were described by Farwell, J, in *Borland's Trustee v. Steel Bros. & Co. Ltd (1901)* as follows:

A share is the interest of a shareholder in the company measured by a sum of money, for the purpose of liability in the first place, and of interest in the second, but also consisting of a series of mutual covenants entered into by all the shareholders inter se.

Note that the word 'interest' here may be confusing. It does not refer to any rate of interest, but to the extent that the shareholder is financially interested in the company. The reward enjoyed by the shareholder for buying a share takes the form of a dividend, which depends upon the type of share held, the profitability of the enterprise and the recommendations of the directors. The interest of a shareholder is the extent to which his ownership of the company extends.

Various terms are used to describe the share capital of a company: the **authorized** or **nominal capital** is the amount that a company may raise ultimately by issuing its shares; the **issued capital** is that portion of the authorized capital which has been issued by the company and the **uncalled capital** is that part of the issued capital which has not been called and/or paid by the shareholders; the **reserve capital** is that part of the uncalled capital which has been set aside by special resolution and will only be called up in the event of the company being wound up (Section 120, 1985 Act).

When a share is issued **at par**, it is issued at its present nominal value. If issued above the nominal value it is said to be issued at a **premium** and if issued below its nominal value it is said to be issued at a **discount**. (Shares may no longer be issued at a discount, even by leave of the court.)

The share capital of a company may consist of different types of shares and the rights of different classes of shareholders will be set out in the company's articles. A company's share capital may consist of:

5.5.1 Ordinary shares

The holders of these shares do not have any special rights apart from voting rights. Companies may issue non-voting ordinary shares. The holders of ordinary shares receive any dividend that the directors may recommend after the preference shareholders have received their dividend. The extent of the dividend paid to these shareholders will vary with the fortunes of the company. Ordinary share capital is also called 'equity' share capital, since all shares participate equally in the profits, or share equally in any losses. Because the risks are greater for equity shares than for preference shares equity capital is also spoken of as 'risk' capital.

5.5.2 Preference shares

The issue of these shares is authorized by the memorandum or the articles and the holders of the shares receive priority over other shareholders of the company. The holders are paid a fixed rate of dividend and usually also have preferential rights to repayment of capital in the event of winding up. The rights of holders of these shares may vary considerably from company to company and they may or may not be eligible to vote at a general meeting. Preference shares may be **cumulative**, in which case, if the preference dividend is passed in a bad year the entitlement will be carried forward to the following year, or the year after that, until the company makes sufficient profits to honour it. When they are **non-cumulative** the shortfall of dividend will not be made good in future years. Holders of **'participating'** preference shares will participate in any further distribution of funds to equity shareholders. Thus if shares are designated as 7 per cent participating preference shares the preference shareholders will first be awarded 7 per cent. If the ordinary shareholders are then awarded 20 per cent the preference shareholders would be entitled to participate in this more extensive distribution of profits and would be entitled to a further 13 per cent dividend.

The 1981 Act repealed Section 58 of the Companies Act (which authorized the issue of **redeemable** preference shares). Instead Section 159 of the 1985 Act permits companies to issue redeemable shares of any type. The shares may only be redeemed out of the distributable profits of the company, or out of the proceeds of a fresh issue of shares made for the purposes of the redemption. Any premium payable on redemption must also be paid out of distributable profits of the company, except where they were originally issued at a premium, when special rules apply. Shares redeemed in this way may be treated as cancelled on redemption, and reduce the amount of the company's issued share capital, but the authorized capital is not reduced – and hence the shares could be reissued at a future date.

Another innovation under Section 162 of the 1985 Act is the power granted to companies to purchase their own shares. Certain safeguards are built into the Act, but the general effect is that the company may use the distributable profits to purchase and cancel shares, if authorized to do so by its articles.

5.5.3 Deferred or founders' shares

The holders of these shares receive a dividend after the declaration of dividends on the preference and ordinary shares. These shares are usually held by promoters and directors of the company and are also known as management shares. The extent of the dividends will vary according to the profits made by the company, and may be very lucrative. The willingness of a founder of a business to accept 'founders' shares in part settlement of the purchase price when selling the business to a company is evidence of his belief in the future viability of the business, since they rank for dividend only after the other shareholders have received some reward.

76 Business Law

5.5.4 Stocks and shares

A company's share capital may consist of stocks and shares. The difference between the two is that whereas stocks are fully-paid and may be assigned in fragments in fractional amounts, shares may have been partly paid and cannot be divided up. Fully-paid shares may be converted by the company into stock, e.g. 100 £1 shares may be converted into four stock certificates of £25.

5.5.5 Debentures

Apart from raising capital through the issue of shares, an important and common means of raising capital for the company is by the issue of debentures. A debenture is a document issued to a person who extends a loan to the company. The document acknowledges the debt owed by the company and the debenture holder becomes a creditor of the company, receiving a fixed rate of interest. The debenture holder, unlike a shareholder, is not a member of the company and hence does not have any voting rights.

A debenture is normally secured by a fixed or floating charge over the company's assets. Where specific assets (e.g. plant and machinery) are given as security the debenture holder is said to have a **fixed charge** over the company's assets. In the circumstances, the company cannot deal with the assets or sell them without the consent of the debenture holder. A **floating charge** exists where the circulating assets (e.g. stock in trade) are given as security. Here the company does not require express permission of the debenture holder in order to deal with or sell the assets charged. Whether a debenture is secured by a fixed charge or a floating charge, the debenture holder has the ultimate power to enforce the security in the event of default by the company on the loan. Section 395 of the *Companies Act, 1985*, requires charges to be registered with the Registrar of Companies within 21 days of their creation. The reason why charges must be registered is to render them matters of public record, which may be consulted by creditors and future debenture holders needing to know whether other creditors with a prior charge exist. Failure to register such charges will mean that the charges will be void against a creditor or a liquidator of the company. The new sections introduced by the 1989 Act are quite complex in this area (see Sections 92–107, 1989 Act).

5.6 The management of companies

Since a company is an artificial legal person it can act only through natural persons – the directors and other officers who are empowered to act on its behalf. The type and extent of these powers will depend on the company's articles. A typical company structure may look something like the one shown in Figure 5.1.

Whereas in a private company the directors and shareholders are usually the same persons, in a public company this is not the case as the officials may hold only a few shares in the company and hence effectively the management is divorced from the ownership of the company. Although the shareholders appoint and can dismiss the directors, once appointed the management of the company rests with the directors. Their powers, contained in the articles of association, must be exercised *bona fide* for the benefit of the company as a whole. The shareholders cannot interfere with the exercise of the directors' powers unless these are exceeded and neither can they interfere with the day-to-day management of the company.

The directors together form a board of directors which then constitutes the governing body of the company. The board may in turn appoint a managing director as provided in the memorandum or the articles. His status depends on the powers conferred on him by the company.

Business entities: limited companies 77

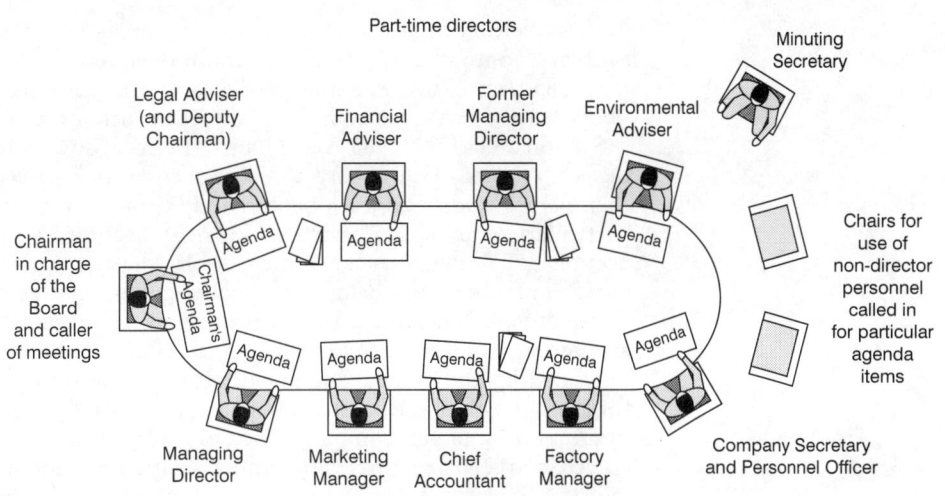

Figure 5.1
A typical company structure

5.7 Company directors

The management of the company is entrusted to a small group of persons called directors. As trustees and agents of the company, onerous liabilities and responsibilities are placed on them. Directors are appointed by the shareholders and hold office in accordance with the terms of the articles. These may require that they hold qualification shares in the company. The minimum number of directors required in a public company is two (Section 282, 1985 Act), while for a private company there need only be one director but he cannot also be appointed as a secretary (Section 283). Certain persons cannot be appointed as directors and these are:

- A person aged 70 or over, with certain exceptions – for example, if the company is a private company, or if the articles otherwise provide, or the appointment is by a resolution in which special notice of the age is given (Section 293, 1985 Act).
- An undischarged bankrupt (Section 302).
- A person convicted of an indictable offence connected with the promotion, formation or management of a company (Sections 295–299). These offences have now been extended to include offences connected with liquidation, receivership or management of a company.
- A person found guilty of fraud or any breach of duty in relation to a company while an officer of the company.
- A person who has been persistently in default of compliance with the Companies Acts (Section 297, 1985 Act).
- A person who is, or has been, a director of an insolvent company and is, or has been, a director of another such company which has gone into liquidation within five years of the first mentioned company and whose conduct as a director in any of those companies makes him unfit (Section 300, 1985 Act).

A director may resign at any time and provision for this is made in the articles. Provision for retirement is also made in the articles, and under Section 303 of the 1985 Act the company can remove a director by ordinary resolution before his period of office has expired, notwithstanding anything in the articles. Provisions may exist in the articles on disqualifications from acting or continuing to act as a director, over and above those contained in the 1985 Act – for example, under Section 302 it is an offence for an undischarged bankrupt to act as a director without authority of the court.

Section 288 of the 1985 Act requires the company to keep at its registered office a register of all its directors and secretaries. The register must contain their names, addresses, nationalities and business occupations and must give particulars of any other directorships held. Section 324 of the 1985 Act and Section 325), oblige a director to notify the company of his interests in shares or debentures held in the company or any associated companies. These must be registered. In this respect, the interests of a director's spouse and infant children are considered that of the director. The 1985 Act has tightened up and extended the law on the disclosure of interests in shares – for example, by requiring disclosure by persons acting together to acquire an interest in a 'target company'. Section 325 of the 1985 Act obliges the company to keep a register containing information about directors' interests in the company or any associated companies. The registers containing information on company directors must be kept at the registered office and be available for inspection by members of the company without any charge and by non-members for a minimal charge.

Also available for inspection must be copies of each of the directors' contracts of service as required by Section 318 of the 1985 Act. Section 323 of the 1985 Act penalizes the directors, and any shadow directors, for any option dealing, i.e. buying or selling any quoted shares or debentures of the company or associated companies. This prohibition is intended to further the interests of fairness by denying directors an opportunity to use 'inside' information which the ordinary members do not possess. It can also be justified as a means of preventing 'insiders' from manipulating the stockmarkets. The primary aim of this section is to protect members.

One of the commonest abuses by directors in the past has been their ability to make profits by 'insider dealing'. This term refers to the fact that a person who is on the Board of a company and knows of secret discussions which will affect the price of the company's shares when the information becomes public knowledge is in a position to take advantage of the time-lag. He might, for example, sell shares which he holds which he knows will fall in price in the near future. He might buy shares cheaply now if the price is expected to rise. The *Criminal Justice Act, 1993* has repealed the *Company Securities (Insider Dealing) Act, 1985* which formerly covered such activities. The changes made in the law are part of the harmonization arrangements within the European Union, and comply with EC Directive 89/592 'Coordinating Regulations on Insider Dealing'. Until 1980 it was not an offence to use inside information to make a profit (or avoid a loss) by dealing in shares. Inside information is defined as information relating to particular securities, which are liable to rise, or fall, if the information becomes public knowledge. The offences arise if the person having the information:

- Deals in the securities, either buying them in expectation of a rise, or selling them to avoid a loss.
- Encourages another person to deal in them, having reasonable cause to believe that the person will act on the suggestion.
- Disclose it to a third party otherwise than in the proper performance of his office or profession.

The punishment for these offences is imprisonment for up to seven years or a fine, or both.

Directors are managers or controllers of the company and normally receive remuneration in accordance with the terms of the articles. Accordingly, directors cannot claim payment for their services unless provision is made in the articles. The remuneration of the directors is normally determined by the company at general meetings. Directors cannot be compensated for loss of office or when retiring unless the amount is disclosed to the members and approved by the company (Section 312, 1985 Act). It is illegal for a company to make tax-free payments to any of its directors as the law considers any such payments made to be subject to tax (Section 311, 1985 Act). Particulars of directors' salaries, pensions, etc., must be mentioned in the company accounts and laid before the company at general meetings (Section 231, 1985 Act). Sections 231 and 237 of the 1985 Act further provide that these accounts must contain certain additional information on the directors' emoluments. Section 330 of the 1985 Act prohibits the company from making a loan to a director of the company or its holding company or to provide guarantee or security for a loan made to a director by any other person.

A company may make short-term loans to directors or provide guarantees or security for them up to a limit of £5000. Loans for company purposes, to finance expenditure incurred on the company's behalf is permitted if approved by the shareholders up to a total of £20 000. If a director acquires from or sells to the company property worth more than £100 000 (or more than 10 per cent of the company's assets if lower than £100 000) the facts must be disclosed in the company's accounts.

Let us now consider the directors' positions and their other duties. As a general rule directors cannot be regarded as servants of the company but there are cases to the effect that a managing director who devotes his full time to the affairs of the company may be regarded as employed by the company (*Trussed Steel Concrete Co. Ltd v. Green (1946)*). It is also recognized that for some purposes a director may be regarded as a servant of the company. For example, in *Lee v. Lee's Air Farming Ltd (1961)* the Privy Council held that a person who happened to hold all the shares except one and to be managing director and pilot of a company engaged in crop-spraying could also be regarded as a servant of the company and his widow could therefore recover under the *Workmen's Compensation Act*, effective at that time.

Essentially directors occupy twin roles within a company as trustees and agents. 'The directors are the mere trustees or agents of the company – trustees of the company's money and property, agents in the transactions which they enter into on behalf of the company' (per Lord Selbourne, LC, in *Great Eastern Railway Co. v. Turner (1872)*). As trustees of the company's money and property they must ensure that these are used solely for the benefit of the company. Any misapplication of funds or property is regarded as a breach of trust for which the directors may be called to account (*Wallersteiner v. Moir (No. 2) (1975)*). In *Maxwell v. Bishopgate Investment Trust (1993) BCLC 1282*, it was held that it was a breach of duty for a director to sign away title to company assets if there was no apparent gain to the company.

A director must not make a profit from his position. In *Attorney General of Hong Kong v. Reid (1993) 3WLR 1143* the Privy Council ruled that not only was a bribe recoverable by the company from the director who had taken it, but profits earned by investing the bribe were also recoverable, while losses made when an investment proved unsatisfactory had to be made good.

As trustees of the powers conferred on them the directors must ensure that these are used *bona fide* for the benefit of the company as a whole

– for example, where powers are given to issue shares, these must be used for raising capital when required by the company and not for the purpose of maintaining control of the company and preventing the election of additional directors (*Piercy v. S. Mills & Co. Ltd (1920)*). As trustees of the powers, they cannot fetter their future discretion, i.e. they cannot contract either with one another or third parties on how they shall vote at future board meetings (*Selangor United Rubber Estates Ltd v. Cradock (1968)*).

As agents of the company directors bind the company on contracts with outsiders. They will not incur personal liability for *intra vires* contracts (*Elkington & Co. v. Hürter (1892)*). Outsiders led by the directors into making contracts which are *ultra vires* the company are now protected, but the *ultra vires* rule still holds directors responsible to the members of the company for acts outside their powers, or the company's powers. Moreover, if the directors were to exceed the authority conferred on them by the articles and memorandum they might be liable for breach of warranty of authority (*Firbank's Executors v. Humphreys (1886)*). *Ultra vires* contracts made by directors can be ratified by a resolution at a general meeting or the articles of the company may be altered retrospectively by a special resolution. However, now that the 1989 Act has introduced the new clauses referred to above (Sections 35A, 35B and 35C) contracts made by the directors cannot be rendered invalid by anything in the objects clause of the memorandum of association and the company will be bound to honour the bargains made. For principles of agency see Chapter 13.

The directors of a company owe the following duties to the company:

(a) *A duty of care and skill*. Directors are required to exercise ordinary care and skill in discharging their duties. They will be held liable for neglecting their duties only if they are guilty of 'gross or culpable negligence in a business sense' (Romer, J, in *Re City Equitable Fire Insurance Co. Ltd (1925)*): on the question of the duties, the judge said that a director is not required to display in performing his duties a greater degree of skill than can reasonably be expected from a person of the director's knowledge and experience, e.g. 'a director of a life insurance company ... does not guarantee that he has the skill of an actuary or physician'. Further, a director is not bound to give continuous attention to the affairs of the company as his duties are of an intermittent nature. Lastly, a director can properly delegate his duties and be justified in trusting that the duties will be performed honestly. In *Re Duomatic Ltd (1969)*, where the directors had compensated a former director for loss of office without notifying the shareholders (Section 191, 1948 Act – now Section 312, 1985 Act), it was held they had acted unreasonably in failing to take legal advice on the point.

(b) *Duty of loyalty and good faith*. Since directors occupy a fiduciary position *vis-à-vis* the company they owe their duties to the whole company as a corporate body. They do not therefore owe a fiduciary duty to any individual shareholder (*Percival v. Wright (1902)*), and neither should the directors when considering what is in the best interests of the company give prominence to their duty to employees only as opposed to their prime duty to the shareholders (*Parke v. Daily News Ltd (1962)*). Directors are barred from any sort of 'insider' dealings, under the *Criminal Justice Act, 1993*.

(c) *A duty to act for a proper purpose*. A director must act in the interest of the whole company, and will be in breach of his fiduciary duty if he acts from an improper purpose. This requirement extends to any aspect of the director's duties. The leading case in this area is *Howard Smith Ltd v. Ampol*

Petroleum Ltd (1974) AC821, where the directors decided to embark upon an issue of shares not because the company needed extra capital, but in order to influence the voting of the shareholders.

Because of their position, directors should not allow themselves to be placed in a situation where their personal interests may conflict with their duties to the company.

> *Transvaal Lands Co. v. New Belgium (Transvaal) Land Co. (1914)*
>
> The articles of T.L.Co. provided that its directors could not vote in respect of contracts in which they had an interest. H was a shareholder in both the companies and a director of T.L.Co. H voted in favour of the purchase but did not disclose his interest in the N.B.Co. as required also by the articles of T.L.Co. **Held**: the contract was voidable.

Section 317 of the 1985 Act provides that 'it shall be the duty of a director of a company who is in any way, whether directly or indirectly, interested in a contract or proposed contract with the company to declare the nature of his interest at a meeting of the directors of the company'. A fine is imposed for failure to comply with this duty and this section in no way prejudices the right of a company to impose a more rigorous penalty in accordance with its articles, nor does it 'prejudice the operation of any rule of law restricting directors of a company from having interests in contracts with the company' (Section 317(9)).

A breach of Section 317 does not mean that the contract is a nullity; it means that the contract is *prima facie* voidable at the option of the company (*Hely-Hutchinson v. Brayhead Ltd (1968)*). Any secret profits made or benefits received by a director on such a contract must be accounted for by the director. In *Boston Deep Sea Fishing & Ice Co. v. Ansell (1888)*. Bowen, LJ, stated:

> *There can be no question that an agent employed by a principal or master to do business with another, who, unknown to that principal or master, takes from that other person a profit arising out of the business which he is employed to transact, is doing a wrongful act inconsistent with his duty towards his master, and the continuance of confidence between them. ... If it is a profit which arises out of the transaction, it belongs to his master, and the agent or servant has no right to take it, or keep it, or bargain for it, or receive it without bargain, unless his master knows of it.*

The facts of the case were that A was a director of B.Co. and on the company's behalf contracted for the building of fishing smacks. Unknown to the company, A was paid a commission on the contract from the other party to the contract. In addition A received a bonus from B.Co. of which he was a shareholder and which supplied ice to the fishing smacks. **Held**: A must account to B.Co. for both the commission and the bonus.

Finally, concerning directors' duties, Section 310 of the 1985 Act provides that any exclusion of liability in respect of a director for 'any negligence, default, breach of duty or breach of trust of which he may be guilty in relation to the company shall be void'.

The 1985 Act embodies numerous measures introduced by Parliament to ensure fair dealing by directors. In particular:

- Directors are required to have regard to employees' interests; employees cannot, however, enforce the duty.
- Service contracts for more than five years require the approval of a general meeting.
- Any 'substantial' property transaction between a director and the company also requires the sanction of a general meeting.
- Increased provisions for disclosure in the accounts of loans and contracts in which directors have an interest are imposed.
- Regarding insider dealings, the exclusion from dealings on the open market now includes a person who is, or during the last six months has been, knowingly connected with a company. Such a person may not deal in the securities of the company, or a related company, or one which the company has had dealings with, if he has unpublished price-sensitive information. Nor may he counsel or procure another to deal, or communicate the information to another. The maximum penalty is two years' imprisonment and/or an unlimited fine.

On the question of enforcing director's duties, the rule established in *Foss v. Harbottle (1843)* and as stated by Lord Davey in *Burland v. Earle (1902)* is that 'in order to redress a wrong done to the company or to recover moneys or damages alleged to be due to the company, the action should *prima facie* be brought by the company itself'. No outsider, member or director of a company may bring an action for an alleged wrong done to the company except the company itself. In *Foss v. Harbottle*, two members of the company had instigated proceedings against the company directors, alleging fraud and mismanagement of the company's assets. Upholding the corporate principle of a company, the court held that in such a case the proper plaintiff was the company and the matter was considered to be a matter of internal management which could have been ratified by a majority of the members.

The rule in *Foss v. Harbottle* has a number of exceptions when a shareholder may sue depending on the situation, either in his personal capacity or in a representative capacity on behalf of the other shareholders, in order to redress a wrong. These exceptions are as follows:

- Where the alleged action is illegal or *ultra vires* since the action cannot be ratified by the members (*Moseley v. Koffyfontein Mines Ltd (1911)*).
- Where a resolution is not validly passed, i.e. a matter has been decided by a simple majority whereas it requires the passing of a special or extraordinary resolution (*Edwards v. Halliwell (1950)*).
- Where personal rights of a plaintiff shareholder have been infringed or are about to be infringed, i.e. rights conferred by the articles (*Pender v. Lushington (1877)*).
- In circumstances where those who control the company are perpetrating a fraud on the minority shareholders. According to Lord Davey in *Burland v. Earle (1902)*, fraud takes place when the 'majority in the company are endeavouring directly or indirectly to appropriate for themselves money, property or advantages belonging to the company or in which other shareholders are entitled to participate'.
- In cases where the interests of justice require departure from the rule in *Foss v. Harbottle* – for example, in *Heyting v. Dupont (1964)* it was intimated that a member might be allowed to sue to restrain misfeasance without alleging fraud.

- Under the statutory provisions of the 1986 Insolvency Act a member of the company can petition the court to wind up the company alleging 'that it is just and equitable that the company should be wound up' (Section 122). Some of the varied circumstances when this would occur would be where the substratum of the company has failed (the company concerned had been unable to obtain a patent essential to its activities) (*Re German Date Coffee Co. (1882)*) or where there is a deadlock in the management of the company (*Re Yenidje Tobacco Co. Ltd (1916)*), or where the petitioner is kept from his rightful share in the management of the company (*Re Westbourne Galleries Ltd (1973)*), or where no *bona fide* intention exists for carrying on business in a proper manner (*Re London & County Coal Co. (1866)*), or where the company was formed for a fraudulent or illegal purpose (*Re Thomas Edward Brinsmead (1897)*). Under Section 459 of the 1985 Act, a member can petition for an alternative remedy to a winding-up where 'the affairs of the company are being conducted in a manner unfairly prejudicial to some part of the membership (including himself) or that any actual or proposed act or omission of the company is, or would be so prejudicial.

The 1985 Act imposes increased penalties for many of the offences in the Companies Acts. There are over 20 pages in schedule 24 of penalties imposed for offences under the Act.

Further provisions in the 1985 Act under which members can bring an action are: Section 5 (where objects are being altered), Section 127 (where class rights are being varied) and under Sections 431 and 442 (where a certain statutory minimum number of shareholders may apply for the Department of Trade to conduct an investigation into the company's affairs).

The principle of limited liability which is such an encouragement to enterprise and industry and makes the limited company such a satisfactory form of business enterprise, is open to abuse. For example, directors may order vast quantities of supplies from unsophisticated suppliers with no intention to pay, leaving the creditors with bad debts which cannot be recovered. The provisions of the *Companies Act, 1985* and the *Insolvency Act, 1985* were consolidated in the *Company Directors Disqualification Act, 1986* to prevent unscrupulous directors from restarting businesses under a new name while other companies were being dissolved with heavy losses to creditors.

Disqualification can be ordered on the following grounds:

- Up to five years' disqualification for general misconduct – for example where a director is convicted of an indictable offence re company promotion, formation, management or liquidation. Where there is persistent default in delivering annual returns to the registrar, or other documents this could also lead to disqualification. You cannot have the privilege of limited liability unless you stick to the rules.
- Disqualification for between two and fifteen years can be ordered against a person who has been a director of a company which has become insolvent.
- Fraudulent practice revealed by a liquidator who has been authorized to wind up a company can lead to the liquidator applying to the court for a declaration that the directors named have been involved in fraudulent trading. Disqualification can then be imposed for up to 15 years.

Directors who ignore the disqualification of the court will be held fully liable for the debts of any company formed.

It is also possible to require the director to pay such a contribution to the company's assets as the court thinks fit.

- 'Wrongful trading' consists of continuing to trade when the company is known to be insolvent. By hanging on, hoping for something to turn up, the directors are making the position worse, week by week, for eventual creditors who are continuing to supply goods or services. Not only can such directors be disqualified from future directorships but they can lose the privilege of limited liability and become personally liable for the debts of the business.

5.8 Other officers of the company

5.8.1 The secretary

The law requires that a company must have a secretary who may be an individual or a corporation. The 1985 Act requires the company secretary of a *public* company to be qualified as a solicitor, barrister, accountant or chartered secretary. In a public company one of the two directors may be the secretary while in a private company a sole director cannot also be the secretary (Section 293, 1985 Act). Being the main administrative officer in the company, he has varied duties and responsibilities depending on the company. He is regarded as an officer of the company, being included in the section of the Act dealing with the officers. A deputy secretary may be appointed. A secretary can sign administrative contracts on behalf of the company (e.g. employing staff, ordering cars, etc.), whereas other contracts require specific authority and hence he cannot bind the company (*Houghton & Co. v. Nothard, Lowe and Willis Ltd* (1928)).

As a clerk, he is present at all meetings of the company and board. He prepares proper minutes of the proceedings and issues all notices to members and others. He is responsible for all matters connected with the shares – for example, he certifies transfers of shares, keeps the register of members, makes returns to the Registrar and maintains the books of the company, etc. As a clerk or servant of the company he is entitled to preferential payment of his salary in the event of a winding-up of the company.

5.8.2 Auditors

They can be appointed by the directors at any time before the first general meeting of the company. If the auditors have not been appointed by the directors, the company can do so at the general meeting (Section 384, 1985 Act). Auditors appointed at a general meeting are to hold office from the end of that meeting until the end of the next (Section 384, 1985 Act). The Secretary of State must be given notice where no auditor is appointed or reappointed at a general meeting and failure to do so makes the company and every officer in default liable to a fine (Section 384(5), 1985 Act). The remuneration of the auditors is fixed by the company at a general meeting. The auditors are required to be independent persons and as such an officer or servant of the company, a body corporate or a partner or employee of an officer or servant of the company cannot be appointed as an auditor. To be appointed an auditor, a person must be a member of a recognized body of accountants. The 1985 Act recognizes the three Institutes of Chartered Accountants (England and Wales, Scotland, and Northern Ireland) and the Chartered Association of Certified Accountants. Alternatively, the person must have been authorized by the Department of Trade. A company can remove an auditor by ordinary resolution before his term of office expires and notwithstanding anything in any agreement with him (Section 386, 1985

Act). An auditor is an officer of the company for some purposes and an agent of the company for other purposes.

The duty of an auditor, depending on the articles, is essentially to examine the company accounts in order to ascertain the true financial position of the company and lay a report before the members of the company. Under the 1989 Act this duty is extended to include consideration of the director's report, and any inconsistencies in that report compared with the published accounts (Section 9, 1989 Act). Where accounts are defective the directors may prepare revisions to the accounts so that they do comply with the requirements of the Companies Acts. The Secretary of State may order such revisions and dissatisfied parties may apply to the courts to require the directors to produce accounts that do comply with the Acts. Section 221 of the 1985 Act requires every company to keep accounting records which must be available for inspection by the company's officers; the form and content of the accounts are prescribed in the Fourth Schedule to the 1985 Act. The auditor's duty is owed primarily to the members of the company and not to the directors as such (*Re London & General Bank (No. 2) (1895)*). Auditors are required to act honestly and with reasonable care and skill in discharging their duties. An auditor will be liable to the company for any loss resulting from negligence or default in the performance of his duties although a court may grant him relief against liability in certain circumstances – for example, where he has acted honestly and reasonably (Section 727, 1985 Act).

5.9 Meetings and proceedings

Section 366 of the 1985 Act requires the company to call an annual general meeting every year and an interval of not more than 15 months should elapse between meetings. Under Section 368 an extraordinary general meeting may be requisitioned, irrespective of anything in the articles, by the holders of at least one-tenth of the paid-up capital with voting rights at a general meeting or members representing one-tenth of the voting rights in the case of a company without share capital.

Notice of the meetings of the company must be given, and should contain the place, date and the time of the meeting. On the question of length of notice for calling meetings, Section 369 requires 21 days' written notice in the case of an annual meeting whereas other general meetings require 14 days' written notice unless a special resolution is proposed, when not less than 21 days' notice is required. The period of notice can be shortened in particular cases if specified in the articles, e.g. with agreement of all members at an annual general meeting. Where the 1985 Act requires special notice then at least 28 days' notice of the meeting must be given (Section 379).

Notice of the meeting must be served on each member of the company (Section 370) and also served on the auditors (Section 387, 1985 Act). Where a notice of such a meeting is not given to every entitled person, any resolution passed becomes a nullity (*Young v. Ladies' Imperial Club Ltd (1920)*). However, company articles can provide that accidental omission does not invalidate the company proceedings at the meeting.

Members themselves have a right to move a resolution or to circulate statements on any proposed resolution at the meeting (Section 376). Proceedings at general meetings will be valid only if an effective quorum is present and this may depend on the articles. However, Section 370(4) of the 1985 Act provides that the quorum duly constituted for both public and private companies is two members personally present.

At the meeting any member can be elected as chairman (Section 370) and the manner in which the meeting is conducted depends on the meeting itself.

Although the chairman cannot adjourn a meeting at his will, he may do so in case of disorder. Voting at the meeting is decided by a show of hands if the articles do not provide otherwise.

Subject to the articles of a company, a poll may be demanded, when every member is normally entitled to one vote per share (Section 370). Section 372 grants a right to vote by proxy in a poll. At the general meetings some matters are decided by ordinary resolution requiring a simple majority while more important matters are decided by extraordinary resolution requiring a three-quarter majority of those present and entitled to vote. Special resolutions require the same majority as extraordinary resolutions but in addition also require the serving of at least 21 days' notice.

A statutory right exists to demand a poll when passing a special resolution or an extraordinary resolution (Section 378(4) and (5)) or where the articles so provide.

Lastly, Section 380 of the 1985 Act requires that copies of certain resolutions and agreements are to be forwarded to the Registrar within 15 days, either in printed form or in a form approved by the Registrar.

5.10 Winding up of a company

Although a company cannot die it will cease to exist if dissolved and removed from the register of companies. The process leading up to dissolution is called winding up or liquidation. All insolvency, whatever the type of business unit, is now covered by the *Insolvency Act, 1986* as amended by the *Insolvency Act, 1994* and the *Insolvency (No. 2) Act, 1994*. For companies, liquidation can take the forms shown below, but before looking at these two methods of winding up we must first say that there are good reasons very often for avoiding the winding up of a company. It may be preferable to seek arrangements which will keep the company operating as a going concern (for example to avoid the mass unemployment that may result from the closure of an important company). It may be preferable to secure a voluntary rearrangement of the affairs of the company – put in a new management, etc. This may resolve the company's difficulties to the satisfaction of its creditors, and thus avoid the expense and adverse social effects of other proceedings. The shareholders may feel that their investment can be rescued more effectively if a less abrupt procedure than winding up is followed. These solutions could be achieved by an **administration order**, whose purpose is to rehabilitate and rescue a company as a going concern.

An administration order appoints an administrator, as a result of a petition to the court from either the directors, or the shareholders or the creditors. The administrator has to formulate proposals for submission to the creditors' meeting, and when approved the administrator becomes the manager of the company, charged with the responsibility of bringing the proposed solution to the company's problems to fruition. Pending the achievement of a successful solution the company's earlier commitments to mortgagors, debenture holders, hire purchase creditors and others are suspended. The administrator is the agent of the company, and does not acquire any personal liability for contracts entered into on the company's behalf. Note that the appointment of an administrator in this way is a serious disadvantage to a mortgagor with a fixed or floating charge on the assets of a company. Such a secured debenture holder might (selfishly) prefer to recover its money from the sale of the assets of the company, whatever its effect on the employees, the shareholders and the unsecured creditors. The holder of a debenture secured by a floating charge can now appoint an

administrative receiver. Such a person has the same powers as an administrator, but only needs to sell off the assets – when the *secured* creditor will have first claim on the proceeds.

The arrangements described above to rescue a company (one might almost say for 'social' reasons) were seriously affected by the decisions in a case which became popularly known as the 'Paramount Airways' case. In this case, *Powdrill v. Wilson (1994)*, the Court of Appeal ruled that where an administrator of a company continues to employ staff of the company for more than 14 days after his or her appointment as administrator and where they are to continue to be paid under their previous contracts, the administrator is deemed to have adopted these contracts. The administrators in the case had agreed to keep pilots and others in employment but had disclaimed responsibility for paying the wages from their own funds pending a resolution of the company's difficulties. Later, when it became clear that no buyer could be found for the company, the staff were dismissed. The Court of Appeal's ruling meant that the administrator's disclaimer was ineffective and the administrator had adopted the contracts and must pay the wages out of the funds available and before claiming their own remuneration. Parliament decided it must rectify the problem, because you cannot sell a company as a going concern if you have dismissed all the staff, and two weeks is not long enough to sort out the problems of any major insolvency. The result was the passing of the *Insolvency Act, 1994*, which reverses the decision, and only makes the administrators liable for wages incurred after their appointment (and not for accumulations of unpaid wages under the contracts of employment, built up before the date of the administrator's appointment).

There is also an *Insolvency (No. 2) Act, 1994*, which deals with a minor difficulty which arises in insolvency cases where interests in property have been acquired by persons otherwise than in good faith and for value.

5.10.1 Compulsory winding up

Under Section 122 of the 1986 Act a company may be wound up by the court. The High Court and in some cases the County Court may make such an order if:

- By special resolution the company has so resolved.
- The company has not been issued with a certificate under Section 117 of the *Companies Act, 1985* (public companies).
- The company does not commence business within a year from its incorporation or suspends its business for a year.
- The minimum membership is reduced below two.
- The company is unable to pay its debts (Section 123 defines what this means).
- The court is of the opinion that it is just and equitable that the company be wound up. The various grounds under this head are mentioned in the first bullet point on page 83.

Petitions for winding up may be presented, depending on the circumstances, by either the company, a creditor, a contributory (those liable to contribute to the assets of the company in case of winding up), the Official Receiver or the Department of Trade. The court controls the winding up and appoints the liquidator, whose role is to dispose of all the remaining assets of the company in order to pay the various creditors in the order of their ranking.

5.10.2 Voluntary winding up

Since the *Insolvency Act, 1986* this can take two forms only:

- *Members' voluntary winding up*. Here the company is able to pay all its debts in full within 12 months and the company directors file a statutory declaration of solvency in accordance with the terms of Section 89 of the 1986 Act. Members of the company appoint a liquidator and the powers of the directors cease forthwith (Section 91).
- *Creditors voluntary winding up*. Apart from the above all other types of voluntary winding up will take this form. The company is unable to meet the creditors' claims in full and they will be able to appoint a liquidator (Section 100) to control the winding up.

Note: The 1985 Companies Act is the most comprehensive restatement of company law for forty years. It has now been joined by the *Companies Act, 1989*. This book is not a 'company law' book and cannot deal with company law in full. Those requiring a really detailed guide to the Acts, apart from reading and studying the Acts themselves, should turn to the publications by ICSA Publishing Ltd, the publishing side of the Institute of Chartered Secretaries and Administrators. Although these volumes (*The Companies Act 1985 and Related Legislation* and *The Companies Act 1989 with commentary and consolidated index*) are expensive, they are invaluable, and should be available in most libraries (and indeed many companies might be prepared to buy them for the use of staff studying company law). They are available from International Book Distributors Ltd, 66 Wood Lane End, Hemel Hempstead, Herts HP2 4RG or from the Institute to personal callers at 16 Park Crescent, London W1.

5.11 Advantages of the limited company as a form of business entity

When compared with a partnership or a sole trader a company has the following advantages:

- Being a separate legal person, the debts of the company can only be claimed against the company. The liability of the shareholders is limited to any outstanding amount of the shares taken. In a partnership the partners are jointly liable for the debts of the firm (except a limited partner) and a creditor can make claim against the personal assets of a partner. The same would also apply to a sole trader who is personally liable for all his debts.
- Once formed, a company enjoys perpetual succession and the death, bankruptcy, mental disorder or retirement of a member does not affect the existence of the company. A partnership dissolves on grounds of death, bankruptcy or insanity of a partner.
- A new partner cannot be introduced in a partnership without the consent of all existing partners whereas in a company shares can be transferred without the consent of other shareholders.
- A company can enter into contracts with its members and can sue and be sued on the contracts. A partner cannot enter into a contract with the firm.
- Since the property of a company belongs to the company, any changes in the ownership of shares does not affect the ownership of the company property. In a partnership, changes due to death or retirement of a partner will result in changes to the ownership of the firm's property.
- Each partner can take part in the management of the firm (except a limited partner) and as an agent of the firm can bind the firm on contracts entered with outsiders. Shareholders of a company are not agents of the company

Business entities: limited companies

and they do not participate in the management of the company; management is entrusted to a body of persons called directors whose status, function and powers are determined by the articles and the memorandum.
- A company can raise large amounts of capital because of its huge membership whereas a firm has to be content with the personal contributions of the individual partners which, due to the restricted membership, cannot be large. A company has greater facilities for borrowing – e.g. through the issue of debentures – than a firm or a sole trader.

5.12 Disadvantages of limited companies

Some of the disadvantages associated with a company are:

- Members who own the company are not necessarily those who run the company and hence management is divorced from ownership. This leaves it open for the directors to abuse their position although safeguards are provided by the *Companies Acts, 1985–89*. It is also possible that since directors do not own the company they may not devote all their energies to the success of the company. A sole trader or a partner, being the owner of the business, would probably work harder to promote that business.
- A company will not be able to preserve the privacy of its business affairs as most of its important documents are filed at the Companies Registry and are available for public inspection. Privacy of business affairs may be considered important to some businessmen and a partnership or sole tradership may appear more attractive in this regard.

Note: A private company can maintain some privacy on its affairs. Under the 1985 Act small companies (those with a turnover less than £2 million and assets of less than £975 000) need not file a profit and loss account, and need only submit a modified Balance Sheet. Medium companies (those with turnover less than £8 million and assets of less than £3.9 million) need not reveal their turnover, and may submit a modified Profit and Loss Account as laid down in Sch. 8, Part 1 of the 1985 Act.

Test your knowledge

Answers	Questions
	1 What is the principle of limited liability?
1 Shareholders cannot be held liable for losses suffered by a company beyond the amount of nominal share capital they agreed to contribute.	2 As a result, on whom do such losses fall?
2 On creditors, who cannot secure payment for goods and services supplied to an insolvent company.	3 What are the three types of company?

90 Business Law

Answers	Questions
3 Chartered, statutory and registered companies.	4 What are the types of registered companies?
4 Public companies and private companies.	5 How is a company formed?
5 By registering with the Registrar of Companies: (a) a memorandum of association; (b) articles of association; (c) a statutory declaration that the requirements of the Companies Act have been complied with; (d) a statement of the capital required, and how it will be contributed; (e) the names and addresses of the first director or directors and first secretary or joint secretaries with their written consent to take office.	6 What is the most important clause in a memorandum of association?
6 The objects clause, because it establishes which activities a company may perform and which acts are *ultra vires*.	7 How does Section 35 of the 1985 Act (as amended by the 1989 Act) affect the *ultra vires* principle in English law?
7 It makes it possible for those who have dealings with a company in good faith to secure redress of any grievance even though the dealing was outside the powers of the company. It reduces the severity of English law.	8 What is the rule in *Royal British Bank v. Turquand* (1856)?
8 The rule is that those dealing with a company can expect that the internal requirements and formalities have been complied with. Thus if the company should have passed a resolution to authorize the directors to act for the company one can assume it has been done.	9 What was *Salomon v. Salomon* (1897) about?
9 It established that the company was a different legal person from the directors of the company.	10 What are the commonest classes of shares?

Business entities: limited companies

Answers	Questions
10 (a) Ordinary shares; (b) preference shares; (c) deferred or founders' shares.	11 What duties do directors owe to the company?
11 (a) A duty of care and skill; (b) a duty of loyalty and good faith; (c) a duty to have regard of the employees' interests; (d) a duty to act for a proper purpose.	12 What was *Foss v. Harbottle* (1843) about?
12 It held that individual members could not sue the directors for fraud and mismanagement for the proper plaintiff was the company itself. However, there are several exceptions to this rule, where a shareholder may sue.	13 In what way has the *Companies Act, 1989* eased the administration of private companies?
13 (a) Resolutions may be passed by correspondence, rather than at formal Board Meetings; (b) it introduces an 'elective' regime where the company can pass a resolution to elect to dispense with certain formalities, such as the holding of AGMs and laying accounts before AGMs.	14 What is insider dealing?
14 Dealing in a company's shares by directors and employees who know of projected developments which have not yet been released to the general public.	15 What Act makes insider dealing an offence?
15 The *Criminal Justice Act, 1993*.	16 On what grounds can a director be disqualified?
16 (a) General misconduct; (b) insolvency of a former company; (c) fraudulent practice revealed at a liquidation; (d) late delivery of returns to Companies House.	17 What Act now controls all insolvencies?

Answers	Questions
17 The *Insolvency Act, 1986*, as amended by the two *Insolvency Acts of 1994*.	18 Go over the questions again until you are sure of all the answers. Then try the written questions in Appendix 1.

Part Three The Law of Contract

6 The nature of contracts

6.1 Agreement as the basis of contracts

The whole basis of the law of contract is agreement. In particular, a contract is an agreement bringing with it obligations which will be enforced by the courts.

Most of the principles of modern contract date from the eighteenth and nineteenth centuries, when great importance was placed upon the commercial freedom of individuals. The concept of a contract at that time was of equals coming together to bargain and reach agreement: an agreement which they would wish to be upheld by the courts. Whilst it is still true that individuals come together to form agreements, it must also be recognized that countless contracts are entered into between parties who are not equals in any way, even if the law may pretend they are. A major criticism of contract law over the years has been that rich, experienced and legally advised corporations have been able to make bargains with many people who are of limited resources, relatively unsophisticated and totally unrepresented legally for fear of incurring costs beyond their means. Because of this the law of contract has gradually moved away from a total commitment to enforce, without qualification, any agreement which has the basic elements of a contract. In particular, Parliament has introduced statutes which are often designed to protect relatively weak consumers from businessmen having greater bargaining power. Despite this, the courts are still reluctant to set aside an agreement having all the elements of a contract and in this respect follow their nineteenth century predecessors.

The form of the contract. A contract may be in any form, which means it may be:

- oral;
- written;
- partly oral and partly written;
- standard – where the contract is of a repetitive nature the written form of the contract may be in a standard form known as a standard form contract;
- formal, i.e. a deed, drawn up by a solicitor and signed and witnessed in a formal manner, under seal.

The different forms of contracts are discussed below.

6.1.1 Oral contracts

Where a contract is made by word of mouth it can only be proved in court if witnesses are available. The second-hand car dealer who calls Joe in from under a lorry and Maria in from the photocopier and says, 'This is Mr Kadar. I am buying his second-hand Volvo car for £850, payable by cheque on his delivering the car to me in its present condition at 4 p.m. today' is making sure he has two witnesses to the agreement. Two minutes later Joe is back under the lorry and Maria is back at the photocopier and Mr Kadar knows he is committed to a bargain and must deliver the car at 4 p.m.

6.1.2 Written contracts

A written contract will embody the terms of the agreement in writing and each party will have a copy. In some apprenticeship agreements, called indentures, the agreement was written twice on a single sheet of paper (or perhaps parchment) and cut apart with a pair of scissors to give a pattern of teeth marks – indentures.

6.1.3 Partly written and oral contracts

Where the parties choose to put the contract into writing the courts used not to allow evidence of any unwritten terms to be given. However, this rule is of little importance now as the courts have created very wide exceptions to it. There is, for example, a 'doctrine of the implied term (a custom or trade usage)'. This is explained later (see Section 9.3). There is sometimes an oral condition precedent, perhaps specified at the time of the offer or acceptance, while sometimes the parties intend the contract to be partly written and partly oral. This last exception has been used in so many cases that the general rule would appear to have lost its original value. For example:

> *S.S. Ardennes (Cargo Owners) v. Ardennes (Owners) (1950)*
>
> The defendants orally promised that their ship would proceed direct to London and in reliance upon this promise the plaintiffs agreed to the shipment of 3000 cases of their mandarins for sale in the London market. The bill of lading provided that the defendants were able to carry the goods to London proceeding by any route, and whether 'directly or indirectly to such port' and were permitted 'to carry the goods beyond their port of destination'. The ship did not sail straight to London but went first to Antwerp and as a result the cargo was delivered later than could have reasonably been expected. The plaintiffs obtained a lower price for their fruit, had to pay a higher import duty and claimed damages for breach of contract in respect of this loss. **Held**: they were entitled to succeed as the bill of lading was not, in itself, the contract between the parties but merely evidence of its terms. The promise to proceed direct to London was part of the contract and the plaintiffs were awarded damages for breach of this provision. (Courtesy of *Cracknell's Law Students' Companion*)

Note that a bill of lading is a typical example of a standard form contract. They are issued by shipping lines and a full set of standard terms and conditions is printed on the back of the document.

6.1.4 Standard form contracts

Where a firm or company repeatedly carries out the same type of transaction (for example the carriage of goods by land, sea or air) it is usual to have a set of standard terms and conditions embodying the contract between the parties. Such standard form contracts are desirable because they can be thought out carefully and legal advice can be taken on them. Often they are provided by trade associations to members (for example the Road Haulage Association's Conditions of Carriage are widely used). Today such contracts are usually approved by the Director General of Fair Trading to ensure that they do not infringe the *Unfair Contract Terms Act, 1977*.

6.1.5 A deed (or specialty)

This is a formal contract required in certain transactions (for example conveyances of land, leases of property for a longer period than three years, deeds of partnership, etc.). A deed may, however, be drawn up for any contract if the parties wish to be formal about the matter and gifts are often given in this formal way because with a gift there is no valuable consideration by the donee to the donor, and to be effective the gift must be made by deed.

The essential characteristics of a deed are that it is signed, sealed and delivered. The signature is usually witnessed by two persons who append their names and addresses but need not know the contents of the document. An illiterate person may 'make his/her mark' – usually a cross. Sealing is now less official than in former times, and merely consists of affixing a red disc to the document which is touched by the person signing the deed. Delivery is the handing of the document to the other party named in it, but this is not physically necessary since it can be done 'constructively'. This word means 'indirectly' or 'by inference'. The person drawing up the deed touches the red seal and says, 'I deliver this as my act and deed' and this may be construed as if it was an actual physical delivery by the drawer to the other party to the contract. The document then goes by post, or may be delivered by messenger, or handed to the other party when he/she calls at the solicitor's office.

Deeds are often made subject to a certain condition and cannot take effect until the condition is fulfilled. They are said to be 'escrows' and are usually kept in the custody of a solicitor until such time as the condition has been fulfilled. For example, a Deed of Gift might only take effect on the donee's 25th birthday, and until such time the deed will be 'in escrow'. With regard to a legal mortgage with a bank, provided the latter's mortgage form contains a circle containing the word 'seal' or 'LS' (*locus sigilli* – the place of the seal) and signature, this makes it a deed (*First National Securities Ltd v. Jones (1978)*). The old formalities for a seal to consist of a wax or waifer-seal and the need for a would-be signatory to touch the seal and solemnly declare, 'This is my word and deed' are no longer strictly required.

6.2 A definition of a contract

A contract has been defined by Sir William Anson as

a legally binding agreement made between two or more parties, by which rights are acquired by one or more to acts or forbearances on the part of the other, or others.

The essential elements of this definition are as follows:

- *Legally binding*. Not all agreements are contracts, for not all agreements are legally binding. In particular we may notice social arrangements, domestic arrangements and agreements specifically stated to be entered into without any intention of creating legal arrangements (see Section 6.5 below.)
- *Two or more parties*. To have an agreement there must be at least two parties. One cannot make bargains with oneself.
- *Rights are acquired*. An essential feature of a contract is that legal rights are acquired. One person promises to do a certain thing, or supply a certain object. The other person promises to pay the price, or do something else in return.
- *Forbearances*. To forbear is to refrain from doing something. It may still be a benefit to one party to have the other promise not to do something. Thus the owner of a right of way across land might agree, in consideration of a payment of £200, to use the footpath only on weekdays, leaving the other party to enjoy the privacy of the land at weekends.

6.3 The elements of a contract

The elements of a contract may be listed as follows:

- Capacity to contract.
- Intention to create legal relations.
- Agreement to the same idea (*consensus ad idem*).
- A clear offer, communicated to the offeree.
- A valid acceptance of the offer.
- Valuable consideration.
- Absence of duress or undue influence.
- Absence of mistake amounting to 'operative mistake'.
- Absence of misrepresentation.
- Legality of the objects of the contract.

A diagrammatic representation of these points is given in Figure 6.1. The chief points about the first three items listed above are raised in this chapter. The rest are dealt with in Chapters 7 and 8.

```
                              Contract
     ┌────────────┬──────────────┬──────────┬──────────┬──────────────────┐
  Agreement   Consideration   Capacity   Intention   Matters relating
     │                                                to the operation
     │                                                of a contract
     │                                                (a) Mistake
  ┌──┴──┐                                             (b) Misrepresentation
 Offer Acceptance                                     (c) Illegality
                                                      (d) Duress or undue
                                                          influence
                                                      (e) Frustration
```

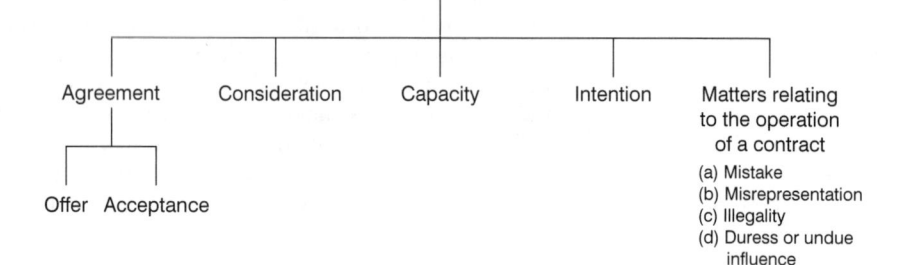

Figure 6.1 The elements of a contract

6.4 Capacity to contract

In general every person has full legal powers to enter into whatever contracts they might choose. There are, however, some exceptions to this general rule and they are:

- Minors (formerly called infants).
- Persons drunk or mentally disordered.
- Corporations.

6.4.1 Minors

The term 'minors' is becoming more usual to describe persons under the age of 18 years, who were formerly called 'infants'. The age of 18 became the age of maturity by Section 12 of the *Family Law Reform Act, 1969* – previously the age was 21 years. The basic intention of the law is to protect minors from exploitation, whilst at the same time to avoid impairing in total their right to enter into contracts. It is possible to put contracts made by minors into three groups: (a) valid contracts; (b) voidable contracts; and (c) controls affected by the *Minors' Contracts Act, 1987*.

(a) Valid contracts

There are two types of contract which the courts will enforce against minors: contracts for necessaries and beneficial contracts (usually contracts of employment).

Contracts for necessaries For a long time it has been the law that a minor is bound to pay a *reasonable* price (not necessarily the contractual price) for necessaries supplied to him. Necessaries may be goods and services and are those things reasonably necessary to maintain the minor in the station in life in which he moves. So far as goods are concerned necessaries have been defined in Section 3 of the *Sale of Goods Act, 1979*, as meaning: 'goods suitable to the condition in life of the minor or other person concerned and to his actual requirements at the time of the sale and delivery.' This means that there are two factors determining whether a particular article is a necessity: the condition in life of the minor and his actual requirements at the time of sale and delivery. Should the minor be sufficiently supplied with goods of the kind in question then, even though the fact is not known to the plaintiff, the price is irrecoverable:

Nash v. Inman (1908)

The plaintiff was a tailor in Savile Row and the defendant an undergraduate at Trinity College, Cambridge. While under 21 (the age has been reduced to 18 since that time) the defendant ordered certain clothes from the plaintiff, including 11 fancy waistcoats at two guineas each, and the plaintiff instituted proceedings to recover the cost of the clothes supplied. Evidence given by the defendant's father showed that the defendant already had an adequate supply of clothes suitable and necessary for his condition in life. **Held**: in view of this fact the goods ordered from the plaintiff were not necessaries and the plaintiff's action must fail. (Courtesy of *Cracknell's Law Students' Companion*)

The tests are the same for necessary services as for goods. Necessary services include education, medical and legal advice. In *Chapple v. Cooper (1844)* it was held that the provision of a funeral service ordered by a minor for her deceased husband was a necessary.

Beneficial contracts of service A contract of employment is binding on a minor if *viewed as a whole when made it is for the minor's benefit*. The court looks at the whole contract, weighs the onerous against the beneficial terms and then decides whether the balance is in favour of the infant. Compare the following cases:

Clements v. London and North Western Railway Co. (1894)

The plaintiff, who was an infant, entered the service of the defendants as a porter and agreed to become a member of the defendants' insurance scheme, to the funds of which the defendants contributed, and to forfeit his right to sue the defendants under the *Employers' Liability Acts*. The insurance scheme did not restrict the payment of compensation to those cases for which the employers would otherwise be liable, but the amount of benefit payable under the scheme was rather less than that which could be recovered under the Acts. The scheme also provided that claims should be forfeited in certain circumstances and that all disputes should be settled by arbitration. The plaintiff was injured in the course of his employment and sued to recover damages from the defendants. **Held**: the action must fail as the plaintiff's contract of service, which contained a clause prohibiting proceedings of this kind, was binding upon him because it was, taken as a whole, advantageous to him. (Courtesy of *Cracknell's Law Students' Companion*)

De Francesco v. Barnum (1890)

An infant and her mother executed a deed whereby the infant, who was to be apprenticed to the plaintiff for seven years with a view to being taught stage dancing, agreed that she would not marry or accept any professional engagements during the period of her apprenticeship without the consent of the plaintiff. The contract also contained terms whereby the infant was to be paid a certain small sum for such engagements as she should fulfil, but there was no stipulation that the plaintiff should provide engagements for the infant or maintain her while she was unemployed. In breach of this agreement the infant signed a contract to dance for the defendant and the plaintiff sought to enforce the provisions of the deed and claimed damages for breach of contract. **Held**: the claim must fail as the provisions of the deed were unreasonable and could not be enforced against the infant or her mother and no action would lie against the defendant for enticing the infant away from the plaintiff's employment. (Courtesy of *Cracknell's Law Students' Companion*)

Benefit to the minor is the vital factor when considering such contracts. However, there is no *general* principle that any kind of agreement is binding merely because it confers benefit upon the infant. For example, it has long been established that a minor is not bound by a trading contract even if it is financially beneficial for him. He is not liable for the price of goods supplied to him in trade; he cannot be made bankrupt for trade debts; and he is not liable for the non-delivery of goods which he has sold as a trader. For example:

Cowern v. Nield (1912)

The defendant, an infant, carried on business as a hay and straw merchant. The plaintiff ordered some clover and hay and sent his cheque in settlement. The goods were never delivered and the plaintiff brought an action to recover the amount which he had paid. **Held**: the plaintiff's claim must fail as the transaction in question was a trading contract and whether or not it was for the benefit of the defendant, in the absence of fraud, he could not be liable under such an agreement. (Courtesy of *Cracknell's Law Students' Companion*)

For a beneficial agreement to be valid it must either be a service or apprenticeship contract or analogous to such a contract. For example:

Doyle v. White City Stadium, Ltd (1935)

The infant plaintiff was a boxer and the terms of the contract with the British Boxing Board of Control by which he was granted a licence to box provided that payment of the money due to a boxer might be withheld if he was disqualified for one of various reasons. The plaintiff took part in a contest for the heavy-weight championship of Great Britain but was disqualified in the second round. The plaintiff sought to recover the amount due to him in respect of the fight and contended that he was not bound by the terms of the contract with the British Boxing Board of Control as he was an infant. **Held**: the plaintiff's action must fail as he was bound by the agreement, which was closely analogous to a contract of employment, because it was, on the whole, for his benefit. (Courtesy of *Cracknell's Law Students' Companion*)

The nature of contracts **101**

(b) Voidable contracts

Contracts falling within this group are voidable in the sense that they are valid and binding upon the minor unless he repudiates them during his minority or within a reasonable time thereafter. The other party cannot repudiate.

Contracts in this category are those which confer a continuous interest on a minor. There are four main kinds:

- Contracts concerning land – particularly contracts to buy or rent land.
- Contracts to subscribe for, or buy in the market, company shares.
- Partnership contracts.
- Marriage settlements.

When a minor repudiates such contracts he is relieved of all liabilities (e.g. rent) which accrue after the repudiation but probably not those which accrued before repudiation.

> *Steinberg v. Scala (Leeds) Ltd (1923)*
>
> An infant applied for and was allotted certain shares. She paid the amount due on allotment and also the first call. Eighteen months later, while still an infant, she purported to repudiate the contract and sought repayment of the money she had paid. **Held**: her claim must fail as there had not been a total failure of consideration, the only ground on which she could have succeeded. (Courtesy of *Cracknell's Law Students' Companion*)

An infant partner is not liable for debts that the firm has acquired during his infancy (*Lovell and Christmas v. Beauchamp (1894)*). However, when he reaches the age of majority, i.e. the commencement of the eighteenth birthday, he is liable for all the debts incurred during the period of his majority unless he takes steps within a reasonable time to avoid the partnership contract (*Goode v. Harrison (1821)*).

(c) The Minors' Contracts Act, 1987

This Act repealed the *Infants Relief Act, 1874*, which for 100 years or so gave minors considerable protection from the activities of such people as money lenders. That Act made all contracts for the loan of money to infants absolutely void, and moneys lent could not be recovered. Under Section 5 of another Act, the *Betting and Loans (Infants) Act, 1892* (also repealed by the new Act) money loaned in infancy could not be recovered even if the infant ratified the contract after reaching his majority. Even a guarantee given by an adult against such a loan could not be enforced against the guarantor. Similarly, goods supplied to a minor which were not 'necessaries' could not be recovered, even though they had not been paid for and were still in the minor's possession. With the increasing sophistication of young people today and the tighter control of credit under the *Consumer Credit Act, 1974* it was felt that these protections could be dispensed with and the position allowed to revert to the old common law position. This was that there was a third group of contracts (besides contracts for necessaries and beneficial contracts) which were neither valid nor voidable. They became binding on the minor only if he ratified them on attaining full age. This is the position under the new Act.

The Act also provides that where a minor has repudiated a contract in which he obtained goods, either by being supplied with them, or (by implication) as a result of borrowing cash which was then used to buy the goods, and these are still in his possession, the court may – if it is just and equitable so to do – order the minor to restore them to the plaintiff.

The Act also provides that where a guarantor has guaranteed a loan to a minor who subsequently repudiates the loan contract on the grounds that he was a minor at the time it was made, the guarantee shall not be unenforceable against the guarantor for that reason alone. This reverses the law usually quoted from the case of *Coutts & Co. v. Browne-Lecky (1946)*, which held that since the underlying loan was void, the guarantee was also void. The underlying loan is not now void by illegality, and therefore the guarantee is not void either.

6.4.2 Persons drunk or mentally disordered

Some persons of unsound mind have their property controlled for them by the courts under Part 8 of the *Mental Health Act, 1959*. Such persons can never make a valid contract.

Other persons of unsound mind and those 'unbalanced' by intoxication are treated alike. Their contracts are divided into two types: those for necessary goods (the situation is as with minors) and other contracts (where the presumption is one of validity unless the person of unsound mind or the drunkard can show: (i) he did not know what he was doing, and (ii) the other party was aware of this). In this case the contract is voidable at the option of the person of unsound mind, or the drunkard. In *Hart v. O'Connor (1985)* the Judicial Committee of the Privy Council held that the validity of a contract entered into by a lunatic *who is ostensibly sane* is to be judged by the same standards as a contract by a person of sound mind and is *not* voidable by the lunatic or his representative by reason of unfairness unless such unfairness amounts to equitable fraud, which would have enabled the complaining party to avoid the contract even if he had been sane.

6.4.3 Corporations

A corporation is a legal entity created by a process of law. It has a separate legal entity from the person or persons who actually represent it in human form. Thus a company which is a corporation has a separate legal entity from the shareholders who own it and the directors of the board that conduct its business. It can own property, employ staff and sue and be sued in the courts under its corporate name. There are two kinds of corporation: **corporations sole** and **corporations aggregate**.

A corporation sole is a high office held by an individual, who therefore has a corporate capacity as well as a personal capacity. Examples are the bishops of the Church of England and the Lord Warden of the Cinque Ports.

A corporation aggregate can be created under:

- Common law.
- Royal charter.
- Special statute. Many early railway companies were set up under private statutes, and in recent times statutes have been passed to set up many public corporations – for example, the Atomic Energy Authority was set up under the *Atomic Energy Act, 1954*.
- The *Companies Acts 1985–9*. As already explained in Chapter 5 this Act has consolidated into a single statute the five Acts of 1948, 1967, 1976, 1980 and 1981. It has now been joined by a further Act, the *Companies Act, 1989*, while one or two specialized items such as the provisions about

business names have been put into separate minor statutes. The two most important were the *Business Names Act, 1985* and the *Company Securities (Insider Dealing) Act, 1985*. However, the latter Act has now been repealed and replaced by the *Criminal Justice Act, 1993* (see page 78).

These changes aside there are detailed provisions in the 1985–9 statutes which contain rules for the formation, registration, conduct and liquidation of limited and unlimited companies. One such provision is that there shall be a memorandum of association in which those wishing to form the company express their willingness to associate together. It contains the **objects clause** which governs the capacity of the company to contract. A company can only contract on matters falling within its objects clause, and since the records of companies are matters of public record available for inspection at Companies House it used to be the case that a company could not have a contract enforced against it if it lay outside its object clause. The presumption was that those entering into contracts with the company knew or ought to have known the contents of the objects clause. Consequently anyone making an *ultra vires* (outside the powers) contract with a company only had themselves to blame. On entry into the European Community in 1973 this *ultra vires* doctrine had to be revised, since it is not followed in the other countries of the Community. This matter has been fully discussed already in Chapter 5 (see page 69) and need not be restated here, except to reiterate that those who enter into contracts with companies can enforce such contracts even though they are outside the objects clause, providing of course that they have acted in good faith themselves. Despite the amelioration of hardship to unsophisticated contractors, the fact remains that the capacity of a company is limited to activities authorized by its objects clause. It has been clearly laid down in *International Sales and Agencies Ltd v. Marcus (1982)* that the clause which is now Section 35 in the 1985 Act was designed to protect innocent third parties dealing with the company unaware of its objects clause. It was not designed to protect sophisticated businessmen, or to defeat the duties of a trustee or constructive trustee (which were the facts in the case).

A more detailed coverage of companies has been given in Chapter 5.

6.5 Intention to create legal relations

As mentioned in Section 6.1 above, merely because there is an agreement it cannot be assumed that an enforceable contract exists. English law requires that the parties to a contract actually intended to enter into legal relations (by which is meant relations actionable and enforceable in the courts). If it can be demonstrated that no such intention existed then the courts will not intervene, despite the presence of agreement and consideration.

When the courts are called upon to examine agreements from the point of view of intention, they classify them into two broad groups:

- Social, family, and other domestic agreements, where the general rule is that the courts presume that there is *no* intention to enter into legal relations.
- Commercial agreements, where the courts presume that the parties *do* intend to enter into legal relations.

Though the above are the general rules it is possible to demonstrate to the court that in the first group of agreements the form of words used, and the circumstances in which they were used, amounted to an intention to enter into legal relations. It is equally possible to rebut the presumption in the second group by showing that in fact the parties clearly expressed their desire to exclude legally enforceable relations.

6.5.1 Social, family and other domestic agreements

The following cases demonstrate the view of the courts in relation to the basic presumption, i.e. lack of intention:

> **Balfour v. Balfour (1919)**
>
> The defendant Balfour, a civil servant, returned to his work in Ceylon leaving his wife in England – doctors advised that her health would not allow her to accompany him. He promised that, whilst away, he would send her £30 per month on which she might live. He did not keep this promise and his wife sued. At first she succeeded but on appeal it was said by Atkin, LJ, that of the forms of agreement which do not constitute a contract one of the most usual consists of arrangements made between husband and wife. They are not contracts because the parties do not intend that legal consequences should follow from them. In this particular case the parties were amicable and living together normally when the arrangements were made and clearly they did not envisage any legal developments.

> **Buckpitt v. Oates (1968)**
>
> The parties were two friends who occasionally rode in each other's cars. Neither had passenger insurance and whilst Oates was driving his negligence caused an accident in which Buckpitt was injured. Prior to the trip Buckpitt had paid Oates 10 shillings (50 pence) towards the fuel costs. Also Oates had displayed on his dashboard a notice disclaiming liability for injuries to passengers. Buckpitt sued Oates, however, (a) for breach of contract and (b) in tort for negligence. He failed in (a) because it was regarded that the carrying of Buckpitt was a friendly gentleman's agreement and there was no intention to enter into legal relations. He also failed in (b) because of the notice disclaiming liability – a situation which has been changed by the *Road Traffic Act, 1972* (Section 148(3)).

The following cases demonstrate how the presumption of non-intention might be rebutted:

> **Merrit v. Merrit (1970)**
>
> The husband left his wife and began living with another woman. The family home was in the names of both Mr and Mrs Merrit and £180 was still owed on the mortgage. A document was signed whereby Mr Merrit agreed to transfer the property into the sole ownership of his wife providing she met all charges associated with the property until such times as the mortgage was discharged. Mrs Merrit paid off the mortgage but her husband refused to transfer the property. **Held**: at the time the agreement was made the pair were not living happily together as man and wife and therefore the usual presumption relating to non-intention did not apply. There was a binding contract and the property must be transferred.

Parker v. Clarke (1960)

The Clarkes, an elderly couple, invited the Parkers to sell their cottage and come to live with them (Mrs Parker was Mrs Clarke's niece). The Clarkes promised that the house and contents would belong to the Parkers once the Clarkes died. The move took place. After two years though the Clarkes asked the Parkers to leave. The Parkers sued for breach of contract and succeeded. An intention to create legal relations was found and was thought to be particularly strong since the Parkers had been induced to sell their own home.

6.5.2 Commercial agreements

The following cases demonstrate the view of the courts in relation to commercial agreements, i.e. that there *is* an intention to create legal relations:

Edwards v. Skyways Ltd (1964)

Skyways made Edwards, a pilot, redundant. They eventually agreed to make all redundant pilots an *ex gratia* payment amounting to the sum each had paid into the pension fund. Skyways then refused to make any payments. Edwards sued for breach of contract. **Held:** in business arrangements it is presumed that the parties intend legal relations, and the use of words such as '*ex gratia*' is insufficient to rebut that presumption.

The following case demonstrates how the presumption to enter legal relations might be rebutted:

Jones v. Vernons Pools Ltd (1938)

Jones claimed to have sent a winning coupon to Vernons who did not receive it. All coupons issued by the company contained the clause 'binding in honour only' and required a signature accepting the clause. Jones agreed that he had signed the coupon (unsigned it would have been invalid). **Held:** there was clearly no intention to enter into legal relations, and there could be no contract.

There are two rather special cases where what appear to be situations involving commercial agreements are in fact regarded as if the parties do not intend to enter into legal relations. They are:

(a) Collective bargaining agreements

Collective bargaining agreements, e.g. *Ford Motor Co. v. Amalgamated Union of Engineering and Foundry Workers (1969)*, where Lane J. held that agreements relating to pay and working conditions arrived at between the company and the trade union were not intended to create legal relations.

The question as to whether a collective bargaining agreement can be held to be binding upon the body of workers on whose behalf it has been negotiated is one which has exercised the minds of employers, trade unions, governments and judges for some years. Whatever the principle is in such matters, and some believe that such an agreement should be as enforceable as any other set of clauses would be in any other commercial agreement, it does appear that the courts will hesitate to find an individual worker liable for breach of the agreement unless its terms have been expressly incorporated into his/her contract of employment. Section 18 of the *Trade Union and Labour Relations Act, 1974* provides that if a collective agreement contains a provision which states that the parties intend that only one or more parts of it shall be a legally enforceable contract, then it will have this effect. Whether this would be sufficient to bind a worker who had not had the term expressly incorporated into his/her contract of service (with all the work, and possible discontent among staff, that such a renegotiation of contracts would involve) seems very doubtful. Any general presumption of legal enforceability on all employees as a result of their intention to create legal relations seems unfounded. It is much more likely that if such cases are brought to court they will be assessed by the judiciary on the basis of their own facts at the time, and each case will be but a poor authority for establishing a general principle of enforceability.

The *Trade Union and Labour Relations Act, 1974* also provides that a 'no-strike' clause shall not form part of the contract between a worker and an employer unless the agreement is in writing, has an express provision that the clause shall be incorporated in the contracts of employment, and is actually incorporated either expressly or implicitly in the worker's contract. Furthermore, the precise terms of the agreement made must be available to the employee for consideration and study, in working hours, at the place of employment. The trade union or unions must also be independent trade unions (which presumably means they are true representatives of the employees and not 'company' unions).

It should be noted that most of the collective agreements contain provisions expressly stating that no legal intention is intended. Those agreements that are silent on the matter are covered by the *Trade Union and Labour Relations Act, 1974* (Section 18), which provided that it will be presumed that no legal intention is intended. Some politicians have called for the enactment of a contrary presumption but this has not transpired to date.

(b) Public body acting under statutory duty

Cases where a public body is acting under a statutory duty, e.g. *Willmore v. S.E. Electricity Board (1957)*. Here it was held that a public body under a statutory duty to supply a service such as electricity and having agreed to supply electricity to a consumer, intends only to fulfil its statutory duty – *not* to enter into legal relations. Hence if the electricity supply fails and chickens die (as did Willmore's) the Electricity Board is not liable for breach of contract.

6.6 Agreement to the same idea (consensus ad idem)

It is said that the UK Cabinet Secretariat was originally set up after a certain Prime Minister had said: 'Well gentlemen, then we are all agreed!' After a chorus of assents had carried this proposition, one diffident voice was heard to say: 'But Prime Minister, on what have we all agreed?' In contract law, no less than in Cabinet, we need to know what we have agreed. It is possible for two parties to use words which are susceptible to interpretation in different ways, so that they do not have the same idea in mind when they 'agree'. If A says 'I will sell you my car for £800 (thinking of his rather battered 1300 cc family saloon) and B replies 'Done!' (thinking of A's vintage Rolls-Royce) they have not agreed to the same idea. The classic case is:

Raffles v Wichelhaus (1864)

The defendants agreed to buy '125 bales of Surat cotton ... to arrive *ex Peerless* from Bombay....' It appeared that the ship mentioned in the agreement was intended by the defendants to be the *Peerless*, which sailed from Bombay in October, whereas the plaintiff ordered 125 bales of Surat cotton from another ship called the *Peerless* which sailed from Bombay in December. **Held**: there was no binding contract between the parties as the defendant meant one ship and the plaintiff another. (Courtesy of *Cracknell's Law Students' Companion*)

Other cases of interest are *Smith v. Hughes (1871)* and *Scriven Brothers v. Hindley (1913)*. The question in each of these three cases was: 'Were the parties in agreement to the same idea' or, in Latin, was there a *consensus ad idem*.

Test your knowledge

Answers	Questions
	1 What is the basis of a contract?
1 Agreement between the parties.	2 Why is *consensus ad idem* important in contract law?
2 It means 'agreement to the same idea'. If the parties have not agreed to the same idea then there is no true agreement. The classic case is *Raffles v. Wichelhaus* (see Question 15 below).	3 How did Sir William Anson define a contract?
3 As 'a legally binding agreement made between two or more parties, by which rights are acquired by one or more to acts or forbearances on the part of the other, or others'.	4 What agreements are not contracts?
4 Social arrangements, domestic arrangements and agreements specifically made without intention of creating legal arrangements.	5 What is capacity?
5 The ability to make a legally binding contract.	6 What is a minor (infant)?
6 A person under 18 years of age.	7 What contracts are binding against infants?

Answers	Questions
7 (a) Contracts for the supply of necessaries; (b) contracts which are beneficial to the infant, i.e. apprenticeships.	8 What is the classic case about necessaries supplied to an infant?
8 *Nash v. Inman (1908)* – the 'fancy waistcoats' case, in which it was held that clothing supplied to an infant who already had adequate clothing was not a necessary.	9 What was *Doyle v. White City Stadium Ltd* about?
9 It was a 1935 case about an infant boxer who was not paid his fee because he struck a low blow and was disqualified. The contract specifically forbade payment if he struck a low blow. **Held**: it was a beneficial contract and he was bound by it.	10 What was the *Infants Relief Act, 1874*?
10 An act to prevent loans being made to infants. It has now been repealed by the *Minors' Contracts Act, 1987*.	11 What about loans made to minors now?
11 They are voidable by the minor until the age of 18. After that they will be valid unless repudiated by the young person within a reasonable time of reaching his/her majority.	12 What is the basis for the legality of the contracts made by corporations?
12 The 'objects clause' of the memorandum of association outlines the objects which the company may pursue. Contracts must be *intra vires*, within the objects clause and therefore 'within the law'.	13 What Act modifies this rule about the objects clause?
13 The new S.35 of the *Companies Act, 1985*, as introduced by the *Companies Act, 1989*, which reduces the severity of the rule to innocent parties who have made contracts with a company not knowing what the objects clause said.	14 What was *Balfour v. Balfour (1919)*?

Answers	Questions
14 A 1919 case between a husband and wife. Its conclusion was that a domestic arrangement is not a contract.	15 What was *Raffles v. Wichelhaus* (1864)?
15 A case in which the parties agreed to ship cotton from Bombay to England in a vessel called SS *Peerless*. There were two ships of that name and the conclusion was that the parties had not agreed to the same idea.	16 Go over the questions until you are sure of all the answers. Then try the written questions in Appendix 1.

7 Offer, acceptance and valuable consideration

7.1 A clear offer, communicated to the offeree

An offer is a promise that the person making the offer (known as the offeror) is prepared to be legally bound upon specified terms. It is susceptible to acceptance by the offeree at any time, unless it is revoked by the offeror.

For example, Jack might offer his car to John providing that John pays £250 for it. Jack is prepared to be legally bound to deliver the car provided that John complies with the specified term of the offer and pays the £250.

It might be thought that the area of offer is one which is simple and clear, but this is not so. A number of situations arise which at first sight appear to be offers capable of being accepted by the offeree, but which the courts have ruled are not 'offers'. These situations are:

- Invitations to treat.
- The supply of information.
- Declarations of intent.

Other matters of interest are:

- That offers must be clear – not vague and uncertain.
- That offers may be specific (addressed to a particular individual) or general (addressed to the world at large).

7.1.1 Invitations to treat

Invitations to treat are not offers. An invitation to treat is an invitation to do business with another party. It is not an offer but an invitation to others to make offers. Examples are:

(a) Display of goods

The display of goods in a shop window or a self-service store is an invitation to the public to buy – in other words, to offer to buy. It is not an offer to sell, which would be immediately susceptible to acceptance. The classic case is:

> **Pharmaceutical Society of Great Britain, Ltd v. Boots Cash Chemists (Southern) Ltd (1953)**
>
> According to the *Pharmacy and Poisons Act, 1933 (Section 18)* specific drugs could only be sold under the supervision of a registered pharmacist. At Boots customers took the goods from a self-service counter and paid for them at a check-out till *supervised* by a registered pharmacist. The point at issue centred upon where the goods were *sold*. If the display constituted an offer, then the goods were sold when customers accepted the offer by placing drugs in their self-service baskets. If the display was an invitation to treat then the customers offered to purchase at the check-out and Boots accepted the offer – sale being supervised by the pharmacist. The court held that the display was an invitation to treat – it solicited offers which the cashier could accept or reject.

Similarly, in *Fisher v. Bell* (*1960*), where a shopkeeper had displayed a flick-knife with a price tag in his shop window, it was held that this did not constitute an offer for sale; the display was merely an invitation to treat.

(b) Invitation for bids

Under the *Sale of Goods Act,* (*1979*) (Section 57) the bids at an auction constitute offers. The auctioneer's invitation for bids is only an invitation to treat, and the bids are offers to buy. Acceptance is completed by the fall of the auctioneer's hammer. Up to that point any offer made can be withdrawn. The case of *Payne v. Cave* (*1789*) illustrates the point.

(c) Circulars and advertisements

These are not considered as offers. This is illustrated by the following case:

> *Partridge v. Crittenden* (*1968*)
>
> P advertised for sale bramblefinch cocks and hens. It is illegal to offer wild birds for sale under the *Wild Birds Act, 1954*. However, on appeal the court held that such an advertisement was *not* an offer for sale but an invitation to treat.

In the above case Lord Parker, LCJ, did make one important qualification, however, and that was that where advertisements or circulars came direct from the manufacturers they can be construed as offers. No doubt the decision in *Carlill v Carbolic Smoke Ball Co.* (*1892*) (see below) brought forth this qualification.

In *Grainger & Son v. Gough* (*1896*) the court held that a price list sent out by a wine merchant to canvas orders amounted to an attempt to induce offers; it was not an offer.

> *Gibson v. Manchester City Council* (*1979*)
>
> Gibson received a letter from the council saying in response to his enquiry about the purchase of his council house that the Council might be prepared to sell it to him, and he should make a formal application to buy. This he did but before the Council could proceed an election changed the character of the Council and the new Council reversed the policy and decided only to proceed where formal offers and acceptances had occurred. The case went all the way to the House of Lords, which applied the rules about offer and acceptance strictly. It held that the application by Gibson was the offer to buy, but there was no acceptance of this offer, and therefore no contract. The Council's original suggestion that Gibson make a formal application could not be regarded as anything other than an invitation to treat. It was not an offer which was susceptible of acceptance.

7.1.2 Supply of information

A supply of information is not an offer. Those who may well decide to sell often provide details of what they might sell without any intention of making a legally binding offer. The following case illustrates the point:

Harvey v. Facey (1893)

The appellants sent a telegram to the respondents: 'Will you sell us Bumper Hall Pen? Telegraph lowest cash price.' The respondents telegraphed back: 'Lowest cash price for Bumper Hall Pen £900.' The appellants then sent a further telegram purporting to accept this 'offer' and when it was ignored, they sued for specific performance. The court held that the respondents' original reply did not constitute an offer – it was merely information about the lowest cash price required if they did decide to sell.

7.1.3 Declaration of intent

Quite often a businessman may make a mistake about matters which, when he makes it, he intends to perform, but which he does not envisage as leading to legal relations. For example, the case of *Harris v. Nickerson (1873)* was as follows:

Harris v. Nickerson (1873)

An auctioneer advertised that particular goods were to be auctioned at a specific time and place. The particular goods were withdrawn from the sale and Harris sued the auctioneer for loss of time and expense incurred in going to the sale. The action failed on the grounds that information about the auction amounted only to a declaration of intent – not an offer which was susceptible of acceptance.

7.1.4 Vague offers

The terms of an offer must be clear and certain, not vague. Where a contract is left deliberately vague, the courts will hesitate to uphold it, since the vagueness must not be interpreted to the benefit of one particular party. However, there is a rule which says 'that is not vague which may be reduced to certainty'. The cases of *Scammell and Nephew Ltd v. Ouston (1941)* and *Hillas and Co. v. Arcos Ltd (1932)* may be contrasted. Both were vague contracts, but in the case of the latter the vagueness could be reduced to certainty by referring to previous transactions, and the customs of business in the trade concerned. Another similar case was *Loftus v. Roberts (1902)*.

Scammell and Nephew Ltd v. Ouston (1941) (House of Lords)

The respondents agreed to purchase a motor van from the appellants but their order was given on the understanding 'that the balance of the purchase price can be had on hire-purchase terms over a period of two years'. **Held**: no precise meaning could be attributed to this clause as hire-purchase agreements varied widely and consequently there was no enforceable contract. There were no previous dealings between the parties or an accepted trade practice to which the court could refer to determine the hire-purchase terms and, in any case, their lordships found that the matter had not passed the stage of negotiation. (Courtesy of *Cracknell's Law Students' Companion*)

Hillas and Co. v. Arcos Ltd (1932) (House of Lords)

There was an agreement in writing for the supply of wood during 1930 and it contained an option to buy more wood during the following year but the option clause did not specify the precise kind or size of timber to be supplied, the ports to which it was to be shipped or the manner of shipment. The suppliers argued that the option clause was not binding as it was intended merely to form the basis of a future agreement. **Held**: the agreement in respect of the supply of timber during 1930 was couched in similar terms and had been duly observed. The option clause showed a sufficient intention to be bound and could create a valid contract, as those points which were not specifically resolved in the option clause could be determined by reference to the previous dealings between the parties and normal business practice in the timber trade. (Courtesy of *Cracknell's Law Students' Companion*)

Loftus v. Roberts (1902)

Roberts engaged an actress for a play 'at a West End salary to be agreed between us'. **Held**: that the reference to salary was too vague to be enforced.

7.1.5 Specific or general offers

An offer may be specific or general (to the world at large). If an offer is made to a specific individual it can only be accepted by that individual. Other offers may be general offers, made to the world at large. The following case is of interest:

Carlill v. Carbolic Smoke Ball Co. Ltd (1893)

The company advertised a promised payment of £100 to anyone who contracted influenza after using the smoke ball as specified. The advertisement further stated that £1000 had been lodged at the company's bank to show their good faith. Mrs Carlill purchased a smoke ball but still contracted influenza. She sued for her £100. In defence the company argued that the advertisement was only an invitation to treat, being made to no specific person. **Held**: the advertisement was an offer to the whole world, the sincerity of which was demonstrated by the £1000 lodged to pay those who accepted the offer and were dissatisfied. Mrs Carlill had accepted the offer by purchasing the article and paying the price. (Courtesy of *Cracknell's Law Students' Companion*)

It should be noted, however, that not all advertisements are serious offers. In this case it was held to be an offer because the defendant company had deposited £1000 with its bankers. In the absence of this deposit the court might well have come to a different conclusion. Hence each advertisement has to be judged individually having regard to the circumstances of each case. It is probably best to say that most advertisements are examples of invitations to treat, as was held in the case of *Partridge v. Crittenden (1968)*.

7.1.6 Communication of the offer

An offer is effective only when it is communicated to the offeree. In *Taylor v. Laird* (1856) a sailor who helped work a ship home failed in a claim for wages due, since the owners knew nothing of the offer and had not accepted it. The so-called 'reward cases' are a further illustration. A person supplying information or returning items cannot 'accept' the offer of a reward if he supplied the information or returned the items without knowledge of the offer of reward.

7.2 Termination of the offer

Once an offer has been made, how long does it remain open? There are several ways in which an offer may cease to be available. Since the primary purpose of an offer is that some other party should accept, the offer ceases as soon as acceptance takes place, and is then said to be 'merged' into the contract. Between the moment of 'offer' and the moment of 'acceptance' the following events might lead to a termination of the offer.

7.2.1 Revocation of the offer

An offeror can withdraw his offer at any time before it is accepted. The revocation must be communicated to the offeree. The offeror cannot just change his mind and not tell anyone about it. Revocation by post is not complete until the letter is received by the offeree. The following case illustrates this:

> **Byrne v Van Tienhoven (1880)**
> Van Tienhoven in Cardiff posted a letter offering to sell goods to Byrne, a New York customer, on 1 October. On 8 October Van Tienhoven posted a letter withdrawing the offer. On 11 October Byrne telegraphed acceptance and this was confirmed with a letter on 15 October. By 20 October the letter of revocation reached Byrne. **Held**: the revocation was ineffective since acceptance took place before the revocation was received by Byrne.

There are however, some exceptions to the rule that revocation must be 'brought to the mind' of the offeree. A withdrawal would be effective if the offeree just neglected to read it after it had reached him. Similarly, a withdrawal sent to the last known address of the offeree would be effective if the offeree had failed to inform the offeror of a change of address. In addition, an offer made to the general public can be withdrawn by taking 'reasonable steps' to bring the withdrawal to the notice of those persons who knew of the offer.

A bid at an auction may be retracted up to the moment when the auctioneer announces the completion of the sale by the fall of the hammer (*Sale of Goods Act, 1979*, Section 57).

Providing the communication of the revocation takes place it need not be communicated by the actual offeror. In *Dickinson v. Dodds* it was established that a third party will suffice providing that a reasonable person would regard the information as true.

> **Dickinson v. Dodds (1876)**
>
> Dodds offered in writing to sell a house for £800, the offer to be kept open to 12 June. On 11 June, a third party informed Dickinson that the house had already been sold. Dickinson then purported to accept the offer. **Held**: that the revocation had been received by Dickinson and he could not accept an offer which had been revoked even though the revocation only reached him indirectly.

One further point about revocation is that a revocation can take place at any time before acceptance, regardless of any *gratuitous* promise to keep the offer open. *Routledge v. Grant* illustrates this point.

> **Routledge v. Grant (1828)**
>
> Grant offered to buy Routledge's house, a definite answer to be given by Routledge within six weeks. He then withdrew the offer before the six weeks ended. **Held**: that Grant could revoke at any time during this six week period – providing that acceptance had not taken place. There had been no consideration for the promise to hold the offer open, and consequently it was not binding on Grant.

7.2.2 Rejection of the offer, or a counter-offer

Once rejection takes place an offer is terminated. The offeree cannot go back at a later date and attempt to accept the 'offer'. Also acceptance must *exactly fit the offer*. An attempt to accept an offer on new terms not contained in the offer amounts to a rejection of the original offer accompanied by a counter-offer. This is illustrated by the following case:

> **Hyde v. Wrench (1840)**
>
> Wrench offered to sell land for £1000. Hyde wrote back offering £950, which was refused. Later Hyde wrote saying he was prepared to pay £1000 and he accepted the original offer. **Held**: the second letter could not accept the original offer since this original offer had been terminated by Hyde's counter-offer.

On the other hand, a request for further information will not amount to rejection of an offer, as in *Stevenson v. McLean* (1880). Details of this case are given in Section 7.3 below.

7.2.3 Lapse of time

An offer may lapse (go out of existence) through the passage of time. Obviously an offer which is expressly stated to run for a fixed period of time cannot be accepted after that time. If there is no time stated in the offer then the offer lapses after a reasonable time. What is reasonable depends upon the facts surrounding each case, in particular with regard to the subject matter of the contract and the means of communication used. In *Ramsgate Victoria Hotel Co. v. Montefiore* (1866), the defendant had intended to purchase shares in the plaintiff company. He applied in June and paid a deposit. Not until the end of November was he informed that he had been allotted shares and that he should therefore pay the balance outstanding on the shares. The defendant's refusal to accept the shares was upheld on the grounds that his offer to purchase the shares in June should have been accepted by the company within a reasonable time. Since the company did not accept the offer until November, his offer had lapsed.

7.2.4 Failure of a condition of the offer

An offer which is expressly or impliedly made subject to some condition cannot be accepted if the condition fails. For example, an offer to buy goods is subject to an implied condition that they will not deteriorate before the offer is accepted.

7.2.5 Death of the offeror

In *Dickinson v. Dodds (1876)* Mellish, LJ, said: 'If a man who makes an offer dies, the offer cannot be accepted after he is dead.' However, in the case of *Bradbury v. Morgan (1862)* the estate of a guarantor was held liable for the guarantee of a deceased man whose promise to honour the debts of another was held to be a standing offer which did not lapse on his death. The plaintiff had no notice of his death and had relied on the guarantee in supplying the goods.

7.3 Acceptance

An acceptance is an assent to all the terms of an offer. As with the offer, acceptance can be either oral, in writing or implied by conduct. The acceptance must exactly fit the offers; additions or qualifications constitute a counter-offer which renders the purported 'acceptance' invalid. We have already seen this in *Hyde v. Wrench (1840)*. However, if the court considers that the offeree is enquiring after details rather than making a counter-offer, then the original offer is not destroyed and is still capable of acceptance, as in *Stevenson v. McLean (1880)*:

> **Stevenson, Jaques & Co. v. McLean (1880)**
>
> The defendant offered to sell iron to the plaintiffs at 40 shillings per ton. The plaintiffs telegraphed to the defendant: 'Please wire whether you would accept forty for delivery over two months, or if not, longest limit you could give.' Later in the day a further telegram was sent to the defendant in which the plaintiffs accepted the original offer and when the plaintiffs sought to recover damages for breach of contract the defendant maintained that the first telegram was a counter-offer which had destroyed the offer which he originally made. **Held:** the plaintiffs' first telegram was not a rejection of the defendant's offer but an inquiry as to whether he would be prepared to modify its terms. (Courtesy of *Cracknell's Law Students' Companion*)

There is no binding acceptance in the following cases:

7.3.1 Acceptance 'subject to contract'

Acceptance is not binding where there is an express statement by the offeree that his acceptance is 'subject to contract'. There are two reasons why this does not create a contract. First, it negates the intention to create legal relations. Second, it is an acceptance which does not correspond with the terms of the offer, because it imposes a further condition.

Branca v. Cobarro (1947)

The parties negotiated for the sale of a mushroom farm and signed a document containing the terms of their agreement which concluded: 'This is a provisional agreement until a fully legalized agreement drawn up by a solicitor and embodying all the conditions herewith stated is signed.' The purchaser sued for the return of his deposit and the vendor contended that their 'provisional agreement' was a binding contract. **Held**: there was *no* immediately binding contract 'until' the document was replaced by one expressed in more precise and formal language. If the parties had used the word 'tentative' instead of 'provisional' it would probably have been held otherwise, but each case depends on the intention of the parties as found by the court. (But see *Chillingworth v. Esche (1924)*.) (Courtesy of *Cracknell's Law Students' Companion*)

7.3.2 Vague contracts

Nor is acceptance binding where the terms of the alleged contract are too vague for the court to ascribe legal meaning to them. However, the court might attempt to make a vague contract certain by implying unstated terms as the basis of:

- Previous dealings between the parties, as in the case of *Hillas and Co. v. Arcos Ltd (1932)* already described.
- Accepted business practice, as in the case of *Foley v. Classique Coaches Ltd (1934)*.

Foley v. Classique Coaches Ltd (1934)

Foley supplied petrol to Classique 'at the price to be agreed by the parties in writing from time to time', with a provision for arbitration in the case of dispute. **Held**: that the lack of a stated price did not invalidate the contract. A term would be implied that the quantity and price of the petrol would be reasonable, and this, together with the arbitration clause, gave the contract its own machinery by which the price could be set.

7.4 Communication of acceptance

The offeree might have decided in his own mind that he will accept the offer, but this is not sufficient to amount to acceptance in law. There has to be some 'external act', words spoken or written which communicate acceptance to the offeror. Communication is said to have taken place when the acceptance is actually brought to the notice of the offeror by the offeree or his authorized agent. The case of *Powell v. Lee (1908)* illustrates this.

Powell v. Lee (1908)

The defendants resolved to appoint the plaintiff headmaster of a school of which they were managers. The terms of the resolution were never communicated to the plaintiff. **Held**: there was no contract between the parties as the defendants' acceptance of the plaintiff's offer of his services had not been communicated to him. (Courtesy of *Cracknell's Law Students' Companion*)

In *Entores Ltd v. Miles Far East Corporation (1955)*, Lord Denning (*obiter*) considered in detail the rule that acceptance must be communicated and said that if he shouted an offer to a man across a courtyard and the reply was drowned by the noise of a passing aircraft then there would be no contract. The rule that acceptance is incomplete until received by the offeror governs conversations over the telephone and all other methods where communication is virtually instantaneous, such as fax. There is one major exception to this rule of communication though, and it relates to the less speedy means of dealing through the post. It is known as the 'postal rule'.

The general rule with regard to postal communications is that acceptance is complete upon posting. For example:

> ### Adams v. Lindsell (1818)
> Lindsell wrote to Adams offering to sell wool and asking for a reply 'in course of post'. Lindsell had wrongly addressed the letter and the acceptance arrived later than they expected. In the intervening period Lindsell had sold the wool elsewhere. **Held**: Lindsell had breached the contract which came into existence when Adam's letter of acceptance was posted.

Note: 'Posted' means put into the control of the Post Office, or one of its employees authorized to receive letters. Posting does not take place at the time when a letter is handed to an employee of the Post Office authorized to deliver letters (*Re London and Northern Bank (1900)*).

The postal rule is obviously in existence because of convenience. It is clearly to the benefit of contracting parties that they know as soon as possible whether or not they have a contract. In this respect the postal rule obviously favours the offeree. The reason for this is that the offeror who chooses to commence negotiations by post takes the risk of delay and accidents in the post, but he can protect himself by stipulating that he is not bound until actual receipt of the acceptance.

The following points are important as regards the postal rule:

- Where a party uses the post as a means of acceptance it must be reasonable to do so. It would not, for example, normally be regarded as reasonable to reply by post to an offer made by telegram or fax. In addition, it would not be reasonable to reply by post if the acceptor knew that the postal service was disrupted.
- A posted acceptance prevails over a withdrawal of the offer which was posted before acceptance, but which has not yet reached the offeree when the acceptance was posted, i.e. acceptance is complete when posted but withdrawal is complete only when received by an offeree.
- A posted acceptance takes effect even though it never reaches the offeror because it is lost through an accident in the post (*Household Fire & Carriage Accident Insurance Co. v. Grant (1879)*).
- The postal rule has been extended as far as telegrams (*Cowan v. O'Connor (1888)*) but not as far as telex.

The postal rule is automatically set aside where a term in the offer stipulates the method of communicating acceptance, e.g. in *Holwell Securities v. Hughes* it was stipulated that the acceptance was to be in writing and communicated 'to the intending vendor (Dr Hughes)'. The court found there was no valid acceptance since the letter containing acceptance was posted and subsequently lost in the post. The stipulation that actual communication was required overruled the ordinary postal rule. The court was merely following the precedent set in the earlier case of *Eliason v. Henshaw* (1819) (see below) where the court had declared no acceptance when the mode of acceptance 'by return of wagon' was not satisfied!

7.5 Other points on acceptance

7.5.1 Silence

You cannot take silence as acceptance. An offeror cannot, without the offeree's consent, put a condition in his offer that silence shall amount to an acceptance. For example:

> *Felthouse v. Bindley* (1862)
>
> Felthouse wrote to a person J offering to buy a horse saying 'If I hear no more about him, I consider him mine'. J did not reply but told the auctioneer B not to sell the horse. B sold by mistake and F sued B for conversion. **Held**: there could be no conversion because there was no contract between F and J since J had not communicated acceptance of F's offer to F.

7.5.2 Waiver of acceptance

The offeror can waive acceptance. While the offeror may not impose a condition on the offeree that silence will amount to acceptance, he may waive the need to communicate acceptance, i.e. he may himself run the risk of incurring an uncommunicated obligation, though he may not impose one upon others. Such a waiver may be express or may be inferred from the circumstances, e.g. *Carlill v. Carbolic Smoke Ball Co.* (1893), referred to earlier.

7.5.3 Manner of acceptance

The acceptance must usually be made in the same manner as the offer. Where an offer explicitly or implicitly calls for acceptance in a certain way, the offeror will not generally be bound unless acceptance is made in that way.

> *Eliason v. Henshaw* (1819)
>
> A offered to purchase flour from B and the letter which contained this offer stipulated the price to be paid and mode of transport, and in a postscript A added: 'Please write by return of wagon whether you accept our offer.' B accepted the offer but in a letter sent by the first regular mail and A contended that it was not a valid acceptance as it was not sent 'by return of wagon'. **Held**: there was no contract as an offer creates no obligation unless it is accepted according to the terms on which the offer was made. Any departure from these terms invalidates the acceptance unless the different mode of acceptance is agreed to by the person who made the offer. (Courtesy of *Cracknell's Law Students' Companion*)

If the requirement is at all tentative, acceptance by some other method may still bind the offeror. The rule is expressed in *Manchester Diocesan Council for Education v. Commercial and General Investments Ltd* (1969) by Buckley, J,

'It may be that an offeror who by the terms of his offer insists upon acceptance in a particular manner, is entitled to insist that he is not bound unless acceptance is affected or communicated in that precise way. Where, however, the offeror has prescribed a particular method of acceptance, but not in terms insisting that only acceptance in that mode shall be binding, I am of the opinion that acceptance communicated to the offeror by any other mode, which is no less advantageous to him, will conclude the contract.'

7.6 Valuable consideration

English law will not enforce a simple contract (a contract that is not signed and sealed, i.e. is not a deed) unless it is supported by a valuable consideration. This rule is based upon the principle that English law enforces bargains, i.e. the exchange of valuable promises, not gratuitous promises.

The question then arises 'What is "consideration"?' The answer is 'anything of value'. The supply of goods; the performance of a service; exercising forbearance from the performance of an act, or promising to act, or forbear can all amount to consideration.

Some confusion might arise here over the status of a promise as regards consideration. The following examples may illustrate the various situations:

- Aunt Julia promises nephew Ben that she will give him a motorcycle. Such a promise is gratuitous and will not be upheld by the courts – Ben did nothing with which to 'buy' Julia's promise.
- Aunt Julia promises to supply Ben with a motorcycle and in return Ben promises to pay Julia £250. Here Julia's promise is 'bought' by Ben's promise of payment. In return of course, Ben's promise of payment is bought by Julia's own promise to deliver the machine.

Although both of the above situations involve promises only the second involves a 'bargain'. Only the second situation will be upheld by the courts, because it alone has consideration, which has been provided by both parties.

- Aunt Julia promises Ben that on his 18th birthday she will give him £5000. The promise is drawn up in a 'deed of gift' and witnessed formally in her solicitor's office. Although there is no valuable consideration from Ben the promise will be binding upon Aunt Julia because of the formality of the promise. A gratuitous promise made in a formal deed will be upheld by the courts.

7.7 General requirements of valuable consideration

7.7.1 Commercial adequacy

Consideration must be real and of some value but it need not be adequate. Some acts or promises are not regarded by the courts as being valid consideration (see below). However, in all other situations where the courts are prepared to find consideration, they will not investigate its commercial adequacy, or even fairness. So long as the consideration has *some* value in the eyes of the law then that is enough.

'The adequacy of the consideration is for the parties to consider at the time of making the agreement, not for the court when it is sought to be enforced.' – Lord Blackburn in *Bolton v. Madden (1873)*.

Were the above rule not strictly followed then the freedom of parties to contract would be very much impaired, and the courts see no reason why an individual who, say, wants to sell his kingdom for a horse, should be prevented from doing so.

A sentimental or similar motive for making a promise will not make that promise binding. Thus in *White v. Bluett (1853)* the facts were:

> ### White v. Bluett (1853)
>
> A father promised not to sue his son on a promissory note provided that the son did not bore his father with complaints. **Held**: that the son had not provided consideration for his father's promise.

In similar vein it has been held that a moral obligation is not good consideration, as in *Eastwood v. Kenyon (1840)*.

> ### Eastwood v. Kenyon (1840)
>
> Eastwood was the guardian of an infant who eventually married Kenyon. Upon coming of age the infant had agreed to repay debts entered into by Eastwood to improve her (the infant's) property – a promise also entered into by her eventual husband, Kenyon. In the event Kenyon did not pay. Eastwood sued, but failed in his case because he had not provided consideration to Kenyon for his promise. Though Kenyon might be morally bound to repay the debt he was not legally bound because of this lack of consideration.

Even trivial acts or worthless items may constitute consideration, e.g. *De La Bere v. Pearson (1908)* and *Chapell & Co. Ltd v. Nestlé Co. Ltd (1959)*.

> ### De La Bere v. Pearson (1908)
>
> A newspaper offered financial advice to its readers. The plaintiff wrote and asked for the name of a good stockbroker. He was supplied instead with the name of an undischarged bankrupt, who made off with the £1400 forwarded to him. The plaintiff sued the newspaper. **Held**: that the plaintiff had provided consideration by paying for his copy of the newspaper.

> ### Chapell and Co. Ltd v. Nestlé Co. Ltd (1959)
>
> Chapell & Co. Ltd owned the copyright in a dance tune. Another firm X made recordings which they sold to the defendants for four pence a copy. The defendants then sold them to the public for 18 pence and three wrappers from their chocolate bars. These were of no value, and were thrown away. A royalty, as required by the *Copyright Act, 1956*, was paid at 6¼ per cent of the 'ordinary retail price'. The defendant's claimed that this was 18 pence, the plaintiffs' that it was 18 pence plus the retail price of three chocolate bars. **Held**: the plaintiffs must succeed. It was unrealistic to maintain that the wrappers were not part of the valuable consideration. 'A peppercorn does not cease to be valuable consideration if it is established that the promisee does not like pepper and will throw away the corn.' (*per* Lord Somervell)

7.7.2 Forbearance to sue

Forbearance to sue may constitute consideration. Suppose G owes H £200 at 12 per cent interest, the money now being due. G says that he will pay H a higher rate of interest providing that H does not sue for the time being. H forbears and this will amount to consideration for G's promise which thereby becomes enforceable.

> **Alliance Bank v. Broom (1864)**
> B owed the bank £22 000 and the bank asked for security, which B promised to give. The bank gave no promise not to sue, but in fact did not sue. **Held**: the bank's forbearance amounted to consideration received by B.

7.7.3 Existing obligations

Existing obligations cannot be consideration for a further promise. In a number of cases the courts have decided that certain acts or promises to perform acts do not constitute sufficient consideration because they believe such acts or promises do not contribute anything to the bargain. These are:

(a) Performance of a public duty

A contracting party cannot claim that he is providing consideration if he is merely performing duties which he is bound to do. For example:

> **Collins v. Godefroy (1831)**
> Collins was subpoenaed to attend court as a potential witness for Godefroy. Collins was not called but demanded payment for his attendance. **Held**: The subpoena put him under a public duty to attend and even if Godefroy had promised him payment, he, Collins, had provided no consideration.

By contrast, in *Glasbrook Brothers v. Glamorgan County Council (1925)* Glasbrook Brothers as owners of a mine asked for police protection during a strike. The police were of the opinion that a small mobile guard would be enough for the task. The mine owners wanted a number of stationary guards posted around the mine. This the police agreed to provide at a total cost of £2200. The company refused to pay, contending that the police had not provided any consideration since they were already obliged by law to provide protection. The House of Lords held that in providing the stationary guards, the police had exceeded their normal duty and this therefore constituted valuable consideration that merited the payment of £2200.

(b) Performance of an existing contractual duty owed to the promisor

It cannot be regarded as consideration if the person receiving the promise (promisee) agrees to perform for the giver of the promise (the promisor) some act which he is *already* contractually bound to perform.

> **Stilk v. Myrick (1809)**
>
> Two members of a ship's crew deserted at a port of call. The captain offered the rest of the crew the deserters' wages – if they worked the ship home shorthanded. When the captain did not pay the crew sued. **Held**: they were already contractually bound to work the ship home in foreseeable emergencies and had therefore not provided consideration.

(c) Part payment of a debt

Part payment of a debt is generally not regarded as consideration for a promise not to sue for the rest. The creditor normally has the option of subsequently suing for the rest of the sum should he so wish. This basic rule was laid down in *Pinnel's case (1602)*, when the court stated that 'payment of a lesser sum on the day (due) in satisfaction of a greater cannot be any satisfaction for the whole'.

Such a view was reinforced by the decision in *Foakes v. Beer (1884)*.

> **Foakes v. Beer (1884)**
>
> Mrs Beer obtained a judgment against Foakes for a sum owed. Mrs Beer allowed time to pay and agreed not to take proceedings on the judgment. Foakes paid the sum, but then Mrs Beer realized she had not charged interest. Foakes refused to pay this and Mrs Beer sued. **Held**: she must succeed. She was entitled to the interest, and payment of the debt *less* interest could not be consideration for a promise not to take proceedings on the judgment.

This view was upheld in *Selectmove Ltd v. Inland Revenue (1993)*.

There are four situations where the creditor might not be able to obtain full payment:

1. Qualifications outlined in Pinnel's case   These are as follows:

- Payment of a smaller sum *before* the due date, at the creditor's request.
- Payment of a smaller sum at a *different* place, at the creditor's request.
- Payment of a smaller sum accompanied by delivery of a chattel (or just delivery of a chattel) 'The gift of a hawk, horse, or robe etc.' at the creditor's request.

The above situations all recognize the fact that the new element must provide some benefit to the creditor and that this benefit will amount to consideration.

2. Composition with creditors   This is an agreement by all creditors of the debtor that they will accept a proportion of what they are owed in full settlement of their claims. A creditor who participates in a composition will fail if he sues separately for the remainder of his debt.

3. Payment of a smaller sum by a third party   For example:

Hirachand Punamchand v. Temple (1911)

Temple owed money to Hirachand. Hirachand accepted a smaller sum from Temple's father in full settlement. **Held**: Hirachand could not subsequently sue Temple for the remainder of the sum.

4. The equitable doctrine of promissory estoppel This is sometimes known as quasi-estoppel, or the 'rule in the High Trees House case'. This rule is a major qualification to *Pinnel's case* and *Foakes v. Beer*. It states that once a person has made a promise to another party, *and that party has acted upon it*, the party making the promise will be prevented in equity – estopped – from going back upon it.

Central London Property Trust Ltd v. High Trees House Ltd (1947)

In 1937 the plaintiffs let a block of flats to the defendants for a term of 99 years at a ground rent of £2500 pa. In 1940, as few of the flats were occupied because of the war the plaintiffs agreed to reduce the rent to £1250 as from the beginning of the term. The defendants continued to pay the reduced rent until 1945, when all the flats were let and the plaintiffs claimed that the full rent was again payable. **Held**: the plaintiffs were entitled to recover the full rent from the time when the flats were again occupied; had they sued for the full rent between 1940 and 1945 they would have been estopped from asserting their strict legal right to demand payment in full, as when parties enter into an arrangement which is intended to create legal relations and in pursuance of such arrangement one party makes a promise to the other which he knows will be acted on and which is in fact acted on by the promisee, the promise is binding on the promisor to the extent that it will not allow him to act inconsistently with it, although the promise may not be supported by consideration in the strict sense. 'I ... apply the principle that the promise, intended to be binding, intended to be acted on and in fact acted on, is binding so far as its terms properly apply. It is binding as covering the period down to 1945, and from that time full rent is payable.' (*per* Denning, LJ).

This principle operates as 'a shield and not a sword' and hence can only be used in defence. It follows that a plaintiff would not be able to plead it when instituting legal proceedings. As Denning, LJ, explained in *Combe v. Combe (1951)*. 'The principle stated in the High Trees case ... does not create new causes of action where none existed before. It only prevents a party from insisting upon his strict legal rights, when it would be unjust to allow him to enforce them, having regard to the dealings which have taken place between the parties...'. (Courtesy of *Cracknell's Law Students' Companion*)

7.7.4 Consideration must not be past

Consideration cannot consist of something wholly performed before the promise which it is seeking to support was made. Consideration must be given in response to the promise. The rule is that past consideration is no consideration. The promise and the consideration must form part of the same transaction.

Roscorla v. Thomas (1842)

Roscorla bought a horse from Thomas for £30. After the sale had taken place Thomas made a promise to Roscorla that the horse was an animal which was sound and free from vice. In fact the horse was not. Roscorla failed in an action for breach of contract since the consideration for the promise (the sale) was past.

There are some exceptions to this rule that past consideration is no consideration. They are:

- If the act was done at the promisor's request *and* it was assumed by both parties that payment would ultimately be made, then past consideration will be good consideration.

Lampleigh v. Braithwait (1615)

The defendant had feloniously slain another and, at his request, the plaintiff did all that he could to obtain the King's pardon for the defendant. This involved 'many days labour' and much 'riding and journeying at his own charges' and in consideration of this the defendant afterwards promised to pay the plaintiff £100. **Held**: there was a binding contract to make this payment as the promise to pay £100 'couples itself' with the request to obtain the King's pardon and the plaintiff's efforts on the defendant's behalf were executed in consideration for the defendant's promise. (Courtesy of *Cracknell's Law Students' Companion*)

- Section 27 of the *Bills of Exchange Act, 1882*, states that a bill of exchange may be supported by an earlier debt or liability.

7.7.5 Consideration must move from the promisee

Consideration must move from the promisee to the promisor or some other party nominated by the promisor. There are two aspects to this rule:

- The promisor cannot escape from the contract by showing that he received no benefit from the promisee (a third party could be beneficiary).
- Only those providing consideration get any rights under a contract. A third party may well be a beneficiary but cannot sue on the contract since he has provided no consideration. This rule is also known as the **doctrine of privity of contract**. It means that a stranger to a contract cannot enforce it although the contract is for his benefit. He can only enforce the contract if he was a party to the contract and has given valuable consideration for the promise. The classic case is:

Dunlop Pneumatic Tyre Co. Ltd v. Selfridge & Co. Ltd (1915)

The defendants, who were large storekeepers and sold tyres retail to the public, ordered tyres made by the plaintiffs from Messrs A. J. Dew & Co., who were motor accessory factors. In accordance with the requirements of a contract between the plaintiffs and Messrs A. J. Dew & Co., an agreement purporting to be made between the defendants and Messrs A. J. Dew & Co. provided that in consideration of Messrs A. J. Dew & Co. allowing them certain discounts off the plaintiff's list prices, the defendants would not sell or offer any tyres made by the plaintiffs at less than list prices. The plaintiffs sued the defendants for breach of this agreement. **Held**: their action could not succeed as 'only a person who is a party to a contract can sue on it' (*per* Viscount Haldane, LC). (Courtesy of *Cracknell's Law Students' Companion*)

126 Business Law

Signed and sealed contracts are not bound by this rule on consideration since you are able to enforce a contract although you have not given any consideration to the other party. Besides, certain statutory exceptions are allowed to the privity rule, e.g. under *The Road Traffic Act, 1972* although the insurance contract is between the car user and the insurer, any other person(s) specified in the motor insurance policy can sue the insurer directly. Also under Section 11 of the *Married Women's Property Act, 1882* where a husband insures his life in favour of his wife (or vice versa) and children, those named in the insurance policy obtain independent capability to sue and claim the benefits of the insurance policy although the insurance contract is between the husband and the insurance company.

7.7.6 The consideration must be lawful

The courts will not uphold a bargain made for an illegal purpose, or where the consideration is unlawful. Thus an action for non-payment of a bribe would obviously never come to court.

Test your knowledge

Answers	Questions
	1 What is an offer?
1 A promise that the offeror is prepared to be legally bound, upon specified terms.	2 What is an invitation to treat?
2 An invitation to do business with other parties. They are invited to make offers which will be considered.	3 What was *Pharmaceutical Society of Great Britain v. Boots* about?
3 It was a 1953 test case about the display of goods in self-service shops. It was held that the display is only an invitation to treat.	4 What was *Fisher v. Bell* about?
4 It was a 1960 case about the display of a flickknife in a shop. It was held to be an invitation to treat, not an offer.	5 Who makes the offers at an auction?
5 The bidder. The fall of the hammer is the auctioneer's acceptance of the highest offer made.	6 What are the requirements for an offer?
6 (a) It must be clear – a vague offer will not be upheld; (b) it must be communicated to the offeree.	7 When does an offer terminate?

Answers	Questions
7 (a) On acceptance – it is merged into the contract; (b) on revocation, but the revocation must be communicated to the offeree; (c) on rejection, or on a counter-offer; (d) after lapse of the stated time, or a reasonable time; (e) on the death of the offeror; (f) on failure of a condition subject to which the offer was made.	8 What is an acceptance?
8 Assent to all the terms of an offer.	9 How may it be made?
9 Orally, in writing or by conduct – such as stepping on a bus at a bus stop.	10 When is an acceptance not binding?
10 (a) When it is expressed 'subject to contract'; (b) where the terms are too vague for the courts to tell what was agreed upon.	11 Contrast *Hillas v. Arcos* and *Scammell & Nephew v. Ousten*.
11 Both were cases about vague contracts. *Hillas v. Arcos* was a 1933 case about the supply of timber. **Held**: 'that is not vague which can be reduced to certainty'. *Scammell & Nephew v. Ousten* was a case about the hire purchase of a car in 1941. **Held**: the matter had not got past the negotiation stage.	12 What are the rules about communication of acceptance?
12 The acceptance must be communicated to the offeror. You cannot take silence as acceptance.	13 What are the postal rules about acceptance?
13 In general acceptance occurs when the letter is put into the pillar box. This rule is defeated if the offeror specified that acceptance must reach him before he would be bound. A withdrawal of an offer must reach the offeree before it	14 What is consideration?

Answers	Questions
takes effect, so an acceptance of the offer posted before the withdrawal is received is binding.	
14 Anything valuable that supports a contract by proving that the parties have struck a bargain.	15 When is valuable consideration not required?
15 When the contract is formal – signed sealed and delivered – rather than a simple contract.	16 What are the rules about consideration?
16 (a) Consideration must be real, but it need not be adequate – it is for the parties to decide what is adequate; (b) existing obligations cannot be consideration for a further promise; (c) consideration must not be past; (d) consideration must move from the promisee.	17 List some important cases about valuable consideration. Make sure you know the facts of each.
17 (a) *Pinnel's case* (1602); (b) *White v. Bluett* (1853); (c) *Glasbrook Brothers v. Glamorgan County Council* (1925); (d) *Stilk v. Myrick* (1809); (e) *Foakes v. Beer* (1884); (f) *Central London Property Trust v. High Trees House Ltd* (1947); (g) *Roscorla v. Thomas* (1842).	18 Go over the questions again until you are sure of all the points. Then try some of the questions in Appendix 1.

8 Circumstances affecting the validity of contracts

8.1 Introduction

Agreements where a valid offer is validly accepted and valuable consideration is present are almost always legally binding, but in certain circumstances the contract may be rendered invalid, and either void or voidable by one of the parties. The most common circumstances may be listed as follows:

- Where either duress, or undue influence is present.
- Where certain types of mistake have been made.
- Where the contract is illegal.

8.2 Duress and undue influence

8.2.1 Duress

Duress is actual or threatened violence to, or restraint of the person of, a contracting party. If a contract is made under duress it is at once suspect, because consent has not been freely given to the bargain supposedly made. The contract is voidable at the option of the party concerned.

Duress is a common law doctrine which relates entirely to the person and has no relation to that person's goods. As such it is a very limited doctrine and is one where cases are rare. However, a case came to the Judicial Committee of the Privy Council in 1975, and this illustrates the principles of duress:

> **Barton v. Armstrong (1975)**
>
> Armstrong was the Chairman and Barton was the Managing Director of a group of property companies in New South Wales. Hostility developed between them in 1966, and Barton and the other directors removed Armstrong from his chairmanship of some of the companies. Armstrong then threatened to withdraw his money from them, and he also told Barton: 'The city is not as safe as you may think between office and home.' He telephoned him on various mornings between 4 and 5 am saying, 'You will be killed' or simply breathing heavily. He told Barton: 'You can get killed.' These threats were issued to make Barton sign an agreement giving Armstrong excessive compensation in return for resigning from the boards of the companies. Barton signed. **Held**: that there had been duress and the agreements entered into by Barton were void. The onus is upon the person uttering threats to prove that the contract was not made as a result of them.

8.2.2 Undue influence

Because of the very narrow application of duress under the common law, equity found it necessary to develop related principles where free will or judgement had been excessively influenced – without threats to the person.

The equitable doctrine of undue influence is extremely difficult to define since a narrow line divides what might be undue influence from what might be mere persuasion.

The common law doctrine of duress and the equitable doctrine of undue influence are in the process of merging to cover all cases where a contract is entered into under compulsion, from physical or moral pressures, which the law considers unfair. The cases where a contract will be regarded as voidable by the party under duress are extended to cover the following cases of undue influence:

- Threatened criminal proceedings.
- Wrongful detention of property.
- A fiduciary relationship (one of trust) between the parties.

In general the requirements relating to undue influence are:

- The plaintiff must prove undue influence if there is no special relationship between the parties. A case illustrating this is:

Williams v. Bayley (1866)

A son forged his father's signature on certain promissory notes. When the forgery, which the son did not deny, was discovered the bankers arranged a meeting with his father and issued veiled threats to the effect that if some settlement was not made the son would be prosecuted. The father thereupon executed an agreement to make an equitable mortgage of his property and the forged promissory notes were returned to him. **Held**: the agreement was invalid as in these circumstances the father could not be said to have entered into it freely and voluntarily.

- Where there is a special relationship between the parties then it is up to the defendant to *disprove* undue influence. There is a presumption in contracts between solicitor and client, religious adviser and disciple, doctor and patient, parent and child, etc., that there is undue influence. It can be rebutted by proof of independent advice. For example:

Lancashire Loans Ltd v. Black (1934)

A daughter married at 18 and after the marriage went to live with her husband. Some time after the daughter came of age her mother, who was very extravagant and a frequent borrower from moneylenders, requested her daughter to raise certain money to pay off her debts, sign promissory notes and give a second charge on a vested interest in remainder without which the moneylenders refused to make any further loans. The only advice which the daughter received was from a solicitor who acted for the mother and the moneylenders. The moneylenders sued to enforce a promissory note given by the daughter. **Held**: so far as the daughter was concerned, the transaction must be set aside. She had given the note under her mother's influence and as the moneylenders had notice of the fact that the mother had exercised undue influence they were in no stronger position than she was. (Courtesy of *Cracknell's Law Students' Companion*)

- The effect of undue influence is to render the contract voidable at the option of the injured party, i.e. they can set it aside if they choose. However, the usual equitable bars to relief apply – for example, there should be no prolonged delay in seeking relief.

Allcard v. Skinner (1887)

When Miss Allcard was about 35 years of age she felt a desire to devote her life to good works. She became associated with the Sisters of the Poor and after a few years became a professed member of that sisterhood and bound herself to observe the rules of poverty, chastity and obedience. The rule as to poverty required a member to surrender all her property either to her relatives, the poor or to the sisterhood itself. The rules also provided that no sister should seek advice from anyone outside the order without the consent of the lady superior. Within a few days of becoming a member Miss Allcard made a will bequeathing all her property to Miss Skinner, the lady superior, and in succeeding years made gifts to the value of about £7000 to the same person. When Miss Allcard left the sisterhood about eight years later she immediately revoked her will but waited a further six years before commencing an action to recover what was left of the money given to Miss Skinner. **Held**: if she had sued to recover the amount of her gifts which had not been expended on the fulfilment of the purposes of the sisterhood at an earlier date she would have succeeded on the ground of undue influence, but as it was her acquiescence rendered her claim barred by laches. ('Laches' is laxity in performing a legal duty.) (Courtesy of *Cracknell's Law Students' Companion*)

An interesting example of undue influence is the case of Barclays Bank v. O'Brien.

Barclays Bank v. O'Brien (1993) The Times, 22 October

O'Brien persuaded his wife to agree to their joint home being used as collateral for loans made to a company in which he had an interest, although his wife had none. As part of the persuasion he said the sum involved was only £60 000, and the duration of the loan was only three weeks. Mrs O'Brien signed documents at a sub-branch of Barclays but the bank's representative did not carry out his instructions, which were to ensure that she knew that the documents put her house at risk and covered the full amount of any advances whatsoever made to her husband – the final amount of which was over £154 000. When the bank attempted to foreclose Mrs O'Brien refused to leave the house, and the bank sought to enforce the charge against her. In the Court of Appeal the court found in favour of Mrs O'Brien. It held that equity treats married women more tenderly than other sureties and the charge was only valid to the extent of £60 000. The House of Lords overruled this argument, holding that there was no special equity for married women. What there was in this case was a situation where the bank must have known that there was a strong possibility that undue influence might have been brought upon Mrs O'Brien to sign, and they should have acquainted her with the full facts in a private interview without the presence of her husband, and should have recommended that she take separate legal advice. The bank were put upon enquiry in the matter, and in fact did not enquire whether the wife had taken separate legal advice. The bank's request for possession of the property was dismissed.

8.3 Mistake

Sometimes parties enter into a contract on the basis of a mistake. At common law mistake is 'operative' (i.e. its presence has an effect on the contract) only in a limited class of cases: a person may enter into a contract under a serious mistake and yet (unless the case is covered by the law relating to **misrepresentation**) have no remedy. The main reason for this is that where mistake is operative at common law it makes the contract void *ab initio* (from the very beginning). This may have a serious effect, not only for the parties to the contract, but also for third parties (see, for example, *Cundy v. Lindsay* below).

Where a mistake is present, but is not such as to make the contract void at common law, *equity* may give relief to a party who would otherwise suffer as a result of the mistake. Both at common law and in equity, only a **mistake of fact** (as opposed to a mistake of *law*) has an effect on the contract. There is a general presumption that everyone knows the law. The rule '*ignorantia juris haud excusat*' (ignorance of the law excuses no one) rules out all mistakes of law except two: one is not expected to know the law of other countries, so *foreign laws* are not regarded as law and have to be proved in court as facts which the court can then take note of; and one is not expected to know *private rights* even when they are legal and these again must be proved in court as facts. Any mistake of private rights or of foreign law is therefore regarded as a mistake of fact and not a mistake of law, and therefore might be an operative mistake.

Ignorantia juris haud excusat also accounts for the rule that a misrepresentation of the law is not actionable. If we are all deemed to know the law, it is not possible for anyone to misrepresent it to us.

The different types of mistake are usually classified as follows:

- **Common mistake**. Here both parties make the same mistake, e.g. A sells B a picture which they both mistakenly believe to be a Warhol.
- **Mutual mistake**. Here the parties are at cross-purposes, e.g. A has two cars, a Ford and a Toyota: he contracts to sell a car to B; A means the Ford, whereas B thinks he means the Toyota.
- **Unilateral mistake**. Here one party is mistaken, and the other knows of his mistake, e.g. A sells B a picture which B mistakenly believes to be a Warhol: A knows the picture is not a Warhol, and knows of B's mistake.

    Note: In common mistake the parties have reached an agreement, but on the basis of a mistake; in mutual and unilateral mistake, there is no agreement at all.

It will be seen from the above that there is an overlap between the law relating to mistake and the law relating to misrepresentation. In cases of common mistake there has been an innocent or negligent misrepresentation (e.g. in *Leaf v. International Galleries*, where the galleries sold what they believed to be a genuine Constable painting to the plaintiff, who discovered five years later that it was not genuine – see below).

In unilateral mistake there has often been a fraudulent misrepresentation (as above). In cases where both mistake and misrepresentation are present, the effect of mistake should be considered first, because if it is operative at common law it makes the contract *void*: thus there will normally be no remedy for misrepresentation, since any misrepresentation made has not induced a contract. However, if the misrepresentation was fraudulent, there may be damages for the tort of deceit. If the misrepresentation was *negligent*, there may be damages for the tort of negligence under the rule in Hedley

8.3.1 Common mistake: the effects at common law

To ascertain the effect of common mistake at common law, the following points are helpful:

(a) Cases of res extincta

These are cases where, unknown to both parties, the subject matter of the contract has never existed, or has ceased to exist at the time when the contract is made.

> **Couturier v. Hastie (1852)**
>
> The plaintiffs, who were merchants, shipped 1180 quarters of Indian corn and the defendants, their *del credere* agents, successfully negotiated a sale. (A *del credere* agent is one who agrees, in return for extra commission, to run the risk of any bad debts.) In fact the corn had to be disposed of before reaching its destination, because it had fermented. The buyer refused to pay, no corn having arrived, and Couturier claimed that Hastie must honour this bad debt. On a technicality, the *del credere* arrangement not being in writing as required by the *Statute of Frauds, 1677*, Hastie denied liability. This argument was rejected by the court, but on appeal the House of Lords rejected the claims of Couturier anyway. It was a case of *res extincta*. The contract contemplated that there was an existing something to be sold and bought and capable of transfer but as the corn had already been sold at the time of the sale by the defendants this was not the case and the defendants were not liable. There was no contract, and consequently no bad debt. (Adapted from *Cracknell's Law Students' Companion*)

(b) Cases of res sua

These are cases where A agrees to sell or lease to B property which already belongs to B.

> **Cooper v. Phibbs (1867)**
>
> The appellant sought to be relieved from an agreement whereby he contracted to take from the respondent a three-year lease of a salmon fishery. At the time of making the agreement the appellant believed that the fishery belonged to the respondent but it afterwards appeared that the fishery was the property of the appellant himself. **Held**: the appellant was entitled to have the agreement for the lease set aside subject to the respondent having a lien on the property in respect of money spent on purchasing certain fishing rights and improving the fishery. (Courtesy of *Cracknell's Law Students' Companion*)

In cases of *res extincta* and *res sua* the contracts have been held to be void. *The reason for this is the absence of any contractual subject matter.*

It is rare for operative mistake to be extended to situations where there is mistake as to the quality of the subject matter of the contract. For example:

> **Leaf v. International Galleries (1950)**
>
> (Court of Appeal) The plaintiff bought an oil painting of Salisbury Cathedral and accepted it as a genuine Constable on the representations of the sellers, the defendants. Five years after the sale the plaintiff discovered that the painting was not by Constable and he claimed rescission on the grounds of innocent misrepresentation. **Held**: his claim must fail as the action had not been commenced within a reasonable time and, further, the mistake in question was not one which would entitle the plaintiff to avoid the contract. (Courtesy of *Cracknell's Law Students' Companion*)

Note that the rescission of a contract entered into after an innocent misrepresentation is now permitted under the *Misrepresentation Act, 1967*, but it is an equitable remedy which will be refused if there has been an undue lapse of time. This would not prevent damages for innocent misrepresentation being given under Section 2(2) of the Act. Whatever the effect of misrepresentation the court ruled that the mistake made was not one which would entitle the plaintiff to avoid the contract.

However, the House of Lords in *Bell v. Lever Bros. Ltd* (1932) did state that it would be possible for a contract to be void at common law for a common mistake as to the quality of the subject matter if the mistake was 'fundamental' to the contract.

(c) The effect in equity

Where the contract is void at common law (e.g. cases of *res extincta* and *res sua*) it is also void in equity. In addition, the court may impose terms on either party (e.g., *Cooper v. Phibbs*, where the respondent was allowed a lien on a property for work done).

Even where the contract is not void at common law, equity may give relief in one of two ways:

- It may set the contract aside, with or without imposing terms. For example:

> **Grist v. Bailey (1966)**
>
> B agreed to sell a freehold house to G at a price of £850, in the belief that the house was subject to an existing statutory tenancy. In fact the house was not subject to a statutory tenancy, and on a vacant possession basis was worth £2250. G sought specific performance of the agreement, and B pleaded the existence of a common mistake of fact, and counterclaimed for rescission of the sale agreement. **Held**: the sale agreement would be set aside for a fundamental common mistake of fact, on terms which gave G the option to buy the house at the vacant possession price. (Courtesy of *Cracknell's Law Students' Companion*)

- It may grant the equitable remedy of **rectification**. Where the parties have made an agreement or reached a common intention, and have attempted to incorporate this in a document, and, because of a mistake, the document does not accurately reflect their prior agreement or intention, then the court may order rectification of the document, and specific performance of it as rectified.

Joscelyne v. Nissen (1970)

J agreed with his daughter (N) that she should take over his car-hire business. Throughout the negotiations it was agreed that she should pay all the household expenses. However, when the written contract was concluded no reference was made to household expenses. **Held**: The court would rectify the document to include the daughter's agreement to pay the expenses.

8.3.2 Mutual mistake

Where the parties are at cross-purposes the court applies an objective test, and tries to determine the 'sense of the promise': i.e. would a sensible third party, looking at the externals of the contract, come to the conclusion that the contract meant what A intended or what B intended? If such a third party could not conclude that the contract meant what A intended or what B intended, then the contract is void. The classic case is *Raffles v. Wichelhaus (1864)* – see page 107.

The effect in equity of mutual mistake Equity follows the common law in holding that, where the sense of the promise can be ascertained, a contract to that effect exists and **specific performance** may be ordered, even though the effect may be harsh. An example is given below:

Tamplin v. James (1880)

'The Ship Inn' and a saddler's shop adjoining were put up for sale by auction and the extent of the property to be sold was clearly marked on plans which were on view in the auction room. At the back of the property were two pieces of garden which originally belonged to the vendors, the plaintiffs, but which were now let to them by the present owners. The tenants of the inn and shop used and enjoyed these gardens and the defendant, who purchased the inn and shop at the auction, refused to complete his purchase on the ground that he believed that he was buying the freehold of all that was in the occupation of the plaintiffs' tenants. The defendant said that he had not seen the plans which correctly delineated the property to be sold. **Held**: the plaintiffs were entitled to specific performance as the fact that the purchaser had made this mistake without any excuse ought not to enable him to escape from his bargain. (Courtesy of *Cracknell's Law Students' Companion*)

8.3.3 Unilateral mistake

Where we are considering whether one party knows of the other's mistake, he is taken to know what would be obvious to a reasonable person. For example, in *Hartog v. Colin and Shields*:

Hartog v. Colin and Shields (1939)

The defendants offered to sell the plaintiff 30 000 Argentine hare skins at certain prices per pound but after the plaintiff had accepted this offer the defendants failed to deliver the skins because they had intended, as was the usual practice, that they should be sold at the specific prices per *piece*. **Held**: the plaintiff's action for damages would not succeed as he must have realized that the offer made by the defendants contained a mistake. (Courtesy of *Cracknell's Law Students' Companion*)

There are several special cases of unilateral mistake:

- mistaken identity;
- mistakes about documents;
- mistakes in equity.

(a) *Mistaken identity*

Cases of mistaken identity usually arise from fraudulent misrepresentation: e.g. R, a rogue, by pretending to be X, a reputable person, obtains goods on credit from O, the owner. R then disposes of the goods for value to T, a third party acting in good faith. O's contract with R is voidable for fraudulent misrepresentation, but this will not enable him to recover the goods from T. This is shown by the case of *Phillips v. Brooks*:

> *Phillips v. Brooks Ltd* (1919)
>
> A man entered the plaintiff's shop and asked to inspect some jewellery. He selected some pearls and rings to the value of £3000 and when he was signing a cheque for that amount he stated: 'You see who I am, I am Sir George Bullough', and he gave an address in St James's Square. The plaintiff knew that there was such a man as Sir George Bullough and reference to a directory confirmed that Sir George lived at the address mentioned. The plaintiff asked the man in the shop if he would like to take the jewels with him but was told: 'You had better have the cheque cleared first, but I should like to take the ring as it is my wife's birthday tomorrow.' The plaintiff let the man have the ring but his cheque was dishonoured. The rogue pledged the ring to the defendants from whom the plaintiff sought to recover either the ring or its value. **Held**: the plaintiff intended to contract with the man who came into the shop although he believed (mistakenly) that he was Sir George Bullough. The property in the ring had therefore passed to the actual purchaser who was able to give a good title to the defendants. For this reason the plaintiff's action failed. (Courtesy of *Cracknell's Law Students' Companion*)

In order to recover property, O must prove that his contract with R is void *ab initio* for operative mistake, with the result that no title can pass to or from R. There is a presumption that a contract exists and the court will not hold it void unless the mistaken party can prove the following four points:

- *That his mistake as to identity was known to the person with whom he dealt.*
- *That he intended to deal with some third person, i.e. some person other than the person with whom he apparently made the contract.* Thus if there is no third person in existence to point to, the contract will not normally be void.

> *King's Norton Metal Co Ltd v. Edridge, Merrett & Co. Ltd* (1897)
>
> Both parties were metal manufacturers and the plaintiffs had received a letter ordering certain goods which purported to come from Hallam & Co., Soho Hackle Pin and Wire Works, Sheffield. At the head of the paper on which the letter was written there was a representation of a large factory with a number of

chimneys and a statement that the firm had depots and agencies in Belfast, Lille and Ghent. The plaintiffs supplied the goods but it afterwards appeared that they had been ordered by a man called Wallis who in turn had sold them to the defendants. The firm Hallam & Co. did not exist but the plaintiffs had received payment in respect of previous orders made in the name of that firm. On the occasion in question Wallis did not pay for the goods and the plaintiffs brought an action for damages for conversion. **Held**: their action must fail as they were found to have contracted with the writer of the letter. The property in the goods had therefore passed to Wallis who was able to give the defendants a good title to the goods when they purchased them. (Courtesy of *Cracknell's Law Students' Companion*)

- *That at the time of negotiating the agreement, he regarded the identity of the other contracting party as a matter of crucial importance.*

Cundy v. Lindsay (1878)

Messrs Lindsay & Co. were linen manufacturers in Belfast and Alfred Blenkarn, who occupied a room in a house looking into Wood Street, Cheapside, wrote to them and proposed buying a quantity of their goods. Blenkarn used the address '37, Wood Street, Cheapside' and signed the letters, without using an initial or Christian name, in such a way that his signature appeared to be 'Blenkiron & Co.'. There was a highly respectable firm of W. Blenkiron & Son carrying on business at 123 Wood Street and Messrs Lindsay & Co., who knew of this firm's reputation but not the number of the premises where they carried on business, supplied the goods ordered by Blenkarn and addressed them to Messrs Blenkiron & Co., 37 Wood Street, Cheapside. Blenkarn did not pay for the goods but disposed of them to the defendants who were sued by Messrs Lindsay & Co. for unlawful conversion. **Held**: no contract had been concluded with Blenkarn who therefore had no property in the goods to transfer to the defendants; consequently the defendants were liable to the extent of their value. (Courtesy of *Cracknell's Law Students' Companion*)

- *That he took reasonable steps to verify the identity of the person with whom he was invited to deal.*

Ingram v. Little (1960)

The plaintiffs, who were two sisters and a third person, advertised for sale the car of which they were joint owners. A man called on them, and agreed to buy the car for £717. In order to persuade the plaintiffs to accept a cheque in payment the man said that he was H, and gave an address in Surrey. Having checked the name and address in the telephone directory, the plaintiffs accepted the cheque and parted with the car. The man, who was not H, sold the car to the defendant and then disappeared, his cheque being dishonoured. The plaintiffs sought to recover the car or its value from the defendant who had bought it in good faith. **Held**: the plaintiff's offer to sell on payment by cheque was made only to H, and could not be accepted by the man representing himself to be H; no contract had been formed, therefore, and the plaintiffs were entitled to recover the car or damages from the defendant. (Courtesy of *Cracknell's Law Students' Companion*)

Some doubt has been cast on the correctness of this decision, because in rather similar circumstances the Court of Appeal refused to follow *Ingram v. Little* and referred in the judgment to 'a presumption that where a transaction takes place between people face-to-face the offer by one person is made to the other, and not to someone he says he is.' The case was:

Lewis v. Averay (1971)

The plaintiff advertised a car for sale. A man telephoned for an appointment to view the car, but did not give his name. He came along and tested the car and the plaintiff took him to a flat to discuss the details. At the flat the potential buyer stated that he was 'Richard Green', the well-known actor, and he agreed to buy the car at £450. He tendered a cheque in payment, signed 'R. A. Green', and on producing evidence of his identity he was allowed to take the car away. The cheque proved worthless. The buyer was a rogue, not Richard Green, and later sold the car to the defendant, who bought it in good faith. The plaintiff sued the defendant in conversion. **Held**: where a transaction takes place between people face to face there is a presumption that the offer by one person is made to the other and not to any person that other says he is, and there was nothing on the facts of the case to rebut this presumption. Thus, the plaintiff's offer was made to the rogue and not to 'Richard Green'. The rogue accordingly got a voidable title to the car, under which he sold the car to the defendant before the contract between the plaintiff and the rogue had been avoided. The plaintiff's claim therefore failed.

(b) Documents mistakenly signed

Often documents are signed by mistake. It may be that one party, A, induces another party, B, to sign a document different in class or contents from that which B contemplated. The question then arises as to B's liability to any third party who might subsequently hold such documents. The matter revolves around the point as to whether the law will allow B to say in his own defence that the document is 'not his act' ('*non est factum*').

The basic position as regards *non est factum* follows from the cases listed below, which rest upon two points:

- Was the document which was signed totally different in nature from the document which the party believed he was signing? If it was, the court may feel that he should be released from his obligations. If it was substantially the same he must honour the contract. This was the case in *Saunders v. Anglia Building Society (1970)*.

Saunders v. Anglia Building Society (1970)

An elderly widow signed without reading a document which X told her was a deed of gift of her house in favour of her nephew. In fact, it was a purported assignment of the leasehold to X, and the old lady would not have signed had she known the facts. X mortgaged the house to the building society, and on his defaulting on the repayments due under the mortgage, they sought possession. **Held**: The plaintiff could not rely on a plea of *non est factum* as against the building society, because on the facts the transaction she intended and what she actually carried out were the same character, and she was bound by what she had signed. (Courtesy of *Cracknell's Law Students' Companion*)

- Was the signee negligent in signing? In *Foster v. Mackinnon* the document was totally different and the feeble-sighted old man was held not to be negligent in signing:

> *Foster v. Mackinnon (1869)*
>
> The defendant, an old man of feeble sight, was induced to sign his name on the back of a bill of exchange by a fraudulent misrepresentation that he was signing a guarantee. **Held**: if the defendant signed without knowing that it was a bill of exchange under the belief that it was a guarantee, and if he had not been guilty of negligence in so signing, he was entitled to be released from liability under the bill. (Courtesy of *Cracknell's Law Students' Companion*)

> *Lloyds Bank plc v. Waterhouse (1990)*
>
> Lloyds Bank obtained a guarantee from a father as security for a loan to his son. The father was illiterate, which the bank did not know, but he did ask what was the extent of the guarantee, and concluded that it covered the mortgage on his son's farm only. In fact it was worded to guarantee all the son's indebtedness to the bank. The son defaulted and the bank sought to recover the full debts, less the amount realized by the sale of the farm. **Held**: the father had not been careless, and had been led into signing something more than what he believed. It was a case of *non est factum* coupled with negligent misrepresentation.

(c) Mistake in equity

Where a mistake occurs as a slip of the pen (or these days as a slip of the keyboard) equity will not allow the error to go uncorrected. In *Webster v. Cecil (1861)* a purported acceptance of an offer to sell land at £1250 when previous offers at £2000 had been rejected was not upheld. The defendant Cecil had intended to offer to sell at £2250. Performance of a sale at £1250 was refused, for Webster must have known it was a slip of the pen.

8.4 Illegal contracts

Any contract where the promise, the consideration or the object of the contract is unlawful will be void and cannot be enforced in the courts. Where a contract is prohibited by statute or contrary to public policy because it encourages immorality, or crime, or is against the public interest in some other way, it is illegal and the courts will not lend their support to anyone on the matter. It is said to be **void by illegality**. Sometimes a contract is merely denied its full validity, because of a technicality, and it is said to be unenforceable. The words illegal, void and unenforceable are often used loosely and precise understanding of what is meant by each is not easy to attain. The general rule is that all illegal contracts are void. The maxim is *ex turpi causa non oritur actio* (no action arises from a base or wrongful cause).

Some writers suggest that there is virtually no difference between illegal and void contracts, others still maintain that the distinction is worth making, especially since a contract void by illegality will render unenforceable any contracts depending upon it, whilst a contract void for other reasons will not.

Illegal contracts may be illegal by virtue of an infringement of a statute or they may be illegal at common law. However, this does not necessarily mean that the courts will view all infringements with equal severity; some contracts may be strictly illegal and the court will not offer redress to either party, while others may be only nominally illegal and the court may sever the illegal part from the legal part.

8.5 Contracts illegal at common law

These include agreements to commit crimes or torts; agreements to defraud the revenue or other public authority; agreements to commit immoral acts or make immoral acts possible and other contracts which are against public policy.

(a) Contracts where the object is the commission of a crime or a civil wrong

Any contract which purports to commit a crime or a tort is illegal and void. Even where the crime is to be committed outside UK jurisdiction it is illegal to make a contract which envisages crime in a foreign and friendly country. In *Foster v. Driscoll* (*1929*) a contract was made to smuggle whisky into the United States during prohibition. It was held to be illegal and void.

(b) Contracts to defraud the revenue or other public authority

Any attempt to defraud the public purse is illegal and cannot be relied upon in a court of law. In *Alexander v. Rayson* (*1936*), 1 KB 169, Alexander and Rayson entered into an agreement whereby the agreed rent was split into two parts, one part declared to be rent and the other declared to be for services to the flat concerned. The object was to reduce the assessment for rates. When A sued R for failure to pay for the 'services' the arrangement was held to be void.

(c) Contracts depending for their performance upon sexually immoral acts

In *Pearce v. Brooks* (*1866*) a prostitute failed to pay a carriage-maker for a coach which had been specially built for the attraction of male customers. It was held to be an illegal contract, and the carriage-maker could not recover the price.

(d) Other contracts against public policy

The term 'against public policy' means that crime would be encouraged, or the public interest would suffer. Thus it is against public policy for a person to be allowed to insure property in which they have no interest, for they might just be tempted to make the event occur which they are insuring against, since they will not suffer if the risk occurs. Thus I may insure my own life, my wife's life or our mutual property, for I have an interest in them and would suffer a loss if they were adversely affected by the risk covered. I am not entitled to insure the property (for example) of others, for I have no insurable interest in it.

It is in general against public policy if private activity is curtailed unnecessarily. Everyone has the right to use his personal talents or skills in any lawful way he chooses. Therefore **contracts in restraint of trade** are *prima facie* illegal. This is such an important topic that it is worth separate consideration.

(e) Contracts in restraint of trade

It is frequently the case that an employee may find out things in the course of his employment that would be helpful to him should he decide to set up in business on his own. This might harm his former employer. Similarly, a vendor of a business is usually paid a sum for goodwill, the money being compensation for the hard work done in establishing a clientèle locally. To set up in business next door to the previous business would clearly be unfair. The question then arises how shall the employer, or the purchaser of a business protect himself from such unfairness? The answer is to insert clauses 'in restraint of trade' in the contract of employment or the agreement to purchase which prohibit the employee or the vendor from setting up in business again. However, it is against public policy to impose such a restriction on the use of one's talents and labours.

The solution is to permit clauses in restraint of trade which are fair and reasonable but to declare unreasonable restrictions against public policy and void. To restrict an employee from setting up next door to his employer might be held reasonable. To restrict him from setting up anywhere in the UK would be unreasonable. The following cases illustrate the problem.

> *British Reinforced Concrete Co. Ltd v. Schelff (1921)*
>
> A company took over the local business of S and included a clause in the agreement restricting him from setting up in business again within 10 miles of any branch of their organization *which was nationwide*. **Held**: it was too wide a restriction and void.

> *Nordenfeldt v. Maxim Nordenfeldt Gun Co. (1894)*
>
> The inventor of a famous machine gun promised that for 25 years he would not make or sell guns or ammunition anywhere in the world. In return he was generously compensated. When he found this restriction irksome and tried to break it the court found it reasonable and binding.

> *Spencer v. Marchinton (1988)*
>
> An employer sought to restrict an employee from setting up in business within 25 miles of the place of former employment. **Held**: it was too wide – the claims made about prospective customers within the proposed area were too insubstantial to be upheld.

8.6 Illegality declared by statute

In modern society a wide range of statutes is passed by the legislative body. They are designed to fulfil a range of purposes and it is often a question put to the judiciary as to what the exact meaning of a statute might be. Some statutes are such that those who neglect their contents render contracts made in that area illegal. Others do not have such a serious impact upon contracts. It is up to the court to interpret and decide in the light of the facts of each case.

Examples of specific declarations about illegality are as follows:

8.6.1 Gaming and Wagering

By Section 18 of the *Gaming Act, 1845* contracts by way of gaming or wagering are null and void and no action can be brought to recover money won upon any wagers. The *Gaming Act, 1968*, drew a distinction between

8.6.2 Restrictive practices

'hard gaming' and 'bingo' and permitted relaxations in the rules about gaming premises when used for this more innocent activity.

The *Restrictive Trade Practices Acts, 1976 and 1977*, and the *Resale Prices Act, 1976*, make it illegal to impose restrictive practices unless these are registered for consideration by the Restrictive Practices Court.

As examples of less specific cases of illegality we may maintain the following:

(a) The ultra vires doctrine

This had already been fully discussed (see pages 69–71). Here it is sufficient to state again that when a company is registered under the *Companies Act, 1985* it includes in its memorandum of association an 'objects clause'. Since this is a matter of public record everybody may be deemed to know what the objects of every company are. If I engage in a contract with a company which is *ultra vires* the company (outside the powers of the company) the contract is strictly speaking illegal. Although Section 35 of the Act (see page 70) now protects innocent third parties who make contracts with companies it still remains a fact that as far as the directors of the company are concerned the contract is illegal, and the *ultra vires* principle is therefore still a good example of a situation where a contract may, in certain circumstances, be held to be void by illegality.

(b) Statutes requiring a licence

Many statutes require a person engaging in certain activities to take out a licence. If contracts are made by unlicensed persons the contract is void *ab initio* (from the very beginning). Neither party can acquire rights, whether there is any intention to break the law or not. However, even where a contract is lawfully formed it is possible that the performance of the contract may be illegal. In *Anderson Ltd v. Daniel (1924)* a statute required that a seller of artificial fertilizers must give the buyer an invoice stating the composition of the fertilizer. The sellers had failed to do this when supplying 10 tons of fertilizer and when suing for the price were held to have no rights or remedies under the contract, which had been illegally performed.

It must be emphasized, however, that a contract is not automatically rendered illegal as performed merely because some statutory requirement has been violated in the course of its completion. It is all a question of the construction of a statute to determine whether it was the express or implied intention of the legislation that such a violation as that which the guilty party has committed should deprive him of all remedies.

The effects of illegality The effect is to render the contract void, and unenforceable. This means that the courts will do nothing to implement the contract, even if unfairness results. Where there is equal wrongdoing the court will do nothing to help either party. Thus the coachmaker in *Pearce v. Brooks* could not obtain either payment or the return of the coach. The rule is 'where there is equal wrongdoing' the position of the defendant is the stronger. Where there is unequal wrongdoing the court may order in favour of one of the parties if there is genuine repentance.

Sometimes a contract may be like the curate's egg – good in parts. In that case the court may try to sever the contract into its good and bad parts, and uphold the good part while rejecting the illegal part. This is called **severance** of the contract.

Test your knowledge

Answers	Questions
	1 What is duress?
1 Actual or threatened violence to the person (or imprisonment of the person).	2 What is undue influence?
2 Excessive influence over the free will or judgement of a party to a contract.	3 What is the presumption where there is a special relationship?
3 That there is undue influence.	4 How can this presumption be rebutted?
4 By proof that independent legal advice was available to the plaintiff.	5 What is an operative mistake?
5 A mistake that goes to the root of the operations following from a contract.	6 What is the effect of operative mistake at common law?
6 It renders the contract void *ab initio*?	7 What are the classes of operative mistake?
7 (a) Common mistake; (b) mutual mistake; (c) unilateral mistake.	8 List common cases of operative mistake?
8 (a) Mistake as to the existence of the subject matter; (b) mistake as to the quality of the subject matter; (c) mistake as to the terms of the agreement; (d) mistake as to the identity of the person dealt with; (e) mistake in equity – a slip of the pen or the keyboard.	9 What is the meaning of *non est factum*?
9 'Not my act.'	10 When is a contract illegal?
10 When it contravenes a statute or the common law.	11 What is the effect of illegality?
11 The contract is void and unenforceable, except in certain cases where severance is possible to sever the illegal part from the part that is legal.	12 Go over the questions again until you are sure of all the answers. Then try some of the written questions in Appendix 1

9 The terms of the contract

9.1 Introduction

The contents of a contract are known as the **terms**. Usually the parties to a contract state the terms *expressly*, and may choose to do so orally, or in writing, or in a combination of these methods. However, as we have already seen, terms can sometimes be *implied* by law into the contract (as for example, in *Hillas v. Arcos* (*1932*) (see page 113) and *Foley v. Classique Coaches* (*1934*) (see page 117). These are instances of judicial implication, but terms are also frequently implied into contracts by Acts of Parliament.

The terms themselves, whether express or implied, have varying degrees of importance and a party will be allowed wider remedies for breach by the other party of an important term than for breach of an unimportant term.

Finally, terms in a contract may not only confer rights on one or both of the parties but may also restrict or exclude a party's rights.

Before considering the terms of a contract in detail we must first distinguish between representations and terms.

9.1.1 The distinction between representations and terms

A term is part of the contract. A representation is not: it is a statement which *induces* the making of the contract. The distinction between a term and a representation is important, because the remedies are different (see Misrepresentation in Chapter 10). Three tests have been used by judges in determining whether a statement made by a party is a term or a mere representation. None of these tests is, by itself, conclusive.

(a) The time test

If the statement was made *at the time the contract was formed*, or shortly before, then it is more likely to be a term than a representation. For example:

> *Routledge v. McKay (1954)*
>
> A Douglas motorcycle combination was first registered in 1930 but when a new registration book was issued the date of original registration was given as '9.9.41'. In October 1949, the seller, who was not responsible for the incorrect entry in the registration book, in answer to a question by the buyer as to the date of the machine, said that it was a late 1941 or a 1942 model and seven days later the buyer and seller entered into a contract of sale. The memorandum of agreement made no mention of the date of the machine. The buyer claimed damages for breach of warranty. **Held**: the incorrect statement in the registration book was a false representation and not a warranty and, in the absence of fraud, the buyer could not succeed. (Courtesy of *Cracknell's Law Students' Companion*)

(b) The writing test

If the terms are in writing, then any oral statement is more likely to be a mere representation. The court infers that the parties considered it insufficiently important to be reduced to writing, and, therefore, regard it as a representation only. For example:

> ### Heilbut, Symons & Co. v. Buckleton (1913)
>
> The appellants' manager had been intructed to obtain applications for shares in the Filisola Rubber and Produce Estates Limited. The respondent telephoned the appellants' manager and said: 'I understand you are bringing out a rubber company', and the manager replied: 'We are.' The respondent asked 'if it was all right' and was told 'We are bringing it out', to which the respondent rejoined: 'That is good enough for me.' As a result of this conversation 6000 shares were allotted to the respondent but they quickly fell in value. The respondent contended that as the company could not be properly described as a rubber company there was a breach of warranty that it was a rubber company whose main object was to produce rubber. **Held**: the words of the appellants' manager constituted a mere representation and not a warranty. (Courtesy of *Cracknell's Law Students' Companion*)

(c) The skill and knowledge test

If the maker of the statement possessed special skill and knowledge compared with the other party, then it is probably a term. This is probably the test to which the courts attach the greatest weight. For example:

> ### Dick Bentley Productions Ltd v. Harold Smith (Motors) Ltd (1965)
>
> The plaintiff told the defendant dealer that he was on the look-out for a well-vetted Bentley car and the defendant truthfully assured the plaintiff that he (the defendant) was in a position to find out the history of cars. Later, the defendant informed the plaintiff that he had just purchased 'one of the nicest cars we have had in for quite a long time', that it had been fitted with a replacement engine and gearbox and (falsely but not fraudulently) that it had done 20 000 miles only since it had been so fitted (the speedometer read 20 000 miles). The plaintiff purchased the car for £1850 but it was a considerable disappointment to him and he brought an action for breach of warranty. **Held**: he was entitled to succeed as the inference that the representation was intended as a warranty had not been rebutted. 'If a representation is made in the course of dealings for a contract for the very purpose of inducing the other party to act on it, and it actually induces him to act on it by entering into the contract, that is *prima facie* ground for inferring that the representation was intended as a warranty. ... But the maker of the representation can rebut this inference if he can show that it really was an innocent misrepresentation, in that he was in fact innocent of fault in making it, and that it would not be reasonable in the circumstances for him to be bound by it' (*per* Lord Denning, MR). (Courtesy of *Cracknell's Law Students' Companion*)

9.2 Express terms: conditions and warranties

An express term is a clear stipulation in the contract which the parties intend should be binding upon them. Traditionally, the common law has divided terms into two categories. First there are **conditions**, which are terms going to the root of the contract, and for breach of which the remedies of repudiation or rescission of the contract *and* damages are allowed. Second, there are **warranties,** which are minor terms of the contract, for breach of which the *only* remedy is damages. The following cases illustrate the distinction.

> ### Bettini v. Gye (1876)
> The plaintiff entered into a contract to sing for the defendant for a certain period and at a fixed salary and agreed to be in London six days before the commencement of his engagement for the purpose of rehearsal. In fact, due to illness, he arrived four days later than he had promised and the defendant refused to proceed with the engagement. **Held**: the provision as to rehearsal was not a condition precedent as it did not go to the root of the matter and for this reason the defendant was not entitled to avoid the contract. (Courtesy of *Cracknell's Law Students' Companion*)

> ### Poussard v. Spiers and Pond (1876)
> The plaintiff agreed with the defendants to sing the chief female part for a period of three months in a new opera which was about to be produced at the defendants' theatre. Owing to illness the plaintiff was not able to attend the final rehearsals or the first four performances and when she offered to take her part in the fifth performance the defendants refused to accept her services and the plaintiff brought an action for wrongful dismissal. **Held**: the plaintiff could not recover as her inability to perform on the opening day and early performances was a breach of a condition precedent which went to the root of the matter and hence entitled the defendants to treat the contract as discharged. (Courtesy of *Cracknell's Law Students' Companion*)

In *Heyworth v. Hutchinson* (1867) Lord Blackburn defined a condition as a term 'going to the essence of the contract' or which 'goes to the root of the matter', and a warranty as a clause 'only collateral to the contract'.

Parliament followed this classification of terms in codifying the law relating to the sale of goods. By Section 11.3 of the *Sale of Goods Act, 1979*, a condition is stated to be a term 'the breach of which may give rise to a right to treat the contract as repudiated', while Section 61 defines a warranty as a term 'collateral to the main purpose of the contract'.

While the basic distinction between a condition and a warranty in a contract still holds good today, there may be circumstances in which the court will find it difficult to assign a term to either category.

Faced with a term which involves several obligations which are actually or potentially of varying importance, the modern tendency of the courts is not to attempt to label the term as a 'condition' or a 'warranty'. Instead, they look to *the effect of the breach*: if it is serious, then the injured party can repudiate and obtain damages. An example was given by Upjohn, LJ in the first case in which this approach was adopted (*Hong Kong Fir Shipping Co. Ltd v. Kawasaki Kisen Kaisha Ltd (1962)*). He said:

> *If a nail is missing from one of the timbers of a wooden vessel ... the owners are in breach of the seaworthiness stipulation. It is contrary to common sense to suppose that ... the charterer should at once be entitled to treat the contract as at an end for such a trifling breach.*

This approach has tended to be followed in the majority of subsequent cases dealing with this point, e.g.

> *Reardon Smith Line Ltd v. Hansen-Tangen (1976)*
>
> The appellants chartered a ship which was described in the charterparty as to be built by a named Japanese shipbuilding company and having a particular hull number. When delivered, the ship had been built by subcontractors under the supervision of the named company, many of whose personnel had been seconded to work on the vessel. The hull number was also different. The appellants appealed against a decision that the ship in fact complied with the description having regard to Japanese custom. They contended that the words specifying the builders and the number were contractual terms forming part of the description and that because of the departure from the description they were entitled to reject the vessel. **Held**: Dismissing the appeal, in reaching its decision the court had to place itself in the same factual position as that in which the parties had been when contracting. The relevant words were only intended as a means of identification. The strict rule of compliance with description which applied in sale of goods cases did not apply to a contract like the present which came under the general law of contract. Even if it did apply, the description had been complied with in the strict sense. The words fulfilled their function of providing a means of identifying the vessel. They could not be read as essential terms of the contract which must be complied with literally. (Courtesy of *Cracknell's Law Students' Companion*)

Apart from this, however, there are three matters which can affect the remedies of the innocent party, in relation to breach of contract:

(a) Acceptance of goods

The right to repudiate a contract for the sale of goods will be lost if the buyer has *accepted* the goods (Section 11(4) of the *Sale of Goods Act, 1979*). 'Acceptance', according to Section 35 of the Act, occurs if he *indicates acceptance*, or if he *retains the goods* beyond a reasonable time, or if he does anything *inconsistent* with the seller's ownership (such as resale). Effectively then, the condition must be treated as a warranty, with a right only to claim damages, e.g. *Leaf v. International Galleries* (see page 134).

(b) Representation becoming a warranty

If a representation becomes a warranty in the contract – which could happen if a statement was made before the contract, and then repeated at the time of the contract – then the innocent party could not only obtain damages if it were untrue, but also obtain rescission of the contract under Section 1 of the *Misrepresentation Act, 1967*. This right will be considered again in Chapter 10 on Misrepresentation.

(c) Waiver

A breach of condition can be waived. This extinguishes the right to repudiate, e.g.

Aquis Estates Ltd v. Minton (1975)

The plaintiff appellants contracted to buy the residue of a lease from the defendants 'subject to no adverse land charge entry'. Unknown to both parties, there was an adverse entry (the property was a 'listed building' for planning purposes) but after discovering it the plaintiffs negotiated (unsuccessfully) with the freeholders for the purchase of the freehold. The court held that the plaintiffs had thereby *waived* the breach of condition of no adverse entries, and so were liable to forfeit their deposit and pay damages for wrongful repudiation. (Courtesy of *Cracknell's Law Students' Companion*)

9.3 Implied terms

Implied terms are those terms which, although not expressly stated by the parties by words or conduct, are by law deemed to be part of the contract.

Terms may be implied into contracts by custom, statute, or the courts.

9.3.1 Terms implied by custom

By custom, a lawyer means an established practice or usage in a trade, locality, type of transaction, or between parties.

If two or more people enter into a contract against a common background of business, it is considered that they expressly intend the trade usage of that business unless they expressly exclude this.

Trade custom is illustrated by the following case:

British Crane Hire Corporation v. Ipswich Plant Hire Ltd (1974)

A crane was hired under an oral agreement between two large companies who were both engaged in the plant hire business. The owner's usual printed conditions of hire, which were standard in the trade, were sent on later. **Held**: the conditions of hire were part of the contract not withstanding that there had been no 'course of dealing'. The standard conditions were fair and reasonable and the hirers knew that the conditions were always applied. (Courtesy of *Cracknell's Law Students' Companion*)

A course of dealing between two parties can also give rise to an implied term in a subsequent contract between two parties, as in *Hillas v. Arcos* (see page 113).

If an express term conflicts with a custom, then the former prevails. For example:

Affréteurs Réunis Société Anonyme, Les, v. Leopold Watford (London) Ltd (1919)

A charterparty provided that commission was due to the charterers' brokers on the signing of the charter whereas by custom commission was only payable if hire was earned. **Held**: commission was payable on the signing of the charter as custom was entirely inconsistent with the plain words of the agreement and therefore, in the circumstances of the case, of no effect. The charterers, as trustees for the brokers, could enforce this provision against the shipowners. (Courtesy of *Cracknell's Law Students' Companion*)

9.3.2 Terms implied by statute

There are many areas of the civil law where Parliament has interfered with the right of parties to regulate their own affairs; this interference mainly occurs where one party has used his dominant bargaining position to abuse this freedom.

Thus, in sale of goods, the general principle *'caveat emptor'* ('buyer beware') has been greatly modified, particularly in favour of the consumer, by the provisions in Sections 12 to 15 of the *Sale of Goods Act, 1979*. These points are dealt with fully in Chapter 14 on the Sale of Goods.

In addition important changes in relation to exemption clauses have been brought about by the *Unfair Contracts Terms Act, 1977*. Such changes are discussed later.

9.3.3 Terms implied by the courts

The court will imply a term into a contract, under **the doctrine of the implied term**, if it was the *presumed* intention of the parties that there should have been a particular term, but they have omitted to state it expressly.

Although the implied term is one which the parties probably never contemplated when making the contract, the courts justify this by saying that the implication is necessary in order to give 'business efficacy' to the contract.

> ### 'Moorcock', The (1889)
> The appellants made an agreement with the respondent for the use of their wharf and jetty for the purpose of loading and storing cargo from the *Moorcock*. The bed of the river adjoining the jetty was vested in a third party: it was beyond the control of the appellants and they had taken no steps to ascertain whether it was a safe place for the *Moorcock* to lie as was inevitable at low water on every tide. The vessel grounded and suffered damages because of the uneven condition of the riverbed. **Held**: the appellants were liable as the jetty could not have been used without the *Moorcock* grounding and in these circumstances they would be deemed to have impliedly represented that they had taken reasonable care to ascertain that the riverbed adjoining the jetty was in such a condition as not to cause injury to the vessel. (Courtesy of *Cracknell's Law Students' Companion*)

> ### Reed v. Dean (1949)
> Reed hired a motor launch which subsequently caught fire. They had to abandon the launch since fire-fighting equipment was out of order. Reed suffered personal injury and loss of belongings. **Held**: that Reed was entitled to recompense since there was an implied undertaking by Dean that the launch was fit for the purpose for which it was supplied; both the (unexplained) fire and the lack of correct fire-fighting equipment amounted to a breach of this implied undertaking.

It is possible to criticize the willingness of judges to imply a term into a contract to give it business efficacy. It is a convenient tool to resolve difficulties, particularly in hard cases. By saying that the parties must have intended the term implied, otherwise the whole contract would not have been sensible, the court is able to cut the Gordian knot, but if it does it too readily, and without paying careful attention to the terms in the contract itself, it does introduce uncertainty. Indeed it should be the case that an express term which is in conflict with a proposed implied term should always override it, for it at least embodies the original agreed intentions of the parties. By contrast the implied term is the expression of the court's interpretation of the intentions of the parties, and may leave at least one party dissatisfied in that he did not get the result he had been expecting when he entered into the contract.

9.4 Excluding and limiting terms

Contractual clauses designed to exonerate a party wholly or partly from liability for breaches of express or implied terms, or for tort, first appeared in the early nineteenth century. The common law did not interfere, but took the view that the parties were free to make a bargain, within the limits of legality, upon such terms as they thought fit.

This is still the general rule today, but the growth and amalgamation of large trading concerns controlling large areas of the market have led to the increase of excluding and restricting clauses – both in number and stringency – to the severe detriment of other parties.

These clauses may be imposed by means of notices, receipts, tickets or other documents which do not contain all the terms of the contract. On the other hand, they may appear in documents which purport to include the whole contract, and which are printed or reproduced in a stereotyped form. The latter are often called **standard form contracts** and Lord Diplock has pointed out that they can be subdivided into those which operate between commercial concerns of roughly equal bargaining power, and those which are imposed by big concerns on consumers on a 'take it or leave it' basis. Unfortunately, the common law does not differentiate between these two kinds of standard form contract.

Many standard form contracts are used in the field of transport, where the common law treated the carrier very harshly, as a person liable for every loss that occurs. Nineteenth- and twentieth-century legislation in this field is very complex (see Chapter 16) and there are at least five international conventions to sort out the problems arising from exemption clauses in carriage contracts. In other areas, until 1977, legislative intervention had been piecemeal and there were still large areas of contract where any party was free to impose total or partial exclusion of his liability on the other, if his bargaining strength permitted. The *Unfair Contracts Terms Act, 1977*, remedied many of these defects and is considered below. First though, it is necessary to consider the ways in which objectionable clauses have been circumvented by the courts using the general rules of contract. These are outlined below.

9.4.1 The writing must be a contractual document

It is assumed that no reasonable man would expect to find contractual terms in a mere receipt for money:

Chapelton v. Barry Urban District Council (1940)

Deckchairs were stacked up on the beach and beside them was a notice which said 'Barry Urban District Council. Cold Knap. Hire of chairs, 2p per session of 3 hours....' The appellant paid for the hire of two chairs and was given two tickets on the back of which was a condition which purported to exclude the respondents' liability for any injury which the hirer should sustain. The appellant did not read this condition. The canvas on one of the chairs was defective and the appellant claimed damages in respect of the injuries which resulted. **Held**: damages would be awarded as the appellant was entitled to assume that the conditions of hire were to be found in the notice near the stack of chairs. The ticket was a mere voucher or receipt to prove payment or the time of commencement of hire. (Courtesy of *Cracknell's Law Students' Companion*)

But a receipt for *goods* would be regarded as a contractual document, as it is frequently evidence of a contract of bailment (i.e. one whereby the possession of goods is transferred by bailor to bailee), and must be produced by the bailor in order to recover the goods. Common examples are receipts for left luggage, car parking tickets, laundry tickets, and tickets for carriage of goods by land or sea.

9.4.2 Reasonable notification

Reasonable steps must be taken to bring the existence of the excepting terms to the notice of the other party. This does *not* mean that he must actually know of the terms. In the case of *Thompson v. LMS Railway (1930)* Mrs Thompson was unaware of the terms, but as the railway company had taken reasonable steps to notify the ordinary passenger (by referring to the conditions on the front of the ticket) Mrs Thompson too was bound. A copy of the full conditions was available on request, but, if it had not been, no passenger would be bound by them.

Where the exclusion sought is of a serious nature, such as liability for death or injury, then the reasonable steps taken to notify on tickets requires that such notices be especially prominent:

Thornton v. Shoe Lane Parking Ltd (1971)

The plaintiff parked his car at the defendants' automatic car-park. On entering the car-park he passed through an automatic barrier, taking a ticket from the machine at the barrier. On the ticket, in small print, it was stated that the ticket was issued subject to conditions displayed on the premises. To find where the conditions were displayed the plaintiff would have to drive the car into the garage and walk around. The conditions were lengthy but included one exempting the defendants not only from liability for damage to cars but also from liability for any injury to a customer, howsoever caused, whilst his car was in the car-park. The plaintiff later returned to collect his car and there was an accident in which he was severely injured. **Held**: the defendants were not protected by the exemption clause. In order to show that the plaintiff was bound by it, it was necessary to show either that he knew of it or that the defendants had done what was reasonably necessary to draw it to his attention. For this purpose, where the clause was exceptionally wide and was one which was not usual in that class of contract, it was not enough to show that the plaintiff had been given notice that the ticket was issued subject to conditions. It must be shown that adequate steps had been taken to draw his attention in the most explicit way to the particular exempting conditions relied on. Here the defendants had failed to show that the plaintiff knew of the condition or that they had taken sufficient steps to draw his attention to it. (Courtesy of *Cracknell's Law Students' Companion*)

Similarly, a notice displayed on premises must be sufficiently prominent for a reasonable man to see it *before* he makes the contract.

There have been many cases where the courts had laid down that the term *must be notified before or at the time of contracting*. Chapelton v. Barry UDC was one, and the most famous case is:

> **Olley v. Marlborough Court Ltd (1949)**
>
> The plaintiff was a guest at the defendant's hotel and during her stay some of her property was stolen. There was a notice in her room which stated that 'The proprietors will not hold themselves responsible for articles lost or stolen...' **Held**: this notice could not be read into the contract between the parties as the contract was concluded before the plaintiff was shown to her room and therefore before she saw the notice which purported to exclude liability. (Courtesy of *Cracknell's Law Students' Companion*)

The question of what are 'reasonable steps' is an objective one, and the answer to the question is ultimately one of fact, based on the circumstances of each case.

Yet, even if a defendant is found to have failed to take reasonable steps, the plaintiff may still be bound by the conditions because he knew them from *previous dealings* with the defendant. However, this method of imposing terms is not often likely to succeed.

9.4.3 Presumed agreement

If the exclusion clause is a document signed by a party, then it is presumed that he has agreed to it, whether or not he has read it. In such a case, it is not easy to escape the effects of the clause.

> **L'Estrange v. F. Graucob Ltd (1934)**
>
> The plaintiff ordered an automatic slot machine by signing a printed form supplied by the defendants for this purpose and on this form in very small print were certain special terms. One of these terms provided that 'any express or implied condition, statement or warranty ... is hereby excluded'. The machine did not work satisfactorily and the plaintiff, who contended that she was not bound by the condition as she had not read it and knew nothing of its contents, claimed damages. **Held**: her action must fail as, having signed the contract, in the absence of misrepresentation, she was bound by its terms and the provision in the contract had successfully excluded the defendants' liability under the implied warranty that the machine was fit for the purpose for which it was sold. (Courtesy of *Cracknell's Law Students' Companion*)

But if the effect of the clause was *misrepresented* to him by the other party, it may only take effect as he understood it at the time of the contract:

Curtis v. Chemical Cleaning and Dyeing Co. Ltd (1951)

The plaintiff took a white satin wedding dress to the defendants for cleaning. She was asked to sign a document which contained a clause that the dress 'is accepted on condition that the company is not liable for any damage howsoever arising' but, before she signed, she was told that the effect of the document which she was about to sign was to exclude liability for damage to beads or sequins. Without reading all the terms of the document the plaintiff then signed as she was asked. The dress was stained due to the negligence of the defendants. **Held**: the defendants were liable as the innocent misrepresentation as to the extent of the exception clause had the effect of excluding the clause from the contract between the parties. (Courtesy of *Cracknell's Law Students' Companion*)

However, while signature of the document containing the clause makes it difficult to show that it was not in a contractual document, yet most of the other methods of avoiding the impact of the clause would still be available (e.g. fundamental breach – see Section 9.4.6 below).

9.4.4 Interpretation of ambiguity

Any ambiguity in the clause will be interpreted against the party who put it forward. It is a general rule of construction of any document that it will be construed '*contra proferentem*' – that is, against the person who prepared the document. As an exclusion clause is invariably drafted by the imposer of it, this is an extremely useful weapon against exclusion clauses.

The effect of the rule is to give the party who proposed the ambiguous clause only the lesser of the protections possible. Thus where an insurance company inserted a clause excluding liability to members of the assured's family (which might mean his wife and children) but they claimed it meant any relative at all (when his sister was injured in a crash) they were held liable. If they wanted the wider meaning of the word 'family' they could easily have chosen words which gave them the wider meaning. They did not, and so much the worse for them. The one who draws up the contract has the choice of words, and must choose them to show clearly the intention he had in mind.

9.4.5 Protection of a third party

The exclusion clause cannot protect a third party: this is an application of the rule of privity of contract, that a third party cannot enforce, or take a benefit from a contract.

Scruttons Ltd v. Midland Silicones Ltd (1962)

The respondents were the consignees and owners of a drum of chemicals shipped in New York for carriage to London on the terms of the shipowners' standard bill of lading, one clause of which had the effect of limiting the carrier's (i.e. the shipowners') liability for damage to the drum to 500 dollars. For some years the shipowners had engaged the appellant stevedores to discharge their vessels at the Port of London and the agreement between them provided that the appellants have 'such protection as is afforded by the terms ... of ... bills of lading'. While lowering the drum into a lorry the appellants negligently dropped it, causing damage to it amounting to £593. The act of lowering the drum into the lorry was one which, by the terms of their agreement with the shipowners, the appellants had contracted with the shipowners to do and which, by the terms

> of the bill of lading, the shipowners had contracted with the respondents to do. The appellants admitted negligence but contended that they were entitled to rely on the provisions in the bill of lading limiting liability to 500 dollars (then £179). **Held**: they were not so entitled as they were strangers to the bill of lading and it is a general principle (to which this case was not an exception) that a stranger cannot rely for his protection on provisions in a contract (i.e. the bill of lading) to which he is not a party. (Courtesy of *Cracknell's Law Students' Companion*)

9.4.6 The doctrine of fundamental breach

This doctrine (which is no longer effective) was developed to prevent anyone relying on an exemption clause if he had failed to carry out the basic purpose of the contract. As Lord Abinger said in *Chanter v. Hopkins* (*1838*): 'If a man offers to buy peas of another, and he sends him beans, he does not perform his contract.... That is not a warranty.'

Such a breach is more serious, or 'fundamental', than a breach of a condition or warranty, and so an excluding clause which protects a party against a breach of condition or warranty, could not shield him from the consequences of a fundamental breach of the contract.

Originally, the doctrine was applied only to the so-called 'deviation cases', where shipowners diverted ships from their agreed course for their own purposes, thereby causing loss to the charterers or cargo-owners whose cargo was delayed.

In *Hain SS Co. v. Tate & Lyle Ltd* (*1936*), where the appellants unjustifiably diverted their ship from its course, causing loss to the respondents in respect of their cargo of sugar on board, Lord Atkin said:

> *The departure from the voyage contracted to be made is a breach by the shipowner of ... such a serious character that however slight the deviation the other party is entitled to treat it as going to the root of the contract, and to declare himself as no longer bound by* any of its terms.

Since then, however, the courts have extended the doctrine to other types of contract. For example:

> ### Karsales (Harrow) Ltd v. Wallis (1956)
> Wallis inspected and agreed to purchase a car in excellent condition. He took finance. On attempted delivery the car was seen to have changed dramatically to be a virtual wreck incapable of moving. Wallis refused delivery, but it was towed to his place of business and left there. The finance company involved assigned its rights to Karsales and they sought to recover the payments relying on the following clause in the agreement assigned to them: 'No condition or warranty that the vehicle is roadworthy ... or of fitness for any purpose is given by the owner or implied herein.' **Held**: exemption clauses only avail the party which included them when they are carrying out their part of the contract in its essential respects. Here breach was such as to amount to non-performance – 'a car which will not go is no car at all' (Birkett, LJ).

Thus the doctrine of fundamental breach was developed by the courts into an extremely effective way of combating exclusion clauses. This was subject nevertheless to two qualifications:

(a) Waiver of the breach

It has always been clear that, in the words of Lord Atkin in *Hain SS Co. Ltd v. Tate & Lyle Ltd (1936)*, 'the innocent party can elect to treat the contract as subsisting: and if he does this with knowledge of his rights he must in accordance with the general law of contract be held bound'. In that case, Tate & Lyle lost their claim because they had earlier waived their rights, and so the charterparty remained in force.

(b) Excluding liability for a fundamental breach

It is possible to frame an exclusion clause in such wide terms that it covers even a fundamental breach. In the *Suisse Atlantique Case (1966)* Viscount Dilhorne stated: 'It is not right to say that the law prohibits and nullifies a clause exempting or limiting liability for a fundamental breach.' The House of Lords laid down that there is no rule of law that an exemption clause is nullified by a 'fundamental breach of contract' or breach of a 'fundamental term'; in each case the question is one of construction of the contract.

Theoretically, therefore, such an exclusion clause is possible, but the courts would be slow to construe a clause so widely that it would protect a party from the lawful consequences of total non-performance of the contract. In the words of Lord Reid in the same case, 'It is generally reasonable to draw the line at fundamental breaches. A case of this type soon followed:

> **Photo Production Ltd v. Securicor Ltd (1980)**
>
> Securicor agreed to carry out a nightly patrol service against burglary and fire at the plaintiff's premises, under standard terms and conditions which stated that Securicor should not be responsible for losses by fire except if caused by the negligence of their servants in the course of carrying out their duties. One of their employees deliberately set fire to the premises which were destroyed. **Held**: on the true construction of the exclusion clause Securicor were not liable – they had chosen words which successfully excluded their liability for the deliberate act of their employee.

The House of Lords in the above case was setting aside the rule that if a defendant committed a fundamental breach he would be precluded from relying on an exclusion clause. So, in theory, an appropriately drafted exclusion clause could exclude liability even for a fundamental breach. However, all this is somewhat academic since the *Unfair Contract Terms Act, 1977* which is described in the section below. Section 11 of this Act has now introduced the statutory requirement of reasonableness to deciding whether a particular exclusion clause is declared valid or set aside. In 1983, in *George Mitchell v. Finney Lock Seeds*, the plaintiff who was seeking damages based his arguments on the common law ground of fundamental breach and the statutory ground of reasonableness. Since the contract was made between 18 May 1973 and 1 February 1978 the test of reasonableness that applied was the one now contained in Section 55 of the *Sale of Goods Act, 1979*. However, the 1977 Act adopted a virtually identical standard for contracts made after 1 February 1978. The court relied exclusively on the latter ground, and Lord Bridge stated categorically that the former doctrine of fundamental breach had been 'forcibly evicted' from our system. (**Note**: for exclusion of liability clauses in sales contracts see Section 14.7 of this text.)

9.5 The Unfair Contract Terms Act, 1977

The efforts of the courts to mitigate the worst effects of objectionable exclusion clauses have been reinforced by the passage of the above Act, which restricts the extent to which liability can be avoided for breach of contract and negligence. The main points of the Act are:

- The Act relates to 'business liability' – that which arises in the course of business or through the occupation of business premises. Transactions between private persons are therefore not covered.
- Liability for death or personal injury resulting from negligence cannot be excluded at all. Attempts to exclude or restrict liability for *other* loss or damage are viewed from the point of view of 'reasonableness'. The party seeking to justify the clause must show that it is fair and reasonable in the circumstances of the contract.
- Where breach occurs and is not a result of negligence (as referred to above), attempts to exclude liability will be interpreted in favour of the party who 'deals as consumer' and against those dealing as businessmen or using 'written standard terms of business'. Once again the 'reasonableness test' is used.
- The 'reasonableness test' is further extended to situations where parties attempt to exclude liability for fundamental breach, i.e. where performance is substantially different from that reasonably expected or there is no performance at all of the whole or any part of the contractual obligations.
  Contracts between business parties not on standard terms or between private parties are not covered here and the doctrine of fundamental breach continues to operate.
- In addition to the above, the following are subject to the Act's provisions:
  – Making liability or its enforcement subject to restrictive or onerous conditions.
  – Excluding or restricting any right or remedy.
  – Excluding or restricting rules of evidence or procedure.
- Any contractual term requiring a party dealing as consumer to indemnify any other person for any liability by reason of the other's negligence or breach of contract is again subject to the test of reasonableness.
- Goods in consumer use and subject to a guarantee cannot have liability for defects excluded by a term of guarantee.
- Evasion of the provisions of the Act by use of a secondary contract is prohibited.

The European Union has now adopted a directive on this subject – the *EU Directive on Unfair Terms in Consumer Contracts* which is in the process of being implemented. Its chief requirement is that 'unfair contract terms used in a contract concluded with a consumer by a seller or supplier shall ... not be binding on the consumer'. Therefore firms who deal with consumers will need to modify their standard form contracts in line with the statutory instrument issued to implement the directive. Traders who do not deal with individuals but only supply trade outlets need not change their standard terms and conditions. A contractual term is to be regarded as unfair if, 'contrary to the requirement of good faith, it causes a significant imbalance in the parties' rights and obligations under the contract to the detriment of the consumer'.

A very important section of the directive requires member states to enact legislation giving persons and organizations interested in consumer protection the right to bring actions before the courts to decide whether a term is unfair. The actions may be against a number of suppliers in the same field, or against a trade association recommending or sponsoring the use of a term. Such representative actions (sometimes called 'class actions') are not allowed in English law at present, but many people feel they should be allowed. It remains to be seen whether steps will be taken to introduce legislation to comply with the directive.

The case law on exclusion clauses is gathering momentum under the influence of the Act. Three typical cases are given below:

Phillips Products Ltd v. Hyland and Another (1984)

Hyland was the driver of a JCB hired by Another to Phillips Products Ltd. Hyland drove the vehicle negligently into Phillips' building and did £3000 damage to it. A clause in the hire contract said that for the period when the driver was operating the JCB he was to be under the hirer (Phillips') direction and was to be regarded as their employee in the event of any claim arising from the operation.

The court found this to be unreasonable. On appeal this opinion was confirmed, and Slade LJ, expressed the view that the meaning of the 'test of reasonableness' is not a general matter that can be interpreted away from the facts of the case. The test is 'Was the clause reasonable in the *particular* contract under consideration?'

Stag Line Ltd v. Tyne Shiprepair Group Ltd and Others (The Zinnia) (1984)

This case was one where repairs to a vessel were defective in quality. When the ship got into difficulty claims were made for various losses including consequential losses, but the case established that the defective repairs played no part in the actual losses which were caused by something else entirely. The point of interest to us is that certain exclusion clauses were considered and in the course of dealing with them Staughton J expressed the opinion that they were in such small print and used such convoluted and prolix language that they might be considered unreasonable from that point of view alone. As one commentator said 'For one judge, apparently, legal gobbledegook is unreasonable'.

Lease Management Services Ltd v. Purnell Secretarial Services Ltd (24 March 1994)

In this case serious misrepresentations by a finance company had been accompanied by exclusion clauses in the contract which purported to exclude most forms of liability, including misrepresentations in the course of negotiations leading to the contract. In this case, the misrepresentations had actually been embodied in the contract as a warranty. The Court of Appeal were in no doubt that these exclusionary clauses failed the test of reasonableness.

Test your knowledge

Answers	Questions
	1 What are stipulations in a contract called?
1 The terms of the contract.	2 What is an express term in a contract?
2 One that is actually stipulated by one of the parties, requiring the other party to do certain things.	3 What is an implied term?
3 A term which will be read into the contract either by custom, or a course of dealing between the parties, or by statute, or under the doctrine of the implied term (where a term has to be implied to give business efficacy to the contract).	4 What is a representation?
4 A statement made in the course of negotiations leading to a contract which induces the other party to enter into the contract.	5 What tests help a judge decide whether a statement is a representation or a term of the contract?
5 (a) The time test; (b) the writing test; (c) the skill and knowledge test.	6 What types of express terms are there?
6 (a) Conditions; (b) warranties.	7 Distinguish between them.
7 A condition goes to the root of the contract and breach of the condition is breach of contract. A warranty is only collateral to the contract, a less serious term. Breach of a warranty is not breach of contract, but it does entitle the disappointed party to damages.	8 What is an exclusionary clause?
8 One which excludes one party to a contract from some legal or statutory duty and forces the other party to trade on unsatisfactory terms.	9 How has the law traditionally reduced the severity of exclusionary clauses?

Answers	Questions
9 (a) By insisting that if they are to be valid they must be in a document which is clearly contractual – not a mere receipt. (b) By insisting that the other party must have notice of the effect of the term and have its importance drawn to his attention. (c) If it is misrepresented to him the clause will only be effective to the extent represented. (d) The *contra proferentem* rule applies. (e) The doctrine of fundamental breach used to apply.	10 What are the chief points made in the *Unfair Contract Terms Act, 1977*?
10 (a) The Act only relates to business contracts. (b) Liability for death or personal injury resulting from negligence cannot be excluded. (c) Other exclusions must be viewed from the point of view of reasonableness. (d) It is for the party inserting the exclusion clause to show that it is fair and reasonable in the particular circumstances of the contract.	11 What are the features of the *EU Directive on Unfair Terms in Consumer Contracts*?
11 (a) A term is unfair if 'contrary to the requirement of good faith, it caused a significant imbalance in the parties rights and obligations to the detriment of the consumer'. (b) It calls for legislation to permit organizations interested in consumer protection to bring 'class actions' to decide if a term is unfair.	12 Go over the questions until you are sure of all the answers. Then try some of the questions in Appendix 1.

10 Misrepresentation

10.1 What is misrepresentation?

Representations are statements made in order to induce a party to enter into a contract. They differ from conditions or warranties in that they do not form part of the contract themselves. However, they are extremely important, for without such representations the contract might not be entered into at all. They may be distinguished from mere puffs, which are statements made in the course of the negotiations which are not intended to be taken seriously but are recognized by both parties as being mere hyperbole (exaggeration for the sake of effect). Thus to say that a horse is 'the finest creature on four legs today' is a mere puff, and not intended to lead to legal action should the other party find a finer animal. A representation does lead to legal relations.

A misrepresentation is a false statement made in the course of negotiations leading to a contract which was intended to induce, and did induce, the other party to enter into that contract.

The various elements of the above definition are considered in detail in Sections 10.1.1–4.

10.1.1 Silence

As a general rule, there must be a positive statement; this is often expressed by saying that *'silence is not a misrepresentation'*. This was shown in the case of *Keates v. Lord Cadogan (1851)*. Here a landlord was held not liable when he failed to inform a tenant that a house being let was in a dilapidated condition – even though he knew that it was required for immediate occupation. In some circumstances this rule operates unjustly, and the courts have long recognized exceptions to it.

- *When silence distorts or falsifies a positive representation.* Thus, if a vendor of land states that the farms are let, he must not omit to state the further fact that the tenants have given notice to quit. This is illustrated by *Dimmock v. Hallet (1866)*.

> *Dimmock v. Hallet (1866)*
> A vendor of farms induced their sale by saying that they were let. Whilst this was true the statement was held to be a misrepresentation because the tenants had given notice to quit.

The principle also applies even if the original statement was full and correct, but subsequent events make it incorrect:

Misrepresentation

With v. O'Flanagan (1936)

In January 1934 a medical practice was represented to the plaintiffs by the doctor selling it as worth £2000 p.a. In May 1934 the plaintiffs contracted to buy, but by then the practice was producing less than £5 p.w. (due to the illness of the defendant). The Court of Appeal held that the duty to disclose had been broken – rescission of the contract was allowed, and so the defendant had to repay.

- *Contracts uberrimae fidei* (see below).
- *Fiduciary relationships* (see below).

10.1.2 Conduct

The statement need not be expressed in words, but can be made by conduct. Thus it could be 'a nod, or a wink, or a shake of the head or a smile' Lord Campbell in *Walters v. Morgan (1861)*.

10.1.3 Fact versus opinion

The statement must be one of fact, and not of law, opinion or intention. However, if a person expresses an opinion *fraudulently*, this is regarded as a statement of *fact*, and therefore actionable. Here we can contrast the cases of *Bisset v. Wilkinson (1927)* and *Smith v. Land and House Property Corporation (1884)*.

Bisset v. Wilkinson (1927)

The appellant sought to recover the purchase money under an agreement for the sale of certain land but the respondents claimed to be entitled to rescind the contract on the ground of misrepresentation. It was shown that the appellant had stated that it was his belief that the land in question would carry 2000 sheep if properly worked but in fact it had never been able to support that number. **Held**: the contract would not be rescinded on the ground of misrepresentation as the statement as to the carrying capacity of the land was merely an opinion which the appellant honestly entertained. (Courtesy of *Cracknell's Law Students' Companion*)

Smith v. Land and House Property Corporation (1884)

In the particulars of sale the plaintiffs said that their hotel was 'now held by a very desirable tenant ... for an unexpired term of twenty-eight years, at a rent of £400 p.a.' The defendants resisted the plaintiffs' claim for specific performance on the ground of misdescription in that it afterwards appeared that the rent was in arrear at the time of the sale and the tenant shortly afterwards filed his petition for liquidation. **Held**: the contract should be rescinded as the description of the tenant as 'very desirable' was not an expression of opinion but a misrepresentation on the faith of which the defendants contracted to purchase the hotel. (Courtesy of *Cracknell's Law Students' Companion*)

In similar fashion a fraudulent statement of intention can lead to misrepresentation. For example:

Edgington v. Fitzmaurice (1885)

The directors of a company issued a prospectus inviting subscriptions for debentures and stating that their purpose in issuing debentures was to complete alterations to the company's premises, purchase horses and vans and develop trade. The plaintiff advanced money on certain of these debentures in reliance upon the statements in the prospectus and in the erroneous belief that the debenture holders would have a charge upon the property, but it turned out that the real object of the loan was to enable the directors to pay off pressing liabilities. **Held**: the mis-statement of the objects for which the debentures were issued was a material mis-statement of fact which rendered the directors liable in deceit although the plaintiff was influenced by his own mistake as to the effect of the transaction. (Courtesy of *Cracknell's Law Students' Companion*)

10.1.4 Induction of the contract

The misrepresentation must at least partly induce the contract.

Smith v. Chadwick (1884)

A prospectus contained a statement that 'the present value of the turnover or output of the entire works is over £1 000 000 sterling per annum'. This statement was ambiguous in that it could mean that in one year the works produced goods worth £1 000 000, in which case it was untrue, or that the works were capable of this output, in which case it was correct. **Held**: in order to succeed in an action of deceit for fraudulent misrepresentation, the plaintiff had to prove that he had interpreted the statement in the sense in which it was false and that he had in fact been influenced by it in making his decision to take shares. The plaintiff failed to satisfy the court on these points. (Courtesy of *Cracknell's Law Students' Companion*)

It would follow that a misrepresentation that does not affect a plaintiff's mind or his judgement (*Attwood v. Small* (*1838*)) or where the plaintiff is aware of the untruth of a misrepresentation (*Jennings v. Broughton* (*1854*)) is legally harmless.

10.2 Types of misrepresentation

There are three types of misrepresentation; innocent, fraudulent and negligent.

10.2.1 Innocent misrepresentation

An innocent misrepresentation is one made honestly, and with reasonable grounds for believing in its truth.

10.2.2 Negligent misrepresentation

A negligent misrepresentation is a statement made honestly, but without reasonable grounds for belief in its truth. It is really a special case of innocent misrepresentation, for although the statement is made in the belief that it is true, insufficient care has been taken to check it. Thus where the plaintiff can show that the statement made was made without reasonable care, and that this negligence resulted to the plaintiff's detriment, he will be able to secure redress of the grievance by an action in tort. The classic case is *Hedley Byrne & Co. Ltd. v. Heller and Partners Ltd (1963)* – see page 376 for details.

10.2.3 Fraudulent misrepresentation

A fraudulent misrepresentation is one made dishonestly, knowing it to be untrue. It was defined in *Derry v. Peek (1889)* by Lord Herschell as a false statement 'made knowingly or without belief in its truth or recklessly, careless whether it be true or false'.

The court must be satisfied, if a statement was made carelessly, that it was so grossly careless that its maker could not honestly have believed it to be true.

Derry v. Peek (1889)

The Plymouth, Devonport and District Tramways Co. was authorized to make certain tramways by special Act of Parliament which provided that the carriages might be moved by animal power and, with the consent of the Board of Trade, by steam or any mechanical power for fixed periods and subject to the regulations of the Board. The company issued a prospectus stating that 'one great feature of this undertaking, to which considerable importance should be attached, is that by special Act of Parliament obtained, the company has the right to use steam or mechanical motive power, instead of horses'. The plaintiff bought shares on the faith of this statement but the Board of Trade afterwards refused their consent to the use of steam power and the company was wound up. At the time of issuing the prospectus the company honestly believed that consent would be granted as a matter of course. **Held**: the plaintiff's action in deceit must fail, as the statement contained in the prospectus was not a fraudulent misrepresentation as the company entertained an honest belief that it was true. (Courtesy of *Cracknell's Law Students' Companion*)

Note: The *Directors' Liability Act, 1890*, altered the law to make directors liable for untrue statements made in prospectuses without reasonable grounds for believing them to be true. This is now contained in Section 43 of the *Companies Act, 1985*.

10.2.4 Non-disclosure

Although as a general rule silence *is not* a misrepresentation, there is a duty in the following kinds of contract to disclose relevant information:

(a) Contracts uberrimae fidei

These comprise contracts which involve one party alone possessing full knowledge of all the material facts, and the other being unable to obtain them from any other source. The law therefore requires *'uberrima fides'* (utmost good faith) from the first party. Examples are contracts of insurance, contracts to take shares from companies and family arrangements. A duty to disclose also arises in fiduciary relationships.

The contract of insurance   The insured must disclose all material facts, i.e. all circumstances 'which would influence the judgement of a prudent insurer in fixing the premium or determining whether he will take the risk'. This definition in Section 18 (2) of the *Marine Insurance Act, 1906*, was held applicable to other types of insurance in:

Locker and Woolf Ltd v. Western Australian Insurance Co. Ltd (1936)

When proposing for fire insurance in respect of their premises the claimants failed to disclose that an insurance on their motorcars had been declined by another company on the grounds of misrepresentation and non-disclosure. **Held**: the non-disclosure of this previous refusal was a material fact in the proposal for fire insurance which entitled the respondents to avoid the policy. In all classes of insurance what constitutes a 'material fact' is decided by reference to Section 18 of the *Marine Insurance Act, 1906*. (Courtesy of *Cracknell's Law Students' Companion*)

But you are not liable to disclose what you do not know (Fletcher Moulton, LJ, in *Joel v. Law Union and Commercial Assurance Co.* (1908).

(b) Contracts to take shares from companies

An omission of a fact from a company's prospectus may be a misrepresentation because it contravenes the *Companies Act, 1985*.

(c) Family arrangements

The classic case here is *Gordon v. Gordon* (1821):

Gordon v. Gordon (1821)

There was an agreement between two brothers, the elder of whom was believed to be illegitimate, for the division of the family estates. It turned out that the younger brother, who had obtained an advantage because of this belief, had known all along that his brother was legitimate. **Held**: even after a lapse of nineteen years, the agreement should be rescinded, because family arrangements of this sort are *uberrimae fidei*. (Courtesy of *Cracknell's Law Students' Companion*)

(d) Fiduciary relationships

This is a relationship of trust – for example, those of doctor and patient, principal and agent, solicitor and client, religious superior and inferior, trustee and beneficiary, parent and child, and guardian and ward. This list is not exhaustive, and if any party to a contract uses his influence, obtained through the confidence necessarily reposed in him by the other, to obtain an advantage at the expense of the confiding party, rescission will be allowed for non-disclosure, or misrepresentation. This is because the first party has been guilty of *fraud* in the equitable sense – unconscionable conduct. For example:

Tate v. Williamson (1866)

Tate was a spendthrift Oxford undergraduate. He relied upon Williamson (his cousin) for financial advice as Tate was estranged from his father because of his extravagance. Williamson, who had been recommended by Tate's great-uncle, advised Tate to sell his estate for £7500 to Williamson (its true value was £20 000), and he duly sold it as advised. **Held**: Williamson's non-disclosure was a misrepresentation and so the sale was set aside.

(Tate's heir was the plaintiff, Tate having died an alcoholic at 24.)

10.3 Remedies for misrepresentation

Under the common law the remedies for misrepresentation were unsatisfactory, in particular with regard to innocent misrepresentation. To correct the position the *Misrepresentation Act, 1967*, removed certain bars to the rescission of a contract for innocent misrepresentation, and also clarified the position about damages.

In general, the plaintiff is interested in three possibilities:

- May he repudiate the contract if it has not yet been executed, and do nothing more about it?
- May he obtain rescission of the contract, if it has been performed and return to the situation before the contract was made?
- Are damages available?

Whether these remedies are available depends upon the type of misrepresentation made, and whether the misrepresentation was embodied as a term in the contract, either as a condition of the contract, or a warranty of the contract. It is in the nature of a representation that it occurs before the contract is finally made, and under the common law if the misrepresentation was embodied in the contract it was only possible to rescind the contract if the plaintiff alleged fraud. This bar to rescission was removed by Section 1 of the *Misrepresentation Act, 1967*. Consequently, whether fraud is alleged or not it is possible to obtain rescission of the contract.

If the misrepresentation has become a term of the contract, then the party who has been deceived has the following remedies:

- *If the term is a condition* he has the right to repudiate the contract if it has not been performed, and the right to have it rescinded if it has been performed. The nature of rescission, which is a discretionary remedy which the courts may, or may not, apply is explained below. Damages will be payable for non-performance.
- *If the misrepresentation is a warranty*, the plaintiff is entitled to damages and, since the *Misrepresentation Act, 1967*, rescission (Section 1 of the Act).

If the misrepresentation has not become a term of the contract, then the remedies available to the innocent party depend on whether the misrepresentation was made to him fraudulently, or negligently, or innocently.

For **fraudulent misrepresentation** the party misled is entitled to damages for the tort of deceit, the measure of damages being the loss incurred as a result, and to repudiate or rescind the contract.

For **innocent misrepresentation** the Act gives the party misled the right to repudiate the contract, or to have it rescinded. Damages may also be payable, depending on the nature of the misrepresentation. The Act says that damages will be payable 'unless the defendant proves that he had reasonable ground to believe, and did believe up to the time the contract was made, that the facts represented were true' (Section 2.1). Note that the usual rule that 'he who alleges must prove' is reversed here; there is a presumption that the misrepresentation was negligent, and the defendant must prove that it was not. Thus, for example, a misrepresentation affecting the state of buildings might be justified if a recent surveyor's report led the defendant to believe that they were in fact in good condition. The Act divides innocent misrepresentation into two categories; namely, negligent misrepresentation and representation which is not negligent. In many cases, negligent misrepresentation is equated with fraudulent misrepresentation.

The working of the Act is illustrated by:

> ### Watts v. Spence (1975)
> The plaintiff, Watts, contracted to buy a house from the first defendant, John Spence who, prior to the contract, told the plaintiff that Mrs Spence (the second defendant) who was a joint owner of the house with her husband, would join in the subsequent conveyance. In fact, she refused to do so. Graham, J in the Chancery Division held that the first defendant was liable to pay damages for *loss of bargain* under Section 2(1) of the 1967 Act.

An interesting example of damages for fraudulent or negligent misrepresentation is provided by the case of *East v. Maurer* (1991) 2 All ER 733. The vendor of a hairdressing business fraudulently misrepresented his intentions by saying that he would not continue in business nearby, and that consequently the clientele of the old business would be fully available to the purchaser. The judge at the Court of First Instance awarded damages on a contractual basis for breach of the warranty that the old clientele would still be available. The Court of Appeal ruled that the damages were to be assessed on a 'tort' basis, as compensation for the losses suffered as a result of the unjustified competition. The aim was to restore the plaintiff to the position he would have been in had the tort not been committed.

Where the innocence of the misrepresentation is established the misled party is in the same situation as before the 1967 Act; he is entitled only to rescission of the contract, with the possible addition of an indemnity for expenses he has *necessarily* incurred under the contract.

> ### Whittington v. Seale-Hayne (1900)
> The plaintiffs, who were lessees of certain premises which they used for breeding prize poultry, alleged that they had been induced to take up the lease by the representations of the defendant's agents, made during oral negotiations for the lease, that the premises were in a sanitary condition and in a good state of repair. The plaintiffs further alleged that in consequence of the insanitary condition of the premises their manager and his family became very ill and the poultry either died or became valueless for the purpose of breeding. The local authority declared that because of defective drainage the premises were unfit for human habitation. The plaintiffs contended that they were entitled to an indemnity against the consequences of entering into the contract, which included losses in respect of stock and medical expenses. **Held**: their claim would fail as it was really a claim for damages which could not be awarded at that time in a case of innocent misrepresentation, but they were entitled to an indemnity in respect of those things which were required to be performed by the terms of the lease and this included rent, rates and repairs. (Courtesy of *Cracknell's Law Students' Companion*)

10.3.1 Exclusion of liability for misrepresentation

Under Section 3 of the *Misrepresentation Act, 1967*, any exclusion clause in a contract which excludes or restricts any liability to which a representor may become liable as a result of misrepresentation, shall be of no effect except in so far as the court or an arbitrator allows reliance on it as being fair and reasonable in the circumstances. This is now the standard of reasonableness in Section 11.1 of the *Unfair Contract Terms Act, 1977*.

Even the right of rescission is subject to the approval of the court, which may hold the contract to be subsisting, and award damages in lieu of rescission. This is explained below.

10.3.2 Limitations on the remedy of rescission

Rescission is a remedy available for all three types of misrepresentation; it has been developed in equity decisions and is limited by general principles common to all the equitable doctrines and remedies (rescission, rectification, injunction and decree of specific performance) with some limitations peculiar to itself. These limitations mean that in some situations a plaintiff will have no remedy. The limitations are:

(a) Discretionary remedy

It is a discretionary remedy. This means that the court will refuse to grant it to a plaintiff who has himself been guilty of inequitable conduct.

(b) Delay

If the plaintiff has been guilty of unreasonable delay (termed laches) in seeking rescission, he will be barred. In *Leaf v. International Galleries* (*1950*) (see page 134) the Court of Appeal decided against Leaf (*inter alia*) because he delayed five years in bringing his action; but in *Gordon v. Gordon* (*1821*) (see page 164) the elder son obtained rescission despite the 19 years which had elapsed, because he had acted as soon as he eventually discovered the truth, and therefore the delay was reasonable.

(c) Affirmation

The representee cannot rescind after expressly or impliedly affirming the contract with full knowledge of the true facts. For example:

> *Long v. Lloyd* (1958)
>
> The defendant advertised for sale a motor lorry which he described as being in 'exceptional condition' and told the plaintiff, who purchased it, that it was capable of 40 mph and did 11 miles to the gallon. Two days later certain defects appeared and the plaintiff accepted the defendant's offer to pay half the cost of a reconditioned dynamo. On the following day the plaintiff's brother set out to drive the lorry to Middlesbrough but it broke down on the way and an expert found that it was not in a roadworthy condition. The defendant's representations concerning the vehicle were untrue, although honestly made, and the plaintiff sought to rescind the contract on the ground of the defendant's innocent misrepresentation. **Held**: the plaintiff had finally accepted the lorry and any right of rescission which he might otherwise have had was lost. (Courtesy of *Cracknell's Law Students' Companion*)

(d) Restitutio in integrum

'Restitutio in integrum' is impossible. Because rescission involves 'a giving back and a taking back on both sides' it clearly cannot apply where the subject-matter of the contract has substantially ceased to exist, or has changed its identity. For example:

Vigers v. Pike (1842)

B had agreed in his lifetime to let mines in return for £165 000. The mines were operated and a part of the payment made. Pike, B's executor, sued the managing director of the company operating the mine for the rest of the money. In defence it was claimed that a number of misrepresentations had been made to induce the lease. **Held**: the lease could not be set aside since the mines had substantially been worked and the parties could not be restored to their original positions.

However, a minor change in subject-matter will not preclude rescission; instead, the court will grant rescission, with an indemnity to compensate for the loss, under the *Whittington v. Seale-Hayne* principle referred to above.

(e) Damages in lieu of rescission

Under Section 2(2) of the 1967 Act, the court *may* declare the contract subsisting, if it would be equitable to do so, having regard to the nature of the misrepresentation, and the loss that would be caused by it if the contract were upheld, as well as to the loss that rescission would cause to the other party. Instead the court will award damages to the victims of the innocent or negligent misrepresentation.

(f) Intervention of third-party rights

It has always been a fundamental principle of equity that it will protect a person who has in good faith and for value acquired rights in property. The effect of a misrepresentation of any kind is to make the contract voidable at the misled party's option, and if he has transferred property under it to the misrepresentor, the title to it will pass to the latter under the voidable contract, and from him to any third party who acquires it in good faith and for value. This was the case in *Phillips v. Brooks* (1919) and *Lewis v. Averay* (1971) referred to earlier (see Section 8.3).

Test your knowledge

Answers

1 It is a false statement made in the course of negotiations leading up to a contract which was intended to induce, and did induce, the other party to enter into the contract.

Questions

1 What is a misrepresentation?

2 What are the three types of misrepresentation?

Answers	Questions
2 (a) Innocent misrepresentation; (b) negligent misrepresentation; (c) fraudulent misrepresentation.	3 When is a misrepresentation innocent?
3 When the representor honestly believes it to be true.	4 What was the case of *Hedley Byrne & Co. v. Heller and Partners Ltd* (1963) about?
4 Heller and Partners were bankers who gave a credit reference on a customer to Hedley Byrne. It proved to be false and the judge ruled there was a duty of care, i.e. a negligent misrepresentation.	5 Why were damages not awarded against Heller and Partners?
5 Because they had disclaimed any responsibility when giving the reference.	6 Is silence misrepresentation?
6 Not generally – there is no general duty to disclose.	7 What special cases are there where silence is misrepresentation?
7 (a) Contracts of the utmost good faith; (b) contracts where a statute calls for disclosure; (c) family arrangements; (d) fiduciary relationships (based on trust).	8 What are the remedies for fraudulent misrepresentation?
8 (a) The right to repudiate the contract and claim damages for loss of bargain; (b) the right to have the contract rescinded and claim damages.	9 (a) What are the remedies for innocent misrepresentation?
9 (a) The right to repudiate the contract; (b) the right to have the contract rescinded (unless damages in lieu of rescission are ordered by the court); (c) the right to damages unless the party at fault can prove that they had reasonable grounds for believing the statement to be true.	10 What is the nature of the remedy 'rescission of the contract'?

Answers	Questions
10 (a) It is an equitable remedy; (b) the court will not exercise it if there has been delay; (c) or if the aggrieved party has reaffirmed the contract after being made aware of the misrepresentation; or (d) if third parties have acquired rights which will be disturbed unfairly.	11 Go over the page again. Then try some of the questions in Appendix 1.

11 The discharge of contracts

11.1 The meaning of discharge

When a contract is entered into it confers upon the parties to it certain rights and obligations. These rights and obligations, though, persist for only as long as the contract is in existence. Once the contract comes to an end (for whatever reason) the rights and obligations are said to have been 'discharged'.

There are four ways in which a contract may be discharged.

- By performance.
- By express agreement.
- Under the doctrine of frustration.
- By breach.

11.2 Discharge of the contract by performance

The normal way in which a contract is discharged is that both parties perform their obligations under it. If only one party performs his obligations, then he alone is discharged, and he acquires the right of action against the other (see later under discharge by breach). *The general rule is that performance must be precise and exact.* This rule is very strict, as is shown by:

> *Cutter v. Powell (1795)*
>
> The defendant agreed to pay Cutter 30 guineas 'provided he proceeds, continues and does his duty as second mate' on a voyage from Kingston, Jamaica, to Liverpool. Cutter began the journey but died when the ship was about one week's sail from Liverpool. His administratrix sought to recover a proportion of the agreed wage in respect of the part of the journey for which Cutter had acted as second mate. **Held**: she was unable to succeed as Cutter had not performed his part of the contract. (Courtesy of *Cracknell's Law Students' Companion*)

For practical reasons the common law has been driven in some circumstances to adopt a lower standard than that of precise and exact performance, and to create exceptions to the general rule in *Cutter v. Powell*. These cover a wide field and represent a considerable inroad upon the doctrine. They all enable a party at fault to recover to the extent of his performance.

11.2.1 Divisible contracts

Most contracts are 'entire' (i.e. indivisible): the obligations of the parties are interdependent: *neither* party can demand performance from the other unless he himself performs or is ready to perform, his obligations.

However, with a contract to work materials into the property of another, or an instalment contract, the presumption is that payment is to keep pace with performance, so that a party can claim a certain sum even though he has not completed his obligations under the contract. Such contracts are said to be divisible.

> ### Roberts v. Havelock (1832)
> The defendant's ship was sailing from Cardiff to Alexandria with a cargo of iron when it was damaged and forced to dock at Milford Haven to allow necessary repairs to be carried out. The plaintiff, a shipwright, was employed and undertook to put the ship into thorough repair. Before the work was completed the plaintiff asked for payment in respect of that part which he had carried out, but when payment was refused he sued to recover the amount to which he maintained he was entitled at that stage. **Held**: the plaintiff would succeed as there was no agreement to the effect that the plaintiff would make no demand for payment until all the repairs were completed. (Courtesy of *Cracknell's Law Students' Companion*)

11.2.2 Prevention from completion

Where a party is prevented from completing his obligations by the action of the other party, he can claim for what he has done:

> ### Planché v. Colburn (1831)
> P agreed to write a book on items of historical interest, and was to be paid £100 on completion of the book. Before he could finish the work the publishers abandoned the idea. P sued and on a *'quantum meruit'* (as much as he has deserved) claim succeeded in getting payment for what he had done.

11.2.3 Partial performance

Where one party has accepted partial performance by the other, that other can claim for the partial performance on the basis of an implied promise of payment, but there must be a true option to accept. This was not the case in *Sumpter v. Hedges, 1898*:

> ### Sumpter v. Hedges (1898)
> The plaintiff, a builder, contracted to build two houses and stables upon the defendant's land for the sum of £565. The plaintiff did part of the work, amounting in value to about £333, and then abandoned the contract. The defendant completed the buildings and the plaintiff claimed payment in respect of that part of the work which he had carried out. **Held**: the defendant was not liable to pay on a *quantum meruit* as there was no inference of a fresh contract to do so. (Courtesy of *Cracknell's Law Students' Companion*)

11.2.4 Substantial performance

At an early point in time the courts developed the **doctrine of substantial performance**, i.e. that a party can claim if his performance has been substantial, even though not exact and literal (although, of course, he cannot claim the full price in such case).

> ### Hoenig v. Isaacs (1952)
> The defendant agreed to pay the plaintiff £750 to redecorate and refurnish his flat. When the job was done he paid only £400, saying there was faulty design and bad workmanship. **Held**: by the Court of Appeal – there were only defects in the furniture and this would cost £55 to remedy. Therefore the defendant was liable to pay £750 less £55.

11.3 Discharge by express agreement

The basic legal rule is 'that which has been created by agreement can be extinguished by agreement'. An agreement to extinguish a contract though is itself a contract, and unless under seal, must be supported by consideration. It is in this area surrounding consideration that difficulties arise. The position as regards consideration depends upon whether discharge is bilateral or unilateral.

11.3.1 Bilateral discharge

Bilateral discharge occurs when both parties to the contract have some rights to surrender. For example, where there has been no performance or only part performance from one or both parties. Agreement in such circumstances can be reduced to one of three possible situations which the parties might intend:

- To rescind the existing agreement. This is called **termination**.
- Rescission plus agreement on the terms of a new contract.
- Variation of the existing contract.

Providing that the original contract is a simple one (where evidence in writing is *not* required), then words of agreement will achieve any of the three situations described above.

With bilateral discharge both parties have rights to surrender and in this way the new agreement generates its own consideration. The consideration given by each party is the surrender of his rights under the contract.

11.3.2 Unilateral discharge

Unilateral discharge occurs where only one party has rights to surrender. For example, where one party has performed his part of the contract he is no longer under an obligation himself but has acquired rights to compel the other party to perform. If for some reason (perhaps out of sympathy) the party with rights agrees not to insist upon them such an agreement will not be enforceable (unless under seal) without the provision of consideration by the party receiving benefit. The process is known as one of 'accord and satisfaction', the accord being the discharge of the obligation, the satisfaction the consideration with which the discharge is 'bought'. An example is:

> ### British Russian Gazette and Trade Outlook Ltd v. Associated Newspapers Ltd (1933)
> Talbot, a director of the Gazette Company, sued the defendants for an alleged libel. A representative of the defendants met Talbot and terms of settlement were arranged whereby Talbot agreed to accept one thousand guineas in full discharge and settlement of his claims and that of his company and undertook to discontinue the action against the defendants. Before the agreed amount was paid Talbot proceeded with the action in breach of the agreement. **Held**: he was not entitled to do so as he was bound by the terms of the settlement, consideration for which was to be found in the executory promises made by the defendants. (Courtesy of *Cracknell's Law Students' Companion*)

There are two further situations where discharge can be by agreement. They are:

- *Novation*. Novation occurs when two existing contracts are replaced by a new one. Suppose one party, X, is involved in two contracts. In one he owes Y £1000, in the other he is owed £1000 by Z. If the parties agree X can be released from his obligation to Y if Z enters into an agreement to pay £1000 directly to Y, by-passing X.
- *Condition subsequent*. Here the parties to a contract agree, at the time of its formation, that in the event of specific things happening the contract will come to an end.

11.4 Discharge of a contract by frustration

At common law, a contract will be discharged if something occurs which is not the fault of the parties, and was not contemplated by them, and prevents the contract from being performed as intended. Generally, where there is a positive contract to do a thing which is not unlawful the promiser must perform the contract or pay damages. This was laid down in:

> *Paradine v. Jane (1647)*
> The defendant was lessee of land and when sued for arrears of rent he contended that he was not liable to pay as the land in question had been occupied by a German Prince who had 'invaded the realm with an hostile army of men', thus preventing the defendant from receiving the profits from the land. **Held**: the plaintiff was entitled to recover as the defendant had covenanted to pay the rent and if he had wished to be excused payment in circumstances such as this he should have inserted a term to that effect in the contract. (Courtesy of *Cracknell's Law Students' Companion*)

Eventually this rule was seen to be harsh and inappropriate to the developing commercial world of the nineteenth century. From *Taylor v. Caldwell (1863)* (see below) the doctrine of frustration was developed. Three requirements must be satisfied for frustration to occur:

- An event has taken place which could not have been foreseen by the parties when they entered into the contract.
- None of the parties to the contract is in any way responsible for the event.
- If the contract was to be performed now despite the event, the contract would be different from the one originally entered into.

There are many areas in which the doctrine of frustration has been held to apply:

(a) Non-availability of subject matter

A contract may be frustrated by the destruction or non-availability of the subject-matter of the contract (i.e. of a thing essential to the performance of the contract):

Taylor v. Caldwell (1863)

The plaintiffs entered into an agreement with the defendants for the hire of a certain music hall for the purpose of giving a series of concerts. Before the series was due to begin the hall was destroyed by accidental fire. **Held**: the plaintiffs could not recover damages as the destruction of the hall excused both parties from the performance of their promises. (Courtesy of *Cracknell's Law Students' Companion*)

(b) Non-availability of a person

The non-availability of a person will frustrate a contract involving personal service – for example, where death, insanity or illness is serious enough to put an end to the contract in a business sense. An example is:

Robinson v. Davison (1871)

The defendant contracted to play in a concert on a particular day but fell ill. **Held**: the performer's illness on that particular day was sufficient to frustrate the contract.

In longer-term contracts the courts are reluctant to find that illness frustrates the contract. For example:

Storey v. Fulham Steel Works (1907)

S was employed by the steel works for five years as a manager. After working for two years he became ill and needed time away from work. Six months later he had recovered, but during his illness his employment had been terminated. S sued for breach and the defendants claimed that S's illness discharged the contract. **Held**: S's absence for six months did not go to the root of the five-year contract and termination could not be allowed.

(c) The non-happening of an event

The most famous cases here arose from the cancellation of the coronation of King Edward VII.

Krell v. Henry (1903)

The processions in connection with the coronation of Edward VII were due to be held on 26 and 27 June 1902, and shortly before this the plaintiff agreed to hire the defendant a flat in Pall Mall along which the processions were to pass. The contract made no mention of the purpose of letting but when the processions were not held on the days originally appointed the defendant refused to pay the balance of the rent. **Held**: the plaintiff's claim to recover such amount would fail as, by a necessary inference drawn from the surrounding circumstances, the holding of the procession on the days planned was regarded by both parties as the foundation of the contract. (Courtesy of *Cracknell's Law Students' Companion*)

Such grounds for frustration, however, are not extended to slight changes in circumstances.

> ### Herne Bay Steam Boat Co. v. Hutton (1903)
>
> The parties entered into an agreement whereby the plaintiffs' ship was to be 'at the disposal' of the defendant on a certain date 'for the purpose of viewing the naval review and for a day's cruise round the fleet'. The Royal review was afterwards cancelled but the fleet was still at Spithead on the day in question. In view of the cancellation of the review the defendant did not use the ship and declined to pay the balance of the hire. The plaintiffs claimed damages for breach of contract. **Held**: the plaintiffs should succeed. The naval review was not the sole foundation of the contract as the object of the voyage was also to cruise round the fleet. (Courtesy of *Cracknell's Law Students' Companion*)

(d) Supervening illegality

This occurs where a contract is entered into the object of which subsequently becomes illegal.

> ### Denny, Mott and Dickson Ltd v. Fraser and Co. Ltd (1944)
>
> In 1929 the two parties made an agreement relating to the sale of timber and the option to purchase or lease a timber yard. Both parties agreed that the sale of timber was frustrated in 1939 by timber control orders. However, in 1941 DM&D attempted to exercise their option to purchase the timber yard. **Held**: that looked at as a whole the main purpose of the contract was the sale of timber and when this had been frustrated the option to purchase no longer existed.

(e) Administrative (governmental) interference

Administrative or (governmental) interference is the most important and frequent example of frustration:

> ### Metropolitan Water Board v. Dick, Kerr and Co. Ltd (1918)
>
> In July 1914 the appellants contracted to construct extensive reservoirs near Staines within six years. The agreement contained a proviso to the effect that if the work should be 'unduly delayed or impeded' an extension of the time for the completion of the work would be granted. War broke out and in February 1916 the Minister of Munitions ordered the work to stop and the plant to be sold. This prohibition was still in force in November 1917. The appellants claimed that the order had put an end to the contract. **Held**: this plea would be upheld as the interruption caused by the prohibition was of such a character and duration as to make the contract when resumed essentially different from that the performance of which was compulsorily brought to an end. (Courtesy of *Cracknell's Law Students' Companion*)

The mere fact that the change in circumstances makes the contract more difficult to execute or less profitable does *not* frustrate the contract:

The discharge of contracts **177**

> *Davis Contractors Ltd v. Fareham Urban District Council (1956)*
> The plaintiffs contracted to build the defendants 78 council houses within eight months for a fixed price. Through no fault of the plaintiffs there was a scarcity of skilled labour and the work took 22 months to complete. The plaintiffs maintained that by reason of the scarcity of labour the contract had been brought to an end and that they were entitled to recover a sum in excess of the contract price on the basis of a *quantum meruit*. **Held**: their claim should fail, as the scarcity of labour had not frustrated the contract and the plaintiffs had not been released from its terms as regards price.

11.4.1 The effects of frustration

The effect is that the contract is ended at once, but for the future only; it is not void *ab initio*, as with mistake. The financial adjustment that is necessary is now governed by the *Law Reform (Frustrated Contracts) Act, 1943*. The effects of the Act are that the payer can recover money prepaid and ceases to be liable to pay, even though there was no total failure of consideration. However, if the payee has incurred expenses the Act says:

- If money has already been paid to him, the court has a discretion to allow him to keep some or all of it;
- If money has not yet been paid to him, the court has a discretion to allow him to claim some or all, but only to the extent that the money was payable before the date of frustration.

The Act further says that if a party has done something in the performance of the contract prior to the frustrating event he may be allowed compensation for any benefit conferred on the other party. This is an exception to the rule, discussed in Section 11.2, that unless performance is *precise and exact*, the plaintiff can recover nothing; formerly this rule applied even though there was frustration.

The Act can be excluded by an express provision in the contract, and it does not apply to the following classes of contract:

- Contracts for the carriage of goods by sea, and charterparties.
- Contracts of insurance.
- Contracts to which Section 7 of the *Sale of Goods Act, 1979*, applies. These are contracts where the specific goods which are the subject matter of an agreement to sell, perish through no fault of either party. The contract is avoided, not frustrated.

11.5 Discharge of a contract by breach

In many respects it is incorrect to say that breach of a contract will bring about that contract's discharge. Breach means the failure of one party to the contract to comply with the terms of that contract. The rights and actions of the innocent party following on from that breach are what will determine if the contract is discharged. We have seen that the terms of a contract fall into two main sections:

- Warranties – those terms which are minor in nature.
- Conditions – those terms which are of greater importance and go to the root of the contract.

Breach of a warranty will not discharge the contract. It merely provides the injured party with the opportunity to sue for damages; in all other respects the contract continues as before.

Breach of a condition gives the injured party the *option* of treating the contract as ended (with the right to sue for damages). However, this is an option and it might be that the injured party sees benefit in continuing with the contract and *then* suing for non-performance. An illustration is:

White and Carter (Councils) Ltd v. McGregor (1961)

The respondent's sales manager, acting within his authority, entered into a contract with the appellants for the fixing to litter-bins of plates advertising the respondent's business. On the same day, upon hearing of the contract the respondent wrote to the appellants to cancel the agreement, but the appellants refused to accept his cancellation. The contract was for a period of 156 weeks and, under the terms of the contract, if any instalment was unpaid for four weeks, the whole of the amount due for the 156 weeks, or the remainder of that period, became due and payable. The respondent did not pay the first instalment within the time allowed and the appellants sought to recover the whole price. **Held**: they were entitled to succeed. 'If one party to a contract repudiates it ... the other party, the innocent party, has an option. He may accept that repudiation and sue for damages for breach of contract whether or not the time for performance has come; or he may if he chooses disregard or refuse to accept it and then the contract remains in full effect. ... It is ... impossible to say that the appellants should be deprived of their right to claim the contract price merely because the benefit to them as against claiming damages and reletting their advertising space might be small in comparison with the loss to the respondent' (*per* Lord Reid). (Courtesy of *Cracknell's Law Students' Companion*)

Those who choose to continue with the contract, though, do face some risk that subsequent events might undermine their position, as in:

Avery v. Bowden (1855)

B chartered a ship from A and agreed to put a cargo on board at Odessa within 45 days. The ship went to Odessa and stood there for almost 45 days without cargo being loaded. B then told the Captain there was no cargo and he ought to go elsewhere. The Captain remained, hoping that the cargo would turn up. Before the end of the 45-day period the Crimean War broke out and performance of the contract would have been illegal. **Held**: A had an option to treat the defendants' refusal to load cargo as anticipatory breach, but this option had been waived by staying on at Odessa. Now the contract was discharged by the outbreak of war.

Whether a particular act of non-performance breaches a warranty or a condition is usually decided by the courts taking into account all the facts surrounding a particular contract. Some outline on this question was given by the Court of Appeal in the case of:

> **Mapleflock Co. Ltd v. Universal Furniture Products (Wembley) Ltd (1934)**
>
> A contract was concluded for the sale and delivery of 100 tons of rag flock to be dispatched in instalments of 1½ tons three times per week. The sixteenth instalment had excessive amounts of chlorine in it and the buyers wished to repudiate stating that the contract had been breached. **Held**: no entitlement to repudiate since the breach bore only a small quantitative ratio to the contract as a whole.

Generally, breaches of contract can be divided into two types: anticipatory breach and actual breach.

11.5.1 Anticipatory breach

Anticipatory breach means a breach which occurs before the date specified in the contract for performance. It can occur in two ways:

- expressly – where the defaulting party notifies his intention not to perform the contract, and
- implicitly – where the defaulting party through some action shows that he will not be performing the contract.

Anticipatory breach given the injured party the *option* of treating the contract as ended.

11.5.2 Actual breach

Actual breach can occur in three ways:

- *Non-performance*, i.e. the due date for performance arrives and the other party does not perform his part of the bargain.
- *Defective performance*. Here performance is not precise and exact. For example, turning up late where time is important.
- *Untruth as regards a term of the contract*. Where the promise made has deliberately concealed the true intentions, as where a cattle truck was sent to do a removal where it was specified that a removal van would be used.

It is cases of actual, as opposed to anticipatory, breach which usually create problems for the courts. As suggested above, the difficulty is in deciding whether a major or minor term of the contract has been breached. With anticipatory breach it is usually the whole of the contract which has been breached.

11.6 Assignment of contracts

It sometimes happens that one party to a contract wishes to dispose of his obligations under it, but the extent to which this is permitted is limited. The other party may have valid reasons why he prefers the obligations to be performed by the original contractor. If I have contracted with Rembrandt to paint my picture it is unlikely that Rembrandt's pupil, or any other acquaintance of Rembrandt, will produce the picture I require. The rule is that liabilities can only be assigned by **novation**. Novation is the formation of a new contract between the party who wishes performance and a new contractor, whom he accepts is as adequately qualified to perform as the original contractor. Liabilities can only be assigned by consent.

By contrast, rights under a contract can usually be assigned without consent of the other party, except where the subject matter involves personal service. Thus if you own me £50, it should not make any difference to you if I say: 'Don't pay me – pay Smith.' This is the basis of many debt collection activities. The debtor who is a slow payer finds that his debt has been sold (at a discount) to a debt collector who specializes in collecting debts and will make clear arrangements about settlement and insist that they are carried out. It is a different matter if personal service is involved. If A engages to teach B the piano, and has been paid for a course of lessons, B cannot say 'Don't teach me – teach C'. C may not have any musical potential. The rights to personal services cannot be transferred without the consent of the person giving the service.

Even if the contract does not involve personal service, but specifically restricts the right to assign the contract or any interest in it to third parties, the assignment of rights will not be permitted. In *Helstan Securities Ltd v. Hertfordshire County Council (1978)* the County Council specifically restricted the right of their contractors to assign the contract in any way. A contractor who got into financial difficulties assigned his rights to the plaintiffs, but payment was refused by the defendants. **Held**: the assignment was invalid.

This case was upheld in the case of *Linden Gardens Trust Ltd v. Lenesta Sludge Disposals Ltd and Others (1993)* where the House of Lords held that a clause in a contract of the type 'neither party shall without the written consent of the other assign this contract', had no 'public policy' overtones. It was not against public policy to restrict a contractor's right to assign the contract; in fact it might be desirable since it is important for everyone to be aware of the onerous obligations which are undertaken when an agreement to procure something is entered into. An attempted assignment of contractual rights in breach of a contractual prohibition of assignment is ineffective to transfer those rights.

Contracts may be assigned in four ways. These are: novation; legal assignment; equitable assignment, and operation of the law.

11.6.1 Novation

This has been referred to above. The old contract is discharged and a new contract is made between one of the original parties (the creditor) to whom the liability (whether goods, services or money) is owed, and the new debtor who has agreed to undertake the obligations. In many cases the matter is quite routine, as where an existing partnership is dissolved and a new partnership is formed. The existing obligations of the old firm are usually honoured by the new firm with the consent of the customers, and no difficulty arises.

11.6.2 Legal assignment

A legal assignment is one made under the *Law of Property Act, 1925*, Section 136. All debts and other things in action (formerly called *choses in action*) may be assigned in the following manner:

- The assignment must be in writing, signed by the assignor;
- It must be absolute, and not by way of a pledge or charge;
- Express notice must be given to the debtor, trustee or other person from whom the assignor is entitled to demand payment or other right. This is to ensure that the debtor knows that the assignor has surrendered his rights completely in favour of the assignee.

Choses in action are rights of property which can only be enforced in the courts, and not by taking possession. A right under a contract is the commonest example of a *chose in action*.

It is not possible to assign part of a debt, for this puts the debtor to the inconvenience of seeking out two creditors.

The effect of a legal assignment are that the assignor transfers the legal rights to the debt, or other *choses in action*, together with the legal and other remedies available, to the assignee, who may demand payment or satisfaction in the agreed manner laid down in the original contract, and sue if dissatisfied in his own name. He is also free to make such arrangements as he wishes to achieve satisfaction and may give a good discharge to the other party without reference to the assignor.

One defect in assignments from the assignee's point of view is that he always takes **'subject to the equities'**. This means that if, on seeking to enforce the assignment, the debtor is able to show that it is inequitable for the full rights to be enforced, the assignee will not be able to enforce them. Thus if a debtor has paid the debt before receiving notice of the assignment, or is able to raise a set-off against the original obligation, the assignee will be able to enforce only the balance and will be thrown back for redress upon the assignor.

11.6.3 Equitable assignments

An equitable assignment is one that will be recognized by equity, even if the common law will not recognize it (because, for example, it lacks the form required by Section 136 of the *Law of Property Act, 1925*). If there has been a clear intention to assign, equity will recognize the assignment and enforce it, even if it is not in writing or only for part of a debt. Thus where K agreed with B, who was his financial backer, that all moneys due to K from customers should be paid direct to B, there was a clear intention to assign. K sold goods to D, who were given notice of assignment by B and asked to pay B. D ignored the request and paid K. When sued by B it was held that D must pay B again, even if they had already paid K. It would be inequitable for B to suffer a loss when they had given clear notice of the assignment (*Brandt v. Dunlop Rubber Co. (1905)*).

This is an example of an equitable assignment of a legal *chose in action*. It must be distinguished from the assignment of an equitable *chose in action* – for example, the assignment of a claim by a legatee on an executor.

11.7 Other assignments

Certain contractual documents are not assigned in the manner laid down in the *Law of Property Act, 1925*, but are governed by special statutes. They include bills of exchange and promissory notes (see Chapter 17), bills of lading, shares in companies, marine insurance policies and life assurance policies.

Assignments by operation of the law occur at death or bankruptcy. At **death** all liabilities and rights on a contract pass to the personal representatives, and are dealt with as part of the estate. Contracts for personal skill and service are not assignable, and terminate at death. At **bankruptcy** the rights and liabilities under a contract pass to the trustee in bankruptcy, and are dealt with as part of the process of settling the bankrupt's affairs.

Test your knowledge

Answers	Questions
	1 How is a contract usually discharged?
1 By performance.	2 In what other ways may it be discharged?
2 (a) By agreement; (b) by frustration; (c) by breach.	3 What are the criteria for discharge by performance?
3 Traditionally performance must be *precise and exact*. More recently the doctrines of *substantial performance*, *divisible contracts* and *quantum meruit* have reduced the severity of the traditional rule.	4 What was the case of *Hoenig v. Isaacs (1952)* about?
4 Substantial performance. Isaacs refused to pay fully for redecoration and refurnishing, but the contract was held to have been substantially performed.	5 What are the rules in discharge by agreement?
5 (a) That which has been created by agreement can be extinguished by agreement; (b) the new agreement is a contract in its own right and requires consideration unless under seal.	6 What is meant by the doctrine of frustration?
6 The doctrine that holds that in certain circumstances a contract may be discharged by events which render it impossible to perform.	7 What are the common instances of frustration?
7 (a) Destruction of the subject matter; (b) non-availability of a person in a contract for personal service; (c) non-occurrence of an event; (d) supervening illegality.	8 What Act of Parliament controls frustrated contracts?
8 The *Law Reform (Frustrated Contracts) Act, 1943*	9 What are its rules?

Answers	Questions
9 (a) Money prepaid can be reclaimed; (b) money not paid need not be paid; (c) if a party has incurred expenses he may retain these out of any repayment, or claim them, if they have conferred a benefit on the other party.	10 What is the result of a breach of a warranty in a contract?
10 The injured party may claim damages, but the contract subsists.	11 What is the result of a breach of condition?
11 (a) The aggrieved party has an option to treat the contract as ended and sue for breach. (b) Alternatively, he may complete the contract and sue for non-performance. In this case he runs the risk that subsequent events may worsen his legal position.	12 What is a legal assignment?
12 The passing of legal rights or obligations on a contract to another party.	13 How are obligations on a contract assigned?
13 By novation with consent of the creditor to whom money, goods or services are due. The old contract ceases and a new contract is made between the new parties.	14 How are rights assigned?
14 By the rules of the *Law of Property Act, 1925,* Section 136.	15 What are these rules?
15 (a) The assignment must be in writing, signed by the assignor; (b) it must be absolute, not by way of charge or pledge; (c) notice must be given to the debtor.	16 What is an equitable assignment?
16 An assignment which equity will recognize even though it lacks the formality required by the *Law of Property Act, 1925.*	17 Go over the questions until you are sure of the answers. Then try some of the written questions in Appendix 1.

12 How the law enforces contractual obligations

12.1 The nature of contractual enforcement

The law of contract is concerned with 'enforceable' agreements. The question then arises as to what 'enforceable' means in this context. It means that should one of the parties to the contract fail to perform his contractual obligations, the courts, at the request of the aggrieved party, will impose conditions upon the defaulting party. These conditions are intended to provide a remedy for the aggrieved rather than a punishment for the defaulter. In this respect the law of contract is quite unlike criminal law; remedies are designed to compensate, not to penalize.

As with many branches of the law, remedies available for those injured by breach of contract fall into two groups:

- Those available at common law.
- Those available in equity.

12.2 Common law remedies

The remedies available at common law are: repudiation of the contract, damages and a *quantum meruit*.

12.2.1 Repudiation of the contract

Where there has been anticipatory breach or breach of a vital condition of the contract, the injured party has the option of repudiating the contract, i.e. treating it as ended. Of course he may decide not to exercise this option (see *White v. McGregor*, page 178). Should he choose to repudiate he will do nothing further on the contract. He will escape from all further contractual obligations and in addition will normally sue for damages. The question arises whether the innocent party should respond positively to the fax or other message making him aware of the breach. In *Vital SA v. Norelf Ltd (1993)* (*The Times*, 20 May) the judge likened the acceptance of an anticipatory breach to the acceptance of an offer. The innocent party could formally acknowledge notification of the intended breach (and possibly assert that legal action would follow). On the other hand acceptance could be inferred by the innocent party's failure to do anything more on the contract. Such passive acceptance has its disadvantages however. For example the breach might be cancelled if the notice of intended breach was withdrawn before any obvious repudiation of the contract had come to the defaulting party's notice. In practice it is rare for a contract to be revived after an anticipatory breach. It is desirable to monitor contracts to ensure that performance is proceeding as planned. Any slippage in delivery dates, time-scales for the performance of work, payment of instalments due, etc., could indicate that breach of contract may be a possible outcome. Prompt action to draw the contractor's attention to the problem may avoid a breach altogether.

12.2.2 Damages

These are available not only to those who have suffered through anticipatory breach or breach of condition, but also those disadvantaged through breach of warranty.

Damages are a money payment designed to put the injured party in the position he would have been in had the contract been performed. Therefore the injured party can never get more in damages than the extent of his loss. If he suffers no loss he may still win his action for breach but will receive only nominal damages (a token payment). He may not recover his costs. The following are the main areas of concern as regards contractual damages:

(a) Remoteness of damage

A situation might arise where a breach of contract leads not only to the loss immediate upon the breach itself, but to further consequences which give rise to additional loss. The question then arises as to whether the injured party can recover for all of these consequences. In other words, how are the damages to be assessed, and how extensive are the consequences to be considered?

The line of demarcation between the losses recoverable through an action for damages, and those not recoverable because the damage is too remote, was laid down in the case of *Hadley v. Baxendale (1854)*. This is the most important case:

> ### Hadley v. Baxendale (1854)
> The plaintiffs were millers and mealmen in Gloucester. The crankshaft of the steam engine which worked their mill was fractured and they ordered another from a firm in Greenwich who asked that the old shaft should be sent to them for use as a pattern. The plaintiffs gave the shaft to the defendants, who were common carriers, and the defendants promised to deliver the shaft on the following day. In fact they took a week to deliver it and because their mill was out of action for longer than would otherwise have been the case the plaintiffs claimed damages for loss of profit. **Held**: the plaintiffs would not succeed as the loss of profit could not reasonably be considered a consequence of the breach of contract which could have been fairly and reasonably contemplated by both parties when they entered into the contract of carriage. 'Where two parties have made a contract which one of them has broken, the damages which the other party ought to receive in respect of such breach of contract should be such as *may fairly and reasonably be considered either arising naturally, i.e. according to the usual course of things, from such breach of contract itself, or such as may reasonably be supposed to have been in the contemplation of both parties, at the time they made the contract, as the probable result of the breach of it.* Now, if the special circumstances under which the contract was actually made were communicated by the plaintiffs to the defendants, and thus known to both parties, the damages resulting from the breach of such a contract, which they would reasonably contemplate, would be the amount of injury which would ordinarily follow from a breach of the contract under the special circumstances so known and communicated. But, on the other hand, if these special circumstances were wholly unknown to the party breaking the contract, he, at the most, could only be supposed to have had in his contemplation the amount of injury which would arise generally, and in the great multitude of cases not affected by any special circumstances, from such a breach of contract. For, had the special circumstances been known, the parties might have specially provided for the breach of contract by special terms as to damages in that case; and of this advantage it would be very unjust to deprive them' (*per* Alderson, B). (Courtesy of *Cracknell's Law Students' Companion*)

The rule in this case has been applied in many subsequent cases and is well established. The following cases further illustrate this rule:

> ### Diamond v. Campbell-Jones (1960)
> The defendants wrongly repudiated an agreement for the sale by the defendants to the plaintiff of a leasehold property in Mayfair and the question arose as to the amount of damages that the plaintiff was entitled to recover. The agreement to purchase the property was linked to the grant of a new lease and a contract which required the premises to be converted by the lessee into ground-floor office accommodation and residential maisonettes. The plaintiff was a dealer in real property but it was not shown that the defendants were aware of this or that he intended to carry out a conversion of the premises. **Held**: the amount of damages should be limited to the difference between the purchase price and the market value at the date of the breach of contract as there were no special circumstances sufficient to impute to the defendants knowledge that the plaintiff intended to convert the property for profit. (Courtesy of *Cracknell's Law Students' Companion*)

> ### Cottrill v. Steyning and Littlehampton Building Society (1966)
> Here it was held that the vendors, knowing that the purchaser intended to develop the land himself, were liable for loss of profits which the purchaser would have made by carrying out the development.

> ### Koufos v. C. Czarnikow Ltd 'The Heron II' (1967)
> A vessel was chartered for a voyage from Constanza to Basrah for the carriage of sugar. She deviated to Berbera to load livestock for the shipowners. If she had not deviated, she would have arrived at Basrah 10 days earlier than she did in fact. The charterers claimed damages for the difference between the market value of the sugar at the due date of delivery and at the actual date of delivery. **Held**: their claim should succeed. Although the shipowners did not know what the charterers intended to do with the sugar, they knew that there was a market for sugar in Basrah. They must have realized that at least it was not unlikely that the sugar would be sold there on arrival, and that in any ordinary market prices were apt to fluctuate daily. It was an even chance that the fluctuation would be downwards. The loss was of a kind which the shipowners, when they made the contract, ought to have realized was liable to result from a breach causing delay in delivery. The Law Lords emphasized that the measure of damages in contract and the measure of damages in tort are not the same. In contract there is opportunity for the injured party to protect himself against risk by directing the other party's attention to it before the contract is made; in tort there is no such opportunity, and the tortfeasor cannot reasonably complain if he has to pay for unusual but foreseeable damage resulting from his wrongdoing.) (Courtesy of *Cracknell's Law Students' Companion*)

(b) Quantification of damages

Once the courts have established the cause for which the injured party may receive damages its attention is turned to the size of those damages, i.e. how to express the loss suffered in terms of money.

Where the contract is for the sale of goods or the carriage of goods the normal way of quantifying damages will be with reference to the market.

This is known as the '**market rule**'. Should a seller fail to deliver goods then the buyer must buy similar goods in the market and his loss will be the difference between the market price and the contract price.

In other cases there are no such specific rules, and often the assessment of damages is reduced virtually to guesswork. The damages which the plaintiff claims may be **liquidated** or **unliquidated**.

Liquidated damages These are a genuine pre-estimate of the loss likely to be suffered by the plaintiff if there is a breach of contract. They are written into the contract itself. For example, if the parties provide in the contract that failure to complete a construction job on time will lead to a claim for damages of £100 a day, this would be a genuine attempt to liquidate (express in money terms) the loss to be suffered. If the sum mentioned is not a genuine pre-estimate of the loss, but is excessive and inserted *in terrorem* (to frighten the other party), it is called a penalty and the law will not enforce it. Thus a claim for £1 000 000 a day would be a penalty, *in terrorem*, and void. If the amount is liquidated damages, the court will enforce it, even though in the event the pre-estimate turns out to have been wrong. If, however, the court comes to the conclusion that the amount is a penalty, then the plaintiff cannot enforce it, but can simply claim unliquidated damages.

Often it is difficult to tell whether an agreed sum is liquidated damages or a penalty; it is a matter of construction. The fact that a sum is described as one thing or another is not conclusive, although there is a rebuttable presumption that the clause is what it says it is.

Willson v. Love (1896)

A tenant farmer agreed to pay the additional rent of £3 per ton by way of penalty for every ton of hay or straw which shall be sold off the premises during the last 12 months of the tenancy. The clause was regarded as penal because at the time hay was worth five shillings a ton more than straw.

Dunlop Pneumatic Tyre Co. Ltd v. New Garage and Motor Co. Ltd (1915)

The appellants, manufacturers of motor tyres, supplied goods to the respondents under a contract which provided that the respondents would not sell tyres at less than the appellants' list price. It was further provided that if the respondents sold a tyre in breach of this agreement they would pay the appellants £5. **Held**: this sum would be regarded as liquidated damages and not as a penalty.

In this case certain rules for guidance were laid down by Lord Dunedin:

- The sum is a penalty if it is greater than the greatest loss which could be suffered from the breach – in other words, if it is 'extravagant and unconscionable'.
- If it is agreed that a larger sum shall be payable in default of paying a smaller sum, this is a penalty.

- If a single sum is payable on different events of varying importance this is *prima facie* a penalty. (But this presumption may be rebutted if it is impossible to prove the exact monetary loss.)

> ### Ford Motor Co. (England) Ltd v. Armstrong (1915)
> A dealer, the defendant, agreed to sell the plaintiff's motorcars and, in the event of his selling any car or parts below list price, to pay £250 for every breach of such undertaking 'such sum being the agreed damages which the manufacturer will sustain'. **Held**: the sum of £250 was a penalty and not liquidated damages.

In *Jobson v. Johnson (1988)* the question arose over whether a clause which required the transfer of property (shares in a company) rather than money could be a penalty clause. It was held that it could, since the value placed upon them bore no relation to the loss suffered by the aggrieved party when the contract was broken, but was excessive.

Unliquidated damages The term means that no attempt has been made by the parties to express the loss in money terms, and the amount payable will be assessed by the court.

(c) Taxation

There are circumstances where the incidence of taxation has to be taken into account when quantifying damages. The guiding case here is:

> ### British Transport Commission v. Gourley (1956)
> Gourley was injured in an accident as a result of the negligence of BTC. His claim for £37 000 loss of earnings for the rest of his working life was reduced to £6000 by the House of Lords since this was the amount he would have received after tax.

The principle behind this decision is that individuals ought not to make a profit out of damages. It is therefore necessary, if the case is to be applied, for there to be a combination of non-taxable damages and a liability for taxation in the earnings which the damages represent. Where the damages will eventually be taxed in the hands of the recipient – for example, where he is a trader, or where they represent a non-taxable item – the court will make no deduction for taxation.

The *Income and Corporation Taxes Act, 1970* (Sections 187 and 188), has slightly modified the position. Damages for wrongful dismissal in excess of £5000 are now taxed in the hands of the recipient: only the initial £5000 is now subject in such cases to the rule in *BTC v. Gourley (1956)*.

(d) Mitigation of damage

It is the duty of the plaintiff to take all reasonable steps to mitigate his loss. In *Brace v. Calder and Others (1895)* four men in partnership agreed to employ Brace for two years in the capacity of manager. Five months later two of the partners retired. The partnership was automatically dissolved but the remaining two partners offered Brace employment on the same terms.

Brace chose to sue for breach and claimed as damages the salary for the remainder of the two year contract period. **Held**: he was entitled to nominal damages only because it was his duty to mitigate his loss which he could easily have done by accepting re-employment.

This rule is subject to two qualifications:

- The burden is on the defendant of proving that the plaintiff has failed to mitigate his damage.

> *Pilkington v. Wood (1953)*
>
> When the plaintiff bought a house in Hampshire he employed the defendant, a solicitor, to act for him. Over a year later the plaintiff decided to sell the house and it was then that a defect in the plaintiff's title came to light. The defendant admitted that he had been guilty of negligence and the question arose as to the amount of damages which he should pay. In addition to the difference between the market value of the house with a good title and its value when the title was defective, the plaintiff claimed certain hotel, travelling and telephone expenses which he would not have incurred if he had been able to sell the house and move to Lancashire, his new place of employment. He also claimed interest on a bank overdraft which would have been paid off when the house was sold. The defendant maintained that it was the duty of the plaintiff to mitigate the damage which he had suffered by suing the vendor in respect of a breach of his implied covenant for title. **Held**: the plaintiff's duty to mitigate the damage did not go so far as to require him to undertake a difficult piece of litigation, but his claim for additional damages would fail as it arose out of facts which could not reasonably be supposed to have been in contemplation of the parties at the time at which the plaintiff bought the house.

- The principle is completely at variance with the rule that, in the case of anticipatory breach, the plaintiff has the option to hold the defendant to his contract and await the date of performance. If he chooses this course, he may well inflate his damages rather than mitigate them (*White and Carter (Councils) Ltd v. McGregor (1962)*). However, it seems he is entitled to do this, since the contract remains alive and the question of damages or of mitigation has not yet arisen.

12.2.3 Quantum meruit

At common law a party injured by breach of contract might be able to make a claim other than for damages. He may be able to claim for what he has done under the contract. This right to sue on a *quantum meruit* does not depend upon the original contract but flows from an implied promise by the other party, who has had executed consideration, that a reasonable sum will be paid for it. Such cases are often described as 'quasi-contractual' (almost contractual). See *Planché v. Colburn* (page 172), and a more recent case *British Steel Corporation v. Cleveland Bridge and Engineering Co. Ltd. (1984)*.

12.3 Equitable remedies

Throughout its development equity has attempted to mitigate the harshness of common law rules to provide for omissions in the common law. In respect to breach of contract the common law remedies of damages and repudiation may not be adequate to compensate the injured party effectively for his loss. Equity therefore developed the equitable remedies of specific performance and injunction.

12.3.1 Specific performance

Specific performance is a decree issued by the court which orders a defendant to perform the promises he has made. Such a decree is likely to be made only where the injured party has no solution to his problem by ordinary dealings in the market. Thus where a contract for the supply of a motor vehicle is broken the court would expect the customer to buy elsewhere and only money damages would be payable. It might be different if the motor vehicle was a unique vintage model which could not therefore be obtained elsewhere.

One of the main difficulties with specific performance is that it involves the courts in the business of supervision and therefore there are many limitations to its application by the courts. The following are the main ones:

- *Where damages is an adequate remedy* specific performance will not be awarded. This means that where the contract is for the sale of goods specific performance is rarely given. For example:

Cohen v. Roche (1927)

Cohen sued for specific performance against Roche, an auctioneer, claiming that he was entitled to a set of eight Hepplewhite chairs after an auction. **Held**: he could have damages, but not specific performance, because the chairs were not special items of interest but ordinary articles of commerce.

Specific performance will be awarded though for an obligation to pay money, where damages would not be an adequate recompense. This is illustrated by:

Beswick v. Beswick (1967)

By a written agreement PB assigned his business as a coal merchant to his nephew, JB. In consideration, JB agreed to employ PB as a consultant at £6 10s. a week for the rest of his life, and further to pay PB's wife an annuity of £5 a week for her life, after PB's death. PB's wife was not a party to the contract. After PB's death, JB paid one sum of £5 to the widow, but refused to pay any more. The widow sought an order for specific performance of the agreement in her capacity as administratrix of her husband's estate and in her personal capacity. **Held**: the widow as administratrix was entitled to enforce the agreement by an order for specific performance in her own personal favour. However, the House of Lords rejected the argument that Section 56, *Law of Property Act, 1925*, applied to such an agreement, and hence the widow would be unable to enforce the agreement in her personal capacity as she was not a party to the original contract. Fortunately she could rely on her position as administratrix of her husband's will.

- *Where the court hesitates to exercise discretion.* As with all equitable remedies, specific performance is not available as of right, but at the court's discretion. In this respect it is unlike damages. The case of *Wood v. Scarth* (1858) illustrates the court's attitude:

Wood v. Scarth (1858)

Wood sued Scarth alleging that Scarth had contracted to grant Wood the lease of a public house but then had refused to convey the property. Scarth acted through an agent and the agent had failed to make clear to Wood the terms which Scarth required. Wood agreed to one set of terms, Scarth to another – in other words a non-identical bilateral mistake. In 1855 Wood sued for specific performance but the court withheld this on the grounds that in view of the mistake performance would be hard on Scarth. In this (1858) action Wood sued at common law for damages and was granted them on the grounds that it was reasonable for Wood to feel that he had entered a contract on the basis of the terms he had agreed.

The principles followed by the court when deciding whether or not to award specific performance depend upon the justness and equity of its application. For example:

Flight v. Bolland (1828)

In this case Sir John Leach, MR, stated that: 'No case of a bill filed by an infant for the specific performance of a contract made by him has been found in the books. It is not disputed that it is a general principle of courts of equity to interpose only where the remedy is mutual.' Since the infant, had he been the defaulting party, would have been insusceptible to legal action, equity felt it would be unfair to grant an equitable remedy in his favour.

- *Where the contract will be difficult to enforce*. There are two areas:
  - Contracts requiring constant supervision by the courts. For example:

Ryan v. Mutual Tontine Westminster Chambers Association (1893)

By the term of a lease of a residential flat the landlords convenanted to provide a porter, who was to be constantly in attendance, or during his temporary absence, a trustworthy assistant. The landlords appointed one Benton to be porter but, while he spent much of his time acting as chef at a neighbouring club, boys and charwomen performed his duties as porter. **Held**: the landlords were in breach of their covenant but the court would not grant an injunction to restrain the continuance of the breach or order the covenant to be specifically enforced. (Courtesy of *Cracknell's Law Students' Companion*)

  - Contracts for personal services, since this would interfere with personal liberty.

12.3.2 Injunction

An injunction is a decree which compels a party to do an act (**a mandatory injunction**) or to refrain from doing an act (**a prohibitory injunction**). In relation to the law of contract it can be used in order to prevent a party from committing a breach of contract, i.e. a negative stipulation. For example, if I enter into a contract promising to take all my electricity supply from you, then I can be prevented from obtaining electricity supply from anyone else (*Metropolitan Electric Supply Co. v. Ginder (1901)*). Negative stipulation applies also to contracts of personal services where an actor or a singer has undertaken to act or sing at the plaintiff's theatre. This actor or singer can be prevented by an injunction from acting or singing for someone else (*Lumley v. Wagner (1852)*; *Warner Bros. v. Nelson (1937)*).

> ### Warner Brothers Pictures Inc. v. Nelson (1936)
> Bette Davis entered into a contract with the plaintiffs, initially for a term of one year, but giving the plaintiffs the option of extending it, whereby she agreed that she would not undertake other film work without obtaining their written consent. The plaintiffs sought an injunction to restrain her from doing film work for another in breach of this agreement. **Held**: the injunction would be granted for the period of the continuance of the contract, or for three years, whichever was the shorter. (Courtesy of *Cracknell's Law Students' Companion*)

However, an injunction will not be granted where the effect is to compel a party to do that which specific performance would not order.

> ### Page One Records Ltd v. Britton (1967)
> By a written agreement made in 1966, the defendants, a group of pop musicians, appointed the plaintiffs as their managers for five years. The agreement was world-wide. The plaintiffs agreed to use their best endeavours to advance the defendants' careers, and the defendants said they would not engage any other person to act as their manager or agent. The plaintiffs were to receive 20 per cent of all moneys earned by the defendants during the currency of the agreement. As a result of the plaintiffs' services, the defendants achieved success, but in 1967 purported to repudiate the management agreement. The court then held that there had been no breaches of duty by the plaintiffs to justify repudiation. The plaintiffs claimed damages for breach of contact and, pending trial, sought an **interlocutory injunction** restraining the defendants from engaging anyone else as their manager. **Held**: dismissing the application, the injunction would be refused because, if granted, it would enforce a contract for personal services of a fiduciary nature to be performed by the plaintiffs and not specifically enforceable by the defendants against them. (Courtesy of *Cracknell's Law Students' Companion*)

12.4 Limitation of actions

Generally speaking, litigation is a costly and time-consuming process which becomes more difficult as the time between the disputed events and the litigation increases. For this reason Parliament has enacted Limitation Acts which set a time limit on the commencement of litigation. The current Act is the *Limitation Act, 1980*.

The right to bring an action can be discharged in three ways:

- The parties to the contract might agree to discharge their rights. This agreement will either be under seal, or through accord and satisfaction.
- Through the judgment of a court.
- Through lapse of time. If an action is not commenced within a certain time the right to sue is extinguished. Specific provision for lapse of time is now governed by the *Limitation Act, 1980*. Actions in simple contract and tort become 'statute barred' after six years. In the case of specialties

(deeds) the time allowed is 12 years. The Act does permit certain extensions to these time limits. For example, where a person is under a disability (he may be unconscious as the result of an accident) the time limit does not begin to run until the disability is removed, or the person dies. These cases are usually concerned with torts, rather than contracts, and are discussed later in this book (see page 364).

A number of international conventions, particularly with regard to the law of carriage, lay down shorter limitation periods for action than those specified in the *Limitation Act, 1980*. For example, in carriage by sea the limitation period is normally one year, but this may be extended by mutual agreement. In carriage by air under the Warsaw Rules the period is two years. Such conventions are enacted into British law in relevant acts of Parliament, in the above cases the *Carriage of Goods by Sea Act, 1971*, and the *Carriage by Air Act, 1961*.

12.5 The *Contracts (Applicable Law) Act, 1990*

When we are almost at the end of a long section of this book about contract law it seems strange to introduce the idea that possibly a contract may not be subject to English law at all. The fact is that we live in a world where international trading is extremely common, and brings with it problems known under the general title of 'conflicts of law'. Where some 200 trading nations are engaged in intricate patterns of trading relationships it would be strange if some conflicts of law did not arise. Often it is necessary to decide before a case can begin which is the law to be applied to this particular contract, and if the court has the jurisdiction to try the case. Over the course of centuries the United Kingdom has laid down certain rules which will decide whether English law applies to a contract, and whether the English courts have jurisdiction (i.e. the right to try the case). These rules are called 'the common law rules for finding the proper law of the contract'.

12.5.1 The common law rules

These rules say that the proper law of the contract is to be discovered in one of three ways:

- Did the parties to the contract select a particular law, and specify it as the proper law of the contract, with some such phrase as 'This contract is subject to the Laws of England.'?
- If they did not make any selection we must look at the circumstances surrounding the contract. For example, if the contract has references to 'Acts of God' it has been held that English law must have been intended, for this phrase is rarely used by other systems of law. If the contract is for the carriage of goods from a port in England to a port in Italy, but the carriage is to be an English ship, and the price is payable in pounds Sterling to a London bank, the court may be influenced into thinking that English law was probably intended as the proper law of the contract.
- If this does not solve the problem it is usual to look for the system of law most closely connected to the contract. Where is the contract to be performed? If it is the building of a dam in the upper reaches of the River Nile, and will be paid for jointly by the Government of Egypt and the Cairo branch of the World Bank (acting on behalf of the Government of Ethiopia) then the fact that it is being built by a German–British consortium will not perhaps dispose the courts to conclude that German or British law will apply, but that Egyptian law exerts the greatest influence.

Obviously such problems are fundamental to good relations between international traders, and the usual method of resolving problems is to hold an international convention at which such issues will be thoroughly discussed. The *Contracts (Applicable Law) Act, 1990* enacts into English law the decisions reached at the *Rome Convention on the Law Applicable to Contractual Obligations* of 1980. The Convention appears as a schedule to the Act, and provides the framework by which all such problems will be resolved by the member states in future. In many ways the rules are not all that different from the 'common law rules' referred to above. Some of the chief points are:

Article 3(1) A contract shall be governed by the law chosen by the parties. The choice must be express (English law, American law, French law, etc.) or demonstrated with reasonable certainty by the terms of the contract or the circumstances of the case.

Article 4(1) If Article 3(1) does not resolve the problem the contract shall be governed by the law of the country with which it is most closely connected. Article 4(2) says that there is a 'presumption that the law of the party which has to effect the performance which is characteristic of the contract' is the law that will apply.

Articles 5 and 6 These articles take note of the fact that consumers and employees are generally speaking less sophisticated and less well-represented than other parties to contracts. Therefore if this is important to a proper understanding of the contract it may be helpful to apply the law with which they are most familiar, and 'at home'.

Article 7 This is about 'mandatory rules'. Some countries feel so strongly about a particular aspect of their law that they specify it to be 'mandatory', i.e. it must be obeyed in every contractual arrangement. Article 7 says that all parties must observe the mandatory rules of a country, even if the law on other points was based upon a different set of laws. For example, when South Africa was practising its Apartheid rule many countries had mandatory rules about the use of South African components or raw materials.

These examples are perhaps enough to show that decisions about the law to be applied to a particular contract can be quite complex, and the only thing to do is to study the Convention in detail. It may be obtained from Her Majesty's Stationery Office by phoning on 0171 873 9090, with either an account number or a credit card number for payment.

Test your knowledge

Answers	Questions
	1 What is meant by 'enforcement of contracts'?
1 It is the imposition of sanctions upon the defaulting party in a contract to compensate the aggrieved other party.	2 What common law sanctions are available?
2 (a) Repudiation of the contract; (b) damages; (c) a *quantum meruit*.	3 What happens with repudiation of the contract?

Answers	Questions
3 The aggrieved party does nothing further on the contract, and may also sue for damages for non-performance.	4 What case laid down the principles on money damages payable?
4 *Hadley v. Baxendale* (1854).	5 What was this case about?
5 A mill owner sent a crankshaft for repair, the carrier promising delivery next day. There was a considerable delay and his factory was idle. He claimed for this loss.	6 What was the principle laid down in the case?
6 Damages would be limited to those naturally following from the breach of contract, or those in the contemplation of both parties when they made the contract.	7 What other rules apply?
7 (a) The rule that the plaintiff must mitigate his losses so far as possible. (b) The rule that taxation may need to be taken into account unless it is taxable on the recipient.	8 What are liquidated damages?
8 Damages laid down as a term in the contract and believed to be a fair pre-estimate of the loss likely to be suffered if a breach of contract occurs.	9 What does *quantum meruit* mean?
9 'How much is it worth?' The aggrieved party sues for the value of the work done.	10 What is an equitable remedy?
10 A remedy given at the discretion of the court to see fair play in a situation where money damages are not a satisfactory remedy.	11 What are the equitable remedies?
11 (a) Specific performance; (b) injunction. The court may also order rescission of the contract.	12 When is specific performance used?

Answers	Questions
12 (a) Where the object of the contract is unique – such as the ownership of a particular parcel of land, or a work of art. (b) Where the supervision required is not great, since the courts hesitate to undertake continuous supervision of any situation.	13 What is an injunction?
13 An order of the court requiring a party to do a certain thing, or to refrain from doing a certain thing.	14 What limitations are placed on ordinary actions by the *Limitation Act, 1980*.
14 (a) Simple contracts, 6 years; (b) torts (civil wrongs), 6 years; (c) specialties (deeds), 12 years.	15 What Act helps us to discover the proper law to be applied to a contract?
15 The *Contracts (Applicable Law) Act, 1990*, which embodies the *Rome Convention on the Law Applicable to Contractual Obligations*.	16 Go over the questions until you are sure of all the answers. Then try some of the questions in Appendix 1 which require a written answer.

13 Agency

13.1 The nature of agency

Any legal person, whether it be an individual, a firm or an incorporation like a company or nationalized corporation can appoint someone to act on his behalf in a particular matter, or in all matters. Thus a householder may appoint an estate agent to sell his property, or an explorer may appoint a friend to act on his behalf in any matters that arise during his absence from home. The essence of agency is that the agent is empowered to make binding contracts between his principal and third parties. The Latin rule *Qui facit per alium, facit per se* ('He who does something by another does it himself') applies, and the principal is bound by the acts of his agent, to the extent that he has authorized them, either expressly or impliedly.

The more sophisticated an economy is the more agency arrangements are made. It is part of specialization into trades and professions that expertise should be developed in special fields, and that the specialists thus developed should act for others who are not knowledgeable in that particular area. Solicitors, estate agents, freight forwarders, bankers, factors, brokers and many others specialize in their fields and offer their services to the business world around them.

The essential aspects of agency may be listed as follows:

- *Appointment.* The agent's appointment determines the extent of his authority and is clearly of crucial importance. There is also an **agency of necessity**.
- *The nature of contracts made under agency.* The relationship is a triangular one, as explained below (see Figure 13.1).
- *Ratification of an unauthorized act.* Sometimes an agent will exceed his authority, but it is always open to the principal to ratify the unauthorized act and thus make it legally binding upon him.
- *Breach of warranty of authority.* In acting with third parties the agent holds himself out as authorized to act for his principal. If this proves to be untrue, and he acts outside his authority, the disappointed third party may sue the agent for breach of warranty of authority.
- *The duties of the agent to the principal.*
- *The duties of the principal to the agent.*
- *The agent as servant, or as independent contractor.* Sometimes servants act as agents of their employers. Other agents are not servants, but independent contractors acting for a principal, but not under the principal's direct control.
- *The doctrine of the undisclosed principal.* Sometimes a principal requires the agent to keep the principal's identity a secret. This presents special problems, and rules have evolved to deal with them.
- *The termination of the agency.* Agencies come to an end in a variety of ways. One is express revocation of the agency by the principal. Agency of necessity comes to an end when the emergency – whatever it was – is over.

All these matters need careful study, and are dealt with below. Before considering them there is an important new body of law arising from the *European Directive on Agent–principal Relationships*. This was drawn up in 1986 and is dated at 18 December 1986, but it took effect on 1 January 1994. A full account of it is given in Section 13.11 below.

13.2 The appointment of agents

Agency relationships can start in a variety of ways. For convenience they are grouped here under the general heading of 'appointments' but not all agency relationships involve a formal or informal appointment of the agent by the principal. If I have your strawberries on my lorry and am unable to reach the market because of floods, I may become your agent of necessity, authorized to do whatever is necessary to ensure that they fetch a reasonable price and do not rot for lack of attention.

The most common types of relationship are as follows:

13.2.1 Express authority

Express authority is given by the principal to the agent. The relationship between a principal and an agent is a contractual relationship. It follows that the parties to it must have the capacity to contract if the relationships between them are to be enforceable. Taking the more usual circumstances, where a principal with full capacity to contract appoints an agent, who also has full capacity to contract, to act for him in some matter, how is the appointment made? No formal appointment is necessary in most cases. An oral appointment will do, even if the agent is to make contracts which by law must be expressed in writing (for example, guarantees). The chief exceptions to this rule about lack of formality are:

- Where the agent is to be authorized to make contracts which are required to be made under seal, the agent's appointment must also be under seal. The actual authority given to such an agent is referred to as the **'power of attorney'**. The law requires certain transactions such as conveyances, legal mortgages and most leases to be by way of a deed. The rules about powers of attorney are laid down in the *Powers of Attorney Act, 1971*. Under the *Enduring Power of Attorney Act, 1985* powers can be given by a donor in a prescribed form and this authority is not relinquished as a result of any subsequent mental incapacity of the donor. The powers are required to be registered with the Court of Protection (an office of the High Court) which has the competence to direct matters in the event of mental incapacity of the donor.
- A statute may require that an agent is appointed in writing. Thus Section 10 of the *Companies Act, 1985*, with regard to the appointment of directors and first secretaries says that if the document required to be registered with the Registrar is provided by an agent for the subscribers to the memorandum it must contain a statement specifying that fact, and giving the agent's name and address. Thus an oral appointment without a written acknowledgement in the registration document would not do.

13.2.2 Implied authority

The term 'implied' in law is the opposite of 'express'. The authority follows not from an express statement in front of witnesses, or a written statement or a formal declaration (in a deed) but from the look of the thing. If I repeatedly send my servant to collect goods from A and in due course settle A's account from time to time, the servant has an implied authority to collect goods from A on my behalf. If I decide to discontinue the man's employment I must not just assume that he will cease to collect goods. I must notify A that the servant is no longer entitled to collect goods on my behalf. Until the implied authority I have conferred on the man is countermanded by an express revocation of authority I shall be liable if he dishonestly obtains further supplies ostensibly on my behalf. The implication is that the servant is my agent and I shall be estopped from denying the fact of this agency (*Ryan v. Pilkington (1959)*).

Similarly, a manager frequently is taken to have implied authority to make contracts on behalf of his employers. It is also unwise to allow letterheads to be in full circulation in an office, where copies could be used by unauthorized persons who would appear, by the use of the letterhead, to have authority.

An example of implied authority is the following case:

> ### Australia and New Zealand Bank v. Ateliers de Constructions Electriques de Charleroi (1966)
>
> The Australian agent of the Belgian company had been in the habit of paying large sums of the company's money into his personal bank account at the Australia and New Zealand Bank. The Belgian company had no bank account in Australia, and had made no previous enquiries about the agent's method of receiving money and making remittances to them. When they did discover how things were being arranged they made no complaint, until the agent went into liquidation and a large sum due to the Belgian company could not be paid. They then sued the bank for conversion of cheques made out to the Belgian company and endorsed and paid into the agent's personal account. The agent had authority to bank cash received in his own account, but had no express authority to bank cheques. **Held**: the Privy Council held that authority could be implied in the agent, and the Belgian company failed in its action.

A particular case of implied authority is agency by **estoppel**. The word 'estoppel' means that a person is prevented from taking a particular course of action because of a previous faulty action of his own. Suppose that a person has allowed another to believe that a certain state of affairs exists, with the result that there is reliance upon such belief. He cannot afterwards be allowed to say that the true state of affairs was far different, if to do so would involve the other person suffering some kind of detriment. Applied to agency this means that a person who by words or conduct has allowed another to appear to the outside world to be his agent, with the result that third parties deal with him as an agent, cannot afterwards repudiate this apparent agency if to do so would cause harm to the third parties. He is treated as being in the same position as if he had in fact authorized the agent to act in the way he had done. Slade, J, in *Rama Corporation v. Proved Tin and General Investment Ltd (1952)*, summed up the requirements for agency by estoppel as follows:

- *A representation.* There must be some statement or conduct on the part of the principal which can amount to a representation that the agent has authority to act on his behalf in the way he is acting.
- *A reliance on the representation.* The representation must be made to the person who relies upon it. This means that it must be made either to the

particular individual who transacts business with the agent, or to the public at large in circumstances in which it is to be expected that the general public would be likely to transact business with the agent.
- *Suffering or 'detriment'*. There must be a suffering or 'detriment' as a result of a change in position because of faith in the representation.

If these requirements are present the principal will be estopped from denying that the agent had authority to act on his behalf. Suppose a partnership has over a period transacted business with a supplier. The partners then quarrel and cease to trade in partnership, but the active partner keeps the name of both partners over the premises and continues to use the partnership letterhead. Suppose now that the non-active partner orders goods from the supplier ostensibly for use in the business. The active partner will be estopped from denying that the purchase has been made on behalf of the business, for he has 'held his former partner out' as being an agent of the firm. An example of estoppel is the following case:

Henderson & Co. v. Williams (1895)

The plaintiffs were sugar merchants and the defendant a warehouseman. The owner of goods lying in the warehouse was induced by the fraud of one Fletcher to instruct the defendant to transfer the goods to the order of Fletcher and the goods were accordingly placed at his disposal. Fletcher sold the goods to innocent purchasers, the plaintiffs, but when Fletcher's fraud was discovered the defendant refused to deliver the goods to the plaintiffs. **Held**: the plaintiffs' action for damages would succeed. The original owners had enabled Fletcher to hold himself out as owner of the goods in such a way as to induce the plaintiffs to enter into a contract and the defendant was estopped from afterwards denying Fletcher's title to the goods. (Courtesy of *Cracknell's Law Students' Companion*)

13.2.3 Agency of necessity

As the name implies, agency of necessity arises out of exceptional circumstances – for example, accidents, fires, flooding, etc. In the commercial field it may be that perishable cargoes are threatened by such developments as strikes, power failures, natural disasters, etc. The emergency must be a genuine one, and actually threaten the goods. It must also be impossible to contact the principal in time to secure proper authority. Thus, in these days of instantaneous communication, it is usually possible to contact the owner of goods by telephone or fax and seek authority for the course of action proposed.

In *Great Northern Railway v. Swaffield* (1874) a horse arrived at a station and there was no one to receive it. The railway company incurred livery stable expenses in accommodating the animal overnight, and were held entitled to recover these charges as agents of necessity.

In *Springer v. Great Western Railway* (1921) the plaintiffs were the owners of tomatoes delayed in Weymouth by a rail strike. The railway's traffic agent decided to sell the whole consignment locally since he believed they could not have reached Covent Garden market in saleable condition. The plaintiffs argued that had the traffic agent contacted them they would have moved the goods by road, and earned the high prices prevailing due to the rail strike. **Held**: There was no agency of necessity, since the traffic agent could easily have communicated with the owners and taken instructions. Damages awarded to the plaintiff.

13.2.4 Agency of the wife

Although usually referred to as agency of the wife, this class of agencies springs from the relationship of a man with those living in the same house, and could equally apply to a common law wife, a housekeeper or a servant. Where a husband actually authorizes a wife to buy goods needed by the family (real authority) or habitually pays for such goods and therefore gives the tradesmen the impression that she has authority (apparent authority) or manifestly cohabits with her (implied authority) the wife will be the agent of her husband.

These authorities may be removed by the husband either by giving notice to traders with whom the wife has had dealings, or by a general notice in the press which is effective against all traders. There is no implied authority where the husband has specifically forbidden his wife to pledge his credit, or where she is adequately provided for or has an adequate allowance. A separated wife has no authority to pledge her husband's credit if she has adequate private means, or is adequately provided for. Third parties must therefore be cautious when assuming that a husband will always stand as principal for the wife's transactions. The assumption may not be well founded.

13.3 The nature of contracts made under agency

When contracts are made by agents on behalf of their principals a triangular relationship results which has legal implications for the three parties. This is most simply illustrated in diagrammatic form, as in Figure 13.1. A note of explanation appears below the diagram.

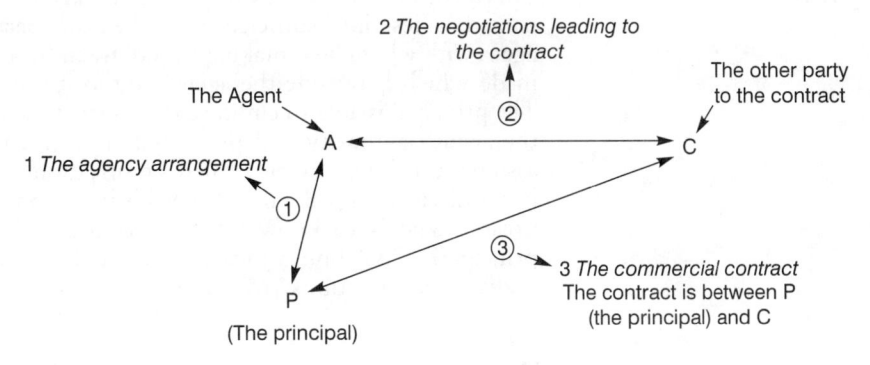

2 The negotiations leading to the contract

The Agent — A

1 The agency arrangement

① ②

C — The other party to the contract

③

P (The principal)

3 The commercial contract
The contract is between P (the principal) and C

Notes
(a) The arrangement is a triangular one in which A, the agent, arranges a contract between P, his principal, and C. (C may be a customer, or a supplier, or the owner of property or a person who performs a service.)
(b) The link between A and P is that of agent and principal. P has appointed A to act for him and their respective rights and duties follow from the appointment. The link is partly contractual and partly fiduciary – a matter of trust between them. The relationship between them is of a confidential nature, and there are other rights and duties between them besides those that follow from the contractual arrangement they have made with one another.
(c) The link between A and C is a nebulous one, since A is acting for P and any contract that results will be between P and C. In acting as agent, A warrants that he has authority, and if this proves to be untrue because A has acted outside his authority C will be disappointed and unable to enforce the contract against P. In this situation C will sue A for breach of warranty of authority. This is explained more fully later in this chapter.
(d) The link between P and C is a binding contract. A has arranged the contract, but the parties to it are P and C. In any dispute about it P will sue C, or C will sue P, but A is not involved in any way. The intermediary drops out of the dispute, leaving the parties to the contract confronting one another.

Figure 13.1 A simple agency arrangement

13.4 Subsequent ratification of an unauthorized act

An agent will usually act within his authority, but if the relationship with his principal is well established he may occasionally act outside it, if he feels that the principal will subsequently ratify it. Imagine A, who is authorized to act for P in the purchase of pre-Columbian artefacts, to a limit of £2500. A particularly beautiful example of Inca gold work is auctioned and although the price climbs above £2500 he continues to bid and secures it for £2900. The principal would be perfectly entitled to reject the artefact, but in fact he ratifies the purchase and adds it to his collection. The unauthorized act has been ratified subsequently, making the contract sound.

The effects of subsequent ratification are as follows:

- The principal and the third party are now in contractual relations with one another and may sue and be sued on the contract.
- The agent cannot be sued by the third party for breach of warranty of authority, for his act has been accorded full authority.
- The principal cannot claim that the agent has exceeded his authority, for the principal has extended the authority far enough to cover the action on *this* occasion.
- The ratification only applies to the act already done, and does not extend the authority to cover a repetition of the act – which would be outside the agent's authority again.
- The agent will be entitled to his remuneration and to indemnity for the expenses incurred.

Some rules about ratification are as follows:

13.4.1

The agent must contract expressly as an agent for a principal who is either named or described sufficiently for the other party to know that it is not the agent with whom he is making the contract. In such circumstances a contract made which is outside the agent's authority may be ratified subsequently. The principal is able to embrace the contract which his former limitation on the agent's authority had prevented, and he enjoys the benefits of it and assumes the duties under it. Such a ratification is not possible if the principal is not disclosed, for if a man keeps his intention to act 'locked up in his own breast', who is to know whether he did in fact act for the undisclosed principal? 'Civil obligations are not to be created by, or founded upon, undisclosed intentions.' (*Keighley Maxstead and Co. v. Durrant (1901)*.)

13.4.2

The principal must exist when the contract is made. It is not possible for an act to be ratified subsequently if the principal did not exist at the time of the act. This frequently presents difficulties when a company is formed to take over an existing business. The benefits of the old business can only be secured for the new business if a management appointed in the interim period carries on the business until the legal formalities can be complete. At the moment of incorporation the company cannot ratify the acts done before incorporation to make them valid, nor can it accept as profits the profits earned in the interim period. The management which has been continuing the business is deemed to have acted as principal, and must make a contract with the new company to hand over its affairs. The profits made in the interim period must be treated as part of the capital transaction on taking over the business and they become part of the capital reserves, which are not available for distribution as profits to the shareholders. They are known as 'profits prior to incorporation'.

13.4.3	In *Kelner v. Baxter (1866)* the proposed directors of a company which had not yet been registered took delivery of wine purported to be sold to the company. They were held liable as principals, since the agents' acts could not be ratified subsequently. Having received the wine, they must pay for it. However, this case was subsequently distinguished by Lord Goddard from a case where the goods had not been delivered. In *Newborne v. Sensolid (Great Britain) Ltd (1954)* Lord Goddard held that a contract made with a non-registered projected company was a nullity, and not susceptible of subsequent ratification. Therefore the person who had signed quite clearly as the representative of the company and who had made it clear that he was not personally a party, could not be forced to accept the goods by the disappointed 'seller'. The situation has now been clarified (but perhaps not improved) by Section 36(4) of the *Companies Act, 1985*, which consolidates the rules of the *European Communities Act, 1972* into company law. It renders the agent liable for contracts made on behalf of an unformed company. This obviously protects innocent third parties, but leans over backwards in their favour. The agent therefore carries a serious personal responsibility in these situations and must be sure that his principal (presumably an intending director) is a worthy individual able to afford to honour the obligations entered into.
13.4.4	The principal must have capacity to contract at the time the act was done by an agent. In *Boston Deep Sea Fishing & Ice Co. Ltd v. Farnham (1957)* the case concerned the tax liability of an English company which was acting as an agent for a French company during the war. It was held that the English company was liable to pay tax locally on the profits accruing to the business, unless the French company as principals could ratify the English company's actions. This the French company could not do as it was considered an alien enemy during the period of the war and lacked capacity to contract.
13.4.5	Subsequent ratification will be implied if a principal who has been informed of an act outside the agent's authority takes no action to reject the bargain made. If he uses goods obtained this will imply ratification of the act which procured them.
13.4.6	Ratification must be of the whole contract, and not just the beneficial parts. The principal ratifies what the agent has done in its entirety. If this were not so, the other party would be left with something less than the bargain he thought he had concluded with the agent.
13.5 **Breach of warranty** **of authority**	An agent who purports to act on behalf of another impliedly warrants that he has the authority to make binding contracts on behalf of his principal. Remember that a warranty is an undertaking which, if broken, can lead to a claim for damages at the suit of the aggrieved party. It follows that if an agent acts without authority, so that there is no contract between his principal and the third party concerned, this third party will be entitled to bring an action for 'breach of implied warranty of authority' against the agent, provided the third party did not know of the lack of authority and has suffered loss as a result. This action is said to be quasi-contractual (*quasi* = almost). It cannot be brought in contract law, because there is no contract between A and C.

The agent's liability is said to be 'strict' – a term which means that he is liable even if he fully believed he had authority, or if the authority had been terminated without his knowledge by some circumstance such as the death or insanity of his principal (*Yonge v. Toynbee, (1910)*).

13.6 The duties of the agent

The relationship between principals and agents is a fiduciary relationship (a relationship based on trust). McCardie, J, pointed out in *Armstrong v. Jackson (1917)* that the position of agent is confidential and readily lends itself to abuse. To meet this special situation the behaviour of the agent must be above reproach, and conform to strict rules. The duties of an agent may be listed as follows:

- To perform his duties in person, using ordinary skill and diligence, or if he purports to have special skills using those special skills as well. The rule which requires the agent to act personally is '*delegatus non potest delegare*' (a delegate cannot delegate). For example, it was held in *John McCann & Co. v. Pow (1974)* that a person who had been appointed a sole agent had no implied authority to appoint a sub-agent. However, this rule is relaxed to permit the agent to delegate for normal business reasons – for example, to a clerk or secretary: he does not have to do everything himself.
- To obey the lawful instructions of his principal, and in so far as he is not instructed on any particular point to act in the principal's best interests. If he fails to act in the best interests of his principal he will be liable to the principal for any loss that is suffered.
- To disclose to the principal all details of the agency, avoiding any conflict of interest with his principal. Thus, unless the principal was fully aware and agreeable to the situation, an agent may not buy the property of the principal.
- To maintain confidentiality about any matters communicated to him as agent, and not to disclose them to prospective third parties or anyone else. The relationship between principal and agent is a fiduciary relationship, depending upon mutual trust.
- To keep proper accounts of all transactions and render them to the principal on request. This includes a duty to keep the principal's property separate. Any failure to do so will raise a presumption that the property is the principal's, and it will be necessary for the agent to prove his ownership of any particular item, or of any money in a mixed account.
- To avoid any secret profits from the transaction. If the agency results in extra profits they must be disclosed to the principal.

13.7 The duties of the principal

The principal's duties may be listed as follows:

13.7.1 Duty to pay the agreed remuneration

A duty to pay the agreed commission or remuneration following from the contract. Where the remuneration is expressly stated it will be payable according to the contract. Where it is not expressly stated the court may imply that payment was intended in order to make the agency effective. This means that if the court holds that the parties could not possibly have intended the agent to act gratuitously, then payment must have been intended and this intention will be implied. The remuneration will then be what is reasonable in the circumstances.

The courts will not override the terms agreed between the parties, even if the terms are extremely unfavourable to one party. Thus where it was agreed that the directors should determine the sum payable, and they failed to determine that any sum was payable, it was held that no remuneration could be claimed (*Re Richmond Gate Property Co. Ltd (1964)*).

13.7.2 Duty to reimburse the agent for expenses

The principal has a duty to reimburse the agent for any expenses, losses or liabilities incurred as a result of the agency. This duty may arise from an express term in the contract or from a term which the court will imply in order to make the agency effective. This duty will require the principal to indemnify the agent for all expenses incurred by the agent acting within the scope of his authority, both actual authority and implied authority. Thus expenses or liabilities incurred as a result of some 'custom of the trade', known to the principal, must be reimbursed to the agent appointed to act for him. The test is whether the principal, had he acted for himself, would have incurred those same costs or liabilities.

The duty does not extend to circumstances where the agent acts outside his authority, or acts negligently or wrongly having failed to exercise the skills he purported to have. Nor will the agent be able to claim reimbursement of expenses incurred when acting in an illegal way.

13.7.3 Agent's commission

The question whether a principal has a duty not to prevent the agent from earning his commission is one that has exercised the courts to a considerable extent. Usually such cases arise in connection with the work of estate agents, where a principal may sell privately and thus prevent the agent earning his commission. The rule is that if such a term is expressed in the contract, or may be implied, the agent may sue his principal for the commission, but the courts will be unwilling to imply such a term (that the principal agrees not to do anything which prevents the agent from earning his commission) unless it is essential to give the contract business efficacy. Most contracts to sell property already have business efficacy without such a clause. The agent agrees to act to try to sell the property for the principal, and if he succeeds a commission will be earned. If the agent wishes to put in a more onerous clause, let him do so; he cannot normally expect the court to imply one for him. This illustrates two very important aspects of English law:

- Words do not always convey a correct impression – in this case the terms 'principal' and 'agent' given an impression that the principal is the stronger of the two. While this is true as far as contractual responsibility occurs, the principal (especially in the sale of landed property) is often less sophisticated than the agent, who handles such transactions every day. It is the agent who lays down the terms of the bargain between them. If he states those terms less clearly than he intended, so much the worse for him.
- In interpreting contracts the courts will always interpret them strictly against the one who drew the contract up. This means they will interpret any clause in favour of this person in the narrower sense, rather than the wider sense. If the agent wishes to be paid commission whether the sale results from his own work or is the result of the principal's private efforts, let him say so in the contract. If he does not say so expressly, he cannot look to the courts to imply it. This is called the 'contra proferentem' rule.

13.8 The agent as servant or independent contractor

An employee frequently acts as an agent for his employer in the course of his employment, and as a result is in a dual capacity; he is both a servant of, and an agent for, the employer. This is important in certain circumstances because an employer is **vicariously liable** for the torts of his employees. The term 'vicariously liable' derives from the Latin (*vicarius* = substitute). The employer is required to substitute himself for the wrongdoer, his servant, as he is generally a more worthy target for a legal action than the servant. The classic case is *Lloyd v. Grace Smith*; the facts were as follows:

> *Lloyd v. Grace, Smith & Co.* (1912)
>
> The appellant, a widow, sought advice from the respondents, a firm of solicitors of high repute, and in fact saw one Sandles, a managing clerk who conducted their conveyancing work without supervision. Sandles advised the appellant to sell two cottages and induced her to sign two documents which he said would enable the properties to be sold. The documents were in fact conveyances to Sandles and he dishonestly proceeded to dispose of the cottages to his advantage. Held: although the fraud was not committed for the benefit of the respondents, they were liable as Sandles had acted in the course of his employment. (Courtesy of *Cracknell's Law Students' Companion*)

The test is whether the servant performed the tort in the course of the employment, and to this extent the matter is really one for the law of master and servant and not the law of agency. The fact that the employee acts as an agent is incidental.

Where the person is an independent contractor, and definitely not the servant of the principal, the principal will not be liable for the torts, and the independent contractor will be the target for legal action brought by any aggrieved person. The test as to whether a person is an independent contractor or not is the question: 'Is this person instructed not only what to do, but how to do it?' If the individual is under the detailed control of the principal as to the manner in which he performs the work concerned he is probably a servant of the principal. If he is instructed what to do, but himself determines completely the manner in which the work should be done and the order of priority to be used between various tasks, he is probably an independent contractor. See *Mersey Docks and Harbour Board v. Coggins* the classic case on this point.

However, the principle outlined above, 'the control test', has been developed by the Court of Appeal ruling in *Lane v. Shire Roofing Co. (Oxford) Ltd* (1995). Mr Lane, a sole trader did building jobs on his own account when he could get them, but at other times he helped Shire Roofing Co. (Oxford) Ltd when they could offer him work. He was seriously injured in an accident and the trial judge ruled that as an independent contractor he could not claim damages. The Court of Appeal extended the test, to decide whether Mr Lane was an employee by asking 'Whose work was it, anyway?' Was it Mr Lane's work or was it one of Shire Roofing Co.'s jobs? Clearly the business was not Mr Lane's, and he was therefore an employee, and entitled to damages.

13.9 The doctrine of the undisclosed principal

Where an agent acts on behalf of a principal three possible situations may exist as to the arrangements between the agent and third parties:

- The agent may say 'In this matter I am acting for B, who is interested in ...' etc. In this situation the third party knows who the other principal is, and is not under any illusions that he is contracting with the agent, for the agent has declared his agency.
- The agent may say 'In this matter I am acting on behalf of a principal, who wishes to remain anonymous.' Here again the third party knows that the agent is acting for someone else, and is not personally a party to any contract that may be concluded. The unsatisfactory part of this situation is that the third party does not know who the other principal is. It may be a little old lady of 90, with nothing but an old-age pension as resources. It may be the most powerful multinational in the country.
- The agent may not say anything at all about his agency, and lead the third party to conclude that he is contracting with a principal. In this situation, should anything go wrong, the third party may find that when he sues on the contract the person he believed to be principal says 'I was only acting as an agent; you must sue X.' The third party may then discover that X is a person of no resources, or (perhaps worse) is the most powerful multinational in the land.

The question arises whether it is fair for this undisclosed principal to become a party to a contract with a person who was ignorant of his existence at the time the contract was made. The courts have justified the view that it is fair, on the grounds of commercial expedience. In many contracts the parties do not mind who assumes the rights and duties upon the contract so long as the bargain made is honoured in every detail. To this extent it would contradict the principle that 'the courts will always uphold the reasonable expectations of businessmen' if the undisclosed principal was not allowed to step in and assume the benefits of, and the duties upon, the contract.

The doctrine of the undisclosed principal holds that where a person has contracted in his own name **in general terms** he may subsequently introduce oral evidence to prove that in fact he did not act on his own behalf but on behalf of some undisclosed principal. The phrase 'in general terms' means that he did not expressly state that he was the real and only principal. If the contract was made in terms which exclude the possibility of any other party being the principal, the undisclosed principal will not be allowed to enforce the contract. For example:

- Where the agent contracts as 'owner', a word without ambiguity, oral evidence cannot be admitted to vary the written evidence. In *Humble v. Hunter* (1848) an agent signed a charterparty in his own name, describing himself as **owner of the ship**. It was held that his undisclosed principal could not sue. If the agent contracts in some more general way – such as 'as a party interested in the ownership of ..., etc.' – the oral evidence would have been permissible to explain the ambiguous term used.
- Where the personality of the parties is important – as where a particular skill is required and the third party contracted with the agent for the use of the agent's personal skills – the agent cannot then claim that he acted on behalf of another.

- Where the third party expressly inquired whether the agent acted for a particular third party, and was misled by a statement to the contrary, the undisclosed principal will not be allowed to enforce specific performance of the contract.

In *Said v. Butt* (*1920*) the defendant had specifically asked the agent whether he acted on behalf of Said, and had been told that he did not. A long-standing dispute between Said and Butt had led Butt (a theatre owner) to regard Said's presence at a 'first night' performance as undesirable. It was held that Said's action must fail; the 'personal element' was strong and Butt had no intention of entering into a contract with the undisclosed principal, who consequently could not intervene.

In all cases where the agent has acted in a manner which is not totally inconsistent with behaviour as an agent, the true principal may emerge from the shadows and exert his rights upon, and assume the duties under, the contract.

In insurance cases it has been held that a policy of insurance is a personal matter, and that the doctrine of the undisclosed principal cannot apply, because it would not be fair for a totally unknown individual to step out of the shadows and claim under the policy. This may certainly be true in life assurance, but it need not be true in all branches of insurance, particularly indemnity insurance, where cover is often arranged by an agent for employers, and so long as it is the employer's situation which is described to the underwriter, the fact that he has not been named makes no difference to the cover provided. In the Hong Kong case of *Sui Yin Kwan v. Eastern Insurance Co. Ltd* (*1994*) *1All ER, 213*, a firm of shipping agents had arranged employer's liability insurance for a firm called Axelson Co. Ltd. Some employees were killed in circumstances which justified a claim but before it could be made Axelson Ltd went into liquidation. Under the Hong Kong law the claimants were entitled to claim directly from the insurance company but it resisted the claim on the grounds that the name of the principal, Axelson Co. Ltd, had not been disclosed. The Privy Council rejected this argument and gave its opinion that an indemnity insurance policy could never be so personal as to deny the doctrine of the undisclosed principal.

Further aspects of these matters are the legal effects that follow from an undisclosed agency. Until the principal is revealed the third party believes the agent to be the principal and may sue the agent. When the true principal is revealed the third party has a right to elect whom he will sue. He will naturally sue the most worthy, and this may not be the principal. If sued by the true principal the third party may set off against the claim all sums owed by the agent, and may use any defences available to him against the agent as defences against the principal.

13.10 The termination of agency

An agency may be terminated in the following ways:

13.10.1 By complete performance of the agent's function

Thus when an estate agent appointed to sell a property completes the sale the agency comes to an end and the commission or other remuneration is paid.

13.10.2 By effluxion of time, when the agency is for a fixed term

Normally a fixed-term appointment is a matter of express agreement between the parties. It is convenient where the parties are uncertain of one another's abilities, or where inflation may erode the arrangements made for remuneration. The expiry of the term gives an opportunity for reappraisal and restatement of the terms of the appointment.

13.10.3 By voluntary discharge of the agency arrangement

This occurs when the parties agree to discontinue the relationship.

13.10.4 By revocation or renunciation

Generally speaking, if the principal gives notice to the agent of his intention to revoke the agency, or if the agent gives notice that he renounces the agency, the agency comes to an end. However, there are special cases where an agency is irrevocable on the part of the principal. For example, where the authority is coupled with an interest having been given to the agent in order that the agent may recover some loss previously suffered or some debt owed to him, the principal cannot revoke the agency. The fact that the authority was granted to benefit the donee in some particular way – and not just by earning a fee or commission for services rendered – means that it would be inequitable to allow the principal to revoke the agency.

13.10.5 By the death or bankruptcy of either party

Agency is a personal contract between agent and principal and except in those cases where the agency is irrevocable the death of either party ends the contract between them. The death of the principal terminates the agent's authority, and even if he is not aware of the death, any subsequent acts on behalf of the principal will lack authority. The agent may still claim from the estate for services rendered before the death occurred, but will not be entitled to commission on services rendered after death, unless the executors subsequently ratify the agent's acts.

Similarly, the bankruptcy of either party normally brings an agency relationship to an end. Bankruptcy is a form of incapacity which precludes the bankrupt from making further contracts, and consequently brings the agency to an end whichever party is affected.

13.10.6 By the mental disorder of either party

The mental disorder of either party automatically ends the agency relationship. A mentally disordered agent can no longer act for his principal while a principal in the same situation is held to be unable to act for himself, and therefore unable to act through an agent. These rules do not present any difficulties, but difficulties can arise where an agent who acts for his principal who has become mentally disordered contracts on the principal's behalf with third parties who are unaware of the principal's disability. In such circumstances the law is somewhat unclear, and is under review at present. The agent has been held, in *Yonge v. Toynbee (1910)*, to be liable for breach of warranty of authority, for in acting for the principal who had become insane they had impliedly warranted that they had authority. An earlier case, *Drew v. Nunn (1879)*, concerned a principal whose wife had purchased goods as his agent during his temporary insanity. It was held that the principal could not claim that his wife's agency ceased entirely on the commencement of his insanity. Though her actual authority had ceased, she still had apparent authority to bind the principal.

13.10.7 By frustration

As with all other contracts, an agency contract is liable to be frustrated by supervening events. Thus where the contract is rendered illegal, or impossible of performance, the agency comes to an end (see Chapter 11 for the doctrine of frustration).

The effects of termination In general, the effects of termination are that the agent's actual authority ceases at once and he may no longer act for the principal. He may claim commission on work already performed before termination.

As explained in Figure 13.1, the agency arrangement is a three-cornered one, in which third parties are brought into legal relationship with the principal as a result of the agent's action. The termination of the agency must be brought to the notice of third parties either known to be involved in negotiations with the agent or potentially likely to be involved. If the principal fails to give notice to third parties, or holds his agent out as having authority in any way on letterheads or similar documents, he will be liable to third parties who are misled.

13.11 The European directive on agent–principal relationships

As part of the procedures for ensuring a level playing field in European Union trading the European Union has harmonized the legal position of agents and principals throughout the Union and the new rules took effect on 1 January 1994.

For the purpose of the directive a commercial agent is defined as a self-employed intermediary who has authority to negotiate the sale or purchase of goods on behalf of another person – the principal. The term does not include an officer of a company acting for his/her company, or a partner acting on behalf of a partnership, or a receiver or liquidator acting in the disposal of a bankrupt's property, or the property of a company in the course of liquidation.

13.11.1 The duties of the agent

In general the agent must act dutifully, in good faith, looking after the interests of the principal and in particular must make proper efforts to negotiate and conclude the transactions he has been asked to handle, keeping the principal informed of all necessary developments and complying with all reasonable instructions.

13.11.2 The duties of the principal

In general the principal must also act dutifully in good faith, and in particular must provide the agent with any necessary documentation and keep the agent informed of his acceptance, refusal or non-execution of any transaction arranged by the agent. He must also forewarn the agent of any falling-off in the level of business to be expected. The parties cannot derogate from the above general requirements.

13.11.3 Remuneration

It is in the remuneration field where the directive has its strongest impact, and improves the agent's situation relative to the principal's situation. The rules are as follows:

Article 6 The agent shall be entitled to the remuneration that commercial agents customarily receive in the place where the agency activities are carried on. If there are no such customary practices an agent must be entitled to a reasonable remuneration. If the reward varies with the volume or value of transactions it is deemed to be commission. This is an important term because Articles 7–12 have important rules regarding commission.

Article 7 The agent shall be entitled to commission during the course of the agency where he/she has arranged the transaction or where the transaction has been concluded with a third party whom the agent secured as a customer at an earlier date.

He/she shall also be entitled to commission on transactions concluded during the period of the agency contract either where he/she is entrusted with a particular geographical area, or group of customers, or where he/she has an exclusive right to a specific geographical area or group of customers.

Article 8 In this article the rights of the agent are extended; the agent being entitled to commission after the agency contract has terminated, if the transaction is mainly attributable to the agent's work while the contract existed, and if the transaction occurred within a reasonable period after termination.

Article 9 Says that a new agent shall not be entitled to a commission if the order is attributable to the previous agent's work, unless it is equitable for the commission to be shared between the agents because of the circumstances.

Article 10 This article deals with the payment of the commission. It becomes payable when the transaction has been executed by the principal or the third party, and is payable before the last day of the month following the end of the quarter when the commission was earned. The parties cannot agree to derogate from this article to the detriment of the agent.

Article 11 Commission cannot be extinguished unless the contract between the principal and the third party is not executed for a reason which is not the fault of the principal. If the fault lies with the third party the agent who introduced the third party loses the commission and must return it if it has been paid.

Article 12 The principal must supply a statement of the commission due by the last day of the month following the end of the quarter when it was earned, and the agent is entitled to demand an extract from the books to check the amount of the commission due. Again, this article cannot be derogated from to the detriment of the agent.

Article 13 Entitles either party to receive from the other on request a signed, written document stating the terms of the agency contract including any other terms subsequently agreed. These measures appear to give the agent a much more favourable legal situation than agents (at least in the United Kingdom) have enjoyed in the past, particularly with regard to remuneration.

The remaining articles in the directive deal with the termination of the agency. They read as follows:

Article 14 If an agency contract for a fixed period is continued after the period has expired it shall be deemed to be converted into an agency contract for an indefinite period.

Article 15 When an agency contract is concluded for an indefinite period either party may terminate it by giving notice. The period of notice is 1 month for the first year, 2 months for the second year and 3 months for the third year (and subsequent years). The parties may not agree to a shorter period of notice. At the discretion of member states notice may be extended up to 6 months for a 6 year contract (and for all subsequent years).

Where the parties agree on longer periods of notice than this the rule is that the period of notice to be observed by the principal may not be shorter than the period to be observed by the agent.

Article 16 says that this directive shall not affect the law of member states where the latter provides for the immediate termination of the agency because (a) of the failure of one party to carry out all or part of his/her obligations, or (b) where exceptional circumstances arise.

Article 17 The member states, in introducing legislation to implement the directive, are to ensure that the commercial agent is indemnified or compensated (as the case may be) in the manner shown below. The reader will note that the treatment accorded takes account of the agent's expenditure in setting up the agency.

(i) If the agent has brought the principal a significantly increased volume of business, which will continue for some time into the future, the agent is entitled to an indemnity. The amount paid should be an equitable amount in view of the agent's loss of commission. It may be further increased if a restraint of trade clause (see Article 20) is to be included in the arrangements for termination.

(ii) The amount would not normally exceed one year's commission calculated as an average over the last five years (or if the agency has not lasted five years the average over the period of the agency). Being given an indemnity does not rule out compensation for damages as well.

(iii) Compensation will be payable if the termination means the loss of commission by the agent or if it means he/she has not had time to amortize the capital expenditure incurred to open the agency. Amortization is the writing off of values out of profits earned – if the agency is terminated unfairly the agent does not have time to earn the profits to write off the assets. Consequently he/she is entitled to compensation.

If the agent dies the indemnity and compensation is still payable and becomes part of the agent's estate.

Article 18 The indemnity and compensation does not become due if the termination results from default attributable to the agent which would justify termination under the national law of the country concerned. If the agent terminates the agreement the indemnity and compensation are not payable unless the fault lies with the principal, or the agent can claim age, infirmity or illness as the reason for termination. If the agent assigns the agency to a third party the indemnity and compensation are not payable.

Article 19 This article states that the parties may not derogate from Articles 17 and 18 to the detriment of the agent.

Article 20 Any agreement restricting the rights of the agent following termination of the agency contract is called a 'restraint of trade' clause. Such a clause is only valid if (i) it is in writing; and (ii) it relates to the geographical territory which the agent covered and the type of goods which the agent handled. Such a clause cannot be valid for more than two years.

We are familiar with clauses in restraint of trade and we can see that Article 2 of the directive is not all that different from the traditional English law. It permits a small element of restraint of trade to protect the principal, but only for a limited period after which the agent is free to pursue his/her legitimate business activities.

The European directive was adopted into English law by a Statutory Instrument S1 1993 No. 3053, *The Commercial Agents (Council Directive) Regulations 1993*. They include the detailed wording of the articles outlined above. There is also a schedule setting out clearly what kind of activities are considered to be commercial agent–principal relationships. They will be arrangements where the principal's business is the sale or purchase of particular goods, which are usually sold or purchased as a result of individual negotiations on a commercial basis – and transactions completed on one occasion are likely to lead to further transactions at a later date, or transactions with other customers in the same geographical area.

Test your knowledge

Answers	Questions
	1 What Latin rule is at the root of the law of agency?
1 *Qui facit per alium facit per se.*	2 What does it mean?
2 He who does something by another, does it himself.	3 What does this mean as far as the law of contract is concerned?
3 A principal can be brought into contractual relationships with another party as a result of the actions of his agent, and will be bound by them just as much as if he had made the contract himself.	4 What are the essential elements of agency?
4 (a) Appointment of the agent by the principal. (b) Negotiations by the agent with a third party. (c) The conclusion of a contract between the third party and the principal. (d) The agent is rewarded for his efforts. (e) Termination of the agency.	5 In what ways may one person become the agent of another?
5 (a) By express appointment. (b) By implication, as a result of repeated behaviour, or holding out of the person by the principal, to give the impression that he has appointed him. (c) By necessity – in a genuine emergency.	6 What was *Great Northern Railway v. Swaffield* (1874) about?

Answers	Questions
6 A horse arrived at a station and there was no one to meet it. The railway company lodged it at a livery stable overnight. **Held**: they were agents of necessity and were entitled to recover their charges from the consignee.	7 What is 'subsequent ratification' in the law of agency?
7 It is the ratification of an act outside the agent's authority, to bring the act within the agency arrangement. The principal who ratifies in this way is bound by the contract made as if he had authorized it originally.	8 What is 'breach of warranty of authority'?
8 An action brought against an agent by a third party who has been disappointed to discover that the agent acted outside his authority and consequently the contract he believed he had made with the agent's principal is not valid.	9 List the duties of an agent to his principal.
9 (a) To perform the duties personally, using that degree of skill he purports to have. (b) To obey the principal's instructions and to act in the best interests of the principal at all times. (c) To disclose to the principal the full facts of the agency, and avoid any conflict of interest. (d) To maintain confidence about any matters disclosed to him. (e) To keep proper accounts and not to make any secret profit. (f) To keep the principal's property separate from his own.	10 What are the duties of the principal to his agent?
10 (a) A duty to pay the agreed remuneration. (b) A duty to reimburse the agent for any expenses incurred.	11 What is the doctrine of the undisclosed principal?

Answers	Questions
11 A doctrine which holds that if an agent has contracted with third parties in general terms he may subsequently introduce oral evidence to prove that he acted for an undisclosed principal, but if he contracts expressly as principal, in terms which do not admit of any ambiguity, he will be precluded from introducing the principal at a later date.	12 How may an agency be terminated?
12 (a) By performance; (b) by effluxion of time; (c) by voluntary discharge; (d) by revocation of the authority; (e) by renunciation by the agent; (f) by death, bankruptcy or mental disorder of either party; (g) by frustration.	13 What effect have the *Commercial Agents (Council Directive) Regulations, 1993* had on agency relationships?
13 They have given agents buying and selling goods on behalf of their principals a very structured and fair system of relationships as far as pay, commission and termination of agency are concerned.	14 Go over the questions until you are sure of all the answers. Then try some of the written questions in Appendix 1.

Part Four Some Specialized Sections of Law

14 Contracts for the sale of goods

14.1 Development of the law of the sale of goods

The sale of goods is a very ancient activity. In a modern advanced society the volume of goods that changes hands daily is enormous. Raw materials flow into our factories and finished goods pour off production lines. The distribution of these goods is a science in itself (physical distribution management) and their exchange, from manufacturer to wholesaler, to retailer, to consumer is the art of commerce.

Naturally disputes arise. The law of 'sale of goods' has a long history, beginning in the merchant courts outside the national systems of laws and later becoming part of English common law under the principle that the courts will always uphold the reasonable expectations of businessmen. Later the many rules of law developed in countless cases over the years were 'codified' by Parliament into the *Sale of Goods Act, 1893*.

14.1.1 The *Sale of Goods Act, 1893*

The test of a good Act of Parliament is that it should last a great many years without major amendment. The 1893 Act was a product of its age, a carefully drawn and fully debated bill became an enduring Act embodying all the rules of law about the sale of goods. Drawn in an age of triumphant capitalism it reflected the principles of that age, that *'laisser faire'* was the wisest policy. If businessmen are largely left to themselves they will do the best both for themselves, and for the nation. Thus the rules embodied in the *Sale of Goods Act, 1893*, could be avoided by contractual stipulations called 'exemption clauses' by which the merchant stated that he exempted himself from any duties implied under the Act. Such clauses were 'fair' because the other party who did not wish to accept them was free to go elsewhere, and obtain goods from the supplier's competitors. The Victorians believed strongly that all were equal before the law, and either party to a contract was free to strike a bargain in the most favourable terms for himself. This philosophy ignores the very real inequalities in bargaining strengths between the parties – for example, between monopolists and their customers who have no chance to go elsewhere. Powerful industrialists may easily escape liability for poor-quality goods supplied to consumers – who are frequently unsophisticated, unrepresented and too poor to employ lawyers to fight cases where the actual sum of money involved is small but the loss in proportion to the individual's total income is great.

Gradually pressure developed for a change of emphasis in the law towards the protection of the consumer, and following the Moloney Commission of 1962, which made 214 recommendations for improvements in the law, a succession of Acts was passed to improve the outdated 1893 Act. Finally the *Sale of Goods Act, 1979*, consolidated the new legislation by re-enacting the 1893 Act *as amended*. That the two Acts are very similar is a tribute to the enduring work of the Victorian legislators, but the modifications reflect the social legislation of the twentieth century and the improved status of the consumer in society.

14.1.2 The *Sale of Goods Act, 1979*

This Act forms the basis of the chapter which follows. As explained above, it is a consolidating Act, which re-enacts most of the rules of the 1893 Act and the new rules of later statutes to give in a single Act all the current statutory provisions. The reader is strongly urged to obtain a copy of the Act itself, although it is extensively quoted in the chapter. It is a particularly good Act to study as an example of the legislative process. Law students must become familiar with the format of Acts of Parliament, and discover for themselves the precision achieved by the legislature even in the most complex matters. Such detailed study highlights the problems faced by the courts in construing legislation and discovering the meaning of Parliament.

14.2 The meaning of 'goods'

The *Sale of Goods Act, 1979*, does not define 'goods', but in Section 61, the 'interpretation' section, it states:

> 'Goods' includes all personal chattels other than things in action and money.

Chattels are items of property, and in law they are divided into 'chattels real' and 'chattels personal'. **Chattels real** refers to 'real estate' (landed property) which means leases of the use of land. **Chattels personal** are all other personal property. Since goods are stated to include all personal chattels other than things in action and money the list of items covered by the word 'goods' is very long – from a million tons of iron ore to a box of chocolates.

The rather awkward phrase 'things in action' means property which can only be recognized as property when it comes up for discussion in court. Thus a debt is a form of property which has no physical existence, though it may be represented by a piece of paper like an IOU or a promissory note. I may sell my debts to a debt collector – but it will not be a sale of 'goods'. 'Things in action' have traditionally been called '*choses in action*' but the 1979 Act set a precedent for doing away with obscure French and Latin terms, as we shall see later.

Money is the means for settling payments, and it would be contrary to common sense to call money 'goods' and talk of 'selling it' to others.

These items aside, all personal chattels are included in the term 'goods'. This is not the end of the definition, for the Act goes on to say that emblements (crops growing on the land which will come to fruition within a year), industrial growing crops (which take longer than a year) and '*things attached to or forming part of the land, which are agreed to be severed before sale or under the contract of sale*' are goods. If I sell you my beech trees, and you fell them and take them away, I have sold you 'goods' under the Act.

14.3 The contract of sale

Section 2(1) of the Act says:

defini'tion properties: word, te definitive

> A contract for the sale of goods is a contract by which the seller transfers or agrees to transfer the property in goods to the buyer, for a money consideration called the price.

Implicit in this definition is the idea that the seller must be the owner of the goods, for no one can transfer the property in goods except the owner, or an agent acting on his behalf. The section goes on to say that there can be a contract of sale between one part-owner and another. A contract of sale may be absolute (**a sale**) or conditional upon the performance of some act, or the passage of time, in which case we have an **agreement to sell**. An agreement to sell becomes a sale after the elapse of the time or the fulfilment of the condition prescribed in the contract.

Capacity to buy and sell is regulated by the general law concerning capacity to contract (see Section 3.1) but the Act makes a special point about necessaries. Even those with no capacity to contract must be able to obtain necessaries. The Act provides that minors, drunkards and those suffering from mental incapacity must pay a reasonable price for necessaries *sold* and *delivered* to them. Consequently such people could not be forced to pay an agreed contractual price if it was an unreasonable price. Necessaries are defined as '*goods suitable to the condition in life of the minor or other person concerned, and to his actual requirements at the time of the sale and delivery*' (Section 3.3). This is of course the rule in the 'fancy waistcoats' case, *Nash v. Inman (1908)* – see page 99. Note that the minor is still not bound by the contract, so that even if goods were delivered to him he could refuse them and send them back. All that the section means is that if he takes delivery and uses the necessaries, he must then pay a reasonable price for them. A minor who is the *seller* cannot be held liable on a contract, for the general rule applies that all contracts made with minors are unenforceable against a minor during his minority, and are only enforceable after the minor reaches the age of 18 if he ratifies the contract.

14.3.1 The form of the contract

There is no special form for contracts of sale, unless required by some Act of Parliament – as, for example, the hire purchase regulations. Ordinary sales contracts may be made by word of mouth, in writing (with or without seal), partly in writing and partly by word of mouth and may be implied from the conduct of the parties.

The following contracts are not contracts of sale:

- *A contract of barter or exchange.* Since the definition of a sale refers to the payment of a 'price', a simple exchange of goods is not a sale of goods. However, since part-exchange is a common practice in some trades like the motor-vehicle trade, the courts have held that part-exchange is a sale if a significant proportion of the consideration is in money form.
- *A contract of hire.* Here the hirer obtains *possession* of the goods, but the property does not pass, and is not intended to pass.
- *A contract of hire purchase.* This is a contract of hire until the clause in the contract which stipulates how the hirer becomes the purchaser is fulfilled. Often this takes place on the payment of the last instalment, or on the payment of a nominal sum of money added to the final instalment. Until that moment the hirer is not the buyer, and the property does not pass, so it is not a sale of goods.
- *A contract for the use of skill and materials*, When a customer approaches a tradesman to carry out work for him, some sort of goods are usually involved. The landscape gardener who lays my patio supplies paving stones and other materials. Am I really paying for these as goods, or as a part of the work at which he is skilled and I am not? Such questions can be difficult to decide, but in general they are not sales of goods, though in some respects – for example, an obligation to supply materials of merchantable quality – they are very similar. In *Robinson v. Graves (1935)* a contract under which Robinson, an artist, was commissioned to paint a

portrait was held to be a contract for the use of skill and materials, and not a sale of goods, even though Robinson supplied the canvas etc.
- *Mortgages, pledges and charges.* Any transaction where goods are used as security for a loan are not 'sales of goods'. The 'seller' never intends to transfer the property in the goods to the person holding them as security, and the money paid is not the 'price' but the return of a loan, with interest.

14.3.2 The subject matter of the contract

In any contract for the sale of goods, the goods which are the subject matter of the contract are prone to the same hazards as all goods. The Act therefore makes several stipulations about them, in Sections 5, 6 and 7.

First, if the goods are actually in existence at the time the sale is made they are called 'existing goods'. If the contract is for the sale of goods which have yet to be manufactured or obtained, these are called 'future goods', and the contract operates as an agreement to sell.

If at the time the bargain is struck the goods in question have already perished without the knowledge of the seller (for example, they may have been lost at sea the night before), the contract is void (Section 6). For example, in *Barrow, Lane and Ballard Ltd v. Phillip, Phillip and Co. (1929)* a contract for the sale of 700 bags of groundnuts was held to be void, since, unknown to the parties, 109 bags had been stolen.

Where the goods are specific goods and the seller has agreed to sell them, but before the time for delivery arrives they perish through no fault of the seller, the contract is again rendered void (Section 7). Specific goods are goods identified at the time the contract of sale is made. Thus if I agree to sell you my Rolls-Royce next week, but it is wrecked before the time arrives, the contract is void. If I agreed to sell you 20 tonnes of wheat which I do not own, and some I am interested in is destroyed, this will not render the contract void for I can still obtain wheat elsewhere. Unless the wheat was actually identified at the time of the contract it will not be 'specific goods'.

14.3.3 The price

The definition of a sale in Section 2 specifically refers to 'a money consideration called the price'. Normally the price will be clearly fixed in the contract, or a manner for fixing it will be agreed. Thus a car might be sold according to the recommended price in a certain popular guide to the values of second-hand cars. A price may be determined by a course of dealing between the parties – though in present inflationary times this is less common than in years gone by. If no method for fixing the price is laid down, the buyer must pay a reasonable price, and this, the Act says (Section 8.3), is always a question of fact dependent on the circumstances of every case.

Section 9 says that where price is to be decided by valuation by a third party, and he cannot or does not make a valuation, the contract is void. If the goods have already been delivered to the buyer he must then pay a reasonable price.

Finally, if the third party cannot make a valuation because of the fault of either the buyer, or the seller, the disappointed party may bring an action for damages against the party at fault.

14.4 Conditions and warranties in the contract

It is this subject area of the Act which has been most subject to modification in recent years. A condition is of course a term in the contract which goes to the root of the contract. If a condition is broken it entitles the disappointed party to repudiate the contract and sue for damages. A warranty is a term in a contract which is not of the essence of the contract, but a less important term. Breach of warranty can lead to an action for damages, but the contract itself is left intact.

The sections of the Act about conditions and warranties are Sections 10–15. They are very detailed, and must be studied from the Act itself. Because certain contracts made before the 1979 Act was passed may still become the subject of disputes in the courts, certain residual features of earlier law are preserved in Schedule 1 of the Act. These features have been ignored in the following description of the Act, the rules of which may be summarized as follows:

14.4.1 The time for performance (Section 10)

Apart from the fact that the word 'month' is defined as meaning *prima facie* a calendar month, it is the terms of the contract which decide whether time for performance of the contract is of the essence or not. However, as regards payment, unless the contract stipulates that the time of payment is of the essence of the contract, it is taken not to be a condition but only a warranty.

14.4.2 Conditions treated as warranties

Those who draw up contracts do not always use the correct terminology and in any dispute it is for the courts to construe the contract. Thus a stipulation that 'It is a condition of the contract, etc.' may in fact prove to be only a warranty, while a stipulation stated to be a warranty may be found by the court to go to the root of the contract, and in fact be a condition. For example:

> *Cehave NV v. Bremer Handelsgesellschaft mbh: The Hansa Nord (1976)*
>
> A written contract stated specifically that a shipment was to be made in good condition. Some of the goods were not in good condition and the buyers rejected the goods for breach of what they held to be a condition of the contract. **Held**: the buyers could not reject the goods as only a breach of warranty had been committed; the buyers were entitled to damages only.

If a contract is conditional upon some act being performed by the seller, and he does not perform it, the buyer may waive the condition, or treat it only as a warranty, and consequently may insist that the seller fulfils the contract.

If a contract of sale is not severable into parts and the buyer has accepted the goods or part of them, the breach of a condition by the seller cannot be used by the buyer as a reason for repudiating the contract, but may only be treated as a breach of warranty, unless the contract is absolutely clear that the buyer is entitled to treat the contract as repudiated.

14.4.3 Implied terms in the contract

By Section 12 of the Act and other sections a number of important terms are implied in the contract. There is an implied condition that the seller has the right to sell, or in an agreement to sell that he *will* have the right to sell, the goods at the time when the property is to pass. Except where the seller only purports to sell such rights as he, or a third person for whom he is acting, has, there is an implied warranty that the goods are free from any charge or encumbrance not disclosed to the buyer, and will remain so. There is also an implied warranty that the buyer will enjoy **quiet possession of the goods**, other than disturbances caused by any encumbrances revealed at the time of the contract. There is an implied warranty that all the encumbrances known to the seller will be revealed to the buyer, and that neither the seller, nor any third party named, nor anyone claiming under them, will disturb the buyer's quiet possession.

This implied condition, that the seller has the right to sell, is commonly broken by someone selling goods which are not his. Very often the seller will have stolen the goods in which case he will normally not be worth suing. However, the condition is also broken when a hirer under a hire purchase agreement sells goods which are subject to the agreement. Another type of case was:

> *Niblett v. Confectioners' Materials Co. (1921)*
>
> An American firm sold to an English buyer a quantity of tins of 'Nissley Brand' condensed milk. These were detained by the Excise authorities in England as constituting an infringement of the Nestlé trade mark. The buyer was forced to remove the offending labels, and re-sold at a loss. **Held**: this constituted a breach of the condition as to title implied by what is now Section 12(1) of the *Sale of Goods Act, 1979*, and the buyer was entitled to damages. (Courtesy of *Cracknell's Law Students' Companion*)

Another interesting case, *Microbeads A.G. v. Vinhurst Road Markings (1975)*, concerned a Swiss firm who had sold road-marking machines to an English firm. It turned out that the machines infringed a British copyright registered at a later date, and the copyright owners threatened to require the delivery-up or destruction of the machines – thus defeating the buyer's quiet enjoyment of the goods for the future. Although the sellers of the foreign machine were quite innocent in the matter, and it was therefore a question of which innocent party must suffer, the court held that the Act threw the load on the vendor.

14.4.4 Sales by description

Where goods are described there is an implied condition that the goods will correspond with the description. If the sale is by sample as well as by description it is not enough if the bulk of the goods correspond with the sample if they do not correspond with the description, and even if the goods are exposed for sale and are selected by the buyer, this does not prevent the sale being a sale by description (Section 13). For example:

> *Beale v. Taylor (1967)*
>
> T advertised a car as a Herald 1961 Convertible, but in fact, unknown to T, it was two halves of wrecks welded together, one a 1961 model and the other of earlier date. **Held**: it did not comply with the description.

14.4.5 Quality and fitness for purpose

The general rule is that there is no implied condition or warranty about the quality or fitness for purpose of goods supplied under the contract of sale. However, under Section 14 there is an implied condition that goods sold *in the course of business* are of merchantable quality, unless defects are drawn to the attention of the buyer at the time, or the buyer examines the goods and ought to have noticed such defects. Where the buyer expressly, or by implication, makes it clear either to the seller, or in the case of hire purchase to the credit broker, that he requires the goods for a particular purpose and relies upon the seller's or credit broker's skill and judgement in choosing the goods, there is an implied condition that the goods supplied are reasonably fit for that purpose. This claim may be rebutted by proof that the buyer did not in fact rely on the seller's skill and judgement, or that it was unreasonable for him to have done so.

Thornett and Fehr v. Beers and Son (1919)

T's representative went to B's factory to inspect glue, and was afforded every facility. He did not actually open any of the drums purchased. When it proved unsatisfactory T and F refused to pay. **Held**: there was no condition that the goods were to be of merchantable quality since an opportunity to examine the goods had been afforded.

In particular trades it is possible for implied conditions about quality or fitness for purpose to be attached to contracts by usage of the trade.

The term 'merchantable quality' means that goods are as fit for the purposes for which such goods are commonly bought as is reasonable in the circumstances, taking any description applied – and the price – into account.

Disputes about merchantable quality frequently arise in the motor trades, where cars are being sold second hand at a wide variety of prices, and where it is a matter of common knowledge that those who drive cars frequently find that breakdowns occur at almost any time. Conceivably a car might be of merchantable quality at the time of the sale and yet break down 200 miles later. In *Bartlett v. Sidney Marcus (1965) 1 WLR 1013*, Lord Denning ruled '... a buyer should realise that when he buys a second-hand car defects may arise sooner or later and in the absence of an express warranty he has no redress.'

Although this case was decided before the *Supply of Goods (Implied Terms Act, 1973)* first enunciated the definition of merchantable quality, which later was embodied in the revised *Sale of Goods Act, 1979*, it has been held in at least one major recent case that Lord Denning's dictum is still persuasive. This case is outlined below:

Business Application Specialists v. Nationwide Credit Corporation Ltd (1989)

The plaintiffs had purchased a 2½-year-old Mercedes with 37 000 miles on the clock, for £15 000. In the next two months it ran 800 miles but then suffered loss of power and excessive oil consumption with loss of oil pressure. Claiming that this should not have happened so quickly and that the car could not have been of merchantable quality, the plaintiffs sued. Both the original trial and the appeal held that, bearing in mind all the facts (the repairs would only cost £600, the car was roadworthy at the time of sale and oil compression was satisfactory), and that some measure of wear and tear must be expected in a second-hand car, the car *was* of merchantable quality at the time of sale.

14.4.6 Sale by sample

Where goods are sold by sample there is an implied condition that the bulk of the goods will correspond to the sample, that the buyer will have a reasonable opportunity to compare the bulk with the sample, and that the goods will be free from any defect rendering them unmerchantable, which would not be apparent on reasonable examination of the sample (Section 15). A case about sale by sample was:

> *Godley v. Perry (1960)*
>
> Perry, who had supplied a defective catapult which injured G, brought in his wholesalers, X, as third parties, who brought in their wholesalers in Hong Kong, Y, as fourth parties. The sale to P had been made by sample. **Held:** X and Y were both in breach of Section 15, the bulk of the goods were not up to the sample.

We see therefore that all these implied conditions and warranties offer some protection to the buyer of goods against unfair trading.

14.5 Effects of a contract for the sale of goods

The whole purpose of a sale of goods is to transfer the ownership of goods from one person to another. There are two reasons why it is important to know when the property passes. First, all goods are at risk to some extent, and Section 20 of the Act says that unless otherwise agreed, the risk passes when the property passes. Goods are at the seller's risk until the property passes to the buyer, and then they are at the buyer's risk, whether the actual delivery of the goods has taken place or not. Second, in normal circumstances the price may only be recovered by the seller once the property in the goods has passed to the buyer. For these reasons the Act tries to pinpoint the moment when the property passes from seller to buyer.

Closely associated with the property (ownership) is the title (right of ownership) which may be exerted in the courts by legal action. Generally speaking, no one can transfer ownership except the true owner or some agent acting on behalf of the true owner. The Latin rule '*nemo dat quod non habet*' (no one can give what he does not have) applies. However, in certain circumstances the transfer of goods to a third party by someone else other than the true owner may transfer a valid right of ownership. These cases are listed in the Act, as shown below.

14.5.1 The transfer of the property

Generally speaking, the property in goods passes from one party to another when the parties intend it to be transferred. The Act lays down a number of rules for determining the intention of the parties, but it first of all says that the property in goods which have not been ascertained cannot pass unless or until the goods are ascertained. Thus a sale of bulk oil stored in a tank at a tank farm with other supplies cannot pass to the buyer until it is separated off and identified as the subject matter of the contract, perhaps by being pumped into a delivery vehicle.

The rules for identifying the intentions of the parties as to the time at which the property is to pass are given in Section 18. They are:

- *Rule 1.* Where there is an unconditional contract for the sale of **specific goods** in a deliverable state, the property passes to the buyer when the contract is made, and it is immaterial whether the time of payment or the time of delivery, or both, is postponed. The important point here, which is not explained until we reach Section 20, is that the risk *prima facie* passes with the property. Thus if goods sold by A to B at noon are destroyed by fire at 1 p.m. the loss is B's, even if the goods were still in A's possession, awaiting delivery. Section 20 goes on to explain that if delivery was delayed due to the fault of a particular party, the risk lies with the party that is at fault. Also the duties of any party as bailee or custodier are not affected by the Act.

- *Rule 2.* If the sale is conditional upon the seller doing something to the goods, the property does not pass until the seller has done it, and the buyer has notice of it.
- *Rule 3.* If the seller has to weigh, measure or do some other act to determine the price the property does not pass until the thing is done and the buyer has notice of it.
- *Rule 4.* When goods are on sale or return or on approval the property does not pass until the potential buyer signifies his approval or does some act adopting the transaction. For example, if A sends goods to B on approval and B sells them to C, this is an act which can be carried out only by the owner, and consequently B must have adopted the transaction. If the buyer does not signify his approval or acceptance of the transaction, but retains the goods without notice of rejection, the property will pass at the end of the time fixed for return of the goods, or – if no time was fixed – at the end of a reasonable time.
- *Rule 5.* Where there is a sale of unascertained or future goods by description, and goods of that description are unconditionally appropriated to the contract by the seller with the assent of the buyer, or by the buyer with the assent of the seller, the property in the goods then passes to the buyer. If the seller delivers the goods to the buyer, or to a carrier, bailee or other custodier for the purpose of delivery to the buyer, and does not reserve the right of disposal, the goods are deemed to have been unconditionally appropriated to the contract, and the property has passed to the buyer.

A particular example of the difficulties in deciding whether the property has passed occurs in the carriage of goods by sea. It is quite common for goods to be shipped under a bill of lading which is made out in favour of the seller or his agent. This is *prima facie* taken to mean that the seller reserves his right to dispose of the goods. Where he then sends the bill of lading, with a bill of exchange drawn on the buyer, to the buyer the understanding is that if the bill of exchange is paid (or accepted for future payment) the property passes to the buyer and he may claim the goods from the ship. If he does not pay the bill of exchange or accept it for future payment, the buyer must return the bill of lading, and the property in the goods represented by the bill of lading does not pass to him.

14.5.2 The transfer of the title

Section 21(1) of the Act embodies two important principles. First, it upholds the rights of the true owner. Anyone else purporting to transfer ownership cannot give a better title to the goods than he has himself (*nemo dat quod non habet*). Second, it seeks to protect commercial transactions by laying down that if the true owner's conduct leads a *bona fide* purchaser to conclude that he is engaging in a *bona fide* transaction he will get a valid title to the goods.

The title to goods is the right of ownership. Only the owner of goods can transfer the title to goods, except in special circumstances, which are listed in the Act. Apart from these circumstances the 'sale' of goods by a person who is not their owner does not transfer to the buyer any better title to the goods than the seller of them had, unless the true owner, by his conduct, is precluded from denying the seller's authority to sell the goods. This situation is called in law 'estoppel'. It is a situation where one party creates an impression which misleads the other party into taking an action which he would not have taken had he known the true facts. If the owner's deliberate conduct makes someone else appear to be the true owner, a person dealing with that 'apparent true owner' will obtain a valid title to the goods.

> ### Eastern Distributors Ltd v. Goldring (1957)
> A person M, who had provided a car dealer C with documents enabling C to appear to be the true owner of a vehicle, was unable to deny the title of Eastern Distributors Ltd, who bought the car from C. M had regained possession of the car by hire purchase from ED Ltd, and sold it to Goldring. ED Ltd sought to recover it from Goldring. **Held**: M had no title to the car, and could not give one to Goldring, who was forced to surrender the car to ED Ltd. (*Note*: Since 1964 the *private buyer* of a motorcar in these circumstances has been protected, and Goldring would not today have to surrender the vehicle.) The case still illustrates the point of title, that he who deliberately creates an impression that another person has a valid title to goods, cannot later deny the title of someone who took the goods from that person in good faith, for value.

It is debatable whether negligent conduct or omission to do what ought to be done is enough to give rise to an estoppel, but it is possible.

The special circumstances listed in the Act in which an innocent third party does receive a valid title to goods transferred by a person who is not the true owner are listed below, but note that rule (d) (sales in market overt) has now been abolished (early 1995) because the Royal Assent has been given to the *Sale of Goods (Amendment) Act, 1994*. The change is explained at (d) below. All the special circumstances outlined below are exceptions to the rule mentioned above '*nemo dat quod non habet*'.

(a) Sales by a factor or other mercantile agent

A factor is defined in the *Factors Act, 1889*, as 'A mercantile agent having in the customary course of business as such agent authority either to sell goods, or to consign goods for the purpose of sale, or to buy goods, or to raise money on the security of goods.' The Act goes on to say that where such a person transfers goods, which are in his possession with the consent of the owner, to another person who acts in good faith, the transfer gives a valid title as if the factor had been expressly authorized to sell the goods.

> ### Folkes v. King (1923)
> F delivered a car to H, a mercantile agent, to sell at a specified price. H sold to K at a lower price, and absconded with the proceeds. F tried to recover the car from K. **Held**: he could not do so. H was in possession as a mercantile agent for the purpose of sale, and when he sold to K he gave K a valid title.

(b) Sales under any other Act

Sale under any Act of Parliament which permits the apparent owner of goods to dispose of them as if he were the true owner, gives a good title to the buyer.

Contracts for the sale of goods **229**

(c) *Sales of goods distrained under a court order*

Auctioneers or bailiffs are clearly not the true owner but their sale of the goods with due authority gives a valid title to the buyer.

(d) *Sales in market overt (open market)*

Sales in market overt have been for centuries an exception to the rule *nemo dat quod non habet*. When a buyer purchases an item in the open market in good faith without any notice of any defect in title of the seller, and paying a fair 'market price', according to the usage of the particular market concerned, and in daylight, between the hours of sunrise and sunset, English law has always presumed that the buyer buys honestly, and gets a good title. A market overt must be recognized by Royal Charter, or by statute, or by prescription (long use). There have been many cases in which the rights of the innocent purchaser have been upheld but as recently as 1973 the Court of Appeal in *Reid v. Commissioner of Police of the Metropolis and Another* returned an object to its rightful owner (Mr Reid) when he proved that at the time the bargain was struck by the innocent purchaser and the stallholder the sun had not yet popped up over the horizon at the New Caledonian Market. However, there is no point in giving the details of 'market overt' cases, for Parliament has abolished the rule with the passage of the *Sale of Goods (Amendment) Act, 1994* which became law in early 1995. The fact is that this 'market overt' rule had become the perfect excuse for those who in other circumstances would be accused of receiving stolen goods. We have so many goods that are worth stealing today that burglary has become very widespread and – it was argued in Parliament – the open market was now a 'thieves kitchen', in which stolen goods were offered for sale to purchasers who could not but know that they must have been stolen. The ordinary person, buying in 'market overt' cannot now presume that he is safe in buying the objects on display, for the title he gets is no better than the title of the stallholder who sells it to him and if the true owner is able to prove his title the stallholder has no title to give. We are back to *nemo dat quod non habet*.

(e) *Sales under a voidable title*

A voidable title is one which is the result of a misrepresentation, mistake as to the identity of the buyer or similar reason. The buyer has a title which can be disturbed by the seller should he discover the misrepresentation or deception. It must be distinguished from a void title, where the so-called seller has no right at all to the goods – as, for example, where he has stolen them. Such a title can never give a third party a valid title, but a voidable title may do so under Section 23 of the Act. The cases of *Cundy v. Lindsay & Co. (1878)* and *Lewis v. Averay (1972)* have already been referred to (see pages 137–8). Sales under a voidable title were at one time thought to be straightforward, since it was thought that the title could only be avoided if the original seller found the original buyer and gave notice that it was avoided. In *Car and Universal Finance Ltd v. Caldwell (1964)*, however, it was held that if the original seller gave notice to the police of the improper conduct of the buyer, and made every attempt to publicize his intention to rescind the contract, the contract would be avoided and the second buyer could not be deemed to have taken the goods in good faith. This leaves the innocent third party in an exposed position. However, the re-enactment of the 1893 Act as the 1979 Act did nothing to remedy the situation and consequently the protection given to the innocent third party by Section 23 is less helpful than formerly supposed.

A decision of the House of Lords in the case of *National Employers Mutual General Insurance Association Ltd v. Jones* (*1988*) appears to have finally decided whether an innocent third party can ever get a good title to stolen goods. Although the appellant, Jones, had bought a car after it had passed through the hands of several dealers the House of Lords held that the title was not a good one, and that the insurance company which had compensated the true owner, and subrogated her rights to the vehicle, was entitled to the value of the car from the appellant. The appellant is left to pursue an action against the person who sold him/her a vehicle with a voidable title.

(f) Resale by a seller in possession

A seller is frequently left in possession of goods, perhaps to repair them, or deliver them. A seller may also be left in possession of the document of title to goods. If the seller then disposes of the goods or the document of title again to an innocent third party taking them in good faith, the third party gets a valid title to the goods, and the original buyer must look to the original seller for satisfaction.

(g) Resale by a buyer in possession after a sale

This section (Section 25) says that if a buyer is in possession of the goods or the documents of title and transfers them to a third party having no notice of a seller's lien or other right, the situation is the same as if the person making the delivery was a mercantile agent in possession of the goods. This is not of much practical interest because it does not really change the legal position. First, a buyer can always sell what he has bought. Second a lien is usually a possessory right to hold onto goods until payment, and is lost when possession is lost to the buyer. The unpaid seller is therefore left in an unsatisfactory position. This also applies to the situation where it is the document of title that is transferred, because Section 47.2 specifically refers to the fact that when a document of title is passed to an innocent third party without notice of any unpaid seller's lien or right to stop the goods in transit, these rights are defeated.

Section 25(2) goes on to say that a buyer under a conditional sale agreement is not to be regarded as a buyer. A conditional sale agreement is one made under the *Consumer Credit Act, 1974*, whereby a sale is made on condition that the property does not pass to the buyer until the last instalment is paid.

We can conclude that if the property in the goods has already passed to the buyer Section 25 does not really have much effect. If the property has not passed, the third party taking in good faith may not get a good title. Since the rule is that the situation is the same as that of a mercantile agent in possession of the goods with the consent of the owner, the third party will only get a good title if he buys in accordance with the rules – i.e. in the ordinary course of business from a person who appeared to be a mercantile agent.

(h) Sale of a vehicle under hire purchase to a private buyer

The *Hire Purchase Act, 1964* (Part III), which is still in force although the rest of the Act has been repealed, gives special protection to innocent third parties who buy a second-hand car unaware that it is not the property of the seller but is in his possession on hire purchase or conditional sales terms. It does not protect motor traders, who are able to check these things out through their professional associations. Where a *private buyer* buys a vehicle in good faith (Section 27 of the Act) the effect is as if the ownership of the vehicle had become vested in the hirer or buyer immediately before the sale to the innocent third party, who thus gets a valid title to the vehicle and quiet enjoyment of it. The finance company or other true owner must now look to the customer who has sold the vehicle for satisfaction.

The provisions of this 1964 Act, with some changes in terminology rather than substance, are now re-enacted in Schedule 4, Para. 22 of the *Consumer Credit Act, 1974*.

Once the good title of an innocent third party has been established, any subsequent action by the third party also gives a valid title:

> *Barker v. Bell (1971)*
>
> A third party sold a car to a dealer, Bell, who sold it to another dealer, Barker, who was found in possession of the car by the original hire purchase company. Barker returned the car to them, and claimed the purchase price from Bell. **Held**: Barker need not have returned the car. The title acquired by Bell was good, and therefore Barker's title was good. The action therefore failed.

14.6 The duties of the seller in the performance of the contract

Section 27 of the Act says 'it is the duty of the seller to deliver the goods ... in accordance with the terms of the contract of sale'. The following points follow from this simple declaration, or from the wider body of law surrounding the sale of goods:

- The seller must fulfil his contractual obligations, both express and implied.
- The word 'delivery' has several implications. Section 61 defines 'delivery' as 'the voluntary transfer of possession from one person to another'. The method of delivery and the place and time of delivery may be important.
- There are other legal aspects of the sale of goods, such as the possibility of tortious liability to third parties not directly involved in the contract, and the need to avoid misrepresentations, or the commission of crimes.

14.6.1 Express contractual duties

A seller may make express promises about quality, delivery and price, and certain other implied terms will be read into the contract under Sections 10–15 of the *Sales of Goods Act, 1979*, as we have seen in Section 14.4 above. Both these sets of promises must be kept.

The seller must do what he promised to do. Express promises must be carried out exactly, unless the contract can be held to have been frustrated (see Section 11.4), but in the absence of frustration any failure to perform the contract to any extent will give a right of action to the disappointed buyer. Whether the breach is of a condition of the contract or only of a warranty is for the court to decide (see Section 14.4 above).

Liability to keep these promises is 'strict'. This means that the seller cannot exempt himself from responsibility by saying it is not his fault that some promise was broken. Even if every precaution is taken the seller will be liable to the buyer for any damage or loss that results, though he may have a right of action subsequently against the person at fault. In *Frost v. Aylesbury Dairy Co. Ltd* the facts were as follows:

> **Frost v. Aylesbury Dairy Co. Ltd (1905)**
>
> The defendant dairy company supplied milk to the plaintiff, using every possible precaution to ensure it was pure. The plaintiff's wife died of typhoid fever as a result of drinking the milk. **Held**: the plaintiff clearly relied on the seller's skill and judgement in supplying milk for domestic consumption. They were in breach of Section 14.1. Although they had taken every precaution they were still liable for all the losses suffered, which included the plaintiff's loss of consortium.

Implied contractual duties. These have already been outlined in Section 14.4 above. Their effect is to ensure that the buyer gets what he wants: goods of merchantable quality fit for the purpose for which they were intended free of any charge or encumbrance.

14.6.2 Statutory requirements about performance of the contract

(a) Delivery

Section 28 of the Act says that unless otherwise agreed delivery of the goods and payment of the price are concurrent conditions of the contract. Each party must be ready and willing to fulfil his part of the bargain at the same time.

Some rules for delivery are laid down in Section 29:

- It is a question of fact in every contract whether it is the buyer who shall collect the goods or the seller who shall send them.
- If no agreement was reached then the place of delivery is the seller's place of business, or his home address, or any other place where the specific goods are known to be.
- If the seller is to send the goods to the buyer but no time limit has been given, then the time allowed is a reasonable time.
- Where the goods are in the hands of a third party there is no delivery to the buyer until the third party acknowledges that he holds the goods on the buyer's behalf.
- Delivery must be made at a reasonable hour.
- Unless otherwise agreed, expenses of delivery must be borne by the seller.

(b) Delivery of the wrong quantity

Where the wrong quantity is delivered the rules are as follows (see Section 30), but if there is a special usage of the trade on such matters it may be held to apply:

- If less than the correct quantity is sent the buyer may reject the goods, but if he accepts them he must pay for them *pro rata*.
- If the seller sends more than the correct quantity the buyer may accept the whole consignment, or accept the correct quantity and reject the rest, or he may reject the whole consignment. If he accepts the whole consignment he must pay *pro rata* for the extra supplies.
- If the seller sends a mixture of goods the buyer may accept only those included in the contract, and reject the rest or he may reject the whole consignment.

(c) Delivery by instalments

On instalment deliveries the Act says (Section 31) that unless otherwise agreed the buyer is not bound to accept delivery by instalments. Where delivery by instalments is agreed, and a dispute arises about non-delivery (or non-acceptance) of one instalment, it is necessary to look at the whole contract to see whether the breach is a breach of the whole contract or a severable breach giving rise only to a claim for compensation.

(d) Delivery to a carrier

If a seller has to deliver the goods to a carrier this is deemed to be (*prima facie*) delivery to the buyer. The contract of carriage is between the carrier and the owner of the goods, and the seller is the agent of the buyer in effecting this contract. He must therefore make the contract in such a way as is reasonable 'having regard to the nature of the goods and the other circumstances of the case'. Failure to do so may lead to the buyer rejecting the idea that the goods were properly transferred to him. If insurance is required for carriage by sea the seller must notify the buyer in time for him to insure, and if not they are at seller's risk during the sea transit.

(e) Goods delivered to a distant place

If the seller agrees to deliver to a distant place at his own risk this does not apply to deterioration of the goods incidental to the transit (unless this is agreed specifically).

(f) The right to examine the goods

A buyer is entitled to a reasonable time to examine the goods, to determine whether they are in accordance with the contract.

14.6.3 Other requirements

(a) Absence of misrepresentation

Misrepresentation has been dealt with elsewhere in this book, but the seller of goods frequently misrepresents them. The difference between a mere 'puff' and a statement liable to mislead the buyer and induce the purchase of goods is a fine one, and an action for misrepresentation is frequently possible.

(b) Tortious liability

Any seller of goods is in a contractual relation with the buyer, but has a general liability in tort to any third party injured or suffering loss as a result of defective goods. Liability in tort is not strict, and therefore the plaintiff must prove the point. The action must also be brought against the negligent person, and this may not always be the actual seller, but someone further back in the chain of production, distribution and exchange. The classic case is *Donaghue v. Stevenson (1932)*, where the person injured was not the buyer, but the buyer's friend, and the negligent person was not the seller, a retailer, but the manufacturer who had supplied the seller. The case is fully discussed later (see page 371).

(c) Criminal liability

Criminal liability for the sale of defective goods exists under a great many Acts of Parliament. It is an offence to sell unsafe motor vehicles under the Road Traffic Acts, or unsafe machinery under the Factories Acts. Under the *Consumer Protection Act, 1987*, the Government is empowered to make regulations about the sale, hire, etc., of any goods which the Secretary of State for the appropriate Department deems to be unsafe. Such regulations are used to prohibit further sales of goods found by experience to be dangerous – such as children's cots which have caused cot deaths. The Act also permits those injured by a breach of safety regulations to recover damages for breach of the statutory duty.

Consumer protection is discussed more fully later in this book (see Chapter 28).

14.7 Exclusionary clauses in contracts

In the *Sale of Goods Act, 1893*, it was possible to exclude any or all of the rights, duties and obligations under the Act by express agreement in the contract or by a custom of the trade. This was in line with the view at that time that both parties to a contract were equally strong in the eyes of the law when making bargains. Today the law has been changed to help consumers in particular, who tend to be the weaker parties in any bargain. Anyone attempting to exclude liability must surmount a number of obstacles placed in his way by the *Sale of Goods Act, 1979*, and the *Unfair Contract Terms Act, 1977*. Section 55 of the *Sale of Goods Act, 1979*, repeats the wording of the 1893 Act but mentions the following points:

- An express condition or warranty does not negative a condition or warranty implied by the 1979 Act unless it is inconsistent with it. An exclusion clause must therefore be worded clearly if it is to negative the intention of the Act.
- Section 55 is stated to be subject to the *Unfair Contract Terms Act, 1977*.

14.7.1 The *Unfair Contract Terms Act, 1977*

This Act gives a considerable protection to consumers who are parties to a contract for the sale of goods, but much less protection to businessmen actually engaged in trade with one another, since here they may be held to be equally sophisticated and legally advised.

Section 6 says that breaches of obligations under Section 12 of the *Sale of Goods Act, 1979* (about title and quiet enjoyment of the goods), and Section 8 of the *Supply of Goods (Implied Terms) Act, 1973* (the same thing in relation to hire purchase), cannot be excluded by an exclusion clause in the contract. Obligations under Sections 13, 14 and 15 of the 1979 Act cannot be excluded as against any consumer, and this also applies to Sections 9, 10 and 11 of the 1973 Act (the same regulations as applied to hire purchase).

As regards other businessmen, Section 12 cannot be excluded but the other sections can be excluded if the seller can show that this is reasonable. Note, however, that these rules only apply to implied conditions and warranties under the Act; express statements can be excluded by a clause, even in a consumer sale – though one wonders why they should be made at all in that case. Even so, they will be caught by Section 2 of the Act, which says that no exclusion clause can operate to exclude liability for negligence causing death or injury, and as far as other loss or damage is concerned only succeeds in excluding liability if it is reasonable in the circumstances.

Section 3 of the Act deals with the situation where one party is a consumer, or deals with the other party under a set of Standard Terms and Conditions. In these circumstances an exclusion clause cannot be inserted to exclude liability for breach of contract, or less than full performance unless it is reasonable. The presumption is that it is invalid unless the seller proves it is reasonable. Although such contracts are not always 'sales of goods' contracts, Section 3 does cover many situations where goods are supplied and attempts are made to exclude liability for breach of express promises made earlier.

Where goods pass as a result of a contract not subject to the law of sale of goods or hire purchase (such as a contract for services and materials) Section 7 says that terms purporting to exclude liability for the quality, fitness for purpose, description or correspondence with sample are void if the contract is with a consumer, and if the contract is with another trader the term is only valid in so far as it is reasonable. Terms about the seller's right to transfer ownership or give possession or give quiet possession are only valid in so far as they are reasonable.

14.8 The duties of the buyer in the performance of the contract

The buyer's duties are to accept the goods and pay for them (Section 27, *Sale of Goods Act, 1979*). He has a right to a reasonable time to examine the goods to determine whether they are in accordance with the contract (Section 34).

Acceptance of the goods is deemed to take place when the buyer intimates to the seller that he accepts them, or (a) when they are delivered to him and he does some act which is inconsistent with the seller's ownership of them (like selling them to someone else) or (b) he retains the goods for a reasonable time but does not intimate to the seller his acceptance of them.

The buyer is not bound to return goods he does not accept; he only needs to intimate to the seller his refusal to accept (Section 36).

The buyer is liable for any costs or losses incurred if he fails to take delivery within a reasonable time from a seller ready and willing to deliver the goods (Section 37).

14.9 The remedies of the buyer

14.9.1 Breach of contract

Failure to deliver the goods is a breach of contract by the seller. The disappointed buyer is entitled to damages for non-delivery, and the measure of damages is the loss directly and naturally resulting from the seller's breach of contract. If there is an available market for the goods the damages is the difference between the price the buyer must pay in that market and the contract price. The time (which may be important when prices are under discussion) is the time when they ought to have been delivered, or if no time was stated the time of refusal to deliver (Section 51, 1979 Act). The market must be available, not half a world away.

14.9.2 Specific performance

Where the goods are specific, or ascertained, goods the court may order specific performance of the contract. This is an equitable remedy which requires the seller to deliver up the goods, and removes his option to retain them and merely pay damages (Section 52).

14.9.3 Breach of warranty

Where there is a breach of warranty, or a breach of condition which the buyer elects to treat as a breach of warranty, the buyer is not entitled to reject the goods, but may commence an action for damages for breach of warranty or for reduction of the price payable. The measure of damages for the former is the estimated loss following from the breach; the damages for the latter is the difference in value between goods in perfect condition and those in the condition as supplied (Section 53).

14.9.4 Breach of condition

Where there is a breach of condition the buyer may treat it as only a breach of warranty, and insist that the contract is still performed. Alternatively, he may reject the goods and treat the contract as terminated. Whether the term was in fact a condition of the contract, or only a warranty, is for the court to decide, but certain implied terms in Sections 12–15 are stated to be conditions, and an express term of the contract which was of a serious nature would be upheld as a breach of condition.

14.10 The remedies of the unpaid seller

The unpaid seller of goods has several rights. The Act defines an 'unpaid seller' to include not only the actual seller, but anyone in the same position, such as an agent of the seller or a consignor or other agent who has become liable for the price.

The position arises when the whole of the price has not been paid or tendered, or when a bill of exchange is dishonoured. In these circumstances the unpaid seller may:

- Exercise a lien on the goods to retain them in his possession until payment is received.
- Stop the goods in transit if the buyer is insolvent. This was formally called 'stoppage *in transitu*' but the 1979 Act has anglicized this to stoppage in transit.
- A limited right of resale.

These points need a little explanation, and a further development (which is not part of the 1979 Act) is the use of:

- Romalpa clauses.

14.10.1 The lien on the goods

(Lien is pronounced to rhyme with the boy's name Ian). A lien is a right to retain possession of the goods until payment or tender of the price. This right may be exercised where no period of credit has been stipulated, or where the period of credit has expired, or where the buyer is known to be insolvent. The right is lost (a) when the goods are delivered to a carrier or other custodier without the rights of disposal being reserved, (b) where the buyer or his agent lawfully obtains possession of the goods, or (c) by waiver.

14.10.2 Stoppage in transit

An unpaid seller who knows that his buyer has become insolvent may stop the goods in transit – that is, resume control over them and retain them until payment or tender of the price. The Act lays down when goods are deemed to be in transit: this is from the time when the goods are handed to the carrier, or other bailee or custodier, until the buyer or his agent takes delivery of them. If the buyer or his agent obtains delivery before their arrival at the stated destination the transit is at an end. If the goods arrive at destination and the carrier acknowledges that he holds them on the buyer's behalf, the transit is at an end even though they are still in the carrier's possession. If the buyer rejects the goods the transit is not at an end. If the carrier wrongfully refuses to deliver the goods to the buyer or his agent the transit is at an end, and the goods cannot be stopped in transit. If goods are delivered to a ship it depends upon the facts of every case as to whether the master holds them as carrier, or as agent for the buyer, as to whether the goods can be stopped. If part of the goods has been delivered the balance can still be stopped in transit, unless delivery of the first part was made in such a way as to show an agreement to give up possession of the whole consignment.

Stoppage is effected by repossessing the goods or by giving notice of the claim to stop the goods to the carrier or other bailee in possession. Notice may be given to the actual custodier or his principal but notice to the principal is ineffective unless, given reasonable diligence, he is able to communicate it to his servant or agent in time to prevent delivery. The carrier of goods stopped in transit must deliver them to, or according to the directions of, the seller, who will bear all the expenses involved.

A sub-sale by the buyer to a third party does not defeat the unpaid seller's right of stoppage in transit, unless the seller has agreed to it. However, where a document of title has been lawfully transferred to an innocent third party acting in good faith and for value, the right to stop the goods is defeated. This means that with such a sale the third party has a valid right to the goods, but where the documents were only pledged the right of lien can still be exercised after the pledgee's rights have been satisfied.

14.10.3 The right of resale

Stoppage in transit or the exercise of a lien does not rescind the contract. If the unpaid seller gives notice to the buyer of his intention to resell, and the buyer does not pay the price within a reasonable time, the seller may resell and claim any difference in proceeds from the buyer. If goods are perishable he may resell at once. If in the original sale the seller reserved the right to resell if the buyer defaulted, the seller may resell at once and still sue the buyer for breach of contract.

Any third party who buys goods from the seller who has exercised a lien or right of stoppage in transit gets a good title to the goods, even though the seller had no right to sell. The seller will be liable to the original buyer for non-delivery if he offers to pay for the goods.

14.10.4 Romalpa clauses

Romalpa clauses take their name from a 1976 case entitled *Aluminium Industrie Vassen B.V. v. Romalpa Aluminium Ltd*. The contract between these two companies had inserted into it a complex clause which entitled the sellers (if unpaid) to claim ownership of the material they had supplied to Romalpa Aluminium Ltd even after the property had passed to the buyer, and even after it had been manufactured into other goods. The rights went even further, stating that even if the goods so manufactured were sold to third parties the debts owed by these customers to Romalpa should be transferred to Aluminium Industrie Vassen, the original suppliers of the materials from which the goods were made. When Romalpa Aluminium Ltd became insolvent all these claims were upheld. It follows that such clauses have now been adopted by many suppliers to give additional rights to the unpaid seller.

This wide adoption of Romalpa clauses has led to several legal actions, often between the seller which inserted the clauses and the receivers of bankrupt firms or the liquidators of companies. Without going too deeply into the case law on this complex issue the following rules seem to have been established:

- If the clauses are worded in such a way as to require the buyer to store the raw materials or finished goods separately, this implies that ownership has not passed until the goods are paid for, and may therefore be recovered by the seller and are not to be included in the realization of the assets by the receiver.
- If the clauses specifically create a fiduciary relationship (one of trust) between the buyer and the seller so that the buyer is under a duty to keep a separate record of goods sold to third parties (either the actual goods supplied by the seller or manufactured products embodying the materials supplied) then this imposes a duty on the buyer to account (for the proceeds of the sub-sales) to the original supplier, and gives a prior claim over other creditors.
- The wording of all such clauses is crucial and varies with every case. A case very relevant to the Sale of Goods Act Section 25 was *Four Point Garage Ltd v. Carter (1985)*. Carter purchased a car from a motor dealer Freeway (Cougar) Ltd, which they had obtained from Four Point Garage Ltd. When Freeway went into liquidation Four Point Garage Ltd tried to reclaim the car from Carter, who had paid for it, on the grounds that Freeway had not paid them, and therefore Carter could not get a good title from Freeway. It was held that the wording of the clauses was inadequate to interfere with the right of title gained by the innocent third party buyer of the car, who had bought in the ordinary course of Freeway's business as a motor dealer. In another case, *Clough Mill v. Martin (1984)*, the Appeal Court decided that the receiver's argument that the Romalpa clause merely established a charge over the materials was incorrect. The clause clearly reserved the property in the materials supplied, and entitled the seller to enter the buyer's premises to repossess the materials if unpaid for. This the receiver refused to allow. The court ordered that they must be allowed to repossess the material.

14.10.5 Other rights of the seller

The seller of goods who has not been paid may bring an action against the buyer for the price. If the price was due to be paid on a certain date the seller may bring an action for the price even though the property has not passed and the goods have not been appropriated to the contract.

If a buyer refuses to take delivery the seller may bring an action for non-acceptance of the goods. The measure of damages is the estimated loss directly and naturally arising from the buyer's breach of contract. If there is an available market it will be the difference between the market price and the agreed contract price.

14.11 The *Trade Descriptions Act, 1968*

Traditionally the sale of goods has been a private contractual matter and the question of liability for selling defective goods was resolved by a civil action brought by the aggrieved party. In recent years a number of Acts of Parliament have made it a criminal offence to supply defective goods, in the interests of public safety. For example, the *Food and Drugs Act, 1955*, makes it an offence to supply food unfit for human consumption, and the *Road Traffic Act, 1972*, makes it illegal to sell a motor vehicle or trailer which is unroadworthy. These are criminal matters for which the offender is prosecuted.

While such Acts deal with particular classes of goods, the *Trade Descriptions Act, 1968* (as amended), is a general Act applying to all who trade in goods (and offer services). Since it is the description of goods which most consumers take into account when making purchases, the misdescription of goods misleads the public, who may be put to considerable expense in bringing a civil action to redress their grievances. To discourage the practice it became a crime, under the 1968 Act, to apply a false trade description to any goods or to supply or offer for sale goods to which such a false description had been applied.

Originally the Act was purely of use to reduce crime; the trading standards officers would initiate prosecutions against offenders, and the result was a fine or imprisonment. This left the victim to sue for the compensation to which he felt entitled. Later, under the *Powers of Criminal Courts Act, 1973*, courts were empowered to make compensation orders up to £1000 to compensate victims and reduce the need for separate civil actions.

14.11.1 Defences to prosecution

It is a defence to any proceedings to show:

- that the description complained of was due to:
  - a mistake,
  - an accident,
  - reliance upon information supplied by another person,
  - the act or default of another person, or
  - some other cause beyond the accused's control; and
- that the person accused took all reasonable precautions and exercised due diligence to avoid the commission of such an offence by himself or any person under his control.

14.11.2 Trade Descriptions (Place of Production) (Marking) Order, 1988

This order requires goods to be marked to show the country of origin where people might otherwise be misled.

14.12 The *Supply of Goods and Services Act, 1982*

This Act might be said to set the seal on recent legislation to control all aspects of the relationships between consumers and those who supply them with goods and services. What it does is carry the ideas developed in recent years about the sale of goods into related fields where similar activities take place, such as the hire of goods and the provision of services. It is concerned with three main areas:

- *The transfer of property in goods* (other than sales of goods, hire purchase of goods, redemption of trading stamps by goods, transfers of goods by deed as a gift and transfers concerned with mortgages, pledges and charges) (Sections 1–5 of the Act).
- *Contracts for the hire of goods.*
- *The supply of services* (but this does not apply to personal service or apprenticeships).

In all these cases the Act provides that the implied terms about title, quality, fitness for purpose, description and sample which we are familiar with in the sale of goods shall also apply to the supplies of goods and services. The effect is that however goods are supplied or transferred in England, Wales and Northern Ireland the implied terms are set out in statutory form and consumers cannot be deprived of their rights in these matters by an exclusionary clause. A contract for the transfer of property in goods is affected even if part of the contract is about services. Furthermore the 1982 Act inserts a new clause 3A into the *1977 Unfair Contract Terms Act* to prevent exclusionary clauses being used to exempt those transferring property from liability for breach of the obligations in the 1982 Act. In the case of services the Act sets out in statutory form certain implied terms which apply to most contracts for the supply of services. These are:

- that the supplier will carry out the service with reasonable care and skill.
- that the supplier will carry out the service within a reasonable time (and what is reasonable is a question of fact in every case).
- that the customer will pay a reasonable charge (and what is reasonable is always a question of fact in every case).

However, in the case of services, it is permissible for the parties to agree that these implied terms shall be excluded or varied by express agreement, or a course of dealing between the parties, or such usage as binds both parties to the contract. However such an exclusionary clause would be subject to the test of reasonableness laid down in the *Unfair Contract Terms Act, 1977*. It is for the trader to prove that the clause is reasonable – not for the consumer to prove that it is unreasonable.

This Act seems to bring to an end the long series of legislation about consumer affairs which began with the Maloney Commission in 1962.

14.13 The *Sale of Goods (Amendment) Act, 1995*

The *Sale of Goods (Amendment) Act, 1995* introduces two improvements when sales are made from bulk. First, amending Section 16, a new rule in Section 18 says that if goods in bulk, as yet not ascertained, fall in quantity, to the point where they are reduced to the level of a customer's outstanding order, they immediately become ascertained goods, appropriated to that contract, and the property passes to the buyer. Second, by a new Section 20A, a buyer who has paid for goods which form part of a bulk supply as yet unascertained becomes at once part-owner (an owner in common) of bulk goods, and the property passes to him. Section 20B then says that it shall be deemed that the other co-owners have consented to any delivery made by a co-owner in so far as it forms part of his share of the bulk.

Test your knowledge

Answers	Questions
	1 Which Act controls the sale of goods?
1 The *Sale of Goods Act, 1979*.	2 What are 'goods'?
2 'Goods' includes all personal chattels other than 'things in action' and money.	3 What is a contract for the sale of goods?
3 One where the seller transfers or agrees to transfer the property in goods to the buyer, for a money consideration called the price.	4 Who has capacity to buy and sell?

Answers	Questions
4 Capacity is the same as for other contracts, but minors, drunkards and those of unsound mind can make valid contracts for necessaries – but they need only pay a reasonable price.	5 What was *Nash v. Inman* about?
5 The 'fancy waistcoats' case, in which it was established that if an infant has adequate clothing, etc., already, such clothing, etc., is not a necessity.	6 Which contracts similar to sales are *not* sales?
6 (a) Barter; (b) hire; (c) hire purchase; (d) contracts for skill and materials; (e) mortgages, pledges and charges.	7 What is Section 12 of the Act about?
7 The seller's right to sell and the buyer's quiet enjoyment of the goods.	8 What is Section 13 about?
8 Sales by description.	9 What is Section 14 about?
9 Quality, fitness for purposes and reliance upon the seller's skill and judgement.	10 What is Section 15 about?
10 Sales by sample.	11 What is meant by 'an implied condition' or 'an implied warranty'?
11 Although the condition or warranty was not actually expressed in the contract the court will infer that it was, because no sensible person would have engaged in the contract unless it had been.	12 When does the property in goods pass?
12 When the parties intended it to pass. It cannot pass until the goods are ascertained goods.	13 What are the five rules for determining the intention of the parties?

Answers	Questions
13 *Rule 1*: Specific goods in a deliverable state pass when the contract is made, even when payment or delivery are postponed. *Rule 2*: If the seller has to do something the property passes when he has done it and the buyer has notice of it. *Rule 3*: If the seller has to weigh, measure, etc., it does not pass until he has done it and the buyer has notice. *Rule 4*: If goods are on approval the property passes when approval is given, or when the buyer does some act only consistent with ownership which adopts the transaction. If the buyer does nothing the property passes at the end of the fixed time, or in a reasonable time. *Rule 5*: If the goods are unascertained or future goods, and they are produced and appropriated to the contract with the knowledge of both parties, the property passes.	14 What is the title to the goods?
14 The right of ownership.	15 Who can transfer the title?
15 Only the owner, except in special cases.	16 What are the special cases?
16 (a) Sales by a factor or mercantile agent; (b) sales under distraint; (c) sales under an Act of Parliament; (d) sales by order of the Court; (e) sales under a voidable title; (f) resale by a seller in possession.	17 What is stoppage in transit?
17 It is the right of an unpaid seller to stop goods in transit and divert them to some other destination than the buyer's premises.	18 What are Romalpa clauses?

Answers	Questions
18 Clauses inserted into a contract which give an unpaid seller rights not only over the goods still unpaid for, but also over any goods into which they have been manufactured, or over the money to be earned from the sale of such goods.	19 Go over the questions again until you are sure of all the answers. Then try some of the written questions in Appendix 1.

15 Insurance

15.1 The nature of insurance

Insurance has an ancient history, but the insurance industry in the last few years has been forced to haul itself into the twenty-first century instead of languishing in the nineteenth. For example in 1978 a United Nations body, UNCTAD (the United Nations Committee on Trade and Development) published a *Report on Marine Insurance* which pinpointed many weaknesses in the ancient document used in marine insurance for over 350 years, and called for an international regime of law and practice in this field. The report, as we shall see, has produced striking improvements in the documents used, though not as yet an international regime of law and practice.

The essence of insurance is that we live in a dangerous world, where 'fate' may at any time knock on our doors. In such circumstances it is wise to reduce risks as much as possible. The best way is to find someone who will bear our risks for us. This is what **insurers** do. **Lloyd's of London**, a particularly experienced institution in the risk-bearing field, calls its risk-bearing members **underwriters**, so that the terms 'insurers' and 'underwriters' have the same meaning. Insurance is the bearing of risks by specialists in risk-bearing, so that ordinary businessmen operate more confidently, 'and losses fall rather easily upon many, than heavily upon a few'.

The main branches of insurance are as follows:

- life assurance
- fire insurance
- marine insurance
- accident insurance
- liability insurance

Some of these will only be dealt with briefly in this book, which is more directly concerned with business aspects of insurance.

The words 'insurance' and 'assurance' are really interchangeable, and at least one London company is seeking to put an end to any confusion by using the word 'insurance' only, and calling the one insured the 'insured' and not the 'assured' – the traditional term. The only difference traditionally is that one event (death) occurs for us all and therefore is assured for everyone. Life assurance is therefore traditionally used as a description for life cover. Other types of loss are not so definite: we may never have a fire, or a burglary, or an accident, but we shall surely die.

The consideration for undertaking to provide cover for any risk is called the **premium**. This may be a lump sum payment or a succession of payments. The premiums form a pool of reserves, which is invested to earn further income that is added to the pool. Valid claims are settled by compensation payments from the pool. The adequacy of reserves is always an important consideration for insurers, but provided reserves are adequate profits may be extracted by the insurers as a reward for their activities. It is the reduction of the heavy losses which fall upon individuals in the real world into a wider loss spread over the whole population in the form of premiums paid, that makes insurance such a sound system for risk-bearing.

Every insurer has a right to insure himself against the chance that the peril he has agreed to insure will occur. This insurance of insurance liabilities is called **reinsurance**, and is governed by the same rules as an ordinary insurance policy. Where this is arranged as a regular thing, one insurer agreeing to reinsure either a particular class of policies for another insurer, or an agreed percentage of that insurer's total business, it is called a 'reinsurance treaty'.

15.2 The principles of insurance

To assume someone's risks is a burden not to be lightly undertaken and there have to be strict rules. These are the **principles of insurance**. They may be listed as follows:

- Insurable interest
- Utmost good faith
- Indemnity
  - Contribution
  - Subrogation

There is also a doctrine, called the **doctrine of proximate cause**. What do these various terms mean?

15.2.1 Insurable interest

This principle holds that no one may insure against any risk unless he/she will suffer loss should the risk insured against occur. Thus I may insure my own life, and my person and my property against accident, fire, flood, tempest, etc., because if I die, or am injured, or my property is damaged or destroyed I shall suffer a loss. I may not insure my neighbour's life, person or property except in very special circumstances, because usually I have no interest in their wellbeing and shall not suffer a loss if they are adversely affected.

A person is considered to have an insurable interest in his/her own life and the life of his/her spouse. Parents do not necessarily have an insurable interest in the lives of their children or vice versa; a pecuniary interest must be shown. This means that the proposer must show that he will suffer financial loss if the person whose life he has insured dies (*Halford v. Kymer (1830)*). Hence a creditor has an insurable interest in the life of his debtor; a guarantor has an insurable interest in the life of the debtor he is guaranteeing and an employer has an insurable interest in the life of his employees and vice versa. Everyone may insure property wholly owned, or jointy owned with another, or where there is an equitable or limited interest in property. A shareholder in a company may insure the shares held, but not the property of the company, for a shareholder has no insurable interest in property owned by the company. The person insured is called the **assured** – a name traditionally used, which has the same meaning as *insured*.

15.2.2 Utmost good faith

This principle holds that all contracts of insurance are contracts *uberrimae fidei* (of the utmost good faith). The proposer of an insurance policy is under a duty to disclose to the insurer all the material facts. Any non-disclosure of a material fact makes the insurance contract voidable at the option of the insurer. This doctrine of disclosure of material facts, which applies to all types of insurance, is well described in Section 18 of the *Marine Insurance Act, 1906*:

> *Subject to the provisions of this section, the assured must disclose to the insurer, before the contract is concluded, every material circumstance which is known to the assured and the assured is deemed to know every circumstance, which, in the ordinary course of business, ought to be known by him. If the assured fails to make such disclosure, the insurer may avoid the contract.*
>
> *Every circumstance is material which would influence the judgement of a prudent insurer in fixing the premium, or determining whether he will take the risk.*

In *Carter v. Boehm* (1766) Lord Mansfield said:

> *Good faith forbids either party, by concealing what he privately knows, to draw the other party into the bargain from his ignorance of that fact and his believing the contrary.*

In *Arterial Caravans Ltd v. Yorkshire Insurance Co.* (1973) where a company seeking fire insurance failed to reveal that another company managed by them had suffered a loss by fire, it was held that this constituted non-disclosure of a material fact. Similarly, a failure to reveal that a motor insurer had refused cover in circumstances reflecting upon the moral integrity of the insured's character was held to be a breach of utmost good faith by an applicant for a fire policy (*Locker & Woolfe Ltd. v. West Australian Insurance Co. Ltd* (1936)).

15.2.3 Indemnity

This principle holds that the duty of the insurer is to indemnify the assured against the loss he has suffered, and thus restore him (so far as money can) to the same position he was in before the loss occurred. Where indemnity is not the purpose of the contract, as with life assurance and accident insurance, the purpose of the contract is to pay the insured a known sum of money (the benefit) on the happening of the event. Indemnity is restoration to the previous situation, not to a better situation. It is against public policy (which means 'crime would be encouraged') for those who might suffer a loss to be in a position where they could profit from it if the loss occurred. Thus the owner of a wrecked vehicle does not receive a new car, but only the value of the car in the condition it was in immediately prior to the accident. Due allowance will be made for depreciation in deciding the value of the vehicle.

(a) Contribution

This subprinciple of indemnity holds that an insured person cannot be allowed to recover more than once for any loss – so that if two policies exist to cover the same risk the insurers will contribute to the loss pro rata, according to the terms expressed in the contracts. Any attempt deliberately to insure to a value greater than the interest existing in the life or property may be void under the *Life Assurance Act, 1774*. In other circumstances – for example, where a 'Contents' policy and an 'All Risks' policy cover the same goods – contribution would apply. Where one insurer pays in full he may recover from the other insurers. The rule does not apply to cases of life assurance, where a person may take out several policies to yield benefits large enough to support his dependants in the event of his death.

(b) Subrogation

To subrogate is to step into the shoes of another individual, and become entitled to every right of that individual, both contractual and in tort, or indeed in any other branch of law. The fact that I have obtained cover against any loss – for example, loss of goods in transit – does not mean that the person who caused the loss escapes liability for his actions, such as dangerous driving, negligent driving, etc. The insurance company is entitled to subrogate into the legal situation of the assured, and to exert the assured's legal rights in its own name. The assured may have been fully compensated, and may no longer be interested, but the insurance company is anxious to restore to the pool of insurance funds what it can recover by way of salvage or from the person at fault. This right is based upon equitable considerations. Since the contract of insurance is a contract to indemnify the assured, once this has been done it would be inequitable if any further sums from the sale of damaged goods, or compensation from those liable for the loss, should also go to the assured. The insurer is entitled to be recouped by having the amount returned to him. However, this recoupment only extends to the limit of the indemnity. In *Yorkshire Insurance Co. Ltd v. Nisbet Shipping Co. Ltd* (1962), where a refund – due to the delay involved – resulted in an exchange profit which exceeded the indemnity, the insurers were allowed to recover only what they had paid.

15.2.4 The doctrine of proximate cause

A policy of insurance provides cover against named risks, a claim being payable only if the named risk occurs as the proximate cause of the loss (closest in effect, or 'efficiency', not in time). Suppose a property is covered against fire, but in view of its proximity to an airfield damage due to an aviation accident is excluded. If an aircraft crashes and causes a fire is the loss covered by the policy? It would appear not, for the proximate cause of the loss is the aircraft accident, and the fire was a consequence of that event. In making a claim it is for the claimant to prove that the loss comes within the terms of the policy. If a *prima facie* case is established the onus shifts to the insurer to raise the question of proximate cause.

The following complex situations may arise:

- The loss was caused by a succession of perils, of which the last one was *the insured peril*. If the others were non-insured perils the loss is covered by the insured peril and the insurers are liable. If the others were excluded perils, see below.
- The insured peril was not the last in the chain of perils, but an earlier link in the chain. The question then arises, did the series of events follow in an unbroken chain? If so, the insured peril is the cause of the loss. If the chain of events was interrupted after the insured peril, and the final event is an uninsured peril, the insurers are not liable, for the cover they provided was not cover for the event that actually caused the loss. This new event is called a *novus actus interveniens* – a new act which intervenes to break the chain of events.
- An insured peril and an uninsured peril occur at the same time. The loss is deemed to be caused equally by the two perils, and hence the insured peril caused the loss and the insurers are liable.
- An insured peril and an *excluded* peril operate separately. Since their separate actions can be distinguished we can determine which caused the loss. Note that an excluded peril is not the same thing as an uninsured peril. If a peril is not insured because neither party at the start of the contract mentioned it, and it clearly falls outside the terms of the contract, its occurrence cannot be the subject of a claim. But if a peril is excluded,

by being specifically mentioned, the insurer clearly stating that he has no intention of bearing such a risk there is a clear refusal to cover the event. The difference is explained in the following point.

- An insured peril and an *excluded* peril operate in circumstances where it is difficult to distinguish their individual effects. If the insured peril was preceded by the excluded peril and followed from it the excluded peril is the proximate cause and the insurers are not liable. If the insured peril came first, and the excluded peril followed from it, the insured peril is the proximate cause and the insurers are liable. If the insured peril came first, and then the excluded peril as a separate and distinct event, the excluded peril caused the loss, and the insurers are not liable. Finally, if the events are concurrent and equally effective in causing the loss, we have what seems to be a strange result: the insurers are not liable. This is because it can truthfully be said that the excluded peril caused the loss, and in such circumstances the insurance company cannot be held liable. They were careful to exclude this peril and it would be wrong to hold them liable.

15.3 Life assurance

Life assurance is a contract by which an insurer undertakes to pay a beneficiary a certain sum of money (or succession of payments of money) on the death of the person whose life is insured.

The *Life Assurance Act, 1774*, rules that any life assurance contract taken out by someone who has no interest in the life assured is null and void. The name of the interested person, or the name of the beneficiary, shall be inserted in the policy. Where the insured has an interest (as where a creditor insures the life of his debtor to the value of his debt) he shall not recover more than the amount of the interest. If a life assurance policy is assigned to a third party (perhaps as security for a debt) it is not necessary for the assignee to have an insurable interest in the life concerned.

In business, life assurance is possible for partners, employers and employees. For example, at the death of a partner the estate of the deceased will perhaps wish to withdraw the deceased's share for distribution to the heirs. It is wise to insure the life of your partner, so that at death a sum of money becomes available to pay out the partner's share. An employer may insure the life of a key employee, and an employee may insure the life of the employer upon whom he depends for employment. In *Hebdon v. West* the facts were:

> ### Hebdon v. West (1863)
> An employee was contracted to serve for seven years at £600 per year to a man named Pedder. He insured Pedder's life for £2500. After two years Pedder died. **Held**: he had an insurable interest in Pedder's life for the amount of unpaid salary (£3000) and the claim would therefore succeed.

15.3.1 Suicide

The general principles of insurance law preclude a claim resulting from a loss deliberately caused by the policy holder. For example, unless the policy expressly provides otherwise the personal representatives of a policy holder who commits suicide while sane will not be able to succeed in a claim. They will succeed if the policy holder committed suicide while mentally disordered since this is not considered a deliberate act, unless the policy provides otherwise.

15.3.2 Cooling-off period

To prevent difficulties caused when a persuasive insurance salesman deals with an unsophisticated client, insurance companies are now required to send a statutory notice when long-term contracts are entered into. These give clients a 10-day cooling-off period during which they may consider the matter again and withdraw from the contract if they so wish (*Section 1 1978 No. 1304 Insurance Companies (Notice of Long-term Policy) Regulations, 1978*).

15.3.3 Assignment of a life policy

If a policy is assigned to a third party the assignment must be in writing, either endorsed upon the policy or in a separate document. The assignee's rights will be subject to defences which would have been valid against the assignor (for example, if the policy excluded payment if the life assured ended by suicide). The assignee should give notice to the insurance company at the place specified in the policy for such notice to be given. Assignments may be made under the general terms for assignment of *things in action* (Section 136 of the *Law of Property Act* 1925) but also under the special terms of the *Policies of Assurance Act, 1867*.

15.3.4 Right of subrogation and life assurance

The right of subrogation does not apply to life assurance, and the company must pay the benefit agreed without any hope of recovery from the offending party if the death was unnatural. The rights of action against anyone concerned lie with the legal representatives of the deceased and any award made will not be subject to any claim for a refund of the benefit paid.

15.3.5 Termination of the contract

Where a life policy is terminated otherwise than by the death of the insured life, two alternatives are usually available. The insured may surrender the policy and instead accept a sum of money called the **surrender value**. This surrender value will be affected by a clawback of tax under the *Finance Act, 1975*. Alternatively, he may agree to accept a **'fully paid' policy**. This means that no further payments are called for, but the policy continues until the death of the insured when a reduced benefit – recognizing the premiums already paid and the deceased's expectation of life at the time the 'fully paid' policy is issued – becomes payable.

15.4 Fire insurance

A fire insurance contract is an indemnity contract where the insurer, in consideration of a premium payable either as a lump sum or at regular intervals, agrees to indemnify the insured against the consequences of a fire happening within an agreed period. In general, such a policy covers fires however caused, even if the insured was negligent (*Harris v. Poland (1941)*), or some third party deliberately caused the fire. Cover does not extend to the **wilful misconduct** of the insured (though wilful misconduct is very difficult to prove), nor to the insured's deliberate **arson**.

Fire is a different risk from explosion, even if the latter is followed by a fire, and it depends upon the wording of clauses about explosions as to what liability the insurers will accept. Usually they will cover damage due to the fire, but not blast damage attributable to the explosion. A fire requires ignition, so that damage due to overheating is not covered by a fire policy if there is no fire.

15.4.1 Insurable interest

The insured must have an insurable interest in the premises or goods insured. Owners of property have an interest; occupiers have an interest and a mortgagee may insure property over which he has a mortgage. A bailee (a person in possession of goods for the purpose of performing some service on them) may insure his customer's goods for the full value, and if a loss occurs the sum payable will be for his benefit to the extent of the work done, and the balance will be held as trustee for the owner.

The interest of a person in buildings must exist at the time of taking out the policy and also at the moment when the loss occurred. If the insured dies, or becomes bankrupt, the insurable interest is assigned by process of law to his legal representatives who may enforce the policy if a fire occurs. If the property is conveyed in other circumstances the policy will continue to be effective only if it is assigned, with the consent of the insurers, to the new owner. If a contract is signed for the conveyance of a property, but the actual conveyance has not yet taken place, the purchaser has an equitable interest in the property to be acquired and may insure it. This is advisable in case there is any defect in the previous owner's policy and the premises are destroyed before the legal conveyance takes place.

Being a policy of indemnity, the amount of the loss only can be recovered, but if the policy is a 'valued policy' which recognizes that the value is a given figure, this sum will be payable even if the true value at the time the loss occurred was different. This is frequently used with marine insurance. Commodities vary in value from day to day and place to place, and the use of valued policies avoids legal disputes over valuations at a particular time or place. One more unusual case – which confirms the rule – was *Elcock v. Thomson*:

> **Elcock v. Thomson (1949)**
>
> A house at Wokingham in Berkshire was insured in 1940 at an agreed valuation in excess of £100 000. It was damaged by fire in 1947, when it was found that the true value was less than £20 000 before the fire and damage amounted to 30 per cent of this value. **Held**: The percentage of depreciation due to the fire should be applied to the agreed value, not the true value, and compensation of more than £30 000 was due.

15.4.2 Reinstatement

An early Act (the *Fires Prevention (Metropolis) Act, 1774*) creates a statutory obligation on insurance companies to reinstate premises damaged by fire at the request of anyone interested in the continued existence of the property. The person interested must serve clear notice upon the insurance company who must then ensure that the insurance moneys are used for this purpose, whoever receives them. In the absence of such notice the insurers are required to pay only money compensation, and it is for the assured to decide whether reinstatement shall be made. Despite its name, this Act applies to the whole country, not just the metropolis.

15.4.3 Inflation and the value of property

Most fire policies have a 'subject to average' clause which limits the liability of the insurers if the property is under-insured. For a fully insured property partially damaged by fire the rule is that the assured is entitled to have the damage made good, and to be restored to the indemnity position. If the property is under-insured, the damage will only be restored to the same extent as the insured value bears to the full value, leaving the assured to find any balance of funds for the repairs.

15.4.4 Contribution and fire insurance

If property is double insured – i.e. insured for more than its true value (Section 32, *Marine Insurance Act, 1906*) – the question of how a claim will be exerted depends upon whether the policy has a contribution clause. This is a clause which prevents the assured from claiming the full amount from any insurer (leaving that insurer to claim contribution) but requires the assured to claim from each insurer the proportion due from him. Thus a property valued at £25 000 and insured for £20 000 with one company and £30 000 with another company would be exerted by claiming £10 000 from one and £15 000 from the other.

15.5 Marine insurance

The law relating to marine insurance was codified in the *Marine Insurance Act, 1906*, but since the individual arrangements are contractual and by long usage have been reduced to a very large number of standard clauses for the vast majority of contracts, the law depends to a considerable extent on judicial interpretation of these clauses.

In this respect recent criticisms of the traditional legal regime have led to a drastic rethink of the terms and clauses used, which have been greatly changed (and very lucidly set out) in the **1982 Policy Forms and Clauses**. The criticism came in the form of a Report on Marine Insurance published on 20 November 1978, by the United Nations Committee on Trade and Development (UNCTAD). This report – which consisted of a major appraisal of the 'English system' of insurance – took objection to this *de facto* world system of insurance, on the following grounds:

- It had become a *de facto* world system, but lacked the authority of an international legal regime.
- It was a unilateral, insurer-developed system, couched in archaic language so that many assureds did not understand the meaning of many of the clauses and terms.
- In particular the new nations, the developing nations and the Soviet bloc had had no chance to influence the system, or reduce the uncertainties in it for them.
- The regime took little account of new developments, particularly multi-modal movements. Being British-based it was preoccupied with transits involving sea movements, but for many countries sea transits did not arise, and long-haul road and rail movements were more important.

Accordingly the report called for an ad hoc working group to study the situation and report on the idea of an International Convention on Marine Insurance to replace the English system. No doubt such a working party is at work, but in the meantime many of the criticisms have been met by a joint working party of the Institute of London Underwriters and the Corporation of Lloyd's. This has produced and implemented the 1982 Policy Forms and Clauses, which are gradually being extended into all the trades with specialist **trade clauses**. These new clauses are illustrated in this chapter. Whether they quite meet the call from UNCTAD for an international legal regime remains to be seen, but they are likely to be the *de facto* regime for many years to come – since international agreement on these matters is not easy to achieve.

(a) Nature of marine insurance policies

A marine insurance contract is one where the insurer (or underwriter) undertakes to indemnify the assured (or insured) to the extent agreed against marine losses incurred in any marine adventure. The marine insurance market is a highly organized market, on which only experts may deal. The expert acting on behalf of the assured is called a **broker**. Some brokers are accredited by Lloyd's of London, and are called **Lloyd's brokers**. Others are members of **BIBA**, the British Insurance Brokers Association. They are not mere agents of the assured, since they are responsible to the underwriters for the payment of the premium. As a result they hold a lien (right of retention) over the policy until such time as the premium they have paid is reimbursed to them by the assured.

The subject matter of marine policies may include the ship itself; the ship's necessaries to be used on the voyage; the cargo and the freight (freight is the reward to a ship-owner for carrying goods); and money lent on a **bottomry bond** (a mortgage on a ship executed by a master in difficulties in a foreign port).

(b) Valued and unvalued policies

Most marine policies are **valued policies** – that is, policies where goods and other items to be covered are expressed at a given value which will be the sum to be repaid in the event of a total loss. If the loss is partial the sum payable will be proportional to the agreed value and the percentage of loss suffered. If a policy is **unvalued** the amount payable to the assured will be the value of the goods at the time and place concerned.

15.5.1
Types of policies

The volume of goods in transit at any time today is so large that it is not possible to arrange cover separately for most routine shipments, which occur repetitively. Consequently a number of different methods of general cover were tried for covering all shipments, but the most usual these days is the 'open cover' (see below). However, particular shipments may call for special negotiation of an agreed premium; a process known as **facultative insurance**. The term means 'cover by permission (of the insurers)'. This is explained more fully below. The various types of general cover were:

- *Voyage policies* cover the subject matter of the insurance policy for a particular voyage 'at and from' port A to port B.
- *Time policies* cover the subject matter of the insurance policy for a stated period of time.
- *Floating policies* were developed in the nineteenth century to save endless renegotiation of insurance cover for repetitive journeys with similar groups of cargo. Under a floating policy an underwriter agrees to cover all sendings, at an agreed rate, the premium being paid in advance. The exact details of the ship's name, value of cargo moving, etc., are notified subsequent to departure in a separate **declaration**. The premium is then adjusted. The trouble with this system is that the insurance policy covers many sendings by many ships, and cannot therefore be assigned to a foreign cargo owner as required in many export transactions. The solution found was to issue a **certificate of insurance** for each consignment which certifies that insurance cover has been arranged for the consignment in question.
- *Open covers*. Floating policies, as described above, had some major disadvantages. To help underwriters the policy was for a fixed amount of cover (say £1 million) and an average premium was agreed and paid in advance. This was a heavy cost to the assured. The fixed amount also meant that as declarations were made against the policy the sum outstanding declined until the full sum had been used up. Note that any adjustment between the average premium and the true premium for each

consignment was adjusted on declaration, a difference either way being paid (or repaid). The difficulty was that if an assured received a spate of urgent orders, the premium falling due at once, he might run out of cover at busy periods. The solution was the introduction of **open covers**. Here the sendings are declared as and when they occur, and the premium is invoiced for on a monthly, quarterly or other agreed basis. All sendings are held covered at a standard premium – which assists costing and quoting to customers – and the insurer has the benefit of a steady stream of business with a residual right of cancellation if required, usually at 30 days notice.

- *Slip policies*. Where insurance is effected facultatively (each cover being decided between the broker and the underwriters rather than by the use of an open cover) the basis for discussion is a slip of paper on which the risk is outlined. The underwriters sign the slip to say what portion of the risk they will accept, and eventually a policy is prepared. The *Marine Insurance Act, 1906*, says that only a policy is evidence for the courts, and other documents like slips, certificates, etc., are not evidence. However, in practice many shipments arrive safely, while many claims are met without dispute, or disputes are settled by arbitration. Therefore the drawing up of many policies is a complete waste of time. In 1972 it was decided that the slip itself should be the policy, and bear a similar wording to the policy itself – but where a formal policy is required one would be issued in substitution for the slip policy, upon request. This resulted in a considerable simplification of arrangements.

15.5.2 The 1.1.82 Policy Forms and Clauses

The 1.1.82 Policy Forms and Clauses replaced the 350-year-old S & G Form (Ship and Goods Form) with its archaic format. Traditionally three main sets of clauses – all risks, WA (with average) and FPA (free of particular average) – had been available. Today there are still three sets of clauses, designated Institute Cargo Clauses (A), Institute Cargo Clauses (B) and Institute Cargo Clauses (C). There is little point in attempting to compare these three sets of clauses with the traditional clauses; suffice to say that the C clauses offer the least cover, the B clauses offer rather more cover, and the A clauses offer something very similar to the all risks cover under the traditional all risks policy. None of the Cargo Clauses offers cover against war, or strikes, and if these risks are to be covered a further set of clauses, the **Institute War Clauses** (there is a choice of three sets) and the **Institute Strikes Clauses** must be adopted (at an extra premium of course).

The new form presents the terms of the contract in a clear format, under eight subheadings. These are:

- risks covered
- exclusions
- duration
- claims
- benefit of insurance
- minimizing losses
- avoidance of delay
- law and practice

The layout of the Institute Cargo Clauses (A) is reproduced on pages 256–9 by kind permission of Witherby & Co. Ltd. Some notes on the various clauses are printed on facing pages, to assist study of the clauses. When reading the clauses please remember that the new format was designed

15.5.3 The Marine Insurance Act, 1906

The *Marine Insurance Act, 1906*, codified the law on marine insurance as it existed at that time, when the old S & G policy had already been in use for over 250 years and a considerable body of case law had grown up. It laid down statutory definitions for many of the phrases used in that policy. Now that the S & G policy is, if not quite dead, at least painlessly laid to rest the wordings have in some cases disappeared, or at least have been expressed in plain modern English. However, the meaning of such words as 'thieves', 'pirates', etc., will still be the same as those laid down in the Act, and the reader is strongly recommended to buy a copy and study it in detail. It is the subject matter for a specialist book on insurance law, rather than a general book like this one.

15.5.4 Claims in marine insurance

Claims may be made by the person with an insurable interest for any loss that is proximately caused by one of the perils insured against. The *doctrine of proximate cause* has already been described, the proximate cause being the one that is *proximate in efficiency*, not necessarily in time. Losses may be total, or partial, as explained below.

As there are frequently many parties involved the settlement between the assured and the insurer is called the **adjustment** and is usually settled on behalf of the assured by the broker, who opens a file on the claim, collects together the various documents and reports and negotiates a settlement. Arrangements are sometimes very complex and – with the losses being suffered around the world – some time is taken in collecting the necessary details. Once the type of loss has been established, settlements are made on the basis of established practice. A broad outline of losses and the settlements that result is as follows:

(a) Total losses

Total losses are divided into **actual total losses** and **constructive total losses**.

An actual total loss is one where:

- The subject matter is actually destroyed, or irretrievably lost, or so badly damaged as to be irreparable.
- The assured is irretrievably deprived of it, because it no longer exists in recognizable form as the object or equipment insured, or
- When a court of competent jurisdiction rules that as a result of the peril insured against it is the property of another, and no longer the insured's property (e.g. sale as a prize by a foreign power).

A constructive total loss is one where the costs of repair (or recovery of a sunken vessel) would exceed its value on repair or recovery. In such cases notice of abandonment must be given, so that the rights of the assured are transferred to the insurers who may then take such action as they think fit to recover or repair the vessel or the damaged goods.

Sections 67–78 of the *Marine Insurance Act, 1906*, are about the **measure of indemnity** payable to the assured by the insurer. The rules are complicated, being based upon case law over more than 250 years, and a detailed study of these sections is essential for those with a particular interest in marine insurance.

Compensation on a ship, subject to any special clauses in the policy, is either at the agreed value for a total loss if it is a valued policy, or if it is an unvalued policy it is the insurable value of the ship at the commencement of the risk, including her outfit, provisions and stores, the money advanced in wages and other disbursements to make the ship ready for the voyage, and the insurance charges (Schedule 1, 1906 Act, rule 15). If a vessel arrives safely after settlement of the claim she is treated as if she had been abandoned and becomes the property of the insurers.

The measure of indemnity for a total loss of goods is payment of the agreed value if it is a valued policy. If unvalued, the figure is once again the insurable value, which is the prime cost of the goods, plus the shipping and insurance charges.

(b) Partial losses

A partial loss may be a **total loss of part** of the goods, or it may be damage to all the goods sent, but not a total loss. In total loss of part of a valued policy the compensation payable is that proportion of the agreed value which the part lost represents of the whole consignment, valued as for an unvalued policy (Section 71, *Marine Insurance Act, 1906*). Thus if the value of the policy is £10 000, and the insurable value according to Section 16 of the Act is £8000, of which half is lost, the compensation payable is half the agreed value, i.e. £5000. If the policy is unvalued, the sum recoverable is the insurable value of the part lost – in the example above it would be £4000.

(c) General average losses

A very ancient body of law relates to the sacrifices made or expenses incurred by some assureds to save the entire project when a ship is in real danger. Thus cargo may be jettisoned to lighten a vessel; or may be used as fuel; or part of the ship may be cut away, etc. The principle of general average (*average* here is from the Arabic word *awariya* meaning 'damaged goods') is that those whose property was sacrificed must be compensated by those whose goods arrived safely as a result of the sacrifice, so that all suffer equally. The sacrifice or expenditure is called a general average loss, and the contributions are called general average contributions. The carrier is legally responsible for collecting the contributions from those whose goods have arrived safely, and to this end has a lien (a right to retain possession until paid) over their goods on arrival. As this can be very inconvenient he will usually release the goods on receipt of a **general average guarantee** from a reputable security such as a bank, or insurance company. The 1.1.82 clauses reproduced on pages 256–259 carry a General Average Clause giving cover against general average charges. The **York-Antwerp rules 1990** cover the internationally agreed rules on general average, and are published by the CMI (The International Maritime Committee). Copies may be obtained from CMI, Mechelse Steen Weg 203-B6, B2018, Antwerp, Belguim.

15.6 Accident insurance

The general heading of accident insurance covers a number of classes of insurance, such as personal accident insurance, motor vehicle insurance and aviation insurance. They may overlap into liability insurance, since accidents often result in liability to other parties. The general principles of insurance apply to all such policies, but they may not all be indemnity policies.

Author's notes

▶ **Risks covered.** The risks clause is clear and unambiguous but it does refer to certain risks which are *not* covered. These are given in detail in Clauses 4, 5, 6 and 7. They include wilful misconduct of the assured, losses due to fair wear and tear, faulty packing, inherent vice, delay, insolvency of the owners or charterers of the vessel, nuclear accident, unseaworthiness, war and strikes.

▶ The **general average clause** (about losses suffered by cargo owners and the owners of vessels where goods are deliberately sacrificed to save the entire venture) says that general average and salvage charges *are* covered. This is explained more fully on page 255.

▶ The **'both to blame collsion' clause**. This is a clause which sometimes arises out of a similar clause in the contract of affreightment. When ships collide and both are to blame the damage suffered by both ships is added together and each carrier is responsible for half. Some contracts of affreightment permit the ship-owner to call on cargo owners to help with such losses. The clause covers the risk that this will occur but also authorizes the insurer to act as agent for the cargo owner in rebutting the claim (at the insurer's expense).

▶ **Exclusions.** These are the clauses referred to above, which list the risks not covered by the policy.

1/1/82 Institute Cargo Clauses (A)
(For use only with the new marine policy form)

RISKS COVERED

1   This insurance covers all risks of loss of or damage to the subject-matter insured except as provided in Clauses 4, 5, 6 and 7 below. — Risks Clause

2   This insurance covers general average and salvage charges, adjusted or determined according to the contract of affreightment and/or the governing law and practice, incurred to avoid or in connection with the avoidance of loss from any cause except those excluded in Clauses 4, 5, 6 and 7 or elsewhere in this insurance. — General Average Clause

3   This insurance is extended to indemnify the Assured against such proportion of liability under the contract of affreightment 'Both to Blame Collision' Clause as is in respect of a loss recoverable hereunder. In the event of any claim by shipowners under the said Clause the Assured agree to notify the Underwriters who shall have the right, at their own cost and expense, to defend the Assured against such claim. — 'Both to Blame' Collision Clause

EXCLUSIONS

4   In no case shall this insurance cover — General Exclusions Clause
   4.1   loss damage or expense attributable to wilful misconduct of the Assured
   4.2   ordinary leakage, ordinary loss in weight or volume, or ordinary wear and tear of the subject-matter insured
   4.3   loss damage or expense caused by insufficiency or unsuitability of packing or preparation of the subject-matter insured (for the purpose of this Clause 4.3 'packing' shall be deemed to include stowage in a container or liftvan but only when such stowage is carried out prior to attachment of this insurance or by the Assured or their servants)
   4.4   loss damage or expense caused by inherent vice or nature of the subject-matter insured
   4.5   loss damage or expense proximately caused by delay, even though the delay be caused by a risk insured against (except expenses payable under Clause 2 above)
   4.6   loss damage or expense arising from insolvency or financial default of the owners managers charterers or operators of the vessel
   4.7   loss damage or expense arising from the use of any weapon of war employing atomic or nuclear fission and/or fusion or other like reaction or radioactive force or matter.

5   5.1   In no case shall this insurance cover loss damage or expense arising from — Unseaworthiness and Unfitness Exclusion Clause
         unseaworthiness of vessel or craft,
         unfitness of vessel craft conveyance container or liftvan for the safe carriage of the subject-matter insured,
         where the Assured or their servants are privy to such unseaworthiness or unfitness, at the time the subject-matter insured is loaded therein.
   5.2   The Underwriters waive any breach of the implied warranties of seaworthiness of the ship and fitness of the ship to carry the subject-matter insured to destination, unless the Assured or their servants are privy to such unseaworthiness or unfitness.

6 In no case shall this insurance cover loss damage or expense caused by   *War Exclusion Clause*
   6.1 war civil war revolution rebellion insurrection, or civil strife arising therefrom, or any hostile act by or against a belligerent power
   6.2 capture seizure arrest restraint or detainment (piracy excepted), and the consequences thereof or any attempt thereat
   6.3 derelict mines torpedoes bombs or other derelict weapons of war.
7 In no case shall this insurance cover loss damage or expense   *Strikes Exclusion Clause*
   7.1 caused by strikers, locked-out workmen, or persons taking part in labour disturbances, riots or civil commotions
   7.2 resulting from strikes, lock-outs, labour disturbances, riots or civil commotions
   7.3 caused by any terrorist or any person acting from a political motive.

▶ **Duration**. Naturally the insurer has to know for how long the policy is to be in existence if a fair premium is to be arranged. Section 8.1 shows that it is a warehouse-to-warehouse arrangement, but Clause 8.1.3 says that if the assured does not take delivery within 60 days of the goods being discharged from the ship at destination the cover ceases. Section 9 and 10 require prompt notice to be given in the special circumstances outlined if the goods are to be held covered, pending movement elsewhere.

DURATION

8 8.1 This insurance attaches from the time the goods leave the warehouse or place of storage at the place named herein for the commencement of the transit, continues during the ordinary course of transit and terminates either   *Transit Clause*
       8.1.1 on delivery to the Consignees' or other final warehouse or place of storage at the destination named herein,
       8.1.2 delivery to any other warehouse or place of storage, whether prior to or at the destination named herein, which the Assured elect to use either
           8.1.2.1 for storage other than in the ordinary course of transit
           or
           8.1.2.2 for allocation or distribution,
           or
       8.1.3 on the expiry of 60 days after completion of discharge overside of the goods hereby insured from the oversea vessel at the final port of discharge, whichever shall first occur.
   8.2 If, after discharge overside from the oversea vessel at the final port of discharge, but prior to termination of this insurance, the goods are to be forwarded to a destination other than that to which they are insured hereunder, this insurance, whilst remaining subject to termination as provided for above, shall not extend beyond the commencement of transit to such other destination.
   8.3 This insurance shall remain in force (subject to termination as provided for above and to the provisions of Clause 9 below) during delay beyond control of the Assured, any deviation, forced discharge, reshipment or trans-shipment and during any variation of the adventure arising from the exercise of a liberty granted to shipowners or charterers under the contract of affreightment.
9 If owing to circumstances beyond the control of the Assured either the contract of carriage is terminated at a port or place other than the destination named therein or the transit is   *Termination of Contract of Carriage Clause*

otherwise terminated before delivery of the goods as provided for in Clause 8 above, then this insurance shall also terminate *unless prompt notice is given to the Underwriters and continuation of cover is requested when the insurance shall remain in force, subject to an additional premium if required by the Underwriters*, either

9.1 until the goods are sold and delivered at such port or place, or, unless otherwise specially agreed, until the expiry of 60 days after arrival of the goods hereby insured at such port or place, whichever shall first occur,

or

9.2 if the goods are forwarded within the said period of 60 days (or any agreed extension thereof) to the destination named herein or to any other destination, until terminated in accordance with the provisions of Clause 8 above.

10 Where, after attachment of this insurance, the destination is changed by the Assured, *held covered at a premium and on conditions to be arranged subject to prompt notice being given to the Underwriters*. Change of Voyage Clause

▶ **Claims.** It is made quite clear that the assured must have an insurable interest at the time of the loss. Three other clauses cover forwarding charges incurred if the goods are discharged elsewhere than at the named destination; what happens when there is a constructive total loss (one where the goods are not lost but so badly damaged that the costs of repair, etc., would be greater than their value when repaired); and what happens when the assured takes out an 'increased value' policy for the cargo in question.

CLAIMS

11 11.1 In order to recover under this insurance the Assured must have an insurable interest in the subject-matter insured at the time of the loss. Insurable Interest Clause

11.2 Subject to 11.1 above, the Assured shall be entitled to recover for insured loss occurring during the period covered by this insurance, notwithstanding that the loss occurred before the contract of insurance was concluded, unless the Assured were aware of the loss and the Underwriters were not.

12 Where as a result of the operation of a risk covered by this insurance, the insured transit is terminated at a port or place other than that to which the subject-matter is covered under this insurance, the Underwriters will reimburse the Assured for any extra charges properly and reasonably incurred in unloading storing and forwarding the subject-matter to the destination to which it is insured hereunder. Forwarding Charges Clause

This Clause 12, which does not apply to general average or salvage charges, shall be subject to the exclusions contained in Clauses 4, 5, 6 and 7 above, and shall not include charges arising from the fault negligence insolvency or financial default of the Assured or their servants.

13 No claim for Constructive Total Loss shall be recoverable hereunder unless the subject-matter insured is reasonably abandoned either on account of its actual total loss appearing to be unavoidable or because the cost of recovering, reconditioning and forwarding the subject-matter to the destination to which it is insured would exceed its value on arrival. Constructive Total Loss Clause

14 14.1 If any Increased Value insurance is effected by the Assured on the cargo insured herein the agreed value of the cargo shall be deemed to be increased to the total amount insured under this insurance and all Increased Value insurances covering the loss, and liability under this insurance shall be in such proportion as the sum insured herein bears to such Increased Value Clause

▶ **Benefit of insurance.** The 'not to inure' clause makes it clear that under no circumstances can the carrier or any other bailee (like a freight forwarder) claim under the insurance since the insurance company, when it settles a claim, subrogates into the assured's legal position and may sue the one at fault (usually the carrier or multimodal operator). It destroys their subrogation rights if these people can claim under the insurance. If found liable to compensate the insurance company the insurance company would then have to compensate them back again, which would be absurd.

▶ **Minimizing losses.** It is a basic rule in insurance that the assured has a duty to do everthing possible to minimize losses. This includes taking what steps are necessary to preserve goods, safeguard them, etc., and any charges incurred are covered by the policy. It also requires the assured to exert all legal rights by giving notice of damage promptly (within the time limits specified in the contract of carriage) and suing promptly (according to the terms of the international convention or other law applicable in the case). Anything done in these respects does not waive any rights of either party, but is simply done to save the goods or recover from the party at fault.

▶ **Avoidance of delay.** This is part of minimizing losses, as explained above.

▶ **Law and practice.** This clause is self-explanatory and simply ensures that English law and practice shall apply, and English courts shall have jurisdiction (though not, of course, exclusive jurisdiction).

total amount insured. In the event of claim the Assured shall provide the Underwriters with evidence of the amounts insured under all other insurances.

14.2 Where this insurance is on Increased Value the following clause shall apply: The agreed value of the cargo shall be deemed to be equal to the total amount insured under the primary insurance and all Increased Value insurances covering the loss and effected on the cargo by the Assured, and liability under this insurance shall be in such proportion as the sum insured herein bears to such total amount insured. In the event of claim the Assured shall provide the Underwriters with evidence of the amounts insured under all other insurances.

BENEFIT OF INSURANCE

15 This insurance shall not inure to the benefit of the carrier or other bailee. *Not to Inure Clause*

MINIMIZING LOSSES

16 It is the duty of the Assured and their servants and agents in respect of loss recoverable hereunder *Duty of Assured Clause*
   16.1 to take such measures as may be reasonable for the purpose of averting or minimizing such loss, and
   16.2 to ensure that all rights against carriers, bailees or other third parties are properly preserved and exercised and the Underwriters will, in addition to any loss recoverable hereunder, reimburse the Assured for any charges properly and reasonably incurred in pursuance of these duties,

17 Measures taken by the Assured or the Underwriters with the object of saving, protecting or recovering the subject-matter insured shall not be considered as a waiver or acceptance of abandonment or otherwise prejudice the rights of either party. *Waiver Clause*

AVOIDANCE OF DELAY

18 It is a condition of this insurance that the Assured shall act with reasonable despatch in all circumstances within their control. *Reasonable Despatch Clause*

LAW AND PRACTICE

19 The insurance is subject to English law and practice. *English Law and Practice Clause*

NOTE: *It is necessary for the Assured when they become aware of an event which is 'held covered' under this insurance to give prompt notice to the Underwriters and the right to such cover is dependent upon compliance with this obligation.*

(Reproduced by courtesy of Witherby & Co. Ltd)

Readers wishing to see the full text of other sets of clauses should obtain the *Annual Reference Book of Marine Insurance Clauses*, obtainable from Witherby & Co. Ltd. They also offer an updating service for new clauses or amended clauses as and when they occur. Their offices are at 32–36 Aylesbury Street, London ECIR OET (Tel 0171 251 5341).

15.6.1 Personal accident insurance

Where an insured arranges cover against the possibility of accidental injury resulting in disablement or death, and the loss of income that results, the policy will not be an indemnity policy, for restoration to the original position is not possible. It will be a benefit policy, securing either a lump sum or a continuation of smaller payments to the policy holder or the dependants.

15.6.2 Motor vehicle insurance

Motor vehicle insurance to cover third parties and passengers is compulsory under the *Road Traffic Act, 1972*. There is a statutory duty to obtain cover and both the owner and the driver are liable to prosecution for failure to obtain cover. Proof of cover being obtained is provided by a **certificate of insurance**, which a police officer may require to be produced for inspection. To give immediate cover a **cover note** will be provided while the insurers are preparing a policy and issuing a certificate of insurance. Many people prefer **comprehensive cover,** which means 'including much', but it still does not cover every possibility. The chief difference is that the driver and his vehicle are covered against injury or damage respectively.

The Act provides that the insurer must pay a third party or passenger who has obtained a judgment against the insured. However, if the terms of policy have been breached the insurers are not compelled to honour the policy. In *Seddon v. Binions* (*1978*) a policy covered the use of the vehicle for 'social, domestic and pleasure purposes' only. The vehicle was being used for business purposes when the accident occurred, and the insurance company was not required to pay.

15.7 Liability insurance

Liability insurance covers the insured person against liability to others by virtue of some tortious act, such as negligence or trespass. It is often part of accident insurance (most notably in the case of motor vehicle insurance) or building insurance. Cover is usually extensive enough to protect the insured even when the law has been broken, as in careless or dangerous driving, but it would not cover deliberate tortious acts such as defamation or deliberate criminal acts. It is even against public policy to allow a claim where the act is foolhardy. In *Gray v. Barr* (*1971*) Gray was the personal representative of a relative who had been shot and killed in a struggle with Barr. Despite Barr's acquittal of murder and manslaughter the action (under the *Fatal Accidents Act, 1959*) sought compensation from Barr. Barr sought an indemnity under his accident liability policy, but he was not allowed to claim under the policy. Those who engage in struggles with loaded guns cannot be allowed to claim that any calamity that results is an accident.

If a third party has a claim against a person who is insured and that person becomes bankrupt, or makes a composition with his creditors, or if the 'person' is a limited company and it goes into liquidation, or its debenture trustees appoint a receiver or manager, the rights of the insured person against the insurers are transferred to the third party and vest in him, and he may claim the compensation directly from the insurance company.

Under the *Employers' Liability (Compulsory Insurance) Act, 1969*, employers must obtain cover against liability for bodily injury or disease sustained by employees in the course of, and arising from, the employment. A copy of the certificate issued by the insurers must be displayed at all premises where workers are employed.

15.8 The Policyholders' Protection Act, 1975

In recent years some spectacular collapses of insurance companies have left both policyholders and those they injure unprotected. The *Policyholders' Protection Act, 1975*, established a fund for UK policies, financed by levies on the insurance companies, to pay claims in full on compulsory insurance policies (for third parties and passengers in motor accident cases and employers' liability cases). Ninety per cent of the value of other claims will also be met.

15.9 The Insurance Companies Act, 1982

This Act confers upon the Department of Trade and Industry powers for the supervision of insurance companies and in particular for reviewing their solvency. Part of the review includes a requirement to keep proper accounts, and to publish annual accounts and balance sheets. An actuarial investigation must be conducted each year into the long-term viability of the business, and reports and accounts must be deposited with the Secretary of State. Copies of such deposited documents must be supplied to shareholders and policy holders who request them.

Test your knowledge

Answers	Questions
	1 What is the main purpose of insurance?
1 The bearing of risks by experienced risk-bearers called insurers or underwriters, so that ordinary businessmen are relieved of uncertainty.	2 What are the chief types of insurance?
2 (a) Life assurance; (b) fire insurance; (c) marine insurance; (d) accident insurance; (e) liability insurance.	3 What are the contributions to the insurance pool called?
3 Premiums.	4 What are the principles of insurance?
4 (a) Insurable interest; (b) utmost good faith; (c) indemnity – with contribution and subrogation; (d) the doctrine of proximate cause.	5 What is insurable interest and why is it important?
5 Insurable interest requires that only those who will suffer a loss if a risk occurs may insure against that risk. It is against public policy (crime would be encouraged) if people who did not suffer any loss could profit from the misfortune of others.	6 Why is utmost good faith essential in insurance?

Answers	Questions
6 Only the insured knows the facts of his own situation. Failure to reveal the true facts would mean that insurers would fix premiums too low, and the pool would be drained of resources fraudulently.	7 What is indemnity?
7 The restoration of an unfortunate victim of fate to the position he/she was in before fate knocked on the door.	8 What is contribution?
8 If double insurance has occurred the insured can only expect to be restored to the indemnity position – the insurers will each contribute to settle the claim.	9 What is subrogation?
9 Taking the place of another. On paying a valid claim the insurer succeeds to all the rights of the insured and may recover what can be recovered by legal action, or by sale of the damaged goods, etc.	10 What is the proximate cause of a loss?
10 The loss *closest in efficiency* to the result that occurred.	11 A ship is struck by a mine in wartime and is unable to answer the helm. A storm blows up and she sinks. What was the proximate cause of the loss?
11 The war risk, not the peril of the seas. From the moment the mine blew up she was in the grip of the war peril, and the storm was only an incidental cause of the loss.	12 What is a *novus actus interveniens*?
12 A new event which intervenes and causes a loss. If the new event was an uninsured peril compensation will not be payable.	13 What are the chief policies offered in marine insurance?
13 (a) Voyage policies; (b) time policies; (c) floating policies; (d) open covers.	14 What are the 1.1.82 Policy Forms and Clauses?

Answers	Questions
14 New policy forms and clauses introduced to meet criticisms of the archaic S & G Form by UNCTAD.	15 What are the chief sets of clauses?
15 Clauses A, B and C, the three sets of Institute War Clauses and the Institute Strikes Clauses.	16 What are the chief features of the new clauses?
16 (a) A clear layout with marginal headings to highlight the main points; (b) a clear statement of the risks covered in plain English; (c) a clear statement of the exclusions; (d) English law and practice is contractually adopted.	17 Go over the questions until you are sure of all the answers. Then try some of the questions in Appendix 1.

16 Law of carriage by land, sea and air

16.1 Carriage and the concept of the common carrier

Carriage is an ancient activity. Since time immemorial carriers have gone over the hills and far away with other people's property, and it was soon established that in these circumstances a carrier was liable for *every* loss that occurred. The common law concept of a **common carrier** is of someone who holds himself out as ready to carry goods for anyone who engages him. Under this concept the carrier is held to be liable as an insurer for every loss that occurs. The severity of this rule was later reduced by the development of five **common law exceptions**. These were:

- Act of God
- Act of the Queen's (King's) enemies
- fault of the consignor
- fraud of the consignor
- inherent vice

An **Act of God** is one so unusual and rare that anything the carrier might do would not have prevented it. To be struck by lightning is an Act of God; a cyclone or hurricane is an Act of God; etc.

An **Act of the Queen's enemies** applies to enemies in time of war, or perhaps to a major insurrection. In *Curtis and Sons v. Matthews* (1919) the acts of rebels in the Dublin insurrection in 1916 were held to be acts of the King's enemies.

Fault of the consignor refers to improper packing and similar faults, while **fraud of the consignor** refers to dishonest behaviour by the consignor – usually failure to declare the true nature and value of the goods. In such circumstances the carrier will not be liable for any loss, however caused.

Inherent vice refers to the nature of goods: strawberries rot, cattle can become frightened, prize bulls develop diseases, etc. Where a consignor sends perishable goods he must himself take the risk that their inherent vices may lead to losses.

Apart from these common law exceptions the common carrier is liable for every loss that occurs. He is also under a **legal duty to carry**, except where the law provides that he may lawfully refuse to carry. These special cases are as follows:

- He need not carry through a riot (and probably not through a war, or a flood or similar natural disaster).
- He need not carry dangerous goods.
- He need not carry goods which are improperly packed.
- He need not carry if his vehicle is full.
- He need not carry if the consignor does not pay the freight in advance.
- He need not carry if the consignor refuses to declare the nature of the goods to be carried.

If a carrier does decide to carry in any of these circumstances he will be under his full liability as a common carrier, unless he makes a special contract with the consignor. Obviously he would usually do so, excluding his liability as a common carrier.

A common carrier holds himself out as being willing to carry for the public at large, though it may be in a restricted field, both as to geographical area and to the class of goods being carried. A carrier of meat cannot be compelled to carry coal, and a carrier offering to carry between Manchester and London cannot be compelled to carry to Glasgow.

A word about this chapter. Underlying the whole relationship between consignors and carriers today is the old concept of the common carrier. The harshness of the ancient rules has made carriers evade them by holding themselves out not as common carriers but as **private carriers**, each using a set of **conditions of carriage** which form the basis of a private contract between the carrier and his customers. It follows that practically every carrier is a private carrier – though since an individual firm may start with as little as one lorry it does happen that some small carriers are unaware of the hazards of being a common carrier and set up with arrangements that leave them vulnerable in this respect. In this chapter the various aspects which affect carriers are dealt with in Section 16.3; the position of the common carrier is outlined first and the improvement in his position (if any) by becoming a private carrier is then explained. The rest of the chapter deals with the various modes of carriage – road, rail, sea and air – and the arrangements under which carriers in the real world actually carry. In the course of these explanations constant references inevitably occur to the common carrier and private carrier situations.

Inevitably in a book of this nature an exhaustive treatment of the law of carriage is not possible. The reader with a particular interest is referred to Glass, David A. and Cashmore, Chris, *Introduction to the Law of Carriage of Goods*, published by Sweet and Maxwell (0 420 39700 4).

16.2 Carrying as a private carrier

Where a carrier does not wish to accept the onerous burdens of the common carrier he can hold himself out as a private carrier, carrying under the terms of private contracts made with his customers, usually based upon a set of conditions of carriage. Under the traditional law of contract all parties were deemed to be equally knowledgeable and equally legally advised, so that any terms in a contract which had been agreed between the parties were perfectly permissible. Early sets of conditions of carriage were therefore frequently very harsh, with the carrier refusing to admit liability of any sort and the less sophisticated customer having to accept the conditions because he could not do anything about them. More recently such Acts as the *Unfair Contract Terms Act, 1977*, have reduced the unfairness in inland carriage. The problem has also been tackled over the years in international trade, and as a result a number of international conventions have been introduced. These are explained in detail later.

The private carrier's position is as follows:

- He is not under a legal duty to carry, but free to pick and choose his customers with whom he makes a private contract.
- He is a bailee of the goods carried, and is liable as such for negligence only, and not as an insurer of the goods, liable for every loss that occurs.
- He may limit or exclude this liability for negligence by a special term in the contract.

As a result of these more favourable terms to the private carrier nearly all carriers today are private carriers, and make it perfectly clear that they are *not* common carriers. A typical clause reads:

1. *The carrier is not a common carrier, and will accept goods for carriage only on these conditions (i.e. the set of standard conditions of carriage of which this is clause 1).*

As the private carrier is liable only for negligence (unless he has excluded this possibility) the proof that he has been negligent lies upon the one alleging this. However, the rule *res ipsa loquitur* (the facts speak for themselves) applies where goods arrive damaged and the onus of proof shifts to the carrier to show that he was not negligent (*Joseph Travers and Sons Ltd v. Cooper* (1915), 1KB 73). Thus he might prove that the damage was the result of an Act of God, or faulty packing, or negligence of some other person.

16.2.1 Conditions of carriage

A set of conditions of carriage which lays down the terms on which a carrier will carry is clearly a very helpful protection for a carrier, including as it usually does clauses dealing with most of the difficulties that have arisen in the past. However there is a problem, for since the *Unfair Contract Terms Act, 1977* it has been essential to ensure that all the clauses are reasonable, and will stand up to the test of reasonableness embodied in that Act. That is why many carriers use the sets of standard conditions of carriage provided by their trade associations, such as the Road Haulage Association or the British International Freight Association. Today these sets of conditions are likely to have been drawn up after extensive negotiations with the Office of Fair Trading.

A further difficulty with conditions of carriage is that it is essential to prove that the conditions were embodied in the contract before it was actually made, if they are to give any protection to the carrier. In these days of electronic data interchange (EDI) orders are often sent electronically, or arrangements are made by EDI for the movement of cargoes, and if accepted equally quickly without any reference to the standard terms and conditions there will be no protection from them. It is essential to insist that all customers have a copy of your standard trading conditions and have signed to say that they agree that these conditions shall govern any movements of cargoes. If conditions are printed on the back of carriage documents it is essential to draw attention to them on the front of the document, in a prominent way which refers to their binding nature.

16.3 Aspects of carriage which are important in law

With whom is the carrier dealing? Traditionally this has always been a point of difficulty. The consignor usually makes arrangements with the carrier but very often is not the owner of the goods, the property in them passing to the buyer (the consignee) at the moment that they are handed to the carrier for carriage. If loss, damage or delay occurs it is usually the consignee who suffers. With a common carrier there is no contract at all; the carrier carries by ancient custom of the realm – a practice which started long before contract law came into existence. Under ancient custom the carrier's liability was in tort to the owner of the goods.

When private carriers began to make contracts with their customers the question arose: who is the other contracting party? The answer is in every case a question of fact. If the consignor unambiguously contracts with the carrier he will be the principal, but more often he contracts as the agent of the owner (*Dawes v. Peck* (*1799*)) and Section 32 of the *Sale of Goods Act, 1979*). The problem is frequently resolved by the carrier covering the point in his conditions of carriage, so as to prevent any difficulty. A typical clause reads:

> 2 (1) *The Trader warrants that he is either the owner of the goods in any consignment or is authorised by such owner to accept these Conditions on such owner's behalf.*
> (Road Haulage Association Conditions of Carriage)

In any difficulty the carrier will thus be able to deal with the owner of the goods, and if the owner is able to reject liability (for freight, for example) the carrier will be able to turn to the consignor for breach of warranty of authority, since he purported to be the owner's agent.

16.3.1 Delay in carriage

Both common carriers and private carriers have a duty to deliver goods within a reasonable time, and what is reasonable depends upon the facts of every case. If the time taken is unreasonable then there has been a delay, and if this can be proved to be due to the carrier's negligence he will be liable. If delay is caused by deviation from the route the carrier will almost certainly be liable.

16.3.2 Deviation from the route

Deviation is departure from the route the carrier has expressly or implicitly agreed to follow. It is also deviation to go past a destination, or to take a vessel in tow at sea. Where no express agreement is entered into about deviation the carrier must carry by his normal route, even if it is not the shortest route. A carrier by sea may depart from his route to avoid imminent peril and to save life, and presumably this would also apply to carriage by land.

The rules about deviation have always been strict. A carrier who deviates is taken to have repudiated the contract *ab initio* and consequently cannot rely upon any clauses in the contract limiting his liability. He is also deemed to be a wrongful possessor of goods, liable for every loss that occurs to them. This is an even more onerous liability than that borne by the common carrier, for to escape liability he must show that the loss was caused by one of the common law exceptions *and also* that it would have occurred even if he had not deviated. In *Morrison v. Shaw, Savill and Albion Co. Ltd* (*1916*) a ship deviated into a French port and was torpedoed as she came out again to resume her voyage. The carriers claimed it was an Act of the King's enemies, but it was held that they must also prove that the ship would still have been torpedoed had she not deviated. This they could not prove, and were held liable for the losses suffered.

Because of the onerous nature of the rules about deviation it is usual in conditions of carriage to have an express term such as the following:

> *The carrier shall be entitled to enter into contracts for the carriage of goods by any route, or by any means.*

16.3.3 Misdelivery

The duty of the carrier is to deliver the goods to the consignee, and if he delivers them to any other person it is a misdelivery. If the carrier has to deliver to a given address it is a misdelivery if he delivers them anywhere else. If he delivers them to the correct address to someone who appears to be entitled to accept delivery he has performed his duty and cannot be held liable if the party who accepted them was not in fact entitled to do so.

If a carrier tries to deliver in normal working hours at the correct address, and is unable to do so for any reason, he is discharged from his duty to deliver and now holds the goods as a warehouseman. In this position he is liable only for negligence. In *Stephenson v. Hart* (1828) a carrier was instructed to deliver goods to a named address. When he arrived there it was clear the premises were deserted. He nevertheless left a card saying that the goods could be claimed at his depot. A person purporting to be the consignee presented the card, collected the goods and could not later be found. It was held to be a negligent misdelivery.

16.3.4 Stoppage in transit

Sections 44–6 of the *Sale of Goods Act, 1979*, re-enacting the *Sale of Goods Act, 1893*, permit an unpaid seller who hears that his customer has become insolvent to stop the goods in transit, and retain them until payment or tender of the price. This naturally raises the question of when goods are in transit – and the Act lays down clear rules for deciding when the goods are in transit. This is from the moment they are given to a carrier or other bailee for the purpose of transit to the buyer until one of the following times:

- The moment when the buyer or his agent takes delivery at destination, or
- The buyer obtains delivery at some other place before the ultimate destination is reached, or
- The carrier acknowledges at the destination end of the journey that he holds them on behalf of the buyer – perhaps for delivery to some further destination, or
- The carrier wrongfully refuses to deliver them to the buyer. In this case the transit is at an end and the carrier will be liable to the buyer if he 'stops' them in transit.

The transit is not at an end – i.e. the goods may be stopped and returned to the seller – if the buyer refuses the goods. When goods are delivered to a ship chartered by the buyer it is a question of fact whether they are held on behalf of the buyer or on behalf of the master of the ship acting as carrier. When a part delivery has been made the balance of goods may still be stopped unless the delivery of the first part was made on the clear understanding that the possession of the whole would be surrendered.

The unpaid seller exercises his right of stoppage in transit by giving notice to the carrier, or to the person actually possessing the goods – usually the driver of a vehicle. If the notice is given to the carrier it must be in time for him to contact the servant or agent in actual possession. The carrier must then redeliver the goods to – or to the order of – the seller, who must pay the costs of redelivery.

16.3.5 The carrier's lien

A lien is a carrier's right to retain the goods in his possession until such time as the charges connected with them are paid. At common law the carrier's lien is a **particular, passive, possessory lien**. In most conditions of carriage the carrier specifies a **general lien**. The differences are as follows:

- A *particular lien* entitles the carrier to retain goods only as long as the charges due on that particular package are not paid. If the customer pays the carriage on the package it must be surrendered, *irrespective of what other sums are owing to the carrier (Prenty v. Midland Great Western Railway Company (1866)).* By specifying a *general lien* the private carrier claims the right to retain goods in his possession until *all* sums owing to him are paid.

- A *passive, possessory lien* confers upon the carrier only the passive right to retain possession of the goods. Some liens specify a right to sell the goods – after due notice to the owner – so that an opportunity is afforded to pay the freight due. When sold, the freight payable may be deducted and the payment of any balance to the owner is full settlement of any claim by him, provided that the goods have been sold at the best price obtainable in the circumstances.

A typical lien clause in a set of conditions reads as follows:

The Carrier shall have a general lien against the owner of the goods for any moneys whatever due from the Trader or such owner to the Carrier. If any such lien is not satisfied within a reasonable time the Carrier may at his absolute discretion, sell the goods, or part thereof, as agent for the owner and apply the proceeds towards the moneys due and the expenses of the retention, insurance and sale of the goods and shall, upon accounting to the Trader for any balance remaining, be discharged from all liability in respect of the goods.
(Road Haulage Association Conditions of Carriage)

16.3.6 Dangerous goods

At common law the consignor of dangerous goods who does not declare their dangerous nature to the carrier is liable for every loss that occurs to persons, goods or the vehicle. If the carrier has a statutory duty to carry, the consignor of dangerous goods is liable whether or not he knew of the danger, or could reasonably have been expected to know of it. With private carriers it is usual for the conditions of carriage to include a clause about dangerous goods, making it perfectly clear that if the carrier agrees to carry them the consignor is responsible for a full and frank declaration of their nature. They must be packed and documented according to law, and the trader must indemnify the carrier against all loss or damage arising out of their carriage. The ADR Convention (*Accord Dangereux Routiers*) is a European convention adopted by the UK which governs the packing, marking and carriage of dangerous goods. It runs to 500 pages and the full text is available from Her Majesty's Stationery Office.

A recent example of the carriage of dangerous goods was *The Giannis, UK*, a 1994 case in which a beetle infestation in a cargo of groundnuts affected other cargo in the vessel. This cargo had to be dumped at sea. The groundnuts cargo was held to be dangerous, in that it caused the loss of the other cargo, and the shipper was held *strictly liable* for it, even though he did not know of the defect and could not have known about it. The damages for loss of cargo and delay were a little over $470 000.

16.3.7 Carriage by two or more carriers

In common law the duty of the carrier is to deliver the goods to the consignee. If he hands the goods over to another carrier and there is a misdelivery or any other loss or damage he will be liable to the owner even though it was the fault of the other carrier. To avoid this liability it is usual to include a clause reading

2 (2) *The Carrier and any other carrier employed by the Carrier may employ the services of any other carrier for the purpose of fulfilling the Contract in whole or in part and the name of every such other carrier shall be provided to the Trader on request.*
(Road Haulage Association Conditions of Carriage)

16.3.8 The measure of damages

The measure of damages at common law is the same as for any ordinary contract, and was laid down in the case of *Hadley v. Baxendale* (see page 185). The damages are limited to those that follow naturally from the breach of duty, or breach of contract, unless the parties noted in advance that special damages would result from any breach by declaring the value of the goods or explaining the consequences of any breach. The parties may of course agree on any sum of liquidated damages they feel is appropriate to offset any loss that may occur, but if this sum is excessive it will be void as constituting a penalty.

In most sets of conditions of carriage the carrier's liability is limited by a special clause to some standard amount. It will never exceed the value of the goods themselves. In most international conventions the difficulties of stating values in money terms have now led to the limitations being expressed in Special Drawing Rights units (SDRs). This is a unit whose value is relatively stable because it is made up of a currency basket. The composition of 1 SDR unit is as follows:

0.45	$US
0.46	Deutschemarks
0.071	£ Sterling
0.74	French Francs
34.00	Japanese Yen

Its actual value in a real settlement currency is recalculated daily by the International Monetary Fund and published in the major financial journals.

Where SDRs are not yet in use and national currencies are used, the limits of liability have traditionally been fixed at £800 per ton. This still applies to road haulage, but British Rail currently quotes £2000 per metric tonne – a figure which appears to take fair account of inflation in the value of goods in recent years.

16.3.9 Himalaya clauses

A celebrated legal case concerning the SS *Himalaya* led to a completely new clause being inserted in contracts of carriage. They were called by the popular name of **Himalaya clauses**. The facts of the case were as follows:

Adler v. Dickson (1954)

The plaintiff was a passenger on the SS *Himalaya* who was injured by a fall which she alleged was due to the negligence of the master and boatswain of the ship. Her ticket bore a clause saying that passengers were carried at their own risk and the company could not be held liable in any circumstances whatsoever, etc. **Held**: the company were protected by their contract, but the master and boatswain were not protected by the contract and the plaintiff's action against them must be allowed to proceed. Considerable damages were received by the plaintiff as a result.

Law of carriage by land, sea and air

The effect has been for nearly all sets of conditions of carriage to carry a Himalaya clause which carries the benefit of the contract over to the servants and agents of the carrier. A typical wording is:

> 2 (3) *The Carrier contracts for itself and as agent of and trustee for its servants and agents and all other carriers referred to in (2) above and such other carrier's servants and agents and every reference in Conditions 3–17 inclusive hereof to 'The Carrier' shall be deemed to include every such other carrier, servant and agent with the intention that they shall have the benefit of the Contract and collectively and together with the Carrier be under no greater liability to the Trader or any other party than is the Carrier hereunder.*
> (Road Haulage Association Conditions of Carriage)

16.4 Statutory modifications to the law of carriage

Before considering the actual laws applicable to each mode of transport it is necessary to make a few points clear. These relate to:

- The development of the law of carriage in various fields.
- The international influences bearing upon the law of carriage.

16.4.1 Development of the law of carriage

Traditionally the law was divided into two parts: inland carriage (which meant carriage by road) and carriage by sea (in ships). However, the Industrial Revolution led to the growth of canals, a new form of inland carriage by inland waterways, which was akin to sea carriage because vessels (barges) were used. Then the railways networks provided a third kind of inland transport. Both of these new networks were open to abuse because they were **natural monopolies**, and the carriers could abuse their monopoly positions by discriminating against particular customers by excessive charges, etc. The result was that Parliament felt it necessary to interfere to ensure fair play, and in particular to see that a proper range of facilities was available to the public and that discrimination was not practised.

16.4.2 International influences

Meanwhile, in sea transport, problems had arisen over the bill of lading, a document used throughout the world, which in some cases was not worth the paper on which it was printed. International trade began to suffer and international agreement was called for. The solution found was to agree an international convention document, the **Hague Rules**, which member states could ratify and enact into their 'national' laws. When a sufficient number of nations had enacted the convention the law in all their countries became the same, and confidence in bills of lading returned. Similar problems arose in air transport, where the need to overfly territory and land anywhere in an emergency called for an international agreement in other ways too. An international convention document, the **Warsaw Rules**, was agreed and implemented in the same way by enactment in Parliament. We see therefore that statutory modifications of the law of carriage became increasingly important. When the movement of goods internationally by road and rail also began, with railway wagons and heavy goods vehicles rumbling across whole continents, even inland carriage became part of an international network. The enactment of conventions for road and rail movements followed.

These statutory modifications of the law of carriage will be explained in each section below at appropriate points.

16.5 Carriage by road

Inland carriage by road is the traditional mode of carriage, and originally all carriers were common carriers subject to the strict rules already described. An early piece of legislation, the *Carriers Act, 1830*, gave statutory recognition to the common carrier's common law right to demand an extra freight for the carriage of valuable goods. It also contained provisions exempting the common carrier from all liability in respect of valuables which were not declared by the consignor. The Act provided that where goods in the valuable class (defined as gold and silver coins, gold and silver in a manufactured or non-manufactured state, precious stones, jewellery, watches, clocks, trinkets, bills of exchange, banknotes, stamps, maps, writings, title deeds, paintings, engravings, pictures, gold-plated or silver-plated articles, china, glass, silks, furs or lace – but later machine-made lace was excluded – worth more than £10) were included in a package, the carrier shall not be liable for loss, except by the felony of his servants, unless the consignor has declared the value and paid an additional sum over and above the freight as insurance money, if the carrier demanded it. The meanings of the words are to be interpreted in the popular use of the word and not strictly. Thus 'valuable paintings' refer to works of art, and not painted patterns belonging to a commercial traveller (*Woodward v. London and North-Western Rly (1878)*). The value is the value to the consignor on sending the goods. The Act is not of great importance now as there are so few common carriers, and the railways are not affected as they have been statutorily declared to be private carriers.

For inland road transport the vast majority of carriers stipulate that they are private carriers, carrying under conditions of carriage which are available on request. Often these are drawn up for them by a trade association, such as the Road Haulage Association.

16.5.1 The Carriage of Goods by Road Act, 1965, and the Carriage by Air and Road Act, 1979

When international road haulage began to develop in the post-war years, it soon became clear that some internationally agreed rules of law were required. The conditions of carriage used by many UK carriers excluded liability, even for negligence, which seemed manifestly unfair to foreign buyers of goods. They were not used to the old figment of English law which held that all the parties to a contract were equally powerful in the eyes of the law. Since in many cases they had not been party to the negotiations when the contract of carriage was concluded it all seemed very nonsensical to them.

The result was an international convention at Geneva, the *Convention de Marchandises par Route* (CMR), which may be freely translated as the convention on merchandise carried by road hauliers. It held that all international carriage except the mails, funeral consignments and furniture removals should be controlled by the provisions of the CMR Convention and be documented by a CMR consignment note. However, Ireland has not ratified the Convention, and Northern Ireland is treated as part of the UK so internal transits to Northern Ireland would not be covered by the Convention. The Convention was embodied in English law by the *Carriage of Goods by Road Act, 1965*. The *Carriage by Air and Road Act, 1979*, changes the basis on which compensation is offered to take account of the use of SDR as the monetary unit in any calculations. The important points of the Convention, which may be read in full in the Acts referred to, are as follows:

- *Basis of legal relationship between the parties.* This is a statutory relationship, based upon the acts mentioned. The Convention overrides what the parties have agreed in their private contracts if it differs from the Convention.
- *The definition of international carriage.* This is defined as 'carriage of goods by road in vehicles for reward, when the place of taking over the goods and the place designated for delivery as specified in the contract, are situated in two different countries, of which at least one is a contracting country (i.e. has ratified the CMR Convention) irrespective of the place of residence and the nationality of the parties.
- *Extent of the carrier's liability.* The hauler is liable for total or partial loss or damage to goods between take-over and delivery, unless he can show fault of the plaintiff, inherent vice or circumstances beyond his own control. He is also liable for delay and failure to collect COD charges (if requested).
- *Official document.* This is the CMR consignment note, which must bear a large sign 'CMR' and the words 'International Consignment Note'.
- *Limitation of liability.* This is limited to 8.33 SDR units of account per kilogram of gross weight, or the full value, whichever is less.
- *Jurisdiction of the courts.* Action may be brought:
  - in any place mutually agreed, or
  - where the defendant is resident or has his principal place of business or an establishment where the contract was made, or
  - where the goods were taken over by the carrier, or
  - in the country of delivery.

  This virtually means that any aggrieved party can have the case tried in his own country, and his courts will have jurisdiction.
- *Time limit on actions.* Action must be brought within one year, but this is extended to three years if wilful misconduct is alleged.

16.6 Carriage by rail

Railways were originally common carriers, and liable to the full extent as common carriers for every loss that occurred except those caused by the common law exceptions listed earlier (see Section 16.1). During the nineteenth century a running battle between Parliament and the monopolist railway companies led to almost annual Railway Acts, with Parliament attempting to load responsibilities onto the companies which they proceeded to evade by clever legal advice. A notable legal rule developed in this period was the '**doctrine of the fair alternative**', which held that railway companies could exclude their liability for negligence in their conditions of carriage if they offered customers a fair alternative. This was carriage at company risk for a slightly higher charge, which amounted to an insurance premium payable by the customer.

Unfortunately, by the time Parliament had really gained control of the railway companies (the actual date was 1 January 1893) the internal combustion engine had arrived to destroy their monopoly, and they had become a high-cost enterprise at just the wrong moment. It has been truthfully said that it takes 60 years for any major development to work its way through the economy; it took 60 years to rivet chains on the railways and make them behave properly, and another 60 years to remove the chains so that they could survive as a transport system. This happened in 1962 when the *Transport Act, 1962*, made them private carriers, carrying by virtue of private contracts with their customers, and relieving them at last of the onerous liabilities of the common carrier.

The carriage of goods by rail is now regulated by five sets of conditions of carriage. These are:

- The general conditions of carriage.
- Carriage by water.
- Carriage of livestock.
- Carriage of coal, coke and patent fuel.
- Warehousing.

They may be obtained on request from the Board of British Rail. Space does not permit the reproduction in full of these conditions, or a detailed discussion of them, but the student with a real interest in the law of carriage will find the study of these sets of conditions very rewarding.

16.6.1 International rail movements

International rail movements were not initially of much interest to the United Kingdom, and the first international convention (signed in 1914) was largely a matter for the continental powers. Later, the United Kingdom did ratify the Convention, called the **CIM Convention**, (a title which may be translated roughly as the Convention on International Merchandise). This name is itself rather illuminating, for at the time it was originally used it was not felt necessary to refer to the fact that it was about rail movements, since in 1914 road transport had not reached the stage where it could carry goods economically internationally. The title 'Convention on International Merchandise' could, therefore, only mean 'merchandise moving by rail'. Today the correct name for the organization which seeks to develop rail movements internationally is OTIF (the initial letters of the French words for the Intergovernmental Organization for International Carriage by Rail). Thirty-three countries have participated in COTIF (the Convention on OTIF). They are called the contracting parties, and include all the European Community countries, most of the former Comecon countries (but not Russia), Iraq, Iran, Algeria, Morocco, Yugoslavia, Syria, Turkey, The Lebanon, Norway, Sweden, Finland and Switzerland.

The aim of the organization is to 'establish a uniform system of law applicable to the carriage of passengers, luggage and goods in international traffic by rail between member states, and to facilitate the application and development of this system.'

Carriage in international through-traffic is subject to two sets of rules: the CIM Rules (uniform rules concerning the contract for International Carriage of Goods by Rail); and the CIV Rules (uniform rules concerning the contract for International Carriage of Passengers and Luggage by Rail). CIV actually stands for the French words for the 'Carriage of International Voyagers'. So, strictly speaking, it is not correct now to talk about the CIM Convention and the CIV Convention – we should instead talk about COTIF (the Convention on OTIF) and the two sets of rules – the CIM Rules and the CIV Rules.

The uniform system of law referred to as the chief aim of OTIF is also intended to apply to goods which travel partly by rail and partly by road, short-sea services and inland waterways.

The COTIF Convention was given effect in the United Kingdom by the *International Transport Conventions Act, 1983*. It is impossible to include the full wording of these Conventions in a book of this sort but some of the chief points in the CIM Rules are as follows:

Law of carriage by land, sea and air

(a) The consignment note	This bears the symbol CIM and is written in three languages: English, French and German. Goods carried under this symbol are regarded as consigned under the Convention and actions may only be brought in accordance with it as required by the 1983 Act. However in the United Kingdom the railway authorities found that the completion of consignment notes at railway stations all over the country was time-consuming and required an excessive amount of training for a multitude of clerks. They therefore set up a special team which makes out all the documents in electronic form; the consignor merely faxing the details of the consignment to the special team and the documentation is prepared centrally, and not in paper form.
(b) Definition of international carriage	Carriage of goods under a through-consignment note for carriage by rail over the territories of at least two contracting states and exclusively over lines listed in Section 59 of the Convention.
(c) Speed of transit	This decides whether delay has occurred. There are two speeds – fast carriage and slow carriage – and within these speeds full wagons are expected to travel faster than part-wagon loads. Full wagon loads at fast carriage must leave within 12 hours and then travel 300 km in the first 24 hours and 400 km in each subsequent 24 hours. Part-wagon loads must leave within 12 hours and then travel 300 km in each subsequent 24 hours. For slow carriage the goods must leave within 24 hours and travel 200 km in the next 24 hours and 300 km per day thereafter. Less than full wagon loads at slow carriage leave within 24 hours and then travel 200 km per day. A red-bordered consignment note is for fast travel, a green note is for slow carriage.
(d) The route	This may be specified by the consignor. If it is not the railway must send the goods by the most favourable route *for the customer.*
(e) Customs	The railway acts as the agent of the sender in clearing the goods through customs. The sender is responsible for the documentation necessary, and a **Simplified Customs Procedure** is available.
(f) The carrier's liability	The carrier is liable for total or partial loss or damage to the goods unless it can prove fault of the claimant, inherent vice or circumstances beyond its own control. Delay is failure to achieve the speeds of transit prescribed above. The carrier may also be held liable for failure to collect COD charges.
(g) Limitation of liability	Liability is limited to 17 European Units of Account per kilogram converted to currency on the date payment is due. The value of an EUA (ECU) is recalculated daily by the European Commission.
(h) Jurisdiction	The plaintiff selects the railway he wishes to sue and brings an action in the courts of the state where the railway is. Thus a consignee could sue his own railway company even if it never received the goods, to enable the consignee

to sue in his country. Claims for delay must be made within 30 days of arrival. One year is allowed for all other claims unless wilful misconduct is alleged, when the time limit is three years.

16.7 Carriage by inland waterways

Canals and inland waterways are not regarded as 'seas' and consequently carriers who use them are treated in law as if they were carriers by road, except that they do use craft which are a form of ship. A ship is defined in the *Merchant Shipping Act, 1894*, as a vessel which is not propelled by oars, so it is incorrect to use the word 'boat' for barges and other river craft. A carrier by inland waterway warrants that his craft is seaworthy – in other words, fit for the purpose for which it is to be used. They are common carriers, but the *Carriers Act, 1830*, does not apply to inland waterways. They may, like all common carriers, make a special contract, and they may hold themselves out as only private carriers if they wish to do so. However, there is a point of difficulty here which concerns the existence of a third type of carrier, which Lord Esher called 'public carriers'.

In *Liver Alkali Company v. Johnson* (1874) Lord Esher took the view that in carriage by sea and inland waterway all those who carry as professional carriers are either **common carriers** or **public carriers**. Common carriers carry under the same rules as common carriers by road, but public carriers are special in that they are not under a duty to carry, and may always refuse to carry if they wish to do so, but if goods are carried the public carrier is liable – like the common carrier – for every loss that occurs, unless it was caused by one of the *six* common law exceptions (for at sea there is a sixth exception – jettison).

Who then is a private carrier by sea or inland waterway? The answer is a person who does not carry on the profession of carrier, but only carries as an ancillary activity to his main business. Thus in *Consolidated Tea and Lands Co. v. Oliver's Wharf* (1910), where the wharfingers had agreed to warehouse items for the company, but only carried in so far as this was necessary to bring the goods to the warehouse, they were held not to be carriers, but only warehousemen, and only carried as an incidental activity to their main business. They were therefore private carriers. Similarly, those who carry for one consignor only are not common carriers or public carriers, for they do not carry for the public at large. Lord Esher's view has been upheld in several cases, so it appears that all who carry as professional carriers are liable as insurers of the goods (unless they have made a special contract to avoid this) but public carriers are not liable in tort for refusal to carry.

16.8 Carriage of goods by sea

A contract for the carriage of goods by sea (a contract of affreightment) may be made in two ways, and there are several bodies of law which apply – most notably the Hague-Visby rules (see below). The two methods are:

- A contract for the carriage of goods in a general ship, the contractual document being a bill of lading.
- A charterparty, which provides for the hiring of the ship itself. A charterer may then carry goods for other people on bills of lading, or may find cargo himself and issue bills of lading referring to these goods, but the charterparty will be the main contractual document between the charterer and the shipowner.

The bodies of law affecting these contracts are as follows:

- In some cases the carrier is a common carrier and the law that applies is the common law.
- In many cases where bills of lading are in use the law that will apply is the *Carriage of Goods by Sea Act, 1971*, which embodies the Hague-Visby rules into English law. This will be explained later.
- Certain statutes have important legal consequences, notably the *Merchant Shipping Acts 1894, 1958 and 1981*.
- The law relating to charterparties.

Once again it is possible in the present text to give only a brief outline – those with a particular interest should read the book recommended in Section 16.1 above.

16.8.1 Historical development of carriage by sea

The reason the law is so involved is that until 1925 it was based upon the common law, and sea carriers were common carriers liable for every loss that occurred, unless the common law exceptions applied. There were six common law exceptions in carriage by sea, **jettison** being added to Act of God, Act of the Queen's enemies, inherent vice, fault of the consignor and fraud of the consignor.

(a) Jettison

This is the deliberate sacrifice of cargo to save a vessel, and the carrier is not liable. Instead the law of general average applies. This has been explained already (see pages 255 and 256).

(b) Warranty of seaworthiness

A carrier warrants that his vessel is seaworthy, and if it is not he is liable (unless the contract expressly excludes this liability). The warranty is that the ship is *reasonably* fit for the *stage* of the voyage that is about to commence. The warranty extends beyond the actual ship's condition to include such things as the adequacy of the crew, illness or drunkenness of the officers, provisions and medicines for the voyage, security of the portholes, etc.

As is usual in such situations, shipowners began to protect themselves from such harsh rules applicable to common carriers by excluding liability in the conditions of carriage written on the back of bills of lading. This had a disastrous effect on the value of bills of lading. Let us stop here to consider the legal aspects of bills of lading.

(a) Bills of lading

A bill of lading is a document given by a shipowner (or a charterer) to a consignor of goods as a receipt for the goods. It is not essential that a bill of lading be issued, but the master of a vessel as the agent of the shipowner will always supply one if requested. It is usual to demand a *shipped* bill of lading, since it confirms that the goods have crossed the ship's rail. A *received for shipment* bill of lading is not so satisfactory, except where the carrier is a multimodal operator assuming the role of **combined transport operator (CTO)** liable for every stage of the journey. An alternative name for CTO is MTO, multimodal transport operator. Even he will hold back the received for shipment bills of lading he normally issues so that they can be stamped **shipped** after the goods are actually on board, if he is requested to do so.

We can list the functions of the bill of lading as follows:

- It is a receipt for the goods shipped.
- It is a document of title, which may be transferred to another person by assignment.
- It is evidence of the contract of carriage.

The chief use of the bill of lading is as a document of title. Since sea journeys take a long time and prices of cargoes fluctuate, the owner of a cargo may wish to sell goods while they are on the high seas. He does this by assigning the bill of lading to the party prepared to buy it, who can then claim the goods by presenting the bill of lading to the master of the vessel on arrival at the destination port. The bill of lading is often said to be quasi-negotiable, which means almost negotiable. It is not fully negotiable – like a bill of exchange – because the assignee does not get a better title than the giver had, but only the same title as the giver had. The assignee always takes subject to the equities, i.e. the equitable rights of others.

The bill of lading is only strong evidence of the contract of carriage, but it is permissible to introduce evidence that in fact the contract was made earlier. Since space has to be booked on ships well in advance in many cases it is likely that the discussions at that time will make a binding contract before the bill of lading has even been completed. In the 'Ardennes' case the facts were as follows:

> *The Ardennes (owners of cargo) v. The Ardennes (owners) (1951)*
>
> In the negotiations leading up to the loading of the cargo the shipowner said that the ship would proceed direct to London. The bill of lading contained a deviation clause which permitted the owner to proceed to ports in any order he chose. By going to Antwerp the vessel was delayed and when it did arrive in London the owners of cargo were charged a higher rate of duty than would have been the case if the vessel had proceeded direct. **Held**: The contract was made earlier than the bill of lading and the safeguarding clause could not protect the shipowner, who was liable for the extra duty charged to the cargo owners.

Returning to the historical aspects, when bills of lading were assigned from one person to another the property in the goods (which were on the high seas) passed to the assignee, but the original contract of affreightment was still between the shipper and the shipowner. This meant, by the strict rules of privity of contract, that the new owners of the goods could not sue the carrier if anything was wrong with the goods on arrival, since they were not a party to the original contract. Also, if clauses were inserted by the shipowners in their bills of lading which denied liability in any circumstances it meant that those who took bills of lading in good faith for value found that when cargoes arrived – if they were damaged or had suffered losses – no redress was available against the carrier. This led to a serious loss of confidence in bills of lading.

Parliament took action by passing the *Bills of Lading Act, 1855*. This Act has recently been repealed and replaced by the *Carriage of Goods by Sea Act, 1992*. However it is worth discussing the 1855 Act because the vital rules in it still apply; the 1992 Act only corrects defects revealed in the 1855 Act during the 140 years since its inception.

Although a very short Act, the *Bills of Lading Act, 1855*, did much to remedy the problems with bills of lading at that time.

(b) Bills of Lading Act, 1855

Section 1 of the Act, which is reproduced below, gave the assignees of a bill of lading the right to sue upon the original contract, which travelled with the bill, giving the assignee the same rights (and the same duties) under the contract of affreightment as were available to the original shipper. The section reads:

> 1. *Consignees and endorsees of bill of lading empowered to sue.* – *Every consignee of goods named in a bill of lading, and every endorsee of a bill of lading, to whom the property in the goods therein mentioned shall pass upon or by reason of such consignment or endorsement, shall have transferred to and vested in him all rights of suit, and be subject to the same liabilities in respect of such goods as if the contract contained in the bill of lading had been made with himself.*

Section 2 made it clear that this new right did not affect the right of stoppage in transit, or the right of the carrier to claim freight against the original shipper.

Section 3, the most important clause, reads as follows:

> *Every bill of lading in the hands of a consignee or endorsee for valuable consideration representing goods to have been shipped on board a vessel shall be conclusive evidence of such shipment as against the master or other person signing the same, notwithstanding that such goods or some part thereof may not have been so shipped, unless such holder of the bill of lading shall have had actual notice at the time of receiving the same that the goods had not been in fact laden on board: Provided that the master or other person so signing may exonerate himself in respect of such misrepresentation by showing that it was caused without any default on his part and wholly by the fraud of the shipper or of the holder or some person under whom the holder claims.*

This has the effect of making the master (or other signatory of a clean bill of lading) liable for goods which are lost or arrive damaged, unless it is possible to falsify the bill of lading by clear proof that the bill misrepresents what was actually loaded without any default on the master's part, but solely because of the fraud of the shipper, or holder, or some person under whom the holder claims.

Although the *Bills of Lading Act, 1855*, did solve some of the problems in carriage by sea it did not say anything about exemption clauses entered into bills of lading and these clauses excluding liability continued to be a cause of trouble. Eventually an international conference held at Brussels in 1922 produced a set of rules which came to be known as the **Hague Rules**. Later these were modified to become the Hague-Visby Rules. Before looking at these rules, which are explained below, we must see what the *Carriage of Goods by Sea Act, 1992* (COGSA 1992) has done to the rules about bills of lading now that the 1855 Act is repealed.

(c) The Carriage of Goods by Sea Act, 1992

In the years since 1855 a number of weaknesses had been revealed in the 1855 Act. The chief of these was in the right to sue upon the bill of lading. The 1855 Act we have seen conferred a right to sue upon assignees 'to whom the property in the goods passes'. This linking of the right to sue to the passing of the property has been a source of difficulty since there are many situations where a person can become a rightful holder of a bill of lading without actually being the owner of the goods. For example where the bill is pledged as security for a debt, the owner does not want to pass the property in the goods to the pledgee, nor does the pledgee want to become liable on the bill (for example for unpaid freight). Similarly if a bill of lading is delayed and a ship has arrived, the *bona fide* owner of the goods wants to take delivery, and it is a common practice to release the cargo in exchange for a letter of indemnity. The consignee agrees to indemnify the shipowner if any other person presents a bill of lading and demands the cargo. In both these cases the person receiving the goods, finding some defect in them, could not sue on the bill because the 1855 Act did not apply, the property in the goods not having passed to them.

COGSA 1992 has resolved the problems referred to by separating the issue of the right to sue from the passing of the property. If the person claiming the goods is a *bona fide* holder of the bill of lading he now has the right to sue upon the bill simply because he is the lawful holder of the bill. This enables the holder to seek legal redress of any breach of contract, loss, damage, delay, etc. A further right is that such a holder may also bring an action in favour of any third party who has an interest in the goods and has suffered loss but who has no right to sue because he/she is not the holder of the bill of lading. Whilst the holder is entitled to do this, he/she is not obliged to do it.

The Act also applies to other documents which are rather similar to bills of lading, which have arisen because of changing practices in shipping. Where the consignor does not wish to sell the goods to a third party while they are in the high seas, there is no point in having a bill of lading. Thus a component manufacturer sending a cargo of parts to a factory in Country A from his factory in Country B has no need of a bill of lading. A document rather like a road haulage consignment note but called a 'sea waybill' is used instead. A ship's delivery order is a similar type of document. *COGSA 1992* says that the holder of such a document can sue upon it if necessary.

Other interesting points of *COGSA 1992* are:

- The Act does apply to a 'received for shipment bill of lading'. Traditionally a received for shipment bill of lading has always been deemed unsatisfactory since it does not signal that goods have actually been shipped on board – as does a 'shipped bill of lading'. However, in these days of multimodal transport, it is common for the consignor to be content with a received for shipment bill of lading since the multimodal transport operator assumes full responsibility for all stages of the transit and once the goods have been taken over by the operator he will be liable for the whole operation. Some major shipping companies acting as MTOs issue a received for shipment bill of lading as soon as goods are put into their hands, but are prepared to overstamp it 'Shipped On Board' once the actual loading has taken place.
- The Act authorizes the Secretary of State to make suitable regulations providing for the Act to cover all situations where paper documents are dispensed with, and the bill of lading or other document exists as an electronic element in some standardized format in a memory bank of someone's information technology network. In such situations the indorsement and assignment would be effected by electronic data interchange (EDI).

The rest of the Act simply re-states the other parts of the 1855 Act, in that:

- the person who acquires the right to sue upon the contract embodied in the bill of lading also assumes any duties stated therein (for example to pay any unpaid freight).
- that the signature of an authorized person evidencing the shipment of goods on board a vessel is conclusive evidence against the carrier that the goods have been shipped as far as the lawful holder of the bill is concerned.

(d) The Merchant Shipping Acts 1894, 1958 and 1981

There are many matters to regulate about the safety of merchant shipping and only one or two affect the law of carriage, but these sections are important.

Sections 492–501 of the *Merchant Shipping Act, 1894*, extend the right of lien of the carrier with regard to warehoused goods. A valuable ship cannot wait around in port for someone to collect his cargo, and the Act permitted a carrier who is delayed for more than three days in this way to unload the goods into the care of a warehouseman empowered to release the goods on payment of the sum the carrier had declared to be due. Exact arrangements for the release of the goods and the payment of the money to the carrier are then laid down.

Section 502 is a re-enactment of a section of an earlier act about fire at sea. Fire at sea is a devastating event and the section says that no British shipowner shall be liable for losses at sea caused by fire unless it can be shown that the fire was actually caused by his 'actual fault and privity'. This means that he is not vicariously liable for the faults of servants or employees, but only liable for his own actual acts or faults.

The *Merchant Shipping Act, 1894*, also introduced a protection for shipowners where valuables had been brought on board undeclared, and were subsequently stolen or made away with secretly. The shipowner is not liable in these circumstances under Section 502 of the Act.

Section 503 of the Act limited the liability of the shipowner for loss of life, injury or damage to goods or other vessels, to an aggregate amount of 3100 gold francs per ton of the ship's tonnage for loss of life or injury, and 1000 gold francs per ton of the ship's tonnage for damage or loss of goods. The use of the gold franc later gave rise to difficulties and this was eventually decided to be the gold franc of $65\frac{1}{2}$ milligrams of gold of millesimal fineness 900. The value of this was published in orders called Sterling Equivalent Orders from time to time but, as we shall see below, the *Merchant Shipping Act, 1981*, has resolved the difficulty.

After the case of *Adler v. Dickson* (1955) referred to earlier, it was resolved to introduce what was virtually a 'Himalaya clause' into the Merchant Shipping Acts to protect the masters and other servants of the shipowner from personal actions brought by aggrieved parties unable to sue the shipowner or carrier because of exclusionary clauses in their contracts. The *Merchant Shipping Act, 1958* provides that they cannot be held liable except in cases of their 'actual fault and privity'. Therefore, while they will always be liable for robbery, theft or secretly making away with valuables, they will not be liable for personal injuries or loss of or damage to goods unless they can be shown to have been personally at fault. The clauses about limitation of liability were also extended to them on the same terms as limitations of the liability of shipowners.

The Merchant Shipping Act, 1981 resolved the old difficulty about the value of the gold franc by replacing it with a designation in SDR units. The Special Drawing Rights unit is a currency basket, made up of a selection of currencies. Its value is more stable than gold, and consequently the problems due to the changing value of gold do not arise. The 3100 gold francs per ton is changed to 206.67 SDRs, and the 1000 gold francs per ton is changed to 66.67 SDRs. For the *Carriage of Goods by Sea Act, 1971*, the figure of 10 000 gold francs per package is changed to 666.67 SDRs, and the figure of 30 gold francs per kilogram is changed to 2 SDRs per kilogram.

16.8.2 Conventions on the carriage of goods by sea

The Convention on the Carriage of Goods by Sea, which came to be known as the **Hague Rules**, was embodied in English law by the *Carriage of Goods by Sea Act, 1924*. Its later revised version, known as the **Hague-Visby Rules**, was embodied in English law by the *Carriage of Goods by Sea Act, 1971*. Like all such Acts it could not commence until the required number of states had ratified it, and the effective date proved to be June 1977. This is now the effective Act, but a new set of rules, the **Hamburg Rules**, have been drawn up by the United Nations. These are slightly more favourable to cargo owners and unfavourable to the carriers, but at present they await ratification.

The essence of the Hague-Visby Rules is that bills of lading for the international carriage of goods shall have such validity that those who wish to buy goods which are on the high seas will not hesitate to buy the bill of lading that represents the goods. To establish this validity the convention makes it clear what are the duties of the shipowner, what faults he can be held liable for, what is the limitation of that liability, etc.

The definition of international carriage is given in Article X as follows:

The provisions of these rules shall apply to every bill of lading relating to the carriage of goods between ports in two different states if:
(a) the bill of lading is issued in a contracting state, or
(b) the carriage is from a port in a contracting state, or
(c) the contract includes a clause that the Rules, or the laws of a country which has ratified the Rules, are to apply to the contract evidenced in the bill of lading, whatever may be the nationality of the ship, the carrier, the shipper, the consignee or any other interested person.

Because this is a rather restrictive definition Parliament enacted in the Act that the rules as far as English law was concerned should also apply to coastal traffic and to the carriage of goods to such places as Northern Ireland, Gibraltar and a few other dependent territories not covered by the definition of 'two different states.' The essential features of the Hague-Visby Rules reproduced in the 1971 Act in full are as follows:

(a) Legal relationships between the parties

The contractual terms of the bill of lading forming the legal relationship between the parties are superseded by the statutory rules now enacted by the inclusion of the Convention Document as a Schedule of the Act. No **clause paramount** (a clause in the bill of lading formally recognizing the existence of the convention rules) is required under the 1971 Act (but the new Hamburg Rules do call for such a clause). As far as the 1971 Act is concerned the rules apply to every bill of lading issued by the master of a British ship under the definitions given in the Act.

Law of carriage by land, sea and air

(b) The liability of the carrier

The shipowner must exercise due diligence in providing a seaworthy and cargo-worthy ship. The absolute warranty of seaworthiness under the common law is therefore reduced to a duty to exercise 'due diligence'. This means that the carrier will be responsible if he is negligent in any way in performing his duty as carrier – and this liability will extend to his servants or agents who perform duties for him *as a carrier*. It does not extend as far as agents who act wrongly outside their terms of reference. In *Leesh River Tea Company Ltd v. British Indian Steam Navigation Co. Ltd (1967)* the action against the shipowner failed because the damage complained of was the result of a theft of a cover from a storm valve by independent stevedores, who in doing so were outside the scope of their employment.

The shipowner must 'properly load, handle, stow, carry, keep, care for and discharge the cargo'. He is not liable for errors in navigation or the management of the ship, nor for fire, perils of the sea and a long list of exceptions which include all the common law exceptions. Notably it is permitted under the rules to save not only life, but also property, at sea. The exclusions are comprehensive because they include 'any other course arising without the **actual fault and privity** of the carrier, his servants and agents'. This makes it clear that the carrier *is* liable for those losses that do arise because of his actual fault or privity (and even more, the Rules make it clear that anyone claiming these exceptions has to prove that the actual fault of the shipowner or his servants *did not contribute to the loss or damage*).

(d) Limitation of liability

The limitation of liability is set under the Rules at 10 000 gold francs per package or 30 gold francs per kilogram, whichever is higher. These figures were agreed in 1968, when the use of currency baskets had not been developed. The *Merchant Shipping Act, 1981*, which still awaits a Commencement Order, will change them to 666.67 SDR units and 2 SDR units respectively. (Note that the Hamburg Rules call for 835 SDR units and 2.5 SDR units respectively.)

(e) Jurisdiction of the courts

The convention is silent about jurisdiction of the courts, which leaves the courts of every country free to decide whether they have jurisdiction in any dispute that arises. Naturally the rules vary from nation to nation, but in England, Wales and Northern Ireland the rules are:

- Original jurisdiction exists in any action where the defendant is present in the country and can be served with a writ.
- Jurisdiction will be assumed where:
  - A contract is governed by English law, or concluded or broken in the English jurisdiction.
  - Where the contract specifies that the English courts shall have jurisdiction.
  - Where an international convention specifies circumstances which bring the case within English jurisdiction (but of course the Hague-Visby rules are silent on this point).
  - Where a foreign partnership or limited company operates within the English jurisdiction. Such an organisation must nominate a person on whom writs may be served.

In any of the above circumstances the courts will give permission for a writ to be served outside the jurisdiction, but reserves the right to refuse this if to do so would be unfair to the defendant by reason of undue difficulty or expense.

| *(f) Time limit on actions* | This is fixed at one year, but may be extended by mutual consent. |

16.9 Charterparties

A charterparty is a contract between a shipowner and a person wishing to use his ship – the charterer. This use may be for a single voyage or a series of voyages (a **voyage charterparty**) or a period of time (a **time charterparty**). There is also a **lump sum charterparty** where a ship is chartered for a particular event, possibly of quite short duration, and the sum payable is decided and paid at once and not based on the time the ship is in use by the charterer. All these are charterparties not by way of demise. With a **demise charterparty** the shipowner surrenders the vessel to become virtually a part of the charterer's own fleet and the master and crew become the servants of the charterer and not the shipowner. In this case the master signing bills of lading signs them on behalf of the charterer, not the shipowner, and the charterer is the carrier of the goods. Where the bill of lading covers the charterer's own goods he is carrying his own goods. In voyage, time and lump sum charters the shipowner is the carrier, the master and crew are his servants and the shipowner is carrying both for the charterer and any other parties who are given bills of lading.

16.9.1 Stipulations in the charterparty

The following stipulations are usually made in a charterparty:

- The name of the ship.
- The nationality of the ship. This is a warranty, and if the shipowner transfers the ship during the lifetime of the charterparty in such a way that its nationality is changed, damages may be claimed.
- The class of the ship, i.e. sailing ship, steamship, etc. This is again a warranty, and may be a condition precedent – though firm legal decision on this is not yet available. (A condition precedent is one which must be met before the contract can commence.)
- The carrying capacity and registered tonnage. These may be conditions precedent, as when the charterparty calls for the charterer to load a full cargo and he needs to know what constitutes a full cargo for the vessel. At other times they may be irrelevant and of no importance.
- The position of the ship at the date of the charterparty. This is a condition precedent. In *Behn v. Burness (1863)* a ship was 62 miles from the place stated and it was held that the charterer was entitled to refuse to load, and could treat the contract as repudiated.
- The date at which the ship will be ready to load at the port of loading. Where there is an express stipulation of this sort it is a condition precedent and if it is not met the charterer may treat the contract as repudiated. If the stipulation is only that she will proceed without delay to the port of loading, and she does delay, there is a breach of warranty only and damages will be awarded.
- A cesser clause. A cesser clause is one which relieves the carrier from the need to pay demurrage (a charge for delaying the vessel longer than the stipulated 'lay days' when she will be available for loading) once he has completed loading. It is a question of construction in every case as to the exact meaning of a cesser clause.

(a) Liability to load

The shipowner wishes to earn a living by carrying goods for others. It is therefore necessary to keep the ship on the move and be perfectly clear what the arrangements are with the charterer as to loading. The master of the vessel must give notice to the charterer that the vessel is actually ready to load; intention to load at a future time is not good enough. In *Christensen v. Hindustan Steel (1971)* it was held that a master who had given notice that a ship would be ready to load on the following day had not given notice that she was ready to load, but only that she was *not* yet ready to load at the time he gave the notice. The notice was one of anticipated readiness.

The charterparty usually contains a stipulation that the charterer will load a full cargo. He will only be excused if it is a fault of the shipowner, or the charterparty has been frustrated, or if the charterparty permits only a partial load in certain circumstances. 'Fault of the shipowner' refers to breaches of a condition precedent. Breach of a mere warranty does not entitle the charterer to refuse to load, it only entitles him to damages.

Usually certain exceptions from liability for failure to load are included in the charterparty at the charterer's request, and as such are interpreted strictly against him as the one who drew them up. They include strikes, lockouts, labour disputes, riots, civil commotions, accidents for which the charterer is not responsible and ice, frost, fog, snow and storm. To illustrate the strictness of the interpretation, it is usual to apply these exceptions only to the actual loading of cargo. If the accident or bad weather prevents goods reaching the port that is not covered by the exceptions unless expressly included in the terms of the charterparty. Similarly, the terms are taken to give excuse only if the events occur during the lay days. If a strike occurs in the demurrage days the charterer will escape liability only if his clause expressly extended the exception from liability into the demurrage days.

Usually the charterer is bound to load a full cargo, and if he does not must pay **dead freight** (an agreed freight for that part of the ship's stowage space which he has failed to utilize). This agreed freight rate must be reasonable, since the shipowner's right is to damages for breach of contract, and if the rate specified was excessive it would be void as constituting a penalty.

(b) Lay days and demurrage

Both loading and discharge are usually required to be carried out within a specified period of time – the lay days. If no lay days are specified the duty of the charterer is to load or discharge in a reasonable time. If the charterer fails to load or discharge within the lay days it is a breach of contract, unless the charterparty also specifies 'demurrage' days. Demurrage days are a further period, after the end of the lay days, in which loading or discharging may be completed on payment of demurrage – an agreed sum for delaying the ship, payable for each day of delay.

The lay days, and consequently the demurrage days as well, run from the time the ship is declared ready for loading or unloading. This does not necessarily mean she has reached a berth and can be unloaded, but that she is an '**arrived ship**', having arrived within the commercial area of the port. This has led to a great deal of dispute, and is frequently crucial in legal cases about demurrage. In *Stag Line Ltd. v. Board of Trade (1950)* the charterparty gave the charterer the right to name a particular berth, and it was held that the ship had not arrived until she actually lay at that berth. No demurrage was payable for the six days she was waiting for a berth. By contrast, in *Shipping Developments Corporation SA v. v/o Sojuzneftenport: The Delian Spirit (1971)* the vessel reached Tuapse on 19 February and her master gave notice of readiness to load. She was directed to her berth on 24 February, and began to load shortly after arrival. She was held to have arrived on 19 February, and the lay days began to run from that time. The charterer was not liable for delaying the vessel until the lay days had expired, but could use his lay days to lie conveniently close until a berth was available. The test of whether a ship is an arrived ship is one of whether she is at the charterer's complete disposal for unloading. If she is, then she has arrived. In the Johanna Oldendorff case, *Oldendorff (E.L.) and Co. v. Trader Export SA (1973)*, it was held that if a ship was lying where the port authorities told her to lie, and was available to be called up for loading directly a berth was available, she had arrived. The test is: 'Had the ship reached a position within the port where she was at the immediate and effective disposition of the charterers?'

The charterparty, or the customs of the port concerned, may determine what 'days' are to be counted as 'days' for the purpose of the contract – whether they are running days, working days or weather working days (days when the weather permitted loading or unloading).

(c) The loading and discharge of the goods

The concept of safe arrival is an important one in transport, and the concept of a 'safe port' is crucial to the relationship between a shipowner and a charterer. It is an implied condition of the contract that the charterer will only use safe ports. If he names an unsafe port he will be liable to the shipowner for any damage caused to the ship, unless the master was at fault in not recognising the danger. In such circumstances the master's duty is to take the cargo to the nearest safe port and unload it there (*The Teutonia (1872)*). If a port cannot be entered without lightening the vessel in the roads, it is not a safe port (*The Alhambra (1881)*).

16.9.2 The Hamburg Rules: the UN Convention on the Carriage of Goods by Sea, 1978

The problem with international trade has always been that 'the strong take what they want, and the weak yield what they must'. Thus the carriers have always been powerful enough to insert clauses restricting their liabilities for losses, etc., and the relatively disorganized owners of cargo have been less well placed to resist such measures. However, the Hague Rules, and today the Hague-Visby Rules, have done a great deal to reduce the severity of such clauses in bills of lading. The United Nations feels that further modifications are required and has proposed the Hamburg Rules. These will strengthen the position of weaker nations, particularly the developing nations. The chief points of interest are:

- The Hamburg Rules will apply to all contracts whether bills of lading are issued or not.
- The courts will be expected to regard foreign decisions as very persuasive (if not binding) precedents.
- The carrier's responsibility is extended to cover all times when the goods are in his care, and not just the time from loading until discharge.
- The carrier's liabilities are clearly stated, and the list of exclusionary clauses is much reduced – in particular he is liable for defects in the management and navigation of the ship.
- The Hamburg Rules call for a paramount clause, specifically stating that the Hamburg Rules apply.
- The limits of liability are expressed in SDRs: 835 SDRs per package or 2.5 SDRs per kilogram of gross weight.
- Unlike the Hague-Visby Rules, which are silent about jurisdiction, the Hamburg Rules (in Article 21) are very clear about the matter.

The adoption of the Hamburg Rules appears as yet to be some distance in the future. The full text cannot be reproduced here but is available from the United Nations Organisation.

16.10
Carriage by air: the Warsaw Rules

Carriage of goods by air began in the years following the First World War, and was soon the subject of an international convention which became known as the Warsaw Rules. These rules have been revised from time to time, and the latest version (the Montreal Version) awaits ratification at present. The original Warsaw Rules were embodied into English law by the *Carriage by Air Act, 1932*. A later version was enacted in the *Carriage by Air Act, 1961*. This became effective in 1967 under the *Carriage by Air Acts (application of provisions) Order, 1967* (SI 1967, No. 480). This order also included a set of Non-International Carriage Rules, which effectively applied many of the international rules to domestic flights. Finally, the *Carriage by Air and Road Act, 1979*, has embodied the Montreal Version of the rules into law, but this Act still awaits a commencement order. From past experience it is usually several years before a quorum of nations ratifies such an international convention.

The situation as regards carriage by air is therefore rather complex and the following list may help the reader:

- When enough nations ratify the Montreal Version this new set of Warsaw Rules will apply to all contracts of carriage by air between the citizens of nations which are high contracting parties.
- Until then the vast majority of contracts for international carriage are covered by the amended convention signed at Guadalajara in 1955, which is embodied in the 1961 Act.
- For the few nations that have not ratified the 1955 Convention, the 1932 Act and the original Warsaw Rules apply.
- For the very few nations that have not ratified any convention, and for domestic flights, the Non-International Carriage Rules, 1967, apply.
- Common law does not apply at all to carriage by air.

In the outline of the law which follows, the Montreal Version, which is likely to be implemented very shortly, has been used as the basis for the statements made, since it best reflects the current position of air carriage. The vast volumes of passenger and freight traffic now moving by air have called for some streamlining of procedures, since aircraft worth millions of pounds cannot be held up by petty bureaucracy, and the increasing use of computerized data instead of documents makes earlier conventions somewhat obsolete. Where necessary a note pointing out differences between earlier conventions and the Montreal Version is included.

16.10.1
International carriage

The definition of international carriage is as follows:

For the purposes of this Convention, the expression international carriage means any carriage in which, according to the agreement between the parties, the place of departure and the place of destination, whether or not there be a break in the carriage or a transhipment, are situated either within the territories of two High Contracting Parties or within the territory of a single High Contracting Party if there is an agreed stopping place within the territory of another state, even if that state is not a High Contracting Party. Carriage between two points within the territory of a single High Contracting Party without an agreed stopping place within the territory of another State is not international carriage for the purposes of this Convention.

Under this definition a flight from London to New York is international carriage, governed by the amended convention of 1955 since both the UK and the USA have ratified the amended convention. A flight between London and Zaire, which has not ratified the amended convention, is governed by the original convention and the *Carriage by Air Act, 1932*. A flight between London and Gibraltar is not international carriage, since Gibraltar is not an independent state. It is therefore governed by the Non-International Carriage Rules.

(a) *The air waybill*

Article V of the amended convention provides that an air waybill shall be delivered to the carrier by the consignor with at least three copies (but in practice there are 12 copies). The carrier's copy must be signed by the consignor; the consignor's copy must be signed by the carrier; and the consignee's copy must be signed by both the carrier and the consignor. The air waybill must include an indication of the places of departure and destination; the place of an intermediate stopping place if departure and destination airports are both in the same country; and an indication of the weight of the consignment.

The earlier conventions held that unless the air waybill complied exactly with the convention the carrier could not rely on the clauses in the convention limiting his liability. This has now been dropped, for it is generally agreed that a mere slip of the typewriter should not disqualify a carrier from receiving the benefits conferred upon him by the convention. The Montreal Version also permits the air waybill to be replaced by electronic data, provided it permits the identification and tracing of a consignment in the electronic records. In general, an air waybill is not negotiable, but there has never been any objection to the issue of negotiable air waybills and they are still possible under the Montreal Version. There is little point in negotiable air waybills as the transit times are so short that the need to sell goods in transit rarely arises.

(b) *Stoppage in transit*

A consignor who has sent goods by air has a copy of the air waybill to prove it. Under Article 12 on production of this copy he may stop the goods in transit and redirect them in any way he likes, up to the moment when they reach the destination airport.

(c) *The rights of the consignee*

These rights start on arrival of the goods at the destination airport. The carrier must notify the consignee of their arrival, and release them on payment of any charges due. If the carrier admits the loss of goods, or if they have not arrived within seven days of the estimated time of arrival, an action may be commenced.

(d) *The liability of the carrier*

The new Rules state quite explicitly that the carrier *is* liable for loss or damage to cargo sustained during the carriage by air, provided the loss was not attributable to inherent vice, defective packing, act of war or act of public authority. The duty of care extends for the whole period of the carriage by air – whether in an airport, on board an aircraft or in an emergency landing in any place whatsoever. It does not cover carriage by land, sea or inland waterway, unless by the nature of the carriage by air such transhipment was essential for loading or delivery and therefore part of the carriage by air.

(e) The limitations of liability

This version of the rules has adopted SDRs as the basis of compensation, and will thus avoid (when implemented) all the problems arising from the use of the gold franc in the original convention. The limits of liability are:

- For destruction, loss or damage to passengers' baggage, 1000 SDRs per passenger. Courts may also award legal costs.
- For loss, damage or delay to cargo, 17 SDRs per kilogram, unless the consignor declared a value to be covered and paid an extra sum by the way of premium.

Under the Amended Convention the limits are 5000 gold francs per passenger and 250 gold francs per kilogram.

Any attempt to reduce the carrier's liability by a clause in the contract is declared null and void, without damaging the remainder of the contract.

There is a 'Himalaya clause' (Article 25A) in the convention to protect servants and agents of the carrier sued personally, provided they have acted within the scope of their employment. They are given the protection of the Convention as to the limitation of liability. Article 24 makes it perfectly clear that however a legal action is brought, whether in contract or tort, any compensation payable is subject to the limitations given above.

(f) Jurisdiction and the time limit for actions

Actions for damages may be brought at the option of the **plaintiff** in the territory of one of the High Contracting Parties, before a court having jurisdiction in the place where the carrier is ordinarily resident, or has his principal place of business, or has an establishment by which the contract was made, or before the court having jurisdiction at the place of destination. It is also possible to bring the case in the country where the plaintiff is ordinarily resident if the carrier has an establishment there.

An action can be brought only if the carrier was given notice of the damage or loss within 14 days of receipt of the cargo, or within seven days of receipt of the baggage. If delay is alleged there are 21 days to notify a complaint.

There is a time limit of two years on the commencement of a legal action, reckoned from the time of arrival, or the time when the aircraft ought to have arrived, or from the date when the carriage stopped.

16.11 Multimodal movements by a Combined Transport Operator (CTO)

In modern transport the economical way to move goods is as unit loads in sealed containers, weighing as much as 32 tonnes. Where a single exporter cannot supply an FCL (full container load) the goods will be sent to a groupage freight forwarder who will make up FCLs from LCLs (less-than-container loads).

The containers travel as multimodal movements, for example road–sea–rail–road, or road–air–road, etc. Many problems can arise on such journeys, for example if the goods on arrival are damaged who is responsible? Clearly an international convention on such matters is essential, and one has in fact been held under the auspices of the United Nations, but to date it has not yet been ratified by sufficient countries for it to be implemented. Meanwhile, the *UNCTAD/ICC Rules for a Combined Transport Document* (ICC publication 481) have formed a useful agreement for the more important trading nations. The rules are available from the International Chamber of Commerce, 14 Belgrave Square London, SW1X 8PS (Tel: 0171 823 2811) (*Continues on page 294*).

Table 16.1 Comparative table on the international carriage of goods: basic concepts

Aspect of law	CMR (International road haulage)	CIM (International rail haulage)	Hague-Visby Rules, Carriage of Goods by Sea Act 1971, also Hamburg Rules awaiting ratification	Warsaw Rules (Carriage by Air) Montreal Version awaiting commencement order	ICC 481 (UNCTAD/ICC Rules for a Multimodal Transport Document)
Basis of legal relationship between the parties	Statutory – by the Carriage of Goods by Road Act, 1965, which enacts the CMR convention. Later amended by the Carriage by Air and Road Act, 1979	Statutory: the COTIF Convention – of which CIM is a part – is given effect by the International Transport Conventions Act, 1983	Statutory	Statutory – by the Carriage by Air Act, 1961. The Montreal Version of the rules is enacted in the Carriage by Air and Road Act, 1979, but awaits a commencement order	Contractual – the UNCTAD/ICC Rules are adopted contractually either orally, or in writing, or in electronic form whenever a combined transport document is issued
The definition used for 'international' carriage	The convention applies to every contract for the carriage of goods for reward by road haulage where the place of taking over the goods and the place of delivery are in two different countries of which one at least is a country which has adopted the convention	The carriage of goods consigned under a through consignment note for carriage by rail over the territories of at least two contracting states and exclusively over lines listed in Article 59 of the convention	The carriage of goods by sea in ships from any port in Great Britain or Northern Ireland to any other port whether in or outside Great Britain or Northern Ireland, provided a bill of lading is issued and goods are not live animals or deck cargo	Carriage between a place of departure and a place of arrival which are in the territories of two different high contracting parties (states which have ratified the convention), or carriage between two places in the same state if there was an intermediate stop in any other state whether a high contracting party or not	These latest rules do not specifically mention 'international carriage'. The earlier '298' rules defined it as: 'The carriage of goods by at least two different modes of transport from a place situated in one country to a place designated for delivery situated in a different country'

Extent of carrier's liability	The haulier is liable for total or partial loss or damage to goods between takeover and delivery, but not where he can prove fault of the plaintiff, inherent vice, or circumstances beyond his own control. He is also liable for unreasonable delay, and for failure to collect COD charges	The railway is liable for total or partial loss of the goods and for damage thereto between takeover and delivery unless it can prove fault of the claimant, inherent vice or circumstances beyond its own control. The time of transit is calculated on one of four formulae. Exceeding this time of transit leads to liability for delay. (See page 275 for details.)	The shipowner must exercise due diligence in providing a seaworthy and cargoworthy ship. He must properly load, handle, stow, carry, keep, care for and discharge the cargo. He is not liable for errors in navigation or management of the ship, nor for fire, perils of the sea, and a long list of exceptions	The operator is liable for loss, destruction or damage to cargo during the carriage by air (whether in an aircraft, or on an aerodrome or in the event of a forced landing anywhere else). The operator is not liable if he can prove that he took all necessary measures, or that it was not possible to take such measures. Nor is he liable if he can prove fault of the claimant. (Montreal Version increases these immunities.) The operator is liable for delay	The MTO (multimodal transport operator) is liable for loss or damage to the goods from time of takeover to time of delivery if the loss was caused by his own, his servants' or his sub-contractors' acts, while acting within the scope of their employment. The operator is liable for delay

Table 16.2 Comparative table on the international carriage of goods: comparison of rules

Aspect of law	CMR (International road haulage)	CIM (International rail haulage)	Hague-Visby Rules, Carriage of Goods by Sea Act 1971, also Hamburg Rules awaiting ratification	Warsaw Rules (Carriage by Air) Montreal Version awaiting commencement order	ICC 481 (UNCTAD/ICC Rules for a Multimodal Transport Document)
Official document. (but all documents may be in electronic form)	CMR consignment note	CIM consignment note	Bill of lading	Air waybill (1961 Act), Air consignment note (1932 Act)	Multimodal Transport Document
Does it have a 'paramount clause'?	The consignment note bears a large sign 'CMR' and the words 'International Consignment Note'	Consignment note bears the sign 'CIM International carriage by rail' – in English, French, and German, and a clause adopting the convention. All UK CIM notes are now in electronic form	The 1971 Act makes no mention of a paramount clause. The Hamburg Rules, when implemented, do require a paramount clause	It bears a warning that if the carriage is international carriage, the convention will apply and limit the carrier's liability	The earlier 298 document required a Paramount Clause. The 481 Rules refer only to a document 'evidencing a multimodal transport contract' and refer to its replacement where required by EDI messages
Limitation of liability. (a) Liability never exceeds the total value (b) Gold franc consists of 65.5 mg of gold of millesimal fineness 900 (c) SDR unit recalculated daily by IMF	8.33 SDR units of account per kg of gross weight	17 European Units of Account (ECUs) per kg converted to currency at the rate prevailing on the date that payment is made	666.67 SDRs per package or 2 SDRs per kg, whichever is higher. The Hamburg Rules will change these limits to 835 SDR units per package or 2.5 SDR units per kg of gross weight	250 gold francs per kg unless a higher value has been declared and a supplementary charge paid. The Montreal version will change this to 17 SDR units per kg and for baggage 1000 SDR units per passenger	Unless a higher value has been declared by the consignor, and recorded on the document, the limit is 666.67 SDR per package, or 2 SDR per kg, whichever is higher. Some special rules apply (see ICC 481)

Jurisdiction of the courts	Action may be brought: (a) anywhere that is agreed, or (b) where the defendant is resident, or has his principal place of business or an establishment where the contract was made, or (c) the place where the goods were taken over by the carrier, or (d) in the place of delivery	The plaintiff must select the railway he wishes to sue, under the rules of Article 43, and must bring his action in the courts of the state to which the railway belongs	The convention does not mention juridiction – so the court would decide whether it was competent to hear a case and which law should be applied. The Hamburg Rules give very clear instructions about jurisdiction	Action must be brought, at the option of the plaintiff in the territory of one of the high contracting parties where the carrier: (a) is ordinarily resident, or (b) has his principal place of business, or (c) has an establishment where the contract was made, or (d) at the place of destination	The Uniform Rules are silent about jurisdiction and therefore it will be for the courts to decide whether they have jurisdiction in a particular case
Time limit on legal action	One year, extended to three years if wilful misconduct is alleged.	One year, extended to three years if wilful misconduct is alleged against the railway	One year normally, but by mutual consent this may be extended	Two years	Nine months after (a) delivery, or (b) date when the goods should have been delivered, or (c) date decided by Rule 5.3 (which says goods are deemed lost 90 days after a reasonable time for delivery has elapsed)

The essence of the arrangements laid down in the rules are as follows:

- A person who is willing to act as a combined transport operator (CTO) assumes responsibility for the whole multimodal transport on a warehouse-to-warehouse basis (i.e. from exporter to foreign importer).
- If any difficulty arises the consignee whose goods are lost, damaged or delayed sues the CTO, who compensates the consignee and then (being well informed about the entire transit) recovers the sum paid from the person actually at fault in so far as this can be discovered (i.e. any subcontractor found to be the actual cause of the loss or delay concerned).
- The goods travel under a Combined Transport Document, which bears a heading revealing its status either as a 'negotiable combined transport document' or a 'non-negotiable combined transport document' subject to the UNCTAD/ICC Rules as laid down in ICC 481.
- The limit of liability of the CTO is fixed at 666.67 SDR per package, or 2 SDRs per Kg, whichever is higher.
- The time limit for the commencement of legal action is set at nine months, which would seem to be a reasonable time bearing in mind that such multimodal transports are frequently concluded in a matter of days, while even those involving long sea voyages rarely take longer than about six weeks.
- The rules are silent about jurisdiction, so that the question of where a case may be brought depends entirely on the arrangements the parties care to make. The courts invited to hear a complaint will decide whether in their opinion they have jurisdiction in the matter, and will proceed accordingly.

16.12 Comparison of conventions on international carriage

To assist the reader in comparing the various conventions on international carriage, Tables 16.1 and 16.2 have been reproduced by courtesy of Woodhead Faulker Ltd, from *Elements of Export Law* (see pages 290–3).

Test your knowledge

Answers	Questions
	1 What is a common carrier?
1 A person who holds himself out as ready to carry for the public at large.	2 What is the extent of the common carrier's liability?
2 He is liable as an insurer for every loss that occurs unless he can show that one of the common law exceptions applies.	3 What are the common law exceptions?

Law of carriage by land, sea and air 295

Answers	Questions
3 (a) Act of God; (b) Act of the Queen's enemies; (c) fault of the consignor; (d) fraud of the consignor; (e) inherent vice.	4 What is a private carrier?
4 One who holds himself out a a carrier, but reserves the rights to choose for whom he will carry – making a private contract with each customer.	5 What form does the private contract take?
5 It incorporates a set of standard *conditions of carriage* into the contract, covering all the points where difficulties usually arise.	6 List these points of difficulty.
6 (a) With whom was the contract made; (b) delay; (c) deviation; (d) stoppage in transit; (e) lien; (f) dangerous goods; (g) carriage by two or more carriers; (h) the measure of damages.	7 What is the *Carriers Act, 1830*, about?
7 Carriage of valuables by common carriers. As it only now applies to road carriage and many carriers make it quite clear they are not common carriers, it is of limited application today.	8 What is the *Carriage of Goods by Road Act, 1965*, about?
8 It implemented the CMR Convention and makes international carriage by road subject to the CMR rules.	9 How does an international convention work?
9 (a) Matters of dispute are discussed at an international meeting and fair rules are agreed. (b) These rules are clearly stated in a Convention document. (c) The delegates go back to their own countries and get their own legislatures to ratify the convention and enact it into national law. (d) When enough countries have ratified it a commencement date is agreed, and from that time the convention overrides unfair terms in private contracts.	10 What are the chief international conventions on the law of carriage of goods?

Answers	Questions
10 (a) The COTIF Convention (on rail carriage); (b) the CMR Convention (on road carriage); (c) the Hague-Visby Rules (on carriage by sea); (d) the Warsaw Rules (on carriage by air); the UNCTAD/ICC Rules for a Combined Transport Document (ICC 481).	11 What are the Hamburg Rules?
11 A United Nations sponsored convention to replace the Hague-Visby Rules on carriage by sea. It is awaiting ratification.	12 List the chief matters requiring harmonization in such conventions.
12 (a) The basis of legal relationships between the parties. (b) The definition of international carriage. (c) The extent of the carrier's liability. (d) Which courts shall have jurisdiction. (e) What is the time limit on legal actions. (f) What currency, or what basket of currencies, is to be used in settling disputes resolved by arbitration or legal decisions in the courts.	13 In this sort of test it is only possible to ask general questions. Students might like to make up their own test on each of the Conventions listed in **10** above, asking questions about each of the points mentioned in **12** above. Then try some of the questions in Appendix 1.

17 Negotiable instruments

17.1 The concept of negotiability

A negotiable instrument is one which passes from hand to hand without notice being given to the party who is liable on it, and without the recipient having to take it 'subject to the equities' (see Section 11.6). Consider an ordinary Bank of England £10 note: on it the Bank of England declares that it promises to pay the bearer on demand the sum of £10. If I transfer this to a shopkeeper to make a small purchase, I do not need to notify the Bank that in future they should pay the shopkeeper and not me (as I would have to do if I transferred an ordinary debt by a legal assignment under Section 136 of the *Law of Property Act, 1925*). Nor is the shopkeeper put upon enquiry as to whether I am the *bona fide* owner of the £10 note. He does not take 'subject to the equities'. So long as the shopkeeper takes the note in good faith, for value, he gets a perfect title to the note, even if I have stolen it. It would be a different matter of course if he took the proceeds of a bank robbery, say 100 000 £10 notes, for 20 pence each. That is not 'in good faith', or 'for value'.

This use of certain documents – particularly bills of exchange and promissory notes – as negotiable instruments arose out of the law merchant. Merchants found that the best way to get round difficulties about notifying the parties liable on such documents, and the risks that a document might have been stolen, was to disregard the difficulty. By custom, or usage, it became generally understood that such documents were freely transferable, the one liable to pay simply honouring the document, whoever presented it, for payment on the due date, provided everything appeared to be in order. The person who took such a document in good faith for value acquired a good title to the document, even if the giver of it had no title. Later this behaviour was recognised in the common law courts as valid behaviour – under the general rule that the courts will always uphold the reasonable expectations of businessmen. Finally, as we shall see, a statutory enactment – the *Bills of Exchange Act, 1882* – put the seal of Parliamentary approval on these arrangements.

The most common negotiable instruments are listed below:

- Bill of exchange (including cheques: a cheque is defined as 'a bill of exchange, drawn on a banker, payable on demand' – *Bills of Exchange Act, 1882*, Section 73).
- Promissory notes (including bank notes).
- Treasury bills.
- Dividend warrants.
- Bankers' drafts.
- Certificates of deposit.
- Bearer bonds of various sorts.

The law is best explained by considering bills of exchange as the typical representative of negotiable instruments, and studying the *Bills of Exchange Act, 1882*.

17.2 Definition of a bill of exchange

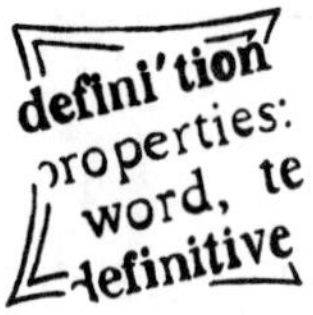

The definition which is given below should be learned by heart, since it is one of the most succinct legal definitions ever drafted. There is not a superfluous word in it, and although it sounds complicated it can easily be committed to memory in five minutes, and clarifies a great many ideas about bills of exchange if it is fully comprehended. Section 3 of the Act reads:

> (1) *A bill of exchange is an unconditional order in writing addressed by one person to another, signed by the person giving it, requiring the person to whom it is addressed to pay on demand or at a fixed or determinable future time a sum certain in money to or to the order of a specified person, or to bearer.*

Considering this definition in relation to the bill of exchange shown in Figure 17.1 we have the following points to note:

- *The bill is an unconditional order in writing*. It says quite clearly 'pay'. It does not say 'provided the good ship *Peerless* arrives safely from Bombay' or put in any other condition about payment; it says 'pay to our order' without any conditions at all.
- *It is 'addressed by one person to another'*. The person who writes the order out is called the **drawer** of the bill because he draws it up. In this case G. M. Whitehead, of Cambridge Educational Supplies (Cambridge) Ltd, is the drawer, and the bill is addressed to another firm, Neanderthal Artefacts Ltd. This company is the **drawee** (the one drawn upon). It is possible to have the drawee a completely fictitious character like 'Robinson Crusoe', but in the vast majority of cases it is a real firm. This is explained below.
- *It is 'signed by the person giving it'*. In this case G.M. Whitehead has signed the bill as the representative of Cambridge Educational Supplies (Cambridge) Ltd. When the drawer signs in this way he immediately becomes liable on the bill (indeed everyone who signs his name on the bill becomes liable on it) and will be obliged to honour it on the due date. The fairness of this arrangement is explained below. Certainly Neanderthal Artefacts are not liable on it yet, for they have not yet signed the bill, and if it had been made out in the name of a fictitious character like Robinson Crusoe we could not have expected him to honour it on the due date.
- *It is for 'a sum certain'*. Note that the Act does not say 'a certain sum', it says 'a sum certain'. The implication is that a clear amount must be stated

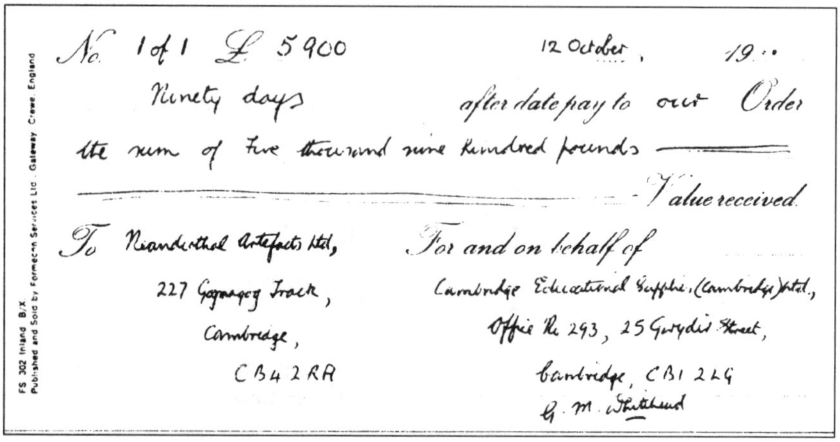
No. 1 of 1 £ 5900   12 October, 19..

Ninety days after date pay to our Order

the sum of Five thousand nine hundred pounds ——

—— Value received.

To Neanderthal Artefacts Ltd,
227 Gogmagog Track,
Cambridge,
CB4 2RA

For and on behalf of
Cambridge Educational Supplies (Cambridge) Ltd.,
Office No 293, 25 Gwydir Street,
Cambridge, CB1 2LG
G. M. Whitehead

FS 302 Inland B/X Published and Sold by Formecon Services Ltd. Gateway Crewe England

Figure 17.1 An inland bill of exchange

– in this case £5900. It would not be a bill of exchange if the bill called for 'the amount my house fetches at auction', for this is an uncertain sum and those handling the bill later, who perhaps do not even know the drawer, would not be able to guess what the value of the bill might be.

- *It is not 'on demand' but it is 'at a fixed or determinable future time'.* The bill reads 'Ninety days after date pay . . .' and the date is 12 October 19 . . (The authors apologize for the use of 19 . . here but this avoids the need to redraw the artwork every year or so; regard this as the year in which you are reading the book.) Ninety days after 12 October is easily determinable; it is 10 January. At one time three days of grace were allowed for the bad conditions of British roads, and such a bill would have been payable on 13 January. This practice has been discontinued, but it may still apply in some countries which have followed British practice and have not discontinued the arrangement.
- *The bill is an 'order' bill.* The definition says that a bill of exchange must order the drawee to pay a sum certain to – or to the order of – a 'specified person, or to bearer'. This bill is not a bearer bill, but it does say 'pay to our order', which means that we will tell them whom to pay, at some time in the future. We shall do this by endorsing the bill. This is also explained later.

This concludes the consideration of how the bill of exchange fits in with the definition of a bill given in the Act. There is still, however, much to say. This is best explained by considering the uses of a bill of exchange.

17.3 The use of bills of exchange

Consider the situation shown diagrammatically in Figure 17.2. Read it carefully now.

This diagram is largely self-explanatory, and illustrates the chief use of bills of exchange as a means of financing business, giving all the parties involved a chance to engage in their particular business activities. All bills should be self-liquidating, which means that by the time the due date arrives the business activity which they fostered has provided the funds to honour the bill. In Figure 17.2 the following situations have been arrived at by the due date:

- Cambridge Educational Supplies have kept their factory going by manufacturing goods which cost them £3500. They have been paid £5667.24, and have thus made a profit of £2167.24.
- Neanderthal Artefacts have obtained supplies three months before Christmas, which they sold for £9300. They have been able to honour the bill for £5900 on 10 January and have £3400 left towards their overheads, and of course their profits.
- The Helpful Bank lent £5667.24 and were repaid £5900, giving interest earned of £232.76. This is an effective rate of 16.66 per cent.
- The ordinary consumers have experienced the satisfactions of the consumer society.

The legal points that need stressing are listed in Sections (a) and (b)

(a) Acceptance of the bill

When the drawer of the bill presents it to the drawee for acceptance he expects the drawee to give his assent to the order it contains by writing *accepted* on it, and signing it. Even just the signature will do. The drawee is now the 'acceptor' and is legally bound to honour the bill on the due date.

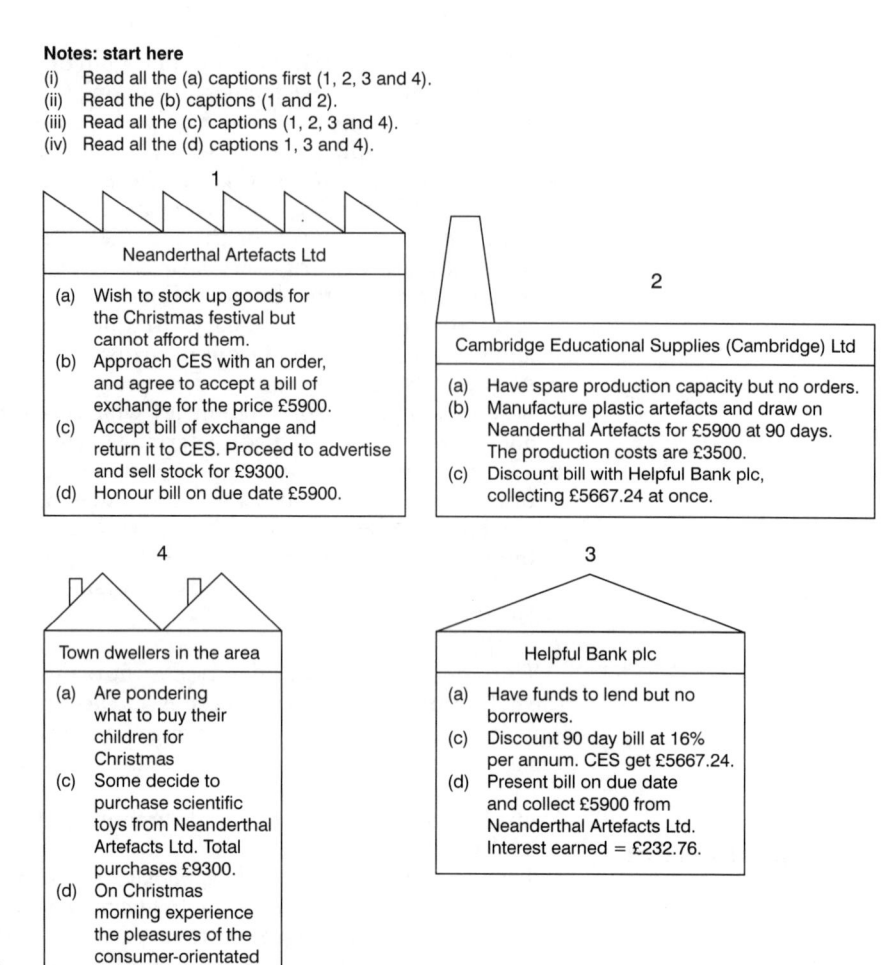

Notes: start here
(i)   Read all the (a) captions first (1, 2, 3 and 4).
(ii) Read the (b) captions (1 and 2).
(iii) Read all the (c) captions (1, 2, 3 and 4).
(iv) Read all the (d) captions 1, 3 and 4).

1 Neanderthal Artefacts Ltd
(a) Wish to stock up goods for the Christmas festival but cannot afford them.
(b) Approach CES with an order, and agree to accept a bill of exchange for the price £5900.
(c) Accept bill of exchange and return it to CES. Proceed to advertise and sell stock for £9300.
(d) Honour bill on due date £5900.

2 Cambridge Educational Supplies (Cambridge) Ltd
(a) Have spare production capacity but no orders.
(b) Manufacture plastic artefacts and draw on Neanderthal Artefacts for £5900 at 90 days. The production costs are £3500.
(c) Discount bill with Helpful Bank plc, collecting £5667.24 at once.

3 Helpful Bank plc
(a) Have funds to lend but no borrowers.
(c) Discount 90 day bill at 16% per annum. CES get £5667.24.
(d) Present bill on due date and collect £5900 from Neanderthal Artefacts Ltd. Interest earned = £232.76.

4 Town dwellers in the area
(a) Are pondering what to buy their children for Christmas
(c) Some decide to purchase scientific toys from Neanderthal Artefacts Ltd. Total purchases £9300.
(d) On Christmas morning experience the pleasures of the consumer-orientated society.

Figure 17.2 The use of a bill of exchange

The drawer is now the holder of the bill (but not a holder in due course – see below). Cambridge Educational Supplies can now do one of the following things:

- *They can keep the bill until maturity, i.e. the due date, and present it for payment.* If they do this they will collect the face value of the bill, £5900, but they will of course have to wait 90 days before they have the use of their money.
- *They can discount the bill with a bank.* If they do this, as in the example given above, they only collect the discounted value of the bill, which at 16 per cent for 90 days is £5667.24. The bank now owns the bill, it having been endorsed to them. When a holder of a bill endorses it to someone else he writes an order on the back of the bill (*in dorso* (Italian) – on the back). (Note that 'endorse' and 'indorse' have the same meaning.) The order might read 'Pay Helpful Bank Plc' and this order would be signed by the drawer – in this case CES Ltd. The drawer has now become the **first endorser**, and the bank has become a 'holder in due course'.

The bank may keep the bill to maturity, or may re-discount it at any time for the number of days it has to run. There is a whole market, the London

Discount Market, for such bills. One of the chief functions of the discount houses is to take from the banks such trade bills as they do not wish to retain in their own portfolios. If they do take such a bill from a bank it will be endorsed over to them, and the bank adds its name to the bill as second endorser. The more names a bill collects in this way the safer it is, for every name on the bill is liable to honour it. Sometimes a bill is completely full on the back, and a piece of paper called an **allonge** has to be stuck on it to take any extra negotiations of the bill to further parties. The word 'negotiation' implies the transfer of a bill of exchange or other negotiable instrument from one party to another, free of the equities.

- *They can negotiate the bill to other third parties for value received.* A third party taking a bill in this way becomes a holder in due course.

(b) Holder in due course

A holder in due course, as defined in Section 29 of the 1882 Act is anyone who holds a bill of exchange under the following conditions:

- That he obtained it before it was overdue and without notice of any dishonour.
- That he took it in good faith, for value, and without notice of any defect in title of the person who gave it to him.
- That the bill is complete and regular on the face of it.

To follow this situation consider what happens if Cambridge Educational Supplies wish to buy raw materials from S for their factory. If S is agreeable, W, for CES Ltd, can endorse the bill to him on some fair basis, taking account of the period before payment is due. S could in turn negotiate it to T, who could negotiate it to X. We can now see why it is fair for the bill to be honoured by the drawer should the acceptor dishonour it. The acceptor's undertaking to honour the bill was made to the drawer, CES Ltd, who subsequently became the first endorser. S became the second endorser, T the third endorser and X the holder of the bill. If X presents the bill to the acceptor on the due date and it is dishonoured, that is no reason why T should not pay X for the value he received from X. Similarly, S must pay T and W must pay S. Ultimately W must honour the bill, because he is the drawer and it is his customer, the acceptor, who has failed to pay. If W honours the bill everyone else is satisfied and W must pursue the acceptor to obtain payment for the goods originally supplied 90 days earlier. The holder of a bill which has been dishonoured may approach anyone higher up on the bill than himself and demand payment, but the most logical person to approach is the drawer, for he must honour the bill in the end. In practice the bill often moves 'backwards to the drawer', each person seeing the person who negotiated the bill to him and demanding payment.

17.3.1 Inland bills and foreign bills

An inland bill is one which is either both drawn and payable within the British Isles, or drawn within the British Isles on some person resident therein. Any other bill is a foreign bill. An important distinction between them is their **treatment on dishonour**. When an inland bill is dishonoured the holder's rights against the drawer and endorsers of the bill are effective at once, but if desired a more formal procedure may establish the fact of dishonour. The bill is taken to a notary public who presents it again, establishes that it is in fact dishonoured and attaches a slip of paper to the bill stating the answer received when presenting the bill, the date and his signature. This is called **noting** and must be done either on the day of dishonour or the next day. Such a 'note' can be turned into a formal protest at any time thereafter (Section 93, 1882 Act).

With foreign bills, and with inland bills where insolvency or bankruptcy of the acceptor takes place before maturity, a more formal **protest** is required. This is a certificate containing a copy of the bill, certifying that the notary presented it for payment and that payment was refused. Such a protest is recognized in international law as proof of dishonour, and binds the drawer and endorsers to honour the bill. Without it they are discharged from liability, and the holder's only recourse is against the acceptor of the bill. A notary public is a solicitor empowered by the courts to act in such matters; not every solicitor is a notary public. In the absence of a notary public any householder or substantial resident may protest a bill, in a form given in Schedule 1 of the 1882 Act.

17.3.2 Sets of bills

In foreign trade bills are sometimes issued in sets, though the practice is reducing as communications improve. The idea is that all the bills in a set constitute *one* bill, and each refers to the existence of the others. The drawee only accepts one of them (if he accepts more he is liable on each one he accepts). The bills could then be sent off by different mails and the first to arrive would be honoured. The others at once become void, but if the copy honoured was not the accepted copy the acceptor could still be liable upon it. If a set of bills is improperly used, and the different copies are negotiated (sold) to different parties, the individual endorsers of them are liable upon them. Figure 17.3 explains the position.

Copy	Drawer	Other holders of the bill				Position on presentation
1	A	A	A	A	A	A – paid by acceptor
2	A	B	D	E	G	J – refused on presentation
3	A	C	C	F	H	K – refused on presentation

Notes
(a) At the beginning all three copies are in A's possession. Copy No. 1 has been accepted.
(b) A negotiates (sells) the other copies to B and C, who negotiate them to other parties as shown.
(c) A presents the accepted copy to the acceptor who honours it. The other bills are now void as far as the acceptor is concerned, and he refuses to honour them.
(d) J may now look to G, E, D, B and A to honour Copy No. 2 and A has the eventual liability on this bill.
(e) K may look to H, F, C and A to honour Copy No. 3, with A having the ultimate liability on it.

Figure 17.3 Improper negotiation of a set of bills

17.3.3 Inchoate instruments

If a bill or cheque is incomplete, with the amount or the name of the payee or some other detail left out, it is said to be inchoate. A person signing such a paper implies authority to the receiver to complete it in the manner agreed between them. If A gives his son B a cheque with no amount filled in to purchase a second-hand car, for example, the son has *prima facie* authority to fill in the amount when he finds a suitable car. The son cannot – even if he completes the document – have the rights of a holder in due course, for he did not take it 'complete and regular on the face of it', but if he negotiates it to someone else for value that person will be a holder in due course and can sue on the bill, since at the time he took it for value it was complete, and not an inchoate instrument.

17.4 The parties to a bill of exchange

These have been referred to above, but to recapitulate they are:

17.4.1 The drawer

The drawer is the person who writes the bill out in the first place and signs it.

17.4.2 The drawee

The drawee is the person drawn upon. If the drawee is the same person as the drawer or if the drawee is a fictitious person, the holder may treat it either as a bill of exchange or as a promissory note. The point is that the person liable on such a bill is the drawer, and therefore he has effectively promised to pay the money to anyone who presents it on the due date. If the drawee is a real person who has been drawn upon in the normal course of business he will usually become in due course the acceptor of the bill.

17.4.3 The acceptor

The drawee who assents to the order in the bill accepts it as already explained, and by accepting it engages that he will honour it on the due date according to the **tenor** of the bill (the period for which it is to run). In doing so he is precluded from denying to any future holder in due course the existence of the drawer, or the genuineness of his signature, or his capacity or authority to draw the bill. If the bill is an order bill, either to the drawer's order or a payee's order, since these parties may endorse the bill to other parties the acceptor cannot deny their right to do so (though he cannot guarantee the genuineness or the validity of their signatures – Section 54).

17.4.4 The payee

The payee is the person to be paid. It is quite usual for this to be the drawer, since the bill may read 'pay me ...' or 'pay to our order ...', but it may be a third person who is to have the benefit of the bill. The Act says that if a bill is made payable to a payee, it must name the payee so that there is reasonable certainty who is intended to benefit on the due date.

17.4.5 Holders

Holders are defined in the Act as 'payees or indorsees of a bill or note who are in possession of it, or the bearers thereof'. It follows that a person could hold a bill – because he had been given it, for example – and yet not be a 'holder in due course'. A holder for value is a person who holds a bill for which value has been given at some previous time, even if not by him. Such a holder for value may look to the acceptor and all prior parties to honour the bill.

17.4.6 Holders in due course

This has been explained in Section 17.3. Their legal position is that they may sue upon the bills in their own names, and may defeat any defences depending on defects of title or depending on the relations between the various parties prior to the bills coming into their possession.

17.4.7 Endorsers

Any endorser of a bill undertakes that it will be honoured on the due date and that if dishonoured he will reimburse the person to whom he endorsed it, or any subsequent endorser who has been obliged to pay it. He is precluded from denying to any holder in due course the validity of the drawer's signature or the signature of any endorser prior to himself.

17.4.8 Bearers

A bearer is a person bearing a bearer bill of exchange (i.e. having it in his possession). A **bearer bill** is one expressed to be payable to bearer, or one which is endorsed 'in blank' by the last endorser. An endorsement is 'in blank' when it consists of the endorser's signature and nothing else. Thus a bill endorsed 'Pay T. Jones, signed J. Blenkinsop', is not endorsed in blank, but a bill endorsed 'J. Blenkinsop' is endorsed in blank, and becomes a bearer bill. Any bearer of this bill may present it for payment on the due date.

17.4.9 Transferor by delivery

Where a bill is a bearer bill the person who transfers it is called the transferor by delivery, and the party to whom it is transferred is the transferee by delivery. Since a bearer bill does not need to be endorsed, the transferor does not sign the bill, and is not liable on it, but he does warrant to the transferee that the bill is what it purports to be, that he has a right to transfer it and that he knows of no defect in it rendering it valueless. The immediate transferee therefore does have a recourse against the transferor should the bill prove defective.

17.4.10 Accommodation parties

An accommodation party is someone who adds his signature to a bill to make it a first-class bill, because he is eminently credit-worthy, to accommodate a friend who is less credit-worthy. He may sign as drawer, acceptor or endorsee. Thus if A, a wealthy businessman, accommodates B, who is in need of funds, by accepting a bill of exchange for £1000 drawn on him at 90 days, he does not receive any value for the bill. He hopes that by the time 90 days has passed B will have funds available to honour the bill. In the meantime A is liable on the bill to the holder of it on the due date, since his intention in accepting it was to give it validity, but he is not liable to the drawer for its value, since he had no benefit from the bill. On the due date, if B is in funds, a holder who presents it to A may be referred to B for settlement. If B is not in funds A must honour it and pursue the settlement of the debt with B.

17.5 The acceptance of a bill

The drawer draws upon the drawee in unconditional terms. Acceptance of these terms unconditionally is called a **general acceptance**. A holder of a bill who presents it for acceptance is entitled to expect a general acceptance and if the drawee offers anything less the holder may treat the bill as dishonoured by non-acceptance. (See dishonour of bills below.) A general acceptance may be given in the following ways by the drawee:

- By merely signing the bill.
- By signing the bill and writing *accepted*.
- By signing the bill, writing *accepted* and also giving the date. The date is essential on any bill expressed to be payable at a certain period 'after sight' for the time cannot begin to run until the bill has been presented for acceptance and the date the drawee sighted the bill has been fixed.
- It is permissible to insert the place where payment will be made, and this is still a general acceptance – but if it is specified that this is the only place where the bill will be honoured the bill is said to be a **'local' bill** and it is not a general acceptance.

17.5.1 Qualified acceptance

A qualified acceptance is one where some qualification is introduced. Examples are:

- *Partial acceptance*, where the drawee undertakes to honour only part of the sum ordered to be paid.
- *Local acceptance*, which is explained above.
- *Qualification as to time*, where the drawee attempts to extend the time available for payment.
- *Conditional acceptance*, where the drawee inserts some condition about the charges, costs, etc., in connection with the bill.
- *Failure of one drawee to sign*. Where two or more drawees are named, it is possible some will refuse to sign. If the holder agrees to accept the signature of the others it is a qualified acceptance.

Section 44 has some important rules regarding qualified acceptances. If the presenter accepts a qualified acceptance the drawers and endorsers who are not a party to the acceptance and have not given authority for it to be taken are discharged from liability on the bill. If they have been given notice, or if they receive notice and do not express their dissent, they are deemed to have assented to it. If a foreign bill is the subject of a partial acceptance it must be protested for the balance of the value (see Section 17.5.3).

17.5.2 Rules about presentation for acceptance

A bill must be presented for acceptance in the following circumstances:

- Where it is payable after sight and must be presented so that the date of sight can be fixed, and hence the date of maturity of the bill can be determined.
- Where it is not payable at the drawee's home, or place of business and consequently the drawee must know what his obligation is and how it is to be fulfilled at the date of maturity.
- Where it is a requirement of the bill.

Apart from these cases a bill need not be presented for acceptance, and the drawer and other endorsers will be liable upon it even if it is not accepted by the drawee.

Presentment must be made in normal business hours, before the bill is overdue. If the bill is addressed to more than one drawee it must be presented to them all, unless one is authorized to accept for all. If the drawee is dead or bankrupt, presentment must be made to the personal representative or the trustee in bankruptcy but the bill may also be treated as dishonoured in these cases. It is also excused where due diligence has been shown in attempting to find the drawee without success, or where the drawee appears to be a fictitious person, or to lack capacity (for example, a minor). Just because you suspect a bill will be dishonoured on presentment is no excuse for not presenting it.

17.5.3 Dishonour by non-acceptance

The holder of a bill which has been dishonoured by non-acceptance, either because the drawee refuses to accept it or because presentment is excused for one of the reasons given above, has an immediate right of recourse against the endorsers or the drawer. The bill may be dealt with in a formal legal manner, by notice or protest, but this is not necessary for an inland bill and the holder's right of recourse is immediate (Section 43, 1882 Act). For a foreign bill protest is essential to establish a proper legal basis for future action. Notice and protest have already been described above.

17.6 Negotiation of a bill

Negotiation is the transfer of a bill in such a way as to constitute the transferee the holder of the bill. Thus a bearer bill may be negotiated by mere delivery; an order bill is negotiated by endorsement and delivery to the transferee. If an order bill is transferred for value without endorsement the transferee has the right to demand endorsement by the transferor.

To be a valid negotiation an endorsement must:

- Be written on the bill, or on an allonge, and be signed by the endorser. Even the signature alone is enough.
- It must be an endorsement of the entire bill. A partial endorsement, or one transferring the whole bill to two or more endorsees severally is not a valid negotiation.
- If there are several payees all must endorse the bill, unless one has authority to act for the rest (as with a partnership).
- If a name is misspelt the endorser should sign with the misspelt name but may add his proper signature if desired.
- An agent may endorse in such a way as to deny any personal liability, e.g. 'T. Green *per pro* Robinson and Co.'.
- A restrictive endorsement is permissible, e.g. 'Pay T. Green only'.
- A conditional endorsement is permissible, i.e. *sans recours* (without recourse to this particular indorser).

17.7 The payment of a bill

A bill must be presented for payment on the due date, and if it is not the drawer and endorsers are discharged. The rules about presentment are as follows:

- If the bill is payable on demand it may be presented at any time, but if the drawer or endorsers are to be held liable on it presentment must be made within a reasonable time. What is reasonable depends upon the facts of every case.
- If it is not payable on demand it must be presented on the due date.
- It must be presented at a reasonable hour on a business day at the specified place, or if no place is specified at the usual business address or the known residence. If these places are not known then it may be presented wherever the acceptor or drawee can be found, or at his last place of address.
- If two or more drawees are named the bill must be presented to both, or all, and the rules already mentioned about death or bankruptcy on presentment apply again.
- If agreement or usage authorizes it presentment may be made through the post.

Presentment is excused where the drawee is a fictitious person, and also where reasonable diligence has failed to find the drawee. It is not excused just because the holder feels it is unlikely to be honoured.

Dishonour occurs when it is presented for payment and payment is refused, or when presentment is excused and the bill is overdue and unpaid. In all these cases the holder has an immediate right of recourse against the drawers and endorsers.

17.8 Dishonour of a bill

Upon dishonour the holder has the right of recourse against all those who have endorsed the bill. He must give notice to the drawer and all endorsers, and any drawer or endorser who is not given notice is discharged from

Case 1	AC,	Dr,	A	B	C	D	E	F	[G]	H
Case 2	AC,	Dr,	A	B	[C]	D	E	F	G	H
Case 3	AC,	[Dr,]	A	B	C	D	E	F	G	H

Notes
(a) In Case 1, H is the holder who presents it to AC for payment. On payment being refused, he immediately gives notice to G, the person who transferred it to him, and G is obliged to honour it. G will then have a right of immediate recourse against all the other parties, i.e. Dr, A, B, C, D, E and F.
(b) In Case 2, H, who knows C, gives him notice of the dishonour. This notice is valid for all endorsers subsequent to C, so D, E, F and G are released from any obligation on the bill as soon as C pays H. C must now look to Dr, A or B for recourse.
(c) In Case 3, H goes direct to the drawer, who has the primary responsibility on the bill. If Dr pays H all the other endorsers are discharged from liability and Dr is left to bring an action against AC to recover the money due to him.
(d) Whoever honours a bill is entitled to receive it at once, and may then take such action as he wishes on it.

Figure 17.4 Notice of dishonour

liability on the bill. The notice must be given by or on behalf of the holder, or an endorser who is liable on the bill, and may be given in any form, orally or in writing, or by the return of the bill itself to any person who is liable on it. When this is done the notice given constitutes proper notice for all parties subsequent to the party to whom the notice is given. For example, consider Figure 17.4. In each case the holder is the last person shown, and the party featured in a box is the one to whom notice is given. AC is the acceptor who has dishonoured the bill and Dr is the drawer of the bill. The other parties are all endorsers of the bill.

17.8.1 The measure of damages on dishonour

The measure of damages in any action on a dishonoured bill of exchange is (a) the value of the bill, plus (b) interest from the time the bill was presented (if a demand bill) or the due date, plus (c) the expenses of noting or protest. If the bill is a foreign bill expressed in a foreign currency the damages is the amount of the re-exchange at the time of dishonour. Thus if a bill for 24 000 Deutschmarks had been discounted at DM4 = £1 (i.e. £6000), but on dishonour the bank sought recourse against the endorser at a time when the rate had hardened to DM3.5 = £1, the bank would require £6857.14, plus interest from the due date, and expenses. The Act does not prescribe a rate of interest but it does say that the court may exercise its discretion to reduce the interest payable if it is deemed fair to do so. A Practice Direction of the Queen's Bench Division dated 24 February 1983, states that the plaintiff may properly ask for a reasonable rate around, or somewhat above base rate – the short term investment account rate is a safe guide.

17.9 The discharge of bills

The discharge of a bill is the cessation of all obligations on the bill and the extinguishment of all rights of action on it.

A bill is discharged normally by payment on the due date by the acceptor to the *bona fide* holder, in good faith without notice of any defect in his title to the bill.

If a bill payable to a third party is honoured by the drawer it is not discharged but the drawer may not reissue it; he may only use it to enforce payment against the acceptor. Similarly, payment by any endorser is not discharge of the bill, since a right of recourse against earlier parties exists.

A bill may also be discharged by the acceptor becoming the holder at maturity, or renunciation, of the holder's rights against the acceptor, or cancellation of the bill by the holder. This involves writing on the bill that it is cancelled, or striking out the acceptor's signature – an action which would automatically discharge all parties to the bill. Similarly, any endorser may be discharged from the bill by striking out his name on the bill, and this will discharge all subsequent endorsers, but it will not discharge the bill itself because all earlier endorsers and the acceptor would still be liable on it.

Material alteration of a bill discharges all parties except the one making the alteration and subsequent endorsers. Material alteration is alteration of the date, the sum payable, the time of payment or the place of payment. Where an alteration is not apparent the innocent holder can also hold endorsers prior to the alteration liable for the *original* sum, so that they are not discharged entirely from the bill.

17.10 Forgeries

Forgery is the act of falsely making or altering any document with the intention of defrauding anyone who takes the document. The forgery of a signature is a special case of forgery. An unauthorized signature, as where an unauthorized director signs on behalf of a company may, or may not, amount to a forgery. The difference is that an unauthorized signature which does not amount to a forgery may be ratified to make it valid.

The effect of both forged and unauthorized signatures is that they are totally inoperative (Section 24, 1882 Act) and no right to retain a bill or enforce payment on it can follow from such a forgery. On a normal bill which has been negotiated via a series of endorsers to an ultimate holder there is an unbroken chain of parties, as shown below:

Acceptor A, Drawer D, Endorsers M, N, O, P, Q, R, S (the holder)

If a forgery appears at any point the effects will be as follows:

- *Forgery of the acceptor's signature.* The only effect is that the bill has not been accepted. When the drawee (who has not signed as acceptor) declares the signature to be a forgery and states that he knows nothing of the bill the holder S may apply to D or any of M, N, O, P, Q and R. There is no break in the chain of responsibility right back to the drawer, who is, as usual, the primary person responsible on an unaccepted bill.
- *Forgery of the drawer's signature.* If it is the drawer's signature that has been forged the document is not a bill at all, because it has not been 'signed by the person giving it'. Forgery of the drawer's signature usually occurs when cheque-books are stolen; there would therefore be no acceptor and the person who takes the forged cheque is the loser. No claim, says Section 24, can follow from a forged signature and the only redress is against the thief, who can usually not be found.
- *Forgery of an endorser's signature.* In this case there is a break in the chain. Suppose O lost the bill, and his signature was forged by the finder in negotiating the bill to P. There is a break in the chain at P and S, the holder, can only claim from P, Q and R. P, the victim of the forger's deception, must be the loser, and his only claim is against the forger. Q, R and S, although they have no valid title to the bill, can rely on Section 55 of the Act to help them, since in each case the person negotiating the bill to them is estopped from denying the validity of the bill. This leaves P as the loser by the forgery.

17.10.1 Estoppel

Estoppel is a legal maxim which prevents a person denying the genuineness of some activity or event because of his earlier failure to do what he should have done. Thus if A, knowing that B regularly writes out cheques in his name in such a way that the paying banker is misled into believing they are genuine signatures, he cannot later claim that they are forgeries and sue the bank for conversion. There are five cases where estoppel may affect bills of exchange:

- Where a person has positively asserted a signature to be genuine or regular (*Bank of England v. Vagliano Bros. (1891)*).
- By failure to fulfil a legal duty. In *Greenwood v. Martins Bank (1933)* Greenwood failed to tell the bank that his wife had forged cheques, and was held to be estopped from denying the validity of her signatures.
- In the case of inchoate instruments, where the bill has been left to be completed by another person. If that person is deceitful the drawer cannot deny the genuineness of the bill.
- Where the drawer or other party complaining has been negligent.
- Under Sections 54 and 55 of the 1882 Act, which hold that the acceptor is precluded from denying the genuineness of the drawer's signature, and the drawer is precluded from denying the identity of the payee and his power to endorse the bill.

17.11 Cheques

A cheque is a bill of exchange, drawn on a banker, payable on demand. Today banks are organizations recognized by the Bank of England, and listed on a register of banks published periodically by the Bank of England, by authority conferred on it by the *Banking Act, 1987*.

Sections 73–82 of the *Bills of Exchange Act, 1882*, deal with cheques, and a later act, the *Cheques Act, 1957*, revises the earlier rules and extends the protection given to paying bankers and collecting bankers. A further Act, the *Cheques Act, 1992* amends the *Bills of Exchange Act, 1882* by enacting an extra Section 81A as explained later in this section.

There is no need for the words 'on demand' to appear on a cheque since by Section 10 of the 1882 Act any bill of exchange is payable on demand if no time for payment is expressed on it. Cheques can be protected by **crossings**. A crossing is an instruction to the banker to pay the cheque only into a bank account, not over the counter. Some common crossings are shown in Figure 17.5, but the *Cheques Act, 1992* has now led bankers to issue the vast majority of cheques to personal customers in the account payee style – see (d) below. Explanations of the cheques illustrated in Figure 17.5 are as follows:

(a) Open cheques and bearer cheques

An **open cheque** (one that has no crossing) can be cashed at the bank by anyone who presents it and claims to be the payee, in this case T. Jones. The cheque must be endorsed (i.e. signed on the back by the person cashing the cheque). Although this is not much of a safeguard it does have a deterrent effect on thieves, because endorsement by a person other than the payee is forgery, which is a serious crime.

There is an even more unsafe cheque, called a **bearer cheque**, which is made out 'pay bearer'. This is very unsafe indeed and does not require endorsement, because the name of the bearer is not important. Anyone who presents it is entitled to payment on it. Generally speaking it is safer to cross a cheque, and banks issue books of cheques that are already crossed for those who prefer to play safe. Any interested party may cross a cheque, so a person receiving an open cheque may draw two lines across it to safeguard the cheque.

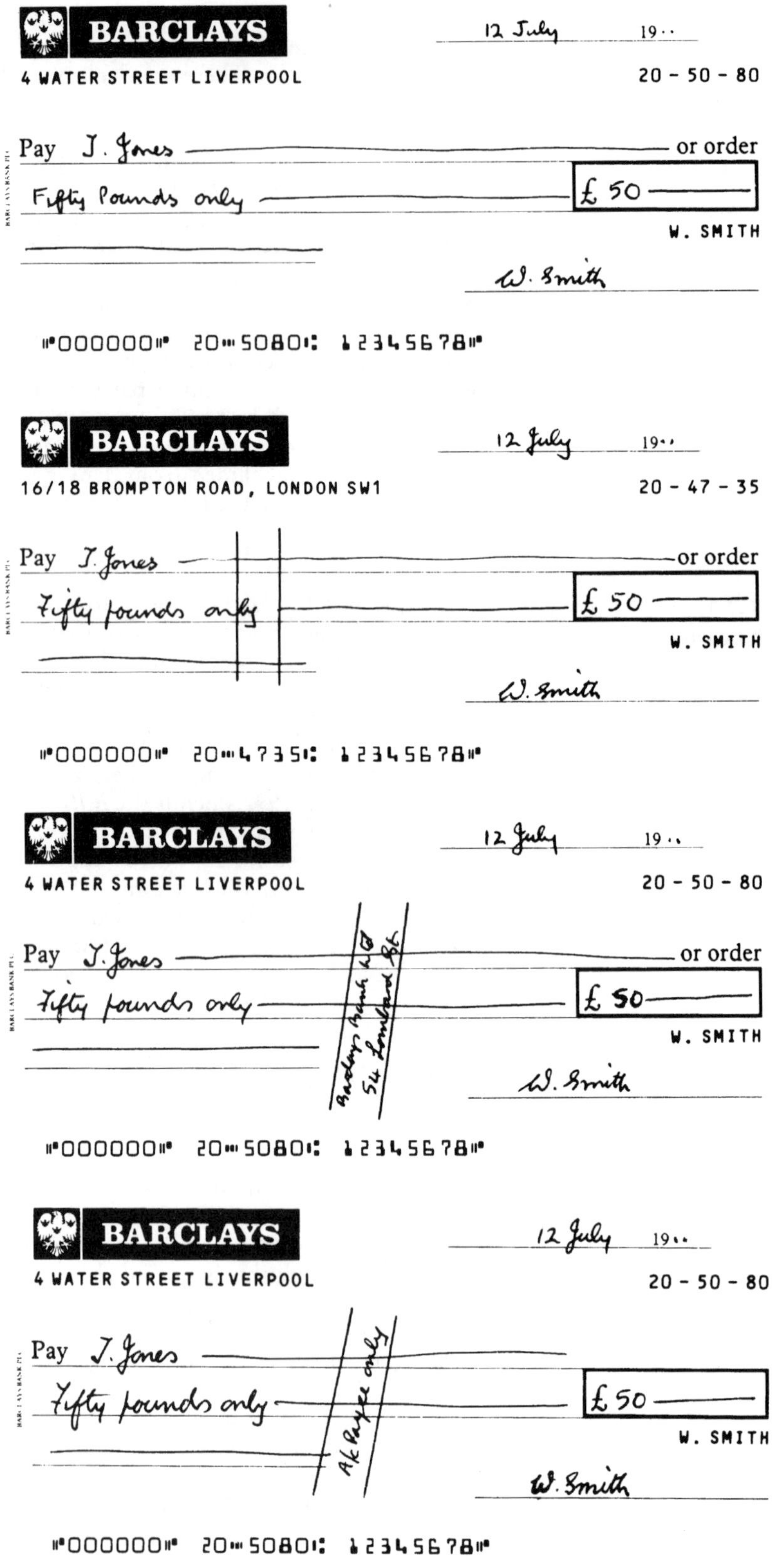

Figure 17.5 Safeguarding a cheque

Negotiable instruments **311**

(b) General crossings   A cheque with two lines across it, with or without '& Co.,' is said to be 'generally' crossed. It will only be cashed across the counter of a bank if the presenter is known to the cashier as the drawer-customer or an accredited representative; otherwise it must be cleared into a bank account. It is therefore much safer than (a) but it can be cleared by anyone so long as T. Jones has endorsed it. Note that it is possible to pay this cheque into any account. It does not have to go into the account of the person named on the cheque, T. Jones. This is because it is an order cheque. At the end of the line it says 'Pay T. Jones … or order'. This means that if Jones endorses it 'Pay R. Brown' and signs the order the bank concerned will obey, and pay R. Brown not T. Jones.

The rules about endorsement are as follows: no endorsement is necessary if the payee pays an order cheque into his/her own account. If a payee orders the bank to pay someone else, the endorsee pays the cheque into his/her own account in due course. An endorsement in blank, i.e. without instructions to the banker, but just signed, say T. Jones, makes the cheque payable to bearer.

(c) Special crossings   Where a cheque has the name of a banker filled in on the face of the cheque it constitutes a crossing and is said to be 'specially' crossed. Such a cheque will normally be cleared into the account of the payee in the bank named on the cheque.

(d) 'A/c payee' cheques   Where a cheque is crossed 'A/c payee' the indication is that the drawer wishes to restrict the cheque. It used to be the case that if such a cheque was paid into any other account the bank was 'put upon inquiry' over the circumstances. The bank must inquire whether the payee has given authority for the cheque to be cleared through the account of the person who has paid it in. However this type of cheque has now become very important because of the *Cheques Act, 1992* (see below).

(e) 'Not negotiable' cheques   Where a cheque is crossed 'not negotiable' it loses the properties of a negotiable instrument, the chief of which is the ability to transfer a better title of ownership than that of the original giver. Any person taking a cheque of this sort from a transferor knows that it is taken subject to any defects in title of the transferor. The transferee must therefore ensure that the transferor really does own the cheque, because if the transferor has no title the transferee will have no title. Even so, the words 'not negotiable' do not mean that the cheque cannot be transferred from one party to another.

Where a cheque appears on the face of it to have been in circulation for an unreasonable length of time it is said to be **overdue** (Section 36, 1882 Act). What is 'unreasonable' is a question of fact in every case. The onus of proving a cheque is overdue rests with the person seeking to avoid paying it. A **stale cheque** is one that has been in circulation for more than six months, and the return of a stale cheque implies that the paying banker prefers not to pay it until it has been confirmed by the drawer as a valid cheque. A **post-dated cheque** is one that has a date on it later than the date it was made out. Post-dating does not make a cheque invalid, but postpones the payment of the cheque until that date. A creditor who has been paid with a post-dated cheque has a valid bill of exchange which is better than nothing at all, but it is obviously less satisfactory than a cheque payable on demand.

The banker has a duty to pay his customer's cheques: the order in the cheque – 'pay . . . ' – gives authority to pay. However, the authority to pay may be countermanded by an express instruction to 'stop' a cheque. It may also be terminated in several other circumstances, as follows:

- By notice of the customer's death or unsoundness of mind.
- By notice that a bankruptcy petition has been presented against him or that a Receiving Order (an order winding up a company) has been made; or in the case of a company that winding-up proceedings have commenced.
- By service of a **garnishee order** attaching the customer's funds for use in the manner directed by the court.
- By injunction.

Where a bank wrongfully dishonours a customer's cheque it is liable in damages for breach of contract and, if the customer's reputation is damaged thereby, for libel. Proof of special damage is not required, damages being assessed without reference to pecuniary loss.

Where a cheque is fraudulently increased the bank will not be liable for paying it if the drawer has negligently left space to permit the alteration (*London Joint Stock Bank Ltd v. MacMillan and Arthur (1918)*).

17.11.1 The Cheques Act, 1957

This Act recognized that over the years since 1882, when the *Bills of Exchange Act* defined a cheque as 'a bill of exchange, drawn on a banker, payable on demand', subtle changes in the use of cheques had occurred. Cheques were no longer used as transferable documents, but simply as a ready method of payment, the payee paying them in for collection by a collecting banker. Therefore the Act sought to abolish the need for endorsement of cheques by payees who were merely paying in the cheques for collection. It also gave some additional protection to paying bankers and collecting bankers in various respects described below.

(a) Protection of the paying banker

A banker who is drawn on in a cheque is required to pay the payee. He is protected as far as this payment is concerned in the following ways:

- *Where an endorsement is forged.* Provided payment is made in good faith, and in the normal course of business, the bank is not liable (Section 60, 1882 Act).
- *Where there is no endorsement or an irregular endorsement.* An irregular endorsement is one where the signature is genuine, but is not in exactly the same style as the designation on the face of the cheque (e.g. where a cheque payable to J. J. Hilbride is endorsed 'James Hilbride') (*Cheques Act, 1957*, Section 1).
- *Where the cheque is crossed and is correctly paid according to the crossing.* Section 80 of the 1882 Act protects a banker who pays a crossed cheque in a proper manner to the true owner.

(b) Protection of the collecting banker

A collecting banker who collects payment on behalf of a customer is liable to be sued for conversion if the customer proves to have had not title to the cheque he paid in for collection. Therefore Section 4 of the *Cheques Act, 1957*, protects the collecting banker who collects in good faith, and without negligence, for a customer. The word 'customer' is important, since the bank may be held negligent if they have accepted a customer without making proper enquiries (*Hampstead Guardians v. Barclays Bank Ltd* (*1923*)). It may also be negligent if it accepts from a customer cheques made out to his employer, or made out in his official capacity, or as agent for someone else, and does not institute enquiries about them. In Marfani's case (*Marfani and Co. v. Midland Bank Ltd* (*1968*)), the bank was held to be protected by Section 4 even though its enquiries were not, according to the evidence, particularly careful.

17.11.2 The Cheques Act, 1992 – account payee cheques

This Act was passed because the growth in the economy in recent years had led to huge volumes of cheques being cleared every day, some of which went astray and got into the hands of unscrupulous people who had them cleared into bank accounts using, for example, forged endorsements. The protections accorded to bankers clearing such cheques in good faith meant that the true owners had no redress and had lost their money.

The *Cheques Act, 1992* enacted a further Section 81A into the *Bills of Exchange Act, 1882* which reads as follows:

> Where a cheque is crossed and bears across its face the words 'account payee' or 'a/c payee', either with or without the word 'only', The cheque shall not be transferable, but shall only be valid between the parties thereto.

As a consequence an a/c payee cheque is not transferable and a bank which did accept it for clearance into an account other than that of the named payee would be negligent. The banks quickly adopted the practice of making the cheque books supplied to personal customers 'a/c payee' crossed cheques, unless specially requested to issue open, or generally crossed cheques. The Act has therefore been generally effective in reducing the mis-use of cheques.

Test your knowledge

Answers	Questions
	1 What is a negotiable instrument?
1 A document which passes from hand to hand without notice having to be given to the party who is liable on it, and without the recipient having to take it 'subject to the equities'.	2 What are the common negotiable instruments?
2 (a) Bills of exchange; (b) cheques; (c) promissory notes; (d) Treasury bills; (e) bankers' drafts; (f) certificates of deposit; (g) divident warrants; (h) various types of bearer bonds.	3 Define a bill of exchange.

Answers	Questions
3 See the definition on page 298.	4 How is a bill of exchange used?
4 As a means of financing business activity in the time interval between production and consumption.	5 What is meant by the phrase 'bills should be self-liquidating'?
5 By the time the bill comes to maturity the business activity which brought it into existence should have provided the funds to honour it.	6 Who are the parties to a bill of exchange?
6 (a) The drawer; (b) the drawee – who becomes the acceptor; (c) the payee; (d) the endorsers; (e) the holder; (f) the holder in due course; (g) accommodation parties; (h) bearers; (i) transferors by delivery.	7 What is acceptance of a bill of exchange?
7 The assent of the drawee to the order in the bill. On signing the 'drawee' becomes the 'acceptor', and is the primary person liable on the bill.	8 What are the types of acceptance?
8 (a) General acceptances; (b) qualified acceptances, which may be: (i) partial; (ii) local; (iii) qualified as to time; (iv) conditional; (v) qualified as to parties.	9 What is negotiation of a bill of exchange?
9 The transfer of a bill in such a way as to constitute the transferee the *holder* of the bill.	10 How is a bill negotiated?
10 A bearer bill is negotiated by mere delivery. An order bill is negotiated by endorsement and delivery.	11 What is a holder of a bill?
11 The payee or endorsee in possession of it, or the bearer of a bearer bill.	12 What is the holder in due course?

Answers	Questions
12 A holder who takes a bill, complete and regular on the face of it, before it was overdue, and without notice of any previous dishonour, in good faith, for value and without notice of any defect in title of the person who negotiated it to him.	13 What are the rights of a holder in due course?
13 (a) He may sue on the bill in his own name; (b) he can defeat any defences based upon defects of title, or relations between earlier parties to the bill, before it came into his possession.	14 What did the *Cheques Act, 1992* do?
14 It introduced an extra clause 81A into the *Bills of Exchange Act, 1882*.	15 What was the point of this clause?
15 It made an 'account payee' cheque not transferable, because it was only to be valid between the two parties concerned.	16 How did this help?
16 It reduced the fraudulent use of cheques, since a stolen cheque could not be endorsed by the thief with a forged signature and paid into his account.	17 Go over the questions again until you are sure of the answers. Then try some of the questions in Appendix 1.

18 Arbitration

18.1 The nature of arbitration

Where a dispute arises in a matter of contract the expenses of a court may be very great, and the law's delay may be tiresome. There are no special arrangements for hearing disputes out of business hours and litigants are often kept waiting around for a previous case to conclude so that the court's time shall not be wasted. Witnesses may need to be brought from around the world, when a simple affidavit would be perfectly satisfactory and infinitely cheaper. A cheaper alternative is arbitration.

Arbitration is the voluntary submission of a dispute to a person qualified to settle it, with an agreement that the arbitrator's decision shall be final and binding.

In many disputes the argument is not a legal matter, but a question of quality, price, delivery, custom of the trade, etc. Judges are experts in law, not in the quality of coffee, etc., and there may be better people to 'judge' the matter in a dispute at the coffee exchange than in the courts of justice. Many contracts consequently provide that any dispute that arises shall be settled by arbitration. An arbitrator may be named, but more usually a method of choosing an arbitrator will be specified, such as 'a senior member from the Board of the relevant Trade Association'.

18.2 The advantages and disadvantages of arbitration

The advantages of arbitration may be listed as follows:

- The arbitrator can be an acknowledged authority on the subject concerned. Thus he may be a technical specialist, a scientist, a financial expert, a transport specialist, etc.
- The evidence can be submitted in writing beforehand, so that all viewpoints have been formally (and thoughtfully) expressed and witnesses' oral evidence is not required. The arbitrator comes to the meeting fully knowledgeable about the dispute, and only needing to hear the personal attitudes of the chief parties concerned.
- The hearing can be at a time and place convenient for the various parties, often after working hours. The hearing is informal and friendly, a resolution of a difficulty rather than a trial.
- Arbitration is private; the press are not entitled to be present as they are in a legal trial, and public attention is not called to the attitudes or behaviour of the parties.
- Foreigners prefer arbitration, which avoids conflicts of law. Decisions of arbitration proceedings are more easily enforced abroad and the enforcement is largely voluntary – to preserve goodwill between trading partners – rather than imposed by an 'external' authority.
- Appeal is possible to the courts on any legal point, and the court does exercise supervision over arbitration proceedings. This is explained in Section 18.3 below.

Against these advantages we may enumerate the following disadvantages:

- There is no judicial precedent created by arbitration decisions, so that every case is said to be 'thrown away'. There is also the possibility that conflicting decisions will be arrived at on the basis of identical sets of facts. Arbitration proceedings are therefore unnecessarily numerous, and there is no certainty about the decisions.
- Although technically a matter of choice between equals, in many standard form contracts the arbitration clause is inserted by a stronger party (for instance, the insurance company) against a weaker party (the assured). Since in many contracts we are statutorily required to take certain actions (for example, to insure) we may in fact be statutorily compelled to contract on another person's terms and thus be forced to accept arbitration when appeal to the courts is a citizen's true birthright.
- Where the matter in dispute involves a legal point we may have to go to the courts for a ruling anyway.
- Arbitration is not all that cheap, especially when every case is 'thrown away' and the point in dispute may need to be settled many times. An interesting case is:

> *International Sea Tankers of Liberia Inc. v. Hemisphere Shipping Co. of Hong Kong (1981)*
>
> During the war between Iraq and Iran certain ships were trapped in the Shatt al Arab. The plaintiffs sought leave to appeal against the decision of an arbitrator who had ruled that the time charterparty had been frustrated. In granting leave to appeal it was held that 'events in this war were likely to give rise to many frustration cases, and the courts ought to give a definitive ruling in order to avoid inconsistent rulings in different arbitrations'.

This illustrates the point that a simple decision on a matter of frustration might be heard many times by countless arbitrators, when one single piece of judicial precedent would resolve them all, and save enormous effort in collecting depositions, writing accounts of events, etc. At the same time certainty would be introduced into the proceedings.

18.3 The Arbitration Acts 1950, 1975 and 1979

The *Arbitration Act, 1950*, is the major statute and controls the general conduct of arbitration proceedings. The 1975 Act gives effect to the New York Convention on Recognition and Enforcement of Foreign Arbitral Awards. The 1979 Act reduces the courts' influence over arbitration proceedings other than by appeal. These Acts will be looked at in reasonable detail below.

18.3.1 Reference to an arbitrator

Matters may come before an arbitrator in three possible ways:

- *By agreement between the parties.* This is the commonest procedure, it having been agreed in the contract that disputes will be settled by arbitration. It is possible that oral agreement is enough but the Acts apply only to written agreements to submit present or future difficulties to arbitration, whether an arbitrator is named therein or not.

- *By order of the court.* The court may refer any matter to an arbitrator, and will tend to do so if the documents under dispute are detailed and need expert investigation – for example, by scientists, accountants, etc. – or if they need local examination. The court may call for a report, or may delegate the trial of the matter to an official or referee.
- *By statute.* Many statutes provide for difficulties that may arise to be settled by arbitration and will usually specify how the arbitration is to be conducted, but if not the Acts of 1950, 1975 and 1979 apply.

18.3.2 Arbitration arrangements

To clarify difficulties that may arise the Act provides that unless the arbitration agreement makes it clear otherwise, the reference to an arbitrator is taken to mean a single individual. If the reference is to two arbitrators, one appointed by either party, there is an implied provision that the arbitrators shall appoint an umpire immediately they have been appointed, and on informing him that they cannot agree the umpire may forthwith enter on the reference in lieu of the arbitrators.

If the reference to arbitration calls for three arbitrators, the award of any two of them shall be binding. If one of them is to be appointed by each party, and the third by the other two, he is treated as an umpire as described above.

All parties to an arbitration must, by the 1950 Act, be prepared to submit to examination under oath, and be prepared to bring before the arbitrator all documents and other evidence as required. The arbitrator is empowered to administer oaths.

The arbitrator must use all reasonable dispatch in making an award, and may make an interim award unless this is specifically excluded by the reference to arbitration in the contract. The arbitrator has the same power as the High Court to order specific performance of the contract (except where an interest in land is concerned). The award is final and binding on both parties.

18.3.3 The control of arbitration by the courts

The usual thing is for an arbitration agreement to exclude an appeal to the courts but the court may become involved in the following circumstances:

(a) Death or unsuitability of the arbitrator

Under the 1950 Act the court may appoint an arbitrator if:

- The arbitrator dies or the formula for his appointment proves for some reason to be inappropriate, or if the parties cannot agree upon an arbitrator (Section 10).
- Where an arbitrator acts improperly (Section 23) the court may remove him and appoint another.

(b) Refusal of a witness to appear

Where a witness fails to appear at an arbitration proceedings any party to the reference may sue out a writ of subpoena and the High Court or judge thereof may order that a writ be issued to compel the attendance of the witness before the arbitrator or umpire.

(c) 'Stay' of proceedings

Where a party to a domestic arbitration agreement (one involving only UK citizens, firms and companies) commences a legal action the other party may at once apply to the courts for a 'stay' of proceedings, provided that he is willing and ready to proceed at once with the arbitration. If the court is satisfied that this is so it will order a 'stay' pending resolution of the problem by arbitration (Section 4, 1950 Act). The requirements for a stay are:

- that the matter comes within the terms of reference of the arbitration clause;
- the applicant has taken no step in the legal proceedings, such as entering a defence to the claims made;
- the applicant must have been ready and willing from the start to proceed with all dispatch to arbitration.

The court will refuse a stay if it believes that the arbitrator will not be impartial or if the dispute alleges fraud, and it is desirable that this allegation is investigated. One of the commonest reasons for an award to be set aside is the fact that the arbitrator has behaved badly, and has failed to listen to the views of one party. Although arbitration is not litigation it is a method of settling disputes which must be conducted fairly, and must be seen to have been conducted fairly. If the arbitrator does not observe the rule, *audi alteram partem* (let the other party be heard), or if he does not allow the parties to express an opinion about vital matters and principles which he is using to decide the case, he is guilty of misconduct. In *Diamond Lock Grabowski v. Laing Investments (Bradnell) 1992*, 60 BLR 112 the arbitrator refused to delay a hearing although the parties had a huge volume of documents to appraise and could not possibly prepare a proper case in the time he was prepared to allow. It was held that the respondent was justified in feeling that the arbitrator would not conduct the hearing fairly, and he was removed from the arbitration.

(d) Rules introduced by the Courts and Legal Services Act, 1990

The *Courts and Legal Services Act, 1990* introduced some new rules about arbitration with some new sections to be inserted into the 1950 Act. These include:

- A new Section 11 which permits an official referee (provided the Lord Chief Justice sanctions the use of his/her time in this way) to be appointed as a sole arbitrator or as an umpire. The activities of such persons as arbitrators or umpires are subject to control by the Court of Appeal, rather than the High Court.
- A new Section 43A to the *Supreme Court Act, 1981* permits the High Court to act as arbitrator in any case coming before it where an arbitration agreement is incorporated, provided both the parties agree.
- Some new subsections in Section 10 of the 1950 Act are inserted to solve difficulties when one party to an arbitration agreement fails to fulfil his/her part of the bargain by appointing an arbitrator. The other party may serve a notice on the other requiring an arbitrator to be appointed within seven days, and if none is appointed his/her arbitrator may act as sole arbitrator (Section 3B) or the court will appoint an arbitrator to act for the party in default (Section 3C).

The *Arbitration Act, 1975*, varies the rules about staying proceedings in non-domestic arbitrations (arbitrations held abroad, involving foreign citizens or foreign incorporations). This Act gives effect to the New York Convention on the Recognition and Enforcement of Foreign Arbitral Awards, dated 25 February 1975. Naturally an international convention should not lightly be displaced by national laws, and the Act therefore says that if a non-domestic arbitration agreement has been made the courts will stay any proceedings commenced by one party in the courts, if the other party requests a 'stay' and it is proved that the arbitration agreement is not null and void, inoperative or incapable of being performed, and that the dispute between the parties comes within the terms of reference of the agreement to arbitrate.

(e) Appeal to the High Court

The High Court may be called upon in numerous situations to make orders in respect of such matters as discovery of documents, giving of evidence by affidavit, examination on oath of witnesses, preservation and sale of goods which are the subject matter of dispute, securing money which is in dispute and bringing it into court, the issue of any interim injunction, or the appointment of a receiver.

(f) Judicial rulings by way of case stated

An interesting situation about judicial control of arbitration proceedings has been changed by the 1979 Act. Until that Act it was the case that under Section 21 of the Act of 1950 an arbitrator or umpire might – or if directed to do so by the High Court must – state a case for consideration by the court on any point of law, or about the amount of any award. The court would then decide the point of law and this decision would be deemed to be a judgment of the court (so that an appeal could be lodged against it). The award could then be remitted to the arbitrator for reconsideration. The principle behind such a procedure was that there could not be any ouster of jurisdiction of the courts on questions of law (in other words, a private agreement to arbitrate could not deprive any citizen of his right to appeal to the courts on a question of law). By the 1979 Act this rule has changed and the stating of cases in this way has been discontinued. Instead, those who feel that an award has gone against them through the arbitrator's misreading of the law may appeal in the following circumstances:

- If all the parties to the arbitration agree to the appeal being made, or
- If the court gives leave to appeal (but the court will not do so if the parties have signed an agreement not to appeal).

If the appeal is allowed the court may confirm, vary or set aside the award, or remit the reward back to the arbitrator for reconsideration, and he shall make a new award within three months after the date of the order.

By Section 2 of the 1979 Act, however, it is possible if the arbitrator, or the umpire, or *all* the parties ask it, for the High Court to give an early decision on any point of law arising, if the court is satisfied that to do so will considerably reduce the costs in any arbitration proceedings.

The rules about 'exclusion agreements' which exclude the right to appeal are complex. As regards non-domestic arbitrations governed by the international convention, the High Court will not exercise its powers under the 1950 Act (Section 24) to take steps to allow the court to determine the matter. For domestic arbitrations the exclusion clause will only operate if it was made *after* the commencement of the arbitration, and for statutory arbitrations an exclusion agreement cannot operate to prevent an appeal on a matter of law, or an award made. There are also special rules about Admiralty matters, insurance and commodity contracts.

Finally, the chief point of the 1975 Act was to implement the New York Convention. Section 3 of the Act says that where there is a convention award made in a foreign country the award must be enforced in the UK courts just as if it was a domestic award. This explains why those engaged in international trade prefer arbitration of disputes, since the awards can be enforced in any country which has ratified the convention.

18.4 The Consumer Arbitration Agreements Act, 1988

It has already been emphasized that where there are contracts in a standard form it frequently occurs that one party to the contract (the consumer) is less sophisticated and less well-advised legally than the other party. The old common law rule that both parties to a contract are equally powerful is, therefore, too harsh where consumers are concerned. Since such contracts frequently include a clause which holds that all disputes must be settled by arbitration, Parliament has enacted in the *Consumer Arbitration Act, 1988* certain protections to consumers.

A consumer is defined in the Act as 'a person who does not make a contract as part of the course of the activities of any business, and the contract is one where the goods are such as are ordinarily supplied for private use and consumption.'

Section 1 of the Act says that an arbitration clause in a contract can only be enforced against a consumer in three situations:

- Where the consumer agrees to arbitration *after* the dispute has arisen, (the original 'agreement' in the contract being overridden by the Act).
- Where the consumer has already submitted to arbitration proceedings under the agreement (Parliament hesitating to set aside a decision already arrived at in the agreed manner).
- Where the court makes an order under Section 4 of the Act that arbitration shall proceed (since in the court's opinion arbitration in the particular case under consideration would be unlikely to affect the consumer adversely).

Apart from these three cases the arbitration clause in an agreement with a consumer (as defined above) is not enforceable, and the consumer is entitled to pursue a solution to the dispute in the ordinary courts.

Test your knowledge

Answers

1 It is the voluntary submission of a dispute to a person qualified to settle it, with an agreement that the arbitrator's decision shall be final and binding.

Questions

1 What is arbitration?

2 What are the advantages of arbitration?

Answers	Questions
2 (a) Usually it is cheaper; (b) delays are reduced; (c) evidence can be submitted in writing; (d) the arbitrator can be a qualified person; (e) Hearings can be at a time convenient to the parties; (f) the hearing is private; (g) foreigners prefer arbitration.	3 What are the disadvantages?
3 (a) No judicial precedent is created and hence every case is 'thrown away'; (b) conflicting decisions may be given on similar sets of facts; (c) often it is not a free choice – arbitration becomes compulsory in many standard form contracts; (d) if a legal point is involved we may have to go to law anyway.	4 How may cases be placed with an arbitrator?
4 (a) By agreement – a clause in the contract; (b) by order of the court – if detailed research or analytical study is required; (c) by statute – many statutes provide for arbitration of disputes arising from the statute.	5 How do the courts control arbitration?
5 They exercise general supervision in any circumstances where difficulties arise, such as the death of an arbitrator, refusal of a witness to appear, etc. They may 'stay' proceeding, in certain circumstances; they may determine points of law in certain circumstances, and aggrieved parties may seek leave to appeal to the High Court against awards made, or on points of law.	6 What is the main Act of Parliament on arbitration?
6 The *Arbitration Act, 1950*.	7 What did the *Arbitration Act, 1975*, do?

Answers	Questions
7 It implemented the New York Convention on the Recognition and Enforcement of Foreign Arbitral Awards.	8 What was the chief purpose of the *Arbitration Act, 1979*?
8 To end the arrangement whereby parties could require the arbitrator to state a case for the High Court, which could then set aside an award or remit it for reconsideration.	9 What must aggrieved parties do now?
9 Seek leave to appeal on a point of law.	10 What does the *Consumer Arbitration Act, 1988* say?
10 That where arbitration clauses appear in agréements with consumers the clause shall only be enforceable in certain circumstances.	11 How does the Act define a consumer?
11 As a person who does not make the contract as part of the transactions of any business, and who is ordering goods or services which are ordinarily used for private consumption or for private purposes.	12 In what circumstances will an arbitration clause be upheld?
12 (a) Where the consumer agrees to go to arbitration *after* the dispute has arisen; (b) where the arbitration has already taken place; (c) where the court believes arbitration should proceed because it could not affect the consumer adversely.	13 If the arbitration clause is ruled invalid what can the consumer now do?
13 Go to court to settle the dispute since he/she is not bound to arbitrate.	14 Go over the questions again. Then try some of the written questions in Appendix 1.

Part Five Public Law

19 Administrative law

19.1 Introduction

Governments have always exercised power. Administrative law has grown up over the centuries to control and supervise the use of government powers. With the advent of the welfare state and its subsequent development, the provision of state services has increased. The progressive development of the mixed economy has ensured that the state plays an important role in an individual's life. The body of administrative law has therefore developed at the same time to control and regulate this relationship between the state and the individual.

Administrative law is concerned with the settlement of disputes between individuals and the various organs of both central and local government engaged in administration. In addition to governing the relationship between various administrative agencies set up to implement public policies and those individuals or private bodies affected, administrative law also regulates and controls the relationship between these various agencies – for example, the relationship between a minister and a local authority.

It is not intended to list all the numerous and varied activities of the state that affect its citizens. Indeed, not all of these state activities are governed by administrative law. To give an idea of the areas that fall under this branch of the law we may list those concerned with the provision of social services, health and education, others with the running of public utilities such as water, gas, postal services, transport and, lastly, the state's involvement with individuals in areas such as immigration control, licensing, town planning, social security, housing, etc.

As far as businesses are concerned their environment is to some extent hemmed in by administrative controls: planning permission, regulations about pollution, noise, dangerous goods and materials, consumer regulations, labelling and similar requirements, health and safety regulations, etc. Whilst endeavouring to meet the requirements of countless laws of this sort, the business person may find that powers are being exceeded or abused. It is in this area that administrative law seeks to control officials acting outside their powers.

The presentation of this section is as follows:

- Controls by the ordinary courts over the activities of public authorities, i.e. the various grounds on which the courts can intervene to question decisions made by public officials.
- A look at the various administrative remedies that are available where a dispute arises which lacks a legal remedy in the ordinary courts. These include the use of administrative tribunals and public enquiries.
- The functions of the Parliamentary Commissioner for Administration (the Ombudsman), and similar officials.

19.2 Judicial control of administrative powers

In the administering of public services, the actions of public authorities directly affect individuals. Their actions in regulating private activities through licensing and other controls confer rights and impose burdens on individuals. While political and administrative control over the actions of public authorities is no less important, judicial control is the most certain and effective way of ensuring that a public authority does not exceed its powers, and enables the rights and duties of an individual to be determined and enforced.

Although Parliament normally provides a right of appeal to an administrative tribunal against an administrative decision with a possible further right of appeal to a court, the courts can nevertheless intervene on various well established grounds to question a decision of a public authority. These grounds are in no way substitutes for other possible remedies available to an aggrieved citizen against the action of a public authority, i.e. an action under tort or contract law. For example, a hospital authority is vicariously liable for the negligence of its servants (nursing staff, physicians, surgeons, etc.) in the performance of their duties (*Cassidy v. Ministry of Health (1951)* and *Roe v. Minister of Health (1954)*). A contract made by a public authority is essentially subject to the same rules that govern contracts between individuals with the exception that where a public authority exceeds its authority in entering a contract, that contract is void and unenforceable (*Rhyl UDC v. Rhyl Amusements Ltd (1959)*).

All remedies are of course subject to whether or not Parliament has conferred immunity on the public authority from being sued or prosecuted. For example, under common law, a sheriff executing a court order is protected from personal liability. Similarly, persons closely involved in the compulsory detention of a mental patient do not incur civil or criminal liability (Section 141, *Mental Health Act, 1959*). Therefore, when Parliament has authorized an action to be taken, that action cannot be wrongful and compensation for any harm that results is payable only if provision for compensation exists under the statute.

The case of *M v. Home Office (1993) 3 WLR 433* has introduced a far-reaching change in the established belief that officers of the Crown are immune from suit under the *Crown Proceedings Act, 1947*. It held that injunctions can be given against ministers and other officers of the Crown where an application is made for judicial review under Section 31 of the *Supreme Court Act, 1981*. It also held that an interim injunction could be granted against a Minister in an appropriate case, pending a full hearing on a matter.

19.3 Grounds for judicial intervention

The action of public authorities may be ruled invalid for a variety of reasons. The courts have consistently upheld the following matters as justifying the control of officials: *ultra vires* actions (actions beyond the powers granted); incorrect procedure; improper purpose; irrelevant consideration; error of law; lack of evidence; and abuse of discretionary powers. It has been suggested that these grounds of judicial intervention are not independent justifications for intervention but merely specialized applications of the *ultra vires* rule or doctrine. Each of these grounds will be considered individually below.

One aspect of administrative law which constantly arises is the **'test of standing'**. If a review of the use of administrative powers is to be held it ought not to be demanded at the whim of any citizen, whether he is affected or not, but should only be undertaken if the plaintiff has a sufficient standing to demand the relief claimed. To pass the 'test of standing' Webster, J, in

Steeples v. Derbyshire County Council (1984) held that if the decision made affected the plaintiff in a way that was over and above the effect on an ordinary member of the public, this would give him the requisite standing to entitle him to claim the relief sought.

19.3.1 The ultra vires rule

Where a public authority is given certain powers and it exceeds those powers then the acts in excess are considered *ultra vires* and invalid. For example, where a public authority is authorized to establish a wash-house where people can wash their own clothes, the installation of a modern laundry to be run as a business is clearly *ultra vires* and a ratepayer would succeed in preventing the public authority from this action (*Att.-Gen. v. Fulham Corporation (1921)*). A further example is:

> **R. v. Minister of Health, ex p. Davies (1929)**
> The minister had power to confirm improvement schemes submitted by local authorities under the *Housing Act, 1925*. A property owner brought an action to prevent the minister approving a scheme submitted by a local authority which did not show how it proposed to develop its compulsorily acquired land. The scheme left the local authority complete freedom to develop, sell or lease the land for any purpose it saw fit. **Held**: since the provisions in the scheme were *ultra vires* the *Housing Act, 1925*, it would have been beyond the power of the minister to confirm it. Hence a prohibition order was issued to prevent the minister from considering the scheme.

In *R. v. GLC and Another (1984)* the right of the GLC to second seven full time members of staff to conduct a political campaign against a particular political proposal (the abolition of the GLC) was challenged. Gildwell, J stated that if the object of the decision was not to discharge local authority functions but to carry out some other purpose then the decision was *ultra vires*. The court was satisfied that the object was to conduct a political campaign which was an irrelevant consideration and outside the powers of the GLC.

The ultra vires rule, estoppel and the Crown Since the Crown cannot, in theory, ever act in an *ultra vires* way, it has long been held that the doctrine of estoppel can only be used in a very limited way against the Crown. In a recent case *Gowa and Others v. Attorney General (1984)* the court held that the Crown was estopped from denying assurances given 30 years earlier by British officials to certain persons that they were British Citizens and need not apply for citizenship. They had relied on the assurances given in error by a senior official and had therefore become statute-barred from making applications for citizenship, through no fault of their own. In order to clarify the position entirely the Appeal Court gave leave to the Attorney General to appeal to the House of Lords.

Where a power that is being questioned comes from the Crown, rather than from Parliament, the question arises whether the action of an official acting for the Crown can ever be queried judicially, since the Crown cannot ever act in an *ultra vires* way. In *Council of Civil Service Unions v. Minister for the Civil Service (1985)* the appeal judges held that judicial review of an individual act by an official purporting to act on behalf of the Crown was possible. This was confirmed in *R. v. Secretary of State for Foreign and*

Commonwealth Affairs (1989) where a renewal of a passport to a citizen living in Spain, against whom a warrant for arrest was outstanding in the United Kingdom, was refused. The court reviewed the decision, but decided it was a perfectly proper use of powers.

Mercy is a royal prerogative and the exercise of that prerogative by the Home Secretary is one that raises the question whether there can be any judicial review of a royal prerogative. In *R v. Secretary of State for the Home Department ex p. Bentley (1993)* the relatives of Bentley, a young man hanged for a crime in which he participated, but did not actually carry out the murder, sought judicial review of the Home Secretary's refusal to recommend a posthumous free pardon, and asked for a writ of mandamus requiring the Home Secretary to reconsider his decision. The claim was made more forcefully in that certain criticisms of the original evidence had led to a widespread belief that the original decision to refuse a reprieve for Bentley was wrong. This was conceded by the court.

Reviewing the development of the law in recent years Watkins, LJ referred to *R v. Secretary of State for Foreign Affairs ex p. Everett (1989) 1 All ER 65* where it was held that a decision to refuse an applicant a passport was reviewable. He quoted the New Zealand case of *Burt v. Governor General (1992)* in which the New Zealand Court of Appeal held the view that the prerogative of mercy was not just an 'arbitrary monarchical right' but 'an integral part of the criminal justice system, and a constitutional safeguard against mistake'.

Drawing support from these authorities Watkins, LJ went on to observe that in the present state of the law it would be regrettable if the action of a Home Secretary was immune from legal challenge. However, the court did not go as far as granting the appellant the writ of mandamus she sought. Instead the court 'invited the Home Secretary to look at the matter again.' No doubt this would be easier, since the then Home Secretary had moved on to a higher post and a new Home Secretary might look at the case with fresh eyes. The court then gave a surprisingly clear idea of what it felt those eyes should see, since it said they 'should examine whether it would be just to exercise the prerogative of mercy in such a way as to give full recognition to the now generally accepted view that this young man should be reprieved'.

19.3.2 Incorrect procedure

Where an Act of Parliament lays down a procedure to be followed before arriving at a decision, failure to follow the procedure may render the decision invalid.

The exercise of power in such circumstances is declared a nullity. Thus, where an Act of Parliament (*Police Act, 1919*) provided that before the dismissal of a chief constable by the police committee, a formal inquiry was required into the charges against him, the failure of the Brighton police committee to hold an inquiry meant that the dismissal was void and ineffective (*Ridge v. Baldwin (1964)*). It must be noted, however, that not every non-compliance with the procedure would render a decision invalid. For a decision to be declared void and invalid there must have been a substantial non-compliance with the procedure and not merely a minor procedural error.

For example, in *Coney v. Choyce and others (1975)* information concerning the proposals to reorganize the Roman Catholic schools in a number of towns was widely circulated in the surrounding areas as required by the *Education Act, 1944*. However, in the case of two schools these requirements were not fully complied with as no notice was posted or displayed at or near the entrances to these schools. An action was brought by the parents of a child to prevent the defendants from implementing the proposals and for a declaration that the Secretary of State's approval of the proposals was invalid on grounds of non-compliance. The court held that there was substantial conformity with the requirements of the 1944 Act and no substantial prejudice was suffered by those for whose benefit the requirements had been introduced. The action of the parents was dismissed. However, in *Bradbury v. London Borough of Enfield (1967)* the decision made by the local authority was affected when in introducing a comprehensive education system for its secondary schools it failed to give public notice in advance of the proposed changes as required by the *Education Act, 1944*. Local ratepayers succeeded in preventing the authority from introducing a comprehensive system in its schools until the procedure was followed.

19.3.3 Improper purpose

If power has been conferred for a particular purpose it must be utilized for that purpose only. The exercise of the power for a different or improper purpose is invalid:

> ### Sydney Municipal Council v. Campbell (1925)
> The Corporation was given powers to acquire land compulsorily in order to improve the infrastructure of the city. The Corporation, however, acquired development land with the intention of making profit when its value increased.
> **Held**: the Corporation could not exercise powers given for one purpose for another.

In *Congreve v. Home Office (1976)*) the Court of Appeal held that there would have been an improper exercise of the Home Secretary's powers of revoking television licences when the Home Secretary threatened to revoke the licences of certain television users if they did not pay the extra £6 (the increase in the licence fee). The court held that the power to revoke licences must be exercised in accordance with the law and it would have been an unlawful exercise of the Home Secretary's discretionary powers of revocation to threaten revocation 'as a means of extracting money'.

19.3.4 Irrelevant consideration

When arriving at a decision public bodies must take into account all the relevant matters. If irrelevant considerations are taken into account in arriving at a decision, that decision is likely to be rendered invalid by the courts. In *R. v. West London Supplementary Benefits Tribunal, ex p. Clarke (1975)* a supplementary benefits tribunal were taking into account irrelevant considerations when assessing the financial resources of a claimant – namely, the financial means of a relative of the claimant who was not legally bound to support the claimant. Similarly, in *R. v. Birmingham Licensing Planning Committee, ex p. Kennedy (1972)* the Birmingham Licensing Planning Committee, as a prerequisite to a hotel company receiving a new licence for a hotel, required the hotel company to make a payment of some £14 500 as a price for obtaining a licence, the sum that would be used to relieve the Birmingham Corporation of the liability to pay compensation to holders of licences in suspense. The court held that the licensing planning committee had taken into account extraneous and irrelevant considerations in arriving at its decision. The committee was accordingly directed to consider the application for a licence on proper grounds.

In *Roberts v. Hopwood (1925)* the House of Lords held that the Poplar Borough Council was guided by irrelevant considerations when it decided to pay its servants minimum wages far in excess of the national average wage for similar workers. The Council was primarily concerned to set an example as a model employer paying generous wages having regard to the efficiency of the work people, the purchasing power of the wages and its duty to both its employees and rate payers. The court was of the opinion that the Council should take into account considerations such as the cost of living, awards of joint industrial councils and wages paid by other similar employers both local and national.

19.3.5 Error of law

If a decision has been arrived at through a misinterpretation of the law or an error of law has been made, the decision can be rendered invalid in a court of law. In *Perilly v. Tower Hamlets Borough Council (1973)* the Borough Council was under a misapprehension that when applications for licences to trade in the Petticoat Lane market were received they were to be dealt with in the strict order of receipt, so that if a market stall became vacant the first person on the waiting list would automatically be entitled to that stall. Perilly's mother had a stall where she had been trading for 30 years, and on her death the council refused a licence to Perilly, the licence being granted to a newcomer to the market. The court ordered that the licence should be issued to Perilly after quashing the licence issued to the newcomer.

19.3.6 Lack of evidence

If a decision arrived at is based on insufficient or lack of evidence, the decision can be quashed in a court of law. In *Coleen Properties Ltd v. Minister of Housing and Local Government (1971)* the minister had agreed to a proposal by a local authority to purchase compulsorily two rows of houses in bad condition. However, the proposal to acquire also related to a first-class modern property at the junction of the houses. The Council took its decision and the minister agreed despite the local inspector's recommendation that it was not necessary to purchase the modern house and hence it should be excused from the order. The owner of the modern property now sought to quash the compulsory purchase order relating to his property only. The Court of Appeal, in complying, held that the Council had not produced satisfactory evidence to show why the modern property should also be compulsorily acquired and hence the minister lacked material evidence to overrule the inspector's recommendation and therefore his decision in relation to the modern property was wrong.

19.3.7 Abuse of discretionary powers

Where a public body is given discretionary powers, these must be exercised properly and all relevant considerations must be taken into account before arriving at a decision. Where a discretion is exercised for an improper purpose contrary to law, the decision arrived at can be questioned in the courts.

In *Padfield v. Minister of Agriculture (1968)*, under the *Agricultural Marketing Act, 1958*, a complaints procedure was laid down under which farmers could complain to a committee of investigation about the workings of the statutory marketing schemes if the minister in any case so directed. The minister refused to refer a complaint made by Padfield, who was a farmer in south-east England, alleging that the 1958 Act had given him unfettered discretion whether or not to refer complaints to the committee of investigation. The House of Lords held that in refusing to refer the complaint, the minister was frustrating the intention and objects of the 1958 Act and hence an order of mandamus lay to compel him to appoint a committee. Lord Reid had the following to say:

> ... *The policy and objects of the Act must be determined by construing the Act as a whole.... If a Minister having misconstrued the Act or for any other reason, so uses his discretion as to thwart or run counter to the policy and objects of the Act, then our law would be very defective if persons aggrieved were not entitled to the protection of the court.*

The court found that the intention of the Act was to provide a machinery by which complaints of farmers could be investigated by a committee which was independent of the Milk Marketing Board. Hence, in refusing to appoint a committee to which complaints could be referred, where it was obvious that people had a grievance, the minister was frustrating the intention of the Act.

Other variations on this theme are instances when a discretion is fettered or surrendered, or where there is an unreasonable exercise of a discretionary power or a complete failure to exercise a discretion. In *Stringer v. Minister of Housing and Local Government (1970)*, an agreement between Cheshire County Council and Manchester University, under which the Council were to exercise its planning powers to discourage development in the neighbourhood of the Jodrell Bank telescope, was held to be *ultra vires*. The agreement prevented the Council from taking into account other relevant considerations and dealing with future planning applications on merit. The Council had basically fettered its discretion.

In *Lavender & Son Ltd v. Minister of Housing & Local Government (1913)* it was held that the minister had failed in the proper exercise of his discretion in acting solely in accordance with his policy of refusing planning permission to extract minerals from any agricultural land where the Minister for Agriculture, Fisheries and Food objected to the proposed use. This was an improper delegation of his duties to another government department. Hence the law of agency *nemo dat quod non habet* applies, i.e. where power is delegated to a body or a person that power cannot be subsequently redelegated. In *Barnard v. National Dock Labour Board (1953)* the suspension of Barnard from work was declared void since the disciplinary powers of suspension delegated to the London Dock Board had unlawfully been delegated to the port manager who had suspended Barnard from work.

The grounds of judicial intervention mentioned above are not the only grounds on which courts may intervene and it was not intended at the outset to list all of them. Besides, there are no constraints on the courts from inventing or adding to the existing list of recognized categories of judicial intervention whenever a situation so demands. It must be stressed that these grounds are not absolutely independent or autonomous categories and hence they may overlap each other and a case may encompass more than one of these grounds. For example, in *Ridge v. Baldwin (1964)* the court found that not only was there a breach of the principle of natural justice but the correct procedure for the dismissal of the Chief Constable was also not followed. One judge or writer may describe a ground as *ultra vires* whereas another may describe it as abuse or excess of power. In one textbook a ground may be described as improper purpose whereas another calls it excess of power.

A ground may be described as frustrating the policy of the statute, as in *Padfield v. Minister of Agriculture (1968)*, or as an abuse of discretionary power. It is obvious that there are no hard or fast rules for categorizing the various grounds of judicial intervention and describing a particular ground in a particular manner is therefore merely a matter of convenience.

In concluding judicial intervention, a recent case having significant bearing on this area is the decision of the House of Lords in *R. v. Greater London Council ex p. Bromley London Borough Council (1981)*. The House of Lords was considering an appeal by the Greater London Council (GLC) against the decision of the Court of Appeal. The issue before the Court of Appeal was that the GLC had made a supplementary rate demand on its ratepayers in order to cover the costs of reduced fares on London Transport's buses and tubes. The Court of Appeal, while allowing an appeal, held that the action of the GLC in requiring the London Transport Executive (LTE) to reduce bus and tube fares by 25 per cent was an abuse of power by the GLC under the *Transport (London) Act, 1969* and therefore *ultra vires*. The Court of Appeal issued an order of *certiorari* to quash the supplementary precept of 6.1p in the pound on the ratepayers. The House of Lords dismissed the appeal, holding that the actions of the GLC and of the LTE were indeed *ultra vires* the 1969 Act. In the opinion of Lord Wilberforce, the GLC had a duty firstly to meet the needs of Greater London transport users and secondly the GLC 'owed a duty of a fiduciary character' to its ratepayers. Therefore in making a grant to support the fares reduction the GLC had acted in breach of its fiduciary duty. Lord Diplock mentioned another ground on which he believed the supplementary precept to be void: namely, that in exercising the collective discretion under Section 11 of the 1969 Act, the members of the majority party had acted 'on an erroneous view of the applicable law' in that 'they regarded the GLC as irrevocably committed to carry out the reduction whatever might be the additional cost to the ratepayers....' Lord Keith was of the opinion that 'it was contrary to the LTE's duties under the Act to submit proposals which involved an arbitrary reduction' of that scale (25 per cent). Lord Scarman was of the opinion that the 'Act required that fares be charged at a level which would, so far as practicable, avoid deficit' and in yielding to policy preference rather than business principles, the GLC was in 'breach of duty owed to the ratepayers and wrong in law'. Lord Brandon said that under the Act it was a matter of administrative discretion as to what extent the passenger services for Greater London was financed by fares paid by passengers and by grants from the GLC. In this case the GLC had not exercised its 'administrative discretion lawfully' in approving a 25 per cent overall reduction in fares.

19.4 Rules of natural justice

A public body, whether exercising judicial, quasi-judicial, administrative or executive functions, is required to act fairly. Hence an underlying and important principle of all judicial review is that all powers given to public officials must be exercised in accordance with the principles or rules of natural justice. Compliance with the rules of natural justice is essential for the interests of justice to prevail and the courts will intervene whenever these rules are not complied with. Two main rules of natural justice are:

- The rule against bias: no man to be a judge in his own cause (*nemo judex in causa sua*), and
- The right to be heard (*audi alteram partem*).

These rules will now be considered individually.

19.4.1 Impartiality, or the rule against bias

For a decision of a court of law or a tribunal to be just, the judge or any other person presiding must be impartial and fair. In *R. v. Rand (1866)* it was laid down that this rule of impartiality is breached (a) where a judge has any pecuniary interest, no matter how small, in the case before him and (b) where there is a real likelihood of the judge being partial towards one of the parties to the case. As Lord Chief Justice Hewart said in *R. v. Sussex Justices, ex p. McCarthy (1924)*: 'Justice should not only be done, but should manifestly and undoubtedly be seen to be done.'

The case concerned an applicant who had applied for a decree of *certiorari* to quash a decision of magistrates in a case when he was successfully prosecuted and convicted of a motoring offence. It was alleged that at the time of his court proceedings, the acting clerk to the court was a member of a firm of solicitors who were to represent the other party involved in the accident. Despite the fact that the clerk had not taken any part in the decision-making process, nor had he given advice or opinion to the justices, the decision of the magistrates to convict the applicant was quashed on grounds of bias. The court was saying that the question of whether there was a bias depends not on what was actually done but upon what might appear to be done. 'Nothing is to be done which creates even a suspicion that there has been an improper interference with the course of justice.'

Similarly, in *Metropolitan Properties Ltd v. Lannon (1969)*, a decision of a rent assessment committee was quashed on the grounds that the chairman of the committee was a solicitor who was living with his father in a block of flats owned by the plaintiff and he was already negotiating rents with the landlords on behalf of all the tenants in the block.

It has been stated in several cases that the test for bias is whether a reasonable man sitting in the body of the court during a trial with only the knowledge that an ordinary member of the public would have would feel that the case might have been wrongly tried. In *R. v. Bristol Crown Court, ex p. Cooper (1989)* an appeal from the licensing committee of justices about the refusal of the justices to grant a licence to sell spirits was under review. One of the magistrates sitting in the Crown Court had also sat in the Magistrates' Court when the licence was refused, although the general public (and our reasonable member of the general public sitting in the body of the court) were unlikely to be aware of it. It was held that there might have been bias, and the applicant might not have had a fair hearing, and the claim for review was granted.

19.4.2 The right to a hearing

This is the second rule of natural justice and embraces the following aspects:

- A right to know the case against oneself.
- A right to fairness in any proceedings.
- A right to be heard.
- A right to know in advance the case one has to meet.
- A right to know the reasons for a decision.

In *Ridge v. Baldwin (1964)* (see page 330), where the Chief Constable of Brighton was dismissed by the Watch Committee, the House of Lords quashed this decision on the grounds that (a) the correct procedure as laid down in the *Police Act, 1919*, was not followed and (b) the rules of natural justice required that the Chief Constable should have been given a hearing by the Watch Committee before being dismissed from the force.

In *Cooper v. Wandsworth Board of Works (1863)* damages were awarded to the plaintiff when the Board demolished his partly-built house because he had failed to notify the Board of his intention to build the house. Although this gave the Board a statutory right to demolish the house, the court held that the Board should have given a hearing to the plaintiff before exercising the right to demolish his house. Accordingly, damages were awarded against the Board.

In *R. v. Aston University Senate, ex p. Roffey (1962)* two students were dismissed from the University on failing their examinations. The court held that this decision was contrary to natural justice and the students should have been given an opportunity to be heard before the final decision was made by the examiners. The decision is in line with another case where a minister, empowered by a statute, dissolved a municipal council without giving the council a hearing. The Judicial Committee of the Privy Council held that the council was entitled to a hearing and the decision made was of no effect (*Durayappah v. Fernando (1967)*).

Rules of natural justice apply to numerous factual situations and it is not proposed to mention all the cases covering these situations. Some of the situations where the courts have insisted on adherence to the rules of natural justice concern, for example, the expulsion of a member from a union, expulsion of students from educational institutions, granting of licences to gaming establishments and the trade unions at GCHQ, Cheltenham, where failure to consult staff rendered the minister's ban 'invalid and of no effect'.

19.5 Methods of judicial review

Apart from the ordinary civil remedies of damages, injunction and specific performance that are normally available and have been mentioned elsewhere in this book, the remedies in Sections 19.5.1–4 are available under judicial review.

19.5.1 Mandamus

This is a peremptory order issued by the Queen's Bench Division of the High Court against a public body or person requiring performance of a public duty imposed by common law or statute. The order is available at the discretion of the court and does not lie against the Crown or its servants except in case of a duty owned to a member of the public, e.g. a statutory duty imposed on a minister or a department as in Padfield's case (see page 332).

19.5.2 Certiorari and prohibition

Certiorari and *prohibition* are normally sought in the same proceedings. Both are issued by the Queen's Bench Division of the High Court, the latter being an order preventing an inferior court from exceeding its jurisdiction or acting contrary to natural justice and the former intended to transfer a case from an inferior court or tribunal to the Queen's Bench Division.

Although they cover broadly the same ground, the main difference between them is that whereas *certiorari* is a means of quashing a decision already arrived at, prohibition is intended to prevent a decision from being made. Originally, both remedies were a means of preventing inferior courts and tribunals from exceeding their jurisdiction. Over the years they have become available against public bodies exercising administrative functions. In the words of Atkin, LJ, in *R. v. Electricity Commissioners, ex p. London Electricity Joint Committee (1924)*, certiorari and prohibition will lie 'wherever any body or persons, having legal authority and having the duty to act judicially, acts in excess of their legal authority ...' Any decision which affects the rights of an individual is a judicial decision for the purposes of issuing *certiorari*. Therefore, a decision made by a legal aid committee is a judicial decision for the purposes of *certiorari* (*R. v. Manchester Legal Aid Committee, ex p. Brand & Co. Ltd (1952)*).

The question of how widely the courts will inquire into an administrative act was considered in *R. v. Norfolk County Council, ex p. M (1989)*. It is clear that the courts will inquire into a case where the legal rights of a party are affected, but should the court go further and inquire into every circumstance that affects an individual? In this case M, a respectable man of good character, was accused of child abuse by a girl of 13, who had been involved in similar cases before and had been pronounced to be in need of psychiatric care. Despite this, M's name was placed on a child abuse register, and he was suspended by his employers. The Council claimed that it was a purely clerical procedure by a conference of case workers. It was held that the Council had a legal duty to act fairly and was in breach of that duty in not letting M know the action it proposed to take and the consequences that might follow.

19.5.3 Injunction

Under private law this remedy is intended to restrain a breach of a contract or the commission of a tort. Under administrative law it is intended to restrain a public body or person from doing a particular act. For example, in *A.G. v. Fulham Corporation (1921)* a ratepayer obtained an injunction restraining the Council from acting *ultra vires*. The remedy is available at the court's discretion and is not available against the Crown or its servants. Since a private individual cannot normally sue for an injunction, the action is commenced by the Attorney-General where public interest is involved. The exception when a private individual may sue is when there is both an interference with a public right as well as the right of the individual concerned – for example, an obstruction placed on a highway affects the rights of the general public as well as in particular the right of the individual in front of whose house the obstruction lies preventing him free access to the house.

19.5.4 Declaration

This is an order of the court which declares the legal rights of the parties concerned. A declaration will normally prevent a public body or official from acting illegally. Apart from other instances, a declaratory order would be particularly convenient in a dispute between a ratepayer and his local authority or between two public authorities. This is a particularly useful remedy for those who are not certain of the legal position and wish to clarify this before embarking on a certain course of action. Once a declaratory judgment is made, any action taken contrary to the declaration is almost certain to be declared null and void in subsequent proceedings.

19.6 Administrative justice

Administrative justice refers to the justice that is the prime concern of those administrative bodies which have been specifically set up to adjudicate disputes between the citizen and the administration; these disputes are specialist in character and cannot normally be settled in the ordinary courts due to lack of jurisdiction. There are four distinct areas of administrative justice. These are:

- Administrative tribunals.
- Public inquiries.
- Tribunals of inquiry.
- The 'Ombudsman' office and the Commissioners for the National Health Service and Local Government.

19.6.1 Administrative tribunals

These could be regarded as specialized courts permanently set up to adjudicate matters which cannot be settled in the ordinary courts (although there may be an ultimate right of appeal to a court of law).

They are administrative bodies set up to deal with disputes involving the rights and duties of citizens and the state. They can also be viewed as specialized courts which stand apart and as an addition to the ordinary machinery of justice provided by the courts.

The Government today plays an important role in all aspects of an individual's life due to its increased involvement with the economic and social life of the community. This relationship is bound to give rise to all kinds of disputes which simply cannot be settled in the ordinary courts of law. The courts are already burdened with their existing legal work and could not possibly take on additional jurisdiction without the risk of a complete breakdown. The court procedure is slow, formal, detailed and costly and may not attract a person seeking quick, cheap and informal settlement of his claim. He may find a tribunal more attractive and, above all, accessible as the legal profession does not have a monopoly of representation. He may prefer his case to be presented by an accountant, a doctor, a trade union official or a social worker rather than a lawyer. Certain matters are more appropriate for a tribunal than a court. For example, a dispute between a citizen concerned with his rights and a minister, Government department, local authority or public official can be settled without recourse to a court. Besides, certain disputes involve specialist knowledge and the courts cannot be expected to provide this. For example, the determination of the extent of disability or injury is a task performed by a doctor on a Pensions Tribunal and this task could not be adequately discharged in a court presided over by a judge.

In comparing tribunals with the courts, the following differences emerge:

- No formal rules of evidence or procedure apply to a tribunal.
- Appointment and dismissal of members is the responsibility of the minister of the department concerned.
- Members need not have legal qualifications and, with the exception of certain tribunals, there is no right of appeal to the ordinary law courts. Nevertheless, the ordinary courts do exercise their supervisory jurisdiction over tribunals and may intervene where there is a clear breach of the rules of natural justice (see page 334) or where one of the grounds (mentioned on pages 328–34) for judicial intervention applies.

There is a Council on Tribunals originally set up by the *Tribunals and Enquiries Act, 1958*; this Act is now re-enacted in the *Tribunals and Inquiries Act, 1971*. The Council is an advisory body which keeps under review the constitution and workings of a large number of tribunals. Some of the listed tribunals under the supervision of the Council which appear in its annual report are the Agricultural Land Tribunals, National Insurance Tribunals, Betting Levy Appeal Tribunal, Commissioners of Income Tax, Industrial Tribunals, Mental Health Review Tribunals, War Pensions Appeal

Tribunals, Rent Tribunals, Value-Added Tax Tribunals, Rate Valuation Courts, Civil Aviation Authority (in its licensing function), Supplementary Benefits Appeal Tribunals and the National Health Service Family Practitioner Committees.

There are bodies which may be regarded as tribunals but which do not fall under the supervisory jurisdiction of the Council on Tribunals. In this category comes the Criminal Injuries Compensation Board, the Gaming Board, the Parole Board, the Legal Aid Committes and many professional disciplinary bodies – for example, the Solicitors' Disciplinary Tribunal and the General Medical Council.

A look into the structure of some of the leading tribunals will convey a better understanding of matters such as their composition, functions, powers and jurisdiction and, lastly, the procedure followed by the tribunal.

(a) National Insurance Tribunals

Various schemes providing insurance against sickness, unemployment, widows' benefits, retirement and industrial injuries have been in existence since the beginning of this century. New schemes for national insurance and industrial injuries were introduced in 1948 to provide a unified scheme of insurance. Today, the important Acts concerning this area are the *National Insurance Act, 1965*, and the *National Insurance (Industrial Injuries) Act, 1965*. Although the *Social Security Acts, 1975–80*, replaced the scheme of contributions and benefits of the two Acts, the tribunal system contained in the Acts has been retained with minor modifications.

Under the *Social Security Acts, 1975–80*, the following procedure applies for claiming benefits. Initially a claim for benefit is submitted to an insurance officer for his decision. Insurance officers are full-time civil servants employed at the local offices of the Department of Health and Social Security. If a claimant disagrees with the decision of an insurance officer, a right of appeal exists to a local tribunal. An insurance officer can, if he so wishes, refer a question to an insurance tribunal for its decision instead of deciding it himself. There are now over 150 local tribunals in England and Wales.

A tribunal consists of a chairman and two members. The chairman is a lawyer appointed by the Secretary of State from a panel drawn up by the Lord Chancellor. The two members are each drawn from two representative panels, one representing employers and insured persons other than those in employment and the other representing employed persons. Members of the tribunal work on a part-time basis and receive allowances for travelling, subsistence and loss of earnings.

From the decision of a local tribunal there is a right of appeal to National Insurance Commissioners. The Commissioners are appointed by the Crown and are barristers or advocates. An appeal is heard by a single commissioner and in exceptional circumstances by three. An appeal can be lodged by the claimant or the insurance officer, or in some cases by an association like a trade union. Although no right of appeal exists from a Commissioner's decision, a decision can be reviewed by the courts.

Hearings before the tribunal and the commissioner are in public except where public security or intimate personal or financial circumstances are involved. An appeal is heard orally, legal representation is allowed and witnesses can be called for questioning. Reasons for a decision are required to be given and, in the interest of consistency, a system of precedent is observed. Once a decision is made it binds all insurance officers and local tribunals. Leading decisions of the commissioners are published and are available to the public.

Although industrial injuries are dealt with by the National Insurance Tribunals, the questions such as the extent of disablement on account of industrial injury are matters for medical boards and medical appeal tribunals. Medical boards consist of two doctors and medical appeal tribunals consist of two doctors and a lawyer who is the chairman. An appeal, on a point of law, lies from a medical appeal tribunal to a national insurance commissioner.

(b) Lands Tribunal

The Lands Tribunal is the creation of the *Lands Tribunal Act, 1949*. The tribunal consists of a president and other members appointed by the Lord Chancellor. The president is a person who either has held a judicial office under the Crown or a barrister of at least seven years' standing. The other members, whose number is determined by the Lord Chancellor according to the circumstances of a particular case, are barristers, solicitors or persons qualified and experienced in valuation work.

The jurisdiction of the tribunal can be enlarged by an Order in Council and at the moment it covers matters such as appeals on rating matters from the local valuation courts. The tribunal's procedures provide for public sitting except in certain circumstances, e.g. cases arising under the *Atomic Energy Act, 1946*. Parties are allowed to appear in person or be represented by a lawyer, a friend or any other person. The tribunal has power to administer an oath and it can also award costs. Its decision is required to be put in writing along with a statement of reasons. There is a right of appeal to the Court of Appeal on a point of law by way of case stated and subsequently to the House of Lords.

(c) The Commissioners of Income Tax

Anyone disputing a decision of the Inland Revenue officials concerning income tax liability can appeal to either the General Commissioners or the Special Commissioners of Income Tax. The General Commissioners are usually local businessmen, magistrates or professional people appointed by the Lord Chancellor and hold office at his pleasure. The Commissioners are not required to possess special knowledge of tax law as they are assisted in their work by a qualified clerk. The jurisdiction of the General Commissioners is local and there are approximately 431 such tribunals with about 4000 General Commissioners.

The Special Commissioners, unlike the General Commissioners, are full-time Crown servants appointed by the Treasury from officials of the Inland Revenue Department or from amongst barristers specializing in taxation work. Once appointed their whole time is devoted to the appellate work and hence they do not perform any administrative duties.

The sittings of both the General and the Special Commissioners are in private. Their main function is to apply revenue law to the facts of individual cases before them. Both can be required to state a case on a point of law for the opinion of the High Court.

(d) Solicitors' Disciplinary Tribunal

The *Solicitors Act, 1974*, set up a Disciplinary Tribunal exercising disciplinary powers over solicitors. Its purpose is to hear applications against solicitors where allegations are made by clients. Being officers of the court, solicitors are required to conform to a public disciplinary code of conduct any breach of which may result in an action before the tribunal. The tribunal is appointed by the Master of the Rolls and when hearing applications a board is convened consisting of two practising solicitors and one layman. The tribunal acts as a judicial body and the legal procedure of a court of law is followed during a hearing. The powers of the tribunal are extensive. It can order suspension from practice, strike a solicitor off the roll, impose a fine and order payment of costs. The hearing before the tribunal is in private although its decisions are made public. There is a right of appeal to the High Court or to the Master of the Rolls.

19.6.2 Public inquiries

These are set up to give the citizen affected by a Government proposal a right to be heard before a final decision is made. They are especially important in relation to the use and development of land. Since Britain is a densely populated country, it is important that all use and development of land is centrally planned and controlled. Although the ultimate decision on use and development of land lies with one of the central government departments, the members of the public affected by such a decision are given a say in the decision-making process. This is achieved by holding public inquiries where those affected can raise reasoned objections before a final decision is made. There are numerous circumstances where a public inquiry becomes an essential prerequisite before a decision is made. An inquiry might be held, for example, when a motorway, a power station or an airport is planned. An inquiry may be held when land is compulsorily acquired, when the use of land has environmental consequences, or following proposed developments under the *Town and Country Planning Act, 1971*, or the *New Towns Act, 1946*.

Public inquiries are an important aspect of the administrative process in addition to the tribunals and both therefore come under the jurisdiction of the Council on Tribunals. According to the Franks Committee, set up to look at the whole area of administrative justice, which reported in 1957, the twofold objects of an inquiry are to protect the interests of the citizens most directly affected by a Government proposal by granting them a statutory right to be heard in support of their objections and to ensure that thereby the minister is better informed of the whole facts of the case before the final decision is made.

Under Section 11 of the *Tribunals and Inquiries Act, 1971*, the Lord Chancellor, after consulting the Council on Tribunals, can make procedural rules for statutory inquiries. These procedural rules provide that:

- Persons affected by an administrative decision must know reasonably in advance of the inquiry the case to be met.
- Departmental representatives must attend such inquiries and disclose the policy of the department concerned.
- On the question of the subject-matter of the inquiry, the inspector in charge of the inquiry is under the control of the Lord Chancellor and not the Government department.
- Reasons for decisions must be given.
- Persons appearing before an inquiry have a right to legal representation or to be represented by any other person.
- Procedures at an inquiry are the concern of the inspector and the degree of formality depends on the circumstances of an inquiry.
- A decision can be challenged in the courts on grounds of jurisdiction and procedure.
- An individual who is dissatisfied with an aspect of a public inquiry can also complain to the Council on Tribunals, which has powers to consider and report on the conduct of public inquiries.

19.6.3 Tribunals of inquiry

A tribunal of inquiry can be set up to inquire into any matter of urgent public importance on the resolution of both the Houses of Parliament (*Tribunals of Inquiry (Evidence) Act, 1921*). Tribunals of inquiry are set up in two circumstances. First, where serious allegations of corruption or improper conduct are made against those in public service – for example, in 1957 a tribunal was appointed to investigate the premature disclosure of information relating to the pending increase in the bank rate. In 1971 a tribunal enquired into the collapse of the Vehicle and General Insurance Company. Secondly, tribunals may be set up to investigate a matter of public concern which may not be adequately dealt with before the ordinary courts. Examples are the inquiries into the Aberfan coal-tip disaster in 1966 and the 'Bloody Sunday' shootings in Londonderry in 1972. The Scarman Inquiry into the Brixton riots was essentially a judicial inquiry under the *Police Act, 1964*, although arguably it assumed tribunal of inquiry proportions.

The overall purpose of a tribunal is to produce an authoritative and impartial account of the facts and attribute responsibility or blame as necessary. The tribunal of inquiry is presided over by a chairman, normally a senior judge, and two members who are often lawyers. In exceptional circumstances an inquiry can be conducted by a single judge. Thus Lord Chief Justice Widgery sat alone on the 'Bloody Sunday' inquiry.

A tribunal has all the powers of a High Court and hence it can compel attendance of a witness or the production of a document. Its proceedings are inquisitorial and, apart from cross-examination of witnesses by a counsel, witnesses may also be questioned by members of the tribunal. Being an inquiry, it cannot impose any penalty or order payment of damages. Any serious breaches before a tribunal may be reported to the High Court for inquiry and punishment. Immunity from criminal prosecution may be granted to a witness by the Attorney-General in respect of matters arising out of his evidence. In addition, witnesses enjoy the same immunities and privileges as in the High Court and hence they cannot be sued for slander for anything said in evidence. Legal representation can be allowed, the cost of which may be met from public funds. Although tribunals sit in public, where public interest requires a tribunal may sit in private.

19.6.4 The Parliamentary Commissioner for Administration

Prior to 1967 the various means of obtaining administrative redress against oppressive or faulty government were the courts, the tribunals, the holding of public enquiries and representation to an MP with a view to obtaining a solution through Parliament. All these approaches were found to be inadequate as they all had limitations, and to give further protection to the citizen in administrative matters, the *Parliamentary Commissioner Act, 1967*, was passed. This Act set up the Office of the Parliamentary Commissioner for Administration (the ombudsman). Although the idea of an ombudsman first developed in Sweden, where it was set up at the beginning of the nineteenth century, and in New Zealand, where it was set up in 1962, the British model is different from these and is essentially based on our existing political institutions.

The Commissioner is appointed by the Crown on the Prime Minister's advice; the first appointment was Sir Edmund Compton, the then retiring Comptroller and Auditor-General. The Commissioner holds office during good behaviour and can be dismissed following addresses by both Houses of Parliament. He is paid out of the Consolidated Fund and his status resembles that of the Comptroller and Auditor-General. He appoints his own staff subject to Treasury approval, almost all of whom are experienced civil servants like the Commissioner himself.

(a) Functions and jurisdiction

The Commissioner's prime function is to investigate complaints from members of the public who claim to have sustained injustice as a result of maladministration by Government departments. The Act does not define maladministration but the term probably means corruption, bias, incompetence, unfair discrimination, neglect, delay or other related administrative sins. His jurisdiction extends to consideration of complaints against nearly all Government departments and a full list in Schedule I of the *Parliamentary and Health Commissioners Act, 1987* replaces the previous list mentioned in Schedule 2 to the 1967 Act. The new list extends the Commissioner's jurisdiction to quasi-autonomous non-governmental organizations (quangos) such as the British Council, the Commission for Racial Equality, the Equal Opportunities Commission, the Charity Commission, etc.

Excluded from his jurisdiction are the local authorities, the police, the Post Office and the nationalized industries. The courts and tribunals were formerly excluded, but in the *Courts and Legal Services Act, 1990* the Parliamentary Commissioners' remit was extended to cover complaints about the administration of courts and tribunals. Certain types of action by departments are excluded from investigation and these appear at Schedule 3 of the Act. Some of the excluded matters are those affecting international relations, diplomatic relations, security of the state and the administration of dependent territories. Others are those under the *Extradition Act, 1870*, and the *Fugitive Offenders Act, 1967*, and appointments, discipline and personnel matters concerning the civil service and the armed forces.

Further limitations on his jurisdiction are that first he cannot investigate a matter in respect of which the complainant has a right of recourse to a court of law or a tribunal and, secondly, he cannot investigate matters in respect of which the complainant allowed 12 months to elapse before making a complaint to an MP.

(b) Powers

The Commissioner has full investigative powers on matters within his jurisdiction. It is for him to determine whether a complaint falls within his jurisdiction and he has complete discretion whether or not to investigate a complaint. He has full access to government departments and can require any minister, officer or member of a department or any other person to furnish any relevant document or information. After completing his investigation he reports the results to the MP through whom the complaint was made. The Commissioner makes an annual report or interim reports, if he thinks fit, to Parliament on his performance in office. He may also make special reports to Parliament upon cases of maladministration where it appears that the injustice complained of has not been or will not be remedied. For the purposes of the law of defamation, anything the Commissioner says in his reports to Parliament or to individual MPs is absolutely privileged.

Although the Commissioner has no executive powers as he cannot alter a departmental decision or award compensation to a citizen, nevertheless ministers are normally under strong pressure to accept his findings to avoid prejudicial political implications. A Select Committee of the House of Commons exists to examine the reports he lays before Parliament and to support the Commissioner in his work.

It is up to the Commissioner to allow legal representation and he may reimburse any legal costs incurred or any other expenses properly incurred as a result of his investigation.

(c) Procedure

A complaint must be made by an individual or any body of persons (corporate or incorporate) in writing to a member of the House of Commons. It is for the MP to decide whether to refer the complaint to the Commissioner. If the MP chooses to refer the complaint, it should include a statement of approval by the complainant for the MP to refer the complaint to the Commissioner; the name and address of the complainant; the identity of the department against which the complaint is made; and, lastly, a statement of the circumstances in which the alleged injustice occurred. The complaint received is examined by the Commissioner to decide whether it falls within his jurisidiction. An investigation is then carried out and the Act requires all the proceedings to be held in private. Finally, a report is sent to the member from whom the complaint was received.

(d) The commissioner's case-work

One of the cases, of which there are many, which supports and justifies the continuing work of the Commissioner was the Sachsenhausen Case in late 1967. The case concerned the question of payment of compensation to victims of Nazi persecution. The Foreign Office had withheld compensation from 12 claimants because in its opinion they did not fall within the criteria laid down for dispensing compensation, since they were detained not in a concentration camp but outside the perimeter of the camp in a special block and hence received better treatment compared to prisoners in the main camp. An independent inquiry was refused and the complaint was referred to the Commissioner. The Commissioner's investigation revealed defects in the administrative procedure by which the Foreign Office reached its decision. His report was debated in the House of Commons and the Foreign Office reviewed the cases and paid normal compensation without at the same time admitting any default or maladministration.

19.6.5 Commissioners for the National Health Service and Local Government

The Health Service Commissioner holds an independent office established under the *National Health Service Reorganization Act, 1973*. His function is to investigate complaints of injustice or hardship from members of the public against the Regional Health Authorities, Area Health Authorities and other bodies under the National Health Service. The Commissioner cannot investigate matters which are solely a consequence of clinical judgements, e.g. the diagnosis of an illness or the treatment of a patient. A special procedure for dealing with such complaints operates from 1 September 1981. This involves a review of the case by two independent consultants in active practice in the appropriate speciality.

Many of the aspects of the Parliamentary Commissioner for Administration apply both to the Health Service Commissioner and the Commissioner for Local Administration, which was set up by the *Local Government Act, 1973*. Statutory provisions encourage various commissioners to cooperate with each other. Complaints of maladministration against local authorities, joint boards, police authorities (other than the Home Secretary) and water authorities can be made by affected individuals to the Commissioner for Local Administration.

19.6.6 Ombudsman services for privatized industries and similar commercial areas

With the privatization of certain nationalized industries and the institution of regulatory controls in other areas such as the financial services industries the ombudsman idea is being extended into new areas.

The Banking Ombudsman has been in existence since 1986 to deal with disputes between banks and their customers. Before a matter is referred to the ombudsman a customer is required to have exhausted all the normal channels for a satisfactory resolution of the dispute. The ombudsman has competence to award up to £100 000 and can deal with any complaints concerning banking business.

The concept of the ombudsman is being introduced into the newly privatized electricity industry as well, and the Oftel Office (the Office of Telecommunications) handles complaints about the telephone system. Its office is at Atlantic House, Holborn Viaduct, London EC4M 7JJ (Tel 0171 822 1600).

There is also a Parliamentary Commissioner for the Rights of Trade Union Members, with considerable powers to investigate abuses of trade union powers. Under the *Employment Act, 1990* the Commissioner can assist trade unionists seeking to bring legal actions against union officials for breaches of the rules.

Further information about these ombudsman offices can be obtained from the following addresses:

- Office of the Banking Ombudsman, Citadel House, 70 Grays Inn Road, London WC1X 8NB (Tel 0171 404 9944).
- The Oftel Office, Atlantic House, Holborn Viaduct, London EC4M 7JJ (Tel 0171 822 1600).
- Office of the Building Society Ombudsman, Grosvenor Gardens House, 35–37 Grosvenor Gardens, London SW1X 7AW (Tel 0171 931 0044).
- Office of Electricity Regulation, 11 Belgrave Road, London SW1V 1RB (Tel 0171 233 6366).
- Office of Gas Supply, Southside, 105 Victoria Street, London SW1 (Tel 0171 828 0898).

Test your knowledge

Answers		Questions	
		1	What is administrative law?
1	It is the branch of law which deals with the control of government power.	2	Why is government power so omnipresent today?
2	Because of the huge part played by the state in the national economy, in particular (a) traditional state functions of defence, law and order, justice, etc., (b) social matters, such as education, health and welfare, (c) nationalization and subsequent privatization of industries in a wide variety of fields, (d) planning, ecological and economic activities.	3	What are the grounds for judicial intervention when an abuse of power may have occurred?

Answers		Questions	
3	(a) The *ultra vires* rule; (b) incorrectness of procedure; (c) improper purpose not sanctioned by Parliament; (d) weight being given to irrelevant considerations; (e) error of law; (f) lack of evidence; (g) abuse of discretionary powers; (h) abuse of natural justice.	4	What are the chief types of abuse of natural justice?
4	(a) Bias – administrators must be impartial; (b) refusal of the right to be heard.	5	What are the methods of judicial review?
5	(a) *Mandamus* – a peremptory order from the court requiring a public body to do what it is supposed to do. (b) *Certiorari* – an order preventing an inferior court from acting outside its jurisdiction or against natural justice, and quashing its decision. (c) Prohibition – an order preventing an inferior court from making a decision outside its jurisdiction, or against natural justice. (d) Injunction – in administrative law this restrains an official body from acting unlawfully. (e) Declaration – an order of the court declaring the rights of individuals in a particular matter.	6	How is administrative justice secured?
6	By (a) administrative tribunals, (b) public inquiries, (c) tribunals of inquiry and (d) the 'ombudsman' office, and similar commissioners.	7	What is the correct title for the ombudsman?
7	The Parliamentary Commissioner for Administration.	8	Go over the page again until you are sure of all the answers. Then try some of the questions in Appendix 1.

Part Six The Businessman and the Law of Tort

20 Introduction to the law of tort

20.1 The nature of the law of tort

A tort is a civil wrong which gives rise to a private, civil action commenced by one party (the **plaintiff**) against another (the **defendant**). The party alleging the wrong normally claims monetary compensation (**damages**) for the harm or loss suffered. The harm alleged may take the form of physical injury, injury to one's character or reputation, financial loss or interference with an individual's right to enjoy his property. Apart from damages other remedies may be appropriate in a particular case – for example, an injunction is more suitable to prevent or restrain someone from committing a tort like nuisance. There is a large number of recognized and listed torts and these will be looked at individually in the following order:

- Negligence.
- Liability of occupiers of premises.
- Strict liability.
- Trespass to property.
- Nuisance.
- Defamation.
- Miscellaneous torts of conspiracy, deceit and injurious falsehood.

Before these we must consider several matters which have a common bearing or application to the whole area of tort.

20.2 Definition of tort

Defining tort is not an easy matter and one has to be careful not to define it too broadly so as to encompass matters other than torts or to define it too narrowly so as to exclude some torts. Two contrasting defintions of tort are offered; one by Salmond, the other by Professor Winfield. They represent different schools of thought.

Salmond defines a tort as:

> *a civil wrong for which the remedy is a common law action for unliquidated damages, and which is not exclusively the breach of a contract or a breach of trust or other merely equitable obligation.*

The late Professor Winfield contended that:

> *all tortious liability arises from the breach of a duty primarily fixed by law; such duty is towards persons generally, and its breach is redressable by an action for unliquidated damages.*

Both these definitions refer to unliquidated damages. Damages are unliquidated when they are not predetermined or pre-estimated (as they are, for example, in an action in contract to recover a debt) but are determined at the absolute discretion of the court.

One school maintains that there is a 'law of torts' which consists of a number of specific torts and to succeed in an action you must show that the alleged wrong falls within the scope of one or more of these torts. The other school maintains that there is a 'law of tort' (not torts) based on a general principle of liability and all harm is actionable *per se* unless the defendant can show a just cause or excuse. There are no inherent contradictions between the two schools of thought as both accept that new categories of torts may be created and the existing law can be expanded to bring new wrongs within its confines. As Professor Glanville Williams puts it: 'To say that the law can be collected into pigeon-holes does not mean that those pigeon-holes may not be capacious, nor does it mean that they are incapable of being added to.'

20.2.1 *Damnum sine injuria* and *injuria sine damno*

Although normally any harm or damage suffered is actionable as a tort, there can be instances when a harm can be done by an individual against another for which the law does not provide a remedy. This is called *damnum sine injuria* (damage without legal wrong). For example, if you suffer bankruptcy as a result of the undercutting of prices by your competitor(s), then you have no legal remedy although your family may suffer as a result:

> **Ajello v. Worsley (1898)**
>
> The defendant had advertised in newspapers the sale of the plaintiff's pianos below their wholesale price. **Held**: no wrong was committed as the defendant was within his legal right to sell at whatever price he wished and to advertise despite the fact that he did not have any of the plaintiff's pianos in stock.

Similarly, there can be instances when although no real damage or harm has resulted to a plaintiff, yet a defendant's acts or omissions may be actionable *per se* (by itself). When you trespass on someone's land this can give rise to an action in tort, although the land owner has not suffered any particular harm or loss. Similarly, a libel is actionable without proof of the fact that the plaintiff has suffered any real loss. The situation where a legal wrong has taken place although no harm or loss is suffered is termed *injuria sine damno* (legal wrong without injury). It must be pointed out, however, that not all torts are actionable *per se* as most require proof of the actual damage or harm suffered by a plaintiff.

20.2.2 Mental element in tort

Injurious conduct is normally actionable as a tort and as a general rule the intention or motive of the defendant is not important. For example:

> **Bradford Corporation. v. Pickles (1895)**
>
> The appellants owned a waterworks and the respondent owned adjoining land from which a valuable supply of water flowed into the appellants' reservoir. It was alleged by the appellants that in order to coerce them into buying the respondent's land at a high price, the respondent commenced harmful activities on his land which resulted in a reduction of the water flow and pollution. The appellants sought an injunction to prevent these activities which it was contended were actuated by malice. The court refused to grant an injunction, holding that the action of the respondent was lawful as he was merely exercising a right over his own property. Hence his motive or intention were irrelevant.

20.2.3 Comparing tort, crime and contract

When comparing a tort to a crime or a breach of a contract, the following distinctions emerge:

Tort	Crime	Contract
1 The rights and duties are the result of the application of civil law made up of statute law and common law	The rights and duties are the result of the criminal law	The rights and duties depend on the obligations undertaken under the contract
2 A civil action is normally commenced by one individual against another. A typical tort case would be cited as *Smith v. Brown (1980)*	The action is brought by the Crown Prosecution Service as agents of the state against the offending person. A typical criminal case would be cited thus *R. v. Brown (1980)*	The action is brought by the party alleging breach of the contract against the other party to the contract. A contract case would have a similar citation to a tort case
3 The successful party is awarded damages or other remedies where applicable, such as an injunction	The guilty party is punished by way of imprisonment, or by fine or other non-custodial sentence	Apart from damages, other remedies like specific performance, injunction, payment on *quantum meruit* and rescission may be available
4 A duty is owed towards persons generally	Criminal conduct is prescribed by the criminal law and a duty is owed to the general public	A duty is owed to a specific person who is a party to a contract. (There may, of course, be more than one person.)

There has for some time been uncertainty in law about whether a person who is in a contractual relationship with another party can also bring an action in tort. The original position was that a tortious action would not be possible, but in *Esso Petroleum Co. v. Mardon, (1976)* and later in *Midland Bank Trust Co. Ltd v. Hett Stubbs & Kemp (1978)* it was clearly stated that a duty of care could exist alongside a contractual duty as far as negligent misstatements by professional advisors were concerned. Other cases have tended to deny the right of tortious action to parties already in contractual relationships with one another, for example in *Reid v. Rush and Tompkins plc* the courts refused to find tortious liability by the employer over and beyond the express and implied terms of the contract of employment. However, in the recent case of *Lancashire and Cheshire Association of Baptist Churches v. Howard and Eddon* which was about work by the defendant architects in constructing a church building, the judge ruled that it was possible for a complaint in tort to arise over negligent professional activity, and he also expressed the view that he could not see why a similar right to action in tort should not also occur in contracts that were not about professional services. These remarks were only *obiter dicta* but they may nevertheless open the door for a wider range of actions in tort by those who are in contractual relationships.

Having mentioned some differences between contract, crime and tort one can come across instances when there may be an overlap between them. For example, if you were travelling in a taxi which, due to the negligent driving of the taxi driver, collides with a lamp-post, this may result in the following actions: a criminal action by the Crown Prosecution Service against the taxi driver for dangerous driving; if you have suffered physical harm an action by you for negligence against the driver; a breach of contract of hire between the taxi driver and the cab owner or between the taxi driver and the passenger. The tort of negligence and the contractual duty to drive carefully overlap. There is also an overlap between the negligent driving of the driver and the crime of dangerous driving or other road traffic offences. So it is apparent that the three are not absolutely exclusive and the same wrong may give rise to all three.

20.3 General defences in tort

In addition to special defences peculiar to particular torts, the following general defences are available, wherever appropriate, to a defendant in an action for any type of tort:

20.3.1 Volenti non fit injuria

Translated this Latin phrase means that in law no wrong is done to a person who voluntarily consents to undergo it. In sports, if you are injured as a result of normal sporting activities, whether you are a player or a spectator, you have no cause of complaint. For example, if, as a boxer, you are punched and injured, no tort is committed; similarly, if you are injured as a spectator as a result of the sporting activity, there is no cause of action:

> **Hall v. Brooklands Auto Racing Club (1933)**
>
> Two spectators died as a result of a racing car colliding, leaving the race track and hitting the spectators. **Held**: in the absence of negligence, the defendants were not liable as the spectators had impliedly consented to the risk inherent in such a sport.

It is important that the consent of the plaintiff to the risks involved must be either written, oral or be able to be implied from the circumstances. The consent must be genuine, obtained without any force or compulsion. Mere knowledge of the risks involved is not enough to constitute consent. In *Smith v. Baker (Charles) & Sons (1891)*, the plaintiff was a workman employed by the defendants on a construction project. While working in a quarry he was aware of the danger from a crane working overhead and had in fact complained along with other workers about this danger. On one occasion he was injured as a result of some stones falling on him because of the activity of the crane. He successfully sued his employers in negligence as the defence of *volenti non fit injuria* did not apply. His awareness of the danger did not make him a volunteer and true consent on his part was lacking.

In *Dann v. Hamilton (1939)*, a girl who was aware of the potential danger posed by a driver's drunkenness, accepted a lift and was subsequently injured as a result of a collision. In an action for negligence against the estate of the deceased driver, the defence of *volenti non fit injuria* failed as she was not a volunteer who had assented to the negligent driving. Today, in such a case since the plaintiff is aware of the driver's state she is considered as having contributed to the negligence and the damages awarded eventually are reduced in proportion to the extent of her own negligence (*Owens v. Brimmell (1976)*).

An extreme example of contributory negligence is the case of *Pitts v. Hunt and Another (1989)*. The plaintiff was the pillion rider of a motorcycle ridden by the defendant. The plaintiff knew the defendant was not licensed to ride a motor cycle and was uninsured. They had been drinking before the ride began. The plaintiff at the start of the ride was encouraging the defendant to ride in a dangerous manner. As a matter of principle the judge ruled that in a case where a crime was being committed (driving while unlicensed and uninsured) the rule *ex turpi causa non oritur actio* (no action can arise from a base cause) applied. As a matter of public policy the court could not recognize that the defendant owed the plaintiff any duty of care. Even if he was wrong in this ruling, the judge went on to say, could the rule of *volenti non fit injuria* (a willing person cannot be harmed) be a defence for the driver of the vehicle? The judge thought not. In that case did the question of contributory negligence apply? The judge concluded that it did, and since both parties were equally responsible for the accident the plaintiff was 100 per cent contributorily negligent and could recover nothing for his injuries.

In *Morris v. Murray (1990) 3 All ER 801* the plaintiff went on a joyride in an aeroplane with a friend with whom he had been drinking. The plane crashed, and the friend, who acted as pilot, was killed. He was found to have been three times over the alcohol limit for driving a car. The plaintiff had also been drinking heavily, but the question was had he consented to the risk of injury by electing to go on the joyride, or was he so drunk himself that he could not tell that the pilot was too drunk to fly. If he had been this drunk he could not be held to have consented to the risk. It was held that he was not so intoxicated as to fail to realize the state of his friend, and had therefore waived his right to a remedy for his injuries.

An employee obeying his employer's instructions will rarely be a volunteer injured in the performance of his duties unless the risk he ran was not connected with his ordinary duties:

Bowater v. Rowley Regis Corporation (1944)

The plaintiff, who was employed as a carter, was injured because the horse he was provided with bolted and ran away. He had on previous occasions complained to his employers about the vicious propensity of the animal, but continued to work under protest. **Held**: He would succeed in an action for damages as the Corporation had been negligent and the defence of *volenti non fit injuria* did not apply as the employee had not truly consented to the risk involved.

We look finally at the defence of *volenti non fit injuria* and its application to a particular set of circumstances commonly known as the **rescue cases**. A dangerous situation is created by the defendant's negligent act and the plaintiff decides to act to save or protect lives or injury to others from the danger created and in doing so is thereby injured. If the plaintiff brings an action for negligence against the defendant, can the latter plead the defence of *volenti non fit injuria*? The law is that where there is an imminent danger to others and a plaintiff who is motivated by a moral and/or legal duty in protecting life or property, acts to protect others, the defence of *volenti non fit injuria* will fail to protect a defendant who claims that the plaintiff acted voluntarily. In these circumstances the knowledge on the part of the plaintiff of the risks involved does not make the plaintiff a *volens* (a party acting willingly).

Haynes v. Harwood (1935)

A two-horse van was left unattended on a crowded street. Due to this negligent action on the part of the defendant's servant, the horses bolted and were brought under control by the courageous action of a police constable on duty who had perceived the danger created. The constable was, however, injured due to this action and sued the defendant successfully in negligence. The defence of *volenti non fit injuria* did not apply as mere knowledge of the risk involved did not make the constable a volunteer who acted willingly.

Baker v. T. E. Hopkins & Son Ltd. (1959)

A doctor died when he went down a well in order to rescue two servants of the defendant company who were engaged in a cleaning operation using a petrol-driven pump. The servants were overcome by the fumes created by a concentration of carbon monoxide and so was the doctor when he went to rescue them. All three lost their lives. The doctor's executors succeeded in claiming damages for the defendants' negligence in creating the dangerous situation. The doctor had acted under a moral compulsion and hence the defence of *volenti non fit injuria* would fail.

In contrast, in situations where no real emergency exists as there is no imminent danger to anyone, then any action of a person is considered gratuitous and voluntary and the defence of *volenti non fit injuria* will succeed.

Cutler v. United Dairies (London) Ltd (1933)

The plaintiff was injured when he tried to stop a bolting horse drawing a milk cart down a quiet country road. There was no danger or urgency demanded by the circumstances and therefore the plaintiff was considered to have acted freely and voluntarily and the defence of *volenti non fit injuria* provided a complete defence.

Sylvester v. Chapman Ltd (1935)

The plaintiff, who was mauled by a leopard when he crossed a barrier to put out a lighted cigarette end, was not entitled to damages as he was considered to be a volunteer; there were keepers available to do the job without risk.

20.3.2 Necessity

This defence is pleaded when a tortious act is done intentionally to avoid a greater harm being done to the defendant himself, to a third party or to the realm. The defence will succeed if the harm or damage done is reasonably justifiable having regard to the circumstances.

> **Cope v. Sharpe (1912)**
>
> The defendant gamekeeper, in order to prevent fire spreading from the adjoining land and engulfing his master's sitting pheasants, went to the plaintiff's land and set fire to some patches of heather. In an action for trespass, the defence of necessity succeeded as the gamekeeper's action was reasonable in the circumstances.

> **Esso Petroleum Co. Ltd v. Southport Corporation (1955)**
>
> A vessel had run aground in a narrow and shallow channel and in order to save the vessel and the crew from grave danger, the master of the ship discharged considerable quantities of oil which polluted the respondent's beaches. The Southport Corporation, who brought an action to recover the costs of clearing the beaches, failed as necessity was a complete defence to any claim based on trespass or nuisance. The action of the master was reasonable in the circumstances and therefore, he was not guilty of negligence.

In the case of *The King's Prerogative in Saltpetre (1606)* necessity was a good defence to an action for trespass in circumstances where it is necessary for the Crown or its subject to trespass onto the land of another in order to erect fortifications for the defence of the realm.

20.3.3 Mistake

As with contract law, ignorance of the law is not accepted as an excuse. The law does not accept either a mistake of law or of fact as a defence in tort. A trespass is actionable even if the trespasser acted in the mistaken belief that the land was his or that he had a right of entry (*Basely v. Clarkson (1682)*). Similarly, an auctioneer is liable for conversion to the true owners of the goods if he auctions goods for a customer in good faith without any negligence (*Consolidated Co. v. Curtis & Son (1892)*).

In certain circumstances, like malicious prosecution or false imprisonment, mistake may provide a defence. For example, where a crime has been committed and an ordinary citizen or a policeman mistakenly arrests an innocent person because there exist reasonable grounds for suspicion that the person arrested has committed the offence, then mistake may provide a defence to an action for false imprisonment (*Beckwith v. Philby (1827)*). Powers of arrest by a citizen or a policeman are covered by Section 2 of the *Criminal Law Act, 1967*, and in certain circumstances statutory protection may be claimed under this section.

20.3.4 Inevitable accident

This is a good defence in circumstances where it can be shown that an accident could not have been prevented by any reasonable precaution, care or foresight:

> ### *Stanley v. Powell* (1891)
> The plaintiff and defendant were both members of a pheasant-shooting party. The plaintiff received injuries from a pellet fired in a proper manner by the defendant when it glanced off a tree and struck the plaintiff. **Held**: the defendant was not negligent. The plaintiff's injury was accidental and the action for damages for trespass to the person must fail.

20.3.5 Statutory authority

Parliament sometimes confers authority on public bodies to act in a manner which may otherwise be considered tortious. The authority, which may be either absolute or conditional, is normally conferred on local councils by an Act of Parliament or subordinate legislation. An **absolute authority** imposes a duty on the public authority to act even if this may cause harm to others, provided it acts reasonably. A **conditional authority** is a power to act provided no harm results to other persons. Whether or not an authority is absolute or conditional is strictly a matter of construction of the relevant statute.

The House of Lords laid down in *Geddis v. Proprietors of Bann Reservoir (1878)* that it was 'thoroughly well established' that 'no action will lie for doing that which the legislature has authorized, if it be done without negligence ... but an action does lie for doing that which the legislature has authorised, if it be done negligently' (*per* Lord Blackburn).

> ### *Vaughan v. Taff Vale Railway Co.* (1860)
> A railway company was authorized by Parliament to operate a railway which ran through the plaintiff's land. Despite all the care taken by the company, a spark from one of their locomotives caused fire which destroyed eight acres of the plaintiff's wood. **Held**: In the absence of any negligence, the railway company was not liable as it had statutory authority.

> ### *Metropolitan District Asylum Board v. Hill* (1881)
> A hospital authority had conditional authority to erect a smallpox hospital. It erected such a hospital in a residential district of Hampstead where it caused danger of infection in the neighbourhood. **Held**: the hospital constituted a nuisance and an injunction was granted restraining the use of the building as a smallpox hospital. The obligation imposed by the statute on the hospital authority was permissive and not imperative.

20.3.6 Self-defence

Where a person commits tort in defence of himself, his family, his property or in defence of persons generally then self-defence may provide a good defence provided the force used is in proportion to the harm or danger threatened. For example, a blow is not proportionate to verbal provocation (*Lane v. Holloway (1967)*). Similarly, to shoot at trespassers or to set up traps or spring-guns to injure them is a disproportionate use of force to the likely harm threatened or done.

Introduction to the law of tort **357**

> *Dale v. Wood (1822).*
>
> In answer to a claim for assault, the defendant proved that the plaintiff had approached him menacingly on horseback, dismounted, held up a stick at him and provoked him. **Held**: The defendant's action was justified in the circumstances.

Similarly, if a neighbour's dog attacks your cattle or sheep, you are justified in shooting the dog if it is the only reasonable way of preventing harm: *Cresswell v. Sirl (1948)* – now replaced on a somewhat wider basis by Section 9 of the *Animals Act, 1971*.

20.3.7 Act of God

This defence applies to circumstances when injury or harm results to others which no human precaution or foresight can prevent.

> *Nichols v. Marsland (1876)*
>
> Due to an exceptionally violent storm, artificial pools on the defendant's land which were well constructed and adequate for normal circumstances, were destroyed and the escaping water damaged bridges belonging to the plaintiff county council. **Held**: In the absence of negligence, the defendant was not liable as the accident was entirely due to an extraordinary act of nature.

20.3.8 Act of State

The *Crown Proceedings Act, 1947*, places the Crown in the same position as a private person or employer for any tort committed by its servants, although the Queen continues to enjoy personal immunity from legal proceedings. However, neither the Crown nor the officials responsible can be sued in tort where the acts concerned are acts of state, i.e. they are official acts either authorized or subsequently ratified by the Crown, if these acts take place outside the territorial jurisdiction of the Crown (*Buron v. Denman (1848)*). This is because acts of state in foreign parts, such as warlike activities or annexation of territories, are not the concern of the English courts. However, the defence of act of state will fail in respect of damage or harm done to British subjects anywhere (*Nissan v. Attorney-General (1969)*), or done to a citizen of a friendly state when he is within the Crown territory (*Johnston v. Pedlar (1921)*). When this defence fails the affected party may be entitled to compensation.

20.4 Capacity of the parties

Although as a general rule any person of full age can sue and be sued in tort, it is necessary to consider the following categories of persons whose capacity is limited.

20.4.1 The Crown

The *Crown Proceedings Act, 1947* (Section 2), places the Crown in the same position as a private citizen for any tort committed by its servants or agents. A servant or an agent of the Crown is one who is directly or indirectly appointed by the Crown and would include Ministers of State, their subordinates and all other persons employed in government departments. The following are excluded:

- *The police.* Although the police are employed by the local authority they are not considered servants of the local authority (*Fisher v. Oldham Corporation (1930)*). The *Police Act, 1964 (Section 48)*, makes the chief police officer for the area vicariously liable for any tort committed by his officers in the course of their employment. Any damages and costs due are paid out of the police fund.
- *Local authorities.*
- *Hospital authorities.* Both the above have a legal personality of their own, and may be held vicariously liable for any tort committed by their servants.
- *Public corporations.* Although basically they are not Crown servants it does depend on the Act which created them. If the Act provides that a corporation acts for the Crown then it will probably be a crown servant. Otherwise it acts on its own behalf although it may be controlled by a government department (*Tamlin v. Hannaford (1950)*).
- *The Post Office.* Although no longer a Government department, it continues to enjoy immunity for any tort arising from any loss or damage resulting from loss or delay in the post, unless the packet has been registered (*Post Office Act, 1969*).

20.4.2 Infants and minors

A minor (a person under 18 years of age) is normally responsible in tort and infancy is not a defence. However, the standard of care expected from a minor is not that expected from an adult, but one that is commensurate with the minor's age. Besides, in torts which require malice or intention an infant defendant may be considered unlikely to have formed the necessary intent.

If an act complained of is a tort as well as a breach of contract, a plaintiff would not be allowed to frame his action in tort to escape the immunity that a minor enjoys under contract law. (For contractual capacity of minors see pages 98–102).

> *Jennings v. Rundall (1798)*
>
> The infant defendant hired a horse for riding and was sued in tort for injuries received to the animal through excessive riding. **Held**: there was no liability for negligence as this was essentially a breach of contract.

However, in contrast, where an alleged act goes beyond the bounds of a contract, as when a child kills a mare by jumping her against express instructions, this conduct may be considered independent of the contract and hence a minor will be liable in tort (*Burnard v. Haggis (1863)*).

Although a parent is not liable for a child's tort, if he or she affords the child an opportunity to commit the tort, there may be liability in negligence. In *Bebee v. Sales (1916)*, despite previous damage done and despite complaints made, a father allowed his son to keep an air-gun with which he caused injury to another boy's eye. The father was held liable in negligence.

Although minors have full legal capacity to sue in tort, they require to be represented by an adult acting as 'next friend'. In principle, an infant can sue his parent (*Deziel v. Deziel (1953)*). The *Congenital Disabilities (Civil Liability) Act, 1976*, gives a child a right to sue those whose intentional act, negligence or breach of a statutory duty results in pre-natal injuries to that child. Although a mother cannot be held liable for negligently causing injuries to the unborn child, a father's liability is not excluded.

20.4.3 Judicial immunity

A judge discharging his judicial function enjoys absolute immunity from any action in tort and so do justices of the peace when acting within their jurisdiction (*Law v. Llewellyn (1906)*). Similar immunity also extends to counsels and witnesses concerning matters relating to a judicial proceeding.

20.4.4 Foreign sovereigns and diplomats

A foreign sovereign is not liable in tort since he is not subject to an English court's jurisdiction unless he waives this immunity and submits to it. Similarly, foreign ambassadors, other diplomats, members of their families and certain categories of employees at foreign embassies enjoy diplomatic immunity and cannot be sued in tort during their terms of office. They become liable immediately after finishing their terms of office, although the alleged tort may have been committed when they enjoyed diplomatic immunity. They can also voluntarily submit to a local court's jurisdiction.

20.4.5 Corporations

A corporation is a legal person and hence it can sue in its corporate name for any tort committed against it. It is also vicariously liable and can therefore be sued for any tort committed by its agents or servants when acting within the scope of their authority. The Companies Act, 1985, is silent about tortious activities and hence a corporation is not liable for a tort committed when a servant or an agent was engaged in an *ultra vires* activity without express authority, whereas it is liable under Section 35 for contractual activities engaged in by staff with third parties unaware of the *ultra vires* nature of the proposed contract.

20.4.6 Trade unions

Trade unions are unincorporated associations and they enjoy certain immunities from actions in tort. A trade union cannot be held liable for torts committed by its members or officials in furtherance of a trade dispute unless the acts involve an 'unlawful act', such as illegal picketing, etc.

20.4.7 Persons of unsound mind

Although, in general, a person suffering from mental disorder is liable for his torts, the state of mind of a person is important in torts requiring a mental ingredient, e.g. malicious prosecution or deceit. A person of unsound mind is considered incapable of forming the necessary intent or malice for committing such torts. Similarly, if it is proved that a person is so insane that his actions cannot be considered to be voluntary, then he may escape liability in tort. It must be shown that he neither knew of the nature and quality of his act nor that what he was doing was wrong (*Morris v. Marsden (1952)*).

20.4.8 Aliens

There are two categories of aliens – namely, enemy aliens and other aliens. The latter are in the same position as ordinary citizens and hence do not suffer any disability or enjoy any immunity. As regards enemy aliens, these are nationals of a state which is at war with the UK. They also include British subjects who voluntarily reside or carry on business in such a state. Enemy aliens have no right to bring an action in tort although they may defend one, if sued.

360 Business Law

20.4.9 Partners, principals and agents

All partners are jointly and severally liable for a tort committed by one of them in the ordinary course of business. A principal is only liable for the tort of his agent as long as it was committed by the agent when acting within the scope of his authority.

20.4.10 Husband and wife

The *Law Reform (Husband and Wife) Act, 1962*, provides that 'each of the parties to a marriage shall have the like right of action in tort against the other as if they were not married'. Thus a wife may bring an action for assault and battery against a husband or vice versa. A court may stay such proceedings if it appears:

- That no substantial benefit would accrue to either party from the continuation of the proceedings; or
- That the question or questions in issue could more conveniently be disposed of under Section 17 of the *Married Women's Property Act, 1882*. This provides a summary procedure for determining questions between spouses concerning title to or possession of property.

Since the *Law Reform (Married Women and Tortfeasors) Act, 1935*, a wife is fully liable for her torts unless there exists an employer/employee or principal/agent relationship, in which case the husband may be vicariously liable for the wife's tort.

20.5 Remedies for torts

Apart from extra-judicial remedies such as abating nuisances or ejecting trespassers, which are mentioned under specific torts, the judicial remedies that are available to a plaintiff are damages, the granting of an injunction and in some cases restitution of property.

20.5.1 Damages

This is monetary compensation awarded to the party that has suffered a wrong and the underlying principle is one of restitution *in integrum*, i.e. to restore a plaintiff as far as possible to the position he would have been in if no wrong had been committed against him. Damages are classified in a number of ways:

(a) General and special damages

General damages are awarded for the mere fact that a tort has been committed and the law presumes that loss or injury automatically follows from the tort. General damages are awarded at the discretion of the court and are also termed **unliquidated damages**. Unlike general damages, for the award of special damages a plaintiff must prove the loss or injury resulting from a tort. Special damages are pleaded specially and the pleading sets out the exact amount being claimed. Special damages are awarded for losses which are exactly calculable, e.g. loss of earnings up to the date of the trial, medical expenses, etc. Damages which cannot be calculated precisely, e.g. damages for loss of future earnings, damages for pain and suffering and damages for loss of expectation of life, are termed general damages.

(b) Nominal and substantial damages

Nominal damages consist of a small sum of money which is awarded, not as compensation, but in mere recognition of the fact that a plaintiff's rights have been infringed. Nominal damages apply to torts actionable *per se*, e.g. trespass to land that involves no physical damage to the land or any other loss to the plaintiff. Substantial damages are normally unliquidated damages awarded for the actual loss or injury suffered by a plaintiff. They are compensatory in nature and are intended to restore a plaintiff to the position he was in before the commission of the tort.

(c) Exemplary damages

These damages are awarded as a means of punishing a defendant rather than compensating a plaintiff. Hence they are also called **vindictive** or **punitive damages**. The House of Lords, in *Rookes v. Barnard* (1964), mentioned the circumstances in which these damages are awarded. These are:

- Where a plaintiff is harmed as a result of oppressive, arbitrary or unconstitutional action of a government servant.
- Where a defendant's conduct was calculated to make a profit which might exceed the compensation payable to the plaintiff.
- Where a statute authorizes exemplary damages.

(d) Aggravated damages

These are awarded in circumstances where a defendant's conduct is wilful and malicious – for example, slapping someone in a public place may cause greater injury to his feelings and the damages awarded would be larger than the sum that would normally be awarded for such an act.

(e) Remoteness of damage

To succeed in obtaining damages it is essential that the defendant's act or omission and the consequence suffered by the plaintiff are not too remote. We are really concerned with the consequences of tortious conduct. Should the defendant be liable for all the consequences that follow his act or omission or should he be answerable only for the immediate consequences? In order to determine this, the rule before 1961 – as established in *Re Polemis & Furness, Withy & Co. Ltd* (1921) – was that a defendant was liable in negligence for all the direct consequences of his act irrespective of the fact that he could not have reasonably foreseen them.

However, as a result of the decision by the Judicial Committee of the Privy Council in *Overseas Tankship (UK) Ltd v. Morts Dock & Engineering Co. Ltd* (1961), a case also known as *The 'Wagon Mound' (No. 1)*, the test that his been established is that a defendant is liable for the consequences of his negligent act or omission only if he could have reasonably foreseen that his tortious conduct would result in those consequences. The test depends on the foresight of a reasonable man. The facts were as follows:

> **The 'Wagon Mound' (No. 1) (1961)**
>
> Through the carelessness of the appellants' servants, a large quantity of bunkering oil was spilt into a bay while a vessel was discharging gasoline products and taking in oil. It was found as a fact that the appellants did not know, and could not reasonably have been expected to know, that the oil was capable of being set alight when spread on water. Molten metal falling from the respondents' wharf set fire to some cotton waste floating in the oil, which in turn ignited the oil itself and caused a serious fire. Considerable damage was done to the respondents' wharf and equipment. **Held**: the appellants were not liable in negligence for the damage because they could not reasonably have foreseen it.

'The authority of *Polemis* has been severely shaken, though lip service has from time to time been paid to it. In their lordships' opinion, it should no longer be regarded as good law ... It is a principle of civil liability, subject only to qualifications which have no present relevance, that a man must be considered to be responsible for the probable consequences of his act. To demand more of him is too harsh a rule ... Thus foreseeability becomes the effective test. In reasserting this principle, their lordships conceive that they do not depart from, but follow and develop the law of negligence as laid down by Alderson, B, in *Blyth v. Birmingham Waterworks Co.*' (per Viscount Simonds).

Although the decision of the Privy Council in the 'Wagon Mound' is of persuasive authority and consequently does not bind an English court, the decision seems to have been accepted by the House of Lords in *Hughes v. Lord Advocate (1963)* and specifically by the Court of Appeal in *Doughty v. Turner Manufacturing Co. Ltd (1964)*.

Damages that are too remote cannot normally be recovered unless the harm or loss was actually intended by the defendant. Harm or loss are presumed intentional when they are the natural and inevitable consequences of a tortious conduct. For example, if A strikes a blow at B intentionally and B suffers a greater harm than an ordinary person because of a previous illness, A nevertheless is fully responsible for the consequences of his act and B's illness cannot be put forward as a defence.

Smith v. Leech Braine & Co. Ltd (1962)

As a consequence of the defendant's negligence, molten zinc hit the lip of the plaintiff's husband and caused a burn. The husband was a galvanizer employed by the defendants. Three years later the husband died as a result of cancer which developed in the burn. **Held**: the defendants were liable for damages to the wife although the death of the husband could not have been reasonably foreseen. (See also *Meah v. McCreamer (1986)*.)

An interesting example of remoteness of damage is *Weller v. Foot and Mouth Disease Research Institute (1966)*. A virus escaped from the Institute and caused the slaughter of many cattle and the closure of markets to contain the spread of the disease. The plaintiffs were auctioneers who could not carry on their business. It was held that their loss was too remote from the original act of negligence, and they were denied any remedy.

(f) Novus actus interveniens (a new act intervening)

Sometimes a loss resulting from an act or omission of a defendant may be too remote (not foreseeable) and therefore may not be recoverable because of the intervention of an extraneous act. This intervention may have broken the chain of causation resulting from the original act or omission. For example:

Cobb v. Great Western Railway (1894)

The plaintiff passenger was hustled and robbed of £89 because the defendants had negligently allowed a railway carriage to become overcrowded. **Held**: the plaintiff could not succeed in recovering the loss as the robbery was a *novus actus interveniens* which broke the chain of causation caused by the defendant's negligence.

Where the intervening act does not break the chain of causation caused by the original act or omission, then the defendant is liable for the consequences:

> ### Scott v. Shepherd (1773)
> The defendant threw a lighted squib into a crowded market. The squib fell on a stall belonging to Yates whereupon a bystander called Willis, in order to protect himself and Yates' stall, seized the squib and threw it across where it fell on the stall belonging to Ryal, who in order to protect his goods, threw the squib to another part of the market where it exploded and caused injury to the plaintiff. **Held**: the defendant was liable as there was no *novus actus interveniens*. The chain of causation resulting from the defendant's action was not broken by the intervening actions of either Willis or Ryal.

20.5.2 Injunction

This is an equitable remedy and is available at the discretion of the court. An injunction will be refused where damages would be an appropriate remedy and the High Court has power to award damages in lieu of an injunction. An injunction may be granted by any division of the High Court and also by the county courts. It may be granted to forbid the commission of a tort (**prohibitory injunction**) or it may be granted to compel the defendant to do something, e.g. to abate a nuisance (a **mandatory injunction**). An **interlocutory injunction** is granted by the court on the basis of a plaintiff's affidavit to prohibit or restrain the activities of the defendant and maintain the status quo, pending a court hearing. **Perpetual injunction** is granted after the case has been tried and is intended either to compel the defendant to do something or to prohibit him from some act.

The courts may suspend the operation of an injunction for a time to enable the defendant to comply with it. For example, in *Pride of Derby and Derbyshire Angling Association Ltd v. British Celanese Ltd* (1953) the court issued an injunction to prevent the activities of the defendant company which resulted in pollution of a river. However, the company was given time to carry out the necessary alterations to its sewage plant in order to comply with the injunction.

20.5.3 Restitution of property

The courts have discretion to order specific restitution of land or goods in cases where a plaintiff has been tortiously deprived of property by a defendant. In addition, a defendant may be called to give an account of the profits made as a result of his wrongful act, i.e. the deception. For example, if you carry on business activities under a business name of an existing and reputable company, you commit the tort of passing off and you can be compelled to refrain from doing so; you can also be called to account for the profits received by you as a result of the deception.

20.6 Limitation of actions

The law on the limitation of actions was consolidated in the second *Limitation Act, 1980*, which now contains the law concerning the period within which an action in tort must commence. The rules are:

- As a general rule, action in tort must commence within six years of the date on which the right of action accrued. In torts actionable *per se*, this

time runs from the date on which the tort was committed. In torts actionable only on proof of damage, the time runs from the moment damage takes place.
- In case of a tort, like nuisance, which consists of a continuing wrong, a new cause of action arises every day.
- If a tort is committed against a party under a disability (e.g. a person of unsound mind or a minor), the actionable period runs from either the time of the cessation of disability or of his death. Where disabilities are successive, time begins to run from the *last* one.
- Where an alleged wrong consists of a fraud or mistake, the beginning of the period of limitation does not begin until the plaintiff discovers the fraud or mistake.

20.6.1 Other statutory limitations

The 1980 Act re-enacts certain earlier measures about the periods during which action must commence from the date of accrual of the cause of action:

- *Personal injuries due to negligence, nuisance or breach of duty (whether statutory, contractual or independent of either)*. Three years (Section 11(1) of the 1980 Act). However the Act does provide in Section 11(4) that if the plaintiff is under a disability (such as being unconscious after an accident) time does not begin to run until the plaintiff's 'date of knowledge' – which under Section 14 means the time the plaintiff became aware that his/her condition was attributable to the acts of the defendant.

  A further difficulty is met in cases of **intentional torts**, where common sense would seem to suggest that if a person is intentionally harmed their rights for a redress of their wrongs should be at least as extensive as those where the harm suffered was due to negligence. In the case of *Stubbings v. Webb* which involved a claim for damages for child abuse, the case being brought many years after the event, the House of Lords clearly stated that such damage was not a 'personal injury' case and therefore the time limit was six years, not three. Unfortunately this had the undesirable result that the clauses which permitted the time to run from the 'date of knowledge' and another Section 33 clause which allowed the court to disregard limitations of time altogether, and hear the case anyway if the circumstances warranted it, could not apply to intentional torts. At the time of writing this means that a child abuser whose offence was committed many years earlier can escape punishment if the case is brought more than six years after the event. *In Stubbings v. Webb* the plaintiff brought the case 22 years after the offences. The result of the House of Lords' decision reveals a fault in 'limitation law' which needs correcting.
- *Fatal Accidents Act*, 1976. Three years.
- *Maritime Conventions Act, 1911, Section 8*. Two years in respect of life or personal injury to persons on board a vessel or damage to a vessel or her cargo.
- *Carriage by Air Act, 1961*. Two years for carriers subject to the Act.
- *Carriage by Sea Act, 1971*. One year, but the time limit may be extended by mutual agreement.
- *Limitation Act, 1980 (Section 10)*. Two years from the date of a judgement for a tortfeasor seeking contribution from a joint tortfeasor.
- *Nuclear Installations Act, 1965* (Section 15). Thirty years in respect of damage arising from nuclear incidents.

- *Proceedings Against Estates Act, 1970.* Actions in tort against the estate of a deceased person must commence within the normal six-year period or three years in respect of personal injuries.

20.6.2 The survival of actions

The *Law Reform (Miscellaneous Provisions) Act, 1934*, provides that a right of action in tort survives in favour of the estate of a deceased plaintiff and against the estate of a deceased defendant. Two exceptions to the rule are: (a) no action in respect of defamation survives after death unless damage is done to the deceased's property; and (b) exemplary damages are not awarded to the estate of a deceased plaintiff. Damages can be recovered in respect of pain and suffering, loss of earnings before death, medical expenses, loss of expectation of life and funeral or mourning expenses.

The *Fatal Accidents Act, 1976*, allows the personal representative of a deceased person to bring an action for damages on behalf of the deceased's dependants if death accrued as a result of a tortious act on the part of the defendant. Action must commence within three years of the death. A plaintiff must show that pecuniary loss (probably loss of financial benefit) has been suffered by the dependants and that the deceased was a breadwinner; damages for mere mental suffering will not be awarded. Dependants include the deceased's wife or husband, parent, child, grandparent, grandchild, step-parent, stepchild, brother, sister, uncle and aunt; also the issue of the latter four and illegitimate and adopted children.

Although claims for the same fatal accident may be brought under both the 1934 Act (for cause of action arising before the death) and the *Fatal Accidents Act, 1976*, a court will ensure that double benefits are not awarded to a defendant. For example, if an award is made to a surviving wife as a result of her husband's death (under the 1934 Act), any benefit she receives under the *Fatal Accidents Act, 1976*, would be reduced accordingly.

20.7 Vicarious liability

This term refers to a situation where a person who has not himself committed a tort is held responsible for the commission of a tort by another. Vicarious liability will be looked at under the following headings:

- Principal and agent.
- Master and servant.
- Liability for the acts of an independent contractor.

20.7.1 Principal and agent (see Chapter 13)

A principal is vicariously liable for all the acts of an agent which he has either authorized originally or ratified subsequently. To incur liability, the agent must have acted on behalf of the principal and either the principal must be aware of the agent's acts or the agent must have complete authority to act.

In *Ormrod v. Crosville Motor Services Ltd (1953)*, it was held that a friend of an owner of a car who drove the car for the owner's purposes, and with his consent, was an agent of the owner, who was therefore vicariously liable for the friend's negligence. However, in *Morgans v. Launchbury (1972)*, the House of Lords held that where a car owner had authorized his or her spouse to drive and the spouse delegated the driving to another person, the owner would not be vicariously liable for the acts of the latter.

20.7.2 Master and servant

The general rule is that a master is vicariously liable for the torts of his servant committed in the course of his or her employment. The court in *Hewitt v. Bonvir (1940)* approved Salmond's definition of a servant as:

any person employed by another to do work for him on terms that he, the servant, is to be subject to the control and direction of his employer in respect of the manner in which his work is to be done.

A servant is one who works under a contract of service, unlike an independent contractor who works under a contract for services. The relationship must be a voluntary one and the following is considered as evidence of this relationship: the power of an employer to select or appoint; the power to dismiss; and the payment of salary or wages. The various guidelines laid down by the courts for deciding whether a person is a servant or not are not principles of law and neither are they conclusive; the courts will therefore reserve their right to decide this question on the merit of the facts of each individual case.

Some of the cases in this area are mentioned below to give an idea of the circumstances where a vicarious liability may or may not be incurred:

Collins v. Hertfordshire County Council (1947)

A hospital authority was held vicariously liable for the negligence of a student and a pharmacist who were both employed by the Council, but not for the negligence of a consultant surgeon as the authority had no control over the way in which the latter carried out his duties.

Roe v. Ministry of Health (1954)

Where the question concerned the vicarious liability of the defendants in respect of acts committed by a visiting specialist anaesthetist, Denning, LJ, had the following to say on the liability of hospital authorities: 'They are responsible for the whole of their staff, not only for the nurses and doctors but also for the anaesthetists and the surgeons. It does not matter whether they are permanent or temporary, resident or visiting, whole-time or part-time ... The only exception is the case of consultants or anaesthetists selected and employed by the patient himself.'

Mersey Docks & Harbour Board v. Coggins & Griffiths (Liverpool) Ltd (1947)

The question concerned the vicarious liability of the Harbour Board who had lent a crane and a driver to the stevedores (Coggins & Griffiths Ltd). A third person was injured due to the crane driver's negligence. The crane driver was paid by the Harbour Board who also had the power to dismiss him. **Held**: the Harbour Board was vicariously liable as employers since they had control over how the work was to be done.

Watkins v. Birmingham City Council (1975)

The Education Authority was not vicariously liable for the negligence of a pupil who helped in the distribution of milk at the school. The boy was not the Authority's servant.

Beard v. London General Omnibus Co. (1900)

The defendants were not vicariously liable for the negligence of a bus conductor who, in the absence of the driver, drove a bus and injured the plaintiff. **Held**: the conductor had not acted within the scope of his employment.

Limpus v. London General Omnibus Co. (1862)

The defendant's driver deliberately obstructed one of the plaintiff's omnibuses, despite specific instructions to the contrary, causing injury and damage to the plaintiff's horses and omnibus. **Held**: The defendants were vicariously liable for all reckless or improper conduct of the driver occurring within the scope of his employment.

Century Insurance Co. Ltd v. Northern Ireland Road Transport Board (1942)

Petrol was being delivered to a garage. When the petrol was being transferred from a lorry to a tank, the respondent's driver threw away a lighted match after lighting a cigarette. This resulted in an explosion and subsequent damage. **Held**: the driver's employers were liable since he was acting within the course of his employment.

General Engineering Services Ltd v. Kingston and St Andrew Corporation (1988)

This was a case before the Privy Council about the actions of a fire brigade in Jamaica which was exercising a go-slow in pursuit of an industrial dispute, and drove 'in fits and starts' to a fire, with the result that the premises of the engineering plaintiffs were totally destroyed. **Held**: This action was a wrongful repudiation of an essential obligation of the staff's contract and they could not be held to have acted in furtherance of their employer's business, which required them to drive to a fire with the utmost expedition conducive with safety. The employer could not be held vicariously liable for such conduct.

For fraud committed by a servant, see Section 13.8 of this book (*Lloyd v. Grace, Smith & Co. (1912)*).

Warren v. Henlys Ltd (1948)

The defendants were not vicariously liable for the assault committed by their petrol pump attendant on a customer. **Held**: The attendant's assault was an act of personal vengeance and therefore not within the scope of his employment.

Poland v. John Parr & Sons (1927)

A servant of the defendants, with a view to protecting his employer's property from theft, struck a boy who then fell off the back of the cart and injured himself. **Held**: Since the servant was acting within the scope of his implied authority, the employers were liable.

It must be noted that in principle both the master and the servant are liable jointly for a wrong committed by a servant, but usually the master is sued since he happens to be the wealthier of the two, and therefore more worthy. If a master is sued he may recover a contribution or indemnity from the servant for the amount paid in damages to a third party.

Lister v. Romford Ice & Cold Storage Co. Ltd (1957)

Both the father and son were employed by the respondent company. Due to the negligent driving of the son, the father was injured. The father obtained damages against the company who were held vicariously liable for the actions of the son. The insurers of the company then sued the son and obtained an indemnity of the amount for which the company had been made liable to the father. **Held**: The appellant was in breach of his duty to the company to take reasonable care in the performance of his duties.

20.7.3 Independent contractors

Unlike a servant who works under the supervision and direction of his master, an independent contractor is more or less his own master. An independent contractor works under a contract for services and has discretion concerning the manner in which the work is to be done and the time of doing it. The general rule is that an employer is not vicariously liable for the torts committed by an independent contractor. However, there are certain exceptions to the rule which are based not on vicarious liability but on a breach by the master of a non-delegable duty of care binding on himself. Some of these exceptions are:

- Where an employer owes a primary duty to a plaintiff, he will be held responsible personally for any tort committed. In *Ellis v. Sheffield Gas Consumers Co. (1853)*, a duty arose because of the employer's wrongful behaviour. A company employed a contractor to dig trenches in a street without proper authority. The company was held liable to the plaintiff who fell and injured himself as a result of the contractor's servants leaving a heap of stones on the road.
- Where a statute imposes an absolute duty upon an individual, he will be liable since the performance of this duty cannot be delegated to an independent contractor, e.g. the duties to fence dangerous machinery and to provide safe means of access imposed on an employer under the *Factories Act, 1961*.
- Where the work concerned involves hazardous operations the employer will be liable and he cannot delegate the responsibility by employing independent contractors. In *Honeywell and Stein Ltd v. Larkin Bros. (1934)*, the plaintiffs were liable to the owners of a cinema for a fire caused by the defendants who were employed by the plaintiffs to take flash-light photographs in the cinema.
- There is liability on an individual under the rule in *Rylands v. Fletcher (1868)* (see page 387) for the acts of an independent contractor.

- Where a master owes his servants a duty concerning their safety, he will not escape liability by delegating its performance to a contractor, e.g. the duty of an employer under the *Employers' Liability (Defective Equipment) Act, 1969*. An employer having to pay damages for the torts of an independent contractor may claim an indemnity from the contractor if an indemnity clause exists in the contract between them (*Hosking v. De Havilland Aircraft Co. Ltd (1949)*). An employer is not liable for the collateral negligence of a contractor, e.g. wrongs committed by servants in the course of the contractor's employment. In *Padbury v. Holliday & Greenwood (1912)*, a hammer left on a window-sill injured a passer-by when a gust of wind blew it down; the defendant employer was not liable.

20.8 Joint tortfeasors

Where A and B commit a tort against C, A and B are said to be joint tortfeasors whose liability to C is joint and several. C has a choice of suing both of them or only one of them. Where C chooses to sue A alone, under the *Civil Liability (Contribution) Act, 1978*, A can claim contribution from B for any damages he pays to C. The amount that A recovers from B is dependent on the discretion of a court and on the extent of B's responsibility in the commission of the tort.

Under the *Law Reform (Husband and Wife) Act, 1962*, since both husband and wife are treated as independent parties for an action in tort, were a third party to sue a husband alone for the negligence of both, the husband can now claim a contribution from the wife for any damages he pays to the third party.

Test your knowledge

Answers	Questions
	1 Define a tort.
1 A tort is a civil wrong, actionable at the suit of the aggrieved party, which is not either a breach of contract, or a breach of trust or other merely equitable obligation (Salmond).	2 What are the chief torts?
2 (a) Negligence; (b) nuisance; (c) trespass; (d) defamation.	3 What is the chief remedy in tort?
3 Unliquidated damages, i.e. damages which are not predetermined, but are at the absolute discretion of the court.	4 What is the meaning of 'actionable *per se*'?
4 It means the tort is actionable merely because the rights of the plaintiff have been interfered with, even though no damage has actually been suffered.	5 Distinguish a tort from a crime.

Answers	Questions
5 (a) Tort is civil law, crime is criminal law. (b) In tort the plaintiff sues the defendant, but in crime the Crown Prosecution Service prosecutes the offender. (c) The unsuccessful defendant in tort must pay damages or observe an equitable remedy such as injunction. The guilty party in a crime is fined, or imprisoned, or some other penalty is imposed. (d) In tort a duty is owed to persons generally and action is at the suit of anyone who is aggrieved. In crime the duty is prescribed by the criminal law and the state will prosecute the offender.	6 What are the defences in tort?
6 (a) *Volenti non fit injuria*; (b) necessity; (c) certain types of mistake; (d) inevitable accident; (e) statutory authority; (f) self-defence; (g) Act of God; (h) Act of State.	7 Are infants liable in tort?
7 In general yes, but the standard of care may be less than for adults.	8 What are the remedies for torts?
8 (a) Damages, either nominal, substantial, exemplary or aggravated; (b) injunction, either prohibitory, mandatory or interlocutory; (c) restitution of property.	9 What is vicarious liability?
9 It is the liability of one person to offer himself as the target for a legal action by another, because the tort was performed by someone acting as his agent, or his servant.	10 What is the test to distinguish a servant from an independent contractor liable for his own torts?
10 Is the person concerned controlled both as to what is being done, and the manner in which the work shall be performed?	11 Go over the questions until you are sure of all the answers. Then try the written questions in Appendix 1.

21 Negligence

21.1 The meaning of 'negligence'

Negligence may be either a mode of committing other torts (e.g. trespass or nuisance) or an independent tort in its own right. Negligence is considered in this chapter in the latter sense.

Negligence is committed whenever any person owing a legal duty of care breaches this duty with the result that damage (physical, mental or financial) is caused to some other person or persons. Negligence has been defined (per Alderson, B, in *Blyth v. Birmingham Waterworks Co. (1856)*) as:

> the omission to do something which a reasonable man ... would do, or doing something which a prudent and reasonable man would not do.

On the meaning of negligence, Lord Wright in *Lochgelly Iron and Coal Co. v. McMullan (1934)* had the following to say: 'In strict legal analysis, negligence means more than heedless or careless conduct, whether in omission or commission: it properly connotes the complex concept of duty, breach and damage thereby suffered by the person to whom the duty was owing.' Hence to succeed in an action for negligence, a plaintiff is required to prove:

- the existence of a legal duty of care,
- a breach of this legal duty of care, and
- the damage suffered in consequence of the breach.

21.2 The duty of care

Before liability for negligence arises it must be shown by the plaintiff that the defendant owed him a duty of care. There is no legal definition of the term duty of care and we may all be as careless as we wish, providing such carelessness does not cause harm, loss, injury or damage to those around us or to those with whom we have business or other dealings. Whether or not a duty of care arises in a particular circumstance is a question of law, to be decided by a judge. In *Donoghue v. Stevenson*, the House of Lords formulated a general principle known as the 'neighbour principle' for determining whether a duty of care was owed. The facts were as follows:

> **M'Alister (Donoghue) v. Stevenson (1932)**
> A shop assistant, the appellant, drank some ginger-beer which had been manufactured by the respondents. The ginger-beer, which was in a dark opaque glass bottle, had been sold by the respondents to a retailer who in turn sold the drink for consumption by the appellant. As a second glassful was being poured out for her the appellant noticed a decomposed snail float out of the bottle. She became seriously ill and claimed damages for negligence. **Held:** the respondents

> owed the appellant a legal duty to take care that the bottle did not contain noxious matter and they would be liable to her if that legal duty was broken as the manufacturer of an article of food, medicine or the like, sold by him to a distributor in circumstances which prevent the distributor or the ultimate purchaser or consumer from discovering by inspection any defect, is under a legal duty to the ultimate purhcaser or consumer to take reasonable care that the article is free from defect likely to cause injury to health. 'You must take reasonable care to avoid acts or omissions which you can reasonably foresee would be likely to injure your neighbour. Who, then, in law is my neighbour? The answer seems to be – persons who are so closely and directly affected by my act that I ought reasonably to have them in contemplation as being so affected when I am directing my mind to the acts or omissions which are called in question' (*per* Lord Atkin). (Courtesy of *Cracknell's Law Students' Companion*)

The case established a new category of duty, a duty between manufacturer and consumer. The lack of privity of contract between the two (see Section 7.7) does not prevent a liability in tort. A consumer suffering physical injury because of a defective product will succeed on proof of negligence. The *Consumer Protection Act, 1987* now allows a consumer to bring an action against the manufacturer of a defective product. (For more on this Act see pages 435–45.) There is now a *Food Safety Act, 1990* which came into effect in April 1991 which seeks to enhance the protection of the consumer in the area of food safety and hygiene. The Act empowers trading standards officers to bring actions against suppliers of food which does not conform with the nature, or substance, or quality demanded by the customer. Thus if a customer asks for minced beef but is given a minced meat which contains small portions of other meat the butcher is liable to face prosecution. The tests involve detailed analysis by the public analyst, and are becoming more sophisticated year by year.

One area where the law is now prepared to recognize the existence of a duty of care owed to a wide range of people is the area known as 'nervous shock'. At first the law hesitated to accept 'nervous shock' as a disease, and the tendency of professional psychiatrists to give conflicting views of the illness in court did not help matters. However as knowledge about such illnesses grew and a more reasonable consensus of professional opinion developed, the courts began to decide in favour of claimants. More recently the body of cases identified as post traumatic stress disorder (PTSD) became increasingly recognized. The trouble is that the courts do not wish to open the doors too widely on such cases, because this permits claims where the sufferer is really too remote from the event. For example, should a person who saw a horrific accident on television be able to claim that a duty of care existed between him and the person who caused the accident? Duties of care have been held to exist in the following cases:

- Where a plaintiff was present at the scene and suffered personal injury, or injury to close relatives.
- Where a plaintiff had a close tie with the victim and saw him/her very shortly afterwards (for example on being called to the hospital).
- Where the plaintiff was a rescuer, either a member of the rescue services or a volunteer who was unhurt in the accident but assisted those injured, or a passer-by who participated out of natural humanity.

The courts are unlikely to admit claims for stress as a result of seeing an accident on television if the normal television rules (which ban close-ups) have been followed. However should a case arise where the normal rules are broken a claim might be made, but it would not be against the person who caused the horrific event, but against the television company for breaking the regulations.

Other recognized duties of care exist in respect of the following situations. It must be emphasized that these categories are not exhaustive and, as Lord Macmillan noted in *Donoghue v. Stevenson*, 'the categories of negligence are never closed'.

(a) Employers

An employer owes his employees a duty of care. He must provide competent staff, ensure a reasonably safe system of work and provide adequate plant and equipment; the employer is liable for any injury received due to defective equipment, supplied by a third party (*Employers' Liability (Defective Equipment) Act, 1969*).

Cases: *General Cleaning Contractors Ltd v. Christmas (1953)* and *Bux v. Slough Metals (1973)*. The *Employers' Liability (Compulsory Insurance) Act, 1969*, requires an employer to insure against physical injury received or disease contracted by employees at work.

(b) Highway users and adjacent occupiers

A road user owes a duty of care to other road users. Similarly, occupiers and landlords owe a duty of care to other road users in respect of man-made structures adjoining the highways.

(c) Professional people

All professional persons (e.g. doctors, dentists, solicitors, bankers, etc.) owe a duty of care to persons having a professional relationship with them. Cases of medical negligence are becoming increasingly common, but fortunately the United Kingdom has not yet seen the frenzied litigation in this field that is such a feature in the USA. A landmark case *Bolam v. Friern HMC (1957)* held that a doctor could successfully claim that there had been no breach of his duty of care if it could be shown that he 'acted in accordance with practices accepted as proper by a responsible body of medical practitioners'.

(d) Occupiers of premises

(see Chapter 22).

(e) Carriers

Carriers of persons or freight, bus companies, railway companies and other transport authorities owe a duty of care to their passengers, and for the goods carried. This duty of care is independent of any contractual liability that may arise as a result of a contract between the carrier and his customer.

(f) Bailees

A duty of care is owned to the bailer of goods independent of the contract of bailment.

(g) The local authority

In exercising its statutory powers e.g. of inspecting building foundations, a local authority owes a duty of care to all future owners or occupiers of the premises whose safety or health is likely to be affected by any defects in the building (*Anns v. Merton London Borough Council (1978) AC 728*; *Dutton's Case (1972) 1 QB 373*).

(h) A driver and his passengers

A driver owes a duty of care to his passengers, and Section 148(3) of the *Road Traffic Act, 1972* says that no agreement between the driver and his passengers can negate this duty of care. However, in *Pitts v. Hunt (1990)* the plaintiff was riding pillion on a vehicle driven by the defendant, and had been heard shouting encouraging remarks to him. The driver was uninsured and not qualified to ride a motorcycle, and both parties were drunk. The injuries arose as a result of the illegal activity and the ruling *ex turpi causa non oritur actio* (no action can arise from a base cause) was applied. There was no duty of care by the driver to his passenger. Both were knowingly engaged in a reckless activity.

21.3 Breach of duty and the standard of care

Having established a duty of care, the second question that must be proved by a plaintiff is that there has been a breach of this duty of care. This is a question of fact to be decided by a judge and it is difficult to lay down rules for deciding whether or not a breach of duty has occurred. In deciding this matter a court may consider a range of factors such as the nature of the activity in question, the feasibility of precautions, the conduct of the plaintiff, the status of the defendant, the level of knowledge at the time of the accident, the personal state of the plaintiff and so on.

In discharging the duty of care, the standard of care that is demanded of a defendant is an objective one, i.e. the standard of care of an ordinary reasonable man. The reasonable man is a fictitious character (the man on the Clapham omnibus) who is considered neither over-confident nor unduly apprehensive. The standard of care required from a person possessing special skill or knowledge is that which is reasonable having regard to the particular profession or occupation that person is engaged in.

For example, in *Roe v. Ministry of Health (1954)*, a specialist anaesthetist administered contaminated nupercaine to a patient who became paralysed as a result. The anaesthetist was not negligent as he had displayed normal competence and the contamination could not have been reasonably foreseen or discovered (see also *Bolam v. Friern Barnet Hospital Management Committee (1957)*).

A selection of cases will illustrate both the existence of a duty of care and breach of that duty.

Cases in which a duty of care existed:

Carmarthenshire C.C. v. Lewis (1955) 1 All ER 565

A mistress in charge of a nursery school was preparing to take children out. While she was dressing one child, another four-year-old child escaped from the school premises via an unlocked gate. He ran down a side lane into a busy highway, and into the path of a moving lorry. The driver swerved in order to avoid the child. In doing so he collided with a telegraph pole and was killed. The widow of the driver brought an action for damages in negligence. **Held**: the defendants were liable for not taking reasonable care to prevent the escape of the child from the school premises; they ought to have foreseen this eventuality and taken precautions against it.

McLoughlin v. O'Brien and Others (1982)

Here the House of Lords was considering an appeal by Mrs Rosin McLoughlin. The facts were that Mrs McLoughlin's family was travelling in a car that was involved in an accident attributed to the negligence of two lorry drivers. Mrs M who was at home at the time, was informed of the tragedy. The family home was two miles away from the scene of the accident. Mrs M later visited the family in hospital and saw the family members in varying degrees of distress and injury. All this caused her shock and she became ill as a result. She sued the drivers for damages in negligence for the harm resulting from the nervous shock. **Held**: Mrs M would succeed in claiming damages as what happened to her was a reasonably foreseeable consequence.

Wilkinson v. Downton (1897)

Here the defendant, as a practical joke, told the plaintiff that her husband had met with a serious accident and lay injured in a public house in Leytonstone. She was to go at once by taxi with two pillows and fetch him home. This caused the plaintiff nervous shock which resulted in severe and permanent physical injury. **Held**: the defendant was liable in damages for the consequences as they could have been reasonably foreseen.

Cases in which no duty of care existed:

Bolton v. Stone (1951)

The plaintiff, who was standing outside a cricket ground where a match was in progress, was hit and injured by a cricket ball. The ball had travelled approximately 100 yards and traversed a 17-foot-high fence. Evidence showed that similar hits out of the ground had occurred on some six occasions in the previous 30 years. **Held**: the defendant was not liable in negligence as the probability of such an occurrence could not have been anticipated by a reasonable man.

Latimer v. AEC Ltd (1953)

Due to exceptionally heavy rain, a factory floor became flooded. The rainwater combined with oil on the floor and caused slippery conditions. The occupier of the factory spread sawdust as far as possible until supplies ran out and some parts of the floor remained uncovered. The plaintiff who slipped and injured himself sued the defendants in negligence. **Held**: since the plaintiff had taken all reasonable steps to prevent injury or harm in the circumstances, they were not liable. It would not have been reasonable to expect them to shut the factory and send the employees home.

King v. Phillips (1953)

A taxi-driver, when reversing his taxi without exercising proper care, ran into a child on a tricycle and injured the child slightly. At the time the mother of the child was in her house some 70 or 80 yards away. She heard a scream and glanced out of the window. She saw the child's tricycle under the cab but not the child. This caused her tremendous nervous shock and she became ill as a result. She sued the taxi-driver for damages in negligence. **Held**: the driver was not liable. He did not owe the mother a duty of care since he could not have reasonably foreseen that his actions would cause her injury.

21.4 Liability for negligent misstatements

Apart from liability for misleading statements that may arise under a contract (see Misrepresentation, Chapter 10), there may be liability in tort for misleading statements. The House of Lords in an important case decided in *Hedley Byrne & Co. Ltd v. Heller & Partners Ltd* (1963) that liability arises not only in respect of negligent acts but also negligent words. The facts of the case were as follows:

Hedley Byrne and Co. Ltd v. Heller and Partners Ltd (1963)

The appellants, becoming doubtful about the financial position of Easipower Ltd asked their bank to communicate with Easipower's bankers, the respondents. This they did by telephone, asking the repondents 'in confidence, and without liability (on the respondents' part) whether Easipower would be good for a contract of £8000 to £9000. The respondents replied that they believed Easipower 'to be respectably constituted and considered good for its normal business engagements'. Six months later the appellants' bank wrote to the respondents to ask whether they considered Easipower trustworthy, in the way of business, to the extent of a £100 000 per annum contract and the respondents replied: 'Respectably constituted company, considered good for its ordinary business engagements.' The appellants relied upon the respondents' statements and as a result lost over £17 000 when Easipower Ltd went into liquidation. The appellants sought to recover this loss from the respondents as damages on the ground that the respondents' replies were given negligently and in breach of the respondents' duty to exercise care in giving them. **Held**: while bankers are under a duty to give honest answers and, perhaps, owe enquirers (such as the appellants) a duty of care, in this case the respondents never undertook any duty to exercise care in giving their replies and it followed that there was no liability on their part. The appellants' bank, who were their agents in making the enquiry, began by saying "they wanted to know in confidence and without responsibility on your part", i.e. on the part of the respondents. So I cannot see how the appellants can now be entitled to disregard that and maintain that the respondents did incur a responsibility to them.' (*per* Lord Reid). (Courtesy of *Cracknell's Law Students' Companion*)

Note: Under the *Unfair Contract Terms Act, 1977*, cases of tortious liability are caught by Section 2, which holds that a person cannot disclaim responsibility (as in the case just quoted) unless it is reasonable to do so. A disclaimer of this type will only be effective if it satisfies the requirement of reasonableness.

Further indications of how the courts will treat clauses which purport to disclaim responsibility for the statements made have come in a number of cases about the surveying of houses by professional surveyors acting on behalf of building societies and other lenders of money on mortgage.

Traditionally surveyors have always claimed that they will only be liable for the statements made to the organization that paid the fee (the building society) and disclaimed all responsibility to third parties – these actually buying the houses. Building societies invariably advised such people to seek independent advice, even though the fee paid to the surveyor was charged on to the applicant for the mortgage. In practice, the majority of buyers relied on the survey report made to the building society. In *Smith v. Eric S. Bush (1989)* a claim by the plaintiff that the surveyor's report was negligent and that the surveyor did owe the plaintiff a duty of care was upheld both at the original trial and on appeal. The Appeal Court held that it would be neither fair nor reasonable to allow a professional person to claim that he/she did not owe a duty of care to a person who had been sent a copy of their report and whom they knew was likely to rely on it.

In another case, *Harris v. Wyre Forest District Council (1989)*, where the same situation arose but the disclaimer had been very clearly spelled out to the applicant, the original decision, that there was a duty of care to the house buyer despite the disclaimer, was reversed on appeal. When both these cases came before the House of Lords the House, after a very full discussion, concluded that a duty of care was owed in both cases. The test of reasonableness was that the disclaimer must be 'fair and reasonable ... having regard to all the circumstances at the time'. Lord Griffiths said the following four factors should be considered in any such case:

- The relative strengths of the bargaining parties.
- Whether it was practicable to obtain alternative advice. (For a poor person, to pay for a second report when he/she had already paid for the first report was not reasonable or practical.)
- How much difficulty was involved in the actual task in hand and whether the task was routine or involved a high degree of risk. (A high degree of risk is not usually involved in a house survey.)
- Whether or not it would involve a fundamental change in society – for example would surveyors go out of business rather than take on the responsibilities involved. His Lordship held that professional people would take insurance cover and spread the extra cost over all the work they do. No abnormal effect on the house purchase system could be envisaged.

Accordingly both cases were held to be caught by the *Unfair Contract Terms Act*, and the plaintiffs were entitled to compensation.

In *Esso Petroleum Co. Ltd v. Mardon (1976)* Lord Denning, MR, explains the rule established in Hedley Byrne & Co. as follows:

> *If a man, who has or professes to have special knowledge or skill, makes a representation by virtue thereof to another – be it advice, information or opinion – with the intention of inducing him to enter into a contract with him, he is under a duty to use reasonable care to see that the representation is correct, and that the advice, information or opinion is reliable. If he negligently gives unsound advice or misleading information or expresses an erroneous opinion, and thereby induces the other side to enter into a contract with him, he is liable.*

For other cases on this area of tort, see *Sutcliffe v. Thackrah (1975)*; *Mutual Life & Citizens Assurance Co. Ltd v. Evatt (1971)*; *Rondell v. Worsley (1967)*; and *Saif Ali v. Sydney Mitchell & Co. (1978)*.

21.5 Res ipsa loquitur (the thing speaks for itself)

Normally the burden of proving negligence is on the plaintiff, who has to prove the existence of a legal duty of care, the breach of that duty of care and the subsequent damage resulting from the breach. However, where the principle *res ipsa loquitur* (the thing speaks for itself) applies, a court will infer negligence from the facts proved in the absence of any explanation by the defendant. *Res ipsa loquitur* is a rule of evidence under which negligence is presumed and hence a plaintiff is entitled to have his case put to the jury. The burden of proof shifts from the plaintiff to the defendant, who must now prove that he was not negligent, but that the events that occurred were caused by some force outside his control.

> **Scott v. London & St Katherine Docks Co. (1865)**
>
> Six bags of sugar fell on the defendant as he was passing in front of the plaintiff's warehouse. **Held**: 'There must be reasonable evidence of negligence, but where the thing is shown to be under the management of the defendant or his servants, and the accident is such as in the ordinary cause of things does not happen if those who have the management use proper care, it affords reasonable evidence in the absence of explanation by the defendant, that the accident arose from want of care' (*per* Erle, CJ). See also *Byrne v. Boadle* (1863).
>
> Where the facts disclosed do not raise a presumption of negligence or the thing causing the accident is not under the defendant's control (*Wilks v. Cheltenham Home Guard Motor Cycle and Light Car Club* (1971)), or where there is an explanation for the accident (*Barkway v. South Wales Transport Co. Ltd.* (1950)), *res ipsa loquitur* will not apply.

21.6 Contributory negligence

Where a defendant who is negligent shows that the plaintiff was also partly responsible for the injury that resulted to him, the damages awarded to the plaintiff will be reduced to take account of the plaintiff's own negligence. This principle; which applies to collisions of ships at sea, is now contained in Section 1(1) of the *Law Reform (Contributory Negligence) Act*, 1945. The section provides that 'where any person suffers damage as a result of his own fault and partly of the fault of any other person or persons, a claim in respect of that damage shall not be defeated by reason of the fault of the person suffering the damage, but the damage recoverable in respect thereof shall be reduced to such extent as the court thinks just and equitable having regard to the claimant's share in the responsibility for damage.'

The adjustment for contributory negligence is usually some simple fraction of the total, for example $\frac{1}{2}$, $\frac{1}{3}$, $\frac{1}{4}$ or $\frac{1}{10}$th of the total damages payable. To take a simple example, suppose a motorcycle rider X who is not wearing a crash helmet collides with a car driven negligently by Z. X sues Z for damages. The court decides that in the circumstances X is entitled to damages of £9000 against Z. However, the court also finds that the extent of the injury received by X could have been reduced had he worn a crash helmet and accordingly he is one third to blame for the consequences. The court will therefore reduce the damages awarded to X by £3000.

In *O'Connell v. Jackson* (1971) a plaintiff moped-rider not wearing a crash helmet was held to have contributed to the consequences caused by the defendant's negligent act and the plaintiff's damages were reduced accordingly.

Similarly, in *Froom v. Butcher* (1975) failure to wear a seat belt constituted contributory negligence and the damages awarded were reduced proportionately to the extent of injury caused through not wearing a seat belt.

In the case of a child plaintiff, the contributory negligence depends on his age and capacity. For example, in *Yachuk v. Oliver Blaise and Co. Ltd (1949)* a child aged nine was held not to have contributed negligence since he was not sufficiently capable of taking care of himself.

21.6.1 The doctrine of alternative danger (the 'dilemma principle')

An act done in the heat of the moment to protect oneself may not be considered contributory negligence. For example, imagine you are a passenger in a bus and are put in a perilous situation due to the negligent conduct of the bus driver. Anticipating an accident, you take evasive action to protect yourself and are injured. Will you succeed in obtaining damages against the driver if it transpires that the crash you anticipated did not materialize and had you remained in your seat you would have been quite safe? The court in *Jones v. Boyce (1816)* held that a plaintiff in a similar situation will succeed if his action is considered reasonable in the circumstances.

21.7 Negligence and economic loss

In many cases of negligence, particularly with regard to building construction, the question arises over to what extent economic losses following from the negligence are recoverable from the defendant. The problem is that in many cases the activities of the parties have been of a contractual nature and the question arises whether the law of tort can be invoked to secure damages when the economic loss resulted from a contractual matter in which, had the plaintiff party been more alert, he/she might have inserted a clause in the contract to cover the matter. It has been clearly established that where a defect in building work causes personal injury or damage to property other than the defective building itself an action in tort will recover damages. The actual defect in the building itself is a contractual matter (*Department of the Environment v. Thomas Bates & Son Ltd (1989)*) and it is no part of the law of tort to fill in the gaps in contracts. It is well-established in law that those who enter into contracts are free to choose the terms on which they contract, and if they leave out something or inadequately express themselves they cannot look to the law of tort to correct their carelessness.

In the famous case of *Hedley Byrne v. Heller and Partners Ltd (1964)* (see page 376) it was held that in general a duty of care does exist by those who give professional advice in the knowledge that people shown the advice may act upon it and suffer economic loss. This case therefore led to an increased number of actions for negligent advice causing economic loss. The number of circumstances in which such losses might arguably be caused is very great, and the question arises as to how far the courts should go before the question of 'remoteness of damage' arises. The duty of care might arise in the following circumstances:

- Where a special relationship exists of a business or professional nature, particularly one where one party is in the business of giving advice.
- Where one party relies on the statement made, and the other party knew that he/she was likely to rely on it. In a number of building society cases where the purchaser has relied upon a surveyor's report to the society even though he had not seen it, but for which he had paid the fee, the courts have held that it is reasonable for the purchaser to rely on the surveyor's report, if the building society did so and sanctioned the mortgage (*Yianni v. Edwin Evans (1982)* and *Harris v. Wyre Forest DC (1989)*). In the latter case a clause excluding liability for negligence in the survey was ruled unreasonable under the *Unfair Contract Terms Act, 1977*.

- Where the advisor knows, or may infer from the circumstances, that the advice given is likely to be communicated to another party, who may act upon it and suffer loss if the advice is given negligently.

Just how far litigants might be disposed to push the boundaries of 'negligence' is illustrated in the case of *Minories Finance Ltd v. Arthur Young* (1988). The Bank of England has a statutory duty to monitor the prudential behaviour of banks and other financial institutions (with a view to ensuring that they do not get into financial difficulties to the detriment of the investing public, whose money they are using). The question which arose, was whether an institution which suffered financial losses due to its own imprudent conduct should be able to claim damages from the Bank of England for failing to detect the indiscretion and advise how to deal with the problem. Saville, J, held that it would be contrary to common sense to infer that Parliament, in enacting the supervisory powers, intended to create any such duty of care to city institutions. It would not be just or reasonable to imply any such duty in the circumstances.

Test your knowledge

Answers	Questions
	1 What is negligence?
1 A breach of a duty of care owed by one person to another, so that the person suffers some damage.	2 What must the plaintiff normally prove to the satisfaction of the court?
2 (a) The existence of a legal duty of care; (b) breach of that duty; (c) damage suffered as a result of the breach.	3 What was the case of *Donoghue v. Stevenson* about?
3 It was the 'snail in the gingerbeer bottle' case. It established the 'neighbour principle'.	4 What is the 'neighbour principle'?
4 The principle that estalished that 'anyone is my neighbour who is so closely and directly affected by my act that I ought reasonably to have them in my contemplation when I direct my mind to acts or omissions which may be called in question'.	5 What is the standard of care required?
5 It is a reasonable one – bearing in mind the profession or occupation concerned.	6 What does *res ipsa loquitur* mean?

Answers	Questions
6 The facts speak for themselves	7 What is the effect of *res ipsa loquitur*?
7 The facts speak for themselves so the plaintiff need not prove that the defendant was negligent. The burden of proof shifts to the defendant, who must show that he was *not* negligent.	8 What is 'contributory negligence'?
8 It is where the damage suffered by the plaintiff is aggravated by his, or her, own negligence. The damages awarded are reduced by some simple fraction to allow for the contributory negligence of the plaintiff.	9 What is the 'dilemma principle'?
9 It is a principle which holds that a person who is placed in a situation of stress by the negligent act of another, and who takes evasive action which results in injury, may claim damages even though the feared event was in fact avoided.	10 What is the attitude of the courts to negligence claims for negligence which causes economic loss?
10 Generally speaking, it is that the law of tort should not be used to fill out gaps in contracts which the parties failed to bear in mind when making the contract. If a thoughtful person could have inserted a clause covering the matter when they made their contract the persons who did not do so have only themselves to blame and should not be allowed to save the situation by claiming that the other party owed them a duty of care.	11 What was *Department of Environment v. Bates & Son Ltd (1989)* about?
11 Economic loss due to a defect in the construction of a building. It was held that this was not a tortious matter – it was a contractual one about 'warranty of fitness'	12 Go over the page again until you are sure of all the answers. Then try some of the questions in Appendix 1.

22 The liability of occupiers of premises

22.1 The Occupiers' Liability Act, 1957

The law concerning the duty of an occupier of premises towards his lawful visitors is contained in the *Occupiers' Liability Acts 1957–84*. The first of these says that an '**occupier**' is not necessarily the owner of a premises but he can be a person with a degree of control over the premises; there can be more than one occupier.

'**Premises**' include land, buildings, fixed or movable structures, vehicles, ships and aeroplanes. '**Visitors**' are those to whom the occupier has either given permission to use the premises or those who are deemed to have this permission. Whether or not a visitor has implied permission to enter premises is a question of fact depending on the circumstances of each case and the burden of proof rests on the person claiming such permission. Visitors can include persons who enter by right of law (e.g. factory inspectors, gas and electricity meter readers, postmen, refuse collectors, etc.), those lawfully on the premises such as customers in shops or those who have implied permission to enter although their presence may be objectionable to the occupier, e.g. door-to-door salesmen.

Under the Act an occupier of premises owes a 'common duty of care to all his visitors, except in so far as he is free to and does extend, restrict, modify or exclude his duty to any visitor or visitors by agreement or otherwise' (Section 2.1).

The extent of the duty is laid down in Section 2.2 of the Act:

> *A duty to take such care as in all the circumstances of the case is reasonable to see that the visitor will be reasonably safe in using the premises for the purpose for which he is permitted by the occupier to be there.*

Although the Act permits an occupier to exclude his liability towards a visitor by framing a suitable notice, the power and extent of excluding liability depend on judicial and legislative restrictions in force. Judicial restriction means whether or not the courts consider an exclusion of liability reasonable in the circumstances. A major legislative restriction on excluding liability is the *Unfair Contract Terms Act, 1977*. According to Section 2 of the Act any liability arising from death or personal injury resulting from negligence cannot be excluded; an exclusion or restriction for other loss or damage will depend on whether or not the courts consider it reasonable. The Act only applies to 'business liability', i.e. liability that arises from the occupation of premises by an occupier who uses the premises for business purposes. Hence trespassers and non-business visitors are excluded from the scope of the Act.

22.1.1 Liability to children

Section 2(3) of the 1957 Act provides that 'an occupier must be prepared for children to be less careful than adults'. An occupier is compelled to ensure that precaution is taken to prevent harm resulting to children from things which conceal danger but which appear attractive or are alluring to children.

> ### Cooke v. Midland G. W. Rly of Ireland (1909)
> The defendants kept a turntable close to a public road. A boy aged four was injured while playing along with other children on the turntable. Although the defendants' servants were aware of the fact that children habitually came on to the land to play with the turntable, the defendants took no action to prevent this. **Held**: they were liable to the child. Because of the defendants' acquiescence in the trespass, the child trespasser was in the position of a lawful visitor.

> ### Glasgow Corporation v. Taylor (1922)
> A child aged seven died, having eaten poisonous berries picked from a shrub growing in a public park belonging to the Glasgow Corporation. It was alleged that despite the fact that the Corporation was aware that these berries were poisonous and children frequented the park, no precaution was taken to warn children of the danger. **Held**: the Corporation was liable to the deceased child's parents since the berries constituted an allurement.

22.1.2 Liability to trespassers

Since the *Occupiers' Liability Act, 1957* only applied to visitors the rules of common law continued to apply to people who were not 'visitors' under the 1957 Act, until the *Occupiers' Liability Act, 1984* revised the law on the matter. The 1984 Act applies to trespassers, and to persons using rights of way, who fall outside the meaning of visitor under the 1957 Act. The tort of trespass is dealt with more fully in Chapter 23. The common law rule about liability to trespassers has for many years been as explained in the following cases.

In *Addie & Sons v. Dumbreck (1929)*, a trespasser was defined as 'one who goes on to the land without any invitation of any sort and whose presence is either unknown to the proprietor, or, if known, is practically objected to'. The general rule was that no active duty of care was owed to a trespasser; a trespasser entered at his own risk and took the premises as he found them. However, if a trespasser's presence was known to an occupier, he was under a duty to refrain from intentionally or recklessly inflicting damage on the trespasser. For example, an occupier could not set up spring-guns to cause physical injury to a trespasser (*Bird v. Holbrook (1828)*). However, reasonable defensive measures in protection of one's property were permitted, e.g. laying broken glass on the top of high walls.

When it comes to child trespassers a much higher duty of care is required of an occupier. The general rules are that an occupier must be prepared for children to be less careful than adults.

In *British Railways Board v. Herrington (1972)*, the plaintiff was a boy aged six. He was playing with his two brothers in a park through which ran an electrified railway. Although there was a fence on both sides of the railway, the fence was in a dilapidated condition. The Board were aware that people (including children) were quite regularly taking 'short cuts' through the broken fence. The plaintiff was seriously injured when after having crossed the fence he came into contact with a live rail. The House of Lords held the Board liable for breaking its duty of care to the child trespasser. The decision also established that the old rules relating to liability towards trespassers no longer applied. Lord Reid laid down the following twofold test on liability towards trespassers:

- Did the occupier know that there was a 'substantial probability' of the presence of trespassers?
- Could a 'conscientious humane man' with that knowledge, and with the skill and resources which the occupier in fact had, be reasonably expected to have done or refrained from doing before the accident something that would have avoided it?

This was the position until the passing of the 1984 Act. The Act does not change the law significantly but it provides as follows:

- The occupier owes a duty of care if:
  - he/she is aware of the danger, or has reasonable grounds for believing that a danger exists; and
  - he/she knows, or has reasonable grounds to believe that someone is in, or may come into, the vicinity of the danger; and
  - the risk is one against which, in all the circumstances of the case, it would be reasonable to offer that person some protection.
- The occupier's liability is for injury to the person. The Act makes it clear that there is no liability for loss of, or damage to, property.
- The duty may be discharged by adequate warning notices, but only in appropriate cases. A notice is regarded as adequate warning to adults, but not to children.
- The defence of *volenti non fit injuria* (a willing person cannot be harmed) is preserved and is still available to occupiers in appropriate cases.

The duty is therefore to take such care as is reasonable in all the circumstances to ensure that the person concerned does not suffer injury on the premises by the danger concerned.

It seems unlikely that any of the cases since the British Rail case referred to above (1972) would have been decided differently under this Act. The courts must still look at all the circumstances. It has been held as follows in various cases:

- That a notice is adequate warning to an adult (*Westwood v. The Post Office (1974)*).
- That children need special protection, such as an adequate lookout – *Pannett v. McGuinness (1972)* or to prevent their entry to a dangerous and tempting place – *Harris v. Birkenhead Corporation (1975)*.

22.2 The Defective Premises Act, 1972

The Act imposes on a landlord a wider duty of care and he cannot restrict or exclude any of the duties imposed by the Act.

Section 4 of the *Occupiers' Liability Act, 1957*, has been repealed and under the *Defective Premises Act, 1972*, a landlord is liable to all persons who it is reasonable to expect will be affected by defects in the premises. These will include, in addition to the tenant, his family and his visitors, also neighbours, passers-by and possibly trespassers. Under the *Defective Premises Act, 1972*, a builder, any specialist subcontractor, the developer and professional people involved with the construction of new houses owe a statutory duty of care to purchasers and their successors.

22.2.1 Defences to an action

An action may be defended by providing that:

- The visitor has been warned of a danger (Section 2.4). This does not in all the circumstances absolve the occupier from liability; it all depends whether in the circumstances the warning was adequate to enable the visitor to be reasonably safe.
- Where damage is caused to a visitor through the faulty workmanship of an independent contractor employed by the occupier, the contractor will be held liable (*O'Connor v. Swan & Edgar and Carmichael Contractors (1963)*).
- Section 2(5) encompasses the principle of *volenti non fit injuria* (see page 352), i.e. risks willingly accepted by a visitor.

22.3 Strict liability

Strict liability is a liability which would arise irrespective of whether a person was at fault or not. There are two types of torts falling under this category – namely, *breach of statutory duty* and *the rule in Rylands v. Fletcher (1866)*.

22.3.1 Breach of statutory duty

An injured party can sue in tort for a breach of a duty imposed by a statute. Most claims in this area concern industrial injuries arising under the *Mines and Quarries Act, 1954*, the *Factories Act, 1961*, and the *Health and Safety at Work Act, 1974*. Whether or not an injured party will succeed in his action depends on the construction of the statute in the context of the circumstances surrounding the case.

Where on construction a statute imposes an absolute duty, then no proof of negligence or wrongful intent is required. In *Groves v. Lord Wimborne (1898)* the plaintiff was injured because of a breach of the defendant's statutory duty to fence dangerous machinery. The defendant was liable because the statute imposed an absolute duty.

If, on the other hand, a statute does not impose an absolute duty, negligence will have to be proved. In *Hammond v. Vestry of St Pancras (1874)*, because the defendants were in breach of their statutory duty to repair sewers, the plaintiff was injured. The defendants were not liable in the absence of proof of negligence.

For a plaintiff to succeed in his action he must prove the following:

- That a statute was broken and the breach was the direct cause of the injury or damage.

> **Bonnington Castings Ltd v. Wardlaw (1956)**
>
> A plaintiff was injured as a result of inhaling silica dust because of the defendant's breach of the Factories Acts. The House of Lords held: for a plaintiff to succeed, it is not enough to prove that there was a breach of a statutory duty; it must be proved in addition that this breach was the direct or material cause of the injury. In the words of Lord Reid: 'The employee must, in all cases, prove his case by the ordinary standard of proof in civil actions; he must make it appear at least that, on a balance of probabilities, the breach of duty caused, or materially contributed to, his injury.'

- The plaintiff was a person or from a class the statute intended to protect:

> **Hartley v. Mayoh & Co. (1954)**
> The plaintiff, a fireman, was electrocuted while fighting an outbreak of fire at the defendant's factory because the defendant was in breach of statutory regulations. **Held:** Since the regulations were expressly for the benefit of the factory employees only and as the fireman did not fall within this category, the plaintiff's action failed.

- The injury complained of is one the statute intended to prevent:

> **Gorris v. Scott (1874)**
> The plaintiff's sheep were washed overboard because the defendant shipowner, in breach of his statutory duty, had not provided pens on the ship's deck. **Held:** the plaintiff would not succeed in his action for breach of statutory duty since the object of the statute was to protect animals from the spread of contagious disease and not to provide protection against sea hazards.

Defences to an action

(a) Volenti non fit injuria

On grounds of public policy this defence is not available to an employer when he is being sued by his employees. However, where an employer is being sued on grounds of vicarious liability for breach of a statutory duty committed by his workmen, this defence is available. In *ICI Ltd v. Shatwell (1964)* two qualified shot-firers were injured when they tried to test a circuit without taking shelter. Both knew the practice to be dangerous and contrary to the company's policy and statutory regulations. When one of the injured sued the company on grounds of its vicarious liability, it was held that *volenti non fit injuria* was a complete defence.

(b) Contributory negligence

This defence is available and the damages may be apportioned under the *Law Reform (Contributory Negligence) Act, 1945*. (*Caswell v. Powell Duffryn Associated Collieries Ltd (1939)*) (see page 378.)

(c) Delegation of statutory duty

Where a statute imposes an absolute duty on an employer it is not a defence to say that it was delegated to a reasonably competent person. However, a workman would be prevented from recovering damages in circumstances where the fault is entirely his.

> **Ginty v. Belmont Building Supplies Ltd (1959)**
> The plaintiff workman failed to use a crawling-board when working on a roof. This was breach of statutory regulations binding on both his employers and himself. When injured he sued his employers for breach of statutory duty. **Held**: the workman's action failed since he had failed to show that his employers had committed any breach of statutory duty other than the one committed by the workman himself.

In cases where a statutory duty has been delegated but in performance of that statutory duty both the employer and the employee are at fault, damages will be apportioned between them. In *Ross v. Associated Portland Cement Manufacturers Ltd (1964)*, the employers were held two thirds liable for the plaintiff workman's injuries since in delegating their statutory duty to the workman, they had not given him proper instructions in the performance of his task and besides the workman was not qualified to perform the task.

22.3.2 The rule in *Rylands v. Fletcher*

The rule as stated by Blackburn, J, in the Court of Exchequer is as follows:

> *The person who for his own purposes brings on his lands and collects and keeps there anything likely to do mischief if it escapes, must keep it in at his peril, and, if he does not do so, is* prima facie *answerable for all the damage which is the natural consequence of its escape.*

The facts of *Rylands v. Fletcher (1866)* were that the defendant mill owner had employed independent contractors to construct a reservoir on his land. The reservoir was to be used for supplying water for the defendant's mill. During the construction work the contractors had found some disused mine shafts. These the contractors had failed to seal as it was not known to them or the defendant that the shafts connected with the adjoining land where the plaintiff had a mine. When the reservoir was filled with water the plaintiff's adjoining coal mine was flooded through the underground mine shafts. The facts did not disclose the defendants to be liable in negligence and for various reasons action could not be brought in trespass or nuisance. The only way the defendant could be held liable was for the plaintiff to establish that the defendant's liability in the circumstances was strict or absolute. This proposition was accepted by the Court of Exchequer and the defendant was held liable. On appeal, the House of Lords upheld the rule, thus establishing an independent form of tortious liability.

The rule can be summarized as follows:

- There must be an escape from the defendant's land of a thing 'likely to do mischief'. If there is no escape beyond the boundaries of the defendant's land the plaintiff will fail under the rule (*Read v. J. Lyons (1947)*).
- The damage arising must be the result of a non-natural use of the defendant's land.
- The rule is a strict liability one and hence no question of intent or negligence arises.
- Although the tort is actionable *per se*, at least some damage must be proved.

- The fact that the defendant employed a competent independent contractor to do the job cannot excuse him from incurring liability.

Although in *Rylands v. Fletcher* the 'thing' escaping was water, since then the following objects have been held by courts to be covered by the rule:

- Electricity – *Eastern & South African Telegraph Co. v. Cape Town Tramways Co. (1902)*.
- Gas – *North Western Utilities Ltd v. London. Guarantee & Accident Co. (1936)*.
- Wire fencing – *Firth v. Bowling Iron Co. (1878)*.
- Sewage – *Jones v. Llanrwst UDC (1911)*.
- Vibration – *Hoare & Co. v. McAlpine (1923)*.
- Explosives – *Rainham Chemical Works v. Belvedere Fish Co. (1921)*.
- Projecting trees – *Crowhurst v. Amersham Burial Board (1878)*.
- Fire – *Musgrove v. Pandelis (1919)* – but the rule does not apply to accidental fires.

Defences

The following defences may be available to an action under the rule in *Rylands v. Fletcher*.

(a) Act of God

If the escape is due to natural causes, such as exceptionally heavy rainfall which could not have been reasonably anticipated, the defendant may escape liability (*Nichols v. Marsland (1876)*).

(b) Statutory authority

In *Green v. Chelsea Waterworks Co. (1894)* the defendants escaped liability arising from a burst main which flooded plaintiff's premises. **Held**: since defendants were under statutory duty to lay the main and to supply water and since they were not negligent, they were not liable.

(c) Consent of the plaintiff

Where a plaintiff expressly or impliedly consents to the presence of the 'thing' on the defendant's land or premises, the defendant will escape liability for any subsequent escape that causes harm or damage to the plaintiff, e.g. the escape of water from the upper floor in a building to lower floors; in the absence of negligence the occupier of the upper floor is not liable. In *Peters v. Prince of Wales Theatre Ltd (1943)*, the plaintiff's shop was flooded because the sprinkler system which the defendant had installed in their theatre to prevent fire had frozen up. **Held**: defendant not liable to the plaintiff tenant.

(d) Act of a stranger

Where an escape is caused by the unforeseable act of a third party (not the occupier's servants, independent contractors, family members or possibly guests), the defendant may escape liability. In *Rickards v. Lothian (1913)*, due to the malicious act of an unknown person a tap in a top floor lavatory of a building leased by the defendant was turned on. The water had overflowed and damaged plaintiff's stock on the bottom floor. **Held**: the plaintiff could not recover, as the defendants were not negligent and the rule in *Rylands v. Fletcher* could not apply.

(e) Default of the plaintiff

Where the escape was due to the plaintiff's own fault, he cannot recover for the subsequent injury. Where a plaintiff is partly to blame, under the *Law Reform (Contributory Negligence) Act, 1945*, damages can be apportioned between the plaintiff and a defendant.

22.4 Liability for animals

A person may incur liability for any damage done by animals either under the *Animals Act, 1971*, or under general principles in trespass, nuisance or negligence. In addition to retaining the common law rule of strict liability for keepers of dangerous animals, Section 4 of the Act imposes a strict liability on a person in possession (not necessarily the owner) of livestock, which includes bulls, cows, sheep, goats, horses and poultry. Liability may arise under the Act for any livestock trespass that causes damage to a plaintiff's chattels or land. A plaintiff cannot recover for any personal injuries.

Although there is still a strict liability for cattle trespass, i.e. no fault need be proved by a plaintiff, it is no longer actionable *per se* and hence damage or loss resulting subsequent to entry must be proved.

A plaintiff must be either in possession of the affected land or he must be an owner not in possession. There is no longer any liability for damage caused by trespassing cattle to the chattels of a person not in occupation of the land (Section 4). A plaintiff is entitled to claim the expenses of detaining and housing the straying livestock until such time as compensation is paid and the livestock can be returned to the owner. The occupier is also given the right to sell the detained animals after 14 days unless proceedings are pending for the return of the animals.

Under Section 8 a duty of care is imposed on occupiers of land in respect of non-dangerous animals straying onto the highway. The rule in *Searle v. Wallbank (1947)* that an occupier was under no duty to fence his land in order to keep his animals off the highway has been abolished.

The various defences available under the Act are:

- The plaintiff was at fault (Section 5.5.1).
- The animal had strayed accidentally from an adjoining highway Section 5.5.5).
- Trespass was the result of the failure of the plaintiff to fence his land adequately (Section 5.5.6).

Section 3 is concerned with damage done by dogs. It provides that 'where a dog causes damage by killing or injuring livestock, any person who is a keeper of the dog is liable for the damage, except as otherwise provided by this Act'. Two exceptions are: damage is done wholly due to the fault of the person suffering it; and where trespassing livestock is killed or injured by a dog belonging to the occupier or authorized to be there by the occupier.

Test your knowledge

Answers	Questions
	1 Which Acts control the liability of occupiers of premises?
1 The *Occupiers' Liability Acts, 1957–84*.	2 What is the occupier's duty?

Answers	Questions
2 A duty to take such care as is reasonable in all the circumstances of the case to see that the visitor will be reasonably safe in using the premises for the purposes for which he is permitted to be on the premises.	3 What is a visitor?
3 A person whom the occupier has permitted to be there, or who may be deemed to have this permission.	4 What is the extent of liability to children?
4 This is a greater liability than to adult visitors. The Act says the occupier must be prepared for children to be less careful than adults.	5 Where is particular care necessary?
5 Where anything constitutes an 'allurement' to children.	6 What is the liability to trespassers?
6 In general there is no duty to trespassers, but there is now a threefold test: (a) does the occupier know that there is a danger; (b) does he/she know that there is a chance that someone will come into the vicinity of the danger; (c) is the danger such that a reasonable person would offer that person, whoever it is, some measure of protection?	7 What is meant by 'strict liability?'
7 It means that the occupier is liable for the loss even if he was not personally at fault because an absolute liability has been imposed on him by law.	8 What are the two cases of strict liability?
8 (a) Breach of statutory duty; (b) the rule in *Rylands v. Fletcher* (1866).	9 What is the rule in *Rylands v. Fletcher* (1866)?

Answers	Questions
9 The person who brings onto his land and keeps there anything likely to do mischief if it escapes must keep it in at his peril, and if he does not do so is *prima facie* answerable for all the damage which is the consequence of its escape.	10 What are the defences to a *Rylands v. Fletcher* action?
10 (a) Act of God; (b) statutory authority; (c) consent of the plaintiff; (d) act of a stranger; (e) default of the plaintiff.	11 Go over the questions again until you are sure of all the answers. Then try some of the questions in Appendix 1.

23 Trespass to property

23.1 Trespass to land

The word 'trespass' means unlawful interference with the rights of another. Trespass to land consists essentially of any wrongful interference with land which is in another person's possession. 'Possession' means the right to exclude all others and it does not matter whether or not the possessor is physically present; possession can be exercised through servants or agents. It is important that the plaintiff is in possession of the land and it is not enough that he is the owner of the land. If land has been leased then the lessee is the person in possession. Mere use of the land – for example, as a lodger – is not possession. Since trespass is a wrong against possession, the defendant cannot raise the defence of *jus tertii*, i.e. that a third party has a better title to the land than the plaintiff.

A trespass to land can take various forms apart from unlawful physical entry upon the land or buildings in possession of another. Some of these forms of trespass are as follows:

- Placing objects on another's land (*Gregory v. Piper (1829)*).
- Discharging oil at sea so that it is subsequently carried onto the plaintiff's foreshore (*Esso Petroleum Co. Ltd v. Southport Corporation (1955)*).
- Blowing carbon monoxide or any other gas onto the property of another may constitute trespass (*McDonald v. Associated Fuels Ltd (1954)*).
- Entry below the surface (tunnelling or mining) is a trespass and so is entry into the airspace of another. In *Kelson v. Imperial Tobacco Co. Ltd (1957)* an advertising sign which projected a few inches above the plaintiff's airspace was held to be a trespass. By virtue of the *Civil Aviation Act, 1982* (Section 76) civil aircraft flying at a reasonable height are exempted from incurring liability for trespass; strict liability is imposed on the owner of aircraft for any damage resulting from things falling from an aircraft. (The Act does not apply to aircraft on Her Majesty's Service.)
- If a right of lawful entry is abused subsequently then this may constitute a trespass (*Harrison v. The Duke of Rutland (1893)*).
- If an entry is authorized for one purpose and that purpose is exceeded on entry, this may constitute a trespass (*Hickman v. Maisey (1900)*).
- Where a person enters as a result of a common law or statutory right but subsequently abuses the right of entry by a wrongful act, he is deemed to be a trespasser *ab initio* (from the beginning), i.e. his trespass begins from his original 'lawful' entry.

The Six Carpenters Case (1610)

Six carpenters, having entered an inn, consumed a quantity of wine and bread. They later refused to pay the price. **Held**: they were not trespassers *ab initio* since their act was a non-feasance (an omission) only. Had their act been a misfeasance then they would have been trespassers *ab initio*.

A trespass to land is actionable *per se* (in itself) and no proof of actual damage is required. Traditionally trespass upon property has not been a criminal offence, although the *Criminal Law Act, 1977* created a criminal offence of using or threatening violence to gain entry to premises occupied by a person who opposes entry. Similarly the law provides punishment for trespass on property for the purpose of committing a crime (e.g. theft or rape).

However *The Criminal Justice and Public Order Act, 1994* has created a number of offences by trespass, including 'collective trespass', 'aggravated trespass', 'trespassory assemblies' and 'adverse occupation of residential premises'. The new Act is a response to the aggressive advantage taken of traditional rules about trespass by groups of people acting as squatters in domestic premises, or as 'travellers' on public or private land, or simply for a bit of fun at festivals and 'raves'.

Section 72 of the 1994 Act modified the 1977 Act by saying that if the person using violence to gain entry to premises occupied by a person who opposes entry is the owner, or occupier, or intending occupier of the property (whose lawful right to enter has simply been hi-jacked by the person squatting in the property) then no offence has been committed. This also applies to anyone acting on behalf of such a displaced owner or occupier. Section 73 goes on to say that it is an offence for the trespasser to refuse to leave the premises when requested to do so, by, or on behalf of the displaced person.

Trespassers of the 'traveller' type who have moved vehicles onto land, and have refused reasonable requests to leave; who are doing damage, or offering threats or violence to those entitled to ask them to leave, may be removed from the land (Section 61). Persons attending or preparing for a rave may also be removed from the land. In appropriate circumstances the police may enter and stop proceedings, seizing public address and sound equipment (which the court may later declare to be forfeit).

Under Section 68 the offence of aggravated trespass is committed when anyone enters upon land to disrupt or obstruct any lawful activity or intimidates those persons carrying out such a lawful activity.

23.1.2 Remedies for trespass

Apart from the criminal law sanctions introduced by the 1977 and 1994 Acts referred to above, the following remedies for trespass to land are available to a plaintiff:

- *Damages*. This is normally the amount necessary to compensate for the diminution in the value of the land.
- *Injunction*. This is used to forbid the continuance or repetition of the trespass.
- *Forcible ejection*. The occupier of land may eject with reasonable force a trespasser after the latter has been requested to leave and a reasonable time has been given for him to leave:

Hemmings v. Stoke Poges Golf Club Ltd (1920)

The plaintiffs, husband and wife, were employed by the defendant golf club. They were provided with a cottage by the defendant. After the termination of their employment, they were given notice to quit the cottage but they refused. The defendant, who forcibly ejected them, was sued in trespass. **Held**: their action must fail, since the defendant had used reasonable force in ejecting them.

- *Distress damage feasant.* Where straying animals have entered and have done damage, an occupier may exercise his right to seize the animals and retain them until such time as compensation is paid.
- *Re-entry.* A person dispossessed from his land by a trespasser may re-enter peaceably to repossess the land (*Hemmings v. Stoke Poges Golf Club Ltd (1920)*).

23.1.2 Defences to trespass

The following defences to trespass exist:

- *Authority of law,* A police officer may enter to arrest or search premises under the *Criminal Law Act, 1967.* Similarly, he may enter to prevent a breach of the peace (*Thomas v. Sawkins (1935)*). A bailiff has a right of entry to distrain for rent or eject a tenant.
- *Entry by licence.* This applies to theatre guests, guests at any other place of public entertainment, and those with a licence – for example, to fell and remove timber from the land of another (*James & Sons Ltd. v. Tankerville (1909)*). When the licence expires the licensee must leave. If he does not leave he becomes a trespasser.
- *Retaking goods.* It is a good defence to show that the defendant entered plaintiff's land to repossess goods that had been wrongfully taken onto the plaintiff's land.
- *Necessity.* It is good defence to show that the defendant trespassed onto the plaintiff's land to avert danger to life (*Esso Petroleum Co. Ltd v. Southport Corporation (1956),* where it was held no trespass was committed when the defendants discharged oil from a tanker to save the crews' lives which were in danger; see also *Cope v. Sharpe (1912),* page 355).
- *The premises occupied are non-residential.* The new criminal measures introduced by the *Criminal Justice and Public Order Act, 1994* particularly addressed to preventing trespassers interfering with the genuine rights of displaced occupiers of domestic property. It is sometimes a defence to such charges if the accused can show that the property in which he is squatting is not a domestic property but a non-residential property (Section 73).

23.2 Trespass to chattels

Chattels are items of personal property. Trespass to chattels consists of unlawful interference (direct and forcible) with chattels in the possession of another. Trespass to chattels is actionable *per se* and hence no need arises to prove that damage resulted; mere proof of direct and unlawful interference suffices. The plaintiff is required to prove intention or negligence on the part of the defendant (*National Coal Board v. Evans (1951)*) and hence unintentional or accidental touching of another's goods is not actionable.

Unlawful interference with chattels in possession of another can take the form of trespass to goods, conversion of goods, negligence – so far as it results in damage to goods or to an interest in goods – and any other tort so far as it results in damage to goods or to an interest in goods (the *Torts (Interference With Goods) Act, 1977*). This Act has abolished the former tort of *detinue* (wrongful detention of goods), which is now treated as conversion. The Act has considerably simplified the law and procedure in this area of tort.

23.2.1 Trespass to goods

Trespass to goods, like trespass to land, is a wrong against possession and not ownership. Thus anyone in rightful possession of goods may sue. A bailee can sue during the term of his bailment, whereas a bailor cannot. Similarly, a hirer or a borrower in whose possession the goods are has the right to sue. So has a master who has given his servant the custody of the goods since legally the master is considered the custodian of the goods. A personal representative of a deceased person in possession of the deceased's goods can also sue. In *Armoury v. Delamirie (1721)*, a goldsmith to whom a boy who had found a jewel took it to be valued, refused to return it. In an action in *trover*, it was held that the boy was entitled to recover by way of damages the full value of the jewel. (**Note**: Section 8 of the *Torts (Interference with Goods) Act, 1977*, allows a defendant to plead that a third party had a better title than the plaintiff in all actions for wrongful interference.)

(a) Defences to trespass to goods

The following defences are available to an action for trespass to goods.

- *Inevitable accident*:

> **National Coal Board v. J. E. Evans & Co. (Cardiff) Ltd (1951)**
> The facts were that while digging Evans and Co. damaged an underground electricity cable belonging to the NCB. Neither the defendants nor the County Council on whose land the work was taking place were aware of the existence of the cable. **Held**: since the presence of the cable was not foreseeable the defence of inevitable accident would protect the defendants from any liability.

- *Exercise of a legal right*. No trespass is committed when something is done in pursuance of any legal right or legal process, e.g. bailiffs exercising a legal right.
- *Protection of persons or property*. It is not trespass when action is taken to avert impending danger to persons or property (*Cresswell v. Sirl (1947)* – see Self-defence, page 356).

23.2.1 Conversion

Salmond in his *Law of Torts* defines conversion of a chattel as:

> *an act, or complex series of acts of wilful interference, without lawful justification, with the right of another, whereby the other is deprived of the use and possession of it.*

The definition consists of the following elements:

- Doing something to the chattel inconsistent with the rights of the rightful owner.
- Intentionally denying a person's right to the chattel.
- Preventing the rightful owner from asserting his right.
- Wrongfully asserting ownership (*Douglas Valley Finance Co. Ltd v. S. Hughes (Hires) Ltd (1967)*).

Any interference that is not wilful and wrongful does not amount to conversion. In *Ashby v. Tolhurst (1937)* it was held that the defendant carpark attendant was not liable in conversion for negligently allowing a stranger to remove the plaintiff's car.

396 Business Law

(a) Who can sue in conversion?

Any person who is in possession or entitled to be in possession of the converted goods can sue. It is not necessary for the plaintiff to be the owner of the goods. Possession is difficult to decide in cases where there are two or more claimants. In the absence of any general rule each case is treated on merit having regard to the circumstances. For example, in *Bridges v. Hawkesworth (1851)* it was held that the plaintiff, who found some bank notes on the floor of a shop, had a good title against everyone except the true owner.

In *Elwes v. Brigg Gas Co. (1886)* the lessor of the land where a prehistoric boat was found had a better title to it than the lessee with a 99-year lease. In *Hannah v. Peel (1945)* it was held that a soldier in a requisitioned house who found a valuable brooch had a better title than the owner of the house, who had never been in physical occupation of the house and did not know of the existence of the brooch, until the soldier found it. A recent case was:

> **Parker v. British Airways Board (1982)**
>
> P found a gold bracelet at Heathrow Airport and handed it in to an official requesting that it be returned to him if not claimed. BAB sold it for £850 and refused to hand the money over to P. **Held**: The finder had a better title than the occupier, unless the occupier could show that it intended to exercise control over the object. The right to exercise control was not enough. £850 + £50 interest awarded to P. (All ER 834.)

(b) Types of conversion

Conversion may take the following forms:

- Where chattels are wrongfully taken from the possession of the rightful owner with the intention of exercising temporary or permanent dominion over them (*Fouldes v. Willoughby (1841)*).
- Wrongful detention of goods with an intention to keep the goods from the person entitled to possess them.
- Wrongful destruction of the goods, whereby the goods either cease to exist or change their identity, e.g. raw material converted into finished product.
- Wrongfully disposing of the goods in such a way as to confer a good title on someone other than the original owner.
- Wrongfully delivering the goods to someone other than the person lawfully entitled to them (*Hollins v. Fowler (1875)*).
- Under Section 11(2) of the 1977 Act 'receipt of goods by way of pledge is conversion if the delivery of the goods is conversion'.
- Although there can only be a conversion of chattels and not documents, e.g. the value on a cheque, the difficulty is overcome by treating the cheque as a chattel, i.e. a piece of paper, which can be converted (*Lloyds Bank v. Chartered Bank (1929)*). The principle can be extended to negotiable instruments, trading stamps, credit cards, book tokens, etc. (For conversion of negotiable instruments, see page 308 and 312.)

(c) Remedies for conversion of goods

The following remedies are available:

- Damages.
- Specific delivery of goods.
- Defendant given a choice of the above two.
- The latter two are discretionary remedies.

Trespass to property

Section 8 of the *Torts (Interference With Goods) Act, 1977*, abolishes the *jus tertii* rule and a defendant can successfully assert that a third party has a better title to the goods than the plaintiff. Section 10 holds that co-ownership is no longer a defence to an action for both conversion and trespass to goods.

(d) Defences to an action for conversion

These include:

- Where a defendant shows that he was merely in possession of the goods without title but he was not withholding possession from the rightful possessor.
- Where a defendant shows that the plaintiff had either no possession or insufficient possession of the goods.
- Contributory negligence was abolished as a defence by Section 11(1) of the 1977 Act, but has been restored in relation to actions in conversion against a collecting banker by Section 47 of the *Banking Act, 1979*.
- A defendant (e.g. a warehouseman) who shows that goods had been merely deposited with him. Blackburn, J, in *Hollins v. Fowler (1875)* said: 'A warehouseman with whom goods have been deposited is guilty of no conversion by keeping them or restoring them to the person who deposited them with him, though that person turns out to have no authority from the true owner.'

(e) Ineffectual defences

Mistake of law or fact is not a defence. It is no defence to claim that loss from the interference was not intended or that it was not the natural or probable result of the act of conversion (*Hiort v. Bott (1874)*). It is no defence to claim that the defendant was acting on behalf of another.

> **Consolidated Co. v. Curtis and Son (1892)**
> A lady who had assigned certain of her furniture to the plaintiffs subsequently ordered the defendants to auction her property. They had no notice of the bill of sale and auctioned the items assigned. **Held**: Curtis and Son were liable for conversion.

Finally, it is no defence to claim that the loss or deprivation of possession by the plaintiff was only temporary.

Test your knowledge

Answers	Questions
	1 What is trespass?
1 Unlawful interference with the rights of another.	2 Give some examples of the forms trespass to land can take?

Answers	Questions
2 (a) Physical entry on another's land; (b) placing objects on it; (c) discharging oil on it; (d) blowing gas over it; (e) entry below or above the land; (f) where the purpose of entry is exceeded or abused.	3 What are the remedies for trespass to land?
3 (a) Damages; (b) injunction; (c) forcible ejection; (d) distress damage feasant; (e) re-entry.	4 What defences can a defendant plead to an action for trespass?
4 (a) Authority of law; (b) entry by licence; (c) re-taking goods; (d) necessity.	5 What is trespass *ab initio*?
5 Trespass from the very beginning; as where a person who lawfully enters another's land then performs an unlawful act (a misfeasance) and becomes a trespasser *ab initio*.	6 Explain trespass to chattels.
6 This consists of any unlawful interference with the chattels in another's possession.	7 Give examples of trespass to chattels.
7 (a) Trespass to goods; (b) conversion of goods; (c) negligence.	8 What important changes has the *Torts (Interference with Goods) Act, 1977*, made in this area of the law?
8 (a) The Act has abolished the tort of detinue and treats it as conversion. (b) The Act has simplified the law and procedure.	9 Explain trespass to goods.
9 Any interference with the goods in lawful possession (not ownership) of another. For example, unlawful interference with goods in possession of a bailee, a hirer, a borrower or a personal representative of a deceased person.	10 What defences are available to trespass to goods?

Answers	Questions
10 (a) Inevitable accident; (b) exercising a legal right; (c) protection of persons or property.	11 Define conversion.
11 'An act, or complex series of acts, of wilful interference, without lawful justification, with any chattel in a manner inconsistent with the right of another, whereby the other is deprived of the use and possession of it' (Salmond).	12 Give examples of conversion.
12 (a) Exercising temporary or permanent dominion over goods belonging to another person. (b) Wrongful detention of goods. (c) Wrongful destruction of goods. (d) Wrongful disposition of goods. (e) Wrongful delivery to another. (f) Under Section 11 (2) of the 1977 Act. (g) There can be conversion of documents, e.g. negotiable instruments, stamps, credit cards, book tokens, etc.	13 What remedies are available for conversion?
13 (a) Damages; (b) specific delivery of goods.	14 What defences are available to an action for conversion?
14 (a) Where it is shown that the possessor did not withhold possession from the rightful possessor. (b) Where a plaintiff has either no possession or insufficient possession over the goods. (c) Contributory negligence (but only in actions against a collecting bank). (d) Where goods are properly deposited with a defendant, e.g. a warehouseman.	15 Now try some of the written questions in Appendix 1.

24 Nuisance

24.1 Types of nuisance

There are two kinds of nuisance: private nuisance and public nuisance. Private nuisance affects only a particular individual, or group, whereas public nuisance affects the general public. Public nuisance is generally a crime, and not a tort, but it may be a tort in certain circumstances, as explained in Section 24.3 below.

24.2 Private nuisance

Private nuisance is an unlawful act or omission which interferes with a man's use of his property or affects his health, comfort or convenience. Any unreasonable interference with a person's use or enjoyment of his property or any unreasonable interference which causes injuries to one's servitudes or easements (e.g. right of way, rights to light, rights to support of walls, etc.) constitutes nuisance.

In the vast majority of cases private nuisances are interferences by owners or occupiers of property with the use and enjoyment of the property in the vicinity. The tort of nuisance is based on the principle of live and let live, i.e. one should use and enjoy one's property in such a way as not to cause harm to one's neighbours. Unlike trespass, nuisance is not actionable *per se* and hence to succeed a plaintiff must show that harm has resulted to him as a result of the nuisance.

The following points are relevant when considering a nuisance:

(a) Unreasonable interference

There must be an unreasonable and substantial interference for an act or omission to constitute a nuisance.

Manchester Corporation v. Farnworth (1930)
Poisonous fumes were emitted from the chimneys of a generating station which was erected by the Corporation. **Held**: Since all reasonable steps had not been taken to prevent the nuisance, the Corporation was liable.

Heath v. Brighton Corporation (1908)
The incumbent and trustees of a church had alleged nuisance in the form of noise from the defendants' electricity works. The noise was not excessive. The congregation had not decreased and neither had the congregation complained. **Held**: in the absence of a sufficiently serious annoyance, the plaintiffs would be refused an injunction.

(b) Varying standards of comfort	The standard of comfort is a variable one. Account is taken of the fact that life in Mayfair, for example, is quiet and peaceful whereas life in, say, Whitechapel may be noisy and bustling. So what may constitute nuisance in Mayfair may not necessarily be considered nuisance in Whitechapel. The only exception to this is interference caused to light. Where actual damage to property is caused as a result of nuisance the question of the area where the property is situated is immaterial.
(c) Indirect injury	It is not necessary to show direct injury to one's health; it is enough that one has been prevented from enjoying the ordinary comforts of life.
(d) Abnormal sensitivity	The abnormal sensitivity of a person or property is not taken into consideration in deciding whether an act or omission is a nuisance:

> ### Robinson v. Kilvert (1989)
> The plaintiff's unusually sensitive paper was stored on the ground floor of the defendants' premises. The defendants were makers of paper boxes and they used a boiler for their purposes in the basement. This resulted in harm to the plaintiff's sensitive paper although in the circumstances no adverse effects would have resulted on any other kind of paper. **Held:** there was no nuisance. Lopes, LJ, said: 'A man who carries on an exceptionally delicate trade cannot complain because it is injured by his neighbour doing something lawful on his property, if it is something which would not injure anything but an exceptionally delicate trade.'

(e) Forms of nuisance	Nuisance can take various forms and may include such things as fumes, smoke, dirt, damp, vibrations, noise, smell, a circus performance, church bell-ringing, use of radios, projecting tree roots or branches on neighbours' land, destructive animals and many others.
(f) Essential activities for the community	Some activities are necessary and useful for the community – e.g. pigsties, quarries, breweries, takeaway food shops – but these activities can still constitute a nuisance if they cause serious or appreciable discomfort to a plaintiff.

> ### Adams v. Ursell (1913)
> The defendant's fried-fish shop allegedly caused odour and vapour to the plaintiff who had a house next to the shop. **Held:** an injunction would be granted to the plaintiff despite the fact that the shop served a working-class area.

This does not mean that a fried fish shop that is a nuisance in one place will be a nuisance in another. Each case is judged on its merits and account is taken of all the circumstances.

(g) Malice

Sometimes malice (i.e. evil motive) may be important in showing whether or not the defendant was acting reasonably and lawfully:

> **Hollywood Silver Fox Farm Ltd v. Emmett (1936)**
> The defendant deliberately and maliciously fired guns on his land to frighten the plaintiff's breeding vixen. **Held**: the defendant was liable in nuisance and damages plus an injunction were granted.

(h) Multiple wrongdoers

Where a nuisance is caused by the acts or omissions of several wrongdoers, a plaintiff may sue them either jointly or he may sue one of the wrongdoers. If the plaintiff sues one of them, the latter has a right to contribution from the other wrongdoers for any damages awarded to the plaintiff.

(i) Instantaneous acts

It is not necessary that the act complained of as nuisance be a continuous one. It may be an instantaneous one, e.g. an explosion (*British Celanese v. Hunt (1969)*). An isolated act cannot constitute nuisance (*Bolton v. Stone (1951)*). Where an act is a temporary one the court may not grant an injunction and award damages only.

(j) Prescription

A person may acquire a right to commit a private nuisance, through **prescription**, i.e. through 20 years' continuous operation since the act complained of first began and first constituted a nuisance. This defence is not available in respect of an act or omission constituting a crime and no length of time can legitimize a crime.

(k) Harassment

The increasing sensitivity of public opinion to the fact of harassment in modern society has revealed a weakness in the law – no authority in English law has yet recognized harassment as a tort actionable in its own right. The facts of *Khorasandjian v. Bush, 1993* illustrate the problem. K was a young lady of 15 who formed an acquaintanceship with B, a young man of 20. The friendship did not last long because of B's odd behaviour and K sought to end the friendship. B then threatened suicide, assaulted the plaintiff and made her life a misery by endless telephone calls to her parents' house where she lived. The plaintiff, who was not married to the defendant, and had never cohabited with him, was not able to seek a remedy under the *Domestic Violence and Matrimonial Proceedings Act, 1976* which only applies to married couples or cohabiting partners. She therefore had to look for redress at common law. A judge granted her an injunction restraining the defendant from 'using violence, harassing, pestering or communicating with her'. The defendant appealed, saying that the judge had no right to use such terms, since harassment was not a form of tortious conduct known to English law.

Could harassment be 'nuisance'? It has been clearly laid down that nuisance is a tort that applies to interests in land, and K did not have any freehold or leasehold interest in her father's house, though her father did. Dillon, LJ, argued that the law of nuisance must move with the times, and recognize that children residing with their parents who were suffering a nuisance should be able to sue.

However nuisance also requires proof of damage. If the law of nuisance is to be extended to allow such actions, is it necessary to wait until some actual damage – for example psychological damage causing ill health – has occurred? Dillon, LJ, argued that since there was a great likelihood that persistent misbehaviour would have this effect eventually, there was no need to wait – the persistent phone calls were enough and an injunction could be granted. He also finally drew attention to Section 37(i) of the *Supreme Courts Act, 1981* which says that the court has the power to grant relief by an injunction on 'such terms and conditions as the court thinks fit'. This does not mean that harassment has actually been recognized as a tort that is actionable in its own right – but it does seem to hint that it is time Parliament made it one.

24.2.1 Parties to an action for nuisance

Although usually it is the occupant of the property affected by a nuisance who has a right to sue (*Malone v. Laskey (1907)*), in some cases a landlord may sue where permanent injury to his property has been or will be caused. As regards the person to be sued, it is normally the person who has created the nuisance even if he has vacated the land. Other persons who may be sued, depending on the circumstances, are:

- A person in possession may be sued unless the nuisance was caused by an independent contractor, a trespasser or where the nuisance existed before the occupier acquired the property. However, the person in possession may be sued despite the fact that the work has been given to an independent contractor if the work necessitates special precautions by the occupier (*Bower v. Peate (1876)*). Similarly, an occupier is liable if he adopts the nuisance committed by a trespasser (*Sedleigh-Denfield v. O'Callaghan (1940)*).
- In a landlord/tenant relationship, the general rule is that the tenant as occupier is liable for any nuisance but the landlord will be liable where:
  – he knew or ought to have known of the nuisance before the tenancy;
  – he was covenanted to repair;
  – he has authorized the nuisance;
  – he has reserved the right to enter and repair.
- An occupier is responsible for nuisance created by his servants, agents or anyone under his control, e.g. family and guests.

24.2.2 Defences to an action for nuisance

The defences are as follows:

- Absolute statutory authority (see page 356).
- Inevitable accident (*Esso Petroleum Co. Ltd v. Southport Corporation (1956)* – see page 355).
- Act of God (see page 357).
- Contributory negligence (see page 378).
- Prescription: a private nuisance is legal after 20 years from the time when the plaintiff becomes aware of it.
- Commission of a nuisance may be in the public interest. There are, however, two conflicting Court of Appeal decisions on this point. In *Miller v. Jackson (1977)*, where cricket balls had hit the adjoining premises, it was held that an injunction would be refused and damages awarded. Public interest prevailed over the hardship of a few householders. However, in *Kennaway v. Thompson (1980)* the court refused to

follow the above case, holding that it was wrong to allow continuance of a nuisance merely because the wrongdoer is able and willing to pay for any resulting harm.

24.2.3 Ineffectual defences

These may be listed as follows:

- If a nuisance injures a particular plaintiff it is no defence that the activity benefits the public generally (*Adams v. Ursell (1913)*, see page 401).
- It is no defence that the defendant used all reasonable care and skill to prevent harm to the plaintiff (*Rapier v. London Tramways, 1983*).
- It is no defence that the plaintiff came to the nuisance:

> **Bliss v. Hall (1838)**
>
> The defendant was a candle-maker and the plaintiff had moved into the adjoining premises. The plaintiff complained that the chandlery emitted noxious vapours and smells and brought an action in nuisance. In defence, the defendant contended that he had been carrying on his business for three years before the plaintiff's arrival. **Held**: in the absence of a right by prescription, the defendants were liable.

- It is no defence to say that one is making a reasonable use of one's property (*A.G. v. Cole (1901)*), nor is it a defence that the place which gives rise to a nuisance is a suitable one for carrying out the activities complained of.

24.2.4 Remedies

Apart from damages and injunction (see pages 360–3) abatement is an important remedy. Through a process of 'self-help' the cause of the nuisance may be removed, e.g. projecting roots and branches from a neighbour's tree may be cut off (*Lemmon v. Webb (1894)*), but they remain at all times the property of the owner of the tree (*Mills v. Brooker (1919)*). Entry into another's land or infringement of another's rights are not permitted. Notice to the occupier of the land where the nuisance arises must be given except in cases of emergency or where it is possible to remove the nuisance without entry.

24.3 Public nuisance

Public nuisance is an unlawful act or omission which interferes or endangers the lives, comfort, property or common rights of the public generally or 'any nuisance which materially affects the reasonable comfort and convenience of life of a class of Her Majesty's subjects …' (*per* Romer, LJ, in *Attorney General v. P.Y.A. Quarries Ltd (1957)*).

A nuisance is public only when the number of people affected is sufficiently large to constitute a class. This is a question of fact depending on the circumstances. In *R. v. Madden (1975)*, where only the police, the telephonist and a few security guards were aware of a telephone call about a bomb at a local steel plant which turned out to be a hoax, it was held that the offence of public nuisance had not been committed since not enough persons were affected. By contrast, when dust, vibration, stones and splinters from a quarry had caused discomfort to the neighbours, it was held a public nuisance had been committed (*A.G. v. P.Y.A. Quarries Ltd (1957)*).

A public nuisance is a crime and criminal proceedings can be taken by the Attorney-General on behalf of the public or by the police. A public nuisance may also be a tort and to prevent a multiplicity of actions, civil proceedings may be started only by a person who has suffered particular damage over and above that suffered by the public at large. In *Benjamin v. Storr (1874)*, where the defendant's horses and vans waiting outside the plaintiff's coffee-house while obstructing the highway at the same time also obstructed light to the plaintiff's shop-window and generated smell, it was held that since the plaintiff had suffered special damage he would succeed in tort.

24.3.1 Acts or omissions constituting public nuisance.

These can take various forms. Some of them are as follows:

- Obstruction of a highway (*A.G. v. Gastonia Coaches (1976)*).
- Dangerous premises (*Wringe v. Cohen (1940)*).
- Dangerous activities carried on or near the highway (*Castle v. St Augustine's Links (1922)*).
- Artificial projections on highways.
- Natural projections which obstruct a highway if the person responsible has known or ought to know that they are in dangerous condition (*Noble v. Harrison (1926)*).
- Keeping a brothel.
- Excessive emission of smoke, fumes or dirt from factories causing discomfort.
- Section 44 of the *Highways Act, 1959*, imposes an absolute duty on the highway authorities to maintain highways, and the *Highways Act, 1961*, by removing any immunity that these authorities may have enjoyed, renders them open to an action for breach of their statutory duty.

24.3.2 Statutory nuisances

There are statutes which forbid nuisances. Some of these are the *Public Health Act, 1936*, the *Clean Air Act, 1956*, the *Noise Abatement Act, 1960*, the *Control of Pollution Act, 1974* and the *Deposit of Poisonous Wastes Act, 1972*.

Test your knowledge

Answers	Questions
	1 What are the two types of nuisances?
1 Public nuisance and private nuisance.	2 What is a private nuisance?
2 Any unlawful act or omission that interferes with a person's use of his property or affects his health, comfort or convenience.	3 Outline the important factors when considering nuisance.

Answers	Questions
3 (a) There must be an unreasonable and substantial interference. (b) The standard of comfort varies from one locality to another. (c) Direct injury to one's health need not be shown. (d) Abnormal sensitivities of a person are not taken into consideration. (e) Essential activities for the community can constitute nuisance, e.g. quarries, breweries, fish-shops, etc. (f) The act constituting nuisance need not be a continuous one, e.g. an explosion. (g) Malice may be important in some cases. (h) A right to commit nuisance may be acquired through prescription.	4 What defences are available to an action for nuisance?
4 (a) Absolute statutory authority; (b) inevitable accident; (c) Act of God; (d) contributory negligence; (e) prescription; (f) public interest.	5 What remedies are available for nuisance?
5 (a) Damages; (b) injunction; (c) abatement.	6 What is abatement?
6 A person against whom nuisance is committed can remove the cause of the nuisance, e.g. any roots or branches projecting on to your land from a neighbour's land may be cut off.	7 What is a public nuisance?
7 An unlawful act or omission which interferes with or endangers the lives, comfort, property or common rights of the public generally or a class of Her Majesty's subjects.	8 What is the main difference between a private and a public nuisance?
8 A public nuisance is a crime and criminal proceedings can be commenced by the Attorney-General or the Crown Prosecution Service.	9 Give examples of public nuisances.

Answers	Questions
9 (a) Obstructing a highway; (b) dangerous premises; (c) dangerous activities on or near a highway; (d) artificial or natural projections on highways; (e) keeping a brothel; (f) excessive emission of smoke, fumes or dirt from factories.	10 What statutes forbid nuisances?
10 (a) *Public Health Act, 1936*; (b) *Clean Air Act, 1956*; (c) *Noise Abatement Act, 1960*; (d) *Control of Pollution Act, 1974*; (e) *Deposit of Poisonous Wastes Act, 1972*.	11 Now try some of the written questions in Appendix 1.

25 Defamation

25.1 What is defamation?

Defamation as a tort consists in the publication of a false statement made without lawful justification concerning a plaintiff's reputation.

According to Lord Atkins in *Sim v. Stretch* (*1936*), a statement is defamatory if the words in the statement 'tend to lower him in the estimation of right-thinking members of the society'. Hence a defamatory statement basically injures a plaintiff's reputation; it tends to make the right-thinking members of society shun or avoid the plaintiff. A statement capable of affecting a plaintiff's reputation would be one that imputed either criminality, dishonesty, immorality, insanity or certain diseases to the plaintiff; one that reflected adversely on the plaintiff's trade, business or profession; and, lastly, one that imputed that the plaintiff has been raped. Defamation is distinguished from mere vulgar abuse, which injures a man's dignity and not his reputation. In *Penfold v. Westcote* (*1806*) it was held that the words 'blackguard, rascal and scoundrel' were mere abuse.

25.2 Forms of defamation

Defamation can take the form of libel or slander. The differences between the two forms are as shown in Table 25.1

25.3 The standard of proof required

In a typical defamation case the function of the judge is to decide as a *matter of law* whether in the circumstances a reasonable man would take the view that the statement allegedly made by the defendant is capable of being defamatory. If a judge is not satisfied he can withhold the case from the jury, whose function is to decide, where a case is submitted to it, whether *on the facts disclosed* the statement is in fact defamatory (*Capital & Counties Bank Ltd v. George Henty & Sons* (*1882*)). For a successful claim in defamation a plaintiff must prove the points made in Sections (a)–(d).

(a) The statement was defamatory

In deciding this the intention of the defendant, although useful in mitigating damages, is not crucial, i.e. innocence is no defence. The test is: what meaning would be imputed by right-thinking members of society from the statement? It follows that a defamatory intention is not significant where others do not reasonably understand the defamatory meaning.

> **Byrne v. Deane (1937)**
>
> The plaintiff had alleged that a typewritten poem on the notice-board of a golf club was defamatory since it showed that he had been disloyal to his fellow members. Earlier the plaintiff had reported to the police that gambling machines were kept on the premises and these had to be removed. **Held**: the statement was not defamatory for although it may lower the plaintiff in the estimation of his fellow-members, right-thinking members would not think less of him because he helped in the process of law enforcement.

Table 25.1 The differences between libel and slander

Libel	Slander
• The defamatory statement is in permanent form, e.g. a written or printed statement, a film (*Yousoupoff v. MGM Pictures Ltd (1934)*), pictures, an effigy, a statue, a caricature, a record, or broadcasting on radio and television (*S.I. Defamation Act, 1952*) Under Section 4 of the *Theatres Act, 1968*, publication of words (including pictures, visual images and gestures) in the public performance of a play is treated as libel	• The statement lacks permanence and is in transitory form, e.g. speech or gesture (**note**: except for broadcast speech, and speech in the public performance of a play – see libel, opposite)
• It is actionable *per se*, without proof of any damage	• Proof of actual financial loss by the plaintiff is required except in cases where a plaintiff is imputed with any of the following: – Crime punishable by imprisonment; – Contagious or infectious disease, e.g. venereal disease, plague or leprosy; – Where the plaintiff is a female and unchastity or adultery are alleged (*Slander of Women Act 1891*) or lesbianism (*Kerr v. Kennedy (1942)*). – Unfitness as regards 'any office, profession, calling, trade or business held or carried on by him at the time of the publication' (*Defamation Act, 1952*)
• Can be a crime as well as a tort if it is a breach of the peace, e.g. sedition or obscene libel	• Can never be a crime

Sometimes words are used in a statement which may not appear at first sight to be defamatory but may carry hidden meaning or implications harmful to the plaintiff. In such a case, if a plaintiff shows that the words defame him by implication (**innuendo**) and that this is also the implication drawn by reasonable persons from the words, he will succeed.

Tolley v. Fry (1931)

The plaintiff, who was a leading amateur golfer, alleged that a published advertisement showing him playing golf with a bar of chocolate in his pocket carried the innuendo that for financial gains the plaintiff had prostituted his amateur golf status. **Held**: the defendants were liable and damages were awarded to the plaintiff.

Cassidy v. Daily Mirror (1929)

The *Daily Mirror* had published a photograph of a couple with a caption that their engagement had been announced. The plaintiff, Mrs C, who was the wife of the man Mr C in the photograph, alleged that the caption by innuendo imputed that Mrs C was 'living in sin' with Mr C. **Held**: the defendants were liable in damages although they had acted quite innocently.

Today the defence of unintentional defamation may be available to a newspaper under Section 4 of the *Defamation Act, 1952*.

(b) The statement referred to the plaintiff

It must be shown that the plaintiff as an individual has been indentified by reasonably-minded persons as being connected with the defamatory statement. It is no defence that the defendant never intended to refer to the plaintiff.

Hulton v. Jones (1910)

There appeared in a newspaper a humorous article describing the immoral life of a fictitious character by the name of Artemus Jones. There was in real life a person by the same name who was a barrister. Evidence was shown that those who knew the real Artemus Jones thought that the article referred to him. **Held**: the newspaper was liable in damages.

Whereas in the above case it was no defence for the newspaper to say they had not intended to refer to the plaintiff, in *Newstead v. London Express Newspaper Ltd (1940)* it was no defence to say that the words were true and intended to refer to a third party and not the plaintiff. It is not necessary that the plaintiff be named or described. Any pointer or indicator to the plaintiff in the statement is sufficient (*Morgan v. Odhams Press Ltd (1971)*).

There cannot be defamation of a class of persons, e.g. lawyers, priests, politicians, etc. However, where a particular ethnic or racial group has been defamed a criminal action may arise under the *Race Relations Act, 1976*

(c) The defamatory statement was published by the defendant

To constitute publication, the statement, whether oral or in writing, must be made known to at least one person other than the plaintiff. The following examples provide more information on published and unpublished statements:

- There is publication when an author of a letter reveals its contents to a secretary.

- When a postcard is sent through the post or a telegram is despatched or a document is printed, it is presumed that there is publication.
- The communication of a statement by a husband to his wife or vice versa about a third party does not constitute publication (*Wennhak v. Morgan (1888)*). However, a statement by a third party to a wife defaming her husband is a publication (*Wenman v. Ash (1853)*).
- Where a servant wrongfully opens his master's letter there is no publication (*Huth v. Huth (1915)*).
- A statement may be published by dictation to a secretary unless the communication is privileged (*Osborn v. Boulter (1930)*).
- There is no publication where a printer returns a defamatory manuscript which he has printed to its author (*Eglantine Inn Ltd v. Smith (1948)*).
- There may be publication when defamatory matter is written or posted on one's premises by an unknown person and the owner of the premises takes no steps to remove it, but the degree of difficulty in removing the offensive matter may be taken into account in mitigation (*Byrne v. Deane, 1937*).

Repetition and dissemination Every repetition of a defamatory statement is a new and distinct publication and hence gives rise to a new cause of action. Where a newspaper or a book is published, the proprietor, editor, publisher and printer may all be sued. However newsagents, booksellers, distributors and libraries are not liable if they are unaware of the defamatory statement and could not have reasonably found out about it; if they are negligent in not discovering the defamatory statement, they are liable (*Vizetelly v. Mudie's Select Library Ltd (1900)*).

(d) The plaintiff suffered damage as a consequence of the publication of the defamatory material

Proof of financial loss is required in respect of slander only, unless one of the four exceptions mentioned in Table 25.1 applies.

25.4 Defences to defamation

Apart from denying that the alleged matter is defamatory, or that there has been any publication, the defences outlined in Sections 25.4.1–25.4.5 are available where appropriate.

25.4.1 Justification

Where a statement is true both in substance and in fact, this is a good defence; small inaccuracies will not be allowed to defeat the defence. For example:

> **Alexander v. N.E. Railway Co. (1865)**
>
> The plaintiff had been convicted of an offence of travelling without paying his rail fare and was sentenced to a fine or two weeks' imprisonment. The rail company had published a poster in which the alternative sentence was given as three weeks. **Held**: the defence of justification was good and the minor inaccuracy about the sentence did not defeat the defence.

Two statutory provisions affecting this area are:

- Section 5 of the *Defamation Act, 1952*, provides that in an action for libel or slander concerning words which contain two or more distinct charges against the plaintiff, the defence of justification will not fail because the truth of every charge cannot be proved, if the charge that is found not to be true does not materially injure the plaintiff's reputation having regard to the true charges. For example, a person has been convicted of murder, or manslaughter, and he brings an action against someone who has called him a thief and a murderer. The action will not succeed since his reputation is hardly tarnished by being called a thief even if in reality he is not.
- Section 8 of the *Rehabilitation of Offenders Act, 1974*, provides that where a defendant maliciously publishes details of a 'spent conviction', the plaintiff may recover damages. Under the Act if a successful rehabilitation period of between five to ten years has elapsed since the conviction for a crime carrying a sentence of 30 months' maximum imprisonment, the convicted person is treated in law as if he had *not* been charged, prosecuted, convicted or sentenced.

25.4.2 Fair comment

This defence applies where the statement made is a fair comment, made in good faith and on a matter of public interest. The statement must be made without any malice or improper motive and the defendant must have honestly believed in its truthfulness. In addition, the statement must be a statement of opinion and not fact, and the facts relied on by the defendant must have existed at the time of the comment and not be facts which may have occurred some time before (*Cohen v. Daily Telegraph (1968)*).

What constitutes matters of public importance or interest is decided by a judge. The following areas would be included: operations of central government and public authorities, conduct of persons in public life, trade unions, the police, matters concerning broadcasting, television, books, plays (*London Artists Ltd v. Littler (1969)*), writing, painting, sculpture, music, etc. However, the private lives of persons involved in the above mentioned areas are excluded.

25.4.3 Privileges

On grounds of public policy and in order to preserve and protect the cherished right of freedom of speech, certain statements which may be defamatory are protected by the law. The public interest in free speech is allowed to override the private right or interest of a person whose reputation has been injured. The two classes of privileges are absolute privilege and qualified privilege:

(a) Absolute privilege

This is a complete defence and it does not matter whether a statement was false or actuated by malice. The following statements would enjoy absolute privilege:

- Anything said in the Houses of Parliament (*Bill of Rights, 1689*).
- Reports of parliamentary proceedings published by order of either House (e.g. Hansard) or any subsequent republication in full (*Parliamentary Papers Act, 1840*).
- Statements made by judges, advocates, jurors, witnesses or parties in the course of judicial proceedings, i.e. civil, criminal or military but not

administrative proceedings at a tribunal (*Royal Aquarium Society Ltd v. Parkinson (1892)*). The privilege extends to tribunals exercising a judicial function, e.g. the Disciplinary Committee of the Law Society (*Addis v. Crocker (1961)*).
- A statement made by one officer of state to another in the course of their official duty (*Chatterton v. Secretary of State for India (1895)*). Officers of state would include ministers, secretaries of state, senior officials communicating with a minister, High Commissioners reporting to the Prime Minister, and a military officer reporting to his superiors, but it is uncertain whether and how far this privilege would extend to those in subordinate ranks.
- Statements between husband and wife.
- Statements made between a client and his solicitor in the course of their professional relationship (*Watson v. McEwen (1905)*).

(b) Qualified privilege

This defence will succeed provided the person making the defamatory statement is not actuated by malice and honestly believes in its truth. Qualified privilege would be available on the following occasions:

- The person making the statement is under a legal or moral duty to communicate it to a person having a similar legitimate interest, e.g. testimonials or references to employers (*Jackson v. Hopperton (1864)*).
- Statements made as a consequence of protecting one's private interests (*Osborn v. Boulter (Thomas) and Sons (1930)*).
- Statements made to public authorities and professional bodies, e.g. a complaint to a local authority or police.
- Communication between a client and his solicitor in the course of their professional relationship. However, it seems that the relationship might also enjoy absolute privilege but this matter has not been absolutely settled (*Minter v. Priest (1930)*).
- Fair and accurate reporting of parliamentary or judicial proceedings. The privilege does not extend to tribunals where members of the public are not admitted, or to domestic tribunals.
- Section 7 of the *Defamation Act, 1952*, confers qualified privilege on fair and accurate reporting in newspapers (including monthly publications) or broadcasting of various matters of public interest and importance, e.g. reports of public meetings or meetings of public companies, public and local authorities, reports of public proceedings of colonial or dominion legislatures, the United Nations Organization, the International Court of Justice and the British Courts-martial.

25.4.4 Unintentional defamation

Section 4 of the *Defamation Act, 1952*, may be invoked by a defendant who alleges that the alleged statement was published innocently and makes an offer of amends. The following conditions of innocence must be satisfied:

- The defendant did not intend to publish the offending words and he was unaware of the circumstances whereby they might be taken to refer to the plaintiff.
- The defendant was unaware of the circumstances by which *prima facie* innocent words might be understood to refer to the plaintiff.
- The defendant exercised reasonable care in the publication.

A defendant relying on Section 4 must plead his offer of amends, submit an affadavit to establish his innocence, offer to publish a suitable correction and lastly take reasonable steps to notify recipients of the offending matter. If the defendant's offer of amends is accepted there will be no further legal proceedings and the court may make an order for the payment of costs and expenses. If, however, the offer is rejected it will be a good defence to prove that the publication was made innocently and that an offer was made without delay.

25.4.5 Apology

This defence is available under the *Libel Act, 1843*. A defendant can plead when sued for libel contained in a newspaper or other periodicals that:

- The publication was not actuated by malice or gross negligence.
- An apology was published at the earliest opportunity.
- A sum of money has been paid into the court.

25.5 Remedies for defamation

The main remedies available to a plaintiff are damages and injunction. As regards damages, a defendant can mitigate these by apology, proof of provocation by the plaintiff and by producing evidence of the plaintiff's bad reputation prior to the publication.

Damages in tort have been discussed earlier (see Section 20.5) but they present special problems in defamation cases, where it is common these days for the 'gutter press' deliberately to invent scurrilous stories about prominent people. Juries may feel the need to award punitive damages to show their contempt for the behaviour of the parties concerned. Addressing this problem in *Cassell v. Broome (1972)* Lord Hailsham said that juries should not be told what level of awards had been given in other cases, but should be given information which would help them appreciate the true value of an award – for example how much an award might earn if invested in a building society account.

The Court of Appeal will hesitate to interfere with the amount of an award unless it feels that the award made was such that no reasonable jury would have awarded that amount. One recent case where an award was reduced concerned the magazine *Private Eye*, which alleged that the wife of Peter Sutcliffe, the Yorkshire Ripper, had sold her story to a newspaper for a considerable sum. She was awarded £600 000 damages which was more than twice as much as the magazine had alleged she had received. This was punitive in the extreme, and the Court of Appeal reduced it to £60 000.

Test your knowledge

Answers	Questions
	1 What is defamation?
1 The publication of a false statement made without lawful justification about a plaintiff's reputation.	2 What forms can defamation take?
2 Libel or slander.	3 What is the essential difference between libel and slander?

Defamation

Answers	Questions
3 Libel is in permanent form, e.g. written statement, while slander is in transitory form, e.g. speech or gesture.	4 What points must a plaintiff prove to succeed in an action for defamation?
4 (a) The statement is defamatory; (b) the statement refers to him; (c) the statement was published; (d) the plaintiff suffered damage as a consequence.	5 Who may be sued if defamatory material is contained in a book?
5 A right to sue arises against the proprietor, editor, publisher and printer of the book.	6 What defences are available when it is alleged that a published statement is defamatory?
6 (a) Justification; (b) fair comment; (c) absolute privilege; (d) qualified privilege; (e) Section 4 of the *Defamation Act, 1952*, for unintentional defamation; (f) apology under the *Libel Act, 1843*.	7 On what occasions would a statement enjoy absolute privilege?
7 (a) Statements in the Houses of Parliament. (b) Reports of parliamentary proceedings. (c) Statements by judges, and other parties during judicial proceedings. (d) Statements made by one officer of state to another in the course of official duties. (e) Statements between husband and wife. (f) Statements between a client and his solicitor in their professional relationship.	8 What do you understand by the defence of justification in defamation?
8 Where a published statement is true in substance and fact, justification offers a good defence (*Alexander v. N.E. Railway Co.* (1865)).	9 Why is Section 8 of the *Rehabilitation of Offenders, 1974*, important?
9 If a defendant maliciously publishes details of a 'spent conviction', a plaintiff can recover damages.	10 What is meant by 'spent conviction' under Section 8 of the Act?

Answers	Questions
10 A sentence is considered spent where a person has undergone a rehabilitation period of between 5 to 10 years since being convicted of a crime carrying a maximum sentence of 30 months.	11 Explain the defence of fair comment.
11 A fair comment, made in good faith and honestly on a matter of public interest without any malice or improper motive.	12 What remedies are available for defamation?
12 Damages and injunction.	13 When will the court interfere with a jury's award of damages?
13 Only when it feels that the award is so extreme that no reasonable jury would have made such an award.	14 Now try some of the written questions in Appendix 1.

26 Miscellaneous torts

26.1 Introduction

Besides the torts already dealt with there are one or two other torts which may be important to businessmen. They may be described as economic torts, in that their effect is to harm the plaintiff economically. They may be listed as:

- Conspiracy.
- Deceit, or fraud.
- Malicious or injurious falsehood.

26.2 Conspiracy

This tort is committed when two or more persons intentionally and without lawful justification combine together to injure the plaintiff, or do unlawful acts that result in injury to the plaintiff. To succeed in an action the plaintiff must prove that the predominant purpose of the defendants was to combine together unlawfully to cause him economic damage. If, however, the defendants had combined together to further their own interests, e.g. to defend the interests of union members, and economic damage was a consequence, no action for conspiracy will succeed. In *Crofter Hand-Woven Harris Tweed Co. Ltd v. Veitch (1942)* it was held that the action of the members of a union to refuse to load cheaper tweed made from mainland yarn in order to protect the members' interests was not a conspiracy to inflict damage on the plaintiffs. If the overall objective of a combination is to put forward or defend the trade of those who enter into it then no wrong results despite damage to the plaintiff (*Sorrell v. Smith (1925)*).

26.3 Deceit or fraud
(for contractual misrepresentation see page 160)

This tort is committed when a person acts to his detriment relying on a fraudulent misrepresentation of another. The essential requirements of deceit are as follows:

- A false representation is made. This must be a statement of fact.
- The person making the representation knows it to be false or does not believe it to be true or is reckless about it, not caring whether it is true or false.
- The misrepresentation is intended to be acted upon.
- The person to whom the misrepresentation is made has acted upon it.

This tort has reduced in importance since recognition by the House of Lords of a duty of care for negligent misstatements in *Hedley Byrne & Co. Ltd v. Heller and Partners Ltd (1963)* – see page 376. In addition to recovering for financial loss, a plaintiff may recover for physical injury (*Burrows v. Rhodes (1899)*). As regards what constitutes false misrepresentation, Lord Herschell's definition of fraud in *Derry v. Peek (1889)* is important:

Fraud is proved when it is shown that a false representation has been made (1) knowingly, or (2) without belief in its truth, or (3) recklessly, careless whether it be true or false.

Hence it is not fraud if the person making the representation honestly believes it to be true.

The tort of deceit has sometimes been used to evade Section 4 of the *Statute of Frauds* (which requires guarantees to be evidenced in writing). By alleging that an oral representation about credit was made fraudulently, and suing in tort for deceit, the requirement about written evidence was evaded. Section 6 of Lord Tenterden's Act, the *Statute of Frauds Amendment Act, 1828*, prevents an action for deceit over a character reference designed to secure credit unless the fraudulent misrepresentation is in writing, signed by the person concerned.

26.4 Injurious falsehood

Whereas in deceit and defamation damage is done to a plaintiff's reputation, in injurious falsehood a tort is committed against the plaintiff's business interests. An injurious falsehood is a false statement, made maliciously about a plaintiff's business interests whereby other persons are deceived, thereby causing damage to the plaintiff. The word 'maliciously' means 'from an improper motive'. Types of injurious falsehoods are as follows:

(a) Slander of title and goods

This arises when doubts are cast through the action of the defendant on the plaintiff's title to real or personal property, patents and copyrights, or the quality of his goods or products (*Wren v. Weild (1869)*). According to Section 3 of the *Defamation Act, 1952*, no special damage need be proved by a plaintiff in an action for malicious falsehood. Puffs and mere sales talk in general terms, although untrue, may not be injurious falsehood, i.e. to say that your products are of a superior quality to those of your competitors. The test is that if a reasonable man takes a statement seriously it is slanderous (*De Beers Abrasive Products Ltd v. International Electric Co. of New York Ltd (1975)*).

(b) Slander of plaintiff's trade or business

It is actionable to imply in a newspaper or other published material that a plaintiff has gone out of business with the result that the plaintiff's trade suffers (*Ratcliffe v. Evans (1892)*).

(c) Passing-off

This consists of a deliberate act of the defendant to mislead others into believing that the defendant's goods are those of the plaintiff. In doing so the defendant takes an unfair advantage of the plaintiff's trade or business. The chief stages leading to an action for passing-off are as follows:

- There is a misrepresentation by a trader in the course of his marketing activities.
- Which will incline his prospective customers for goods or services.
- To select his terms or services instead of those of an established trader in such a way as to harm that trader's business or goodwill.
- And does in fact injure that business or goodwill, or will probably do so.

The tort may take the form of:

- A statement that the business or merchandise of the plaintiff is the defendant's.
- Marketing under the plaintiff's trade name (*Reddaway v. Banham (1896)*).
- Using the plaintiff's trade mark – especially unregistered trade marks, since statutory protection is given to registered trade marks under the *Trade Marks Act, 1938* and the *Trade Marks (Amendment) Act, 1984*.
- Imitating the presentation or appearance of the plaintiff's goods (*J. Bollinger v. Costa Brava Wine Co. Ltd (1960)*).

The remedies for torts of this kind are injunctions to restrain the falsehood or unfair practice and/or damages. Damages will reflect not only the economic loss (if any) suffered, but also compensation for loss of reputation and ill-will caused by the behaviour of the defendant in misleading potential customers.

In the case of *Bostik Limited v. Sellotape GB Ltd (1994)* the plaintiff sought an injunction to prevent Sellotape passing off its product Sello–Tak for Bostik's established product Blu-Tack, claiming that the product looked exactly the same. This was true when the two products were in use as a re-usable self-adhesive putty. The court considered that the time to view the 'passing-off' of a product was at the point of sale, where the public exercised choice between the two products. At this point the two packages looked very different, and no confusion could exist except by the use of the terms 'Tak' and 'Tack' in the name. There was no real confusion at the point of sale and the application was dismissed.

Test your knowledge

Answers		Questions	
		1	What is conspiracy?
1	It is where two parties conspire together to take actions which injure the plaintiff.	2	When is a combination of this sort not conspiracy?
2	When it is a combination to promote the interests of the combining parties rather than to injure the plaintiff.	3	What is a fraudulent misrepresentation?
3	A false representation knowingly or recklessly made by the defendant which the plaintiff was intended to act upon, and did act upon:	4	What is injurious falsehood?
4	A false statement, maliciously made, about a plaintiff's business interests which deceives others and consequently causes the plaintiff loss.	5	What are the chief types of injurious falsehood?

Answers	Questions
5 (a) Slander of title; (b) slander of goods; (c) slander of trade or business; (d) passing-off.	6 At what point should products be compared if passing-off is alleged?
6 The moment of sale is the moment when the passing-off would be considered – is the purchaser misled by similar appearance at the point of sale? (*Bostik Limited v. Sellotape GB Ltd* (1994)).	7 Go over the list again. Then try the written questions in Appendix 1.

Part Seven Business Property

27 The law of property

27.1 Ownership and possession

As far as English Law is concerned the concept of property is a relatively recent development, dating from the emergence of the capitalist system in the Industrial Revolution. Prior to that time (say, AD 1760) the rights of landowners were based on possession, and we commonly hear, even today, the expression 'Possession is nine tenths of the law'. The concept of ownership grew out of this earlier concept of possession and gradually extended to cover other types of property besides landed estates. Ownership has been defined as 'the entirety of the powers of use and disposal allowed by law (Pollock: *First Book of Jurisprudence*).

Property is anything that is capable of being privately owned by an individual (or other legal person). Such an owner has the legal right to deal with his property as he wishes, he may use it, alter it, sell it, give it away, destroy it, discard it or otherwise dispose of it subject only to such legal barriers as the law of nuisance, planning, litter, etc.

We may acquire ownership in three different ways: originally, derivatively or by succession.

(a) Original ownership

This may be ownership achieved by creating the thing in the first place, as where an artist paints a picture or a manufacturer produces a product. Original ownership may also be achieved by occupation; taking possession of land or goods not owned by anyone else, or abandoned by a previous owner. Finally original ownership can be achieved by accession, as where a mare has a foal, and the foal becomes the property of the mare's owner.

(b) Derivative ownership

This is ownership derived from the previous owner, either by purchase, or by gift or process of law – as where a bankrupt's property is sold, or where a prisoner's effects are forfeited and auctioned by order of the court.

(c) Ownership by succession

This is ownership achieved as the result of the death of the former owner. The new owner may be a beneficiary under a will, or a person entitled to claim in an intestacy (a death where the deceased left no will).

While ownership involves all the powers of use and disposal, possession is based upon fact. If A owns a motor car and allows his son B to tour the Lake District in it, B has possession of the car and exercises temporary control over it. If C steals the car he has of course no rights to ownership, but he is in possession, and may exercise the rights of possession to the exclusion of everyone else except the true owner and his son. A finder of goods may retain them against the claims of everyone except the true owner.

When we say that 'possession is nine tenths of the law' we recognize that the law gives the person in possession considerable credibility as far as ownership is concerned. Possession is *prima facie* evidence of ownership (though not conclusive evidence). Even wrongful possession of goods for six years, or land for twelve years, may defeat the rights of the previous owner and constitute the possessor the lawful owner.

27.2 Types of property

Property is of two kinds, real property and personal property. The term 'real' refers to land, and the two kinds of property are sometimes referred to as realty and personalty. The essential feature of real property is that in a dispute over it the law will restore the thing itself (in Latin *res*) to the true owner. This is true of landed property, but not of personal property where payment of a sufficient sum of money will almost always give sufficient satisfaction to the owner (though equity will sometimes order specific performance of a bargain). Real property is immovable; a particular part of the earth's surface or property actually fixed to a particular part of the earth's surface. Thus a piece of land or a house built upon a piece of land is real property. Today real property is called freehold property. Leasehold property, where the freeholder has granted a lease for a number of years to a leaseholder, is not real property in the true sense of the word, but a special type of chattel. Chattels are movable property, things that we own which are not fixed to a particular spot on the earth's surface. Leasehold property is a sort of halfway product – it is a right which can be exercised over a piece of land, but only for a short period (many leases are on a week-by-week basis). In classifying property leases are referred to as **chattels real**, to distinguish them from all other types of chattel, which are called **chattels personal**.

The chart shown in Figure 27.1 shows the various types of property. Note that chattels personal are divided into two classes, **choses in possession** and **choses in action**. 'Choses' is just the old Norman French word for 'things'. Things in possession are items of personal property that we physically possess, such as a student's clothes, books, writing materials, personal transport, etc. Things in action are rights which we can exert by legal action in the courts (though the threat of such action is enough in most cases to persuade the parties concerned to recognize our rights). Thus debts, bills of exchange, cheques and patent rights will usually be honoured without legal enforcement being necessary.

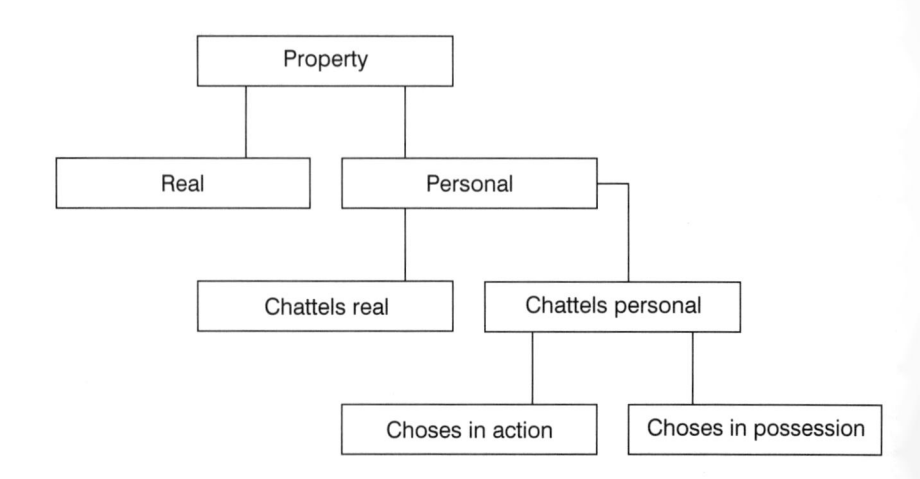

Figure 27.1 Types of property

27.3
Rights over land

Land law in the United Kingdom developed from the feudal system imposed by William the Conqueror, in which he seized all the land and portioned it out to his nobles who held it as his vassals. They in turn subinfeudated it to lesser men who owed them loyalty in return. It gave a strong, centralized form of government which lasted for several centuries but was eventually eroded so that private ownership of land became possible. After 850 years land law had become so excessively complicated – with so many people having such a variety of interests in any particular piece of land that some pieces of landed property could never be transferred. It was essential to sort the muddle out, and five Acts (loosely called by the general term – the Property Acts) were passed in 1925. They were:

- The *Law of Property Act, 1925*.
- The *Settled Land Act, 1925*.
- The *Administration of Estates Act, 1925*.
- The *Land Charges Act, 1925*.
- The *Land Registration Act, 1925*.

There is no need in *Business Law* to go into the many old wrongs which these five Acts put right, or to detail their many provisions for cutting the numerous Gordian knots that had been tied in almost a thousand years of legal and Chancery Court proceedings. The final result was this; the only two legal estates that could exist after 1925 were freehold estates and leasehold estates. An estate is a right in relation to land. It need not be extensive parkland like a stately home – a council tenant has only a small right in relation to land, but it is an 'estate' nevertheless.

A freehold estate is a 'fee simple absolute in possession'. The phrase means:

- A *fee*: a right to the land which may be passed on to one's heirs.
- *Simple*: it may be passed on to the general heirs and is not entailed – i.e. bound to pass to any particular person – like the eldest son.
- *Absolute*: there is no time limit on the right – it continues forever.
- *In possession*: the estate holder is entitled to immediate possession (though he may let someone else live there and just take the rents and profits to signify 'possession' of the property).

The freeholder is therefore the owner of the property – the rights extend down to the centre of the earth and up to the sky – though practical considerations mean that aircraft may fly over and occasionally an Act of Parliament will give authority to someone to tunnel under land or lay pipelines etc. Such matters aside, the freeholder is free to use his land as he likes subject to by-laws, laws of nuisance, planning, etc.

A leasehold estate is called 'a term of years absolute'. It is grant by a freeholder (the landlord) to a tenant (the leaseholder) of exclusive possession of the property leased for a stated period. The term of years includes fractions of a year, so that weekly, monthly and quarterly tenancies are possible (periodic tenancies) but long leases of 99 years and 999 years are also common. We can also have tenancies at will and tenancies at sufferance.

Besides these legal estates in land, freehold and leasehold, there are a number of interests or charges over land which can be created and conveyed at law. They are:

- An easement, right or privilege attaching to the land and enduring as long as the freehold (for ever) or the lease (the term of years agreed). Such an

easement could be a right of way to one tenement (the dominant tenement) across another piece of land (the servient tenement). A right of support, and a right to light are similar easements. Similar to an easement are profits a prendre (the right to take something that is growing or a natural product of the land e.g. fishing rights, turf cutting, firewood, etc.).
- A rentcharge – a right entitling the owner to a sum of money payable periodically.
- A mortgage – which prevents the sale of the property until such time as a loan of money has been repaid.
- A land tax created by statute.
- A right of entry in respect of a lease (for the purpose of inspecting the upkeep of the property).

These are the only interests which the *law* will recognize – the only legal interests – but *equity* may recognize other interests (called equitable interests). Thus the deposit of deeds with a bank as security for a loan gives the bank an equitable interest in the property, but not a legal interest.

Business premises Although the purchase of business premises involves many problems, of site selection, suitability, change of use, etc., the legal problems associated with the property itself have special importance. They will either involve the purchase of a freehold property, or the purchase of a lease. These are difficult matters and require professional guidance and assistance not only in the actual purchase but in the general field of legal obligations.

27.4 The purchase and sale of landed property

There are two elements in the purchase of landed property, the contract of sale and the delivery of the land and the transfer of title to it. As far as the contract of sale is concerned the usual rules of contract apply. The parties must have capacity to contract, there must be an offer to sell, an agreement about the price, etc., and an unconditional acceptance of the offer. It is usual for a short time for the initial acceptance to be 'subject to contract', in other words a conditional acceptance, subject to a detailed contract being drawn up by the solicitors of the parties. There is no agreement at this stage, until the contracts are exchanged between the solicitors, when the contract becomes a binding contract. Under Section: 40 of the *Law of Property Act, 1925*, contracts for the sale of land had to be evidenced in writing. Either a written contract or a memorandum or note was required. It did not matter if all the relevant information was spread over more than one paper or document – in other words joinder of documents was permitted. However, the *Law of Property (Miscellaneous Provisions) Act, 1989* which came into force on 27 September 1989 has now repealed Section 40 of the *Law of Property Act, 1925* and replaced it with Section 2. This section provides that all contracts for the sale of estates or interests in land must be in writing and incorporate all the agreed terms in one document. The alternative evidence in writing, i.e. a memorandum or a note, has been dispensed with.

The stages of the purchase of landed property are therefore as follows:

- The agreement, subject to contract, after inspection of the property and a certain amount of haggling over price.
- The preparation of the contract by the parties' solicitors.
- The exchange of contracts between the solicitors, at which point the purchaser pays a deposit – usually 10 per cent.

- Delivery by the vendor's solicitors of an 'abstract of title'.
- Comparison of this abstract of title with the deeds to the property, by the purchaser's solicitor. This may require the purchaser's solicitor to deliver sets of questions to the vendor's solicitor on any points that are not clear.
- Searches by the purchaser's solicitor at the Land Registry and with the local authority to discover any encumbrances or restrictions on the use of the property which may affect the purchaser.
- Preparation of a conveyance and its completion by signature and delivery. This usually takes place at the vendor's solicitor's office, the purchaser's solicitor paying the balance of the price and receiving in exchange the conveyance and the deeds. The purchaser is then entitled to immediate possession of the property.

As mentioned above the *Law of Property (Miscellaneous Provisions) Act, 1989* has also introduced new rules about the form of, and execution of, deeds (see Section 1 of the Act and Section 36A of the *Companies Act, 1985*, as inserted by Section 130(2) of the *Companies Act, 1989*). This has presented a particular difficulty to the Land Registry, because where land is registered it is essential to establish before registration that the documents provided do constitute valid deeds. Under Section 1 of the Act the requirements for a document to be a deed are:

- that it is in writing,
- that it includes on its face a clear intention by the person making it to create a deed, and
- that it must be executed as a deed.

As regards the second point above the inclusion of some such words as 'executed as a deed' or 'signed as a deed' would be a suitable declaration. Alternatively to declare that the document is a type of instrument which must by law be a deed, such is 'this legal mortgage' or 'this conveyance', would also be adequate proof of intention.

As regards the third point above an individual who desires to execute a document as a deed must sign it in the presence of one witness, who also signs and inserts his/her name on the deed. A deed which is signed by another person authorized to sign on behalf of the true executor must be signed in the presence of two witnesses who must both sign to attest the signature and append their names and addresses. Since these deeds which are executed under powers of attorney are only valid if the power of attorney itself is valid the person registering the deed must also submit either the original power of attorney or a certified copy of it signed on every page by a solicitor to attest that it is a complete copy.

There are numerous other points about the registration of land which are too detailed to give in the present volume, but the Land Registry supplies a Practice Leaflet which should be referred to whenever documents are submitted for land registration purchases.

The directors and secretaries of companies should study Section 130(2) of the *Companies Act, 1989* and comply with its requirements about deeds.

27.5 Acquiring leasehold premises

The procedure for acquiring leasehold premises is in many ways similar to the procedure already described if the lease is for more than three years and therefore has been created by deed. Once again professional advice is desirable since the terms of a lease can be onerous if not properly discussed by a knowledgeable legal representative. There will usually be a number of express convenants about taking the premises in their existing state, undertaking to pay rent and service charges agreed, to pay the rates and taxes, to repair as necessary and premit inspection of the premises at reasonable hours, to insure against fire, etc. There is often a stipulation that the lessee may not assign or underlet without consent, and that the landlord's permission must be sought for any change of use.

In return the lessee gets quiet enjoyment of the premises, and the lessor must not derogate from his grant (i.e. he must not do anything which renders the property unsuitable for the purpose for which it was leased – for example use adjoining property in such a way as to spoil the lessee's quiet enjoyment of the property).

Where an existing lease is being assigned by an existing leaseholder it is essential to check that the business the purchaser proposes to engage in does not constitute a change of use, or that the landlord has given permission for any proposed change of use before the agreement goes beyond the 'subject to contract' stage. This 'change of use' must also be the subject of a planning application to the local authority. The assignee is bound to observe all the convenants binding on the assignor.

27.6 Restrictive covenants

A restrictive covenant is one which restricts the use of freehold land by agreement with the original developer, but which can be enforced against future assignees even though they were not party to the original contract. The case for such enforcement is that a person who enters into an agreement knowing that an earlier party had rights under it ought not in equity, to disregard those rights but is in conscience bound to observe them. In *Tulk v. Moxhay (1848)* land sold by Tulk to a purchaser who agreed not to build on it was later sold to Moxhay at a cheap price because of the restrictive covenant, which he promptly disregarded; he started to use the land for building purposes. The site happened to be the centre of Leicester Square in London. Moxhay was held to be bound by the covenant. Under the *Land Charges Act, 1925*, all restrictive covenants entered into after 1 January 1926 are registerable as land charges. As such they become matters of public record of which everyone is deemed in law to have notice so that a purchaser cannot claim that he bought the property without notice of the restrictive covenant.

27.7 Mortgages

When money is borrowed it is usual to give some sort of security, as for example when a pawnbroker agrees to advance £20 against the 'pledge' of a gold watch. When the £20 is returned with interest the watch will be restored to its owner. When we wish to 'pledge' our landed property it is not so easy for we cannot physically deliver it to the pawnbroker nor move out of it with any convenience. The ancient solution was to provide a mortgage (a dead pledge in Norman French) by which the property was conveyed to the mortgagee on a promise of re-conveyance when the loan was repaid with interest. Failure to repay meant that the land was forfeit and the loan was still repayable with interest. The resultant hardship can be imagined, and Chancery Court devised various equity rulings to reduce it.

Today there are two forms of mortgage, legal mortgages and equitable mortgages. In both cases the mortgagee (who is the person making the loan) acquires an interest in the property but not an estate. The legal mortgage gives a *legal* interest which the courts will recognize; the equitable mortgage gives an equitable interest, which will be recognized by the courts in equity.

Legal interests are rights *in rem*, i.e. they are against the land itself and hence are enforceable against the whole world. Equitable interest are rights *in personam* and are therefore enforceable against those who are aware of them but not against a *bona fide* purchaser for value who has no notice of them. The usual remedy of the mortgagee in the event of non-payment is the sale of the property, out of which the loan with interest is redeemed, the expenses of the sale are paid and the balance (if any) is paid over to the mortgagor.

27.7.1 The Property Misdescriptions Act, 1991

This Act sought to reduce the deceptions practised in estate agency and property development by the use of misleading descriptions. It declares the use of false and misleading statements to be an offence by the person carrying on the business, and by any employee where the statement is due to the act or default of an employee.

There is a *defence of due diligence* available to an accused who can show that he took all reasonable steps to avoid committing the offence. It is not a defence to say the offending statement was based on another person's information, unless due diligence can be shown in checking out the statements made.

Enforcement of the Act and of any Order made by the Secretary of State in furtherance of the act is given to the local Weights and Measures Authorities in Great Britain and to the Department of Economic Development in Northern Ireland.

27.8 Patents, trade marks and copyrights

The law gives protection to those who make new inventions, create original works or develop business activities which are unique in some way. Thus inventions may be patented, trade marks and service marks may be registered, designs may be registered and original writing is copyright from the moment pen is put to paper. The following points are of interest:

27.8.1 Patents

Patents may be registered on application to the Patent Office by the inventor, or his employer if the invention was the result of the inventor's employment. Such an invention belongs to the employer, but the *Patents Act, 1977* gives a statutory right to employees to participate in an award scheme; the award being a fair share in the proceeds to the employer. A clause in the employee's contract of employment seeking to reduce the employee's right is void under the Act. After an administrative procedure involving the filing of a **complete specification** and **claims to originality**, the testing of the claims for novelty and inventiveness and the publication of the specification, **letters patent** are issued, and infringement of them gives a right to sue.

27.8.2 Trade marks and service marks

Under the *Trade Marks Act, 1938* and the *Trade Mark (Amendment) Act, 1984* both trade marks and service marks may be registered at the Patent Office, Concept House, Cardiff Rd. Newport, Gwent NP9 1RH (Tel. 01633 814 000).

The word 'mark' includes a device, brand, heading, label, ticket, name, signature, word, letter, numeral or any combination thereof.

The procedures are not involved, and there is a Trade Mark Protection Society at Celcon House, 289–293 High Holborn, London WC1V 7HV

(Tel. 0171 405 2174) which is prepared to offer a professional service to those wishing to register marks. They also have a Liverpool Office at Coopers Buildings, Church Street, Liverpool L1 3AB (Tel: 0151 709 3172).

There is a trade and professional organization for those active in the trade mark registration field called the Institute of Trade Mark Agents, 4th Floor, Canterbury House, 2–6 Sydenham Road, Croydon CR0 9XE. The Institute is prepared to provide a list of firms dealing with trade marks, and also enrols student members from firms active in this area (Tel: 0181 686 2052).

When infringement of a registered mark occurs the owner of the registered mark is entitled to an injunction and to damages for loss of profits. An order for modification of any goods, publicity material etc., or if necessary for their destruction, may be made.

27.8.3 Copyright

The *Copyright, Designs and Patents Act, 1988* is a massive Act of Parliament which codifies and updates the law on all aspects of copyright, designs and patents. The Act defines a copyright as a right which subsists in original literary, dramatic, musical or artistic works, sound recordings, films, broadcasts or cable programmes and the typographical layout of published editions. The owner of the copyright has the exclusive right to copy the work, to issue copies to the public, to perform or show the work in public, to broadcast it, and to adapt it. Copyright is infringed by a person who does any of these things without a licence from the copyright owner. Copyright lasts until 70 years after the end of the calendar year in which the death of the 'author' who originated the work occurred. The period of 70 years harmonizes United Kingdom practice with other EU countries. After that time works enter the public domain.

There is no copyright in a title, or in a pseudonym, but an author who has written under a pseudonym in one journal may use it elsewhere provided no agreement has been made to the contrary.

No formalities have to be observed in countries where the Berne Copyright Convention applies, and copyright exists immediately a work is written.

An author also acquires certain moral rights under the Act. These are:

- *The right of paternity.* This is a right to be identified whenever the work is published, performed or broadcast.
- *The right of integrity.* This is a right to object to 'derogatory' treatment of the work, for example its distortion or mutilation in such a way as to be prejudicial to the honour or reputation of the author.
- *The right not to have other work falsely attributed to the author.*

Test your knowledge

Answers	Questions
	1 What is ownership?
1 It is the entirety of the powers of use and disposal allowed by law.	2 How may ownership be acquired?

Answers	Questions
2 Either originally, or it may be derived from a previous owner by gift, or purchase, or by succession on the death of the previous owner.	3 What is possession based upon?
3 It is based upon fact. The one in possession, and with the intention to exercise control over the property to the exclusion of others has a powerful right recognized by law.	4 What are the two types of property?
4 Realty and personalty. Realty is freehold property. Personalty is chattels, either chattels real or chattels personal.	5 What are chattels real?
5 Leases, which give control over land for a stated period of time.	6 What are chattels personal?
6 They may be *choses in possession* (personal belongings of all types) or *choses in action* (rights enforceable at law, such as patents, debts, bills of exchange and copyrights).	7 What are the two legal estates in land?
7 (a) Freehold and (b) leasehold	8 What is the full legal definition of these legal rights?
8 (b) Freehold land is a fee simple absolute in possession. (b) Leasehold land is 'a term of years absolute'.	9 Explain 'fee simple absolute in possession'.
9 It is a legal right which may be passed on to one's general heirs, for ever, and gives the freeholder immediate rights to possession of the property.	10 Explain 'term of years absolute'.

Answers	Questions
10 It is a grant of rights by a freeholder (the landlord) to a leaseholder (the tenant) of exclusive possession and quiet enjoyment for the period of time stated in the lease.	11 What other legal interests are there? (Interests that will be recognized by common law rather than in equity.)
11 Easements, profits à prendre, rent charges, mortgages, land taxes imposed by statute and rights of entry.	12 How is ownership of freehold land transferred?
12 By conveyance; the deeds are transferred with a legal document (the conveyance) detailing the contractual arrangements.	13 What exactly is a mortgage?
13 The word means a 'dead pledge', and it is a way of pledging a property, either freehold or leasehold, as security for a loan. A variety of rights are secured by the mortgagee but the usual right to be exercised in the event of non-payment is the sale of the property, the balance of the loan being redeemed out of the proceeds.	14 Go over the page again until you are quite sure of all the answers. Then try the written questions in Appendix 1.

Part Eight Consumer Protection

28 The law and consumer protection

28.1 Introduction

Consumer protection is as old as law itself, yet it is also the latest fad of legislators which is spawning not only frequent Acts of Parliament but a mass of delegated legislation. Almost every week there is some new statutory instrument (SI) seeking to control the sale of dangerous goods of one sort or another. From the medieval 'Assize of Bread and Ale' which in 1266 established a system for ensuring that weights and measures were not false and fraudulent, to the establishment of an Office of Fair Trading with a Director General of Fair Trading in 1973, consumer protection legislation has always been with us. It reflects the concern of administrators that the weak and vulnerable (the consumers) should not be held to ransom by the rich and powerful producers of goods and services.

Whether such legislation is always justified is debatable, but this is a political and economic controversy rather than a legal one. The law is simply the way control (once its desirability is established) is administered and enforced. A balance has to be struck between enterprise (and a fair reward for enterprise) and exploitation (where unfair trading creams off excess profits to monopolists and oligopolists). That some controls are necessary is clear – but excessive control can kill the goose that lays the golden eggs.

A brief account of the development of consumer protection law is helpful. From 1760 to 1895 the development of capitalist society in the United Kingdom took place in a highly competitive and largely uncontrolled way. Adam Smith's philosophy of *laissez-faire* (let things work themselves out) meant that free enterprise flourished, but high social costs were borne by the general public. Some of these included polluted atmosphere, disfigured countryside, etc., but a major disadvantage was adulterated food and poor quality goods. Cut-throat competition led to deterioration in quality.

In 1895 a chemist, Glyn Jones, who had a shop in the East End of London devised Resale Price Maintenance (RPM) as a way to prevent price cutting. He persuaded suppliers of chemists' sundries to put RPM clauses in their contracts of sale. It was made a major condition of the contracts that the goods should not be sold below the price laid down by the manufacturer, and retailers who were in breach of this contractual clause could be sued. The price had to be maintained at the 'fair' retail price.

In practice the manufacturers also developed the custom of refusing to supply anyone who cut their prices, so that he/she could not obtain replacements for the stock sold. It might be thought that there is little point in the manufacturers doing this, since it will make little difference to them whether their goods are sold at cut prices or not. In fact, it does affect them because retailers who are being forced to sell goods at cut prices owing to fierce competition soon turn on the manufacturer and insist that he cuts his profit margins too. If he then has to cut quality in order to make a living the public are not really benefiting from the cut price at all. Also there is a tendency for cut prices to force some retailers out of business, with a consequent reduction in the number of selling points for a manufacturers' goods, and a decline in convenience to the shopper.

For many years the manufacturers successfully defeated the attempts of some retailers to increase their share of any given market by cutting prices. From 1895 to 1948, in a period of stable money values, the general lack of prosperity kept profit margins and business activity down.

In 1948 the Royal Arsenal Cooperative Society opened the first specially designed self-service store in the UK. Customers selected the goods they required, took them to the cashier and paid for them, surrendering their ration coupons at the same time. This proved to be highly popular with busy workers, and highly profitable to the Cooperative Society, which made the full RPM profit on all goods sold. The retailing revolution had arrived. The idea was soon copied, in many ways more extensively, and more intensively, by free enterprise (non-cooperative) traders. They made fortunes, for price cutting was still forbidden, and it became obvious that the resale price maintenance system was a serious disadvantage to consumers, who would have preferred to shop at the newer, private-enterprise stores with cut prices at the point of sale rather than take a Cooperative dividend at six-monthly intervals.

In 1956 the Restrictive Trade Practices Act started to restrict the RPM system. Prices could only be maintained if the restrictive clauses were taken before a Restrictive Practices Court which would rule whether they were in the public interest. Thousands of products were set free from the RPM system and competition flourished.

In 1962 the Moloney Commission on the Protection of Consumers made 214 recommendations to protect the consumer, particularly in the fields of hire purchase, consumer credit, false trade descriptions, unfair trading practices, weights and measures, dangerous goods and many other areas. It has taken 25 years to bring all these under control, with major Acts such as the *Trade Descriptions Act, 1968*, the *Fair Trading Act, 1973*, the *Consumer Credit Act, 1974*, the *Consumer Protection Act, 1987*, and many other Acts.

Finally, European Community directives also have a part to play in bringing the United Kingdom arrangements on these matters into harmony with those of other member countries.

We must now consider the various Acts of Parliament that have implications for businesses supplying customers with goods and services. Some of the Acts listed below have been dealt with elsewhere, and need not be referred to here, other than to give the page references. The others have not been dealt with in chronological order but in order of importance since in some cases an Act has been introduced to bring a number of other earlier Acts into a major statute; the earlier Acts being repealed. The total list of measures includes the following:

- The *Trade Descriptions Act, 1968* (see Section 14.11).
- The *Unsolicited Goods and Services Acts, 1971 and 1975*.
- The *Fair Trading Act, 1973*.
- The *Consumer Credit Act, 1974*.
- The *Policyholders' Protection Act, 1975* (see Section 15.8).
- The *Unfair Contract Terms Act, 1977* (see Sections 9.5 and 14.7).
- The *Sale of Goods Act, 1979* (see Chapter 14).
- The *Estate Agents Act, 1979*.
- The *Supply of Goods and Services Act, 1982* (see Section 14.12).
- The *Insurance Companies Act, 1982* (see Section 15.9).
- The *Data Protection Act, 1984*.
- The *Weights and Measures Act, 1985*.
- The *Financial Services Act, 1986*.
- The *Consumer Protection Act, 1987*.
- The *Consumer Arbitration Agreements Act, 1988* (see Section 18.4).

28.2 The Consumer Protection Act, 1987

This Act implements a European Community Directive (No. 85/374/ EEC) dated 25 July 1985 which harmonizes the laws, regulations and administrative procedures of member states on matters protecting the consumer. In passing the Act, Parliament seized the opportunity to tidy up United Kingdom law on aspects of consumer safety and protection, repealing a number of earlier Acts.

There are three main streams of policy in this Act. They are:

- Liability for defective products.
- Consumer safety.
- Misleading price indications.

The necessary orders to bring these aspects of law into effect have been introduced, and these three aspects are now controlled as outlined in Sections 28.2.1–3.

28.2.1 Liability for defective products

The Act says that if a product sold to consumers causes damage, the person responsible for the damage is the producer of the product, or the importer who brought it into the member state. If a product has a brand name applied to it, even if the brand name is only an 'own-brand' name and it was actually produced by someone else, the brander is responsible, because the brand-owner has held himself/herself out as the producer. The supplier is not liable, but can become liable if they refuse to give the injured party the name of the producer, brander or importer. Premises are not products, and neither are unprocessed agricultural produce, but all other products, building materials, components, raw materials, semi-manufactures and manufactured goods are products under the Act.

The 'damage' referred to is death, personal injury or damage to property, including land. Damage to the item itself is not 'damage'. As the Act only protects consumers there is no liability for damage to property that is not for private use, occupation or consumption.

One very controversial part of this section of the Act, which some people believe the EC did not intend to include in the Directive, but which the Parliamentary draughtsmen incorporated into the bill and Parliament enacted, is a section which makes a new defence available to producers – the 'state of the art' defence. This may enable producers to escape liability for the damage done by claiming that the state of scientific and technical knowledge at the relevant time was such that the producer could not have been expected to discover the defect in the product while it was under development and in his/her control. This is clearly a very valuable defence, but it remains to be seen to what extent the courts will allow it to succeed.

Other defences are:

- The defect was not in the product at the time of supply (the purchaser or the retailer having handled it wrongly). Anyone who has tried to assemble some of the packaged furniture that is available today will know this is all too easy – especially with the poor instructions often available.
- The product was designed to the customer's specifications, and the fault is the result of defective specifications.
- The article was not the product of the producer, but a counterfeit product using substitute materials etc. and made by unskilled persons.
- The product was the result of compliance with the law. Presumably such a situation could arise, but the exact meaning is a little obscure.

There is a time limit on legal action or it will become statute barred. Action must be started within three years of the injury and within ten years of purchasing the product.

28.2.2 Consumer safety

The Act lays down a *general safety requirement*. It is an offence to supply consumer goods which fail to comply with this general safety requirement, defined as 'being reasonably safe', having regard to all the circumstances, and to whether they contain any defective substances, or infringe any regulations about goods of that class, or could have been made safer (at reasonable cost).

This is a very tentative safety requirement – one wonders how judges will be able to decide what 'reasonable cost' means for some of the complex equipment used in homes today – with every nursery having its electronic miracles. Clearly it is important that regulations for many household articles should be made without delay so that manufacturers know what standards of safety are required. Hence the plethora of statutory instruments appearing in the 'Consumer Protection' field.

The Act suggests certain actions by all firms, including:

- A regular review of company policy on product safety, including the review of management procedures at all stages of production to ensure the safety of the final product.
- Checking that any existing safety standards are being met, and taking action to meet any new proposals for safety requirements as they are promulgated.
- Consulting the British Standards document BS 5750 for an appropriate system of documentation and record keeping for product quality control. If necessary, consultancy advisory services should be used to obtain an objective view.
- Keeping records of all component failures and arranging contractual terms, when making contracts with suppliers, for the liability of the supplier if quality is not up to standard.

28.2.3 Misleading price indications

The Act makes it an offence to give misleading price information, by whatever means, to consumers. The rules apply to the sale of goods, the supply of services, the provision of accommodation or any facilities. There is a Code of Practice which guides suppliers. The chief point of this section of the Act is that it is an offence to give misleading price indications which assert that:

- the price is less than it really is;
- the price is independent of any other facts or circumstances when in fact it is not (thus to say that the rent of a room was £x but in fact lighting, heating etc. were extras might infringe the rules);
- the price will be reduced, or increased, or maintained when in fact it will not be;
- the facts the consumer is relying upon are not in fact what they purport to be.

The Code of Practice is widely available from local Trading Standards Offices (in some areas called Consumer Protection Offices) and students might do well to study the code to follow its full implications for traders.

There have been many successful prosecutions for misleading price indications, and many famous names have been forced to pay heavy fines. In one promotion MFI, a furniture supplier, claimed customers would make savings of up to 30 per cent, but the prices were no lower than ones it had been charging in various promotions over the previous six months. In one case the charge was £100 more than had previously been charged. They were fined £18 000 and costs.

An important rule here is the '28 day rule'. If a price tag says £50 off, it should mean £50 less than the price that has been charged in the same store for 28 consecutive days prior to the sale. If this is not true an offence has been committed.

Consumer Protection (Cancellation of Contracts concluded away from Business Premises) Regulations, 1987 This regulation reinforces the rules under the *Consumer Credit Act, 1974* about the so-called 'doorstep sales'. It provides for a seven-day cooling-off period during which consumers have the right to cancel a contract entered into during an unsolicited visit by a trader to their home or place of work.

28.3 The Consumer Credit Act, 1974

This Act was passed at a time when the whole consumer system was becoming more sophisticated with a wider and wider range of credit facilities being offered to simplify the provision of credit to ever-larger circles of consumers. The result was that the possibilities of abuse by credit-providers increased, and the chances of unsophisticated borrowers getting into financial difficulties also rose. The Act has been extremely effective in improving the behaviour of credit-providers and raising their professional standards, while at the same time avoiding too tight-fisted a regime in the provision of credit with all the frustrations that result when mature people are denied access to funds they require, and are capable of managing. It has taken years to achieve control of all the various types of credit, but the Act has now been fully implemented under the control of the Office of Fair Trading, whose Director General has seen the whole process through.

Under the Act a regulated agreement is required to comply with the style and content of the Act and any subsequent rules made by the Director General. A regulated agreement is one where a borrower is not an incorporated body (e.g. a company) but is an individual, sole trader, partnership, etc. and the total advance does not exceed £15 000, excluding any bank charges and interest.

There are about six types of credit which concern the Director General. Some of them are:

- *Running accounts credit*, such as bank overdrafts, credit card facilities, budget accounts and ordinary trade credit from business to business.
- *Fixed sum credit* where the sum borrowed is gradually repaid – for example personal loans from banks, hire purchase credit from finance houses, pledges with pawnbrokers and voucher trading by tally-men.
- *Restricted use credit* where the money is made available not to the borrower, but to the person supplying the borrower with goods. Examples are loans from finance houses for motor vehicles, store credit from department stores, etc.
- *Unrestricted use credit* – this may be in the form of a debtor–creditor arrangement without reference to the supplier of any goods or services, the debtor being free to spend the money in any way he/she likes. It may

be a three-way arrangement with the supplier involved as a matter of convenience not only to supply the goods but also to collect the repayments weekly or monthly as they fall due.

28.3.1 Duties of the Director General

Control has been established in the following ways:

- By licensing all credit outlets, so that the **credit-brokers** thus authorized to provide credit are people of good standing. Anyone who is operating in the credit supply field, from the largest bank to the part-time agent who introduces consumers to a source of funds must register (though the Director General may exercise discretion where the part played is relatively trivial).
- By the issue of regulations about the way in which credit is made available and the supervision of arrangements to ensure they do comply with the regulations.
- By drawing to the attention of ministers any developments in the credit field which may need to be brought under control.
- By disseminating information and advice to traders, credit brokers and the public at large.

28.3.2 Comparing credit sources – the annual percentage rate (APR)

The most far-reaching reform introduced by the Director General has been the concept of **annual percentage rate**, or **APR**; a term which has entered all our lives. By requiring all those who make credit available to quote the true annual percentage rate the consumer is able to see exactly how expensive the borrowing of money is. Whereas between 1760 and 1946 the cost of borrowing money was about 2½ per cent, rising to 5 per cent on the more risky transactions, today money rarely costs less than about 14 per cent and the vast majority of consumer credit is in the 20 per cent to 40 per cent region. Despite the fact that some of the price paid reflects inflation (borrowers are really paying back in money that is worth less than the money they borrowed) the fact remains that some interest rates are excessive. The wise consumer borrows from the source demanding the smallest APR.

It is an offence to trade without a licence, punishable by a fine, or imprisonment, or both. The unlicensed credit provider is also denied the legal right to enforce the contract for repayment of the money (unless the Director General permits).

Besides credit brokerage the Act also recognizes debt-adjusting, debt-counselling, debt-collecting and credit reference agencies as businesses which are subject to control. They all require a licence and unlicensed trading is an offence.

28.3.3 Advertising controls

All advertising must be fair and give a comprehensive account of the nature of the services available. It is an offence to publish a misleading advertisement. The *Control of Misleading Advertisement Regulations Act, 1988* enables the Director General of Fair Trading to seek a court injunction to prevent the publication of a misleading advertisement where the normal methods of control have failed, or where a matter is one of extreme urgency. It is an offence to send correspondence about credit availability to a minor, and cold-calling and canvassing is also forbidden. Credit must only be discussed with a consumer in the consumer's home if a prior request in writing has been made by the person visited.

A very important set of Trader Guidance Booklets was issued by the Office of Fair Trading in 1984, preparatory to the implementation of the remaining sections of the Act in May 1985. The four booklets cover:

- Cancellable agreements.
- Non-cancellable agreements.
- Hire agreements.
- Matters arising during the lifetime of an agreement.

They cannot be described fully in a book of this sort, but students with a particular interest in consumer law should obtain copies from their local Trading Standards Office or from the Consumer Affairs Division, Office of Fair Trading, Field House, Breams Buildings, London EC4 1PR (Tel: 0171 242 2858).

28.4 The Unsolicited Goods and Services Acts, 1971–5

These Acts entitle anyone who receives unsolicited goods to retain them as a free gift provided that he/she has kept them for six months so that the sender could retake possession of them if desired and that, not less than 30 days before the expiry of the period the recipient gave notice to the sender in writing by post of their whereabouts. The Act also makes it an offence to demand payment for unsolicited goods, or to claim payment for directory entries. The Secretary of State is also empowered to make regulations about the contents and form of notes of agreement, invoices and similar documents.

28.5 The Fair Trading Act, 1973

This Act established the post of Director General of Fair Trading and set up the Office of Fair Trading which has been so influential in securing closer control of many aspects of consumer affairs. In the wider field its influence in the field of competition law which, while not directly affecting consumers, is very important in keeping industry and commerce competitive, rather than monopolistic or oligopolistic. A 'monopoly' is defined as a situation where a single producer has more than 25 per cent of the trade in a particular sector of industry or commerce and the Director General may refer to the Monopolies and Mergers Commission any takeover bid or acquisition situation which he believes may exceed this 25 per cent limit. The Commission will then conduct an enquiry and rule whether the merger is in the public interest or not.

28.6 The Estate Agents Act, 1979

This Act, and the regulations which have been published as a result of the Act, protect the individual house buyer and seller from unsavoury practices in estate agency. They bring the establishment of estate agent business under the general control of the Director General of Fair Trading who is empowered to make orders prohibiting unfit persons from doing estate agency work. Apart from persons who have been involved in fraud, dishonesty or violence, orders might be made against people who show discrimination in the course of estate agency work, or any other undesirable activity, prohibition of which has been laid down by statute. The Director General may issue 'warning orders'. The Act also lays down rules for handling clients' money and requires prior information to be given to buyers and sellers of the estate agent's scale of charges.

28.7 The Data Protection Act, 1984

The Act is designed to regulate records of personal data on living individuals kept by electronic methods on personal computers, word processors and mainframe computers. The Act imposes certain duties known as **data protection principles** on data users. These state that:

- information is to be obtained fairly and lawfully;
- the data must be accurate;
- the data must not be disclosed or used for any unauthorized purpose;
- the data must be kept secured and the individual concerned will have reasonable access to any personal information kept on him/her.

Data users are required to register on the Data Protection Register kept at the Data Protection Registry. Any data user who contravenes any of the basic duties will be removed from the Register and thereafter will not be allowed to keep any information on individuals on data banks. The Act exempts accounting records, matters concerning national security, payroll or pension records, sales and purchase of goods records, records concerning financial or management forecasts and (since 1987) personal data on persons held under the *Financial Services Act, 1986* by statutory bodies e.g. the Securities and Investment Board, whose function is to protect the public from dishonesty, incompetence and malpractice of those engaged in investment business (*Data Protection Order 1987*).

28.8 The Weights and Measures Act, 1985

This Act makes it an offence to fail to weigh the contents of a range of prepacked goods, or to fail to mark the weight on the packet or container. It is an offence to give short measure, or to use measuring equipment which has not been properly inspected and approved by an Inspector of Weights and Measures.

28.9 The Financial Services Act, 1986

Although the inclusion of this Act in a section on consumer law may appear to stretch the meaning of the word 'consumer' it is a fact that as far as financial services go there is a vast body of unsophisticated customers whose savings are at risk if the financial services industry is unprofessional in its approach towards them. While competition is *prima facie* desirable in this sort of business it does lend itself to abuse – particularly by 'insider dealing'. This is dealing where those who know of some impending change in a business are able to make profits or avoid losses by buying or selling shares before the general investing public know what is happening (see page 78). The Act is a long and complex one and too advanced for this book, but a few helpful ideas about it are worth mentioning at this stage.

(a) The regulation of investment business

Investment business is business concerned with shares, debentures, government and public securities, dividend warrants, units in collective investment schemes such as unit trusts, options, futures, long-term insurances having a surrender value, etc. Dealings in these assets by way of either buying, selling, underwriting, participating in their issue, managing portfolios or giving investment advice are all controlled under the Act. No person shall carry on such a business unless he/she is authorized to do so.

A Securities and Investment Board has been set up and some of the responsibilities of the Secretary of State have been delegated to the Board. Investment business can only be conducted provided an authorization has been obtained by direct application to the Board, or the financial consultant concerned is a member of one of the self-regulating organisations e.g. FIMBRA (The Financial Intermediaries, Managers and Brokers' Regulatory Organization) or LAUTRO (The Life Assurance and Unit Trust Regulatory Organization) etc. Some insurance companies, friendly societies, banks etc. are authorized, as are some professional bodies such as the Institute of Chartered Accountants, the Law Society and the Institute of Actuaries.

Foreign persons and corporations recognized in their own countries as competent to engage in investment activities are permitted to trade in the United Kingdom.

Certain bodies are exempt from the rules, for example the Bank of England, recognized investment exchanges and clearing houses and overseas investment exchanges. Bodies wishing to be recognised as exempt must apply to the Secretary of State.

(b) The conduct of investment business

It is an offence to make a statement, promise or forecast which is known to be misleading, false, or dishonestly conceals material facts. The Secretary of State may make rules about the extent of the financial resources required by investment businesses, and regulations about the notification to him of any events he deems important. He may also make rules about indemnity for any claims etc. He may also set up a compensation fund for compensating investors, and for the safe-keeping of clients' moneys. Unsolicited calls on customers about investments will be unenforceable in the courts and restrictions on advertising may be imposed. The Secretary of State has powers to intervene for the protection of investors and may restrict individuals from engaging in business or dealing in assets.

(c) The Financial Services Tribunal

This is a tribunal set up under the Act to whom people served with a notice under the Act may apply for review of the restriction imposed upon them. The Tribunal will hear the case and report back to the Secretary of State.

(d) Takeover offers

Schedule 12 of the Act is a detailed revision of the law on takeovers, to replace relevant sections of the *Companies Act, 1985*. It particularly refers to the rights of minority shareholders.

To conclude on consumer protection, the question arises how far should bureaucracy be allowed to grow in seeking to protect the consumer. It is becoming a fetish in our society that the consumer is so naïve, so unsophisticated and so helpless that he has to be protected by an army of guardian angels. Are we forgetting that the consumer has common sense too, and can often protect himself? Regulators are a fertile breed, and multiply at an alarming rate. They cast ever-widening nets, and in the end destroy confidence to such an extent that they make things worse. A blizzard of regulations may discourage inventiveness, experimentation and innovation to the detriment of our lifestyle.

Test your knowledge

Answers	Questions
	1 Why do we need consumer protection legislation?
1 Because consumers are more vulnerable than ordinary business people and may be persuaded to sign contracts unwisely, or may be over-charged or cheated by the sale to them of poor quality goods.	2 What are the chief areas where control is necessary?
2 (a) Consumer credit; (b) the sale of goods; (c) the marking and pricing of goods; (d) the field of financial services; (e) the trade descriptions area.	3 What measures have been introduced in the consumer credit field?
3 (a) The licensing of credit brokers; (b) the need to give the annual percentage rate (APR) on every credit transaction; (c) the control of advertising and doorstep sales; (d) the use of 'cooling-off periods' to enable consumers to cancel contracts made away from trade premises.	4 What are the chief areas covered by the *Consumer Protection Act, 1987*?
4 (a) Liability for defective products; (b) consumer safety; (c) misleading price indications.	5 Who is liable if a product causes injury or damage to persons or property?
5 (a) The producer; or (b) the importer; or (c) the brandowner who holds himself/herself out as being the producer.	6 What new defence does the Act give to those claimed to be liable for the defects?
6 The 'state of the art' defence which claims that in the light of what was known at the time the product was safe.	7 What is the requirement as far as consumer safety is concerned?

Answers	Questions
7 All goods must comply with the 'general safety requirement' which is defined as 'being reasonably safe', having regard to all the circumstances and to whether they contain any defective substances or infringe any regulations, or could have been made safer at reasonable cost.	8 What does the Act say about misleading price indications?
8 It is an offence to give misleading price information whether about the sale of goods, the supply of services, the provision of accommodation or the use of any facilities.	9 What is the law about unsolicited goods and services?
9 (a) It is an offence to demand payment for them; (b) it is an offence to demand payment for unsolicited directory entries; (c) the recipient may regard unsolicited goods as a free gift after giving notice to the owner and allowing six months' delay before using them.	10 What is the Director General's power with regard to estate agents?
10 (a) He may make orders prohibiting unfit persons from running estate agencies; (b) proper accounts must be kept for clients' moneys; (c) prior information about charges must be provided in advance of any contractual arrangement.	11 What sort of regime operates in the financial services industry?
11 Basically it is a self-regulating regime, with all members of the industry belonging to one or other of the professional bodies and liable to be disciplined for improper conduct.	12 Go over the questions again until you are sure of all the answers. Then try some of the written questions in Appendix 1.

Part Nine Employment Law

29 Employment law

29.1 The field of employment law

Employment law is a very wide field of business law and in a general book of this sort it is impossible to cover the various parts in any real depth. For those especially interested it is worthwhile subscribing to one of the popular handbooks which give monthly updates, such as *Croner's Reference Book for Employers*, or *Croner's Employment Law Guide*. There is also a Croner's Employment Law Line, which will answer particular enquiries on tricky points faced by subscribers. All these guides are available on annual subscriptions, and subscribers have confidence that they are always up-to-date in legal requirements.

Law impinges on employers in countless ways – there is hardly anything we do when employing people to work in our offices, factories and plants that has not its own specialist controls and regulations. The chief areas are regulations about manpower itself, health and safety at work, the payment of wages, industrial relations, pensions, social security and data protection. It is essential for all employers, particularly large scale employers, to bear in mind the wide variety of legal responsibilities imposed upon them by Parliament and the general legal framework of common law and equity. References to new legislation in trade journals should be followed up, and for the more important developments it may be wise to appoint a senior individual to study the new legislation and perhaps act as team leader for a small *ad hoc* committee formed to implement the legislation as it comes into force.

It is also worthwhile opening an account with Her Majesty's Stationery Office so that copies of relevant legislation can be obtained without delay by a single phone call. This is a simple procedure, and once agreed you will have no difficulty in getting any piece of legislation you require. Accounts can be arranged by phoning 0171 873 8382 and, once opened, orders may be placed by phoning 0171 873 9090. Payment is by direct debit – usually two weeks after a monthly statement has been submitted. This gives you time to query an account before you actually have the money taken from you by the direct debit system.

29.2 Manpower

We all need a labour force, with a variety of skills and abilities and in general we may employ anyone we like who seems to be suitable and is willing to take employment with us. Taking employment, and offering employment, are serious matters, and should not be entered into casually. Both parties at once acquire certain rights and undertake certain responsibilities, which are outlined in this chapter. There should therefore be certain formalities observed to get the new relationship off on a sound footing – interviews should be arranged, references taken up and a formal appointment offered by the employer and accepted by the employee. An induction procedure should be followed and if a probationary period is featured as part of the earlier discussions the completion of the probationary period should be formally recognized. This may be by a brief interview which reviews the start made by the employee and confirms the appointment as a permanent one – subject to notice on either side. More of this later.

This general rule, that we may employ anyone we like, is subject to one or two restrictions. Some of these are:

(a) Children

A child is a person under the current school leaving age, which is at present 16. No child may be employed in any industrial undertaking. No child may be employed elsewhere if they are under 13 years of age, and those over 13 may not be employed before 7 am or after 7 pm, or for more than 2 hours on any school day, or on Sunday. The Secretary of State for Employment may make regulations on a wide variety of matters (such as the employment of children in any particular trade). The employment of child actors in performances requires a licence from the local authority.

(b) EU nationals

Under Article 48 of the Treaty of Rome nationals of other EU countries have the right to travel to the UK to take up employment or look for employment without any permission from the Employment Department. This is also true of nationals from the residue of EFTA countries, Iceland and Lichtenstein, under the European Economic Area Agreement. Certain family members are also free to enter.

(c) Work permits

Nationals of other countries not mentioned above must have a work permit obtained by their prospective employer *before* they enter the United Kingdom. This will only be issued if there is a shortage of resident labour of the type seeking entry and usually the permit will not exceed four years. Employers should check whether such potential employees require immigration clearance, and should make the offer of employment subject to clearance being obtained before entry. Entertainers and sportsmen/women do not need permits if they fall within a range of categories. The whole subject of work permits is a difficult and detailed area which cannot be fully explained in the present volume.

(d) Disabled persons

In order to assist the employment of persons registered as disabled, the *Disabled Persons (Employment) Acts, 1944* and *1958* impose certain duties on firms with 20 employees or more. Such firms will be required to employ a quota of disabled persons. This quota will take into account the number of employees and the nature of the work (since some work may be too heavy for any disabled person). The Acts also give the minister powers to designate certain classes of employment as 'disabled employments'. An employer must employ a disabled person for these types of work, unless he/she has a permit from the Employment Service accepting that no trained disabled person is available for the post.

(e) Employees with convictions

Employers are naturally hesitant to employ a person who has been convicted of an offence, and will normally ask a prospective employee whether he has any convictions. It is an offence not to reply truthfully to such a question, but under the *Rehabilitation of Offenders Act, 1974* the vast majority of convictions do become 'spent' after a time and the offender is allowed to treat it as if it had never occurred. Such an employee may answer 'No' to the question 'Have you ever been convicted of a crime?' An employer may not ask 'Have you any spent convictions?'

The rehabilitation periods vary between 10 years (for imprisonment between six months and 2½ years) and six months for a person given an absolute discharge. The periods are halved for offenders below the age of 17 years. The period runs from the date of the sentence.

A conviction can never become 'spent' if the term of imprisonment exceeded 2½ years, or was a life sentence, or preventive detention. Nor does the Act apply if the person is a professional person, doctor, dentist, accountant, teacher, etc.

The question of references sometimes raises difficulties, but it is permissible for an employer to omit any reference to a 'spent' conviction. If an employer does mention a 'spent' conviction it is a question of fact in every case whether the former offender may sue. In general it will not give rise to a successful action unless the 'spent' conviction was revealed maliciously (which means 'from an improper motive' – for example out of spite, or to take revenge on the employee for leaving the employment).

These few restrictions are relatively trifling compared with the general principle that employers may employ anyone they like who has the requisite skills and qualifications for the employment proposed.

29.3 The rights of employees

It is only in recent years that employees have had any statutory rights. Prior to about 1960 the struggle for their rights to be recognized was a source of strife between managements and employees, and sufficiently bitter at times to be described in 'class' terms as the 'class struggle'. Today we can recognize two sets of rights, individual rights and collective rights.

29.3.1 Individual rights

The *Employment Protection (Consolidation) Act, 1978* (EPCA) consolidated all the legislation on the individual rights of employees. It has been amended in a series of later statements, notably the *Employment Acts of 1980–1990* (five Acts) and the *Trade Union Reform and Employment Rights Act, 1993*. It is therefore usual to refer to the main Act as the *Employment Protection (Consolidation) Act, 1978, as amended*.

29.3.2 Collective rights

Besides the individual rights which employees have been accorded over the years both by common law and by statute, they have also 'collective rights'. There are representative organizations on both sides of the industrial scene who are active in the field of industrial relations; employers have their trade associations which act as pressure groups on behalf of the industries they represent and the workers have their trade unions and professional bodies. The history of trade unionism has been in former times largely confrontational – even Adam Smith in the early days of the Industrial Revolution wrote 'we have many laws to prevent workers combining to raise wages but few to stop employers combining together to lower them'. In more recent times legislation has attempted to establish a more equal balance of power between employees and employers, but as – by now – it was the unions which were more powerful, the effect of the legislation has been remarkably the same as it was in the early years – designed to reduce the influence of the trade unions. Certainly there have always been abuses of power on both sides.

The current Act is the *Trade Union and Labour Relations (Consolidation Act) 1992*, which consolidates the various Acts passed in the 1980s. These were mainly concerned to make the arrangements for industrial relations more reasonable; for example the 'closed shop' was abolished so that workers could not be forced to join a union of which they disapproved, or be dismissed for lack of a union card. Employees cannot now be forced to strike without having a chance to ballot in the workplace to ensure there is a majority in favour. Collective rights are discussed more fully later in this chapter.

29.4 The individual rights of employees

The individual rights of employees may be listed as follows but there are many qualifying rules about these rights:

- A right to receive a written statement of the particulars of his employment.
- A right to an individual written notice of any change in the particulars of employment.
- A right to an itemized pay statement, on or before each pay day.
- A right to 'guarantee pay' where work was not provided throughout the day.
- A right to pay during medical suspension (a situation where for some reason the worker is not allowed to work because of hazardous substances).
- A right to time off work for trade union duties, or public duties, or to look for other work when in a redundancy situation. A pregnant employee is entitled to time off for ante-natal care.
- A pregnant employee is entitled to time off work, and to statutory maternity pay, and also has a right to return to work after confinement to the same job, with the same rights. She also has a right not to be dismissed for being pregnant.
- A right not to be dismissed unfairly and to a minimum period of notice on dismissal.
- A right to redundancy payments in a redundancy situation.

Amplifying some of these rights we may list some of the important details at the time of writing as shown below. However this is a very dynamic area of law, with Acts of Parliament, codes of conduct, etc., appearing almost monthly, so that reference to a loose-leaf updating service is very desirable.

29.4.1 The written statement of particulars

The main Act for employment legislation is the *Employment Protection (Consolidation) Act, 1978* (which is abbreviated to EPCA). Later legislation tends to amend ECPA by substituting new sections in it, and the most recent batch is in the *Trade Union Reform and Employment Rights Act, 1993*. This Act says that certain information must be given to employees in a written statement, but divides the information into groups, some of which must be given in the 'principle statement' to anyone who works more than eight hours per week, within two months of starting work. Items under this grouping include:

- The names of both parties – the employer and the employee.
- The date of commencement.
- The date on which the employee's period of continuous employment began.
- The scale, or rate of pay, or the method of calculating the remuneration payable.
- The intervals at which remuneration is paid, weekly, monthly, quarterly, etc.

- Any terms and conditions relating to the hours of work.
- The title of the job, or a brief description of the work the employee is required to do.
- The address of the place of employment or the various places of employment if the employee is expected to work at a number of places.

There are numerous other headings which need to be covered, though not necessarily in the principle statement, and yet more which must be drawn to the employee's attention, but may be given by reference to the place where they are published – for example in pension scheme booklets, sickness regulations, manuals of health and safety at work, discipline manuals of procedure, etc.

As with all statutory regulations new regulations can appear at any time and employers must keep *au fait* with legislation.

29.4.2 Changes to the written 'statement of particulars'

Where there is a change in the written statement of particulars the employee is entitled to a written notification of the proposed changes. If the employer's name changes it is possible that the *Transfer of Undertakings Regulations, 1981* are likely to apply. If there has been a 'transfer of undertakings' then the contracts of employment of relevant employees transfer to the new employer, and the old employer's rights and obligations are also transferred. The law on such cases is somewhat uncertain and can only be resolved by developing case law. In *Allen v. Stirling District Council (1994)* some dismissed employees were found to have been unfairly dismissed by a tribunal, but their claim to be compensated by Stirling District Council was dismissed since the obligations of the Council had been assumed by the new employer.

29.4.3 The written pay statement

Since almost all employees are taxed under the PAYE (Pay-As-You-Earn system) it is convenient to provide a pay slip which follows the basic statutory system, which is built up along the following lines:

- Give the separate types of pay (wages, commission, etc.) and total them as gross pay.
- Deduct from this gross pay any sums paid by the employee which are not taxed (for example superannuation). This gives the gross pay less superannuation.
- We now use the PAYE tables provided which show the tax-free pay to date. When this is deducted from the gross pay less superannuation figure we have the taxable pay to date, and the tables tell us the total tax due so far in the tax year. By deducting the total tax paid up to last week (or last month) we arrive at the tax that needs to be deducted from this week's (or month's) pay packet.
- We now deduct this tax, national insurance contributions and any other voluntary deductions (charities, etc.) to give the final net pay. This will be the amount put in the pay packet, or more likely credited in the employee's bank account.

The statutory sick pay (SSP) and statutory maternity pay (SMP), payable originally from government funds, may be shown as part of the pay due. The employer used to be able to deduct these sums from the tax and national insurance contributions it had collected on the Government's behalf, but the Government is gradually withdrawing from such responsibilities, leaving the

29.4.4 Time off work

Under the 1978 Act (EPCA) certain employees are allowed time off work for the performance of public duties. They include justices of the peace, members of local authorities, statutory tribunals, NHS trusts, prison visitors, school governors, members of river authorities, etc.

Time off work is also allowed for ante-natal care and in a redundancy situation an employee may take time off in the 'notice' period to find and train for a new job.

The rights to maternity leave and to return to work are best described in the current literature, since the arrangements vary from time to time.

29.4.5 Minimum periods of notice

Employees who have worked for 16 hours per week or more for at least one month (or who have worked at least eight hours per week for five years) are entitled to one week's notice if the period of employment is less than two years. If an employee has been continuously employed for two years or more they are entitled to one week's notice for each year, up to a maximum of 12 years. Employees who have been employed for one month or more need to give only one week's notice.

29.4.6 Summary dismissal

Summary dismissal is only possible for gross misconduct (defined as misconduct so grave as to go to the root of the contract, and such that no reasonable employer could tolerate the continued employment of the employee). Even so it is essential to go through a proper disciplinary procedure, because a claim for unfair dismissal could be made.

Today in the United Kingdom a considerable legal apparatatus exists to ensure that employees are protected against arbitrary dismissals by employers. Alleged unfair dismissals can be brought before an industrial tribunal. Representation at such tribunals and the preparation of a defence can be quite expensive to an employer, and it is better to avoid such hearings if at all possible. Certainly evidence of the existence of fair arrangements about dismissal procedures is the best rebuttal of claims about unfair dismissal. The basic requirement is that the laws of natural justice should have been followed. The two main rules of natural justice are:

- the rule against bias: no man should be a judge in his own case; and
- the right to a hearing

The rules will generally have been met provided there is some right of appeal to senior management against the allegedly unfair dismissal, and the employee has had a full opportunity to explain the case from his/her own point of view, or has been allowed to be represented by a friend or colleague, trade union representative, etc. There will be less question of unfairness if an employee has been warned on previous occasions that similar behaviour was not approved of and might lead to dismissal. In general, summary dismissals should not be made except for the most serious offences, theft of money or stock, serious assaults on other workers, etc. In all other cases the employee should be given a chance to state a defence and should be warned about the consequences of any repetition. Formal notice of intention to dismiss should be given if persistent misbehaviour, unpunctuality, absenteeism, etc., occurs. Policy on these matters should be published and drawn to the attention of all staff.

The right to a hearing embodies several points: a right to know the nature of the complaint; a right to prepare a defence in advance of any hearing; a right to be heard; a right to be represented if necessary; and a right to know not only the decisions made, but the reasons for the decision. Generally speaking a breach of natural justice makes the decision taken by management ineffective – the employee is entitled to re-instatement and if this is refused considerable compensation will be payable.

29.4.7 Constructive dismissal

Constructive dismissal occurs when an employer changes the terms of employment without warning or consultation in such a way that the employee suffers serious disadvantage. Thus increased hours, or decreased pay, or the cancellation of free transport, or overbearing conduct entitle the employee to leave the employment and claim unfair dismissal.

The remedies for unfair dismissal are re-instatement, compensation, or special awards where the dismissal arose out of membership of a trade union.

29.4.8 Employer's references

An employee has a right to an accurate reference, and the employer has a duty of care to ensure that any reference given gives a true picture of the employee's abilities and skills. A disclaimer of liability on the reference will be of no avail if the reference is not accurate and the employee suffers loss thereby. In *Spring v. Guardian Insurance plc and Others (1994) (The Times*, 8 July) the House of Lords held that as employers had a special knowledge of an employee's skills and diligence there was an implied term in the contract of employment that the employer owed a duty of care when giving a reference, and the employee must be able to rely on the employer to use skill and care in expressing himself in the reference. This decision has left employers very much exposed to claims for damages if a reference has been carelessly prepared without investigating the truth of the statements made.

29.4.9 The Race Relations Act, 1976

This makes it unlawful to discriminate against a person, directly or indirectly, in the field of employment, on racial grounds. Direct discrimination means treating a person, on racial grounds, less favourably than other people. Indirect discrimination is not clearly defined but might, for example, include less favourable treatment because the employee had a poor command of English when this was not required for the job concerned. What was fair treatment on language grounds for a person with poor English seeking a post as a telephone operator might be discrimination against a seamstress whose command of English was weak.

The Code of Practice for the Elimination of Racial Discrimination and the Promotion of Equality of Opportunity in Employment recommends that all employers should adopt, implement and monitor an equal opportunity policy which should be communicated to all employees, through the usual channels (notice boards, written particulars of employment, written notifications, etc.).

Particular care has to be applied when advertising vacancies, or when using the services of employment agencies, and it is unlawful to give instructions to discriminate or to bring pressure on such agencies to exclude certain groups. Similarly, recruitment from the friends of existing staff where this is likely to produce a disproportionate number of people from a particular racial group may amount to discrimination.

Victimization is discrimination against a person on the grounds that he/she has brought action on the grounds of racial discrimination, or is to give evidence or has made allegations of racial discrimination.

29.4.10 The Sex Discrimination Act, 1975 (as amended by the Sex Discrimination Act, 1986)

These Acts make it unlawful to discriminate against women by treating them less favourably than men. It also applies to men if they are treated less favourably than women and to married persons of either sex if they are treated less favourably than a single person. Exceptions apply in a number of situations where sex is a genuine occupational qualification. A related matter, sexual harassment, can constitute sexual discrimination where it can be proved that the claimant has been treated in a way which would not have applied to someone of the opposite sex, or where it led to constructive dismissal (where the employee resigns rather than endure the harassment). As with the *Race Relations Act*, discriminatory advertisements, instructions and pressure to discriminate are unlawful.

The subject of employment law is a full time study in its own right and a general book of this type can only refer to a small part of the detailed regulations in this field.

29.5 The collective rights of employees

What is a trade union? The 1992 Act defines a trade union as an organization which:

- consists wholly or mainly of workers of one or more descriptions and is an organization whose principal purposes include the regulation of relations between workers of that description or those descriptions and employers or employers' associations; or
- consists wholly or mainly of:
  - constituent or affiliated organizations which fulfil the conditions specified in the paragraph above (or themselves consist wholly or mainly of constituent or affiliated organizations which fulfil those conditions), or
  - representatives of such constituent or affiliated organizations;

  and in either case is an organization whose principal purposes include the regulation of relations between workers and employers or between workers and employers' associations, or include the regulation of relations between its constituent or affiliated organizations.

The statutory rights given to trade unions are dependent on them being independent representatives of the employees – not 'company' unions dominated or controlled by an employer. An independent union can apply to the Certification Officer appointed by the Secretary of State for Employment for a certificate of independence. His function is to maintain a list of trade unions and a list of employers' organizations. Only those bodies listed as such can receive help with the costs of balloting members. They must also maintain proper accounting records and provide copies of rule books, annual returns, etc., for public inspection.

All employers of more than 250 persons must include in their annual directors' report an account of the company's activities during the year to introduce, maintain or develop arrangements which help the workforce understand, participate in and further the activities of the company.

29.5.1 Collective bargaining

In many countries in the European Union the unions are actively engaged with management in negotiations about pay and conditions of work, and collective agreements arrived at are legally enforceable. There is no such requirement in English law, and in general, collective agreements arrived at are not legally enforceable at common law, but are 'binding in honour only'. However the *Trade Union and Labour Relations (Consolidation) Act, 1992* does say that a collective agreement is legally enforceable if it is both in writing and states that the parties intended it to be legally enforceable. Also, where a collective agreement becomes part of an employee's personal contract of employment it will become enforceable because the contract of employment is legally enforceable. However a 'no-strikes' clause is not legally enforceable unless it satisfies certain conditions. These are:

- it must be in writing;
- it must expressly permit the agreement to be incorporated into personal contracts;
- the agreement must be accessible to all employees;
- the trade union must be independent; and
- the individual contract must expressly or impliedly incorporate the clause into the contract.

29.5.2 Codes of practice on industrial relations

The industrial relations scene has changed considerably in recent years, due to government legislation introduced to curb the abuse of powers by trade unions themselves. Initially designed to reduce the exploitation of working people by unscrupulous entrepreneurs, the trade union movement in some areas had become an arbitrary power in its own right, to such an extent that managements have in some situations been quite unable to manage, and whole industries had collapsed because of their inability to react and adjust to new situations in a competitive world. The position now is that firms and trade unions act within a tight framework of employment law. Where an established trade union does act reasonably and management can, through some sort of joint consultation procedure, draw up a code of practice acceptable to both parties this is much the best procedure. Under the *Employment Act, 1988* the Secretary of State may take steps leading to the issue of codes of practice in certain areas of industrial relations, for example about the conduct of union elections and ballots, or about disciplinary action against members acting in good faith in alleging union misconduct. Whether this process has gone too far remains to be seen, but the law at present has removed many of the powers of the unions and readjusted the balance of power between management and staff.

29.5.3 Right to disclosure of information

Under the 1992 Act the employer must make available to the representatives of the trade union information which they require for proper collective bargaining – but there are some grounds for refusing to disclose: where injury would be caused to the employer's business, or the national security, etc. The Advisory, Conciliation and Arbitration Service (ACAS) has issued a Code of Practice which emphasizes that the information to be disclosed depends upon the purpose for which it is required, and should include such information as, if not disclosed, would impede the collective bargaining process. For example information about pay, benefits, conditions of service, productivity, the order book, cost structures, profits, etc., are likely to be the main headings.

There are a lot of detailed regulations about trade disputes, picketing, secondary industrial action (action at related plants, depots, etc., which are not part of the main centre of unrest but might be used to bring pressure on managements elsewhere). The right of anyone to take steps to prevent unlawful industrial action (i.e. asking for an injunction to restrain secondary industrial action) is specifically authorized by the *Trade Union Reform and Employment Rights Act, 1993*.

Test your knowledge

Answers	Questions
	1. What is the effect of employment law on employers generally?
1. It provides a very tight framework for all their activities and imposes many costs and obligations upon them.	2. What assumption of law requires employers to be vigilant in legal matters?
2. The rule '*ignorantia juris haud excusat*'. Ignorance of the law is no excuse, and the law assumes that we all know everything about every new law as soon as it is passed. Of course we don't, but it is a figment of law that we do.	3. What are the important points about offering employment to anyone?
3. There are special rules about (a) children; (b) disabled persons; (c) EU nationals; (d) work permits for other nationals; (e) racial balance in the workforce, and (f) sexual balance in the workforce.	4. What are the classes of rights enjoyed by employees?
4. There are two types; individual rights and collective rights.	5. List the chief individual rights.
5. (a) A right to a written statement of the particulars of employment, and any change in those particulars; (b) a right to an itemized pay statement, and the net pay that results; (c) rights to time off work in certain circumstances; (d) a right not to be dismissed unfairly and to a minimum period of notice on dismissal; (e) a right to redundancy payments in a redundancy situation.	6. What are the collective rights of employees?

Answers	Questions
6 (a) A right to belong to a trade union; (b) a right not to belong to a trade union; (c) a right to a ballot in the workplace before being called out on strike; (d) a right to be informed and to make plans for redundancy situations; (e) a right not to have action taken against them as individuals for refusal to participate in collective activities; (f) a right to time off for certain trade union activities, training, etc.; (g) a right to appeal to the Commissioner for the Rights of Trade Union Members.	7 Go over the page again. Then try some of the questions in Appendix 1.

Appendix 1 Questions

Chapter 1:
Elements of
English law

1 Define law. What are the essential institutions if laws are to be promulgated and the 'rule of law' sustained?
2 Distinguish between 'public law' and 'private law'. The ABCD Company plc is in difficulties. First, its managing director after a business luncheon has driven the firm's car into a lamp-post, been breathalysed and told that action will certainly follow. Second, the company's most important customer has complained about serious defects in a recent contract and has informed ABCD that he is seeing a solicitor. What will be the effect of these two potential brushes with 'the law' upon ABCD?
3 What are the chief sources of law? Explain two of these sources in detail, with particular reference to the impact of law upon businesses.
4 Explain statute law, using as your example any statue with which you are familiar.
5 'The Secretary of State, in exercise of the powers conferred by Section 1(3) of the *Merchant Shipping (Liability of Shipowners and others) Act, 1958*, hereby makes the following order.
  'For the purposes of Section 1 of the Act named above £133.66 and £42.12 are hereby specified as the amounts which shall be taken as equivalent to 3100 and 1000 gold francs respectively.'
  Explain the purpose of orders such as this.
6 What are the chief institutions of the European Union? Describe the part played by any two of them.
7 Explain 'subsidiarity' as used in the European Union.
8 An Act of Parliament which is very controversial was passed after the Government imposed a 'guillotine' procedure, so that discussion on the last quarter of the bill was cut off. The bill passed in its draft form and a dispute has now arisen about the meaning of several sections. What are the rules which would guide the courts in the interpretation of this statute?

Chapter 2:
The courts of law

1 Describe the composition and jurisdiction of the County Courts. A plaintiff wishes to bring an action to recover £150 from a tenant for unpaid rent. How will this matter be dealt with?
2 An action for recovery of £175 000 allegedly lost as a result of a breach of contract is brought in the High Court. Explain the likely composition of the court, and its general procedure.
3 Explain the doctrine of binding precedent. How is precedent effective in civil matters?
4 Explain the provisions of Article 177 of the Treaty of Rome with regard to preliminary rulings on the interpretation of the Treaty and Community Law.
5 Describe the composition and jurisdiction of *two* of the following courts: (a) Crown Courts; (b) Magistrates' Courts; (c) County Courts; (d) the High Court; (e) the Court of Appeal; (f) the House of Lords.

6 What is meant by the phrase 'a divided profession' when referring to the legal profession? Explain the steps taken in the *Courts and Legal Services Act, 1990* to ameliorate the divisions in the profession.
7 How would an aggrieved person seeking redress of a civil wrong obtain financial assistance from official resources to bring an action in the courts?

Chapter 3: The legal environment for business entities

1 Explain the concept of business entity. What is the position of a sole trader and a partner as far as business entity is concerned?
2 A sole trader uses the firm name 'Gimmicks Electronics'. How is this name brought to the attention of the public in compliance with the law?
3 Discuss the advantages and disadvantages of forming a partnership, with particular reference to the legal position of partners (a) *inter se* and (b) with regard to the world at large.
4 B, who is about to set up in partnership with A, has been told that a simple handshake is enough. Advise him.
5 What are the most important features of partnership law on the dissolution of a partnership? Y, who is a junior partner, feels he is unfairly treated by his senior partners who do not let him see the books and overrule his view on many matters he feels to be important. He wishes to know how to bring an end to the partnership and retrieve the capital he has contributed to it. Advise him.
6 Write notes on *two* of the following: (a) relation of partners with third parties; (b) the rights and duties between partners; (c) limited partnership; (d) dissolution of partnership; (e) advantages and disadvantages compared with other business entities.
7 What Act of Parliament deals with bankruptcy? What solutions are available to the partners of a partnership business which is getting into financial difficulties?

Chapter 4: Business entities: unincorporated associations

1 What is an unincorporated association? Who is in charge of such an association and what legal liabilities are faced by such persons?
2 A croquet club finds itself unable to attract members and proposes to sell its valuable land. How will this be arranged and how will the money provided be disposed of?
3 A is the secretary of a club. He asks B to redecorate the premises at a fee of £500. After the work has been completed it appears that the treasurer is unable to pay the bill, and claims that the work was not authorized by the committee. Advise B.
4 Why is the constitution (or rule book) of a club important? A, who has been banned from the club by S, the secretary, for rowdy behaviour, claims that he has been given no opportunity to explain his behaviour. Advise him.
5 What is the situation of (a) a club, (b) a trade union and (c) a partnership with regard to actions against them for tort. Who is likely to be held liable?
6 A, an innocent passer-by, has been seriously hurt by a missile thrown by B, a member of the Merry Revellers Wine Club. The Annual Club Dinner, was in progress at the time, and the missile emerged from the club premises after breaking a window. Advise A.

Chapter 5: Business entities: limited companies

1. What is the meaning of limited liability? Why is it such an important concept and how is it obtained by business persons?
2. Compare and contrast the different forms of business units, i.e. companies, partnerships and sole traders.
3. What are the formalities involved in registering a public company?
4. What are the basic differences between a public company and a private company under the *Companies Act, 1985*?
5. Explain the contents and purpose of: (a) a memorandum of association; (b) a set of articles of association.
6. Explain the *ultra vires* rule and the changes that have been effected in it by the *Companies Acts, 1985–9*.
7. What are the important legal consequences of incorporation of a company? Give cases where applicable.
8. What are the duties of directors of a company.
9. Explain the various forms of winding up a company.
10. Describe a typical structure for a public limited company. What is the relationship between the company and (a) its shareholders, (b) its directors and (c) its employees?
11. Discuss the proposition that 'worker' directors should be appointed to the boards of public companies. What conflicts of interest might a worker-director face?
12. Why are auditors appointed? What is their legal position relative to (a) the company and (b) the shareholders?
13. What is 'compulsory winding up'? In what way is it different from voluntary dissolution of the company?
14. What is 'insider dealing'? How is it controlled?
15. On what grounds might a director be disqualified from future participation in the formation and running of limited companies?
16. What do you understand by the terms (a) Administration Order, (b) Voluntary Arrangement and (c) Administrative Receiver under the *Insolvency Act, 1986*.
17. What do you understand by the notion that a company is a legal person in its own right? Are there any exceptions to this rule?

Chapter 6: The nature of contracts

1. Define a contract. Who may make contracts? N, a school leaver aged 16, undertakes to work for B 'in the course of learning the trade of automobile mechanic' for a payment of £50 a week in the first three years, and £80 a week in the remaining two years. Discuss whether this contract is binding upon N.
2. What is a contract for necessaries? B, a student aged 17, is supplied with (a) groceries, (b) wines and spirits and (c) an optical telescope by Supermarkets Ltd, the account to be settled at the end of the month. B does not pay. Advise M, the supermarket manager.
3. What is the importance of the concept 'intention to create legal relations' in contract law? Refer in your answer to the following two cases:
   (a) A asks B to redecorate his premises 'from top to bottom, inside and outside'. He is amazed at the size of the bill, which is completely documented and does not appear to contain any extravagant use of materials.
   (b) C agrees with D to complete a football pools coupon regularly and hand it to him with the cash invested, after completing the coupon in the usual way, and signing his name on the part which reads. 'It is agreed that this coupon is binding in honour only'. D absconds with C's money each week, but this is not discovered until C 'wins' a large prize.

4 Balfour agrees with his wife that he will pay her £80 a week if she agrees to separate from him and live in rented accommodation. Some time later he is made redundant and is unable to keep up the payments. Advise Mrs Balfour of her legal rights in this matter.
5 Explain the term *consensus ad idem*. A agrees to buy B's camera, which B said was referred to in the Ornithological Society as being capable of taking long-distance colour photographs. He gives a £20 deposit, but when the camera is produced it proves to be quite a different model and not worth the price discussed earlier. Advise A (a) about the bargain made and (b) about the prospects of recovering his deposit.
6 (a) What various forms can contracts take? (b) Arthur has to sell his car due to a family crisis. He approaches Lovely Motors Ltd and in the presence of several members of their staff agrees to sell the car at 5 p.m. that evening for £1500. He goes on to a meeting at which a colleague offers him £2000 for the car. Advise Arthur.

Chapter 7: Offer, acceptance and valuable consideration

1 Mrs A selects certain items in a supermarket, takes them to the checkout and offers to pay for them. The total bill is more than she has in her purse, and she regretfully has to leave two items behind. These are returned to the shelves by an assistant. Explain the following terms by reference to the above events: (a) invitation to treat; (b) offer; (c) acceptance; (d) valuable consideration; (e) revocation of offer.
2 A announces that an auction will be held in his sale rooms commencing at 2 p.m. on 14 November. B, who is interested in this type of sale, travels 50 miles to attend the sale, only to discover that it is cancelled because the items have been sold privately. Advise B.
3 X offers Y his horse for £900. Y faxes, 'Would you be prepared to take £600 and my stallion Pericles.' X replies 'No'. Y then faxes, 'Very well, accept your offer to sell at £900,' but X has already sold it to Z for £950. Advise Y.
4 Peter offers Paul an editorial post at 'a Mayfair salary'. Paul accepts this offer, but no starting date is arranged and Peter takes no further action. Advise Paul.
5 'The rules about postal offers and acceptances can be very confusing.' What are these rules and what justification is there for them?
6 Discuss the concept of 'lapse of time' on offer and acceptance.
7 'A smaller sum will not satisfy a larger sum.' Explain this principle, outlining the cases which illustrate it.
8 What is meant by 'quasi-estoppel', or the 'rule in the High Trees House case'? Explain in detail the facts and *ratio decidendi* of this case.
9 What is meant by the doctrine of privity of contract?

Chapter 8: Circumstances affecting the validity of contracts

1 Distinguish between the various types of mistake.
2 In what ways might a contract be rendered illegal? What is the effect of illegality?
3 What are the 'presumptions' normally associated with undue influence?
4 M, the mother of S, who is over 18 years of age, persuades him to sell some shares and use the money to pay off her mortgage. Before S's stockbroker can make the sale S contacts him to cancel the arrangement. M asks whether, in your opinion, she can force S to carry out his promise. Advise her.
5 Define duress. What is the effect of duress upon a contract?

6 A offers to sell his car to B for £4000. B has seen A driving an impressive modern vehicle which he considers well worth £4000, and accepts the offer. On delivery the vehicle proves to be a different vehicle altogether. B refuses to take delivery, or to pay the price. Advise A.

Chapter 9: The terms of the contract

1 (a) What are the main differences between representations and terms in relation to a contract? (b) B states early in the negotiations leading to the sale of a second-hand machine that it has been in regular use up to the time of sale. On delivery the machine is found to be rusted solid in one essential area and clearly has not been used for many years. Discuss the remedies available to A, the purchaser.

2 (a) Distinguish between express and implied terms in a contract. (b) B contracted to deliver goods to A, the contract expressly stating that the concrete posts required were essential for erection on 5 May, when contractors had agreed to do the job. They arrived on 6 May, due to a breakdown in B's vehicle, but by then the contractors had used their own supplies at a higher price per unit. Advise A.

3 The *effect* of a breach of contract is helpful to the courts in deciding whether a term in a contract is a condition or a warranty. Explain, referring in your answer to the case below.

P undertakes to deliver material to Z, the contract stating 'it is a condition of the contract that delivery be made by 3 p.m., Friday January 19'. The reason for this is that Z's religion forbids him to work after 5 p.m. on Friday, and a major contract is to start at his clothing factory on Monday. P's vehicle breaks down, but delivery is made early on Monday morning, the lorry being available at the opening of the factory and taking only half an hour to unload.

4 (a) What are 'standard trading conditions'? (b) B hires a machine from A, another plant-hire company, so that he can fulfil a contract made with C. The machine B hoped to hire to C had broken down, and could not be repaired in time. A's terms and conditions were sent on at a later date and contained a clause stating 'the cost of transport of machines hired is for the hirer's account'. B maintains that this was not part of the bargain. Discuss.

5 (a) A term in a set of standard trading conditions reads: 'If the customer sends any dangerous goods without notification to the carrier for carriage, and these goods cause damage to other goods or to the vehicle, the customer will indemnify the carrier and all claimants for the damage caused.' Is this term binding on the carrier's customers?

(b) A, who sends goods he believes to be harmless by the carrier mentioned in (a) above, does not know that when in contact with flour the product produces a dangerous effect. The carrier loads the goods next to a sack of wholemeal flour destined for a health-food shop. Three deaths occur and numerous other people are taken ill. No similar case has been recorded. Discuss the liability of A.

6 How have the courts mitigated the most onerous aspects of exclusion clauses used in contracts?

7 What have been the main effects of the *Unfair Contract Terms Act, 1977*?

8 What does the law provide for testing the validity of clauses seeking to exclude liability for a fundamental breach of contract?

9 What is a 'representative action'? Explain how the Society of Furniture Manufacturers would contest a clause in a set of road haulage conditions which purported to exclude road hauliers for liability for damage to furniture, howsoever caused.

Chapter 10: Misrepresentation

1 Why is it necessary for the law to draw up rules relating to misrepresentation?
2 What are the various types of misrepresentation, how do they differ and what remedies are available to injured parties?
3 What are the essential elements of a misrepresentation?
4 (a) Distinguish between a puff and a misrepresentation. (b) X says: 'This is the finest little car in England.' Y says: 'I will take it in part exchange for my own vehicle, which is a two-year-old Ford Sierra, and £800 to settle the rest.' X agrees. Both statements about the cars prove to be untrue. Advise X of his legal position.
5 'Negligent misrepresentation is closer to fraudulent misrepresentation than it is to innocent misrepresentation.' Discuss this statement, referring in your answer to the following cases:
  A, who is selling Tumbledown House, refers untruthfully to its 'complete freedom from woodworm or other pests'.
  B, who is selling a similar property, replies to the question 'Is there any woodworm?' by saying 'I've never seen any.' Woodworm is found later to be present.
  C, who is selling a similar property, warrants that it is free from woodworm, and produces a recent surveyor's report. Despite this, woodworm is found to be present.
6 'Silence is not misrepresentation.' Discuss this statement. M completes an application form for life assurance which asks the question: 'Has any insurance company ever refused to cover you?' In fact, many years ago as a young motorcyclist who had bought a high-powered motorcycle, cover had been refused. M does not answer this question, leaving the space blank. Despite this a premium is agreed and paid for several years, when M is killed in a road accident. The insurance company refuses to pay, claiming misrepresentation. Advise M's wife, the beneficiary.

Chapter 11: The discharge of contracts

1 How is a contract normally discharged? A, an author, contracts with P, a publisher, to write a travel book. He goes to some expense to collect pictures and other material, only to be told that P is no longer able to proceed with publication. Advise A.
2 What is meant by the doctrine of substantial performance? J, a joiner, fulfills a contract to install guard rails around a staircase and landing, but fails to use a certain type of countersunk washer on the bolts concerned. These were specified in the contract, but are no longer manufactured. A perfectly serviceable type of non-countersunk washer was used instead. P, the property owner, refuses to pay the price. Advise J.
3 Discuss the importance of valuable consideration in any contract to discontinue one bargain and replace it by another. Mrs A sues her doctor for negligence in prescribing a wrong dose of drugs and the court awards her £2000. She agrees with the doctor to accept £500 on 1 January for the next four years. Later she asks for interest at 5 per cent on the outstanding balance to be added to each payment except the first. The doctor refuses. Advise Mrs A.
4 A contract to carry goods to India has just been concluded at a fair price when the Suez Canal is closed by military action. Discuss whether this frustrates the contract, which is much less lucrative if it is to be fulfilled by the long journey around southern Africa.
5 A contract between A and B for the construction of a major engineering works is affected by the outbreak of war, which requires A to divert his labour force to other projects in the national interest. The order

requisitioning his men and plant is made under an Act entitled the Outbreak of Hostilities Act. Advise B, who feels that alternative labour is available, especially as a large exporter has discharged staff in the locality.

6 'Breach of contract does not necessarily discharge the contract.' Explain this statement. In your answer refer to a breach of contract by a fashion designer, whose factories supply 12 000 garments to a major fashion house in four colours – cream, maroon, blue and grey. The contract called for cream, maroon, blue and green garments.

7 What is meant by a legal assignment of a contract? A, who has contracted to do work for B, is so busy that he cannot perform it. He asks B to allow C to take over the contract. Advise B of the legal position, and explain what will be the legal effect of any decision to assent to the proposal.

8 X, who is owed money by Z, agrees orally with Y to assign Z's debt to him. Y accordingly notifies Z that he must pay him (Y) and not X. Is this a legal assignment? If Z ignores the request, can Y sue Z, and will the courts uphold it if he does?

Chapter 12: How the law enforces contractual obligations

1 What remedies are available (a) at common law, (b) in equity, to an aggrieved person disappointed by the failure of another person to perform a contract? C, who has agreed to lay a patio for D, is offered a more lucrative contract with E and tells D he is not able to perform the contract as arranged. What should D do, and what remedies are available to him for C's breach of contract?

2 What is 'repudiation of a contract?' X promises Y that he can get him a reconditioned engine within two days. Seven days later X is still waiting and is offered a similar engine for immediate delivery by Z. X badly needs his car. Advise him.

3 'The case of *Hadley v. Baxendale* (1854) is one of the most important in contract law.' What was the case about and why is it important?

4 Distinguish between liquidated damages, unliquidated damages and a penalty. B agrees to build a turnstile for A at the entrance to his stately home, by a given date. Failure to do so will result in damages of £20 per day until completion. This is an estimate of the extra cost required in employing staff to supervise those seeking entry through an uncontrolled entrance area. B does not complete the work in time but refuses to pay damages. Advise A.

5 What is a *quantum meruit*? A starts to erect a house for B but gets into difficulties financially and B is forced to employ another builder to complete the work. X starts to erect a house for Y but after a while Y, who is disappointed with the quality of X's work, tells him to leave the house unfinished and he will seek a better workman. Discuss whether either, both or neither of these is entitled to be paid on a *quantum meruit*.

6 When will the courts grant a decree of specific performance? Why do they sometimes refuse to exercise discretion in this respect?

7 What is meant by the term 'statute-barred'? Why is it desirable that some time limit is set on legal action, particularly in such matters as the carriage of goods by sea and air?

8 (a) What does the *Contracts (Applicable Law) Act, 1990* say are the methods to be used to decide which is the proper law of a contract?

(b) Baltimore Fred has entered into a contract for the supply and delivery of tobacco from the USA harvest to Liverpool Sean. They did not discuss the question of which law would govern the contract, only specifying that the product was to be best Virginia tobacco and the packing and dispatch would be the responsibility of Baltimore Fred. Payment is to be made in dollars through the Washington branch of Bank of America. Advise Liverpool Sean, who is questioning the quality of the product.

Chapter 13: Agency

1. 'He who acts by another, acts for himself.' Explain this legal maxim, referring in your answer to common examples from business life where a businessman acts through another person.
2. 'Agency involves a tripartite arrangement.' Explain the tripartite arrangement and the legal relations of all these parties.
3. (a) Explain the term 'subsequent ratification of an unauthorized act'. (b) A who has been acting on behalf of B in the purchase of a vintage motorcar from C accepts C's offer to sell at £5000 although he knows he has only authority to go as far as £4500. C hears that A has exceeded his authority, and tells him that he is commencing an action against him for breach of warranty of authority. What is the position of A in these circumstances?
4. B appoints A to act as his agent in the purchase of a piece of property. What are A's duties to his principal, and what rights has he against the principal?
5. Define agency of necessity. A, the servant of Transporters (Wilbraham) Ltd, is the driver of a container lorry taking tomatoes from Southampton to Birmingham. He is involved in an accident and to preserve the fruit he sells them at a very low price to Chutney-makers Ltd. His travel documents include a 'case of need' address and telephone number for the South of England agents of the owners, B Ltd. Discuss the legal position of B Ltd, who have suffered considerably by the driver's action.
6. A is the agent for B in the sale of B's paintings, on a continuing basis. B dies, but before A has heard of this he disposes of an important painting to C. The executors refuse to ratify the agent's act, or to pay him commission on the sale. Discuss A's legal position with respect to C.

Chapter 14: Contracts for the sale of goods

1. (a) Define a contract for the sale of goods. (b) Explain whether each of the following is a sale of goods: (i) A transfers his motor vehicle to B for £1000, payable on the last day of the present month. (ii) A transfers his motor vehicle to B in exchange for shares in the General Electronic Ltd valued at £1000. (iii) A hires his motor vehicle to B for £65 per week during the long vacation. (iv) A agrees to leave his motor vehicle with B as security for a loan of £1000, repayable at the end of the long vacation.
2. (a) What is the special position of a minor under the *Sale of Goods Act, 1979*, with regard to the purchase of necessaries? (b) M, who is 17 years of age, lives in a rural area where there is no public transport. He is about to start a technical course at a college in a nearby town and 'buys' a motorcar for £485, payable when he receives his grant. A friend tells him the vehicle is not worth more than £130. Advise M.
3. (a) List the terms which are implied into a contract under Sections 12–15 of the *Sale of Goods Act, 1979*. (b) Choose any one of these implied terms and explain in detail what the implications are.
4. (a) What is meant by the term 'merchantable quality'? (b) M, who is thinking of buying a large quantity of paint thinners from Cautious Ltd, asks for proof of its quality. Cautious Ltd states that they have never been asked for such proof before, and suggest that they will provide a single

drum, randomly selected by M, for test purposes, free of charge. M asks his chemist D to select a specimen drum. He does so, but finds his own test facilities inadequate and does not test it other than superficially, by appearance, etc. A large order is placed, but it proves to be unsatisfactory. Advise M.

5 What are the rights of an unpaid seller? Basics plc, who supply chemical raw materials to Doubtful Ltd, are anxious to write the contract in such a way as to ensure payment, even when the property passed to Doubtful Ltd has been mixed with other materials to produce quite different products. Advise Basics plc.

6 M Ltd have placed an order for 5000 sacks of potting compost. What is the legal position in each of these cases: (a) a lorry arrives with 2000 sacks; (b) a lorry arrives with 6500 sacks; (c) a lorry arrives with 5000 sacks of a totally unsuitable mixture; (d) a lorry arrives with 5000 sacks of a different material, which will do at a pinch, but the price quoted for the original material is excessive for this material.

Chapter 15: Insurance

1 What is the nature of insurance? How would A, who wishes to obtain fire insurance cover for his factory, set about obtaining it? In the event that cover is arranged, what would be the procedure should a fire occur?

2 Explain the term 'insurable interest'. What persons might have an insurable interest in the safe arrival of a ship, loaded with containerized cargo, setting off from Southampton on a journey to Perth, Western Australia?

3 Why is a contract of insurance a contract *uberrima fides*? What statements would you expect to have to make in completing a proposal form for life assurance on your own life?

4 What is subrogation in insurance? A, who has insured goods sent by a carrier against all risks, hears that the carrier's driver has had an accident and is to be charged with drunken driving. The goods are seriously damaged and the insurance company agrees to pay full compensation. Where does subrogation enter into this scenario?

5 Explain each of the following terms: (a) indemnity; (b) measure of indemnity (in marine insurance); (c) benefit payable.

6 What are the 1.1.82 Policy Forms and Clauses? Why were they introduced, and to what extent are they an improvement on former practice?

7 A ship is in a dangerous situation and the master takes the following actions: (a) road haulage vehicles and containers on deck have shifted position – their restraining cables are severed and they fall overboard; (b) fuel in transit as deck cargo is used to feed the ship's engines; (c) damaged superstructure is hacked free and jettisoned. The ship and the rest of the cargo arrive safely. How will these losses be dealt with?

Chapter 16: Law of carriage by land, sea and air

1 (a) What is a common carrier? (b) What are the common law exceptions? (c) A, who is a lorry driver, set up in a business as a haulier without any special arrangements. He is carrying a load to the west country when a heavy storm sweeps away a bridge he is crossing, and he barely escapes with his life. Advise B, the owner of the goods, which are irretrievably lost.

2 (a) What is a private carrier? (b) How does a haulier usually make it clear that he is a private carrier, not a common carrier? (c) T, who is a private carrier, states that he will not be liable for losses sustained in transit, however caused. P's goods are stolen by T's driver, who is sent to prison. Advise P.

3 What is stoppage in transit? Why is it fair that the right of stoppage in transit should exist?
   A has sent goods by B to C. B arrives with the goods and C asks him to hold them at his depot until next day, and to deliver them to D, who will pay B the extra freight charges. B agrees. On arriving back at his depot he receives a telephone call from A telling him to stop the goods in transit, as A has heard that C is insolvent and about to call in the receivers. Advise B.
4 What is a lien? Why does a haulier insert in his conditions of carriage a statement that he is entitled to a general lien on all goods carried?
5 What is the CMR Convention? What difference would it make to A who has sent goods by B, a haulier, under a contract which says that B will not be liable for any loss, howsoever caused? B's vehicle is in poor repair, and due to handbrake failure on a French mountain road falls into a ravine where A's goods are a total loss.
6 What is the CIM Convention? How is it incorporated into English law? What does it say about: (a) contractual documents, (b) the liability of the carrier for loss, damage or delay?
7 What is a bill of lading? What functions does it serve and how is it affected by the Hague-Visby Rules?
8 A carrier by sea is invited to carry hazardous cargo and agrees to do so – on deck. During a storm the container in which this cargo is packed begins to smoke. It is jettisoned. Advise A, the owner of the cargo disposed of.
9 Why is a definition of international carriage important in any international convention about the law of carriage? How is a sender of goods by air freight warned of the existence of clauses in the Warsaw Rules limiting the carrier's liability? What is the limit specified in the Rules?
10 ICC Publication No. 481 is about the carriage of goods by a multimodal operator under a Multimodal Transport Document. What is the purpose of this body of uniform rules, and how is it made effective in law?

Chapter 17: Negotiable instruments

1 What is 'the concept of negotiability'? A takes a £5 note in a shop from B, a complete stranger, supplying goods and change to the full value. Later C enters, claiming that he lost the note, and that D, who has come along with C, saw B pick it up and make off with it in the direction of A's shop. D is a convincing witness. Advise C.
2 What is the definition of a bill of exchange? M orders P to sell his motorcar at auction, to keep 10 per cent for himself, pay 50 per cent to R and return any balance left. Discuss whether this order is a bill of exchange.
3 What is meant by the term 'acceptance' of a bill of exchange? What are the legal implications of acceptance and what are the consequences of failing to observe the legal requirements?
4 Write short explanations (5–8 lines) about each of the following: (a) the holder of a bill; (b) a holder in due course; (c) endorsement of a bill; (d) bearer bills.
5 What is the liability of the drawer upon a bill? M has drawn on N for £1000 for goods supplied. N accepted the bill; M discounted it with a bank B, who subsequently passed it to C. It then moved to E, F, G and H. H presented it on the due date but N regretted his inability to pay. H, who knows M as a business acquaintance, approaches M for payment. Explain why M should pay. If M cannot pay, who must pay H the value of the bill?

6 Define a holder in due course. What are his rights on a bill? R is the holder in due course of a bill of exchange, which on presentation proves to have been stolen earlier by T, a thief. T as a 'favour' endorsed it and gave it to S, who used it to buy goods from R. T has since disappeared and the acceptor has already honoured a substitute bill made out when the first bill disappeared. Who must pay R, and who stands the loss on the bill?

7 Write short explanations of the following terms: (a) open cheque; (b) crossed cheque; (c) bearer cheque; (d) special crossing; (e) 'not negotiable'; (f) account payee.

8 Define a cheque. What protection is given to bankers who pay cheques under the *Cheques Act, 1957*?

9 What protection is given to a collecting banker by the *Cheques Act, 1957*? When does a collecting banker lose protection?

Chapter 18: Arbitration

1 What is arbitration? What are its advantages? Are there any disadvantages?

2 Explain the terms 'arbitrator' and 'umpire' in arbitration proceedings. An arbitration clause says: 'In any dispute the matter shall be settled by the opinion of two arbitrators, one of whom – for the carriers – shall be a member of the sea freight trade association. The other shall be appointed by the cargo owners.' In such a situation who is the umpire?

3 'In arbitration proceedings every case is thrown away, and of no legal effect whatsoever.' Appraise this statement using an imaginary situation in which a war closes both ends of the Suez Canal, trapping 18 vessels chartered by various charterers from various owners.

4 Under arbitration proceedings held in New York which included an agreement by the parties 'not to appeal to any court of law in any country, but to rely solely on the decisions of the arbitrators concerned', A must pay B 100 000 dollars. B, a British citizen, considers the award to have been unfair and the arbitrators biased. What will be the attitude of a British court?

5 What is the situation if X, a party who believes a point of law has been incorrectly viewed in domestic arbitration proceedings, wishes to bring the matter before the courts? Y, the other party, is not prepared to agree to the matter being referred to the courts, on the ground that the costs will be out of all proportion to any possible change in the award.

6 (a) What is the effect of the *Consumer Arbitration Agreements Act, 1988* on clauses inserted into contracts by which the parties agree to let all disputes be settled by arbitration? (b) Penniless purchased furniture for his bed-sit from Unscrupulous Ltd, using money borrowed on personal loan. The furniture falls to pieces within a few months and Penniless is told by Unscrupulous Ltd that legal action will not avail him of any remedy, since the contract contains a clause 'All disputes whatsoever are to be settled by an arbitrator from the Furniture Makers Trade Association Ltd'. Advise Penniless.

Chapter 19: Administrative law

1 Explain briefly some of the grounds on which courts may intervene to set aside an administrative decision.

2 What do you understand by the concept of natural justice?

3 Write notes on at least *three* of the following methods of judicial control: (a) *mandamus*; (b) *certiorari*; (c) prohibition; (d) injunction; (e) declaration.

472 Business Law

4 Explain what administrative justice is and discuss the workings of at least *two* administrative tribunals.
5 Compare and contrast public inquiries and tribunals of inquiry.
6 The office of the Parliamentary Commissioner for Administration (the Ombudsman) is an important means of redress against oppressive or faulty government. Discuss.
7 Explain fully, with case law examples, at least three grounds on which the courts may intervene to set aside an administrative decision.
8 The concept of ombudsman seems to be working and is therefore being introduced in new areas. Do you consider this to be a good development?

Chapter 20: Introduction to the law of tort

1 What is tort and how does it differ from a crime or a breach of a contract?
2 Explain *three* of the following general defences available to an action for tort: (a) *volenti non fit injuria*; (b) necessity; (c) mistake; (d) inevitable accident; (e) statutory authority; (f) self-defence; (g) Act of God; (h) Act of State.
3 What do you understand by vicarious liability in relation to the liability of: (a) principal and agent; (b) master and servant; and (c) an independent contractor?
4 Explain the various remedies available to an action for tort. M has attended an ice hockey match and been injured in the eye by a flying puck. He gained admission on a ticket bearing a warning: '*Note*: The management cannot accept responsibility for injury to members of the public attending this match.' Advise M.
5 T has been injured by a vehicle driven by X, the employee of Y. X was intoxicated, having spent his lunch-time in a bar. Y, who knows that X likes a drink, has specifically forbidden him to enter a bar during his lunch period. Advise T.
6 Distinguish between nominal, substantial and aggravated damages. Z has been injured in an accident due to the negligence of a crane driver in a port, who is the employee of the Port Authority. The injuries were made worse by Z's failure to wear a hard helmet provided to all visitors. Discuss what sort of damages are payable to Z.

Chapter 21: Negligence

1 Define negligence. It has been said that 'the categories of negligence are never closed'. Explain this statement, referring in your answer to a case in which people were made ill, and some died, because a carrier placed a sack of wholemeal flour alongside a sack of a new type of adhesive. Neither the manufacturer nor the carrier knew of the potentially dangerous nature of the new material. The baker, who is being sued by the relatives of deceased customers, seeks advice.
2 What do you understand by a 'duty of care'? To whom is a duty of care owed?
3 Explain the doctrine of *res ipsa loquitur*. A receives a crate of crockery which is smashed to pieces, although packed by professional packers. It was delivered by T Ltd, a multimodal transport operator, whose conditions of carriage state that he will be liable for damage not attributable to fault of the consigner. Advise A (i) as to his need to provide proof of damage, (ii) as to any defences the carrier may raise to deny liability.

4 Why is the House of Lords' decision in *Hedley Byrne and Co. Ltd v. Heller and Partners Ltd* (*1963*) important?
5 What is contributory negligence? A was seriously injured while sitting in the front passenger seat of a car driven by B who has been found guilty of careless driving. A's seat belt was not in use at the time although it was available and in good condition. A does not believe people should be forced to wear seat belts. B was not seriously injured in the crash, yet the impact the car sustained was on the driver's side. Discuss the 'negligence' implications in this case.
6 What is the 'neighbour principle'? Discuss whether A, who has a miscarriage when B's car collides with C's car in the street outside her house, is a neighbour of B or C.
7 (a) What is the meaning of the term 'economic loss' in the law of tort? (b) Market Gardeners Ltd have an oral agreement with Country Transporters Co. that the road haulage firm will carry their goods to the railway depot as and when required – a system which has worked well for some years. The haulier's vehicle had a slow puncture in one tyre, but to meet an unexpected request from Market Gardeners Ltd they decided to pump it up hard and trust to luck that it would last long enough to complete the journey. It didn't and they missed the train. Market Gardeners Ltd threaten to sue for economic loss due to missing the market. Advise Country Transporters Co.

Chapter 22: The liability of occupiers of premises

1 What is the liability of an occupier of premises towards: (a) visitors; (b) children; (c) trespassers?
2 What are the main provisions of the *Occupiers Liability Act, 1957*, concerning the liability of an occupier of premises? Can an occupier exclude his liability?
3 What is meant by 'a breach of statutory duty'? To succeed in his action what must a plaintiff prove? Outline the defences available.
4 What is the rule in *Rylands v. Fletcher*? What defences are available?
5 Explain the important provisions of the *Animals Act, 1971*, concerning: (a) livestock; (b) animals straying on highways; (c) keepers of dogs.
6 What is the liability of a landowner to trespassers on his/her property?

Chapter 23: Trespass to property

1 Explain what you understand by trespass to land, giving cases. Give examples of the forms trespass to property can take.
2 (a) What is trespass to land? (b) Explain some of the forms it takes. (c) What defences can be pleaded to an action for trespass to land?
3 Explain: (a) trespass to goods; (b) conversion.
4 Define conversion and explain the various types of conversion.
5 Write notes on *three* of the following: (a) trespass *ab initio*; (b) *Esso Petroleum Co. Ltd v. Southport Corporation* (*1955*); (c) remedies for trespass to land; (d) defences to trespass to goods; (e) ineffectual defences in conversion.
6 What new types of trespass are made offences under the *Criminal Justice and Public Order Act, 1994*? Explain each type.

Chapter 24: Nuisance

1 Explain private nuisance and public nuisance.
2 What is a private nuisance and what factors are important when considering it?

474 Business Law

3. What is meant by abatement of a nuisance? B uses a malodorous substance to manure his fields. At a public meeting he agrees to spray the substance on only once a month, but always chooses a day before a weekend. Advise A, who is unable to enjoy his garden.
4. Compare private and public nuisance. What defences are available to an action for private nuisance?
5. Write notes on *three* of the following: (a) the standard of comfort varies in private nuisance; (b) *Robinson v. Kilvert* (*1889*); (c) prescription; (d) ineffectual defences in private nuisance; (e) *R. v. Maddox* (1975); (f) the forms public nuisance can take.

Chapter 25: Defamation

1. (a) Distinguish between a libel and a slander. (b) What defences are available when sued for defamation?
2. Explain, giving cases, what a plaintiff must prove to succeed in a claim for defamation.
3. Write notes on *two* of the following defences in defamation: (a) justification; (b) fair comment; (c) absolute privilege; (d) qualified privilege; (e) unintentional defamation; (f) apology.
4. Explain the differences between libel and slander. What is meant by innuendo?
5. What do you understand by the defences of absolute and qualified privilege in defamation?

Chapter 26: Miscellaneous torts

1. Explain the tort of conspiracy. A and B, the employees of C, join a union to seek wage increases for themselves and their fellow employees. The resulting strike seriously affects C's business, not so much by the disruption it causes but by the publication of the wages paid to employees, which are abysmally low. Advise C.
2. A has been misled by B into purchasing shares in a company which subsequently collapsed. He has now discovered that A's statements were made the day after a crisis board meeting which A had attended in which the possible voluntary liquidation of the company was discussed. Before the discussion could be completed by a further meeting the company became insolvent. Advise A.
3. Distinguish between defamation and injurious falsehood. G, whose business has suffered by unfair adverse criticism in a magazine which confused his product with one with a similar name, is seeking damages for injurious falsehood. What would be the measure of damages in such a case?
4. J advertises a blend of synthetic alcohols and home-brewed wine as 'Scotch Heather Whisky'. A firm of Scottish whisky distillers markets a brand of Scotch whisky under the brand name 'Purple Heather'. What actions might they be able to bring against J?

Chapter 27: Property

1. What is property? What is ownership? What is possession?
2. List the different types of property and give three examples of each.
3. What is the difference between a legal interest in land and an equitable interest in land? In your answer refer to (a) rights of way; and (b) the deposit of deeds with a bank as security for a loan.
4. (a) What is a lease? (b) What is a covenant in a lease? (c) Tailor, who makes made-to-measure suits, buys the lease of shop premises with living accommodation above. A clause in the lease requires the lessee to live over

the premises, and not to use the domestic part of the premises for trade purposes. Advise Tailor, whose wife does not like the arrangements and who would like to expand his business by employing several apprentices.
5 State the case for and against do-it-yourself conveyancing of business premises.
6 What is a trade mark? What is a service mark? Why is it advisable to register such marks?
7 (a) What is the right of paternity in authorship and similar activities? (b) Composer has written the musical score of a television production and is credited with this on the list of credits at the end of the film. A video is released but due to the length of the film the credits have been cut and no attributions appear to any of the performers or other personnel involved. Advise Composer.
8 How has Section 40 of the *Law of Property Act* been modified by Section 2 of the *Law of Property (Miscellaneous Provisions) Act, 1985*?

Chapter 28: The law and consumer protection

1 Why do consumers need protection? List five Acts of Parliament which come into this area of law.
2 Who is liable when a defective product causes injury to a child? Refer in your answer to the supplier, and any other parties to whom the child may look for compensation.
3 (a) What defences are available to a person held liable for a defective product? (b) Drugmaker is sued because a child is born with a deformity. Advise Drugmaker about possible defences to the allegation.
4 (a) What is the legal position about a price indication which proves to be misleading? (b) Rackman, who lets out property in a slum area, charges very low rents. At the same time he has arranged for gas and electricity to be supplied through coin meters at an excessive price, and he also bills tenants monthly for security, waste disposal and similar services. Advise Student, who has signed a one-year tenancy agreement.
5 What is an APR? Explain why an APR enables borrowers to compare the following situations: (a) A television set available at a cash price of £100; (b) a television set available for a £20 deposit and 24 monthly instalments, the balance of £80 being charged interest at a flat rate of 15 per cent per annum; (c) a television set paid for with a credit card at a price of £100 repayable at the buyer's discretion with interest at 2.35 per cent per month.
6 What are the basic principles one is required to abide by when storing personal electronic data on others?
7 In what ways does the *Financial Services Act, 1986* regulate investment business in this country?

Chapter 29: Employment law

1 What is the position of a Spanish engineer who wishes to work in the United Kingdom? Contrast with this the position of a Romanian welder, experienced in bridge construction, who wishes to do the same thing.
2 What is a 'spent' conviction? Advise A, who is preparing to attend an interview and was fined 15 years ago for knocking off a policeman's helmet in a demonstration.
3 What matters should appear in a 'written statement of the particulars of an employee's employment'?
4 What is statutory sick pay? How is it paid?

5 What is 'summary dismissal'? Arthur, who is the living image of Henry, is met in the corridor by his employer who accuses him of leaking secrets to a competitor. Security is called and he is escorted off the premises. When he asks for his hat and coat and other personal things they are thrown out of the gate to the factory. Arthur suspects he has been mistaken for Henry. Advise Arthur.
6 What sort of information must a Board of Directors disclose to the staff representatives of a joint consultation committee?

Appendix 2   Glossary of Latin terms

ab initio	from the beginning
actio personalis moritur cum persona	a personal action dies with the person
ad litem	with respect to a suit at law
administrator cum testamento annexo	administrator with the will annexed (which the court appoints him to administer)
administrator durante minor aetate	administrator during infancy (of the true appointee)
administrator pendente lite	administrator during the litigation (of a disputed will)
animus manendi	the intention to remain in that place or country
animus revocandi	the intention to revoke
audi alteram partem	hear the other side
bona fide	in good faith
bona vacantia	ownerless property
caveat emptor	let the buyer beware
certiorari	to be informed (an order of *certiorari* is explained on page 336)
cestui que trust	the person for whose benefit a trust is created; a beneficiary
chattels personal	personal goods
chattels real	a lease, forming part of personalty
chose in action	a thing in action; a personal right of property which can only be claimed or enforced by an action at law and not by taking physical possession
chose in possession	a thing that is the subject of physical possession (contrast with chose in action)
consensus ad idem	mutual agreement on the same point
cujus est solum ejus est usque ad coelum	the owner of land owns all the land below the surface and all the space above the land
cum testamento annexo	with the will attached
Curia Regis	the King's Court
cy-près	so near; as nearly as possible
damnum sine injuria	damage without legal wrong
de facto	existing in fact
del credere	in the belief that (the buyer is solvent)
delegatus non potest delegare	one to whom power has been delegated cannot delegate that power to another
de minimis non curat lex	'the law takes no notice of trifles'

de novo	anew
distress damage feasant	the right of an occupier of land to seize animals doing damage thereon
donatio mortis causa	a gift in anticipation of death
durante minore aetate	during infancy
ejusdem generis	of the same kind, or nature
equitas sequitur legem	equity follows the law
escrow	a sealed writing delivered conditionally, which condition being performed it operates immediately as a deed
estoppel	a rule of evidence whereby a party is precluded by some previous act to which he was party or privy from asserting or denying a fact. For example, a party cannot aver that a state of things is different from what he has led the other party to believe if the other party has acted upon such belief and changed his position to his detriment
ex gratia	as a matter of favour
ex nudo pacto non oritur actio	a bare promise (without consideration) does not give rise to any action
ex officio	arising from an official position, by virtue of his office
ex parte	on the application of (an *ex parte* hearing is one at which only one side is represented)
ex post facto	after the event
expressio unius est exclusio alterius	the express mention of one thing implies the exclusion of another
ex turpi causa non oritur actio	no action arises out of a base cause
ibid. = *ibidem*	in the same place
ignorantia juris haud excusat	
ignorantia juris neminem excusat	ignorance of the law excuses no one
ignorantia juris non excusat	
in consimili casu	in similar case to
in extremis	in imminent peril of death
in personam	against a person (as distinct from the whole world)
in pari delicto potior est conditio possidentis	where two parties are equally in the wrong, the condition of the possessor is the stronger
in pari delicto potior est conditio defendentis	of two wrongdoers it is better to be the defendant
in personam	an act, proceeding or a right in land which is good against a specified person who is aware of it – but not valid against any other person – such as a buyer of the property who is not aware of the right
in re	in the matter of

Appendix 2 Glossary of Latin terms

in rem	against a thing; a right *in rem* is a right in property such as land which is good against the whole world
in terrorem	as a threat, to cause fear
indenture	a deed to which there are two or more parties
injuria sine damno	legal wrong without damage
inter alia	among other matters
inter se	among themselves
inter vivos	during life
just accrescendi	right of survivorship
jus tertii	the right of a third party
laches	delay, e.g. in pursuing a remedy at law
lex loci contractus	the law of the place where the agreement was made
locus sigilli	the place of the seal
mandamus	we command (an order of *mandamus* is explained on page 336)
Magnum Concilium	the Great Council
mens rea	guilty mind
mesne	intermediate
nec per vim, nec clam, nec precario	peaceably, openly and as of right
nemo dat quod non habet	no one can give what he does not have
nemo judex in causa sua	no one shall be a judge in his own case
non est factum	'not my act'
noscitur a sociis	the meaning of a word can be gathered from its context
novus actus interveniens	a new development intervening (to change the legal situation)
obiter dicta	sayings by the way
overt	open
pendente lite	during the litigation
per incuriam	by oversight (of a judge)
per se	by itself, by *or* through himself
per subsequens matrimonium	by subsequent marriage
per capita	by the number of individuals
prima facie	at a first view
puisne	lesser in importance
pur autre vie	for another's life
quantum meruit	as much as he has deserved
quasi	as if, as it were
quid pro quo	a mutual consideration; tit for tat
qui facit per alium facit per se	he who does a thing through another does it himself

ratio decidendi	the reason for the decision
res	thing
res extincta	the thing having ceased to exist
res ipsa loquitur	'the thing speaks for itself'
res sua	the thing being his own property
restitutio in integrum	restoration to the original position
sans recours	without recourse
sciens	knowing
scienti non fit injuria	one who knows cannot be harmed
seisin	effective possession of land by a freeholder
sic utere tuo ut alienum non laedas	so use your own property as not to injure your neighbour's
sine die	without fixing a day
stare decisis	to stand by past decisions
status quo	the state in which a thing exists
sue	to take proceedings in a civil action
sui juris	of full legal capacity
surrogate	deputy
tortfeasor	a person liable on a civil wrong other than a contractual or trust matter
trover	an early form of conversion in which a finding (*trover*) of the goods was alleged
uberrimae fidei	of the utmost good faith
ubi jus ibi remedium	where there is a right there is a remedy
ubi remedium ibi jus	where there is a remedy there is a right
ultra vires	beyond the powers of
viva voce	by word of mouth
volens	willing
volenti non fit injuria	no wrong can be done to one who consents to what is done

Appendix 3 Table of cases

Case	Page
Adams v. Lindsell (1818) 1 B & Ald 681	118
Adams v. Ursell (1913) I Ch 269	401, 404
Addie and Sons v. Dumbreck (1929) AC 358 (H of L)	383
Addis v. Crocker (1961) 2 All ER 629	413
Adler v. Dickson (1954) 3 All ER 396 (C of A)	281
Affréteurs Réunis, SA Les, v. Leopold Watford (London) Ltd (1919) AC 801 (H of L)	148
Ajello v. Worsley (1898) I Ch 274	350
Alexander v. NE Railway Co. (1865) 6 B & S 340	411
Alexander v. Rayson (1936) I KB 169	140
Alhambra, The, (1881) WR 655	286
Allcard v. Skinner (1887) 36 Ch D 145 (C of A)	131
Allen v. Gold Reefs of West Africa Ltd (1900) All ER 746	71
Alliance Bank v. Broom (1865) 34 LJ Ch 256	122
Aluminium Industrie Vassen BV v. Romalpa Aluminium Ltd (1976) WLR 676	237
Anderson Ltd v. Daniel (1924) I KB 138	142
Anns v. Merton London Borough Council (1978) AC 728	374
Aquis Estates Ltd v. Minton (1975) I WLR 1452	148
Arbuckle v. Taylor (1815) 3 Dow 160	54
Ardennes, SS (Cargo Owners) v. Ardennes (Owners) (1950) 2 All ER 517	96, 278
Armoury v. Delamirie (1721)	395
Armstrong v. Jackson (1917) 2 KB 827	204
Arterial Caravans Ltd v. Yorkshire Insurance Co. (1973) 1 LI Rep. 169	246
Ashbury Railway Carriage & Iron Co. v. Riche (1875) LR7 HL653 (H of L)	69
Ashby v. Tolhurst (1937) 2 All ER 837	395
Att. Gen. v. Cole (1901) 1 Ch 205	404
Att. Gen. v. Fulham Corporation (1921) 1 Ch. 440	329, 337
Att. Gen. v. Gastonia Coaches (1976) RTR 219	405
Att. Gen. v. Great Eastern Railway (1880) 5 App Cas 473	69
Att. Gen. v. P.Y.A. Quarries Ltd (1957) 1 All ER (C of A)	404
Att. Gen. of Hong Kong v. Reid (1993) 3 WLR 1143	79
Attwood v. Small (1838) 6 C1 & Fin 232	162
Australia and New Zealand Bank v. Ateliers de Constructions Electriques, de Charleroi (1966) 1 AC 86	199
Avery v. Bowden (1855) 6 E & B 953	178
Baker v. T. E. Hopkins and Sons Ltd (1959) 3 All ER 225	354
Balfour v. Balfour (1919) 2 KB 571 (C of A)	104, 108
Bank of England v. Vagliano Bros. (1891) AC 107	309
Barker v. Bell (1971) 1 WLR 983	231
Barclays Bank v. O'Brien (1993) 3 WLR 786 (H of L)	131
Barkway v. South Wales Transport Co. Ltd (1950) 94 SJ 95	378
Barnard v. National Dock Harbour Board (1953) 2 QB 18	333
Barrow, Lane and Ballard Ltd v. Phillip, Phillip and Co. (1929) 1 KB 574	222
Bartlett v. Sidney Marcus (1965), 1 WLR 1013	225
Barton v. Armstrong (1975) 2 All ER 465	129
Baseley v. Clarkson (1681) 3 Lev 37	355
Beale v. Taylor (1967) 3 All ER 253 (C of A)	224
Beard v. London General Omnibus Co. (1900) 2 QB 530	367
Bebee v. Sales (1916) 32 TLR 413	358
Beckwith v. Philby (1827) 6 B & C 635	355
Behn v. Burness (1863) 3 B & S 751	284
Bell v. Lever Bros Ltd (1932) AC 161	134
Benjamin v. Storr (1874) LR9 CP400	405
Bentley v. Craven (1853) 18 Beav 75	55

Beswick v. Beswick (1967) 2 All ER 1197 (H of L) 190
Bettini v. Gye (1876) 1 QBD 183 146
Bevan v. The National Bank Ltd (1906) 52
Bevan v. Webb (1905) I Ch 620 55
Bird v. Holbrook (1828) 4 Bing 628 383
Bisset v. Wilkinson (1927) Ac 177 (Privy Council) 161
Bliss v. Hall (1838) 4 Bing NC 183 404
Blyth v. Birmingham Waterworks Co. (1856) 11 Exch 781 .... 362, 371
Bogel v. Miller (1903) 54
Bolam v. Friern Barnet Hospital Committee (1957) 2 All ER 118 .... 373, 374
Bollinger J. v. Costa Brava Wine Co. Ltd (1961) 1 All ER 561 419
Bolton v. Madden (1873) LR 9 QB 55 120
Bolton v. Stone (1951) 1 All ER 1078 .... 375, 402
Bonnington Castings Ltd v. Wardlaw (1956) 1 All ER 615 385
Borland's Trustee v. Steel Bros & Co. Ltd (1901) Ch 279 74
Bostik Limited v. Sellotape, GB Ltd (1994) *The Times* January 11, 1994 419
Boston Deep Sea Fishing and Ice Co. v. Ansell (1888) 39 CHD 339 81
Boston Deep Sea Fishing and Ice Co. v. Farnham (1957) 1 WLR 1051 203
Bowater v. Rowley Regis Corporation (1944) 1 All ER 465 353
Bower v. Peate (1876) 1 QBD 321 403
Brace v. Calder and Others 2 QB 253 188
Bradbury v. London Borough of Enfield (1967) 3 All ER 434 331
Bradbury v. Morgan (1862) 1 H & C 249 116
Bradford Corporation v. Pickles (1895) AC 587 (H of L) 350
Branca v. Cobarro (1947) 2 All ER 101 (Court of Appeal) 117
Brandt's v. Dunlop Rubber Co. (1905) AC 454 181
Bratton Seymour Service Co. Ltd v. Oxborough (1992) BCE 471 72
Bridges v. Hawkesworth (1851) 21 LJ QB 75 396
British Celanese v. A. H. Hunt (1969) 2 All ER 1252 402
British Crane Hire Corporation v. Ipswich Plant Hire Ltd (1974) 1 All ER 1059
    (C of A) 148
British Railways Board v. Herrington (1972) AC 877 383
British Reinforced Concrete Co. v. Schelff (1921) 2 Ch 563 141
British Russian Gazette and Trade Outlook Ltd v. Associated Newspapers Ltd (1933)
    2 KB 616 CA 173
British Steel Corporation v. Cleveland Bridge and Engineering (1984) All ER 504 189
British Transport Commission v. Gourley (1956) AC 185 HL 188
Brown v. Lewis (1896) 12 TLR 566 63
Buckpitt v. Oates (1968) 1 All ER 1145 104
Bulmer H. P. v. Bollinger J. SA (1974) FSR 334 37
Burland v. Earle (1902) AC 83 82
Burnard v. Haggis (1863) 14 CB (NS) 45 358
Buron v. Denman (1848) 2 Exch 167 357
Burrows v. Rhodes (1899) 1 QB 816 417
Burt v. Governor General of New Zealand (1992) 330
Business Application Specialists v. Nationwide Corporation Ltd (1985) *The Times* April
    27, 1988 225
Bux v. Slough Metals (1973) 1 WLR 1358 373
Byrne v. Boadle (1863) 2 H & C 722 378
Byrne v. Deane (1937) 2 All ER 204 .... 408, 411
Byrne v. Van Tienhoven (1880) 5 CPD 344 114

Capital and Counties Bank Ltd v. George Henty & Sons (1882) 7 App Cas 741
    (H of L) 408
Car and Universal Finance Ltd. v. Caldwell (1964) 1 All ER 290 (C of A) 229
Carlill v. Carbolic Smoke Ball Co. (1892) 1 QB 256 (C of A) 111, 113, 115
Carmarthenshire C.C. v. Lewis (1955) 1 All ER 565 (H of L) 374
Carmichael v. Evans (1904) 1 Ch 46 57
Carter v. Boehm (1766) All ER 183 246
Cassell v. Broome (1972) 2 WLR 645 414
Cassidy v. Daily Mirror (1929) 2 KB 331 (C of A) 410
Cassidy v. Ministry of Health (1951) 1 All ER 574 (C of A) 329
Castle v. St Augustine's Links (1922) 38 TLR 615 405
Caswell v. Powell Duffryn Associated Collieries Ltd (1939) 3 All ER 722 (H of L) .. 386
Cehave NV v. Bremer Handelsgesellschaft mbh, The Hansa Nord (1976) QB 44 222
Century Insurance Co. Ltd v. Northern Ireland Road Transport Board (1942)
    AC 509 367

Central London Property Trust Ltd v. High Trees House Ltd (1947)
    1 All ER 256 .... 124, 128
Chanter v. Hopkins (1838) 4 M & W 399 154
Chapell and Co. Ltd v. Nestlé Ltd (1959) 2 All ER 701 121
Chapelton v. Barry UDC (1940) 1 All ER 356 150–1
Chapple v. Cooper (1844) 13 M & W 252 99
Chatterton v. Secretary of State for India (1895) 2 QB 189 (C of A) 413
Chillingworth v. Esche (1924) 1 Ch 97 117
Christensen v. Hindustan Steel (1971) 1 WLR 1369 285
Citizens Life Assurance Co. v. Brown (1904) AC 423 73
Clements v. London and North Western Railway Co. (1894) 2 QB 482 (C of A) 99
Clough Mill v. Martin (1985) 1 WLR 111 238
Cobb v. Great Western Railway (1894) AC 419 362
Cohen v. Daily Telegraph (1968) 2 All ER 407 412
Cohen v. Roche (1927) 1 KB 169 190
Coleen Properties Ltd v. Minister of Housing and Local Government (1971)
    1 WLR 433 332
Collins v. Godefroy (1831) 1 B & Ad 950 122
Collins v. Hertfordshire County Council (1947) 1 All ER 633 366
Combe v. Combe (1951) 1 All ER 767 124
Coney v. Choyce and Others (1975) 1 WLR 422 330
Congreve v. Home Office (1976) QB 629 331
Consolidated Co. v. Curtis and Son (1892) 1 QB 495 .... 355, 397
Consolidated Tea and Lands Co. v. Oliver's Wharf (1910) 2 KB 395 276
Cooke v. Midland G.W. Railway of Ireland (1909) AC 229 383
Cooper v. Phibbs (1867) LR 2HL 149 .... 133, 134
Cooper v. Wandsworth Board of Works (1863) 14 CB (NS) 180 336
Cope v. Sharpe (1912) 1 KB 496 .... 355, 394
Cottrill v. Steyning and Littlehampton Building Society (1966) 2 All ER 295 186
Council of Civil Service Unions v. Minister for the Civil Service (1985) ICR14 329
Coutts & Co. v. Browne-Lecky (1946) 2 All ER 207 102
Couturier v. Hastie (1952) 8 Exch 40 133
Cowan v. O'Connor (1888) 20 QBD 640 118
Cowern v. Nield (1912) 2 KB 419 100
Creasey v. Beechwood Motors Ltd (1992) BCC 638 73
Cresswell v. Sirl (1948) 2 All ER 730 .... 357, 395
Crofter Hand Woven Harris Tweed Co. Ltd v. Veitch (1942) 1 All ER 142 (H of L) . 417
Crowhurst v. Amersham Burial Board (1878) 4EX D5 388
Cundy v. Lindsay (1878) 3 App Cas 459 (H of L) 132, 137, 229
Curtis v. Chemical Cleaning and Dyeing Co. Ltd (1951) 1 KB 805 153
Curtis and Sons v. Matthews (1919) 1 KB 425 264
Cutler v. United Dairies (London) Ltd (1933) 2 KB 297 (C of A) 354
Cutter v. Powell (1795) 6 Term Rep 320 171

Daimler Co. Ltd v. Continental Tyre & Rubber Co. (Gt Britain) Ltd (1916)
    2 AC 307 73
Dale v. Wood (1822) 7 Moore CP 33 357
Dann v. Hamilton (1939) 1 All ER 59 351
Davis Contractors Ltd v. Fareham Urban District Council (1956) 2 All ER 145
    (H of L) 177
Dawes v. Peck (1799) 8 TR 330 267
De Beers Abrasive Products Ltd v. International Electric Co. of New York Ltd (1975)
    2 All ER 599 418
De Francesco v. Barnum (1890) 45 Ch D 430 100
De La Bere v. Pearson (1908) 1 KB 280 121
Denny Mott and Dickson Ltd v. Fraser & Co. Ltd (1944) AC 265 176
Department of Environment v. Thomas Bates & Sons Ltd (1989) 1 All ER 1075 . 379, 381
Derry v. Peek (1889) 14 App Cas 337 (H of L) 163, 417
Deziel v. Deziel (1953) 1 DLR 651 358
Diamond v. Campbell-Jones (1960) 1 All ER 583 186
Diamond Lock Grabowski v. Laing Investments (Bradnell) (1992) 60 BLR 112 319
Dick Bentley Productions Ltd v. Harold Smith (Motors) Ltd (1965) 2 All ER 65
    (C of A) 145
Dickinson v. Dodds (1876) 2 Ch D 463 (C of A) 114–15, 116
Dimmock v. Hallet (1866) 2 Ch App 21 160
Donoghue v. Stevenson (1932) AC 562 (H of L) 233, 371, 373, 380
Doughty v. Turner Manufacturing Co. Ltd (1964) 1 All ER 98 (C of A) 362

Douglas Valley Finance Co. Ltd *v.* S. Hughes (Hires) Ltd (1966) 2 All ER 214 395
Doyle *v.* White City Stadium Ltd (1935) 1 KB 110 .... 100, 108
Drew *v.* Nunn (1879) 4 QBD 661 209
Dunlop Pneumatic Tyre Co. Ltd *v.* New Grange & Motor Co. Ltd (1915) AC 7
  (H of L) 187
Dunlop Pneumatic Tyre Co. Ltd *v.* Selfridge & Co. Ltd (1915) AC 847 (H of L) 125
Durayappah *v.* Fernando (1967) 2 AC 337 336
Dutton's Case (1972) 1QB 373 374

Earl of Oxford's Case (1616) 1 Rep Ch 1 11
East *v.* Maurer (1991) 2 All ER 733 166
Eastern and South African Telegraph Co. Ltd *v.* Cape Town Tramways Co. (1902)
  AC 381 388
Eastern Distributors Ltd *v.* Goldring (1957) 2 QB 600 228
Eastwood *v.* Kenyon (1840) 11 Ad & EC 438 121
Edgington *v.* Fitzmaurice (1885) 29 Ch D7 C of A 162
Edwards *v.* Halliwell (1950) WN 537 82
Edwards *v.* Skyways Ltd (1964) 1 WLR 349 QB 105
Eglantine Inn Ltd *v.* Smith (1948) NI 29 411
Elcock *v.* Thompson (1949) 2 KB 755 250
Eliason *v.* Henshaw (1819) I Wheaton 225 (Supreme Court of the USA) 119
Elkington & Co. *v.* Hurter (1892) 80
Ellis *v.* Sheffield Gas Consumers Co. (1853) 2 E & B 767 368
Elwes *v.* Brigg Gas Co. (1886) 33 Ch D 562 396
Entores Ltd *v.* Miles Far East Corporation (1955) 2 QB 327 118
Esso Petroleum Co. Ltd *v.* Mardon (1976) 2 All ER 5 (C of A) 351, 377
Esso Petroleum Co. Ltd *v.* Southport Corporation (1955) 3 All ER 864
  (H of L) 355, 392, 394, 403

Featherstonhaugh *v.* Fenwick (1810) 17 Ves 298 55
Felthouse *v.* Bindley (1862) 11 CBNS 869 119
Finney Lockseeds *v.* Mitchell George (1979) 2 L1R 301 155
Firbank's Executors *v.* Humphreys (1886) 18 QBD 54 80
First National Securities Ltd *v.* Jones (1978) 2 All ER 221 97
Firth *v.* Bowling Iron Co. (1878) 3 CPD 254 388
Fisher *v.* Bell (1960) 3 All ER 731 111
Fisher *v.* Oldham Corporation (1930) 2 KB 364 358
Flight *v.* Bolland (1828) 298 Chancery 191
Floydd *v.* Cheney (1970) Ch 602 55
Foakes *v.* Beer (1884) 9 AC 605 .... 123, 124, 128
Foley *v.* Classique Coaches Ltd (1934) 2 KB 1 .... 117, 144
Folkes *v.* King (1923) KB 282 228
Ford Motor Co. *v.* Amalgamated Union of Engineers (1969) 2 QB 303 105
Ford Motor Co. (England) Ltd *v.* Armstrong (1915) 31 TLR 267 CR 188
Foss *v.* Harbottle (1843) 2 Hare 461 .... 82, 91
Foster *v.* Driscoll (1929) 1 KB 470 (C of A) 140
Foster *v.* MacKinnon (1869) LR4 CP 704 139
Fouldes *v.* Willoughby (1841) 8 M & W 540 396
Four Point Garage Ltd *v.* Carter (1985) 3 All ER 12 238
Froom *v.* Butcher (1975) 3 All ER 520 378
Frost *v.* Aylesbury Dairy Co. Ltd (1905) 1 KB 608 231–2

Garner *v.* Murray (1903) 1 Ch 57 58
Geddis *v.* Proprietors of Bann Reservoir (1878) 3 App Cas 430 356
General Engineering Services Ltd *v.* Kingston and St Andrew Corporation (1988) 3 All
  ER 867 367
General Cleaning Contractors Ltd *v.* Christmas (1952) 2 All ER 1110 (H of L) 373
George Mitchell *v.* Finney Lock Seeds, 1 All ER 108 155
Gibson *v.* Manchester City Council (1979) 1 WLR 294 111
Ginty *v.* Belmont Building Supplies Ltd (1959) 1 All ER 414 387
Glasbrook Brothers *v.* Glamorgan County Council (1925) AC270 (H of L) 122, 128
Glasgow Corporation *v.* Taylor (1922) 1 AC 44 383
Godley *v.* Perry (1960) 1 All ER 36 226
Goode *v.* Harrison (1821) 5 B & Ald 147 101
Gordon *v.* Gordon (1821) 3 Swan 400 .... 164, 167

Gorris *v.* Scott (1874) LR 9 Exch 125 386
Gowa and Others *v.* Attorney General (1984) 1 WLR 1003 329
Grainger & Son *v.* Gough (1896) AC 325 111
Gray *v.* Barr (1971) 2 QB 554 260
Great Eastern Railway Co. *v.* Turner (1872) 8 Ch App 149 79
Great Northern Railway *v.* Swaffield (1874) All ER 1065 .... 200, 213
Green *v.* Chelsea Waterworks Co. (1894) 70 LT 547 388
Greenwood *v.* Martin's Bank (1933) A.C. 51 309
Gregory *v.* Piper (1829) 9 B & C 591 392
Grist *v.* Bailey (1966) 2 All ER 875 134
Groves *v.* Lord Wimborne (1898) 2 QB 402 385

Hadley *v.* Baxendale (1854) 9 Exch 341 .... 185, 270
Hain S. S. Co. *v.* Tate & Lyle Ltd (1936) 2 All ER 597 154
Halford *v.* Kymer (1830) 10 B & C 724 245
Hall *v.* Brooklands Auto Racing Club (1933) 1 KB 205 352
Hamlyn *v.* Harston & Co. (1903) 1 KB 81 54
Hammond *v.* Vestry of St Pancras (1874) LR9 CP 316 385
Hampstead Guardians *v.* Barclay Bank Ltd (1923) 39 TLR 229 313
Hannah *v.* Peel (1945) KB 509 396
Harris *v.* Birkenhead Corporation (1975) 1 WLR 279 384
Harris *v.* Nickerson (1873) LR 8 QB 286 112
Harris *v.* Poland (1941) 1 KB 462 249
Harris *v.* Wyre Forest District Council (1989) 17 EG 68 HL 377, 379
Harrison *v.* Duke of Rutland (1893) 1 QB 142 (C of A) 392
Hart *v.* O'Connor (1985) 2 All ER 580 102
Hartley *v.* Mayoh & Co. (1954) 1 QB 383 386
Hartog *v.* Colin and Shields (1939) 3 All ER 566 135
Harvey *v.* Facey (1893) AC 552 112
Haynes *v.* Harwood (1935) 1 KB 146 354
Heath *v.* Brighton Corporation (1908) 98 LT 718 400
Hebdon *v.* West (1963) 3 B & S 579 248
Hedley Byrne & Co. Ltd *v.* Heller and Partners Ltd (1923)
    AC 465 .... 133, 163, 169, 376, 379, 417
Heilbut, Symons & Co. *v.* Buckleton (1913) AC 30 H of L 145
Helston Securities Ltd *v.* Hertfordshire County Council (1978) 3 All ER 262 .. 180
Hely-Hutchinson *v.* Brayhead Ltd (1968) 3 All ER 98 81
Hemmings *v.* Stoke Poges Golf Club Ltd (1920) 1 KB 720 .... 393, 394
Henderson & Co. *v.* Williams (1895) 1 WB 521 C of A 200
Herne Bay Steamboat Co. *v.* Hutton (1903) 2 KB 683 CA 176
Hewitt *v.* Bonvir (1940) 1 KB 188 365
Heyting *v.* Dupont (1964) 1 WLR 843 82
Heyworth *v.* Hutchinson (1867) LR 2 WB 447 146
Hickman *v.* Maisey (1900) 1 QB 752 392
Higgins *v.* Beauchamp (1914) 3 KB 1192 53
Hillas & Co. *v.* Arcos Ltd (1932) 38 Com Cas 23 (H of L) ... 112, 113, 117, 127, 144, 148
Hiort *v.* Bott (1874) LR 9 Exch 86 397
Hirachand Punamchand *v.* Temple (1911) 2 KB 330 CA 124
Hoare & Co. *v.* McAlpine (1923) 1 Ch 167 388
Hoenig *v.* Isaacs (1952) 2 All ER 176 CA 173, 182
Hollins *v.* Fowler (1875) LR 7 HL 757 .... 396, 397
Hollywood Silver Fox Farm Ltd *v.* Emmett (1936) 2 KB 468 402
Holwell Securities *v.* Hughes 1 All ER 161 118
Honeywell & Stein Ltd *v.* Larkin Bros (1934) 1 KB 191 368
Hong Kong Fir Shipping Co. Ltd *v.* Kawasaki Kisen Kaisha Ltd (1962) 1 All ER
    474 CA 146
Hosking *v.* De Havilland Aircraft Co. Ltd (1949) 1 All ER 450 369
Houghton & Co. *v.* Nothard, Lowe & Willis Ltd (1928) AC 1 84
Houldsworth *v.* City of Glasgow Bank (1880) 5 AC 317 73
Household Fire and Carriage Accident Insurance Co. *v.* Grant 1879 4 ExD 216 .. 118
Howard Smith Ltd *v.* Ampol Petroleum Ltd (1974) AC 281 80–1
H. P. Bulmer *v.* J. Bollinger SA (1974) Ch 401 2 All ER 1226 37
Hughes *v.* Lord Advocate (1936) AC 837 362
Hulton *v.* Jones (1910) AC 20 410
Humble *v.* Hunter (1848) 12 QB 310 207
Huth *v.* Huth (1915) 3 KB 32 411

Hyde v. Wrench (1840) 3 Bear 334 .... 115, 116
ICI Ltd v. Shatwell (1964) 2 All ER 999 386
Ingram v. Little (1960) 3 All ER 332 (C of A) 137
International Sales and Agencies Ltd v. Marcus (1982) 3 All ER 551 103
International Sea Tanker Inc. of Liberia v. Hemisphere Shipping Co. of Hong Kong
    (1981) Com LR 157 317
Introductions Ltd v. National Provincial Bank Ltd (1969) 2 WLR 791 70

Jackson v. Hopperton (1864) 16 CB (NS) 829 413
James & Sons Ltd v. Tankerville (1909) 394
Jennings v. Broughton (1854) 162
Jennings v. Rundall (1799) 8 Term Rep 335 358
Jobson v. Johnson (1988) 4 BCC 488 188
Joel v. Law Union and Commercial Assurance Co. (1908) 2 KB 813 164
John McCann & Co. v. Pow (1974) 1 WLR 1643 204
Johnston v. Pedlar (1921) 2 AC 262 357
Jones v. Boyce (1816) I Starkie 493 379
Jones v. Llanrwst Urban District Council (1911) 1 Ch 393 388
Jones v. Vernons Pools Ltd (1938) 2 All ER 626 105
Joscelyne v. Nissen (1970) 135
Joseph Travers & Sons Ltd v. Cooper (1915) 1 KB 73 266

Karsales (Harrow) Ltd v. Wallis (1956) 2 All ER 866 .... 154, 155
Keates v. Earl of Cadogan (1851) 10 CB 951 160
Keighley Maxstead & Co. v. Durrant (1901) AC 240 202
Kelner v. Baxter (1866) LR 2 CP 174 203
Kelson v. Imperial Tobacco Co. Ltd (1957) 2 QB 334 392
Kendall v. Hamilton (1897) 4 App Cas 504 54
Kennaway v. Thompson (1980) 3 WLR 361 403
Kerr v. Kennedy (1942) 1 KB 409 408
Khorasandjian v. Bush (1993) 402
King v. Phillips (1953) 1 All ER 617 375
Kings Norton Metal Co. Ltd v. Edridge, Merrett & Co. Ltd (1897) 14 TLR 98
    (C of A) 136
King's Prerogative in Saltpetre (1606) 355
Koufos v. C. Czarnikow Ltd, The Heron II (1967) 3 All ER 686 HL 186
Krell v. Henry (1903) 2 KB 740 CA 175

Lampleigh v. Braithwait (1615) 80 All ER 255 125
Lancashire & Cheshire Assoc. of Baptist Churches v. Howard and Eldon 351
Lancashire Loans Ltd v. Black (1934) 1 KB 380 C of A 130
Lane v. Holloway (1967) 3 WLR 1003 356
Lane v. Shire Roofing Co. (Oxford) Ltd (1995), *The Times* February 22 206
Latimer v. AEC Ltd (1953) 2 All ER 449 375
Lavender & Son Ltd v. Minister of Housing and Local Government (1970)
    1 WLR 1231 333
Law v. Llewellyn (1906) 1 KB 487 359
Leaf v. International Galleries (1950) 1 All ER 693 C of A 132, 134, 147, 167
Lease Management Services Ltd v. Purnell Secretarial Services Ltd, 1994 *The Times*
    April 1 157
Lee v. Lee's Air Farming Ltd (1961) AC 12 79
Leesh River Tea Co. v. British Indian Steam Navigation Co. Ltd (1967) 2 QB 250 ... 283
Lemmon v. Webb (1891) AC 1 (1894) 3 Ch 1 404
L'Estrange v. F. Graucob Ltd (1934) 2 KB 394 152
Lewis v. Averay (1971) 3 All ER 907 (C of A) 138, 168, 229
Limpus v. London General Omnibus Co. (1862) 1 H & C 526 367
Linden Gardens Trust Ltd v. Sludge Disposals and others (1993) 180
Lister v. Romford Ice and Cold Storage Co. Ltd (1957) AC 555 368
Liver Alkali Co. v. Johnson (1874) LR 9Ex 338 276
Lloyd v. Grace Smith & Co. (1912) AC 716 HL 206, 367
Lloyds Bank v. Chartered Bank (1929) 1 KB 40 396
Lloyds Bank Ltd v. Waterhouse (1990) 139
Lochgelly Iron & Coal Co. v. McMullan (1934) AC 1 371
Locker and Woolf Ltd v. Western Australian Insurance Co. Ltd (1936) 1 KB 408
    (C of A) 164, 246
Loftus v. Roberts (1902) 18 TLR 532 113

London Artists Ltd v. Littler (1969) 2 All ER 193	412
London Joint Stock Bank Ltd v. MacMillan and Arthur (1918)	312
Long v. Lloyd (1958) 2 All ER 402 (C of A)	167
Lovell and Christmas v. Beauchamp (1894) AC 607	101
Lumley v. Wagner (1852) 1 De GM & G 604	192
M v. Home Office (1993) 3 WLR 433	328
McDonald v. Associated Fuels Ltd (1954) 3 DLR 775	392
McLoughlin v. O'Brien and Others TLR 5/5/82	375
M'Alister (Donaghue) v. Stevenson (1932) AC 562 (H of L)	233, 371, 373, 380
Malone v. Laskey (1907) 2 KB 141	403
Manchester Corporation v. Farnworth (1930) AC 171	400
Manchester Diocesan Council for Education v. Commercial and General Investments Ltd (1969) All ER 1953	119
Mapleflock Co. Ltd v. Universal Furniture (Wembley) Ltd (1934) 1 KB 148	179
Marfani & Co. v. Midland Bank Ltd (1968) 1 WLR 956	313
Marr (Pauline) re Marr (Robert) re (1989) v. Commissioners of Customs and Excise (1989) 3 WLR 674	57
Maxwell v. Bishopsgate Investment Trust (1993) BCLC 1282	79
Meah v. McCreamer and others (1986)	362
Mercer v. Denne (1905) 2 Ch 528	9, 23
Merritt v. Merritt (1970) 1 WLR 1121 CA	104
Mersey Docks & Harbour Board v. Coggins & Griffith (Liverpool) Ltd (1946) 2 All ER 345 HL	176, 206, 366
Metropolitan District Asylum Board v. Hill (1981) All ER 536	356
Metropolitan Electric Supply Co. v. Ginder (1901) 2 Ch 799	191
Metropolitan Properties Ltd v. Lannon (1969) 1 WB 577	335
Metropolitan Water Board v. Dick, Kerr & Co. Ltd (1918) AC 119 HL	176
Microbeads AG v. Vinhurst Road Markings (1975) 1 WLR 218	224
Midland Bank Trust Co. Ltd v. Hett, Stubbs and Kemp (1978) 3 WLR 167	351
Miliangos v. Frank (Textiles) Ltd (1976) AC 443, 465	38
Miller v. Jackson (1977) QB 966	403
Mills v. Brooker (1919) 1 KB 555	404
Minories Finance Ltd v. Arthur Young (1988) The Independent July 20, 1988	380
Minter v. Priest (1930) AC 558	413
Moorcock, The (1889) 14 RD 64	149
Morgan v. Odhams Press Ltd (1971) 1 WLR 1239	410
Morgans v. Launchbury (1972) 2 All ER 606	365
Morris v. Marsden (1952)	359
Morris v. Murray (1990) 3 All ER 801	353
Morrison v. Shaw, Savill and Albion Co. Ltd (1916) 2 KB 783	267
Moseley v. Koffyfontein Mines Ltd (1904) 2 Ch 108	82
Musgrove v. Pandelis (1919) 2 KB 43	388
Mutual Life & Citizens' Assurance Co. Ltd v. Evatt (1971) AC 793	377
Nash v. Inman (1908) 2 KB 1 C of A	5, 99, 241
National Coal Board v. Evans (1951) 2 All ER	395
National Employers General Insurance Association Ltd v. Jones (1988) 2 WLR 952	230
Newborne v. Sensolid (GB) Ltd (1954) 1 QE 45	203
Newstead v. London Express Newspaper Ltd (1940) 1 KB 377	410
Niblett Ltd v. Confectioners' Materials Co. (1921) 3 KB 387 CA	224
Nichols v. Marsland (1976) 2 Ex D1	357, 388
Nissan v. Attorney General (1969) 2 WLR 926	357
Noble v. Harrison (1926) 2 KB 332	405
Nordenfeldt v. Maxim Nordenfeldt Gun Co. (1894) AC 535 (H of L)	141
North Western Utilities Ltd v. London Guarantee & Accident Co. (1902) AC 381	388
O'Connell v. Jackson (1931) All ER 129	378
O'Connor v. Swann & Edgar and Carmichael Contractors (1963) 107 SJ 215	385
Oldendorff (EL) & Co. v. Trader Export SA (1973) 3 WLR 382	286
Olley v. Marlborough Court Ltd (1949) 1 All ER 127	152
Ormrod v. Crosville Motor Services Ltd (1953) 1 WLR 1120	365
Osborn v. Boulter (Thomas) and Sons (1930) 2 KB 226 CA	411, 413
Overseas Tankship (UK) Ltd v. Morts Dock and Engineering Co. Ltd (1961) AC 388	361
Owens v. Brimmell (1976) 2 All ER 765	353

Padbury v. Holliday & Greenwood (1912) 28 TLR 494 369
Padfield v. Ministry of Agriculture (1968) 1 All ER 694 .... 332, 334
Page One Records Ltd v. Britton (1967) 3 All ER 833 192
Pannett v. McGuinness (1972) 2 QB 599 384
Paradine v. Jane (1647) 82 ER 897 174
Parke v. The Daily News Ltd (1962) Ch 972 80
Parker v. British Airways Board (1982) 2 WLR 503 396
Parker v. Clarke (1960) WLR 286 105
Partridge v. Crittenden (1968) 2 All ER 111, 113
Payne v. Cave (1789) 3 Terms Rep 148 111
Pearce v. Brooks (1866) LR1 Exch 213 140
Pender v. Lushington (1877) 6 Ch D 70 82
Penfold v. Westcote (1806) 2 B & P (NR) 335 408
Pepper v. Hart & Others, 1992 STC 898 .... 14, 16
Percival v. Wright (1902) 2 CH 421 80
Perilly v. Tower Hamlets Borough Council (1973) QB 9 332
Peters v. Prince of Wales Theatre Ltd (1943) KB 73 388
Pharmaceutical Society v. Boots Ltd (1953) 2 All ER 456 .... 110, 126
Phillips v. Brooks Ltd (1919) 2 KB 243 .... 136, 168
Phillips Products Ltd v. Hyland and Another (1985) 129 SJ 47 157
Photo Production Ltd v. Securicor (1980) 155
Piercey v. S. Mills & Co. Ltd (1920) 1 Ch 77 80
Pilkington v. Wood (1953) 2 All ER 810 189
Pinnel's Case (1602) 5 Co Rep 117a 123, 124, 128
Pitts v. Hunt and Another (1989) 3 WLR 795 353
Planché v. Colburn (1831) 8 Bing 14 All ER 94 172
Poland v. John Parr & Sons (1927) 1 KB 236 368
Poussard v. Spiers Pond (1876) 1 QBO 410 146
Powdrill v. Wilson (1994) *The Times* March 23 1995 8
Powell v. Lee (1908) 99 LT 284 117
Prenty v. Midland Great Western Railway Co. (1866) 14 WR 314 269
Pride of Derby and Derbyshire Angling Association Ltd v. British Celanese Ltd (1953) Ch 149 363
Prole v Allen (1950) 1 All ER 476 63

R. v. Aston University Senate *ex.p*. Roffey (1962) 2 All ER 430 336
R. v. Birmingham Licensing Planning Cttee *ex.p*. Kennedy (1972) 1 All ER 739 331
R. v. Bristol Crown Court, ex parte Cooper (1989) *The Times* August 23, 1989 335
R. v. Electricity Commissioners *ex.p*. London Electricity Joint Comm. (1924) 1 KB 171 336
R. v. Greater London Council *ex.p*. Bromley LBC (1981) *The Times* December 18, 1981 334
R. v. Greater London Council and Another *The Times* December 27, 1984 329
R. v. I.C.R. Haulage Ltd (1944) 1 All ER 691 73
R. v. Madden (1975) 1 WLR 1379 404
R. v. Manchester Legal Aid Cttee *ex.p*. Brand & Co. Ltd (1952) 1 All ER 480 337
R. v. Ministry of Health *ex.p*. Davies (1929) 1 KB 619 329
R. v. Norfolk County Council, ex parte M (1989) 2 All ER 359 337
R. v. Rand (1866) LR 1 QB 230 335
R. v. Secretary of State for Foreign and Commonwealth Affairs, ex parte Everett (1989) 2 WLR 224 330
R. v. Secretary of State for the Home Department *ex.p*. Bentley (1993) 4 All ER 442 DC 330
R. v. Sussex Justices *ex.p*. McCarthy (1924) 1 KB 256 335
R. v. Taylor (1950) 2 KB 368 28
R. v. West London Suppl. Ben. Tribunal, *ex.p*. Clarke (1975) 3 All ER 513 331
Raffles v. Wickelhaus (1864) 33 LJ (NS) 160 .... 107, 108, 135
Rainham Chemical Works v. Belvedere Fish Co. (1921) 2 AC 465 385
Rama Corporation v. Proved Tin and General Investment Ltd (1952) 2 QB 147 194
Ramsgate Victoria Hotel Co. v. Montefiore (1866) LR 1 EX 109 112
Rapier v. London Tramways (1893) 2 Ch 588 404
Ratcliffe v. Evans (1892) 2 QB 524 413
Re City Equitable Fire Insurance Co. Ltd (1925) Ch 407 86
Re Duomatic Ltd (1969) 2 Ch 365 86
Re F.G. Films Ltd (1953) 1 WLR 483 72
Re Garwood's Trust, Garwood v. Paynter (1903) 1 Ch 236 5
Re German Date Coffee Co. (1882) 20 Ch D 169 8

Re Jon Beaufort Ltd (1953) Ch 131 70
Re London & County Coal Co. (1886) LR 3 Eq 355 83
Re London & General Bank No. 2 (1895) 2 Ch 166 85
Re London and Northern Bank (1900) 1 Ch 220 118
Re Polemis & Furness Withy and Co. Ltd (1921) 3 KB 560 361
Re Richmond Gate Property Co. Ltd (1964) 1 WLR 335 205
Re Thomas Edward Brinsmead (1897) 1 Ch 45 83
Re Westbourne Galleries Ltd (1973) AC 360 (Ebrahimi v. Westbourne Galleries) 83
Re Yenidje Tobacco Co. Ltd (1916) 2 Ch 426 .... 57, 83
Read v. Lyons (1947) AC 156 387
Reardon Smith Line Ltd v. Hansen-Tangen (1976) 3 All ER 570 147
Reddaway v. Banham (1896) AC 199 (H of L) 419
Reed v. Dean (1949) 1 KB 188 149
Reid v. Commissioners of Police for the Metropolis and Another (1973) 2 WLR 576 . 229
Reid v. Rush & Tompkins plc 351
Rhyl UDC v. Rhyl Amusements Ltd (1959) 1 All ER 257 328
Richardson v. Pitt-Stanley and Others (1994) *The Times* August 11 1994 73
Rickards v. Lothian (1913) AC 23 388
Ridge v. Baldwin (1964) AC 40 .... 330, 333, 335
Roberts v. Havelock (1832) 3 B & Ad 404 172
Roberts v. Hopwood (1925) 1 All ER 24 332
Robinson v. Davison (1871) LR 6 Ex 269 175
Robinson v. Graves (1935) 1 KB 579 221
Robinson v. Kilvert (1889) 41 Ch D88 401
Roe v. Minister of Health (1954) 2 All ER 131 .... 328, 366, 374
Rondell v. Worsley (1967) 3 All ER 993 377
Rookes v. Barnard (1964) AC 1129 361
Roscorla v. Thomas (1842) 3 QB 234 .... 125, 128
Ross v. Associated Portland Cement Manufacturers Ltd (1964) 1 LR 768 387
Routledge v. Grant (1828) 4 Bing 653 115
Routledge v. McKay (1954) 1 All ER 855 (C of A) 124
Royal Aquarium Society Ltd v. Parkinson (1892) 1 QB 431 (C of A) 413
Royal British Bank v. Turquand (1856) 6 E & B 327 .... 71, 90
Ryan v. Mutual Tontine Westminster Chambers Association (1893) 1 Ch 116 CA 191
Ryan v. Pilkington (1959) 1 WLR 403 199
Rylands v. Fletcher (1868) LR 3HL 330 .... 368, 387, 388, 390, 391

Said v. Butt (1920) 3 KB 497 208
Saif Ali v. Sydney Mitchell & Co. (1978) 3 All ER 774 377
Salomon v. Salomon & Co. Ltd (1897) AC 22 .... 72, 90
Saunders v. Anglia Building Society (1971) 3 WLR 1078 138
Scammell & Nephew Ltd v. Ousten (1941) 1 All ER 14 (H of L) ... 112, 127
Scott v. London and St Catherine Docks Co. (1865) 3 H & C 596 377
Scott v. Shepherd (1773) 2 WB1 892 363
Scriven Bros. v. Hindley (1913) 3 KB 564 107
Scruttons Ltd v. Midland Silicones Ltd (1962) 1 All ER 1 (H of L) 153–4
Searle v. Wallbank (1947) 1 All ER 12 389
Seddon v. Binions (1978) RTR 163 260
Sedleigh-Denfield v. O'Callaghan (1940) AC 880 403
Selangor United Rubber Estates v. Cradock (1968) 2 All ER 1073 80
Shipping Development Corporation SA v. v/o Sojuzneftenport: The Delian Spirit (1971)
    1 QB 103 285
Sim v. Stretch (1936) 2 All ER 1237 (H of L) 408
Six Carpenters Case, The (1610) 8 Rep 146a 392
Smith v. Baker (Charles) & Sons (1891) AC 325 352
Smith v. Chadwick (1884) 9 App. Cas 187 (H of L) 162
Smith v. Eric S. Bush (1989) 17 EG 68 HL 377
Smith v. Hughes (1871) LR 6QB 597, 607 107
Smith v. Land and House Property Corporation (1884) 28 CH D7 (CA) 161
Smith v. Leech, Braine & Co. Ltd (1961) 3 All ER 1159 362
Sorrell v. Smith (1925) AC 700 417
Spencer v. Marchington, 1988 *The Times* February 1, 1988 141
Spring v. Guardian Assurance plc & Others (1994) 3 All ER 129 455
Springer v. Great Western Railway (1921) 1 KB 257 200
Stag Line Ltd v. Board of Trade (1950) 2 KB 149 285
Stag Line Ltd v. Tyne Shiprepair Group Ltd and Other (The Zinnia) (1984) 2LL,
    RP 211 157

Case	Page
Stanley v. Powell (1891) 1 QB 86	356
Steeples v. Derbyshire County Council (1984) 3 All ER 501	329
Steinberg v. Scala (Leeds) Ltd (1923) 2 Ch 522 (CA)	101
Stephenson v. Hart (1828) 4 Bing 476	268
Stevenson, Jacques & Co. v. McLean (1880) 5 QBD 346	115, 116
Stilk v. Meyrick (1809) 2 Camp 317	123, 128
Storey v. Fulham Steelworks (1907) 24 TLR 89	175
Stringer v. Minister of Housing & Local Government (1970) 3 All ER 871	333
Sui Yin Kwan v. Eastern Insurance Co. Ltd (1994) 1 All ER 213	208
Suisse Atlantique Société D'Armement Maritime SA v. NV Rotterdamsche Kolen Centrale (1966) 2 All ER 61 (H of L)	155
Sumpter v. Hedges (1898) 1 QB 673 (C of A)	172
Sutcliffe v. Thackrah (1974) AC 727	377
Sydney Municipal Council v. Campbell (1925) AC 426	331
Sylvester v. Chapman Ltd (1935) 79 Sol Jo 777 (C of A)	354
Tamlin v. Hannaford (1950) 1 KB 18	358
Tamplin v. James (1880) 15 Ch D 215	135
Tate v. Williamson (1866) 2 Ch App 55	164
Taylor v. Caldwell (1863) 3 B & S 826	174, 175
Taylor v. Laird (1856) 1 H & N 266	114
Teutonia, The (1872) LR 4 PC 171	286
Thomas v. Sawkins (1935) 2 KB 249	394
Thompson v. London, Midland and Scottish Railway (1930) 1 KB 41	151
Thornett and Fehr v. Beers & Son (1919) 1 KB 486	225
Thornton v. Shoe Lane Parking Ltd (1971) 1 All ER 686 CA	151
Tolley v. Fry (1931) AC 333 (H of L) AC 333	410
Tomlinson v. Broadsmith (1896) 1 QB 386	54
Tower Cabinet Co. Ltd v. Ingram (1949) 2 KB 397	54
Transvaal Lands Co. v. New Belgium (Transvaal) Land Co. (1914) 2 Ch 488	81
Trussed Steel Concrete Co. Ltd v. Green (1946) 1 Ch 115	79
Tulk v. Moxhay (1848) 18 LJ Ch 83	428
Unit Construction Co. Ltd v. Bullock (1960) AC 351	73
Vaughan v. Taff Vale Railway Co. (1860) 5 H & N 679	356
Vigers v. Pike (1842) 3 Cl & Fin 562 HL	168
Vitol S.A. v. Norelf Ltd 1993 2 LIR 301	184
Vizetelly v. Mudie's Select Library Ltd (1900) 2 QB 170	411
Wagon Mound, The (No. 1) (1961) AC 388	361
Wallersteiner v. Moir (1974) 1 WLR 991	73
Wallersteiner v. Moir (No. 2) (1975) QB 373	79
Walters v. Morgan (1861) 3 De G F & J 718	161
Warner Bros. Pictures Inc. v. Nelson (1936) 3 All ER 160	192
Warren v. Henlys Ltd (1948) 2 All ER 935	367
Watkins v. Birmingham City Council (1975) *The Times* August 1, 1975	366
Watson v. McEwan (1905) AC 480	413
Watts v. Driscoll (1901) 1 Ch 294	56
Watts v. Spence (1975) 2 All ER 528	166
Webster v. Cecil (1861) 30 Beav 62	139
Weller v. Foot and Mouth Research Institute (1966) 3 All ER 560	362
Wenman v. Ash (1853) 13 CB 836	411
Wennhak v. Morgan (1888) 20 QBD 635	411
Westwood v. The Post Office (1974) AC1 (1974)	384
White v. Bluett (1853) 23 L5 Ex 36	121, 128
White and Carter (Councils) Ltd v. McGregor (1961) 3 All ER 1178 HL	178, 184, 189
Whittington v. Seal-Hayne (1900) 82 LT 49	166, 168
Wilkinson v. Downton (1897) 2 QB 57	375
Wilks v. Cheltenham Home Guard Motor Cycle & Light Car Club (1971) 1 WLR 668	378
Williams v. Bayley (1866) LR 1 HL 200	130
Willmore v. SE Electricity Board (1957) 2 LI Rep 375	106
Willson v. Love (1896) 1 QB 626	187
With v. O'Flanagan (1936) Ch 575 CA	161

Wood v. Scarth (1858) 1 F X F 293 190–1
Woodward v. London and North Western Railway (1878) 3 Ex D 121 272
Wren v. Weild (1869) LR 4 QB 730 418
Wringe v. Cohen (1939) 4 All ER 241 (C of A) 405

Yachuk v. Oliver Blaise Co. Ltd (1949) 2 All ER 150 379
Yianni v. Edwin Evans (1982) 3 WLR 843 379
Yonge v. Toynbee (1910) 1 KB 215 .... 204, 209
Yorkshire Insurance Co. Ltd v. Nisbet Shipping Co. Ltd (1962) 2 QB 330 247
Young v. Bristol Aeroplane Co. Ltd (1944) KB 718 28
Young v. Ladies Imperial Club Ltd (1920) 2 KB 523 85
Yousoupoff v. MGM Pictures Ltd (1934) SO TLR 581 409

Appendix 4 Table of statutes

Administration of Estates Act, 1925 .... 15, 425
Administration of Justice Act, 1969 27
Administration of Justice Act, 1970 25
Agricultural Marketing Act, 1958 332
Animals Act, 1971 389
Appellate Jurisdiction Act, 1876 25
Arbitration Act, 1950 .... 317, 318, 319
Arbitration Act, 1975 .... 317, 319, 321
Arbitration Act, 1979 .... 317, 320
Atomic Energy Act, 1946 340
Atomic Energy Act, 1954 102

Banking Act, 1987 53
Betting & Loans (Infants) Act, 1892 101
Bill of Rights, 1689 .... 16, 412
Bills of Exchange Act, 1882 .... 13, 125, 297–315
Bills of Lading Act, 1855 .... 278, 279
Business Names Act, 1916 .... 48, 53
Business Names Act, 1985 .... 48, 53

Carriage by Air Act, 1932 .... 287, 288
Carriage by Air Act, 1961 .... 193, 287, 290, 364
Carriage by Air and Road Act, 1979 .... 272, 290
Carriage of Goods by Road Act, 1965 .... 272, 290
Carriage of Goods by Sea Act, 1924 282
Carriage of Goods by Sea Act, 1971 .... 193, 277, 282, 364
Carriage of Goods by Sea Act, 1992 .... 278, 279–80
Carriers Act, 1830 276
Cheques Act, 1957 312
Cheques Act, 1992 .... 311, 313
Civil Aviation Act, 1982 392
Civil Liability (Contribution) Act, 1978 .... 54, 369
Clean Air Act, 1956 .... 405, 407
Companies Acts, 1985–9 ...... 14, 47, 52, 53, 66–89, 91, 102, 142, 163, 164, 198, 359, 427
Company Directors' Disqualification Act, 1986 83
Company Securities (Insider Dealing) Act, 1985 .... 78, 103
Congenital Disabilities (Civil Liability) Act, 1976 358
Consumer Arbitration Agreements Act, 1988 .... 321, 436
Consumer Credit Act, 1974 .... 101, 230, 231, 436, 439–41
Consumer Protection Act, 1987 .... 233, 372, 436, 437–9, 444, 445
Contracts (Applicable Law) Act, 1990 .... 7, 193–4
Control of Pollution Act, 1974 .... 405, 407
Copyright Act, 1956 127
Copyright, Designs and Patents Act, 1988 430
County Courts Act, 1846 37
County Courts Act, 1959 37
Courts Act, 1971 .... 25, 36
Courts and Legal Services Act, 1990 .... 40, 319, 34.
Criminal Appeal Act, 1966 27
Criminal Appeal Act, 1968 .... 27, 28
Criminal Justice Act, 1960 26
Criminal Justice Act, 1993 .... 78, 80, 91, 10.
Criminal Justice and Public Order Act, 1994 .... 393, 394
Criminal Law Act, 1967 .... 355, 39.
Criminal Law Act, 1977 39
Crown Proceedings Act, 1947 .... 328, 35.

Data Protection Act, 1984 .... 436, 442
Defamation Act, 1952 .... 409, 410, 412, 413, 418
Defective Premises Act, 1972 384
Dentists Act, 1957 35
Deposit of Poisonous Wastes Act, 1972 .... 405, 407
Directors' Liability Act, 1890 163
Disabled Persons (Employment) Acts, 1944 and 1958 450
Domestic Violence and Matrimonial Proceedings Act, 1976 402

Education Act, 1944 .... 330, 331
Emergency Powers Act, 1920 14
Employers' Liability (Compulsory Insurance) Act, 1969 .... 74, 99, 373
Employers' Liability (Defective Equipment) Act, 1969 .... 260, 369, 373
Employment Act, 1980 .... 64, 451
Employment Act, 1982 .... 64, 451
Employment Act, 1988 457
Employment Act, 1990 345
Employment Protection (Consolidation) Act, 1978 .... 451, 452
Enduring Power of Attorney Act, 1985 198
Estate Agents Act, 1979 .... 436, 441
European Communities Act, 1972 .... 17, 21, 36
European Communities (amendment) Act, 1986 .... 17–18, 203
Extradition Act, 1970 343

Factories Act, 1961 .... 368, 385
Factors Act, 1889 228
Fair Trading Act, 1973 .... 35, 436, 441
Family Law Reform Act, 1969 98
Fatal Accidents Act, 1959 260
Fatal Accidents Act, 1976 .... 364, 365
Finance Act, 1975 249
Financial Services Act, 1986 .... 436, 442
Fires Prevention (Metropolis) Act, 1774 250
Food and Drugs Act, 1955 238
Food Safety Act, 1990 372
Fugitive Offenders Act, 1967 343

Gaming Act, 1845 141
Gaming Act, 1968 141

Health and Safety at Work Act, 1974 385
Highways Act, 1959 405
Highways Act, 1961 405
Hire Purchase Act, 1964 230
Housing Act, 1925 329

Income and Corporation Taxes Act, 1970 188
Income and Corporation Taxes Act, 1988 16
Infants' Relief Act, 1874 101
Insolvency Act, 1986 .... 83, 86, 88, 92
Insolvency Act, 1994 .... 86, 87
Insolvency (No. 2) Act, 1994 .... 86, 87
Insurance Companies Act, 1982 .... 261, 436
International Transport Conventions Act, 1983 .... 274, 290
Interpretation Act, 1889 4
Interpretation Act, 1978 .... 4, 14

Judicature Acts, 1873–5 .... 11, 27
Justices of the Peace Act, 1949 34

Land Charges Act, 1925 425
Land Registration Act, 1925 425
Lands Tribunal Act, 1949 340
Law of Property Act, 1925 .... 63, 180, 181, 249, 297, 425, 426
Law of Property (Miscellaneous Provisions) Act, 1989 .... 426, 427
Law Reform (Contributory Negligence) Act, 1945 .... 378, 386, 389
Law Reform (Frustrated Contracts) Act, 1943 .... 177, 182

Law Reform (Husband and Wife) Act, 1962 .... 360, 369
Law Reform (Married Women and Tortfeasors) Act, 1935 360
Law Reform (Miscellaneous Provisions) Act, 1934 365
Legal Aid Act, 1974 41
Legal Aid Act, 1988 41
Libel Act, 1843 414
Life Assurance Act, 1774 .... 246, 248
Limitation Act, 1980 .... 192, 193, 196, 363, 364
Limited Partnership Act, 1907 56
Local Government Act, 1973 344

Marine Insurance Act, 1906 .... 246, 251, 253, 254, 255
Maritime Conventions Act, 1911 364
Married Women's Property Act, 1882 .... 126, 360
Medical Act, 1978 35
Mental Health Acts, 1959–83 .... 34, 102, 328
Merchant Shipping Act, 1894 .... 276, 277, 281
Merchant Shipping Act, 1958 277
Merchant Shipping Act, 1981 .... 277, 282, 283
Mines and Quarries Act, 1954 385
Minors' Contracts Act, 1987 98
Misrepresentation Act, 1967 .... 134, 147, 165, 166, 168

National Health Service Reorganisation Act, 1973 344
National Insurance Act, 1965 339
National Insurance (Industrial Injuries) Act, 1965 339
New Towns Act, 1946 341
Noise Abatement Act, 1960 .... 405, 407
Nuclear Installations Act, 1965 364

Occupiers' Liability Acts, 1957–84 .... 382, 383, 384, 389
Opticians Act, 1958 35

Parliament Act, 1911 13
Parliament Act, 1949 13
Parliamentary Commissioner Act, 1967 342
Parliamentary and Health Commissioners Act, 1987 343
Parliamentary Papers Act, 1840 412
Partnership Act, 1890 .... 13, 47, 51, 52–7, 64
Patents Act, 1977 429
Pharmacy and Poisons Act, 1933 110
Police Act, 1919 .... 330, 335
Police Act, 1964 .... 342, 358
Policies of Assurance Act, 1867 249
Policyholders' Protection Act, 1975 .... 261, 436
Post Office Act, 1969 358
Powers of Attorney Act, 1971 198
Powers of Criminal Courts Act, 1973 239
Proceedings Against Estates Act, 1970 365
Prosecution of Offences Act, 1985 3
Provisions of Oxford, 1258 11
Public Health Act, 1936 .... 405, 407

Race Relations Act, 1976 410
Registration of Business Names Act, 1916 48
Registration of Business Names Act, 1985 48
Rehabilitation of Offenders Act, 1974 .... 412, 415, 450
Resale Prices Act, 1976 35
Restrictive Practices Court Act, 1976 35
Restrictive Trade Practices Act, 1956 .... 35, 436
Restrictive Trade Practices Act, 1976 .... 35, 142
Restrictive Trade Practices Act, 1977 142
Road Traffic Act, 1972 .... 126, 238, 260, 374

Sale of Goods Act, 1893 .... 13, 219
Sale of Goods Act, 1979 .... 13, 99, 111, 114, 149, 155, 177, 219–42, 268, 436
Sale of Goods (Amendment) Act, 1994 .... 228, 229

Appendix 4 Table of statutes **495**

Sale of Goods (Amendment), Act, 1995 240
Settled Land Act, 1925 425
Sex Discrimination Act, 1975 456
Sex Discrimination Act, 1986 456
Slander of Women Act, 1891 409
Social Security Acts, 1975–80 339
Solicitors Act, 1974 340
Statute of Frauds, 1677 418
Statute of Frauds Amendment Act, 1828 418
Statute of Westminster II, 1285 11
Supply of Goods (Implied Terms) Act, 1973 .... 225, 234
Supply of Goods and Services Act, 1982 .... 239, 436
Supreme Court Act, 1981 .... 25, 30, 319, 328, 403

Theatres Act, 1968 409
Torts (Interference with Goods) Act, 1977 .... 394, 395, 397
Town and Country Planning Act, 1971 341
Trade Descriptions Act, 1968 .... 238, 436
Trade Marks Act, 1938 .... 419, 429
Trade Marks Amendment Act, 1984 .... 419, 429
Trade Union and Labour Relations Act, 1974 106
Trade Union and Labour Relations (Consolidation) Act, 1992 .... 451, 457
Trade Union Reform and Employment Rights Act, 1993 .... 451, 452, 458
Transport Act, 1962 273
Transport (London) Act, 1969 334
Tribunals and Inquiries Act, 1958 338
Tribunals and Inquiries Act, 1971 .... 338, 341
Tribunals of Inquiry (Evidence) Act, 1921 342

Unfair Contract Terms Act ... 96, 149, 150, 155, 159, 234, 265, 266, 376, 377, 379, 382, 436
Unsolicited Goods and Services Acts, 1971–5 .... 436, 441

Weights and Measures Act, 1985 .... 436, 442
Wild Birds Act, 1954 111

Index

Abatement, 404
Absolute privilege, 412
Acceptance:
    bills of exchange, of, 299–304
    contracts, of, 98, 116–20
    goods, of, 147
Acceptance of offers, 116–20
    communication of, 117–19
    contracts, and, 116
    definition of, 116
    manner of, 119–20
    postal rules about, 118–19
    silence and, 119
    subject to contract, 116–17
    vague contracts, 117
    waiver of, 119
Acceptor, 303
Accident:
    defence in tort, as, 355
    insurance, 244, 255, 260
Accommodation parties, 304
Accord and satisfaction, 192
Account payee, 310–11
Accused, 8
Act of God, 264, 357, 388
Act of State, 357
Act of a stranger, 388
Acte claire, 37
Administration order, 86
Administrative law, 4, 6, 7–8, 327–46
    abuse of discretionary powers, 332
    administrative justice, 337
    bias and, 335
    certiorari, 336–7
    Commissioners of Income Tax, 340
    Council on Tribunals, 338
    declaration of legal rights, 337
    error of law, and, 332
    estoppel and the Crown, 329
    hearing, right to, 335
    impartiality, 335
    improper purpose and, 331
    income tax commissioners, 340
    incorrect procedures in, 330
    injunctions and, 337
    introduction to, 327
    irrelevant consideration, 331
    judicial control of powers, 328–34
    lack of evidence, 332
    Lands Tribunal, 340
    Local Government Commissioners, 344
    mandamus, 336
    National Health Service Commissioners, 344
    national insurance tribunals, 339
    natural justice and, 334–6
    Ombudsman, 325
    Ombudsman system, 343–5
    Parliamentary Commissioner, 342
    prohibition, 336–7
    public inquiries, 341
    Solicitor's Disciplinary Tribunal, 340–1
    test of standing, 328
    tribunals, 338
    tribunals of inquiry, 342
    'ultra vires' rule, 329
ADR, 269
Advertisements:
    controls over, 440–1
    offers and, 111
Affreightment, contract of, 276
Agency, 197–215
    appointment, 197, 198–200
    breach of warranty of authority, 197, 203–4
    commission payable, 205
    contracts made under, 201
    diagram of, 201
    duties of agent, 197, 204
    duties of principal, 197, 204
    enduring power of attorney, 198
    estoppel and, 199–200
    European Directive on, 198
    express authority, 198
    frustration and, 210
    implied authority, 198–9
    independent contractors and, 197, 206
    nature of, 197–8, 201
    necessity, of, 200
    power of attorney, 198
    ratification of unauthorized acts, 197, 202–3
    remuneration, 210–12
    restraint of trade and, 212
    servants and, 197, 206
    subsequent ratification of, 202–3
    termination of, 197, 208–10
    tort, 360
    undisclosed principal and, 197, 207
    vicarious liability and, 206
    warranty of authority, 203
    wife, of, 201
Agreement:
    contracts and, 95, 98, 106–7
    discharge, to, 173
    to sell, 221
Air, carriage by, 287–9
    consignee's rights, 288
    development of, 287
    documentation, 292

Air, carriage by – *continued*
  international carriage, 287–8, 290
  jurisdiction, 289
  liability of carrier, 288, 291
  limits of liability, 288, 291, 292
  paramount clause and, 292
  SDRs, 289, 292
  stoppage in transit, 288
  time limit for actions, 289, 293
  Warsaw rules, 271, 287–9
  waybill, 288
Aliens:
  partnership and, 52
  torts and, 359
Allonge, 301
Animals, liability for, 389
Anticipatory breach, 185
Apology, 414
Appeal Court, 27–8
  Civil Division, 27
  Criminal Division, 27–8
Appeals:
  by way of case stated, 26, 34
  chart of, 26
  magistrates courts, and, 34
Appointment of agents, 197, 198–200
APR, 440
Arbitration, 316–23
  Acts, 317
  advantages of, 316
  arrangements, 318
  Consumer Arbitrations Agreement Act, 1988, 321
  control of, 318
  Courts and Legal Services Act, 1990, 319
  definition of, 316
  disadvantages of, 317
  exclusion agreements, and, 320
  nature of, 316
  reference to an arbitrator, 317–18
  stay of proceedings in, 319
Arrived ship, 285
Arson, 249
Articles of association, 71–2
Articles of partnership, 52
Assignments, 179–81
  contracts of, 179–81
  equitable, 181
  legal, 180–1
  life policy, of, 249
  partnerships and, 56
  statutes and, 181
Auctions, 111
Auditors, 84–5
Authorship, 430
  right of integrity, 430
  right of paternity, 430

Bankers:
  protection of, 312
Banking Ombudsman, 345
Bankruptcy:
  agency and, 209
  partnership and, 57
Barter, 221
Bearer bills, 304

Beneficial contracts, 99–101
Bias in law, 335
BIBA, 252
Bids, offers, as, 111
Bilateral discharge, 173
Bills of exchange, *see* Negotiable instruments
Bills of lading, 277–81
  Act, 1855, 278–9
  COGSA, 279–81
  functions of, 277–8
  Hague–Visby rules, 282
Binding precedent, 5, 38–9
  case law and, 5
  chain of, 38
  hierarchy of courts, and, 26, 38
  obiter dicta and, 38
  ratio decidendi and, 38
Books of authority, 8, 22
Both-to-blame collision clauses, 256
Bottomry bond, 252
Breach:
  anticipatory, 185
  contract, 155, 177–9
  duty of care, of, 374–6
  sale of goods, in, 235
  statutory duty, 385
  warranty of authority, of, 197, 203–4
Brokers, insurance and, 252
Business efficacy, 149
Business entities, 47–92
  clubs, 62–5
  concept of, 47–8
  corporations, 66–92
  limited companies, 66–92
  names of, 48–9
  particulars of ownership, 48–9
  partnerships, 51–9
  public corporations, 47
  sole traders, 48–51
  unincorporated associations, 62–5
Business law, definition of, 3–4
Business names, 48
Business property, 423–32
Buyer:
  duties of, 235
  remedies of, 235–6
  sale while in possession, 230
Bye-laws, 14

Canon law, 22
Capacity, 98–103
  corporations and, 98, 102–3
  drunkards and, 98, 102
  infants and, 98–102
  mental patients and, 102
  minors and, 98–102
  sale of goods and, 221
  tort and, 357–60
Care:
  duty of, 371–4
  occupiers of premises, 382
  standard of, 374–6
Carriage, law of, 264–96
  Act of God, 264
  ADR, 269

affreightment, contract of, 276
air, by, 287–9
air waybill, 288
bills of lading, and, 276, 277–81
Carriage by Road Act, 1965, 272
Carriers' Act, 1830, 272
carrier's liability, 273, 275, 288, 291
charterparties, 276, 284–6
CIM, 274
CIV, 274
clause paramount, 292
CMR, 272–3
combined transport operator, 294
common carrier, concept of, 264
common law exceptions, 264
comparative charts, 290–3
conditions of carriage, 265, 266
consignee's rights, air, 288
consignment notes, 273, 274, 275
consignor's fault, 264
consignor's fraud, 264
contract of, with whom made, 266
conventions on, 271, 272, 274, 279, 282, 287
COTIF, 274
customs procedures, 275
damages and, 270
dangerous goods, 269
delay, 267
demurrage, 285–6
deviation, 267
documentation of, 273, 275, 292
duty to carry, 264
fair alternative, doctrine of, 273
Hague rules, 271, 282
Hague–Visby rules, 282
Hamburg rules, 282, 286
Himalaya clauses, 270, 281
inherent vice, 264
inland waterways, 276
international carriage, 271, 273, 274–6, 287–8, 290
jettison, 277
jurisdiction in, 273, 275–6, 283, 289
legal relations in, 273, 282, 290–3
liability of carrier, 273, 275, 288, 291
lien, 268–9
limitation on actions 273, 284, 289, 293
limitations of liability, 273, 275, 283, 289, 292
measure of damages, 270
misdelivery, 267–8
MTO, 280
multi-modal movements, 280, 289–94
paramount clauses, 292
private carriers, 265–6
public carriers, 276
Queen's enemies and, 264
rail, by, 273–6
repudiation ab initio, 267
res ipsa loquitur, 266
road, by, 272–3
route, 275
SDRs, 282, 292
sea, 276–86
seaworthiness, 277
special drawing rights, 282, 292
speed of transits, 275
standard conditions, 265, 266
statutory modifications to, 271–2
stoppage in transit, 268, 288
two or more carriers, 269–70
Warsaw rules, 271, 287–9
waybill, air, 288
Cases, 5
ratio decidendi, and, 5
Certificate:
incorporation of, 68, 72–3
insurance, of, 260
trading, of, 68
Certiorari, 336–7
Cesser clause, 284
Chancery:
Court, 11
Division, 29–30
Chartered companies, 66
Charterparties, 284–6
arrived ship concept, 285
cesser clause, 284
dead freight, 285
demise, 284
demurrage, 285–6
discharge, 286
Hamburg rules, 286
laydays, 285
liability to load, 284
loading, 286
lump sum charter, 284
nature of, 284
stipulations in, 284
time charters, 284
voyage charters, 284
Chattels:
personal, 220, 424
real, 220, 424
trespass to, 394
Cheques, 309–13
account payee, 310–11
Act, 1957, 309
Act, 1992, 311, 313
collecting banker, and, 312
crossed, 310–11
garnishee order, 312
not-negotiable, 311
open, 309–10
overdue, 311
paying banker and, 312
post-dated, 311
specially crossed, 310–11
stale, 311
Children:
employment law and, 450
occupier's duty of care to, 382–3
Choses in action, 181, 220, 424
Choses in possession, 424
CIM, 274
Circuit judges, 31, 32
CIV, 274
Civil law, 8
Civil wrong, 140
Claims, insurance, in, 254
Clause paramount, 292
Clubs, *see* Unincorporated associations
CMR, 272–3

Codification of law, 13
COGSA (1992), 279, 281
Collecting banker, protection of, 312
Collective bargaining, 105–6, 457
Collective rights, 451–2, 456–8
Combined Transport Operator, 294
Commercial Agents (Council Directives)
  Regulations 1993, 213
Commercial Court, 29
Commission, European, 20
Commission for NHS and Local
  Government, 344
Committee of Permanent Representatives,
  20
Common carrier:
  concept of, 264
  duty to carry, 264
Common law, 8, 10
  conflict with equity, 11
  defects of, 10
  exceptions, 264
  illegal contracts and, 140–1
Communication:
  acceptance, of, 117–19
  offer, of, 114
  revocation, of, 114–15
Companies, see Limited companies
Comprehensive cover, 260
Conditions, 145–7
  contract, in, 145–7
  definition of, 146
  precedent, 284, 285
  sale of goods in, 222–3
  subsequent, 174
  waiver, 147–8
Conditions of carriage, 265, 266, 274
Consensus ad idem, 98, 106–7
Consideration, see Valuable consideration
Conspiracy, 417
Constitutional law, 6, 7–8
Constructive dismissal, 455
Constructive total loss, 258
Consumer credit, 439–40
Consumer protection, 435–45
  Act of 1987, 437–9
  advertising controls, 440–1
  APR and, 440
  cancellation of contracts, 439
  consumer credit, 439–40
  consumer safety, 438
  data protection, 442
  defective products, 437–8
  Director General of Fair Trading, 439–40
  estate agents, 441
  fair trading, 439–41
  financial services, 442–3
  general safety requirement, 438
  introduction to, 435–6
  misleading prices, 438–9
  resale price maintenance, 28, 435
  unsolicited goods, 441
  weights and measures, 442
Consumer safety, 438
Contra proferentem rule, 153
Contracts, 6
  acceptance, 98, 116–20
  accord and satisfaction, 192

advertisements and, 111
agency and, 201
agreement and, 95, 98, 106–7
ambiguity in, 153
anticipatory breach, 185
Applicable Law Act, 193–4
assignment of, 179–81
auctions and, 111
bargains, as, 91
beneficial, 99–101
bilateral discharge, 173
breach of, 155, 177–9
cancellation of, 439
capacity, 98
carriage, of, 266
'choses in action', 181
clubs and, 63
collective bargaining and, 105–6
commercial agreements, 105–6
common law and, 140–1
condition subsequent, 174
conditions in, 116, 145–7
consensus ad idem, 98, 106–7
consideration and, 98, 120–6
constructive total loss, 258
contra proferentem rule, 153
conventions on, 194
corporations and, 98, 102–3
counter offer, 115
customary terms, 148
damages, 165, 168
declaration of intent, and, 110, 112
deeds, 96–7, 120
definition of, 97
discharge of, 171–83
divisible, 171
doctrine of the implied term, 149
domestic arrangements and, 104
drunkards and, 98, 102
duress and, 98, 129
elements of, 98
enforcement of, 184–96
equitable assignments, 181
equitable remedies, 189–92
equity and, 134, 135, 139
estoppel and, 124
exclusionary clauses, 150–5, 166–7
express terms, 145–7, 173
forbearance and, 122
forms of, 95–7
frustration, 98, 174
fundamental breach, 154
gaming, 141
illegal, 139–42
implied terms, 148–50
infants and, 98–102
injunctions, 191–2
intention to create legal relations, 98, 103–6
invitations to treat, 110–12
laches and, 131
legal assignments, 180–1
legal relationships, 98, 103–6
legality and, 98, 126
licensing, 142
lien, 236, 268–9
limitation of actions, 192–4
mental incapacity and, 98, 102

minors and, 98–102
misrepresentation, 98, 160–70
mistake, 98, 132–9
necessaries, 99
notice of exclusion clauses, 151–2
novation, 174, 180
offer, 98, 110–16
operative mistake, 98, 132
oral, 95
partnerships as, 52
performance, 171–3
postal rules about, 118–19
privity of contract, 125
public policy and, 140
quantum meruit and, 189
rectification, 134
remoteness of damage, 185–6
representations in, 144–5, 147
repudiation of, 165, 184
rescission of, 134, 165, 167
restraint of trade and, 140–1
Rome Convention on, 194
sale of goods as, 220–2
severance, 142
silence and, 119
skill and knowledge test, 145
social arrangements and, 104
specialities, 96–7
specific performance, 11, 135, 190–2
standard form, 96, 150
statutory duty and, 106
statutory implied terms, 148, 149
subject to contract, 116–17
substantial performance, 172–3
supervening illegality, 176
termination, 173
terms of, 144–59
ticket cases, 150–1
time test and, 144
torts and, 351
undue influence and, 98, 129–31
unenforceable, 142
unfair terms, 150, 156
unilateral discharge, 173
unincorporated associations and, 63
vagueness of, 110, 112–13, 117
valid, 98–9
validity of, 129–43
valuable consideration, 98, 120–6
void, 132, 139
voidable, 101
wagers, 141–2
waiver, 119, 147–8
warranties in, 146
writing test, 145
written, 96
written terms, 145
Contribution:
  general average in, 255
  insurance, in, 245, 246, 251
Contributory negligence, 378–9, 386, 403
Conventions system, 271, 272, 274, 282, 287
Conversion, 395–7
  defences to, 397
  remedies for, 396–7
Conveyancing Ombudsman, 40
Convictions, employment and, 450

Copyrights, 430
Coreper, 20
Corporations, 47–8
  aggregate, 102
  companies as, 66
  contracts and, 98, 102–3
  public, 47
  sole, 102
  torts and, 359
COTIF, 274
  CIM and, 274
  CIV and, 274
  international rail movements, 273–6
Council of Ministers, 20
Council on Tribunals, 338
Counter offer, 115
County Court, 31–2
  chart of, 32
  circuit judges and, 31
  district judges and, 32
  jurisdiction, 31–2
  registrars and, 31
Court of Appeal, 27–8
  binding nature of decisions, 28
  civil division, 27
  criminal division, 27–8
  jurisdiction of, 27–8
Court of Auditors, 20
Court of First Instance, 18
Court order, sale under, 229
Courts of law, 25–43
  Appeal Court, 27–8
  Chancery, 11
  Chancery Division, 29–30
  chart of, 26
  Commercial Court, 29
  County Court, 31–2
  Court of Protection, 198
  Crown Court, 30–1
  Divisional Courts, 28–9
  European Court of Justice, 20, 36–7
  Family Division, 30
  hierarchy of, 26, 27, 38
  High Court, 29–31
  House of Lords, 25–7
  Judicial Committee of the Privy Council, 34–5
  magistrates, 33–4
  Queen's Bench Division, 29
  Restrictive Practices Court, 35–6
  Small Claims Court, 32–3
  structure of, 25
  system (chart), 26
Credit brokers, 440
Crime:
  contracts and, 140
  sale of goods and, 233
  torts and, 351
Criminal law, 6
Crown:
  Prosecution Service, 1
  tort, and, 357
Crown Court, 30–1
  chart showing, 26, 31
  jurisdiction of, 30–1
  structure of, 30
  tiers of, 30

CTO, 294
Curia Regis, 25
Custom of the realm, 8–9
Customary terms, 148
Customs procedures, 275

Damages, 9, 185–9, 270
  aggravated, 361
  carriage and, 270
  civil cases, in, 9
  contracts and, 185–9
  definition of, 185
  dishonour, on, 307
  exemplary, 361
  general, 360
  liquidated, 187
  misrepresentation, for, 165, 168
  mitigation of, 188–9
  nominal, 360
  penalties and, 187
  punitive, 361
  quantification of, 186
  quantum meruit, 189
  remoteness of, 185–6, 361
  special, 360
  specific performance and, 190–2
  substantial, 360–1
  taxation and, 188
  torts and, 360–3
  trespass and, 393
  unliquidated, 188, 360
  vindictive, 361
Damnum sine injuria, 350
Dangerous goods, 269
Data protection, 442
Dead freight, 285
Death:
  agency and, 209
  offer and, 116
  partnership and, 52
Debentures, 76
Deceit, 417
Declaration of intent, 110, 112
Declaration of legal rights, 337
Deed of partnership, 52
Deeds, 96–7, 120
Defamation, 409–16
  absolute privilege, 412
  Act, 1952, 410
  apology, 414
  defences to, 411–13
  definition of, 409
  dissemination of, 411
  fair comment and, 411
  forms, of, 409
  innuendo, 410
  justification, 411
  libel, 408–9
  privilege, 412
  proof required, 409–11
  qualified privilege, 413
  Rehabilitation of Offenders Act, and, 412
  remedies for, 414
  repetition of, 411
  slander, 408, 409, 418
  Theatres Act, 1968, and, 409
  unintentional, 413

Defective products, 437–8
Defendant, 8
Defrauding the revenue, 140
Delay, 267
Delegated legislation, 14
Delivery of goods, rules about, 232–3
Demise charterparty, 284
Demurrage, 285–6
Description, sale by, 224
Deviation, 267
Dilemma principle, 379
Diplomats, torts and, 359
Director General of Fair Trading, 35, 439–40
Directors of companies, 77, 84
  disqualification of, 83–4
  duties, of, 80
  insider dealing, and, 78, 82
Disabled persons, employment and, 450
Discharge:
  bills of, 307–8
  breach of contract and, 177–9
  contracts of, 171–83
  vessel, of, 286
Disclosure of information, 457–8
Discounting, 300
Discretionary powers, abuse of, 332
Dishonour:
  bills of, 305, 306–7
  damages in, 307
Dismissal, 454
Dissolution of partnership, 56–7
Distress damage feasant, 394
District Judge, 32
Divisional Courts, 28–9
Doctrine:
  fair alternative, of, 273
  fundamental breach, of, 154
  implied term, of, 149
  proximate cause, of, 245, 247–8, 254
Drunkards, 98, 102, 221
Duress, 98, 129
Duty:
  assured, of, 259
  care, of, 371–4
  to carry, 264

Easements, 425
Economic law, 4
Economic loss, 379–80
Emblements, 220
Employment law, 449–59
  children and, 450
  collective bargaining, 457
  collective rights, 451–2, 456–8
  constructive dismissal, 455
  convictions and, 450
  disabled persons and, 450
  disclosure in, 457–8
  dismissal, 454
  EU nationals, and, 450
  field of, 449
  individual rights, 451, 452
  industrial relations, 457
  manpower, 449
  natural justice and, 454

Index **503**

notice, 454
pay and, 453–4
PAYE and, 453
Race Relations Act and, 455
references, 455
rights of employees, 451
Sex Discrimination Act, and, 456
summary dismissal, 454
time off, 454
trade unions and, 456–7
work permits, 450
written particulars, 452
Enduring power of attorney, 198
Equitable:
    assignments, 181
    estoppel, 124
    remedies, 189–92
Equity, 8, 17–22
    contracts and, 134, 135, 139
    historical development of, 10–12
    mistakes and, 139
    remedies, 11
Error of law, 332
Estate agents, 441
Estoppel:
    agency and, 199–200
    bills of exchange and, 308–9
    contracts and, 124
    Crown and, 329
European Court of Justice, 20, 36–7
    jurisdiction of, 36–7
    preliminary rulings, 37
    references to, 37–8
European Parliament, 20
European Union law, 6, 8, 17–22
    chart of, 19
    companies and, 69, 70
    decisions, 17
    direct application, 21
    Directive on Agent–Principal Relationships, 210–13
    Directive on Unfair Terms in Consumer Contracts, 437
    directives, 17
    employment, and, 450
    institutions of, 18, 19
    Maastricht Treaty, 18
    primacy and, 21
    regulations, 17
    Single European Act, 17
    subsidiarity, 18
    treaties, 17
Ex turpi causa non oritur actio, 139
Exclusionary clauses:
    ambiguity and, 153
    arbitration and, 320
    contra proferentem rule, 153
    contracts, in, 150, 155, 166–7
    doctrine of fundamental breach, 154
    insurance in, 256
    misrepresentation, 166–7
    notice and, 151–2
    receipts and, 151
    sale of goods, in, 234
    signature and, 152
    standard form contracts, 90, 150
    third parties, and, 153–4

ticket cases, and, 150–1
unfair contract terms, 150, 156
Exemption clauses, *see* Exclusionary clauses
Express:
    authority, 198
    terms, 145–7, 173, 231

Fact, mistake of, 132
Factor, sales by, 228
Fair comment, 411
Fair trading, 441
Family Division, 30
Fee simple, 425
Fiduciary arrangements, misrepresentation in, 164
Financial services, 442–3
Fire insurance, 244, 249–51
Firm, 51
Fitness for purpose, 224–5
Floating policies, 252
Forbearance, 122
Forcible ejection, 393
Foreign bills, 301
Foreign law, 22, 132
Foreign sovereigns, 359
Forgeries, 308
Forwarding charges, 258
Fraud, 418
Fraudulent misrepresentation, 165
Freeholds, 425
Frustration, 174–7
    agency and, 210
    discharge by, 174
    effects of, 177
Fundamental breach, 154
Future goods, 222

Gaming contracts, 141
Garnishee order, 312
General average, 255, 256
    clause, 256
    contribution, 255
    losses, 255
    York–Antwerp Rules, 255
General safety requirement, 438
Golden rule, 15
Goods:
    definition of, 220
    sale of, *see* Sale of goods
    trespass to, 394–5
Goodwill:
    partnerships and, 52

Hague Rules, 271, 282
Hague–Visby Rules, 282
Hamburg Rules, 282, 286
Harassment, 402
Heads of agreement, 51
Hearing, right to, 335
High Court, 29–31
    Chancery Division, 29–30
    Commercial Court, 29
    Divisional Court of, 28–9
    Family Division, 30
    Queen's Bench Division, 29

Himalaya clauses, 270, 281
Hire:
  goods, of, 221
  purchase, 221, 230
Holder in due course, 301, 303
House of Lords, 25–7
  binding nature of decisions, 27
  Court of Appeal, as, 25
  Curia Regis, and, 25
  jurisdiction of, 27
  legislative capacity, 25
  Lords of Appeal, 26
  Treaty of Rome and, 27
Husband and wife, torts and, 360

Identity, mistake of, 136
Ignorantia juris haud excusat, 132
Illegal contracts, 139–42
  civil wrong, and, 140
  common law, and, 140, 141
  crime and, 140
  defrauding revenue, 140
  effects of, 142
  ex turpi causa non oritur actio, 139
  gaming contracts, 141
  immorality and, 140
  licensing and, 142
  public policy and, 140
  restraint of trade, and, 140–1
  restrictive practices and, 142
  revenues and, 140
  severance, and, 142
  sexual immorality and, 140
  statutes and, 141–2
  ultra vires contracts, 142
  void nature of, 139
Impartiality, 335
Implied authority, 198–9
Implied terms, 148–50
  business efficacy and, 149
  contracts in, 148
  course of dealing and, 148
  custom and, 148
  doctrine of, 149
  sale of goods, in, 223
  statute and, 149
Improper purpose, 331
Inchoate instruments, 302
Income tax commissioners, 340
Incorrect procedures, 330
Indemnity, 245, 246
Independent contractors, 197, 206, 368
Individual rights, employment and, 451, 452
Industrial relations, 457
Inevitable accident, 355, 395
Infants, *see* Minors
Inherent vice, 264
Injunctions, 11, 191–2
  abuse of administrative powers, 337
  interlocutory, 192
  mandatory, 191, 363
  perpetual, 363
  prohibitory, 191, 363
  torts and, 363, 393
Injuria sine damno, 350

Injurious falsehood, 418
Inland waterways, 276
Innocent misrepresentation, 162, 165
Innuendo, 410
Insider dealing, 78, 82
Insolvency:
  Act, 1986, 83
  companies, 83
  partnerships, 57
Insurance, 244–63
  accident, 244, 255, 260
  Act, 1982, 261
  adjustment, 254
  arson, 249
  assignment of life policy, 249
  assurance, 244
  benefit of insurance, 259
  BIBA, 252
  both-to-blame collision clause, 256
  bottomry bond, 252
  brokers, 252
  certificates, 260
  change of voyage clause, 258
  claims, 254
  comprehensive cover, 260
  constructive total loss, 258
  contribution, 245, 246, 251, 255
  cooling-off period, 249
  cover notes, 260
  doctrine of proximate cause, 245, 247–8, 254
  duration of cover, 257
  duty of assured clause, 259
  English law and practice clause, 259
  exclusion clauses, 256
  fire, 244, 249–51
  floating policies, 252
  forwarding charges, 258
  fully paid policy, 249
  general average, 255, 256
    clause, 256
    contribution, 255
    guarantee, 255
    losses, 255
    York–Antwerp Rules, 255
  increased value clause, 258
  indemnity, 245, 246
  inflation, 250
  insurable interest, 245, 250, 258
  Insurance Companies Act, 1982, 261
  liability, 244, 260
  life, 244, 248–9
  Lloyds of London, 244
  marine, 244, 251–9
  Marine Insurance Act, 1906, 251, 254
  measure of indemnity, 254
  minimizing losses, 259
  misrepresentation in, 163–4
  motor vehicle insurance, 260
  nature of marine policies, 251–2
  not-to-inure clause, 259
  open covers, 252
  partial losses, 255
  personal accident cover, 260
  Policy Forms and Clauses (1982), 251, 253–9
  policy-holders' protection, 261

premium in, 244
principles of, 245–8
proximate cause, 245, 247–8, 254
reasonable dispatch clause, 259
reinstatement, 250
reinsurance, 245
risk bearing, 244
risk clause, 256
slip policies, 253
slips, 253
strikes exclusion clause, 257
subrogation, 245, 247, 249
suicide and, 248
surrender value, 249
termination of, 249, 257
time policies, 252
total loss of part, 255
total losses, 254–5
trade clauses, 251
transit clause, 257
underwriters, 244
unseaworthiness, 256
unvalued policies, 252
utmost good faith, 245
valued policies, 252
voyage policies, 252
waiver clauses, 259
war exclusion clauses, 257
wilful misconduct, 249
Intention to create legal relations, 98, 103–6
Interlocutory injunction, 192
International carriage:
  air, by, 287–9
  CIM, by, 273–6
  CMR, by, 272–3
  multi-modal movements, 280, 289–94
  sea, by, 276–86
International conventions:
  comparison charts, 290–3
International law, 6
Interpretation of statutes, 14–16
  ejusdem generis rule, 15
  four corners rule, 14, 16
  golden rule, 15
  interpretation section, 14
  literal rule, 15
  mischief rule, 15
Invitation to treat, 110–12
Irrelevant consideration, 331

Jettison, 277
Joint tortfeasors, 369
Judicial:
  control of powers, 328–34
  immunity from actions in tort, 359
Judicial Committee of the Privy Council, 34–5
  Curia Regis, and, 34
  jurisdiction of, 35
  Supreme Court and, 35
Jurisdiction:
  carriage and, 273, 275–6, 283, 289
  County Court, of, 31
  Court of Appeal, of, 27
  Crown Court, of, 30–1
  European Court, of, 36–7
  House of Lords, of, 27
  Judicial Committee of the Privy Council, 35
  Magistrates Court, of, 34
  Small Claims Court, 32
Jus tertii, 392
Justices of the peace, 33
Justification, 411

Laches, 131
Land:
  easements, 425
  fee simple absolute in possession, 425
  freehold, 425
  land tax, 426
  leasehold, 425, 427–8
  mortgages, 428
  ownership, by clubs, etc., 63
  property, as, 425–6
  purchase of, 426–8
  restrictive covenants and, 428
  sale of, 426–8
  right of entry, 426
  term of years, absolute, 425
  trespass to, 392–4
  tribunal, 340
  unincorporated associations and, 63
Law:
  administrative, 4, 6, 7–8
  Applicable Law Act, 1990, 193–4
  assignments by, 180–1
  books of authority and, 8, 22
  branches of (chart), 6
  Canon, 22
  cases, 5
  chart of, 6
  civil, 8
  codification of, 13
  common, 8, 10
  Community, 6
  constitutional, 6, 7–8
  contract, 6
  criminal, 6
  custom and, 8–9
  definition of, 3
  delegated legislation, 14
  divisions of, 6–8
  economic, 4
  elements of, 3–24
  equity, and, 8, 10–12
  European Community, 8, 17–22
  foreign, 22
  international, 6
  merchant, 8, 12–13
  mistake of, 132
  municipal, 6, 7
  personnel of, 39–40
  private, 6, 7
  property, 6
  public, 6, 7
  Roman, 22
  sexism and, 4
  sources of, 8–22
  statute, 8, 13–16

Law – *continued*
  succession, 6
  tort, 6
  trust, 6
Laydays, 285
Leaseholds, 425, 427–8
Legal:
  aid, 40–1
  assignments, 180–1
  relations in contract, 98, 103–6
  rights, declaration of, 337
  Services Ombudsman, 40
Liability insurance, 244, 260
Libel, 408, 409
Licences, 140, 394
Licensing, 142
Lien, 236, 268–9
  carriers and, 268–9
  clause, 269
  general, 268
  particular, 268
  passive, 268
  possessory, 236, 268
  sale of goods, and, 236, 269
  waiver of, 236
Life assurance, 244, 248–9
Limitation of actions, 192–4, 273, 284, 289, 293, 363–5
Limited companies, 66–92
  advantages, 88–9
  articles of association, 71–2
  auditors, 84–5
  capital of, 74–6
  certificate of incorporation, 68, 72–3
  certificate of trading, 68
  chartered, 66
  corporation, as, 66
  debentures and, 76
  directors, 77–84
  disadvantages, 89
  disqualification of directors, 83–4
  elective regime and, 67
  European Communities Act and, 69–71
  formation of, 67–8
  incorporation of, 72–3
  insider dealing and, 78, 82
  Insolvency Act, and, 83
  legal personality and, 72
  limited liability, 66
  management of, 76–88
  meetings, 85–6
  Memorandum of Association, 67, 68–71
  nature of, 66
  objects clause of, 69–71
  private, 67
  public, 67
  registered, 66–7
  secretary and, 84
  share capital of, 74–6
  statutory, 66
  structure of, 77
  torts and, 73–4
  types of, 66–7
  ultra vires acts, 69–71
  winding up, 86–8
Limited liability, 66
Limited partnerships, 56

Liquidated damages, 187
Literal rule, 15
Lloyds of London, 244
Loading, 284, 286
Local Government Commissioners, 344
Lord Chancellor:
  Advisory Committee on Legal Education and Conduct, 40
Losses:
  general average, 255
  minimizing, 259
Lump sum charters, 284

Maastricht Treaty, 18–19
Magistrates Courts, 33–4
  appeals and, 26
  chart of, 26, 33
  clerk to the justices, 34
  jurisdiction, 34
  lay magistrates, 33
  personalities, 33–4
  stipendiary magistrates, 33
Malice, 379, 402
Mandamus, 336
Mandatory injunction, 191, 363
Manpower, 449
Marine insurance, 244, 251–9
Market overt, 229
Memorandum of association, 67, 68–71
Mental incapacity:
  agency and, 209
  contracts and, 98, 102
  partnerships and, 52
  sale of goods and, 221
Merchant Law, 8, 12–13
  history of, 12
  'nation state' and, 12
Merchant Shipping Acts, 281–2
Merchantable quality, 225
Minors, 98–102
  beneficial contracts, and, 99–101
  contracts and, 98–102
  guarantees on behalf of, 102
  loans to, 101–2
  necessaries and, 99
  partnerships and, 52
  sale of goods and, 221
  torts, and, 357
  voidable contracts and, 101–2
Mischief rule, 15
Misdelivery, 267–8
Misleading prices, 438–9
Misrepresentation, 98, 160–70
  damages and, 165, 168
  definition of, 160
  exclusionary clauses about, 166–7
  family arrangements and, 164
  fiduciary arrangements and, 164
  fraudulent, 165
  innocent, 162, 165
  insurance and, 163–4
  nature of, 160
  negligent, 162–3
  non-disclosure, 163
  remedies for, 165

Index

repudiation of the contract, 165
rescission of the contract, 165, 167
restitutio in integrum, 167
sale of goods, in, 233
shares and, 164
silence and, 160
third parties and, 168
types of, 162–4
uberrimae fidei contracts, 161, 163
Mis-statements, negligent, 376–7
Mistake, 98, 132–9
  common, 132, 133
  documents signed in, 138
  equity, and, 134, 135
  equity, in, 139
  fact, in, 132
  foreign law and, 132
  ignorantia juris haud excusat, 132
  law, of, 132
  mistaken identity, 136
  mutual, 132
  non est factum, 138
  operative, 132
  private rights and, 132
  rectification, 134
  res extincta, 133
  res sua, 133
  rescission, 134
  specific performance, 135
  torts and, 355
  unilateral, 132
Mitigation of damages, 188–9
Moloney Commission, 219
Mortgages, 222, 426, 428
Motor vehicle insurance, 260
MTO, 280
Multi-modal transport, 280, 289–94
Municipal law, 6, 7

Names, business and, 48–9, 53
National Health Service Commissioners, 344
National insurance tribunals, 339
Natural justice, 334–6, 454
Necessaries, contracts for, 99
Necessity:
  agency of, 200
  torts and, 355, 394
  trespass and, 394
Negligence, 371–81
  alternative danger, doctrine of, 379
  breach of duty of care, 374–6
  carriers, 373
  contributory, 378–9
  definition of, 371
  dilemma principle, 379
  drivers, 374
  duty of care, 371–4
  economic loss and, 379–80
  employers and, 373
  highway users, 373
  local authorities, 373
  mis-statements, 376–7
  professional people and, 373
  res ipsa loquitur, 378
  standard of care, 374–6
Negligent misrepresentation, 162–3

Negotiability, concept of, 297
Negotiable instruments, 297–315
  acceptance, 299, 304
  acceptor, 303
  accommodation parties, 304
  allonge, 301
  bearer bills, 304
  Bills of Exchange Act, 1882, 297
  cheques, 309–12
  concept of negotiability, 298
  damages on dishonour, 307
  definition of a bill, 298
  discharge of bills, 307–8
  discounting of bills, 300
  dishonour, 305, 306–7
  drawee, 303
  drawer, 303
  endorsers, 303
  estoppel, 308–9
  foreign bills, 301
  forgeries, 308
  general acceptance, 304
  holder, 303
  holder in due course, 301, 303
  illustration, 298
  inchoate instruments, 302
  indorsers, 303
  inland bills, 301
  negotiability, concept of, 298
  negotiation of a bill, 302, 306
  noting, 302
  order bills, 299
  parties to a bill, 303–4
  payee, 303
  payment of a bill, 306
  presentation for acceptance, 305
  protesting a bill, 302
  qualified acceptance, 305
  sets of bills, 302
  tenor of a bill, 303
  transferor by delivery, 304
  use of bills, 299–300
Negotiation, bills and, 302, 306
Non-disclosure, 163
Non est factum, 138
Notice, employment and, 454
Novation, 174, 180
Novus actus interveniens, 362
Nuisance, 400–7
  abatement, 404
  abnormal sensitivity and, 401
  actions in tort for public nuisance, 405
  contributory negligence, 378, 403
  defences to, 403
  definitions of, 400, 404
  forms of, 401
  harassment, 402
  indirect injury, 401
  malice and, 402
  parties to an action, 403
  prescription, 402
  private, 400
  public, 400, 404–5
  remedies for, 404
  statutory authority, 403
  types of, 400
  unreasonable interference, 400

Obiter dicta, 38
Objects clause, 69–71
Occupiers' liability, 382–91
    Act, 1957, 382, 384
    Act, 1984, 382
    Act of God, and, 388
    Act of a stranger, 388
    animals and, 389
    breach of statutory duty, 385
    children and, 382–5
    common duty of care, 382
    consent of the plaintiff, 388
    contributory negligence, 386
    default of the plaintiff, 389
    Defective Premises Act, 1972, 384
    defences to, 385–6
    definition of occupier, 382
    delegation of statutory duty, 386–7
    Rylands v. Fletcher, 387
    statutory authority, 388
    statutory duty, 382
    strict liability, 385–9
    trespassers and, 383–4
    Unfair Contract Terms Act, 1977, 382
    visitors, 382
    volenti non fit injuria, 386
Offenders, 8
Offers, 110–16
    advertisements as, 111
    bids as, 111
    clarity of, 110
    communication of, 114
    conditional, 116
    counter offer, 115
    death and, 116
    declarations of intent, 110, 112
    definition of, 110
    display of goods, 110–11
    general offers, 110, 113
    invitations to treat, and, 110
    lapse of time and, 115–16
    price lists and, 111
    rejection of, 115
    revocation of, 114–15
    specific, 110, 113
    statements of intention and, 110, 112
    supply of information and, 110, 111–12
    termination of, 114–15
    vagueness of, 110, 112–13
Ombudsman, 325
    Banking, 345
    Building Societies, 345
    Conveyancing, 40
    Electricity, 345
    Gas, 345
    Legal Services, 40
    system, 343–5
    Telecommunications, 345
    Trade Union members, 345
Open covers, 252
Operative mistake, 132
Oral contracts, 95
Order bills, 299
Orders in Council, 14
Ownership, particulars of, 48–9, 220–1, 423–4

Paramount clauses, 292
Parliamentary Commissioner, 342
Partial losses, 255
Partnerships, 51–9
    Act of 1890, 51
    advantages, 58–9
    aliens and, 52
    articles of, 52
    assignment of share in, 56
    bankruptcy and, 57
    contracts, as, 52
    death and, 52
    deed of, 52
    definition of, 51
    disadvantages, 59
    dissolution, of, 56–7
    duration of, 53
    firm, as, 51
    formation of, 51–2
    goodwill and, 52
    insolvency, 57
    inter-relationship, 54–5
    liability of partners, 54
    limited, 56
    mental incapacity, and, 52
    minors and, 52
    name of, 53
    nature of, 51
    other organizations and, 51
    property of, 55
    termination of, 52
    third parties and, 53–4
    torts and, 54, 360
Passing off, 418–19
Patents, 429
PAYE, 453
Paying banker, protection of, 312
Payment of wages, 453–4
Penalty, 187
Per incuriam, 27
Performance of contract, 171–3, 190–2
    discharge by, 171
    partial, 172
    sale of goods, in, 231–4
    specific, 190–2
    substantial, 172–3
Personnel of the law, 39–40
    barristers, 39
    Ombudsman, 40
    QCs, 40
    solicitors, 39
Piepowder courts, 12
Plaintiff, 8
    consent of, 388
    default of, 389
Pledges, 222
Police and torts, 358
Possession, 423–4
Postal rules, contracts for, 118–19
Power of attorney, 195
Precedents, 5, 38–9
Premiums, 244
Prescription, 402, 403
Price, 222
Principal:
    duties of, 197, 204
    torts and, 360

Private:
  law, 6, 7
  nuisance, 400
  rights, 132
Private carrier, 265–6
  conditions of carriage and, 265
  inland waterways, 276
  negligence and, 373
Privatization, 47
Privilege in defamation, 412
Privity of contract, 125
Prohibition, 336–7
Prohibitory injunction, 191
Promissory estoppel, doctrine, of, 124
Property, 6
  chattels personal, 424
  chattels real, 424
  'choses in action', 424
  'choses in possession', 424
  copyrights, 430
  freehold, 425
  land, as, *see* Land
  leasehold, 425
  mortgages, 426, 428
  ownership, 423–4
  partnership, 55
  patents, 429
  personal, 424
  possession, 423–4
  Property Misdescriptions Act, 1991, 429
  real, 424
  restrictive covenants, 428
  service marks, 429–30
  trade marks, 429–30
  transfer of, 226–7
  trespass to, 392–9
  types of, 424
Prosecution of Offences Act, 1
Protesting a bill, 302
Proximate cause, doctrine of, 245, 247–8, 254
Public:
  carriers, 276
  companies, 67
  corporations, 47, 358
  enquiries, 341
  law, 6, 7, 325–46
  nuisance, 400, 404–5
  policy, 140
Puisne judges, 29

Qualified acceptance, 305
Qualified majority voting, 18–19
Qualified privilege, defamation in, 413
Quality, sale of goods in, 224–5
Quantum meruit, 189
Queen's Bench Division, 29
Queen's enemies, 264
Qui facit per alium, facit per se, 197
Quiet possession, 223

Race relations, employment and, 455
Rail carriage, 273–6
  BR conditions of carriage, 274
  carrier's liability, 273
  CIM, 274
  CIV, 274
  conditions of carriage, 274
  consignment notes, 275
  COTIF, 274
  customs and, 275
  doctrine of fair alternative, 273
  documentation, 275
  history of, 273
  international carriage, 274
  jurisdiction, 275
  liability of carrier, 275
  lien, 268–9
  OTIF, 274
  paramount clause and, 292
  route, 275
  Simplified Customs Procedure, 275
  speed of transit, 275
  time limit on litigation, 293
  Transport Act, 1962, and, 273
Ratification of unauthorized acts, 197, 202–3
Ratio decidendi, 5
Real property, 424
Recodification of law by statutes, 13
Rectification of contract, 134
References, 455
Registered companies, 66–7
Registrars, county court, 31–2
Reinsurance, 245
Remoteness of damages, 185–6, 361
Remuneration of agents, 210–12
Representations, 144–5
  contract, in, 144–5, 147
  skill and knowledge test and, 145
  time test and, 144
  writing test, and, 145
Repudiation of contracts, 165, 184
  ab initio, 267
Res extincta, 133
Res ipsa loquitur, 266, 378
Res sua, 133
Resale of goods, 230, 237
Resale price maintenance, 28, 435
Rescission of contract, 134, 165, 167
Restitution of property, 167, 363
Restraint of trade, 140–1
  agency and, 212
Restrictive covenants, 428
Restrictive practices, 142
Restrictive Practices Court, 35–6
  Director General Fair Trading and, 35
Revision tests:
  acceptance, 126–8
  administrative law, 345–6
  agency, 213–15
  arbitration, 321–3
  business entities, 59–61
  carriage, law of, 294–6
  clubs, 64–5
  companies, 89–92
  consideration, 126–8
  conspiracy, 419–20
  consumer protection, 444–5
  contract, terms of, 158–9
  contracts, nature of, 107–9
  contracts, validity of, 143
  court system, 41–3

Revision tests – *continued*
  deceit, 419–20
  defamation, 414–16
  discharge of contracts, 182–3
  duress, 143
  elements of English law, 22–4
  employment law, 458–9
  enforcement of contracts, 194–6
  fraud, 419–20
  illegal contracts, 143
  injurious falsehood, 419–20
  insurance, 261–3
  limited companies, 89–92
  misrepresentation, 168–70
  mistake, 143
  nature of law, 22–4
  negligence, 380–1
  negotiable instruments, 313–15
  nuisance, 405–7
  occupiers' liability, 389–91
  offer, 126–8
  partnerships, 59–61
  property, 430–2
  sale of goods, 240–3
  sole traders, 59–61
  terms of contract, 158–9
  tort, 369–70
  trespass, 397–9
  undue influence, 143
  unincorporated associations, 64–5
  validity of contracts, 143
  valuable consideration, 126–8
Revocation of agency, 209
Revocation of offer, 114–15
Rights of employees, 451
Risk-bearing, 244
Road haulage, 272–3
  basis of relationship, 273, 290
  carrier's liability, 273, 292
  CMR, 272, 290–3
  documentation, 273
  inland, 272
  international, 273
  jurisdiction, 273
  paramount clause and, 292
  private carriers, and, 272
  time limit on litigation, 273, 293
Romalpa clauses, 237–8
Roman Law, 22
Rome, Treaty of, 17
Rylands *v.* Fletcher, 387

Sales of Goods, 220–43
  Act, 1893, 219
  Act, 1979, 219–20
  (Amendment) Act, 1995, 240
  agreement to sell, 221
  barter and, 221
  breach of contract in, 235
  buyer in possession, by, 230
  buyers' duties, 235
  buyers' remedies, 235–6
  capacity and, 221
  choses in action and, 220
  conditions and, 222–3
  contract for, 220–2
  court order, under, 229
  criminal liability in, 233
  definition of goods, 220
  delivery and, 232–3
  description, by, 224
  distraint and, 229
  drunkards, and, 221
  effects of contract for, 226
  emblements and, 220
  examination of, 233
  exchange and, 221
  exclusionary clauses in, 234
  express contractual duties, 231
  factor, by, 228
  fitness for purpose, 224–5
  form of contract, 221
  future goods and, 222
  goods, defined, 220
  hire and, 221
  hire purchase and, 221, 230
  implied terms in, 223
  intentions of the parties, 226
  lien and, 236
  market overt, abolition of, 229
  mental incapacity and, 221
  mercantile agent and, 228
  merchantable quality, 225
  minors and, 221
  misrepresentations in, 233
  Moloney Commission and, 219
  mortgages and, 222
  ownership and, 220–1
  performance of contract in, 231–4
  pledges and, 222
  price and, 222
  quality and, 224–5
  quiet possession, and, 223
  re-sale and, 230, 237
  Romalpa clauses, 237–8
  Sale of Goods Act, 1893, 219
  Sale of Goods Act, 1979, 219–20
  Sale of Goods (Amendment) Act, 1995, 240
  sample, by, 226
  seller in possession, by, 230
  seller's duties, 231
  seller's remedies, 236–8
  skill and materials, 221–2
  specific goods and, 222
  specific performance, 235
  stoppage in transit, 236
  Supply of Goods and Services Act, 1982, 239–40
  things in action, 220
  time for performance, and, 223
  title and, 227–8
  tortious liability in, 233
  Trade Description Act, 1968, 238
  transfer of property, 226–7
  transfer of title in, 227–8
  unascertained goods, 227, 240
  Unfair Contract Terms Act, 1977, 234
  vehicles on HP and, 230
  voidable title and, 229–30
  warranties and, 222–3
Samples, 226
SDRs, 282, 292

Sea, carriage by, 276–86
  actual fault and privity, 281
  affreightment, contract of, 276
  bill of lading, 277–81
  Bills of Lading Act, 1855, 278, 279
  charterparty, 276, 284–6
  clause paramount, 292
  combined transport operator, 277, 294
  conventions on, 279
  demurrage, 285–6
  development of, 277
  documentation, 292
  duties of the carrier, 283
  fire, 281
  general average, 255, 256
  Hague Rules, 271, 282
  Hague–Visby Rules, 282
  Hamburg Rules, 282, 286
  Himalaya clauses, 270, 281
  historical development, 277
  international carriage, 287–8
  jettison, 277
  jurisdiction, 283
  liability of carrier, 283
  Merchant Shipping Acts, 281–2
  MTO, 277
  paramount clause and, 292
  SDRs, 282
  seaworthiness, 277
  stages of voyage, 277
  time limit on actions, 284, 293
  warranty of seaworthiness, 277
Secretary, company, 84
Self-defence, torts and, 356
Seller:
  duties, of, 231
  remedies, for, 236–8
  resale by, 230
Servants:
  agents, as, 197, 206
  vicarious liability for, 206
Service marks, 429–30
Severance of contracts, 142
Sexism and law, 4
Shares, companies in, 74–6, 164
Slander, 408–9
  business, of, 418
  goods, of, 418
  title, of, 418
  trade, of, 418
Slip policies, 253
Small Claims Court, 32–3
Sole traders, 48–51
  advantages, 50
  business names and, 48–9
  disadvantages, 50–1
  organization of, 50
  personality of, 48
Solicitors' Disciplinary Tribunal, 340–1
Sources of law, 8–22
  books of authority, 8, 22
  canon law, 22
  common law, 8–10
  custom of the realm, 8–9
  delegated legislation, 14
  equity, 8, 10–12
  European Community law, 8, 17–22

  foreign law, 22
  merchant law, 8, 12–13
  Roman law, 22
  statute law, 8, 13–16
Specialties, 96–7
Specific:
  goods, 222
  offers, 110, 113
  performance, 11, 135, 190–2
Standard form contracts, 96, 150
Standing, test of, 328
Statute law, 8, 13–16
  implied terms and, 148, 149
  interpretation of, 14–16
  recodification of, 13
Statutory authority for tort, 356, 388
Statutory companies, 66
Statutory duty of care, 382
Statutory instruments, 14
Statutory nuisance, 403
Stipendiary magistrate, 33
Stoppage in transit, 236, 268, 288
Strict liability, 385–9
Strike clauses, 257
Subject to contract, 116–17
Subrogation, 245, 247, 249
Subsequent ratification of unauthorized acts, 197, 202–3
Subsidiarity, 18
Substantial performance, 172–3
Succession law, 6
Summary dismissal, 454
Supervening illegality, 176
Supreme Court, 27
Surrender value, 249

Tenor of a bill, 303
Term of years absolute, 425
Termination:
  agency of, 197, 208–10
  contract, of, 173
  contract of insurance, 249, 257
  offer, of, 114–15
  partnership, of, 52
Things in action, 424
Things in possession, 424
Ticket cases, 150–1
Time:
  charters, 284
  contracts and, 144
  immemorial, 9
  lapse of, 115–16
  limit on actions, 192, 273, 284, 293, 294
  off work, 454
  performance of contract, for, 223
  policies, 252
  sale of goods, and, 223
  test and, 144
Title, transfer of, 227–8
Tort, 6, 349–420
  accident, 355
  Act of God, 357, 388
  Act of a stranger, 388
  Act of State, 357
  actionable per se, 350
  agents by, 360

Tort – *continued*
  aliens and, 359
  capacity, 357–60
  clubs and, 63
  companies and, 73–4
  conspiracy, 417
  contract and, 351
  contributory negligence and, 378–9, 386
  corporations and, 359
  crime and, 351
  Crown, and, 357
  damages, 360–3
  damnum sine injuria, 350
  deceit, 417
  defamation, *see* Defamation
  defences in, 352–7
  definition of, 349–50
  diplomats and, 359
  duty of care, 371–4
  exemplary damages, 361
  foreign sovereigns, 359
  fraud, 417–18
  hospital authorities, 358
  husband and wife, 360
  independent contractors, 368
  inevitable accident, 355
  infants, and, 357
  injunction in, 363
  injuria sine damno, 350
  injurious falsehood, 418
  joint tortfeasors, 369
  judicial immunity, 359
  libel, 408, 409
  limitation of actions, 363–5
    other statutes, 364
    survival of actions, 365
  malice and, 379
  mental element in, 350
  minors, and, 357
  mistake, 355
  nature of, 349
  necessity and, 355
  negligence, *see* Negligence
  novus actus interveniens, 362
  nuisance, *see* Nuisance
  occupiers' liability, *see* Occupiers' liability
  partners and, 54, 360
  passing off, 418–19
  police, and, 358
  Post Office, 358
  prescription, 403
  principals and, 360
  public corporations, 358
  remedies for, 360–3
  remoteness of damage, 361
  res ipsa loquitur, 378
  rescue cases, 353
  restitution of property, 363
  Rylands *v.* Fletcher, 387
  sale of goods and, 233
  self-defence, 356
  slander, 408–9
  slander of title, 418
  statutory authority, 356
  strict liability, 385–9
  trade unions and, 359
  trespass, *see* Trespass to property

trespassers, 383–4
unincorporated associations and, 63
unliquidated damages, 360
unsound mind and, 359
vicarious liability:
  agency and, 365
  independent contracts and, 368–9
  servants, for, 365–7
  volenti non fit injuria, 352–4
wife and, 360
Total loss of part, 255
Total losses, 254–5
Trade marks, 429–30
Trade unions:
  clubs as, 64
  employment and, 456–7
  torts and, 359
Transit clauses, 257
Treaty of Maastricht, 18
Treaty of Rome, 27
  House of Lords and, 27
Trespass to property, 392–9
  chattels, and, 394
  conversion, 395–7
  damages, 393
  defences to, 394
  distress damage feasant, 394
  forcible ejection, 393
  goods, and, 394–5
  inevitable accident and, 395
  injunction, 393
  jus tertii, and, 392
  land, and, 392–4
  lawful authority to, 394
  licence, 394
  necessity, 394
  non-residential premises, 394
  re-entry for repossession, 394
  remedies for, 393–4
  wooden lie and, 8
Tribunals, 338
Tribunals of inquiry, 342
Trust, 6

Uberrima fides contract, 161, 163
Ultra vires:
  companies and, 69–71
  European Communities Act, and, 69–71
  illegal contracts, 142
  rule in administrative law, 329
  rule in Royal British Bank *v.* Turquand, 71
Unascertained goods, 227, 240
UNCTAD/ICC Rules, 290, 294
Underwriters, 244
Undisclosed principal, doctrine of, 197, 207
Undue influence, 98, 129–31
Unenforceable contracts, 142
Unfair Contracts Terms Act, 156–7
  European directive on, 156–7
  test of reasonableness, 156
Unilateral discharge, 173
Unincorporated associations, 62–5
  actions against, 64
  clubs as, 62
  constitution of, 63

contracts and, 63
definition of, 62
heads of agreement and, 51
land ownership and, 63
legal liability of, 63
nature of, 62
organization of, 62–3
rules of, 62
torts and, 63
trade unions as, 64
Unseaworthiness, 256
Unsolicited goods, 441
Utmost good faith, 245

Vacher's Parliamentary Companion, 30
Valuable consideration, 120–6
adequacy and, 120–1
composition with creditors, 123
contractual duty and, 122
debts and, 113
deeds and, 120
definition, 120
estoppel and, 124
existing obligations and, 122
forbearance and, 122
lawful nature of, 126
moral obligations and, 121
movements from promisee, 125
must be real, 120
past events and, 124–5
privity of contract and, 125
public duty and, 122
requirements of, 120–6
simple contracts and, 120
Valued policies, 252
Vehicles, sale of, 230
Vicarious liability, 206, 365–9

Visitors, 382
Void contracts, 132, 139
ab initio, 132
res extincta, 133
res sua, 133
Voidable:
contracts, 101
title, 229–30
Volenti non fit injuria, 352–4, 386
Voyage:
charters, 284
policies, 252

Wagering contracts, 141–2
Waiver:
acceptance of, 119
condition, of, 147–8
insurance clauses, 259
War exclusion clauses, 257
Warranty:
authority, of, 203
contract, in, 146
seaworthiness, 222–3
Warsaw Rules, 271, 287–9
Waybill, air, 288
Weights and measures, 442
Wife:
agency, and, 201
torts, and, 360
Wilful misconduct, 249
Winding-up of companies 86–8
Witenagemot, 9
Wooden lie, 8
Work permits, 450
Written particulars:
employment of, 452
York–Antwerp Rules, 1974, 255